Harden's

BEST UK RESTAURANTS 2017

SURVEY DRIVEN REVIEWS OF OVER 2,800 RESTAURANTS

ISBN 978-0-9929408-4-3

British Library Cataloguing-in-Publication data: a catalogue record for this book is available from the British Library.

Printed in Britain by Wheatons Exeter

Client Relations Manager: Clare Burnage
Assistant editors: Karen Moss, Bruce Millar, Clodagh Kinsella
Designers: (text) Paul Smith, (cover) Calverts Coop

Harden's Limited
The Brew, Victoria House, 64 Paul Street, London, EC2A 4NG

Would restaurateurs (and PRs) please address communications to 'Editorial' at the above address, or ideally by email to: editorial@hardens.com The contents of this book are believed correct at the time of printing. Nevertheless, the publisher can accept no responsibility for errors or changes in or omissions from the details given.

Celeste, The Lanesborough

Paradise Garage

The Cinnamon Club

This edition of the Harden's guide is the fifth to include restaurants' Food Made Good sustainability stars alongside their score for the food, service and ambience.

Just ten years ago, this might have seemed 'out there'. How times have changed. In fact it's diners' appetites for an all-round good experience that's driving that change. You only have to look at the results of the survey of Harden's readers to see the shift. Ninety three per cent of you said that you considered issues like sourcing local and seasonal produce, high welfare meat and sustainable fish, as well as water and energy saving and treating staff fairly, more now than you did five years ago. And more than 80% said these issues had been a deciding factor when you choose a restaurant.

Perhaps most revealing of all was the finding that 75% of you said you valued the ethical and sustainable achievements of a restaurant more than a 10% discount.

Rather than having to navigate your way through the minefield that is deciding what fish you can eat and when, whether your waiter will receive their fair share of the tip you leave and the etiquette around asking for a doggy bag, just look for the Food Made Good stars.

That way, you can then concentrate on what's really important when you go and eat out – the food, service and ambience – because everything else has been take care of.

One Star - Good Sustainability
Two Stars - Excellent Sustainability
Three Stars - Exceptional Sustainability

Winners at the 2016 Food Made Good Awards include:

Lussmanns Fish and Grill – People's Favourite Restaurant
Poco – Food Made Good Restaurant of the Year
Captain's Galley – Food Made Good Scottish Restaurant of the Year
The Gallery, Barry – Food Made Good, Welsh Restaurant of the Year
Arbor Restaurant – Food Made Good Environment Award

www.foodmadegood.org @FoodMadeGood

CONTENTS

Padella

Restaurant Ours

RATINGS & PRICES

Ratings

Our rating system does not tell you – as most guides do – that expensive restaurants are often better than cheap ones! What we do is compare each restaurant's performance – as judged by the average ratings awarded by reporters in the survey – with other similarly-priced restaurants.

This approach has the advantage that it helps you find – whatever your budget for any particular meal – where you will get the best 'bang for your buck'.

The following qualities are assessed:

F — Food
S — Service
A — Ambience

The rating indicates that, ***in comparison with other restaurants in the same price-bracket***, performance is...

5 — Exceptional
4 — Very good
3 — Good
2 — Average
1 — Poor

NEW SINCE 2015!

Regular readers remember we've turned our marking system on its head. 5 is the new 1!

Prices

The price shown for each restaurant is the cost for one (1) person of an average threecourse dinner with half a bottle of house wine and coffee, any cover charge, service and VAT. Lunch is often cheaper. With BYO restaurants, we have assumed that two people share a £7 bottle of off-licence wine.

Telephone number *– all numbers are '020' numbers.*

Map reference *– shown immediately after the telephone number.*

Full postcodes *– for non-group restaurants, the first entry in the 'small print' at the end of each listing, so you can set your sat-nav.*

Website and Twitter *– shown in the small print, where applicable.*

Last orders time *– listed after the website (if applicable); Sunday may be up to 90 minutes earlier.*

Opening hours *– unless otherwise stated, restaurants are open for lunch and dinner seven days a week.*

Credit and debit cards *– unless otherwise stated, Mastercard, Visa, Amex and Maestro are accepted.*

Dress *– where appropriate, the management's preferences concerning patrons' dress are given.*

Special menus *– if we know of a particularly good value set menu we note this (e.g. "set weekday L"), together with its formula price (FP), calculated exactly as in 'Prices' above. Details change, so always check ahead.*

'Rated on Editors' visit' *– indicates ratings have been determined by the Editors personally, based on their visit, rather than derived from the survey.*

SRA Star Rating *– the sustainability index, as calculated by the Sustainable Restaurant Association – see page 10 for more information.*

FROM THE EDITORS

Welcome to our 26th anniversary edition of what you users and diners have helped to make the UK's most authoritative restaurant guide.

As ever, Harden's is written 'from the bottom up' based on the results of the survey conducted in late spring 2016. It is completely rewritten each year, with the selection of restaurants based on that unique annual poll of thousands of restaurant-goers, in which you are most welcome to take part. (Further details of this are given overleaf.)

Unlike any other national UK restaurant guide – certainly of a print variety – reviews and ratings in the book are primarily statistically derived and driven from our user-survey. This is a much more direct, and we believe democratic use of user feedback than the processes of some competing publications, particularly those who solicit reader feedback, but where the linkage between such feedback and the reviews and ratings in the guide is much less clear-cut.

The survey methodology is also a very different kettle of fish from the modus operandi of user-review sites such as TripAdvisor. The latter has been put under the spotlight as never before in recent times with questions raised over the veracity of a huge number of reviews. With the Harden's survey however, because we don't publish the raw reviews supplied by the dining public, but only a summary based on the careful curation of those raw reviews, it is a much harder ballot to stuff. Of course, restaurants do still try to stuff the ballot in their favour – or less often to disadvantage their competitors – but the presence of so many diners who have participated in the survey for many years provides a good sanity check on the veracity of reviews from more recent sign-ups.

This guide includes the full content of our separately-published London guide, as well as coverage of cities, towns and villages across the whole of the UK. We recognise that the result is a guide somewhat skewed to London. We urge readers, though, to think of this extensive London coverage as a bonus rather than a defect. After all, our out-of-London coverage alone exceeds the headline number of reviews in the whole of *The Good Food Guide* including London. Add in our London coverage and there are more than double the number of entries than the rival publication.

It is certainly no longer true, as one could have said as recently as five years ago, that large areas of the UK are pretty much restaurant deserts, devoid of almost anything of interest to the discerning visitor. This ongoing transformation is perhaps most obvious in the great regional centres – even Manchester, a 'second city' which has been a laggard until very recently, seems finally to be getting its act together!

We urge all our readers to help us do even better justice to the restaurant scene outside the capital. If you think your area is under-represented, the answer is largely in your own hands – take part in our annual survey, and make sure your friends do too!

We are very grateful to each of our thousands of reporters, without whose input this guide could not have been written. Many reporters express views about a number of restaurants at some length, knowing full well that – given the concise format of the guide – we can seemingly never 'do justice' to their observations. We must assume that they do so in the confidence that the short – and we hope snappy – summaries we produce are as fair and well-informed as possible.

You, the reader, must judge – restaurant guides are not works of literature, and should be assessed on the basis of utility. This is a case where the proof of the pudding really is in the eating.

All restaurant guides are the subject of continual revision, and the more input we have, the more accurate and comprehensive future editions will be. If you are not already signed up, please do join the www.hardens.com mailing list – we will then ensure that you are invited to take part in future surveys.

Harden's, Shoreditch, November 2016

HOW THIS BOOK IS ORGANISED

The guide begins in London, and contains the full text of the guide already published as *London Restaurants 2017*. Thereafter, the guide is organised strictly alphabetically by location, without regard to national divisions – Beaumaris, Belfast and Birmingham appear together under 'B'.

For *cities and larger towns*, you should therefore be able to turn straight to the relevant section. In addition to the entries for the restaurants themselves, cities which have significant numbers of restaurants also have a brief introductory overview.

In *less densely populated areas*, you will generally find it easiest to start with the relevant map at the back of the book, which will guide you to the appropriate place names.

If you are looking for a specific restaurant, the alphabetical index at the very back of the book lists all of the restaurants – London and UK – in this guide.

YOUR CONTRIBUTION

This book is the result of a research effort involving thousands of 'reporters'. As a group, you are 'ordinary' members of the public who share with us summary reviews of the best and the worst of your annual dining experiences. This year, over 7,500 of you gave us some 50,000 reviews in total.

The density of the feedback on London (where many of the top places attract several hundred reviews each) is such that the ratings for the restaurants in the capital are almost exclusively statistical in derivation. (We have, as it happens, visited almost all the restaurants in the London section, anonymously, and at our own expense, but we use our personal experiences only to inform the standpoint from which to interpret the consensus opinion.)

In the case of the more commented-upon restaurants away from the capital, we have adopted an essentially statistical approach very similar to London. In the case of less visited provincial establishments, however, the interpretation of survey results owes as much to art as it does to science.

In our experience, smaller establishments are – for better or worse – generally quite consistent, and we have therefore felt able to place a relatively high level of confidence in a lower level of commentary. Conservatism on our part, however, may have led to some smaller places being under-rated compared to their more-visited peers.

LONDON INTRODUCTION & SURVEY RESULTS

SURVEY MOST MENTIONED

RANKED BY THE NUMBER OF REPORTERS' VOTES

These are the restaurants which were most frequently mentioned by reporters. (Last year's position is given in brackets.) An asterisk* indicates the first appearance in the list of a recently-opened restaurant.

1 J Sheekey (1)
2 Clos Maggiore (2)
3 Le Gavroche (3)
4 Chez Bruce (5)
5 The Ledbury (4)
6 Scott's (6)
7 Gymkhana (7)
8 The Wolseley (10)
9 Brasserie Zédel (11)
10 The Cinnamon Club (13)

11 The Delaunay (8) *
12 Fera at Claridges (9)
13 La Trompette (16)
14 Gauthier Soho (22)
15 The River Café (18)
16 Andrew Edmunds (33)
17 Pollen Street Social (14)
18 The Ivy (-)
19= Galvin La Chapelle (15)
19= La Poule au Pot (19)

21 Bocca Di Lupo (-)
22 Medlar (28)
23 Benares (26)
24 Gordon Ramsay (20)
25 Marcus (32)
26 Pied à Terre (25)
27= Galvin Bistrot de Luxe (27)
27= Bleeding Heart Restaurant (31)
29 The Square (17)
30 Le Caprice (23)

31 Dinner (12)
32 Moro (35)
33 The Palomar (24)
34 The Ivy Chelsea Garden (-)
35 Zuma (30)
36= The Berners Tavern (-)
36= Sexy Fish (-)
38 Murano (-)
39 Amaya (29)
40 A Wong (-)

J Sheekey

Fera at Claridges

Pied à Terre

The Ivy Chelsea Garden

Top gastronomic experience

1. The Ledbury (2)
2. Le Gavroche (1)
3. Chez Bruce (3)
4. Fera at Claridges (4)
5. Gauthier Soho (-)
6. Pollen Street Social (8)
7. Pied à Terre (7)
8. La Trompette (-)
9. The River Café (-)
10. Story (9)

Favourite

1. Chez Bruce (1)
2. Le Gavroche (4)
3. The Ledbury (9)
4. J Sheekey (5)
5. Gauthier Soho (6)
6. Moro (10)
7. The Wolseley (3)
8. La Trompette (8)
9. Medlar (-)
10. River Café (-)

Best for business

1 The Wolseley (1)
2= Bleeding Heart Restaurant (10)
2= The Square (3)
4 The Delaunay (2)
5 Scott's (9)
6 City Social (4)
7 The Don (8)
8 L'Anima (6)
9 1 Lombard Street (-)
10 Galvin Bistrot de Luxe (-)

Best for romance

1. Clos Maggiore (1)
2. La Poule au Pot (2)
3. Andrew Edmunds (3)
4. Bleeding Heart Restaurant (4)
5. Le Gavroche (6)
6. Galvin at Windows (-)
7. Gauthier Soho (10)
8. Le Caprice (9)
9. Chez Bruce (5)
10. Gordon Ramsay (-)

Best breakfast/brunch

1. The Wolseley (1)
2. The Delaunay (2)
3. Cecconi's (7)
4. Caravan N1 (-)
5. Duck & Waffle (3)
6. Roast (5)
7. Balthazar (10)
8. Providores (Tapa Room) (-)
9. Riding House Café (4)
10. 45 Jermyn St (-)

Best bar/pub food

1. The Anchor & Hope (1)
2. Harwood Arms (2)
3. The Ladbroke Arms (4)
4. Bull & Last (3)
5. The Camberwell Arms (9)
6. Pig & Butcher (8)
7. The Jugged Hare (5)
8. The Guinea Grill (-)
9. The Wells (-)
10. The Lighterman

Most disappointing cooking

1. Oxo Tower (Rest') (2)
2. The Chiltern Firehouse (1)
3. Gordon Ramsay (7)
4. Pollen Street Social (3)
5. Benares (-)
6. Sexy Fish (-)
7. The Ivy Chelsea Garden (-)
8. The Ivy (-)
9. Dinner (6)
10. Dabbous (9)

Most overpriced restaurant

1. Sexy Fish (-)
2. The River Café (1)
3. Oxo Tower (Rest') (2)
4. Gordon Ramsay (4)
5. Marcus (6)
6. The Chiltern Firehouse (3)
7. Pollen Street Social (8)
8. Le Gavroche (-)
9. Alain Ducasse at The Dorchester (7)
10. Hutong (-)

SURVEY HIGHEST RATINGS

£95+

	FOOD		SERVICE
1	The Araki	1	The Araki
2	The Ledbury	2	Le Gavroche
3	Le Gavroche	3	The Ledbury
4	The Clove Club	4	Pied à Terre
5	Pied à Terre	5	The Ritz Restaurant

£70-£94

	FOOD		SERVICE
1	Hunan	1	The Five Fields
2	The Five Fields	2	Chez Bruce
3	HKK	3	The Goring Hotel
4	Gauthier Soho	4	Seven Park Place
5	Chez Bruce	5	Typing Room

£54-£69

	FOOD		SERVICE
1	Sushi Tetsu	1	Sushi Tetsu
2	Chotto Matte	2	Oslo Court
3	St John	3	Bonham's
4	Zelman Meats	4	Quo Vadis
5	Café Spice Namaste	5	Enoteca Turi

£40-£54

	FOOD		SERVICE
1	Honey & Co	1	Caraffini
2	Jin Kichi	2	The Lighterman
3	Taberna Do Mercado	3	Jin Kichi
4	José	4	Lamberts
5	Potli	5	Brawn

£39 or less

	FOOD		SERVICE
1	The Begging Bowl	1	A Wong
2	Silk Road	2	Paradise Hampstead
3	A Wong	3	Department of Coffee
4	Blanchette	4	Golden Hind
5	Tayyabs	5	Blanchette

AMBIENCE

1. The Ritz Restaurant
2. Sketch (Lecture Rm)
3. Galvin at Windows
4. Le Gavroche
5. The Ledbury

1. Clos Maggiore
2. Hutong
3. Rules
4. Scott's
5. Chutney Mary

1. La Poule au Pot
2. Petersham Hotel
3. Dean Street Townhouse
4. Bob Bob Ricard
5. Summerhouse

1. The Lighterman
2. Andrew Edmunds
3. Brasserie Zédel
4. José
5. Joe Allen

1. The Begging Bowl
2. Blanchette
3. Churchill Arms
4. Department of Coffee
5. Princi

OVERALL

1. The Ledbury
2. The Ritz Restaurant
3. Le Gavroche
4. Sketch (Lecture Rm)
5. The Araki

1. The Five Fields
2. Gauthier Soho
3. Chez Bruce
4. The Guinea Grill
5. Scott's

1. Sushi Tetsu
2. Oslo Court
3. Chotto Matte
4. Quo Vadis
5. Café Spice Namaste

1. The Lighterman
2. José
3. Jin Kichi
4. The Palomar
5. Andrew Edmunds

1. The Begging Bowl
2. Blanchette
3. A Wong
4. Department of Coffee
5. Paradise Hampstead

SURVEY BEST BY CUISINE

These are the restaurants which received the best average food ratings (excluding establishments with a small or notably local following).

Where the most common types of cuisine are concerned, we present the results in two price-brackets. For less common cuisines,we list the top three, regardless of price.

For further information about restaurants which are particularly notable for their food, see the cuisine lists starting on page 158.These indicate, using an asterisk*, restaurants which offer exceptional or very good food.

British, Modern

£55 and over

1 The Ledbury
2 The Five Fields
3 Chez Bruce
4 The Clove Club
5 Trinity

Under £55

1 The Dairy
2 Lamberts
3 The Anglesea Arms
4 Rabbit
5 Oldroyd

French

£55 and over

1 Gauthier Soho
2 Le Gavroche
3 La Petite Maison
4 Pied à Terre
5 Sketch (Lecture Rm)

Under £55

1 Brawn
2 Blanchette
3 Casse-Croute
4 Cigalon
5 Comptoir Gascon

Italian/Mediterranean

£55 and over

1 Bocca di Lupo
2 The River Café
3 Assaggi
4 Murano
5 Locanda Locatelli

Under £55

1 Dehesa
2 L'Amorosa
3 Opera Tavern
4 Princi
5 500

Indian & Pakistani

£55 and over

1 Trishna
2 Tamarind
3 Café Spice Namaste
4 Gymkhana
5 Amaya

Under £55

1 Ganapati
2 Potli
3 Lahore Kebab House
4 Dishoom
5 Hoppers

Chinese

£55 and over

1 Hunan
2 HKK
3 Yauatcha W1
4 Min Jiang
5 Royal China Club

Under £55

1 Silk Road
2 A Wong
3 Royal China W2
4 Shikumen
5 Yming

Japanese

£55 and over

1 The Araki
2 Sushi Tetsu
3 Zuma
4 Dinings
5 Umu

Under £55

1 Jin Kichi
2 Kurobata W2
3 Tsunami SW4
4 Shackfuyu
5 Sticks n Sushi SW19

British, Traditional

1 St John
2 Wiltons
3 Scott's

Vegetarian

1 The Gate EC1
2 Vanilla Black
3 Mildred's

Burgers, etc

1 Tommi's
2 Patty & Bun W1
3 Honest Burger SW9

Pizza

1 Santa Maria
2 Pizza Pilgrims W1
3 Franco Manca SW9

Fish & Chips

1 Olympus
2 Golden Hind
3 The Sea Shell

Thai

1 The Begging Bowl
2 Sukho Fine Thai Cuisine
3 Smoking Goat

Steaks & Grills

1 The Guinea Grill
2 Hawksmoor W1
3 Goodman W1

Fish & Seafood

1 One-O-One
2 Outlaw's
3 Wiltons

Fusion

1 Chotto Matte
2 Bubbledogs (Kitchen Table)
3 Sushisamba

Spanish

1 Barrafina
2 José
3 Donostia

Turkish

1 Oklava
2 Kazan
3 Haz

Lebanese

1 Mezzet
2 Meza
3 Arabica

THE RESTAURANT SCENE

Another stellar year: is this as good as it gets?

This year we list a record 200 newcomers – the largest ever in the 26-year history of the guide, comfortably overtaking last year's record of 179.

Closings – muted in recent years – also grew significantly to 76. Although this is well below the record of 113 seen in 2004, it is the third-highest level we have recorded.

Combining the two factors, the level of net openings this year (openings minus closings) set a new peak (just!): at 124, the figure exceeds last year's record total of 123 by 1!

Although the proportion of openings to closings, at 2.6:1, remains historically high – in fact, the fifth highest on record – this ratio is a good deal lower than last year's spike of 3.2:1. If you put these figures on a graph, then despite this year's record figures (as detailed above) it is not hard to paint a picture of a peak being passed.

Brexit being the hot topic it is, it would be tempting to see the record figures noted above as proof of the resilience of the London restaurant market to Brexit. It is no such thing of course. The time it takes to cook up a new restaurant is at least nine months (securing the site, recruiting staff, etc).

It will take till next year to have any idea whether Brexit is going to hit the confidence of restaurant investors. And even if there is a decline, there will be many factors in play. For example, Brexit aside, many in the trade are already worried about a potential over-supply of new openings, and perhaps rightly so given the rising number of closures.

"Without Europeans, we're f##ked"

These memorable words were spoken by Bruce Poole, at the inaugural Harden's London Restaurant Awards, held at the Hippodrome Casino on 12 September 2016.

In receiving his lifetime achievement award, the proprietor of Chez Bruce used his time on the stage to stress the vital contribution made by migrants from Europe in both boosting the quality of London dining, but also in providing the unskilled foot soldiers on which the trade depends.

Another attendee at the awards who employs 60, noted that in the last 15 years of running restaurants, perhaps 5% of his job applications for the post of kitchen porter had come from UK citizens. Where will they come from in future?

The restaurant trade is no stranger to friction with the home office. Never mind European migrants: any restaurateur involved with cuisine from further afield will attest to the difficulty in getting chefs into the country.

Of course, some will argue that catering to such sybaritic whims are elite concerns. But tourism accounts for about 10% of UK GDP and the importance of having an improving reputation for gastronomy – and cosmopolitan gastronomy at that – shouldn't be understated in building London to being the world's leading in-bound tourist destination. Let's hope the efforts to cope with the referendum result and underlying immigration concerns don't screw up this 'crown-jewel' feature.

East End Meat Feast

When it comes to migration within London, then – after Central London – the East End continues to be the destination of choice for restaurant openings. That noted, West London did stage something of a fight-back this year, with 3/4 the number of openings to the East. North London remains the laggard with the lowest level of activity.

According to our categorisations, Modern British and Italian cuisines remain the most popular for newcomers. But if you lump various categories such as "American", "Burgers" and "Steak & Grills" into a single meatylicious one, then this eco-unfriendly cuisine is as popular as Italian for new openings, and more so in the hipster-heavy eastern postcodes.

The popularity of Japanese cuisine also continues to be a major trend. Nipponese openings again exceeded those of the next most popular cuisines: French, Indian and Spanish.

Despite the huge Chinese community in London and China's immense culinary traditions, its cuisine continues to be poorly represented, especially in fashionable new openings. This remains a massive opportunity for anyone who can dream up winning Chinese-inspired formats.

The hottest of the hot

Every year, we choose what to us seem to be the most significant openings of the year. This year, our selection is as follows:

Anglo	Frenchie
Black Axe Mangal	Hoppers
The Barbary	Padella
Clipstone	Som Saa
Elystan Street	Vineet Bhatia

Prices

The average price of dinner for one at establishments listed in this guide is £51.37 (compared to £50.51 last year). Prices have risen by 1.7% in the past 12 months: again, a lower rate than in the preceding 12 months. This continues a 3-year trend of a slowing rate that nevertheless exceeds the very low rate of inflation generally (effectively zero). This year's real level of above inflation restaurant price rises is very similar to last year's.

OPENINGS AND CLOSURES

Openings (200)

Ahi Poké
Albion Clerkenwell (EC1)
Anglo
Anzu
Aquavit
Assaggi
Le Bab
Bánh Bánh
Bao Fitzrovia (W1)
The Barbary
Barbecoa, Nova (SW1)
Berber & Q Shawarma Bar
Bernardi's
Billy & The Chicks
Bird Camden (NW1)
Black Axe Mangal
Black Roe
Blanchette East (E1)
Blandford Comptoir
Bob Bob Exchange
Bombetta
Boondocks
Bronte
Bukowski Grill (W1, SW9)
Buoni Amici
Cacio & Pepe
Café Monico
Canto Corvino
Caravan Bankside (SE1)
Casita Andina
Céleste, The Lanesborough
Chicama
The Chipping Forecast
Chriskitch (N1)
Chuck Burger
Chucs (W11)
Clipstone
CôBa
Cocotte
Coin Laundry
The Collins Room
Corner Kitchen
Counter Culture
Curio + Ta Ta
Dalloway Terrace, Bloomsbury Hotel
Darbaar
Dickie Fitz

Dip & Flip (SW17)
Dominique Ansel Bakery London
Duende
Dynamo
Elystan Street
Eneko at One Aldwych, One Aldwych Hotel
Enoteca Turi
Escocesa
Estiatorio Milos
Farang
Farley Macallan
Farmacy
La Ferme
Figlio Del Vesuvio
Flora Indica
Foley's
Foxlow (W4)
Frenchie
The Frog
Fumo
Galley
Galvin HOP
Gotto Trattoria
Gourmet Goat
Gunpowder
Hanger
The Harcourt
Hatchetts
Hill & Szrok Public House (N1)
Homeslice (EC1)
The Hour Glass
Humble Grape
Ichiryu
The Ivy Brasserie, One Tower Bridge
The Ivy Café (NW8, SW19)
Jamavar
Jikoni
Joe Public
Kanada-Ya (SW1)
Kiln
Kiru
Kojawan, Hilton Metropole
Kricket (W1)
Legs

The Lighterman
Little Taperia
Lotus
Lucky Chip
MacellaioRC (SW7, EC1)
Maison Eric Kayser
Mamie's
Mangal 1.1 (EC2)
Margot
Martha Ortiz
MEATliquor (SE22)
MeatUp
Mere
Mister Lasagna
MNKY HSE
Morito (E2)
Mr Bao
Mustard
Nanban
Native
The Ninth
Nirvana Kitchen
No 197 Chiswick Fire Station
Noble Rot
Oklava
Oliver Maki
On The Bab (EC4)
100 Wardour Street
Orée
Ormer Mayfair, Flemings Mayfair Hotel
Osteria, Barbican Centre
Osteria 60
Ostuni (N6)
Padella
Parabola
Park Chinois
El Pastór
Patty and Bun (E2)
Pear Tree Cafe
Perilla
Petit Pois Bistro
Peyotito
Pharmacy 2, Newport Street Gallery
Picture Marylebone (W1)
Pidgin
Pique Nique

Pitt Cue Co
Poco (E2)
Poppies (W1)
Rail House Café
Randy's Wing Bar
Restaurant Ours
Rök (N1)
Romulo Café
Rubedo
Sagardi
Saint Luke's Kitchen, Library
Sakagura
Salut
Samarkand
Santa Maria (SW6)
Sardine
Savini at Criterion
Shepherd Market Wine House
Shuang Shuang
Six Portland Road
Smoke and Salt (Residency)
Smokestak (E1)
Som Saa
Sosharu, Turnmill Building
Spring Workshop
Squirrel
The Stable
Strut & Cluck
Sushi Masa
Sushisamba (WC2)
Sutton And Sons (N16)
Sutton And Sons (E8)
Tabun Kitchen
Takahashi
Talli Joe
Tate Modern Restaurant, Switch House
temper
Theo's
Theo's Simple Italian
Tokimeite
Tommi's Burger Joint (W1)
Uli
Upstairs at John the Unicorn
Urban Coterie, M By Montcalm
Veneta
Viet Food
View 94
Vineet Bhatia
VQ (W11)
Walter and Monty
Wazen
The Woodford
Xi'an Impression
Yard Sale Pizza (N4)
Yumi Izakaya
Zayane
Zelman Meats (W1, SW1)
Zia Lucia
Zima

Closures (76)

Abbeville Kitchen SW4
Amico Bio WC1
Apollo Banana Leaf SW17
Arbutus W1
Bangkok SW7
Blackfoot EC1
Bonnie Gull Seafood Bar EC1
Bouillabaisse W1
Brasserie Chavot W1
Bumpkin W11
Bunnychow W1
Canta Napoli W4, TW11
Carom at Meza
Ceru SE1
Chez Patrick W8
Copita del Mercado E1
Cuckoo N1
Delancey & Co W1
Dub Jam WC2
Fabrizio EC1
Garnier SW5
Gin Joint EC2
Green's SW1
Harbour City W1
Hibiscus W1
Izgara N3
Inside SE10
Joint W1
Kateh SW1
Kopapa WC2
Linnea TW9
Little Bay EC1
Lockhart W1
Lolo Rojo SW11
Megan's NW8
Mill Lane Bistro NW6
Mishkins WC2
Morden & Lea W1
Moti Mahal WC2
Newman Street Tavern W1
Nozomi SW3
Old Tom & English W1
One Sixty Smokehouse NW6
Only Running Footman W1
Pescatori W1
Piquet W1
Poissonnerie de l'Avenue SW3
Princess Garden W1
Rasoi SW3
Rex & Mariano W1
Rextail W1
Rocket W1 & WC2
Rooftop Café, The Exchange SE1
Roots at N1
Sackville's W1
Sea Cow SE22
Sesame WC2
Shanghai Blues WC1
Shoe Shop NW5
Source SW11
Stock Pot W1, SW1
Strand Dining Rooms WC2
Suk Saran SW19
Sushi-Say NW2
Tentazioni SE1
Terra Virgine SW10
The Terrace W8
Tinello SW1
Truscott Arms W9
Truscott Cellar NW3
Verden E5
White Rabbit N16
Zucca SE1

Anglo

Aulis, Fera at Claridge's

Chick 'n' Sours

LONDON DIRECTORY

A Cena TW1 £50 333
418 Richmond Rd 020 8288 0108 1–4A
"Original cooking and an interesting wine list" combined with "efficient and friendly service" have long made this St Margaret's local a fave rave. "Good pre-rugby as well" if you're Twickers-bound. / TW1 2EB; www.acena.co.uk; @acenarestaurant; 10 pm; closed Mon L & Sun D; booking max 6 may apply; set weekday L £29 (FP).

A Wong SW1 £35 554
70 Wilton Rd 020 7828 8931 2–4B
"Breathtakingly skilful" dim sum – "a very exciting and intriguing mix of the traditional and innovative" – win huge esteem for Andrew Wong's "jammed-to-the-rafters" Pimlico canteen. "It's great to eat Chinese with such friendly staff" too. Top menu tip – "duck egg custard buns TO DIE FOR!" / SW1V 1DE; www.awong.co.uk; @awongSW1; 10.15 pm; closed Mon L & Sun; credit card deposit required to book.

The Abingdon W8 £62 333
54 Abingdon Rd 020 7937 3339 6–2A
"Totally reliable" and "always a treat", this stalwart, posh gastropub in an agreeable Kensington backstreet gets "very busy, so allow time for your order". Top Tip – nab a booth for the best seats. / W8 6AP; www.theabingdon.co.uk; @TheAbingdonW8; 10.30 pm, Fri & Sat 11 pm, Sun 10 pm; set weekday L £33 (FP), set Sun L £35 (FP).

About Thyme SW1 £52 333
82 Wilton Rd 020 7821 7504 2–4B
"The Spanish-orientated cuisine (including the wine list) remains reliable and interesting" at this Pimlico stalwart. "Amiable service and ambience" ensure that it's popular with locals as well as visitors. / SW1V 1DL; www.aboutthyme.co.uk; 10 pm; closed Sun.

L'Absinthe NW1 £49 232
40 Chalcot Rd 020 7483 4848 9–3B
Run by ebullient Burgundian Jean-Christophe Slowik, this popular corner bistro in Primrose Hill serves "traditional French cuisine", "Franglais-style". Not all reporters are impressed, but for a majority it's "delightful". / NW1 8LS; www.labsinthe.co.uk; @absinthe07jc; 10 pm, Sun 9 pm; closed Mon D.

Abu Zaad W12 £23 332
29 Uxbridge Rd 020 8749 5107 8–1C
"Delicious Middle Eastern cuisine" at very affordable prices makes it worth remembering this "authentic" Syrian café, near the top of Shepherd's Bush Market. / W12 8LH; www.abuzaad.co.uk; 11 pm; no Amex.

Adams Café W12 £33 353
77 Askew Rd 020 8743 0572 8–1B
"Tagines to die for in very generous portions" are the surprise in store at this Shepherd's Bush caff when it "turns into a North African restaurant by night". "It's the most friendly, hospitable, inexpensive place". / W12 9AH; www.adamscafe.co.uk; @adamscafe; 10 pm; closed Sun.

Addie's Thai Café SW5 £34 443
121 Earl's Court Rd 020 7259 2620 6–2A
"It's very cheap and we're very cheerful afterwards!" say fans of this "pretty authentic" Earl's Court café. Top Menu Tip – "especially recommended are the sizzling dishes". / SW5 9RL; www.addiesthai.co.uk; 11 pm, Sun 10.30 pm; no Amex.

The Admiral Codrington SW3 £57 123
17 Mossop St 020 7581 0005 6–2C
This popular, backstreet Chelsea boozer is still "a good old pub" to its fans, but an increasing number of regulars are calling time on its food. "I made the mistake of having a burger, once a Cod speciality. It isn't now", moaned one. "How can a place go downhill so quickly?" asked another. / SW3 2LY; www.theadmiralcodrington.co.uk; @TheAdCod; 10 pm, Thu-Sat 11 pm, Sun 9 pm; no trainers.

Afghan Kitchen N1 £28 322
35 Islington Grn 020 7359 8019 9–3D
"Very good value" Afghan café, by Islington Green where you squash into one of its two miniature floors, decorated Ikea-style, to enjoy a small menu of simple stews. / N1 8DU; 11 pm; closed Mon & Sun; cash only.

Aglio e Olio SW10 £43 432
194 Fulham Rd 020 7351 0070 6–3B
This "everyday Italian" near Chelsea & Westminster Hospital is "a firm favourite" with "very reasonable prices for the area". "The food is exceptionally consistent – as it should be since the menu doesn't seem to have changed in 14 years!" / SW10 9PN; 11.30 pm.

Ahi Poké W1 £11
3 Percy Street no tel 3–1D
New, little (25-cover) café/takeaway in the streets near Tottenham Court Road catering to London's latest food craving: Hawaiian-style raw fish (poké). It opened in mid 2016. / W1T 1DE; www.ahipoke.co.uk; @ahipokelondon; 8 pm.

Al Duca SW1 £49 343
4-5 Duke of York St 020 7839 3090 3–3D
This low-key Italian is a well-established fixture – particularly on the St James's business lunch scene – with a "mainstream, satisfying" menu of modern classics that "never disappoints", and which is "good value" for this part of town. / SW1Y 6LA; www.alduca-restaurant.co.uk; 11 pm; closed Sun; set pre theatre £33 (FP).

Al Forno £34 244
349 Upper Richmond Rd, SW15
020 8878 7522 11–2A
2a King's Rd, SW19 020 8540 5710 11–2B

"Rustic and delicious Italian cooking" including "terrific pizzas" plus a "wonderful atmosphere" make these "fun" locals across southwest London a good bet for a "great night out". / 10 pm-11 pm.

Alain Ducasse at The Dorchester W1 **£129** 2 4 3
53 Park Ln 020 7629 8866 3–3A
"3 stars .... not in my eyes!" – Michelin continue to mis-rate the world-famous Gallic chef's Mayfair temple. True, fans do wax lyrical over its "easy luxury" and cuisine with "perfect balance", and the "un-snooty" service in particular is "exceptional". But there are too many doubters who find it feels "corporate" with "inspiration-free" cooking, and "you need to bring ALL your money!" / W1K 1QA; www.alainducasse-dorchester.com; 9.30 pm; closed Mon, Sat L & Sun; jacket required; set weekday L £84 (FP).

Albertine W12 **£38** 2 4 4
1 Wood Ln 020 8743 9593 8–1C
A perfect escape from the nearby Westfield shopping centre – this "traditional wine bar" is the antithesis of the shiny retail complex opposite, and provides a "good, descriptive list", "knowledgeable service and great cheeses", plus some light, "home-cooked" dishes. / W12 7DP; www.albertinewinebar.co.uk; @AlbertineWine; 11 pm, Thu-Sat midnight; closed Sat L & Sun; no Amex.

Albion **£51** 2 2 2
NEO Bankside, Holland St, SE1
020 3764 5550 10–3B
2-4 Boundary St, E2 020 7729 1051 13–1B
63 Clerkenwell Road, EC1
020 3862 0750 10–1A
"A borderline entry" – Sir Terence Conran's group of all-day pit-stops in Shoreditch, Clerkenwell and Bankside are "relaxed and agreeable" venues, but it's "hard to be fantastically enthusiastic – they're not overpriced but a bit bland". / 11 pm.

The Albion N1 **£48** 2 1 3
10 Thornhill Rd 020 7607 7450 9–3D
"Very handsome" Islington neighbourhood gastro-boozer with "lots of outdoor space" that's long been a "Sunday lunch favourite". "Dire service" too often ruins the experience however: "the staff are positively hostile, especially if you are stupid enough to complain". / N1 1HW; www.the-albion.co.uk; @thealbionpub; 10 pm, Sun 9 pm.

Ali Baba NW1 **£25** 3 2 4
32 Ivor Pl 020 7723 5805 2–1A
"If you want the food and ambience of an Egyptian cafe, you'll find it here", at this living-room-style operation behind a Marylebone takeaway ("the TV is likely to be on only if there is an important football game in Egypt"). "Interesting" home-cooked fare, and you can BYO. / NW1 6DA; midnight; cash only.

Almeida N1 **£63** 3 2 2
30 Almeida St 020 7354 4777 9–3D
This long-running D&D London venue opposite the eponymous theatre nowadays serves modern British cuisine (rather than its old Gallic-style fare). It's a dependable rather than an exciting choice, most notable for its "excellent pre-theatre menu". / N1 1AD; www.almeida-restaurant.co.uk; 10.30 pm; closed Mon L & Sun D; set weekday L & pre-theatre £25 (FP).

Alounak **£33** 3 2 4
10 Russell Gdns, W14 020 7603 1130 8–1D
44 Westbourne Grove, W2
020 7229 0416 7–1B
"Wonderful Persian food at very reasonable prices" keeps these bustling and atmospheric cafés in Bayswater and Olympia busy throughout the week. "Bring your own bottle works well", too. / 11.30 pm; no Amex.

Alquimia SW15 **£51** 3 3 2
30 Brewhouse Ln 020 8785 0508 11–2B
"Shades of Pamplona rather than Putney" attract diners to this tapas bar in a newish Thames-side development by the bridge. There are some gripes that the "more limited" menu's "not as exciting as it was" ("too many old favourites"), but even so "the standard's still pretty good". / SW15 2JX; www.alquimiarestaurant.co.uk; @Alquimia_RestUK; 11.30 pm, Sun 10.30 pm.

Alyn Williams, Westbury Hotel W1 **£93** 4 5 3
37 Conduit St 020 7183 6426 3–2C
"Consistently punching above its weight" – Alyn Williams's "inventive" cuisine and "the most charming service" are often "in excess of expectations" at this windowless hotel dining room, off Bond Street, whose "widely spaced tables are ideal for a discreet business meal". / W1S 2YF; www.alynwilliams.com; @Alyn_Williams; 10.30 pm; closed Mon & Sun; jacket required; set weekday L £53 (FP), set always available £65 (FP).

Amaya SW1 **£78** 5 3 3
Halkin Arc, 19 Motcomb St
020 7823 1166 6–1D
"As far from your local cuzza as Buckingham Palace is from a bedsit!" This stylish Belgravian – with "theatrical" open kitchen – provides tapas-style cuisine that, "even for London, is amazingly sophisticated", and "with a superb variety of flavours". Top Menu Tip – "amazing grilled meats". / SW1X 8JT; www.amaya.biz; @theamaya_; 11.30 pm, Sun 10.30 pm.

Ametsa with Arzak Instruction, Halkin Hotel SW1 **£90** 4 3 2
5 Halkin St 020 7333 1234 2–3A
"The strange taste combinations always work better than you expect" – "incredible" – and

come with "very good wine pairings" ("interesting Spanish wines never seen or heard of before") at this Belgravia outpost of star Basque chef, Juan Mari Arzak. A disgruntled minority of reporters deliver the opposite verdict however, and the setting is "rather dull". / SW1X 7DJ; www.comohotels.com/thehalkin/dining/ametsa; @AmetsaArzak; 10 pm; closed Mon L & Sun.

L'Amorosa W6 £43 **443**
278 King St 020 8563 0300 8–2B
"How lucky we are that Andy Needham decided to open an accessible, neighbourhood Italian on the Hammersmith/Chiswick borders!" "Service shines", and the realisation of the "short but tempting" menu is "extremely competent" – in particular the "brilliant pasta – consistently al dente and combined with strong, gutsy flavours". And all at "sensible prices" too. / W6 0SP; www.lamorosa.co.uk; @LamorosaLondon; 9.30 pm, Fri & Sat 10 pm; closed Mon & Sun D.

Anarkali W6 £36 **343**
303-305 King St 020 8748 1760 8–2B
"Freshly cooked food by chef Rafiq is always a pleasure – fairly standard Indian, but done so well", say fans of this age-old, comfortably traditional Hammersmith curry house. "Great service" too ("attentive when they needed to be, otherwise left us alone"). / W6 9NH; www.anarkalifinedining.com; midnight; closed Mon L & Sun L; no Amex.

The Anchor & Hope SE1 £52 **433**
36 The Cut 020 7928 9898 10–4A
"The gastropub against which all others are judged!" – the survey's No. 1 boozer, a short walk from Waterloo, continues to wow with its "confident, robust, mostly meaty cooking", often enjoyed "at shared table so you meet interesting people". On the downside, it can be a "scrum", with no bookings (aside from Sunday lunch) leading to "endless waits". Top Menu Tip – "the shared lamb for five is divine!" / SE1 8LP; www.anchorandhopepub.co.uk; @AnchorHopeCut; 10.30 pm; closed Mon L; no Amex; no bookings; set weekday L £29 (FP).

Andina E2 £48 **434**
1 Redchurch St 020 7920 6499 13–1B
This "café-style" Shoreditch hotspot serves "wonderful, intriguing Peruvian tapas for sharing". It can be "extremely busy and noisy", but when all is considered the staff "manage to do an excellent job". / E2 7DJ; www.andinalondon.com; @AndinaLondon; 10.30 pm; booking max 6 may apply.

The Andover Arms W6 £46 **355**
57 Aldensey Rd 020 8748 2155 8–1B
"I may have had better food elsewhere, but haven't enjoyed a meal more" – this "well-managed and run", "traditional pub" in Brackenbury Village is "extremely friendly, cosy and welcoming" and "you couldn't get a better neighbourhood pub". Don't go expecting gastro fireworks though, despite its "bizarrely positive TripAdvisor ratings". / W6 0DL; www.theandoverarms.com; @theandoverarms; 10 pm, Sun 9 pm; no Amex.

ANDREW EDMUNDS W1 £52 **345**
46 Lexington St 020 7437 5708 4–2C
"To 'seal the deal' with a date", this "old world", "rickety" Soho "haunt" – "all flickering candlelight and rustic Bohemian style" – has few equals. The "ever-changing", "simple", "seasonal" fare is "honest" and "always reliable", but "the wine makes a meal exceptional" – "an amazing choice" from arguably "the best-value list in London". / W1F 0LW; www.andrewedmunds.com; 10.45 pm, Sun 10.30 pm; no Amex; booking max 6 may apply.

Angelus W2 £68 **343**
4 Bathurst St 020 7402 0083 7–2D
"A good find in an otherwise uninspiring area" – Thierry Tomassin's "classy and serious" venture – "a grown-up, converted pub with white tablecloths" – is an unexpected find near Lancaster Gate tube. The Gallic cooking can be "divine" (although "prices are high"), but the prime attraction is the "wine buff's" wine list one might expect of Le Gavroche's ex-sommelier. / W2 2SD; www.angelusrestaurant.co.uk; @AngelusLondon; 11 pm, Sun 10 pm; set weekday L £44 (FP).

Angler, South Place Hotel EC2 £84 **333**
3 South Pl 020 3215 1260 13–2A
Despite the odd quibble that it feels "corporate", this D&D London rooftop venture near Moorgate leaves most reporters "very surprised by how good it is" – "a lovely setting, with lots of windows and sunshine" and "beautifully cooked and presented" fish. / EC2M 2AF; www.anglerrestaurant.com; @southplacehotel; 10 pm; closed Sat L & Sun.

The Anglesea Arms W6 £51 **344**
35 Wingate Rd 020 8749 1291 8–1B
"Panic set in when it closed for a while", but this "top-class neighbourhood gastropub" near Ravenscourt Park is "in great form" again according to most (if not quite all) reports, combining "hospitable" service with a "charming" setting and "interesting" cooking. / W6 0UR; www.angleseaarmspub.co.uk; @_AngleseaArmsW6; 10 pm, Sun 9 pm; closed weekday L; no bookings.

Anglo EC1 £69 **432**
30 St Cross Street 020 7430 1503 9–4D
"If Noma were to move to London... this is it!" Most early reports on Mark Jarvis and Jack Cashmore's Hatton Garden newcomer – on the modest site vacated by Fabrizio (RIP) – describe "a superb dining experience", particularly the "INCREDIBLE tasting menu of beautifully presented dishes"

(anchored in British ingredients and cuisine). Its ratings are capped by a minority of refuseniks though who just decry "ridiculously small portions… at a price". / EC1N 8UH; www.anglorestaurant.com; 10.30 pm; closed Mon, Sat L & Sun; booking max 4 may apply.

L'Anima EC2 £74 333
1 Snowden St 020 7422 7000 13–2B
"Crisp, all-white" City venue near Liverpool Street – "echoey" when full but "a bit of a mausoleum" at quiet times – that's "perfect for a business lunch", especially "if someone else is paying". The Italian cooking can be "superlative", but since Francesco Mazzei left in 2015 "its precision has declined". / EC2A 2DQ; www.lanima.co.uk; @lanimalondon; 11 pm, Sat 11.30 pm; closed Sat L & Sun; set weekday L & dinner £59 (FP).

L'Anima Café EC2 £53 323
10 Appold St 020 7422 7080 13–2B
"Hearing is easier, and it's more relaxed" than at its namesake restaurant around the corner, but this "busy and bustling" café/deli near Liverpool Street is "pretty slick in terms of overall quality", serving simple southern Italian dishes, snacks and coffee in an "industrial"-style setting. / EC2A 2AP; www.lanimacafe.co.uk; @LAnimacafe; 10 pm; closed Sat & Sun.

Anima e Cuore NW1 £44 421
129 Kentish Town Rd 020 7267 2410 9–2B
This tiny shopfront in Kentish Town "couldn't be more basic", but the "authentic Italian food" and home-made gelato served from a blackboard menu are "absolutely fantastic". Better still, "you bring your own wine, which keeps the total bill down considerably". / NW1 8PB; @animaecuoreuk; 9 pm, Sun 2.30 pm.

Annie's £46 234
162 Thames Rd, W4 020 8994 9080 1–3A
36-38 White Hart Ln, SW13
020 8878 2020 11–1A
A "cosy atmosphere in a pretty room", plus "warm, welcoming, flexible staff", and "great-value" prices create a winning combination for this pair of neighbourhood faves in Barnes and Strand-on-the-Green. The food's only "standard", but there's "plenty on offer" from brunch to supper, and its quality is "reliably consistent". / www.anniesrestaurant.co.uk; 10 pm, Sat 10.30 pm, Sun 9.30 pm.

The Anthologist EC2 £47 223
58 Gresham St 0845 468 0101 10–2C
"Bustling", large bar/restaurant near the Guildhall, whose "different" look for the Square Mile "makes for a good atmosphere". The food's somewhere between "just right for a business meeting" and "pretty average", and service-wise it can be "a slight case of it just being plonked down". / EC2V 7BB; www.theanthologistbar.co.uk; @theanthologist; 11 pm, Thu & Fri 1 am; closed Sat & Sun; SRA-2 star.

L' Antica Pizzeria NW3 £37 433
66 Heath St 020 7431 8516 9–1A
"Permanently heaving with Italians", this "cramped and buzzy little pizzeria on Hampstead High Street" serves "fantastic wood-fired pizza", and you catch "wafts of the most delicious smells whenever the oven opens". / NW3 1DN; www.anticapizzeria.co.uk; @AnticaHamp; 10.30 pm; Mon-Thu D only, Fri-Sun open L & D.

Antico SE1 £47 343
214 Bermondsey St 020 7407 4682 10–4D
"Makes up for the sad demise of Zucca (RIP)"! A "great neighbourhood Italian spot" in Bermondsey, with "consistent food" and "particularly good risottos". It's "family-friendly" too, if "rather noisy" when lunch is in full flow. / SE1 3TQ; www.antico-london.co.uk; @AnticoLondon; 10.30 pm, Sun 9.30 pm; closed Mon.

Antidote W1 £62 222
12a Newburgh St 020 7287 8488 4–1B
"Lovely, cosy but airy wine bar that's a welcome retreat from the bustle of Carnaby Street's environs". "It's great for a glass of wine and some charcuterie/cheese" (the wine list is excellent), but since Mikael Jonsson stopped consulting here, recommendations for the more ambitious fare in the slightly "dreary" upstairs dining room have become mixed: to fans "exceptional", to sceptics "a bit overpriced and not all dishes work". / W1F 7RR; www.antidotewinebar.com; @AntidoteWineBar; 10.30 pm; closed Sun.

Anzu SW1
St James's Market, 1 Norris Street no tel 3–3D
From the owners of Tonkotsu – the ramen bar group – a new format: a Japanese brasserie, inspired by contemporary Tokyo dining, which is expected to open in St James's Market in autumn 2016 (alongside a raft of other eateries, including Aquavit London and Duck & Waffle). / SW1Y 4SB.

Applebee's Café SE1 £56 442
5 Stoney St 020 7407 5777 10–4C
"The best fish pie ever…", "The best scallops ever…", "The best fish 'n' chips ever…" – this "vibrant" café and fish shop provides "memorable" dishes. It's "excellent value" too, even if "it's edged upmarket since Borough Market became so highly fashionable". / SE1 9AA; www.applebeesfish.com; @applebeesfish; Mon-Wed 10 pm, Thu-Sat 11 pm; closed Sun; no Amex.

Apulia EC1 £39 333
50 Long Ln 020 7600 8107 10–2B
This "straightforward, good-value Puglian" local is

a popular option near the Barbican – useful for a working lunch or pre-show supper, with a "great menu of delicious" southern Italian dishes. / EC1A 9EJ; www.apuliarestaurant.co.uk; 10 pm, Sun 3.30 pm; closed Sun.

aqua nueva W1 **£66** [1][2][2]
240 Regent St (entrance 30 Argyll St)
020 7478 0540 4–1A
This "impressive" nightclubby rooftop (with terrace) Spanish venue near Oxford Circus has "changed for the worse", losing ratings across the board. "The bars have become the focal point, food that was good now seems nothing special", and "the music is cranked up too high". (Little feedback this year on the adjoining Japanese, aqua kyoto). / W1B 3BR; www.aqua-london.com; @aqualondon; 10.30 pm, Thu-Sat 11 pm, Sun 8.30 pm.

Aqua Shard SE1 **£95** [1][1][3]
Level 31, 31 St Thomas St
020 3011 1256 10–4C
"Only go for the view!" (admittedly "spectacular") to this swish (but "soulless") chamber on the Shard's 31st floor, where "average food is indifferently served" at extortionate expense. "If you go, go on a deal". / SE1 9RY; www.aquashard.co.uk; @aquashard; 10.45 pm.

Aquavit SW1
1 St James's Market, 1 Carlton St awaiting tel 3–3D
Manhattan's famous Nordic fine dining restaurant (est. 1987), with an emphasis on tasting and prix-fixe menus, is opening a London outpost in Haymarket's new St James's Market development in autumn 2016. Exec chef is Emma Bengtsson, whose claim to fame is being the second US female chef to win two Michelin stars. / SW1Y 4QQ; www.aquavitrestaurants.com; @aquavitlondon.

Arabica Bar & Kitchen SE1 **£49** [3][3][3]
3 Rochester Walk 020 3011 5151 10–4C
"Excellent Middle Eastern fare" – "delicious, authentic and good value" – can be found at this bustling Lebanese outfit in the "great location" of foodie Borough Market. / SE1 9AF; www.arabicabarandkitchen.com; @ArabicaLondon; 10.30 pm, Thu 11 pm, Fri & Sat 11.30 pm; closed Sun D.

The Araki W1 **£380** [5][5][4]
Unit 4 12 New Burlington St
020 7287 2481 4–3A
"Peerless" (and that goes for the bill too…). Given the bankruptcy-inducing set price of a meal – half as expensive again as a meal at The Fat Duck – it would be easy to feel let down by this Mayfair 9-seater, where "world-leading expert in his field Chef Mitsuhiro Araki" (who earnt three Michelin stars in Tokyo, and gave them up to move to London) "prepares and serves the sushi, right in front of you". However, not one of the reports we received on this "stunning, intimate, authentic, and completely unique experience" were anything other than totally rapturous, and it scored the survey's highest food mark this year: "bliss… if at a cost". / W1S 3BH; www.the-araki.com; 8.30 pm; D only, closed Mon; booking essential.

Ariana II NW6 **£30** [3][2][2]
241 Kilburn High Rd 020 3490 6709 1–2B
This "family-run" Kilburn BYO is popular for a "cheap and cheerful" bite, and "handy for the Tricycle Theatre" – "simple Afghan food (grilled meat or veg with rice and salad) at amazing prices". / NW6 7JN; www.ariana2restaurant.co.uk; @Ariana2kilburn; midnight.

Ark Fish E18 **£44** [4][4][2]
142 Hermon Hill 020 8989 5345 1–1D
This South Woodford chippy serves "good fresh fish in casual surroundings", and provides "excellent value". "I go there when I need cheering up – the staff are all mates and seem to be having a good time!" / E18 1QH; www.arkfishrestaurant.co.uk; 9.45 pm, Fri & Sat 10.15 pm, Sun 8.45 pm; closed Mon; no Amex; no bookings.

Artigiano NW3 **£48** [2][3][3]
12a Belsize Ter 020 7794 4288 9–2A
You'll find "excellent service and a very good ambience, with high ceilings and large windows", at this friendly Italian local in Belsize Park. "For the price, the food is good but not great". / NW3 4AX; www.etruscarestaurants.com; @artigianoesp; 10 pm; closed Mon L.

L'Artista NW11 **£37** [2][4][4]
917 Finchley Rd 020 8731 7501 1–1B
"The best pizzas for miles around" draw a family crowd to this festive Italian in the railway arches near Golders Green tube station. There's "always a friendly welcome for children of all ages, and they're very accommodating in adapting the menu". / NW11 7PE; www.lartistapizzeria.com; 11.30 pm.

L'Artiste Musclé W1 **£49** [2][2][5]
1 Shepherd Mkt 020 7493 6150 3–4B
This "perfect French bistro" in Shepherd Market is arguably "a bit of a parody of itself", but reporters young and old "love the place": "I've been going back for 45 years and am never disappointed!" The wine is "well-priced" and "you can drink all afternoon!" / W1J 7PA; @lartistemuscle; 10 pm, Fri-Sun 10.30 pm.

Artusi SE15 **£46** [3][3][3]
161 Bellenden Rd 020 3302 8200 1–4D
"The menus are short, the food excellent" at this two-year-old Italian, seemingly "home-from-home

for Peckham hipsters: last time I dined there, twice as many men had beards as were clean-shaven!" / SE15 4DH; www.artusi.co.uk; @artusipeckham; Mon-Sat 10 pm, Sun 8 pm; closed Mon L.

Asakusa NW1 **£36** 5 3 2
265 Eversholt St 020 7388 8533 9–3C
"Really authentic" Japanese, set in beamed, mock-Tudor premises near Mornington Crescent, impressively highly rated by its fans for outstanding sushi and other fare. / NW1 1BA; 11.30 pm, Sat 11 pm; D only.

Asia de Cuba, St Martin's Lane Hotel WC2 **£88** 1 2 2
45 St Martin's Ln 020 7300 5588 5–4C
"The food is a pale reflection of what it used to be" in the ever-more "canteen-like" dining space of this glossy West End boutique-hotel, where the "overpriced" Cuban-Oriental fare has been "lost in translation" – a "fusion which doesn't fuse"; "good cocktails though". / WC2N 4HX; www.morganshotelgroup.com; @asiadecuba; 11 pm, Fri & Sat midnight, Sun 10.30 pm; set pre-theatre & Sun L £52 (FP).

Assaggi W2 **£73** 4 4 3
39 Chepstow Pl 020 7792 5501 7–1B
"We were thrilled when it re-opened last November!" This "perfect, rustic Italian" in a simple upstairs dining room above a converted Bayswater pub has recently been resurrected, and most reporters are "so glad it's back" as it's just "as good as ever!" – "Pietro is gone, but it's still the same old Assaggi": "warm and welcoming" staff and "authentic south Italian food" ("wonderful, simple but fresh ingredients, deliciously prepared"), "albeit at authentic London prices". / W2 4TS; www.assaggi.co.uk; 11 pm; closed Sun; no Amex.

Assunta Madre W1 **£106** 2 2 2
8-10 Blenheim St 020 3230 3032 3–2B
While diners generally give this Mayfair branch of a Roman seafood specialist the benefit of the doubt on the food front, its "ridiculous" prices remain a major brake on all-round enthusiasm levels. / W1S 1LJ; www.assuntamadre.com; @assuntamadre; midnight.

Atari-Ya **£30** 4 2 2
20 James St, W1 020 7491 1178 3–1A
7 Station Pde, W3 020 8896 1552 1–2A
1 Station Pde, W5 020 8896 3175 1–3A
595 High Rd, N12 020 8446 6669 9–1B
31 Vivian Ave, NW4 020 8202 2789 1–1B
75 Fairfax Road, NW6 020 7328 5338 9–2A
The sushi is "exceptional" ("every piece is delicious!") and comes "at a reasonable cost" at these "authentic" outfits, operated by a Japanese food importer, and scattered around the parts of London frequented by Nipponese expats ("they're always heaving with folks from Japan"). On the downside, "service is woolly", and "they're not the most glamorous" places ("St James's is basically a takeaway with a waiting room, with service on a plastic tray!"). / www.atariya.co.uk; W1 8 pm, NW4 & NW6 9.30 pm, W9 9 pm; NW4, NW6 closed Mon.

L'Atelier de Joel Robuchon WC2 **£112** 2 2 3
13-15 West St 020 7010 8600 5–2B
"Gorgeously decorated" Covent Garden outpost of the star Parisian chef's global empire, which offers a "sumptuous" experience, from cocktails in the plush, rooftop bar and terrace to the exquisite series of "little taste bombs" served in either of the two luxuriously appointed dining rooms. (On the darker ground floor you perch on high stools, and there's a counter where you can watch the kitchen – the second floor is more conventional). Its culinary performance is "average compared to the past", however – even some who say their meal "was not bad by any measure" feel "the taste of the dishes didn't match their looks", or feel its mega prices are "not worth it". / WC2H 9NE; www.joelrobuchon.co.uk; @latelierlondon; 11.30 pm, Sun 10 pm; no trainers.

The Atlas SW6 **£48** 4 4 4
16 Seagrave Rd 020 7385 9129 6–3A
A "hidden gem tucked away at the back of West Brompton tube" – "a fantastic pub (and yes, it's still a pub)", with "outstanding" Med-influenced cuisine, "lots of great ales" and staff who are "soooo friendly"; terrace garden in summer. / SW6 1RX; www.theatlaspub.co.uk; @theatlasfulham; 10 pm.

Augustine Kitchen SW11 **£46** 3 4 2
63 Battersea Bridge Rd 020 7978 7085 6–4C
A "great little gem of a French bistro in Battersea" specialising in "high-quality" Savoyard dishes, such as fera fish from Lake Geneva: "the smoked variety is to be recommended"; "fair prices" too. / SW11 3AU; www.augustine-kitchen.co.uk; @augustinekitchen; 10.30 pm; closed Mon & Sun D.

Aurora W1 **£52** 3 4 4
49 Lexington St 020 7494 0514 4–2C
This low-profile stalwart makes a particularly "cosy" choice for a sociable meal in central Soho and provides "very enjoyable" modern European dishes ("though the menu could vary more often"); cute rear courtyard too. / W1F 9AP; www.aurorasoho.co.uk; 10 pm, Wed-Sat 10.30 pm, Sun 9 pm.

L'Autre Pied W1 **£80** 4 4 2
5-7 Blandford St 020 7486 9696 2–1A
"The more casual baby sister of Pied à Terre" is "everything a top restaurant should be, but with no fuss" – providing "outstanding cuisine" at "a very reasonable price", plus "professional yet informal service". But not everyone's wowed by the "slightly cramped" and low-key interior. / W1U 3DB;

www.lautrepied.co.uk; @LAutrePied; 10 pm; closed Sun D.

L'Aventure NW8 £67 335
3 Blenheim Ter 020 7624 6232 9–3A
"Magnifique!" – Catherine Parisot's "special" St John's Wood treasure is "so French, fun and romantic" and continues to deliver "dependable, high-quality" cuisine bourgeoise. Service from La Patronne and her team can be "attitude-y" or slow, but on most accounts: "who cares?" / NW8 0EH; 11 pm; closed Sat L & Sun.

The Avenue SW1 £63 122
7-9 St James's St 020 7321 2111 3–4D
D&D London's spacious Manhattan-esque brasserie in St James's is tipped by fans as a "stunning and comfortable" business venue, and also for pre-theatre dining. It is perennially accused of being "soulless and overpriced" however, and one or two meals here this year were "a fiasco". / SW1A 1EE; www.avenue-restaurant.co.uk; @avenuestjames; 10.30 pm; closed Sun D; set always available £36 (FP).

Awesome Thai SW13 £28 343
68 Church Rd 020 8563 7027 11–1A
"Super-fresh, very tasty cooking at good prices" has made this "authentic Thai" opposite Barnes's popular Olympic Studios cinema a long-time favourite among local families. "The set lunch is excellent value", too. / SW13 0DQ; www.awesomethai.co.uk; 10.30 pm, Sun 10 pm; Mon-Thu D only, Fri-Sun open L & D.

Le Bab W1 £42 543
2nd Floor, Kingly Ct 020 7439 9222 4–2B
"Just what street food crossovers should be like"; this "gourmet take on the kebab" – now permanently housed at the top of the food court off Carnaby Street – is "awesome". The "owners are engaging and passionate" and the food's "a wonderful seasonal and flavourful twist on an old favourite". / W1B 5PW; www.eatlebab.com; @EatLeBab; 11 pm, Sun 7 pm.

Babaji Pide W1 £39 223
73 Shaftesbury Ave 020 3327 3888 5–3A
Hakkasan founder Alan Yau's year-old concept on Shaftesbury Avenue already "seems to have lost its first flush of fine food and enthusiasm". Fans do still say its "filled Turkish pizza (pide) are really quite special", but even they can find it "less memorably original" than it first was, and service can be "terrible" ("you just get forgotten!") / W1D 6EX; www.babaji.com.tr; 11 pm, Fri & Sat 11.30 pm, Sun 10 pm.

Babur SE23 £53 554
119 Brockley Rise 020 8291 2400 1–4D
It's "worth the trek" across south London to this "sensory experience" in Forest Hill. The modern Indian cuisine – amongst London's best – has huge "subtlety of flavour" and the "unfailingly friendly and positive staff" are "exceptional". / SE23 1JP; www.babur.info; @BaburRestaurant; 11.30 pm.

Babylon, Kensington Roof Gardens W8 £72 223
99 Kensington High St 020 7368 3993 6–1A
"Wonderful views over west London" are a pull at this "specially situated" and "moodily decorated" Kensington penthouse, where you can cap off a meal with a stroll around the incredible roof gardens. Reactions to the modern British cuisine are mixed – to fans "ambitious and well executed", to foes "pretentious style over substance". / W8 5SA; www.virginlimitededition.com/en/the-roof-gardens/b; 10.30 pm; closed Sun D; set weekday L £46 (FP), set Sun L £51 (FP); SRA-3 star.

Bacco TW9 £49 333
39-41 Kew Rd 020 8332 0348 1–4A
This "unpretentious" Italian local is "convenient for both the Orange Tree and Richmond theatres" – as well as being close to the station. "Unfortunately, it's not always consistent", but "homemade pasta is a strong suit", and "when on form it's fabulous". / TW9 2NQ; www.bacco-restaurant.co.uk; @BaccoRichmond; 11 pm; closed Sun.

Bageriet WC2 £14 343
24 Rose St 020 7240 0000 5–3C
"Swinging a cat would be hard" at this "tiny" Swedish café in Covent Garden with "excellent coffee", "incredible cakes and pastries"… and just eight chairs: "I just wish I could get a seat more often!" There's always take-away, and "the loaves they sell are pretty good, too". / WC2E 9EA; www.bageriet.co.uk; @BagerietLondon; 7 pm; closed Sun.

The Balcon, Sofitel St James SW1 £65 222
8 Pall Mall 020 7968 2900 2–3C
As a "good bet for a business lunch" or other West End rendezvous, this ex-bank off Trafalgar Square offers "wonderful architecture" and "a posh French bistro-style menu", which most – if not all – reporters say is "better than your typical, upmarket, chain-hotel brasserie". / SW1Y 5NG; www.thebalconlondon.com; @TheBalcon; 10.45 pm, Sun 9.45 pm.

Balthazar WC2 £69 113
4-6 Russell St 020 3301 1155 5–3D
"Riding the wave of its superior NYC cousin", Keith McNally's "buzzy" Grand Café in Covent Garden "could never live up to the hype that was built up around it, and it consistently falls flat". Sure, the "ornate" interior looks "spectacular", but the brasserie fare – no better than "fine" – is "horrendously expensive", and the room can

become "chaotic and noisy", not helped by "service that manages to be simultaneously over-pushy and neglectful". Top Tip – "a classic for brunch". / WC2B 5HZ; www.balthazarlondon.com; @balthazarlondon; midnight, Sun 11 pm.

Baltic SE1 **£54** **344**
74 Blackfriars Rd 020 7928 1111 10–4A
"Don't be distracted by the large list of homemade flavoured vodkas" and you can enjoy some "surprisingly interesting and varied Polish and Eastern European food" ("a cut above the usual stodge") at this "deceptively spacious" venue ("cocktail bar at the front, more formal dining area beyond"), whose "high ceilings and sparse modern look" result from the conversion of a Georgian factory near The Cut. / SE1 8HA; www.balticrestaurant.co.uk; @balticlondon; 11.15 pm, Sun 10.30 pm; closed Mon L.

Bandol SW10 **£67** **332**
6 Hollywood Rd 020 7351 1322 6–3B
"High quality" Niçoise and Provençal sharing plates with wine from the region are the draw at this Chelsea yearling (from the people behind nearby Margaux). "Always great for delicious, light food – I could go back every week!" / SW10 9HY; www.barbandol.co.uk; @Margaux_Bandol; 11 pm, Sun 10 pm.

Bánh Bánh SE15 **£33** **453**
46 Peckham Rye no tel 1–4D
"Beautifully prepared Vietnamese food" from "a well-executed short menu" has won instant raves for this "absolutely charming" Peckham Rye newcomer – "only recently evolved from pop-up to permanent" and run "exceptionally well" by five siblings from the Nguyen family (plus mum). "Delicious cocktails too". / SE15; www.banhbanh.com; @BanhBanhHQ; 10 pm, Fri & Sat 10.30 pm, Sun 9 pm; closed Mon, Tue-Fri D only, Sat & Sun open L & D.

Banners N8 **£43** **345**
21 Park Rd 020 8348 2930 1–1C
This hallowed all-day Crouch End stalwart majors on "big portions and big flavours", with a strong Caribbean bias on its menu of world food. It's particularly "great for breakfast/brunch" (perhaps less distinguished at other times), and has "a wonderful community feel". / N8 8TE; www.bannersrestaurant.com; 11 pm, Fri 11.30 pm, Sat midnight, Sun 10.30 pm; no Amex.

Bao **£28** **422**
31 Windmill St, W1 01442 510 520 5–1A
53 Lexington St, W1 awaiting tel 4–2C
"Pillowy-soft" and "very more-ish" Taiwanese steamed buns – "sublime pockets of taste" filled with "fabulously spiced meats" – justify the ever-present queues for this Soho phenomenon. "They like you in and out quickly", and "the tiny premises and jam-packed tables don't encourage lingering". (A second Fitzrovia branch opened in mid-2016 in the premises that were Boopshis.)

Baozi Inn WC2 **£24** **422**
26 Newport Ct 020 7287 6877 5–3B
This "cheap, kitsch and wacky" Chinatown caff "hung with Chairman Mao memorabilia" serves "great steamed buns, dandan noodles and dumplings" and "is ideal both for a snack or to fill up". Disclaimers: "you may have to wait", "it will never win points for service or comfortable chairs", it's "cash only, and don't expect to linger". / WC2H 7JS; www.baoziinnlondon.com; 10 pm, Fri & Sat 10.30 pm; cash only; no bookings.

Bar Boulud, Mandarin Oriental SW1 **£71** **233**
66 Knightsbridge 020 7201 3899 6–1D
"The gourmet burgers are worth all the hype" at this relatively "casual" Belgravia outpost of the NYC super-chef, and although it's "full of suits and monied types", other dishes on the "Lyon-via-Manhattan" menu are "reasonable value for the ultra-luxe location" (in the basement of a super-swanky Knightsbridge hotel). / SW1X 7LA; www.barboulud.com; @barbouludlondon; 10.45 pm, Sun 9.45 pm; set weekday L & dinner £37 (FP).

Bar Esteban N8 **£39** **444**
29 Park Rd 020 8340 3090 1–1C
"Fabulous, lip-smacking tapas and great service" bring the Crouch End crowd to this "busy, fun" local – "we're so lucky to live nearby!" / N8 8TE; www.baresteban.com; @barestebanN8; Mon-Thu 9.30 pm, Fri & Sat 10.30 pm, Sun 9 pm.

Bar Italia W1 **£32** **235**
22 Frith St 020 7437 4520 5–2A
"When in London, I just HAVE to go for my espresso fix!" – this legendary Italian pitstop in the heart of Soho is "not the absolute best for coffee, nor the best for service, but still the winner on ambience, style and history", and rammed at all hours. / W1D 4RF; www.baritaliasoho.co.uk; @TheBaristas; open 24 hours, Sun 4 am; no Amex; no bookings.

Bar Termini W1 **£35** **345**
7 Old Compton St awaiting tel 5–2B
"What it lacks in size it makes up in for in substance..." Tony Conigliaro's "tiny" Soho joint is "a reminder of how bars work in Italy – great cappuccino in the morning and then exquisitely prepared aperitifs, digestivi and cocktails". "The bar food's authentic and the Negronis short and sharp as they should be!" / W1D 5JE; www.bar-termini.com; @Bar_Termini; Mon-Thu 11.30 pm, Fri & Sat 1 am, Sun 10.30 pm.

The Barbary WC2 **£44**
16 Neal's Yard awaiting tel 5–2C
From the team behind smash-hit, The Palomar, comes a new summer 2016 venture celebrating the tastes of the Barbary Coast, from North Africa to Jerusalem. The tiny, 24-cover venue in Neal's Yard doesn't take bookings, unfortunately: we suggest you start queuing now. / WC2H 9DP; www.thebarbary.co.uk; no bookings.

Barbecoa **£66** **222**
Nova, Victoria St, SW1 no tel 2–4C
194-196 Piccadilly, W1 awaiting tel 4–4C
20 New Change Pas, EC4
020 3005 8555 10–2B
For "a good, if expensive" business lunch, numerous expense accounters recommend Jamie Oliver's "rather American-feeling shed of a space, in a shopping centre, overlooking St Paul's" (with branches in Victoria and Piccadilly), whose speciality is US style BBQ. Even some fans feel "it's really not worth the price you pay" however, and to sceptics it's just totally "uninspiring and average". / @Barbecoa_london.

La Barca SE1 **£75** **222**
80-81 Lower Marsh 020 7928 2226 10–4A
An "unassuming-looking" age-old trattoria near Waterloo station capable of some "quality, traditional Italian" cooking; even fans advise care when ordering however – "order a pasta and a glass of decent vino and you can escape with a modest bill", otherwise it can be "ridiculously expensive". / SE1 7AB; www.labarca-ristorante.com; @labarca1976; 11.30 pm; closed Sat L & Sun.

Il Baretto W1 **£74** **222**
43 Blandford St 020 7486 7340 2–1A
Despite pukka backing and high prices, this "noisy" basement Italian in Marylebone continues to inspire a mixed rep. As a business venue it has its fans, but scores are mixed given a pizza and pasta offering that can seem "hideously expensive for what it really is". / W1U 7HF; www.ilbaretto.co.uk; @IlBarettoLondon; 10.15 pm, Sun 9.45 pm; set weekday L £50 (FP).

Barnyard W1 **£44** **233**
18 Charlotte St 020 7580 3842 2–1C
Ollie Dabbous's "deliberately barn-like" Fitzrovia "novelty" hasn't particularly made waves of late, but escaped the harsh critiques of last year, with fans "more than impressed" by its eclectic comfort-food small plates (although they're too small for some tastes… especially at the price). / W1T 2LZ; www.barnyard-london.com; Mon-Wed 10 pm, Thu-Sat 10.30 pm, Sun 8.30 pm.

Barrafina **£42** **555**
54 Frith St, W1 020 7813 8016 5–2A
10 Adelaide St, WC2 020 7440 1456 5–4C
43 Drury Ln, WC2 020 7440 1456 5–2D
"It's a theatrical experience to watch your food being prepared with such artistic delicacy and loving care" at the Hart Bros' "rightly celebrated" bars, whose "utterly brilliant" tapas is "better even than in Barcelona". Despite "a queue visible from the space station" (at W1 especially), the food is "totally worth the wait every time" and the "terrific and very kind" staff add to the "wonderfully dynamic" atmosphere. "Exceptionally, the spin-offs are as good as the original" (each is "subtly different"), but in autumn 2016, change is afoot, as the original Frith Street branch moves site into the redeveloped ground floor of nearby Quo Vadis (see also). Top Menu Tip – "everything is bloomin' marvellous and fresh, but anything out of the sea most especially so". / www.barrafina.co.uk; 11 pm, Sun 10 pm; no booking.

Barrica W1 **£55** **333**
62 Goodge St 020 7436 9448 2–1B
"Utterly reliable Goodge Street tapas and wine bar, serving much more interesting and substantial offerings than the norm". With "scrumptious plates and a strong wine list", it's "as close to authentic as you'll get". / W1T 4NE; www.barrica.co.uk; @barricatapas; 10.30 pm; closed Sun.

Barshu W1 **£56** **422**
28 Frith St 020 7287 6688 5–3A
"If you like really good spicy food, look no further" – this Sichuan café in Soho shows a "rare fidelity" to the fiery cuisine, and provides "a good alternative to the standard Chinese in nearby Chinatown". "Favourites include numbing and hot dried beef, and dry wok pig intestines". / W1D 5LF; www.barshurestaurant.co.uk; 10.30 pm, Fri & Sat 11 pm.

Bbar SW1 **£54** **343**
43 Buckingham Palace Rd
020 7958 7000 2–4B
"A handy pitstop within the Victoria area" – overlooking the Royal Mews – this bar/restaurant "provides a good selection of South African wines and tasty bar snacks", with "great moist burgers" the highlight of the "South African-inspired menu". / SW1W 0PP; www.bbarlondon.com; @bbarlondon; 10 pm; closed Sun D; no shorts.

Bea's Cake Boutique WC1 **£39** **323**
44 Theobalds Rd 020 7242 8330 2–1D
"The best cupcakes in London", swoon fans of the Bloomsbury original – a cosy café near Gray's Inn. Naturally it's "absolutely fantastic for afternoon tea". / WC1X 8NW; www.beasofbloomsbury.com; @beas_bloomsbury; 7 pm; L only.

Beast W1 **£115** **222**
3 Chapel Pl 020 7495 1816 3–1B
"Huge" portions of high-quality surf 'n' turf – served in "the most dramatic setting" of candlelit communal

tables – is the bold proposition of this Goodman-owned two-year-old off Oxford Street. But even if "the food is excellent, prices are way OTT", and very "hard to justify". And it's not a place for an "intimate date" – more of an "expensive team night out" if you've got a boss with deep pockets. / W1G 0BG; www.beastrestaurant.co.uk; @beastrestaurant; 10.30 pm; closed Mon L, Tue L, Wed L & Sun.

Beer & Buns EC2 **£36** **334**
3 Appold St 020 7539 9209 13–2B
"A wide selection of Japanese beers with the musical backdrop of heavy rock" sets the scene at this (permanent) 'pop up izakaya', above K10 – "so much fun", with buns and spicy wings that are "so tasty". / EC2A 2AF; www.beerandbuns.co.uk; @Beer_And_Buns; Mon-Fri 11 pm; closed Mon L, Tue L, Wed L, Sat & Sun.

The Begging Bowl SE15 **£37** **543**
168 Bellenden Rd 020 7635 2627 1–4D
"Way above the level of anything else Thai for miles around Peckham" – this no-booking hotspot may be "more cramped than a hamster's cage thanks to its popularity" (and "is not cheap") but provides "friendly, accommodating service" and superbly "tasty, spicy food". / SE15 4BW; www.thebeggingbowl.co.uk; @thebeggingbowl; Mon-Sat 9.45 pm, Sun 9.15 pm; no bookings.

Bel Canto, Corus Hotel Hyde Park W2 **£58** **234**
1 Lancaster Gate 020 7262 1678 7–2C
Expect to have your dinner punctuated by professionally sung operatic arias if you dine at this Bayswater basement dining room, solidly-rated (albeit on limited feedback) in all aspects of its operation. / W2 3LG; www.belcantolondon.co.uk; 10.30 pm; D only, closed Mon & Sun.

Bellamy's W1 **£61** **343**
18-18a Bruton Pl 020 7491 2727 3–2B
"The tucked-away location adds to the charm" of Gavin Rankin's "very clubbable", "art-lined" brasserie, in a "picturesque mews" – "a delightful choice for a civilised lunch, whether for business or pleasure", serving "a limited choice" of "very good, bistro-style dishes", which are "reasonably priced… for Mayfair". (One of a handful of London restaurants ever visited by The Queen.) / W1J 6LY; www.bellamysrestaurant.co.uk; 10.30 pm; closed Sat L & Sun.

Bellanger N1 **£58** **223**
9 Islington Grn 020 7226 2555 9–3D
"Finally a 'grown-up' restaurant on Upper Street" – fans of Corbin & King's replacement for Browns (RIP) on Islington Green adore this "elegant", large yearling, with its "enveloping wood and brass interior". "The hype is a little overdone" though – the "kind-of-Alsatian menu" (lots of tartes flambées and choucroute) can seem "a tad underwhelming" (and "if you don't like this style of food, you have to pick your way through the menu") and all-in-all standards seem "reliable but unremarkable". / N1 2XH; www.bellanger.co.uk; @BellangerN1; 11 pm, Sun 10.30 pm.

Belvedere W8 **£69** **224**
Holland Pk, off Abbotsbury Rd
020 7602 1238 8–1D
"Nothing beats this venue" – a grand 17th-century former ballroom inside Holland Park – "for a summer lunch, it just has all the ingredients". But even fans concede that it's "not cheap" and that "the food won't blow your mind", and sceptics say "it should be wonderful, but needs a relaunch". / W8 6LU; www.belvedererestaurant.co.uk; 10.30 pm; closed Sun D.

Benares W1 **£95** **112**
12a Berkeley Square House,
020 7629 8886 3–3B
Fans still laud the "subtle, gorgeous flavours" of Atul Kochar's cuisine which have made this "classy" if slightly "oddly furnished (shades of the '70s)" gourmet Indian, in rambling first-floor premises by Berkeley Square, one of London's best-known dining destinations. However, its ratings have cratered in recent times due to too many experiences of "Keystone Kops" service and food that just seems "expensive and very average". / W1J 6BS; www.benaresrestaurant.co.uk; @benaresofficial; 10.45 pm, Sun 9.45 pm; closed Sun L.

Bentley's W1 **£82** **344**
11-15 Swallow St 020 7734 4756 4–4B
"Steeped in history", this 100-year-old institution near Piccadilly Circus is "most atmospheric in the downstairs oyster bar" (there's also a more stately first-floor restaurant). Richard Corrigan presides over "a fab choice of the finest fish, with oysters to die for". / W1B 4DG; www.bentleys.org; @bentleys_london; 10.30 pm, Sun 9.30pm; no shorts; booking max 8 may apply; set weekday L & pre-theatre £57 (FP).

Berber & Q E8 **£42** **435**
Arch 338 Acton Mews 020 7923 0829 14–2A
"It looks like style-over-substance, but it's the real deal!" – this "simply brilliant" North African-inspired grill in an oh-so-hip Haggerston railway arch continues to surf the zeitgeist with its lovely cocktails and "amazing, smoky, unctuous meat and stunning vegetable sides" (and, sadly, also its no bookings policy). / E8 4EA; www.berberandq.com; @berberandq; 10.30 pm, Sun 9.30 pm; D only, closed Mon.

Berber & Q Shawarma Bar EC1 **£30**
Exmouth Market 020 7837 1726 10–1A
From Hackney's Berber & Q founders, Josh & Paul Katz and Mattia Bianchi, this Exmouth Market

shawarma bar specialising in slow cooked, spit-roasted lamb and Middle Eastern-style rotisserie chicken opened post-survey in June 2016. / EC1R 4QL; www.berberandq.com; @berberandq; Tue-Sat 10.30 pm, Sun 9.30 pm; closed Mon; no bookings.

Bernardi's W1 £60 343

62 Seymour Street 020 3826 7940 2–2A

"There's a lot to like about this smart but fairly traditional Italian newcomer" in the calm corner of Marylebone off Seymour Place: "a great neighbourhood spot" where "everything is done properly" in a "modern Italian classic style without pretentions or a big bill". It's "huge" however, and when busy "would be transformed enormously by installing carpets to deaden noise", and "when empty has no atmosphere". / W1H 5BN; www.bernardis.co.uk; @BernardisLondon; 10.30 pm, Fri & Sat 11 pm, Sun 9 pm.

The Berners Tavern, London EDITION W1 £73 224

10 Berners St 020 7908 7979 3–1D

"A wow of a space" ("formerly a vast, voluminous banking hall") provides "a sunning backdrop" to a meal at what fans say is "London's chicest dining room", north of Oxford Street. It can seem like a case of "style over substance" though – the food (overseen by Jason Atherton) is "good but not amazing", and at the punishing price can seem "a huge let down". / W1T 3NP; www.bernerstavern.com; 11.45 pm, Sun 10.15 pm.

Best Mangal £36 432

619 Fulham Rd, SW6 020 7610 0009 6–4A
104 North End Rd, W14
020 7610 1050 8–2D
66 North End Rd, W14 020 7602 0212 8–2D

"Not your average kebab joints" – this Turkish trio in west London are popular "cheap 'n' cheerful" pitstops due to their "very good charcoal-grilled meats and super-fresh salads", in "very generous" portions. / www.bestmangal.com; midnight, Sat 1 am; no Amex.

Bibendum SW3 £76

81 Fulham Rd 020 7581 5817 6–2C

"One of London's great dining spaces" – this "spacious room in an iconic site" (the old Michelin Building on Brompton Cross) is best enjoyed at lunchtime when "the daylight filtering through the skylight is lovely". Its "refinement and elegance" and "very fine" wine list make it a still-popular business treat, but – in contrast to the physical refurbishment this year – "a shake-up of the kitchen is overdue": the food is too often "rather ordinary", especially at the "OTT prices". STOP PRESS – the longed for shake-up is coming soon – chef Claude Bosi is rumoured to be moving here in February 2017! / SW3 6RD; www.bibendum.co.uk; @bibendumltd; 11 pm, Sun 10.30 pm; booking max 12 may apply.

Bibendum Oyster Bar SW3 £53 424

81 Fulham Rd 020 7589 1480 6–2C

This "wonderful tiled room" off the foyer of Michelin House is a well-known Chelsea rendezvous for "good seafood and a glass of wine". "The shellfish platter is still superb, as is their petit pot de chocolat". STOP PRESS – the Claude Bosi managed makeover of the main restaurant is likely to involve this ground floor space: details are as yet unknown. / SW3 6RD; www.bibendum.co.uk; @bibendumrestaurant; 10 pm; no bookings.

Bibimbap £29 222

10 Charlotte St, W1 020 7287 3434 2–1C
11 Greek St, W1 020 7287 3434 5–2A
39 Leadenhall Mkt, EC3
020 7283 9165 10–2D

"Grab a cheap, fast bite in a spendy part of town", at these "bustling no-frills Korean canteens" in Soho and Fitzrovia (plus 'To Go' in the City). There's the odd cautionary report though: "I've been coming for years and am really disappointed with my last 2 visits – dry rice in the signature dish, and heavy handed on the soy!"

Bibo SW15 £51 333

146 Upper Richmond Rd
020 8780 0592 11–2B

"Interesting Italian food" (for example, "spicy n'duja croquettes, rabbit ragu and Amalfi lemon doughnuts") make this Putney sibling to Sonny's in Barnes "a high-end and accomplished" modern Italian: "not just the usual pasta but proper cooking". / SW15 2SW; www.biborestaurant.com; @biborestaurant; 10.45 pm.

Big Easy £54 223

12 Maiden Ln, WC2 020 3728 4888 5–3D
332-334 King's Rd, SW3 020 7352 4071 6–3C
Crossrail Pl, E14 020 3841 8844 12–1C

Fans report "an adequate meat-fest" and "great lobsters and shrimp" too at these "fun" US-style BBQ shacks, although "given the proliferation of other smokehouses nowadays" even supporters acknowledge "there's better BBQ elsewhere". Both Covent Garden and the Chelsea original outscore their huge new Canary Wharf sibling, which divides opinion; enthusiasts say "it's a great night out, with a stunning bar and top live music" – sceptics just feel it provides "horrible everything". / www.bigeasy.co.uk; @bigeasytweet; Mon-Thu 11 pm, Fri-Sat 11.30, Sun 10.30 pm.

Bill or Beak NW1 £14 44

Inside King's Boulevard 07791 787567 n/a–n/a

"Worth a detour and a rain-soaked lunch" – these habitués of (amongst other venues) Street Feast, Model Market, and Kerb stand out for reporters: "the Vietnamese pork and duck burger with truffle and Parmesan fries is worth a trip alone!" / NW1; www.billorbeak.co.uk; @BillorBeak.

Billy & The Chicks W1 £29 332
27-28 St Anne's Ct 020 7287 8111 5–2A
More "nicely seasoned fancy chicken" in Soho (opposite Zelman Meats) – this time deep-fried by Billy Stock (latterly of St John and Salt Yard Group), and as is now de rigueur using only free-range British birds (in this case Cotswold Whites). / W1F 0BN; www.billyandthechicks.com; @Billyandthechix; 11 pm; closed Sun.

The Bingham TW10 £66 344
61-63 Petersham Rd 020 8940 0902 1–4A
"Always a joy", this "delightful restaurant in the elegant surroundings" of a Richmond boutique hotel "has a balcony overlooking the garden and the River Thames" – "a treat for lunch or evening romance". There's also "afternoon tea to match anything in central London!" / TW10 6UT; www.thebingham.co.uk; 10 pm; closed Sun D; no trainers.

Bird £38 322
81 Holloway Rd, N7 020 3195 8788 9–2D
21-22 Chalk Farm Rd, NW1
020 3195 4245 9–2B
Westfield Stratford, Montfichet Road, E20 no tel 14–1D
42-44 Kingsland Rd, E2 020 7613 5168 13–1B
"You get exactly what you'd expect – tasty chicken, nothing more!" – at this "fun fried-chicken place" in Shoreditch (now with branches in Islington, Camden and Westfield). "The beer on hand isn't bad, either..."

Bird in Hand W14 £46 334
Brook Green 020 7371 2721 8–1C
"The pizzas are wonderful" ("if hardly cheap") and "the setting even better" at this "fun and lively" backstreet haunt in Olympia (sibling to The Oak in W11 and SW12). / W14 0LR; www.thebirdinhandlondon.com; @TBIHLondon; 10 pm, Sun 9.15 pm.

Bird of Smithfield EC1 £64 222
26 Smithfield St 020 7559 5100 10–2B
"It's popular with business lunchers", but this five-storey Georgian townhouse in Smithfield (with summer roof terrace) attracts somewhat mixed reviews ("OK"... "fine but unremarkable"). "Nice bar though". / EC1A 9LB; www.birdofsmithfield.com; @BirdoSmithfield; 10 pm; closed Sun.

Bistro Aix N8 £54 433
54 Topsfield Pde, Tottenham Ln
020 8340 6346 9–1C
"When you walk through the door you feel as though you're in France" at this small Crouch End bistro where "the cuisine is always good and the service exceptional". Fans agree it's "one of the best locals" – "I've been going for years and always get the same good quality food". / N8 8PT; www.bistroaix.co.uk; @bistroaixlondon; 10 pm, Fri & Sat 11 pm; Mon-Thu D only, Fri-Sun open L & D; no Amex.

Bistro Union SW4 £46 333
40 Abbeville Rd 020 7042 6400 11–2D
Adam Byatt's bistro spinoff from Trinity in Clapham is a "relaxed place for good British food" – "terrific value, great for the kids, excellent food and friendly staff". Top Tip – "Their Sunday Supper offering is a huge winner", BYO and kids eat free. / SW4 9NG; www.bistrounion.co.uk; @BistroUnion; 10 pm, Sun 8 pm.

Bistrotheque E2 £58 334
23-27 Wadeson St 020 8983 7900 14–2B
Critics may say it's "trading on its five minutes of fame as the original hipster hangout ten years ago", but most reports say this East End warehouse-conversion is "hard to find, but worth the effort" – "a light and airy space, with a solid range of offerings (particularly drinks...)" / E2 9DR; www.bistrotheque.com; @bistrotheque; 10.30 pm, Fri & Sat 11 pm; closed weekday L; set pre theatre £39 (FP).

Black Axe Mangal N1 £50 532
156 Canonbury Road no tel 9–2D
"Heavy metal kebabs!" – "The soundtrack is not for everyone" but "if you can handle the loud metal and strong spices", you can enjoy some "mindblowingly good" and unexpectedly audacious cooking at KISS-fan and owner Lee Tiernan's (ex-head chef of St John Bread & Wine) tiny, off-the-wall Highbury Corner newcomer. "Amazing" flatbread starters are followed up with extremely "different" kebab mains, many featuring offal. / N1; www.blackaxemangal.com; @blackaxemangal; Tue-Sat 10.30 pm, Sun 3 pm; closed Mon, Tue L, Wed L, Thu L, Fri L & Sun D; no bookings.

Black Roe W1 £66 333
4 Mill Street 020 3794 8448 3–2C
"Kicking off a new London craze for poké (a Hawaiian raw fish dish)" – Kurt Zdesar's (of Chotto Matte fame) "on-trend" newcomer in the heart of Mayfair also provides more substantial fare from a Kiawe (mesquite tree) wood grill. It's "very expensive", but "the food is zingy and fresh" and it has a good "clubby vibe". / W1S 2AX; www.blackroe.com; @blackroe; 10.45 pm; closed Sun.

Blacklock W1 £35 544
25 Great Windmill St 020 3441 6996. 4–2D
"The best chops in London", draw devotees to this "simple but winning" two-year-old in a bare-brick Soho basement that sells very little else. "Meat overload (in a good way)" – "smokey grilled chops, chips and wine: what's not to like?" The no-reservations policy is "a hassle, but they send you a text to come back from the pub when they're ready". / W1D 7LH; www.theblacklock.com; @blacklocksoho; 11.30 pm; closed Sun; may need 6+ to book.

Blanchette £39 445
9 D'Arblay St, W1 020 7439 8100 4–1C
204 Brick Lane, E1 020 7729 7939 13–1C
"A touch of France in the centre of London" – this

"buzzing" two-year-old "feels like it's been in Soho for years" and is "an excellent place for the price". "Traditional-ish Gallic dishes with a tapas twist" – "rustically presented and packed with flavour" – include "a good selection of regional French cheeses and charcuterie". 'Blanchette East' opened in mid-August 2016 on east London's curry mile, with a similar menu, but also new Southern French and North African dishes.

Blandford Comptoir W1 £53 444
1 Blandford Street 020 7935 4626 2–1A
"A superb wine list, well laid out, and fairly priced" (with 250 bins and 50 champagnes) is the cornerstone of this small Marylebone newcomer – from Texture and 28°-50° co-founder Xavier Rousset – but its varied menus of small and large plates gets a strong thumbs up too. / W1U 3DA; www.blandford-comptoir.co.uk; @BlandfordCompt; 10 pm.

Bleecker Street Burger E1 £16 522
Unit B Pavilion Building, Spitalfields Mkt
077125 40501 13–2B
"Undeniably the best burger in London, if not the UK and/or world!" – so claim devotees of former New York corporate lawyer Zan Kaufman's "basic" pop-up-gone-permanent in Spitalfields (and still also trading at various market locations). Their "simple, juicy beef patty in a bun doesn't try to be fancy or different, but ticks all the burger boxes". / E1 6AA; www.bleeckerburger.co.uk; @bleeckerburger; 9 pm.

Bleeding Heart Restaurant EC1 £64 335
Bleeding Heart Yd, Greville St
020 7242 8238 10–2A
"Time just flows away irrelevantly" at this "olde-worlde" warren, "hidden away in a yard" on the fringe of the City. Its "dark", Dickensian interior has "bucket loads of charm" and provides both "a propitious atmosphere for client deals" over "a lengthy lunch", and also a perfect spot "for a quiet tryst". The "fabulous wine list" ("with an Antipodean twist") outshines what is nevertheless "solid" French cuisine, delivered by "proper French waiters". / EC1N 8SJ; www.bleedingheart.co.uk; @bleedingheartyd; 10.30 pm; closed Sat & Sun.

Blixen E1 £52 344
65a Brushfield St 020 7101 0093 13–2B
This all-day Spitalfields brasserie (no relation to the Out of Africa writer) offers a "very enjoyable" menu from brunch to dinner, with "entertaining and helpful service". "The basement private dining area feels like a retro drinking den". / E1 6AA; www.blixen.co.uk; @BlixenLondon; 11 pm, Sun 8 pm.

Bluebird SW3 £64
350 King's Rd 020 7559 1000 6–3C
"Never again!" is still too often the verdict on this prominent D&D London landmark of nearly 20 years' standing on the King's Road whose airy interior should be "good for all occasions", but too often falls short when it comes to the "snooty" service or "limited and mediocre" food. In September 2016 it relaunched after a £2m refit – perhaps they will have finally sorted this one out. / SW3 5UU; www.bluebird-restaurant.co.uk; @bluebirdchelsea; 10.30 pm, Sun 9.30 pm.

Blueprint Café, Design Museum SE1 £51 225
28 Shad Thames, Butler's Wharf
020 7378 7031 10–4D
"The setting has lost none of its wow-factor" at this "river-view" dining room – a stunning vantage-point (binoculars are provided!) Since Jeremy Lee left a couple of years ago, some reports suggest the cooking has "lost its pizazz", but ratings aren't so bad, and in truth the food's never been the main point here. / SE1 2YD; www.blueprintcafe.co.uk; @BlueprintCafe; 10.30 pm; no bookings.

Bob Bob Exchange EC3
122 Leadenhall Street no tel 10–2D
This sibling to Soho's Bob Bob Ricard is to open in April 2017, occupying the entire third floor of 'The Cheesegrater'. More 'press for champagne' buttons are promised, alongside grills, bites, wine auctions and a sushi bar. One thing we know already: it won't be understated. / EC3V 4PE.

Bob Bob Ricard W1 £66 345
1 Upper James St 020 3145 1000 4–2C
"An emergency champagne button.... what more can you ask for!?" – Leonid Shutov's splendidly "OTT" Soho venue, with its conspiratorial and "romantic" booths, provides a "gorgeous setting for a fun night out" or "enjoyable brunch". Critics fear its "comfort" food is "expensive and ordinary", but most reporters feel it's "very enjoyable". / W1F 9DF; www.bobbobricard.com; @BobBobRicard; Sun-Fri 11.15 pm, Sat midnight; closed Sat L; jacket required.

The Bobbin SW4 £46 344
1-3 Lillieshall Rd 020 7738 8953 11–1D
This sidestreet gastropub "caters charmingly to everyone from the Clapham cool crowd to mums and dads with buggies". A "lovely little garden" and airy conservatory are ideal for "long and chilled Sunday lunches", but there's "plenty of vibe on Friday nights". / SW4 0LN; www.thebobbinclapham.com; @bobbinsw4; 10 pm, Sun 9 pm.

Bobo Social W1 **£45** **4 4 3**
95 Charlotte St 020 7636 9310 2–1C
"Highest quality" rare-breed burgers – "I am American, so you must take it as an article of faith that the Bobo burger is the best burger ever" – win high praise for this small town-house conversion in Fitzrovia. Critics say the decor is "too try-hard" but fans find it "refreshing". / W1T 4PZ; www.bobosocial.com; @BoboSocial; 10.30 pm; closed Sun.

Bocca Di Lupo W1 **£59** **5 4 4**
12 Archer St 020 7734 2223 4–3D
"Discover what REAL Italian food is all about" at Jacob Kennedy and Victor Hugo's "buzzing and exciting" venue, a short walk from Piccadilly Circus: its "inventive" tapas-style plates – an ever-changing selection "from the remotest corners of Italy" – are "unbelievably good" and backed up by a "gorgeous" wine list "full of regional gems". Sitting it at the bar, "watching the skill and intensity of the chefs" is a favourite perch. / W1D 7BB; www.boccadilupo.com; @boccadilupo; 11 pm, Sun 9.30 pm; booking max 10 may apply.

Bocconcino W1 **£72** **3 3 3**
19 Berkeley St 020 7499 4510 3–3C
"A real sensibly priced gem in Mayfair" – who'd have thought a Russian-owned yearling in this eurotrashiest heart of town would be this "very pleasant venue with good pizza and pasta"? "You could pay a lot more for poorer quality food just around the corner". / W1J 8ED; www.bocconcinorestaurant.co.uk; @BocconcinoUK; 11.30 pm, Sun 10.30 pm.

Al Boccon di'vino TW9 **£68** **4 4 5**
14 Red Lion St 020 8940 9060 1–4A
"Lucky Richmond" to have this "memorably amazing culinary experience" – "fabulous Italian food", but "no menu, no choices, no prices", just "a wild ride with a surprise for every course". "Only visit when you're hungry" – "you get a lot of food"; and "be prepared to share your happiness with the strangers at adjoining (very closely adjoining) tables". / TW9 1RW; www.nonsolovinoltd.co.uk; 8 pm; closed Mon, Tue L & Wed L; no Amex.

Bodean's **£44** **2 2 2**
10 Poland St, W1 020 7287 7575 4–1C
25 Catherine St, WC2 020 7257 2790 5–3D
4 Broadway Chambers, SW6
020 7610 0440 6–4A
348 Muswell Hill Broadway, N10 no tel 1–1C
225 Balham High St, SW17
020 8682 4650 11–2C
169 Clapham High St, SW4
020 7622 4248 11–2D
201 City Rd, EC1 020 7608 7230 13–1A
16 Byward St, EC3 020 7488 3883 10–3D
"A carnivore's paradise", these Kansas City-style BBQ joints have become a fixture after more than a decade in London, and they're still "great fun" if "a tiny bit formulaic" – even those who say the food's "only OK" say "it'll win you over if you're a meat-lover". / www.bodeansbbq.com; 11 pm, Sun 10.30 pm; booking: min 8.

La Bodega Negra W1 **£51** **3 3 4**
16 Moor St 020 7758 4100 5–2B
"Fun", "low-lit" basement Mexican in Soho – it gets mixed reviews for its food, but is "so funky that you almost forget about it". / W1D 5NH; www.labodeganegra.com; 1 am, Sun midnight.

Boisdale SW1 **£63** **2 2 3**
13-15 Eccleston St 020 7730 6922 2–4B
Ranald Macdonald's "civilised and fun" Belgravia bastion – if you like all things hearty and male – is known for its meaty Scottish fare ("splendid grouse" and other game in season), marvellous wines and whiskies, "excellent cigar terrace", and live jazz. Even those who feel prices are excessive, or have encountered "poor service", say they use "superb quality meat" and admit that results are "pretty good". / SW1W 9LX; www.boisdale.co.uk; @boisdaleCW; midnight; closed Sat L & Sun.

Boisdale of Bishopsgate EC2 **£66** **2 2 2**
202 Bishopsgate, Swedeland Ct
020 7283 1763 10–2D
"Down a narrow alley" near Liverpool Street, this City-outpost of the Victoria original has a ground floor bar, and below it "a very red, almost gothic-themed banquette-style dining room". Most often tipped as a business venue: even those who felt "the bill was rather high", say "the food was generally good, and steak excellent". / EC2M 4NR; www.boisdale.co.uk; @Boisdale; 11 pm, Sat midnight; closed Sat & Sun.

Boisdale of Canary Wharf E14 **£67** **2 2 3**
Cabot Pl 020 7715 5818 12–1C
The Canary Wharf spin-off from the Belgravia original is a popular expense-accounter choice thanks to its views, meaty Scottish fare ("not complex but good"), spacious interior and Thames-side cigar terrace. It does have its critics though, who say it's "hyped", or "OK but nothing special". / E14 4QT; www.boisdale.co.uk; @boisdaleCW; 11 pm; closed Sun D.

Bombay Brasserie SW7 **£60** **3 3 3**
Courtfield Road 020 7370 4040 6–2B
This "still stylish" South Kensington stalwart – known for its "bright and airy" conservatory – remains a "benchmark" for its fans, with its "subtle use of spices" and "comfortable" colonial decor. Its recent refurb doesn't wow everyone though, and some long-term fans feel "it's a shadow of its former self".

/ SW7 4QH; www.bombayb.co.uk; @bbsw7; 11 pm, Sun 10.30 pm; closed weekday L.

Bombay Palace W2 £49
50 Connaught St 020 7723 8855 7–1D
"Will it ever re-open?", sigh fans of this beloved – if monumentally dull-looking – Bayswater Indian. After a summer 2015 fire, its website has continued to promise that it will... and a date we understand has now been set as this guide goes to press (in autumn 2016). / W2 2AA; www.bombay-palace.co.uk; @bombaypalaceW2; 11 pm.

Bombetta E11
Station Approach 020 3871 0890 1–1D
A group of local foodies (including food writer Suzannah Butcher) have teamed up with owners of online Italian food suppliers The Chef's Deli, to open this new grill a short walk from Snaresbrook tube station, named for the Pugliese cheesy-meat street food bites that form part of its menu. It opened post-survey, but initial feedback suggests it's worth a try... especially if you're in Wanstead! / E11 1QE; www.bombettalondon.com; @bombettaLondon.

Bone Daddies £34 444
Nova, Victoria St, SW1 no tel 2–4C
14a, Old Compton St, W1
020 7734 7492 5–2B
30-31 Peter St, W1 020 7287 8581 4–2D
Whole Foods, Kensington High St, W8
020 7287 8581 6–1A
The Bower, Baldwin St, EC1
020 7439 9299 13–1A
"Power-packed flavours" ("you'll never be able to touch Wagamama noodles again!") inspire drooling reviews for these "very hip Japanese-Western hybrids" in Soho, in High Street Ken's Whole Foods, and now also in Shoreditch and Victoria. "Service is by staff who are laid-back, but still know their stuff". / www.bonedaddies.com; –.

Bonhams Restaurant, Bonhams Auction House W1 £69 453
101 New Bond St 020 7468 5868 3–2B
"Such a delight in a surprising location" – this "top-class" two-year-old sits off the back of the famous Mayfair auction house (with its own entrance). It's "a quiet and spacious" room in which to enjoy both Tom Kemble's accomplished cuisine and a "fantastic all-round wine list". / W1S 1SR; www.bonhams.com/locations/res; 8.30 pm; closed Sat & Sun.

Bonnie Gull W1 £59 443
21a Foley St 020 7436 0921 2–1B
"There's a real seaside feel to this small and cramped Fitzrovia dining room", whose "lovely and relaxed service", "casual, low-key appearance and nautical clichés belie the very tasty and sophisticated seafood that's served". / W1W 6DS; www.bonniegull.com; @BonnieGull; 9.45 pm, Sun 8.45 pm.

The Booking Office, St Pancras Renaissance Hotel NW1 £67 224
Euston Rd 020 7841 3566 9–3C
A "fantastic location" in the beautifully converted former St Pancras station ticket office, with a "quiet and comfy lounge" attached makes this a "great place to start the day with brunch" or for business meetings. The food? – "nothing exotic" but "reasonable". / NW1 2AR; www.bookingofficerestaurant.com; 11 pm.

Boondocks EC1
205 City Rd 07912 345678 13–1A
A follow-up to Bea Vo's Stax (which opened in Carnaby Street's Kingly Court last year) – this sizeable, two-floor newcomer north of the Old Street roundabout offers more American diner fare, and opened in late summer 2016. / EC1V 1JT; midnight.

Boqueria SW2 £34 344
192 Acre Ln 020 7733 4408 11–2D
"Bustling and busy" tapas bar between Clapham and Brixton, now with a Battersea offshoot. Both offer a "jolly" and "fun-packed" destination for "interesting tapas, drawing inspiration from the traditional (patatas bravas and tortilla) and beyond (tuna with almond and soy sauce)". / SW2 5UL; www.boqueriatapas.com; @BoqueriaTapas; 11 pm, Fri & Sat midnight, Sun 10 pm; closed weekday L.

Il Bordello E1 £51 345
81 Wapping High St 020 7481 9950 12–1A
"Cosy, friendly, lively, jolly" – this "quintessential neighbourhood Italian restaurant in Wapping is always overcrowded (a good sign)" and has particularly "enthusiastic" service. "It churns out huge portions of wholesome grub" (in particular "brilliant pizza") – "even when you are at your hungriest, you will find it hard to finish your plate!" / E1W 2YN; www.ilbordello.com; 11 pm, Sun 10.30 pm; closed Sat L.

Boro Bistro SE1 £42 333
Montague Cl, 6-10 Borough High St
020 7378 0788 10–3C
Limited reports on this small Gallic bistro (with outside terrace), by picturesque Southwark Cathedral – all are positive however on its food offering, which includes charcuterie boards and cheese platters. / SE1 9QQ; www.borobistro.co.uk; @borobistro; 10.30 pm.

The Botanist £64 212
7 Sloane Sq, SW1 020 7730 0077 6–2D
Broadgate Circle, EC2 020 3058 9888 13–2B
Attractive bar/restaurant on Sloane Square inspiring very mixed feelings: fans say it delivers "a buzzy atmosphere and surprisingly good food"

but for its harshest critics "it's a package made in hell": "slow, crowded, with indifferent service" and "awful, expensive cooking". (Limited feedback on its Broadgate sibling). / thebotanist.uk.com; @botanistchester; –.

Boudin Blanc W1 £59 234
5 Trebeck St 020 7499 3292 3–4B
The "magical" Shepherd Market location "guarantees it will be full most of the time" and – "if you can get an outside table in the sunshine" – this "very very French" bistro is "hard to beat". Its cooking is quite well-rated, but "the menu could do with a refresh", and "there's little sign of flair". / W1J 7LT; www.boudinblanc.co.uk; 11 pm.

Boulestin SW1 £70 222
5 St James's St 020 7930 2030 3–4D
Mixed views on Joel Kissin's St James's two-year-old, which revives the name of a famous French basement in Covent Garden and serves classic Gallic dishes. Fans proclaim it a "surprisingly chirpy and casual venue for SW1" with a "lovely courtyard" (and "excellent breakfasts" too), but one or two reports are dire, citing "dismal" results. / SW1A 1EF; www.boulestin.com; @BoulestinLondon; 10.30 pm; closed Sun; no trainers; set weekday L, dinner & pre-theatre £45 (FP).

The Boundary E2 £64 113
2-4 Boundary St 020 7729 1051 13–1B
"There's an amazing roof terrace, but the basement space is wonderful too" at Sir Terence Conran's Shoreditch operation. Supporters claim the food is likewise "excellent, with interesting combinations", but a worrying number just find it "boring and badly presented". / E2 7DD; www.theboundary.co.uk; @boundaryldn; 10.30 pm; D only, ex Sun L only.

The Brackenbury W6 £53 343
129-131 Brackenbury Rd
020 8741 4928 8–1C
"It's good having the Brack' back", say locals who love Ossie Gray's relaunched "perfect local" in the backstreets of Hammersmith, with its "interesting French/Italian dishes" and attractive summer terrace. It was refurbished this year, to make one of the two rooms a more informal, tapas-style bar. / W6 0BQ; www.brackenburyrestaurant.co.uk; @BrackenburyRest; 10 pm; closed Mon & Sun.

Bradley's NW3 £60 322
25 Winchester Rd 020 7722 3457 9–2A
"A mildly posh place, really convenient for Hampstead Theatre" – this backstreet stalwart in Swiss Cottage "lacks buzz" but its cooking is "worthwhile" and very "reliable". / NW3 3NR; www.bradleysnw3.co.uk; 10 pm; closed Sun D.

Brady's SW18 £34 333
Dolphin Hs, Smugglers Way
020 8877 9599 11–2B
"A great, local 'upmarket' fish 'n' chip restaurant" – "standards have stayed high at the Brady family's newish, much larger location near the river" in Battersea, which is "less manic" than its old longstanding home (which it vacated a couple of years ago). / SW18 1DG; www.bradysfish.co.uk; @Bradyfish; 10 pm; closed Mon, Tue L, Wed L, Thu L & Sun; no Amex; no bookings.

La Brasserie SW3 £56 224
272 Brompton Rd 020 7581 3089 6–2C
An "excellent French brasserie in the heart of Chelsea" – "reliable, unflashy and cosy", although even fans admit it's "not cutting-edge" and "the food quality could be improved". And it's "not the cheapest" either, but "stop complaining – you'd pay more for less in Paris!" / SW3 2AW; www.labrasserielondon.com; @labrasserie272; Mon-Sat 11.30 pm, Sun 11 pm.

Brasserie Blanc £52 122
"How does Raymond Blanc put his name to cooking of this quality?" This bland modern brasserie chain does have its fans as a business standby, but "it's gone downhill" in recent times – the food can be "very ordinary", service "perfunctory" and "there's no sense of emotional ownership". / www.brasserieblanc.com; most branches close between 10 pm & 11 pm; SE1 closed Sun D, most City branches closed Sat & Sun; SRA-2 star.

Brasserie Gustave SW3 £62 343
4 Sydney St 020 7352 1712 6–2C
"Interesting variations on French classics" and "a really warm welcome from the owners and wait staff" help this Chelsea brasserie two-year-old draw "a lively and eclectic crowd". Named for Gustave Eiffel – he of the famous Parisian tower – it happily plays up to the national stereotype. / SW3 6PP; www.brasserie-gustave.com; @brassergustave; 10.30 pm; closed weekday L; set weekday L & pre-theatre £38 (FP).

Brasserie Toulouse-Lautrec SE11 £45 333
140 Newington Butts 020 7582 6800 1–3C
"Solid" Gallic bistro cooking founds the appeal of this oasis in a gloomy quarter of Kennington; it also has "a superb little jazz bar upstairs", and "if you're lucky enough to sit on the tiny roof terrace, then it's like a tiny slice of Paris". / SE11 4RN; www.btlrestaurant.co.uk; @btlrestaurant; 10.30 pm, Sat & Sun 11 pm.

BRASSERIE ZÉDEL W1 £40 135
20 Sherwood St 020 7734 4888 4–3C
For "glamour on-the-cheap", nowhere matches Corbin & King's "so dazzling", gilded Art Deco

basement – "an approximation to a huge Paris brasserie" just seconds from Piccadilly Circus, where "keen prices for this location" amount to "unbeatable value". It is a trade-off though – service can be "rushed" and the brasserie fodder is "so mediocre". / W1F 7ED; www.brasseriezedel.com; @brasseriezedel; 11.45 pm.

Bravas E1 **£44** **3 3 2**
St Katharine Docks 020 7481 1464 10–3D
A "favourite" choice in St Katharine Docks for all who report – a Hispanic two-year-old, with dependable tapas and the picturesque backdrop of boats in the marina. / E1W 1AT; www.bravastapas.co.uk; @Bravas_Tapas; 10 pm.

Brawn E2 **£51** **5 4 4**
49 Columbia Rd 020 7729 5692 13–1C
Ed Wilson's "intelligently thought-out" dishes "always give the same hearty, down-to-earth impression" ("simple, with no pretension, but clearly demonstrating a superb level of skill and creativity, and great ingredients") at his East End venture (nowadays under his sole ownership). "It's a light and bright room" epitomising "the best of East London design hype – an ex-workshop, with exposed brick, and zinc things", and "those who dine in the back room have the benefit of being able to see the open kitchen". The "unusual and intriguing" wine list "is not a brief read, but it rewards those who select 'off piste' options". / E2 7RG; www.brawn.co; @brawn49; 11 pm; closed Mon L & Sun D; no Amex.

Bread Street Kitchen EC4 **£68** **2 2 3**
10 Bread St 020 3030 4050 10–2B
A "stylish" space and "lovely" breakfasts are two winning features of Gordon Ramsay's "enormous", "bustling" venue in a City shopping mall, most popular with expense-accounters. Scores have improved across the board in the last year, but there are still a fair few reporters who find it "noisy, expensive and totally uninspiring". / EC4M 9AJ; www.breadstreetkitchen.com; @breadstreet; 11 pm, Sun 8 pm.

Breakfast Club **£27** **3 3 2**
33 D'Arblay St, W1 020 7434 2571 4–1C
2-4 Rufus St, N1 020 7729 5252 13–1B
31 Camden Pas, N1 020 7226 5454 9–3D
12-16 Artillery Ln, E1 020 7078 9633 13–2B
"Quirky, retro-fit" '80s-nostalgia diners which seem to be "popping up all over the capital". They do have their critics ("can't even pull off being a funky greasy spoon") but for most reporters the main problems are crazy waits and being "squeezed-in". "So long as you get there early – before the queues form round the block – you'll find easy and informal service and enough tasty scoff to last you a whole day" – "everyone happy!" /

Briciole W1 **£40** **3 3 3**
20 Homer St 020 7723 0040 7–1D
A "favourite discovery", this "small slice of Italy" in Marylebone (little brother of Latium), is a "deli with a relaxing restaurant" serving "hearty dishes from delicious ingredients". / W1H 4NA; www.briciole.co.uk; @briciolelondon; 10.15 pm.

Brick Lane Beigel Bake E1 **£6** **4 1 1**
159 Brick Ln 020 7729 0616 13–1C
"Hectic at weekends but great fun" – this legendary 24-hour Brick Lane takeaway is redolent of a vanished East End… as are its prices. / E1 6SB; open 24 hours; cash only; no bookings.

The Bright Courtyard W1 **£60** **5 3 2**
43-45 Baker St 020 7486 6998 2–1A
The food at this modern Marylebone outfit "is absolutely epic" – "up there with the best Chinese in London, and much more reasonably priced than Hakkasan, etc". Dim sum are "very good and not very expensive", but the room is "a bit antiseptic" and the service "hit and miss". / W1U 8EW; www.lifefashiongroup.com; @BrightCourtyard; 10.45 pm, Thu-Sat 11.15 pm.

Brilliant UB2 **£38** **3 4 3**
72-76 Western Rd 020 8574 1928 1–3A
"Authentic dishes from the Punjab" draw fans from far and wide to the distant 'burbs of Southall, and this big and "buzzy" institution of over 40 years' standing. This family catering outfit was founded in Nairobi, adding a "heavy East African bias" to the cooking. / UB2 5DZ; www.brilliantrestaurant.com; @brilliantrst; 11 pm, Fri & Sat 11.30 pm; closed Mon, Sat L & Sun L.

Brinkley's SW10 **£57** **1 2 3**
47 Hollywood Rd 020 7351 1683 6–3B
A very "Chelsea crowd" is a defining feature of this "lively" bar/restaurant (near the C&W Hospital), as is John Brinkley's "excellent wine list", which is notably reasonably priced. No great prizes for the "brasserie-type fare" however – "it can be terrible". / SW10 9HX; www.brinkleys.com; @BrinkleysR; 11 pm, Sun 10.30 pm; closed weekday L.

Bronte WC2
Grand Buildings, 1-3 Strand awaiting tel 2–3C
On the site of the Strand Dining Rooms (RIP), this large newcomer has recently debuted off Trafalgar Square. It opened too late for survey feedback: early reviews suggest that despite a fairly wacky-sounding Pacific-fusion menu, the food is eclipsed by the dazzling Tom Dixon interior design. / WC2N 5EJ; www.bronte.co.uk; @bronte_london; no bookings.

The Brown Dog SW13 £51 322
28 Cross St 020 8392 2200 11–1A
"On a pretty terraced backstreet in Barnes", this countrified pub is packed out on Sundays for "the best roasts in the vicinity, and one of the best sticky toffee puddings anywhere". "As the name suggests, it helps to like hounds as customers bring 'em in". / SW13 0AP; www.thebrowndog.co.uk; @browndogbarnes; 10 pm, Sun 9 pm.

Brown's Hotel, The English Tea Room W1 £70 344
Albemarle St 020 7493 6020 3–3C
"Let yourself be transported away from the madding crowd to this peaceful haven of afternoon tea!", say fans of this very "traditional" hotel lounge, "with the tinkling piano in the background". "It may not be the most innovative, but the quality and quantity is second to none, and they really look after you". / W1S 4BP; www.roccofortehotels.com; 6.30 pm; no trainers.

Brown's Hotel, HIX Mayfair W1 £72 233
Albemarle St 020 7518 4004 3–3C
For "a grand hotel dining room experience", this "civilised" Mayfair landmark fits the bill, and its "well-spaced tables" and "professional" service add to its appeal "for a discreet business conversation". Its "classic British cuisine" is dependable for fans, but to critics it's "disappointing". / W1S 4BP; www.thealbemarlerestaurant.com; 11 pm, Sun 10.30 pm; set weekday L & dinner £55 (FP).

Brunswick House Café SSW8 £48 235
30 Wandsworth Rd 020 7720 2926 11–1D
"A huge, OTT architectural salvage and antiques shop" in a massive Georgian house in Vauxhall makes "a quirky and unusual setting" for this modern bistro. Service can be "a bit slow" and even fans find the food "variable", but hit lucky and a meal here is "fantastic". / SW8 2LG; www.brunswickhouse.co; 10 pm; closed Sun D.

Bubbledogs, Kitchen Table W1 £104 543
70 Charlotte St 020 7637 7770 2–1C
11/10 for originality to James Knappett and his "amazing" chef's table, tucked away at the back of his and his wife's adjoining hot dog place. "What an experience" – "a floor-show, gastronomical extravaganza and a bit of a mystery tour all combined. You'll find out what the main ingredient in each course is, but not know what you'll eat until it is presented to you by the chef". "Seeing it prepared is revelatory" and the flavours "jump out on your tongue!" / W1T 4QG; www.kitchentablelondon.co.uk; @bubbledogsKT; 6 pm & 7.30 pm seatings only; D only, closed Mon & Sun; credit card deposit required to book.

Buddha-Bar London SW1 £70 223
145 Knightsbridge 020 3667 5222 6–1D
With its "hip club" vibe, this Knightsbridge outpost of a Paris-based franchise is "let down a little by the pan-Asian food, but the atmosphere makes up for it"; "amazing cocktails (including one that arrived still smoking!)" too, along with "Asian afternoon tea that's a delicious alternative to the traditional variety". / SW1X 7PA; www.buddhabarlondon.com; @BuddhaBarLondon; 10 pm.

Buen Ayre E8 £53 422
50 Broadway Mkt 020 7275 9900 14–2B
"Steaks as good as some of the opulent chains, but served with authentic Argentinian flair and taste", can be found at this Hackney 'parilla'. The décor is simple and there's a "good wine list", but "the focus is the food". / E8 4QJ; www.buenayre.co.uk; 10.30 pm; no Amex.

The Builders Arms SW3 £48 224
13 Britten St 020 7349 9040 6–2C
Generous ratings this year for this attractively modernised pub in a cute Chelsea backstreet – fantastic atmosphere and acceptable scoff. / SW3 3TY; www.geronimo-inns.co.uk/london-the-builders; @BuildersChelsea; 10 pm, Thu-Sat 11 pm, Sun 9 pm; no bookings.

Bukowski Grill £38 432
10-11 D'Arblay St, W1 020 3857 4756 4–1C
Brixton Market, Unit 10 Market Row, SW9 020 7733 4646 11–2D
Boxpark, Unit 61, 4-6 Bethnal Green Rd, E1 020 7033 6601 13–2B
"Good burgers, ribs, shakes and no vitamin C in sight" pretty well sums up the appeal of this highly rated US-style mini-chain, with grills in Brixton, Shoreditch and Soho.

The Bull N6 £46 234
13 North Hill 020 8341 0510 1–1C
This "revived microbrewery" pub in Highgate is particularly known for being "great for a family Sunday lunch" – even the only reporter who found the food "disappointing" said "the atmosphere, service and beer filled the gap". / N6 4AB; thebullhighgate.co.uk; @Bull_Highgate; 10 pm.

Bull & Last NW5 £61 323
168 Highgate Rd 020 7267 3641 9–1B
"For a hearty meal after a walk on the heath", this "beaut' of a local" in Kentish Town, with its "spacious, shabby-chic interior" is a classic. However, even some who say "it sets the standard for revived north London boozers" feel "it's getting expensive now"... "a safe bet, but it doesn't reach the heights it once did". / NW5 1QS; www.thebullandlast.co.uk; @thebullandlast; 10 pm, Sun 9 pm.

Bumpkin £53 222
119 Sydney St, SW3 020 3730 9344 6–2B
102 Old Brompton Rd, SW7
020 7341 0802 6–2B
Westfield Stratford City, The Street, E20
020 8221 9900 14–1D
"Some days are really good, other days distinctly ordinary" at this rustically styled chain, where the odd report is of total disaster, but the best praise a "buzzy" atmosphere, plus "good and typically British" dishes. / www.bumpkinuk.com; 11 pm; closed Mon.

Buona Sera £42 333
289a King's Rd, SW3 020 7352 8827 6–3C
22 Northcote Rd, SW11
020 7228 9925 11–2C
"Perfect for a quick plate of pasta" or pizza – this "still reliable (and cheap)" Clapham café is "as lively as ever" after all these years. Less feedback on its "cosy" Chelsea spin-off with fun double-decker seating, but what we have says it is likewise "dependable and very noisy!" / midnight; SW3 11.30 pm, Sun 10 pm; SW3 closed Mon L.

Buoni Amici W12 £42 333
170 Goldhawk Road 020 8743 7335 8–1C
Trying hard in an under-developed corner of Shepherd's Bush: this Italian newcomer – a simple but attractive shop conversion – offers "a large menu (though not everything seems to be 'on' all the time)" and "pleasant service that's keen you should have a good time". / W12 8HJ; www.buoniamici.co.uk; @BuoniAmici; closed Mon; set weekday L £14 (FP).

Burger & Lobster £45 333
Harvey Nichols, 109-125 Knightsbridge, SW1
020 7235 5000 6–1D
26 Binney St, W1 020 3637 5972 3–2A
29 Clarges St, W1 020 7409 1699 3–4B
36 Dean St, W1 020 7432 4800 5–2A
6 Little Portland St, W1 020 7907 7760 3–1C
High Holborn, WC1 020 7432 4805 2–1D
40 St John St, EC1 020 7490 9230 10–1B
Bow Bells Hs, 1 Bread St, EC4
020 7248 1789 10–2B
"If you have the lobster, it's a top deal", according to the massive fanclub of this "so simple, so well-executed" concept. "It's less of a bargain for the burger", but they're "surprisingly good" too. / www.burgerandlobster.com; @Londonlobster; 10.30 pm; Clarges St closed Sun D, Bread St & St John St closed Sun.

Busaba Eathai £39 223
What Alan Yau did next after Wagamama: these handsome, communal Thai canteens remain an "easy" and "reliable" cheap 'n' cheerful choice. On the food front, "compromises over the years have resulted in less authenticity", but they are "approachably priced". / www.busaba.co.uk; 11 pm, Fri & Sat 11.30 pm, Sun 10 pm; W1 no booking; WC1 booking: min 10.

Butler's Restaurant, The Chesterfield Mayfair W1 £82 343
35 Charles St 020 7958 7729 3–3B
Perhaps it is "sedate" and old-fashioned in its styling, but this Mayfair dining room inspires a dedicated fanclub with its "informative" service and Ben Kelliher's quality, traditional British cuisine. / W1J 5EB; www.chesterfieldmayfair.com; @chesterfield_MF; 10 pm; jacket required.

Butlers Wharf Chop House SE1 £60 222
36e Shad Thames 020 7403 3403 10–4D
"Pleasant enough by the side of the Thames" – a harsh but fair verdict on this D&D group property near the better-known Pont de la Tour. The focus is on "fairly straightforward" grills, which are most "acceptable as long as you aren't paying". / SE1 2YE; www.chophouse-restaurant.co.uk; @bwchophousetowerbridge; 11 pm, Sun 10 pm.

La Buvette TW9 £42 333
6 Church Walk 020 8940 6264 1–4A
This "small neighbourhood bistro" attractively "out of the way" off the alleys surrounding St Mary Magdalene has become a fixture in the old heart of Richmond, serving a "limited but nicely prepared menu" of "heavily French-accented" regional cuisine (with occasional forays into Spain, Italy or Switzerland). Top Tip – "good value set menu". / TW9 1SN; www.labuvette.co.uk; @labuvettebistro; 10 pm.

Byron £38 233
"Still love it when a burger is needed!"; the leading 'posh patties' chain is "not what it was" when it first started, but the styling of its individually-designed branches are "a cut above other burger bars" and – while "it offers nothing mindblowing, it's the best failsafe" for its huge armies of fans. / www.byronhamburgers.com; most branches 11 pm.

C London W1 £102 113
25 Davies St 020 7399 0500 3–2B
"The crowd is from another planet" at this eurotrashy Mayfair haunt, which can seem "fun" if you've money to burn. The "simple" cooking isn't so much bad as "massively overpriced" – "service on the other hand is truly dreadful" – "do they have to train the staff to be so inattentive?" / W1K 3DE; www.crestaurant.co.uk; 11.45 pm.

C&R Cafe £35 422
3-4 Rupert Ct, W1 020 7434 1128 5–3A
52 Westbourne Grove, W2
020 7221 7979 7–1B
"I get frustrated if people want to eat anywhere else!" – its small fanclub adores this little, "cheap 'n'

cheerful" Malaysian café in Chinatown (its glossier Bayswater offshoot never inspires much feedback). Top Menu Tip – "fabulous Laksa". / www.cnrrestaurant.com; 10.30 pm; W2 closed Tue.

Caboose, The Old Truman Brewery E1 £31 234
Ely's Yd, Brick Ln 07437 209 275 13–2C
"Great fun" street food BYO, with burgers (and a few other dishes) served from a custom-built railway cabin outside Brick Lane's Old Truman Brewery. Get together a dozen or so friends, and you can have it to yourself for a 3-courser. / E1 6QR; www.wearecaboose.com; @WeAreCaboose; 11 pm.

Cacio & Pepe SW1 £54 444
46 Churton Street 020 7630 7588 2–4B
"In an underserved backwater of Pimlico", "a fine new addition to the ever-improving local restaurant scene", on the former site Mekong (RIP). Owned and run by former Fiorentina footballer Mauro Della Martira (father of 2013 Italian MasterChef winner Enrica Della Martira), it provides "excellent food with a Roman accent" and a "bustly and friendly atmosphere" (although the basement is "a little dark and less atmospheric"). / SW1V 2LP; www.cacioepepe.co.uk; 11 pm.

Café Below EC2 £40 223
St Mary-le-Bow, Cheapside
020 7329 0789 10–2B
"Simple, cheap, good-quality" cooking is on the menu at this "delightful" venue – but the trump card is its "setting in the atmospheric crypt of Bow Bells church". "When busy, conversation can be hard". / EC2 6AU; www.cafebelow.co.uk; 9 pm; closed Mon D, Tue D, Sat & Sun.

Café del Parc N19 £43 554
167 Junction Road 020 7281 5684 9–1C
"This tiny Tuffnell Park spot is an absolute winner", serving "interesting North African/Spanish tapas-style food". "No menu to speak of", "but you're in safe hands with a really confident and inspired chef" who sends out "a splendid succession of delicious and very varied surprises". / N19 5PZ; www.delparc.com; 10.30 pm; closed Mon, Tue, Wed L, Thu L, Fri L, Sat L & Sun L; no Amex.

Café du Marché EC1 £56 334
22 Charterhouse Sq 020 7608 1609 10–1B
"A cosy, candlelit piece of France" – this "delightfully atmospheric building", "tucked away" off Charterhouse Square, is "particularly lovely when there's live music at night", and even if its "traditional, French-bistro-style cooking" can seem "a bit old-fashioned", it's "honest" and "appetising". Still tipped for business lunching, but its prime forte nowadays is being "great for a date". / EC1M 6DX; www.cafedumarche.co.uk; @cafedumarche; 3.30 pm; L only, closed Sat & Sun.

Café East SE16 £23 422
100 Redriff Rd 020 7252 1212 12–2B
"Wonderful, fresh and healthy Vietnamese food" makes this Bermondsey canteen a regular stop for devotees of pho and other Viet classics. "It's the real thing and at a very reasonable price" – "certain dishes are just in a league of their own". / SE16 7LH; www.cafeeastpho.co.uk; @cafeeastpho; 10.30 pm, Sun 10 pm; closed Tue; no Amex.

Café in the Crypt, St Martin's in the Fields WC2 £33 224
Duncannon St 020 7766 1158 2–2C
The self-service crypt of St Martin-in-the-Fields, right on Trafalgar Square, makes a "delightful place to stop for a quick lunch in this busy part of London". It's "always buzzy, and so much better than a lot of the chains nearby" – and even if its soup, sarnies and light dishes are "not very special" they come in "good-sized portions", "and at very reasonable prices". / WC2N 4JJ; stmartin-in-the-fields.org/cafe-in-the-crypt; @smitf_london; 8 pm, Thu-Sat 9 pm, Sun 6 pm; no Amex; no bookings.

Café Monico W1 £61 234
39-45 Shaftesbury Avenue
020 3727 6161 5–3A
Soho House's latest West End foray in the thick of Theatreland aims to look like its been there for decades, with its carefully distressed, vintage looks, and brasserie menu overseen from afar by Rowley Leigh. "Its feel is not dissimilar to Les Deux Salons, but the food is much better and cheaper". / W1D 6LA; www.cafemonico.com; @cafemonico; midnight, Fri & Sat 1 am.

Cafe Murano £54 333
33 St James's St, SW1 020 3371 5559 3–3C
34-36 Tavistock St, WC2
020 3371 5559 5–3D
"Straightforward cooking, with a twist beyond the staple dishes" and "professional" service – all "without the mothership's high prices" – win high popularity for Angela Hartnett's spin-offs in St James's and Covent Garden. Some reports are sceptical though: "sure the food's fine, but mainstream, and do we need another star chef's standard West End option where the biggest excitement is their name?" / www.cafemurano.co.uk;

Café Pistou EC1 £46 322
8-10 Exmouth Mkt 020 7278 5333 10–1A
"Very enjoyable Provençal food" makes this all-day bistro a handy option even in happening Exmouth Market. The service is "very friendly", "even when the place is crowded". / EC1R 4QA; www.cafepistou.co.uk; @CafePistou; 10.30 pm.

Café Spice Namaste E1 £57 554
16 Prescot St 020 7488 9242 12–1A
Cyrus Todiwala's "genuine, exotic and intriguing"

Parsi cuisine "relies on spices rather than heat (though you can get that too)" and delivers some "perfect flavours". "The man himself is very jolly as he works the room" at his Whitechapel HQ, where there's "always a cheerful welcome, and great service". / E1 8AZ; www.cafespice.co.uk; @cafespicenamast; 10.30 pm; closed Sat L & Sun.

Caffè Caldesi W1 £61 333
118 Marylebone Ln 020 7487 0754 2–1A
"Wonderful, authentic Italian food" with an emphasis on robust Tuscan flavours makes this "no-nonsense" Marylebone fixture "a treat". "It's always full of Italians, which speaks volumes for the quality on offer". / W1U 2QF; www.caldesi.com; 10.30 pm, Sun 9.30 pm.

La Cage Imaginaire NW3 £49 223
16 Flask Walk 020 7794 6674 9–1A
"Such a pretty", "tiny bistro on a Hampstead backstreet"; try it in a forgiving frame of mind however – the "traditional Gallic cuisine" is "not the most exciting" (and can be "terribly bland" nowadays), and service is "friendly", but can have "shades of Fawlty Towers". / NW3 1HE; www.la-cage-imaginaire.co.uk; 11 pm.

Cah-Chi £37 342
394 Garratt Ln, SW18 020 8946 8811 11–2B
34 Durham Rd, SW20 020 8947 1081 11–2B
In the Korean enclaves of Raynes Park and Earlsfield, these "buzzy venues" are "very popular with ex-pats". Their "fresh" cooking delivers "super flavours" at "reasonable prices"; BYO. / www.cahchi.com; SW20 11 pm; SW18 11 pm, Sat & Sun 11.30 pm; SW20 closed Mon; cash only.

The Camberwell Arms SE5 £56 433
65 Camberwell Church St
020 7358 4364 1–3C
"A good reason to go to Camberwell!" – this Anchor & Hope sibling goes "from strength to strength", with fans even "daring to suggest" it outshines its stablemate. Not only do you get "excellent, well-sourced, seasonal British food", but "as a bonus, you can even get a table!" / SE5 8TR; www.thecamberwellarms.co.uk; @camberwellarms; closed Mon L & Sun D.

Cambio de Tercio SW5 £70 343
161-163 Old Brompton Rd
020 7244 8970 6–2B
"Superb, modern Spanish cooking complemented by an astonishing wine list, full of mouthwatering options" – plus notably "charming" service – maintain Abel Lusa's "fun and inviting" Earl's Court venture as "one of London's best". On the downside though, it can seem "too crowded" and "expensive". / SW5 0LJ; www.cambiodetercio.co.uk; @CambiodTercio; 11.15 pm, Sun 11 pm.

Camino £47 333
3 Varnishers Yd, Regent Quarter, N1
020 7841 7330 9–3C
The Blue Fin Building, 5 Canvey St, SE1
020 3617 3169 10–4A
15 Mincing Ln, EC3 020 7841 7335 10–3D
33 Blackfriars Ln, EC4 020 7125 0930 10–2A
"A good standby!" – these "fun" tapas stops (they can be "loud") offer "well-prepared dishes" ("sometimes way above average"), and a "decent modestly priced list of wines", beers and sherries. / www.camino.uk.com; EC3 & EC4 closed Sat & Sun.

Canada Water Cafe SE16 £39 343
40 Surrey Quays Road 020 3668 7518 12–2B
Very handy for Canada Water tube – an "efficient and friendly" (and "family-friendly") café, most popular for its "great sourdough pizzas" (though other fare is available). / SE16; www.canadawatercafe.com; 10.30 pm, Mon Sat, Sun 9 pm.

Cannizaro House, Hotel du Vin SW19 £58 233
West Side, Wimbledon Common 0871 943 0345 11–2A
This "romantic" and "plush" venue on the edge of Wimbledon Common, nowadays part of the Hotel du Vin group, offers dining in its bistro or Orangerie. Opinion is split on the experience, ranging from "very enjoyable" to "terrible". / SW19 4UE; www.hotelduvin.com/locations/wimbledon; @HotelduVinBrand; 10 pm.

Cantina Laredo WC2 £53 323
10 Upper St Martin's Ln 020 7420 0630 5–3C
"Upmarket" Mexican operation in Covent Garden, with "very fresh-tasting" dishes (guacamole a speciality); reporters do gripe however that it's "pricey". / WC2H 9FB; www.cantinalaredo.co.uk; @CantinaLaredoUK; 11.30 pm, Fri & Sat midnight, Sun 10.30 pm.

Canto Corvino E1 £62 444
21 Artillery Lane 020 7655 0390 13–2B
This "bright and sparse modern Italian", with its "very posh" decor is "a superb addition to the restaurant scene" around Spitalfields Market. The cooking – "an excellent range of small plates" – is "very fine", and service is "top class". Top Tip – "highly recommended for larger groups looking for a special dining experience". / E1 7HA; www.cantocorvino.co.uk; @cantocorvinoe1.

Canton Arms SW8 £48 434
177 South Lambeth Rd
020 7582 8710 11–1D
"Be prepared to wait for a table and then possibly to share it", if you visit this "jammed" Stockwell gastropub (sibling to the epic Anchor & Hope) – "it still feels like a proper pub", and serves "huge

portions of rustic hearty cuts of meat" and other "distinctive British dishes". / SW8 1XP; www.cantonarms.com; @cantonarms; 10.30 pm; closed Mon L & Sun D; no Amex; no bookings.

Canvas SW1 £71 232
1 Wilbraham Pl 020 7823 4463 6–2D
Limited feedback nowadays on this ambitious basement off Sloane Street (once Le Cercle, RIP). Fans still say it's "romantic" and rate its contemporary cuisine highly, but some reports are of "bizarre dishes that do not work". / SW1X 9AE; www.canvaschelsea.com; @CanvasbyMR; 9.30 pm, Fri & Sat 10 pm; D only, closed Mon.

Capote Y Toros SW5 £49 344
157 Old Brompton Rd 020 7373 0567 6–2B
"The croquetas are the best this side of the Pyrenees", claim fans of Cambio de Tercio's perhaps "over-noisy" but "superbly atmospheric" neighbouring bar, serving "delightful" tapas, with "a joy" of a "comprehensive (if, to be fair, not cheap) wine list and gin menu". / SW5 0LJ; www.cambiodetercio.co.uk; @CambiodTercio; 11.30 pm; D only, closed Mon & Sun.

Le Caprice SW1 £75 344
Arlington Hs, Arlington St
020 7629 2239 3–4C
"The magic never fades" at this "island of casual sophistication and understatement" near the Ritz – "still wonderfully fashionable after all these years", and charmingly presided over by "the amazing Mr Jesus Adorno". That said, while the cooking has always been "nursery" style, it has become more "unexciting" during the tenure of current owner, Richard Caring. / SW1A 1RJ; www.le-caprice.co.uk; @CapriceHoldings; 11.30 pm Mon-Sat, Sun 10.30 pm.

Caraffini SW1 £54 354
61-63 Lower Sloane St 020 7259 0235 6–2D
"Marvellous, long-surviving, honest Italian", near Sloane Square, "which can be recommended without fear of disappointment". The "home-cooked" food "never shines but never misses", while "it's the service that lifts the experience to the next level" and lends the place its "happy" atmosphere – "even first-timers are greeted as regulars", and "waiters are equally charming with your 12-year-old as with your gran". / SW1W 8DH; www.caraffini.co.uk; Mon-Fri 11.30 pm, Sat 11 pm; closed Sun.

Caravaggio EC3 £62 233
107-112 Leadenhall St 020 7626 6206 10–2D
This "City lunchtime favourite" (a spacious Italian, near Leadenhall Market) scored hits and misses this year – some disappointments were recorded, but other reports applaud its "well-cooked fare and very efficient service". / EC3A 4DP; www.etruscarestaurants.com; 10 pm; closed Sat & Sun.

Caravan £52 323
1 Granary Sq, N1 020 7101 7661 9–3C
Metal Box Factory, Great Guildford Street, SE1
no tel 10–4B
11-13 Exmouth Mkt, EC1
020 7833 8115 10–1A
"Crazy eclectica rubs shoulders with family favourites" on the sometimes "bizarre" menu of these "bustling" "cheek-by-jowl" fusion haunts, whose "phenomenal coffee by itself would score a 6/5!" and helps establish them both as major brunch hangouts. Nowadays the "ever-busy" Exmouth Market branch is eclipsed by its huge, "super-cool" Granary Square sibling in King's Cross, where "media types from The Guardian and students from adjacent St Martin's" bolster the "hip and trendy" vibe. Stop Press – a third branch is to open on Bankside. / www.caravanonexmouth.co.uk; EC1 10.30 pm, Sun 4 pm; closed Sun.

Carob Tree NW5 £35 353
15 Highgate Rd 020 7267 9880 9–1B
"The terrific fish is the thing to go for" (although the meat is "well cooked" too) at this very busy local Greek in Dartmouth Park, where "the owners treat you as a long-lost friend even if you have never been in their place before". / NW5 1QX; 10.30 pm, Sun 9 pm; closed Mon; no Amex.

Carousel W1 £54 454
71 Blandford St 020 7487 5564 3–1A
"A different guest chef every week" makes this "engaging and informal" ("shared trestle tables") Marylebone merry-go-round a "fabulous way to try new cuisines" from around the world; on a good night here, the food is "a revelation!" / W1U 8AB; www.carousel-london.com; 11.30 pm.

Casa Brindisa SW7 £46 222
7-9 Exhibition Rd 020 7590 0008 6–2C
"Convenient for the museums", this outpost of the Brindisa group near South Kensington station offers a menu of Spanish small plates, wines and sherries familiar from the Borough Market original, but as a tapas bar it feels a bit "formulaic", and its marks lag behind accordingly. / SW7 2HE; www.brindisatapaskitchens.com/casa-brindisa; @TapasKitchens; 11 pm, Sun 10 pm.

Casa Cruz W11 £48 244
123 Clarendon Rd 020 3321 5400 7–2A
This lavish pub conversion with a copper bar and "shiny gold mirrors" on the edge of Notting Hill was opened last year by Argentinian restaurateur Juan Santa Cruz. While reporters generally favour its performance including the Argentinian-inspired European food, even fans can find it "overpriced". / W11 4JG; www.casacruz.london; @CasaCruzrest; 12.30 am, Sun 5 pm; closed Mon.

Casa Malevo W2 £57 342
23 Connaught St 020 7402 1988 7–1D
"Very good steaks" headline the Latino menu at this cosy, tucked-away Argentinian, in Bayswater; also praised for its "very good service". / W2 2AY; www.casamalevo.com; @casamalevo; 10.30 pm, Sun 10 pm.

Casita Andina W1
Great Windmill Street 020 3327 9464 4–3D
Martin Morales (the restaurateur behind Ceviche and Andina) launched a fourth London Peruvian post-survey in Soho in summer 2016. Apparently it's inspired by Peru's 'picanterias': family-run, traditional restaurants, serving Andean dishes and small bites. / W1F 9UE; www.twitter.com/casitaandina; @CasitaAndina.

Casse-Croute SE1 £45 434
109 Bermondsey St 020 7407 2140 10–4D
"Are you sure this isn't really in a French suburb?" – this "real Gallic bistro in Bermondsey" serves "classic bistro fare with a twist" from a "simple and well-executed menu" on "a daily changing blackboard". "You'll have to breathe in to sit down in this tiny place when it's busy, but it's worth it!" / SE1 3XB; www.cassecroute.co.uk; @CasseCroute109; 10 pm, Sun 4 pm; closed Sun D.

Cau £49 122
10-12 Royal Pde, SE3 020 8318 4200 1–4D
33 High St, SW19 020 8318 4200 11–2B
1 Commodity Quay, E1
020 7702 0341 10–3D
Ratings have dipped at this national Argentinian-themed steakhouse chain, of which the Wimbledon Village branch is by far the best known. Some "yummy steaks" are reported, but there are a concerning number of let-downs ("it looked great, but wasn't properly prepared"). / @CAUrestaurants;

The Cavendish W1 £60 333
35 New Cavendish St 020 7487 3030 2–1A
With its comfortable leather banquettes, upmarket brasserie menu, cigars and cocktails, this Marylebone pub-conversion is consistently well rated as a "pricey-but-good" experience. / W1G 9TR; 35newcavendish.co.uk; @35newcavendish; 10.30 pm, Sun 5.45 pm.

Caxton Grill SW1 £75
2 Caxton St 020 7227 7773 2–4C
Adam Handling's brief stint in the "glorious" dining room of this tucked-away Westminster Hotel has at least put it back on London's culinary map – after his May 2016 departure, whether it stays remains to be seen… / SW1H 0QW; www.caxtongrill.co.uk; 10.30 pm.

Cây Tre £36 433
42-43 Dean St, W1 020 7317 9118 5–2A
301 Old St, EC1 020 7729 8662 13–1B
"Fresh, zingy Vietnamese food" makes these "affordable" Soho and Shoreditch venues a "trusty option", especially for an "excellent-value set lunch" or "quick pre-theatre meal". / www.vietnamesekitchen.co.uk; 11 pm, Fri & Sat 11.30 pm, Sun 10.30 pm; booking: min 8.

Cecconi's W1 £78 223
5a Burlington Gdns 020 7434 1500 4–4A
"Always buzzing with pretty and interesting people" – Richard Caring's "classy" Venetian brasserie near Old Bond Street is a "classic" Mayfair rendezvous, especially for schmoozing by Hedge Fund types. Expansion to Miami, LA etc has done nothing for standards though, and a "slide downhill" this year has tipped the always precarious balance here towards seeming complacent and overpriced. Breakfast though is "superior to other meals" and amongst the best in town: "truffled scrambled eggs – yum!" / W1S 3EP; www.cecconis.co.uk; @SohoHouse; 11.30 pm, Sun 10.30 pm.

Céleste, The Lanesborough SW1 £100 232
Hyde Park Corner 020 7259 5599 2–3A
"Refurbished along very classic lines" (part of a £60m refit of the whole property) – the "grand but soulless" atrium dining space of this luxurious Hyde Park Corner hotel perennially "promises great things" but never quite gets its act together. This latest incumbent (overseen by the management of Paris's Le Bristol) seems cut from the same cloth: "there are some glimmers of Frechon's signature dishes but it doesn't quite make the grade". / SW1X 7TA; www.lanesborough.com/eng/restaurant-bars/celeste; @TheLanesborough; 10.30 pm.

Cellar Gascon EC1 £33 333
59 West Smithfield Rd 020 7600 7561 10–2B
The little sibling of Smithfield stalwart Club Gascon, next door, still wins fans with its "stand-out regional French wines" and elegant (slightly "tired"?) style. One or two reporters feel that "some dishes don't quite hit the mark", but it's overall still well rated. / EC1A 9DS; www.cellargascon.com; midnight; closed Sat & Sun; no Amex.

Ceviche £46 333
17 Frith St, W1 020 7292 2040 5–2A
Alexandra Trust, Baldwin St, EC1
020 3327 9463 13–1A
"Bring your tastebuds alive!", say fans of the "great food and even better Pisco sours" at these "cool" and "lively-if-noisy" hangouts ("like a holiday in Peru!"), in Soho and near Old Street. But while "interesting, not all dishes are entirely successful". / www.cevicheuk.com; @cevicheuk; –.

Chakra W8 £56 423
33c Holland Street 020 7229 2115 7–2B
"Absolutely stunning food in a perfect (Notting Hill) location" (complete with chandeliers) is "not what you would normally get in an Indian restaurant", although it's sometimes let down by "disappointing" service. / W8 4LX; www.chakralondon.com; @ChakraLondon; 11 pm, Sun 10.30 pm.

Chamberlain's EC3 £63 232
23-25 Leadenhall Mkt 020 7648 8690 10–2D
The "lovely fish" at this seafood specialist in Leadenhall Market comes at very City prices – "I almost choked on the bill!" But it has its fans, who praise the "great location, happy staff and interesting food" (if from an "essentially static" menu). / EC3V 1LR; www.chamberlains.org; @Chamberlainsldn; Mon-Sat 9.30 pm; closed Sun.

Champor-Champor SE1 £52 445
62 Weston St 020 7403 4600 10–4C
This "ever wonderful" outfit (the name means 'mix and match'), tucked away behind London Bridge station, is adored by its small fanclub for its funky decor as much as the distinctive Thai-Malay cooking. / SE1 3QJ; www.champor-champor.com; @ChamporChampor; 10 pm; D only.

The Chancery EC4 £66 443
9 Cursitor St 020 7831 4000 10–2A
Graham Long's "very interesting, high quality" and "always reliable" cuisine is the hallmark of this "friendly but formal enough" fixture near Chancery Lane – tipped as often as a gastronomic destination as it is for its natural business appeal. / EC4A 1LL; www.thechancery.co.uk; @chancerylondon; 10.30 pm; closed Sat L & Sun.

Chapters SE3 £51 222
43-45 Montpelier Vale 020 8333 2666 1–4D
"A great choice of brekkies"… "lovely steaks from the Josper grill" – this longstanding modern brasserie by Blackheath Common remains a popular and useful local amenity. / SE3 0TJ; www.chaptersrestaurants.com; @Chapters_ADD; 11 pm, Sun 9 pm.

Charlotte's £52 353
6 Turnham Green Ter, W4
020 8742 3590 8–2A
"For excellent casual dining" this "cosy" (tightly packed) Chiswick haunt hits the spot, boosted by a cute bar by the entrance; value-wise, "you get what you've paid for and more". No feedback on its laid-back W5 sibling, but see also Charlotte's Place W5. / www.charlottes.co.uk; –.

Charlotte's Place W5 £55 333
16 St Matthew's Rd 020 8567 7541 1–3A
Fans of this "favourite local" say it's "the best in Ealing by far" – a "lovely place" where "high-quality produce and cooking" are complemented by "attentive, friendly service". See also its spin-offs Charlotte's in W4 and W5. / W5 3JT; www.charlottes.co.uk; @CharlottesW5; 10.30 pm, Fri & Sat 11 pm, Sun 9 pm.

Cheneston's Restaurant, The Milestone Hotel W8 £88 234
1 Kensington Ct 020 7917 1000 6–1A
"Charming", traditional dining room, offering a tranquil refuge from Kensington. It is particularly recommended for its "feast" of a breakfast and splendid afternoon teas ("scones are perfect – crisp on the outside and fluffy on the inside!") / W8 5DL; www.milestonehotel.com; @milestonehotel; 10pm; no jeans.

Chettinad W1 £38 423
16 Percy St 020 3556 1229 2–1C
"Not a standard Indian restaurant by any means", this Fitzrovia venue named after a village in Tamil Nadu features a "delicious" menu "almost entirely based on southern Indian dishes" (including dosa pancakes). It's "always busy", with "quite a few Indian diners". / W1T 1DT; www.chettinadrestaurant.com; @chettinadlondon; 11 pm, Sun 10 pm; no Amex.

Cheyne Walk Brasserie SW3 £68 333
50 Cheyne Walk 020 7376 8787 6–3C
"Where the beautiful people go" near the Thames in Chelsea, this chic Gallic brasserie serves "delicious BBQ" – most notably "meat grilled on the wood fire in the open restaurant". "Surprisingly family-friendly, too, at least at lunchtime" – although it's certainly "not for anyone who counts their pennies". / SW3 5LR; www.cheynewalkbrasserie.com; @CheyneWalkBrass; 10.30 pm, Sun 9.30 pm; closed Mon L.

Chez Abir W14 £38 323
34 Blythe Rd 020 7603 3241 8–1D
"Tabbouleh as good as I've ever tasted" typifies the "wonderfully tasty and fresh" Lebanese cuisine at this backstreet café – "not to be missed" if you're near Olympia. It made its reputation as Chez Marcelle (she retired a couple of years ago), and is still "well up to snuff". / W14 0HA; www.chezabir.co.uk; 11 pm; closed Mon.

CHEZ BRUCE SW17 £74 554
2 Bellevue Rd 020 8672 0114 11–2C
"You can see why people rave!"; Bruce Poole's "casual yet elegant" neighbourhood classic by Wandsworth Common is – for the umpteenth year – the survey's No. 1 favourite by dint of doing "everything effortlessly… and just right", all at a price that makes it "6/5 for value". The modern British cuisine is "unfailingly outstanding, but never over-elaborate: it just tastes intensely of what it is".

Service is *"first class, helpful and welcoming", the interior is "stylish, but not over-styled", and there's an "enormous, eclectic and excellent wine list".* / SW17 7EG; www.chezbruce.co.uk; @ChezBruce; 10 pm, Fri & Sat 10.30 pm, Sun 9 pm; set weekday L £33 (FP), set Sun L £39 (FP), set dinner £53 (FP).

Chicama SW10
383 King's Road 020 3874 2000 6–3C
From the team behind Marylebone's Pachamama, a new Peruvian seafood restaurant opened in Chelsea in mid-summer 2016. Chef Erren Nathaniel (who has worked at Viajante, as well as Maido in Peru) heads up the kitchen. As well as a 72-cover dining room there's a 16-seater chef's table in the kitchen and 30-cover terrace. / SW10 0LP; www.chicamalondon.com; @chicamalondon.

Chick 'n' Sours E8 £32 3 2 3
390 Kingsland Rd 020 3620 8728 14–2A
"Crispy and spicy Korean-style fried chicken" and "well-considered cocktails" are the deal at this Dalston joint with "all the hipster credentials – dark interior, bearded staff and mono menu". Portions are "surprisingly big". / E8 2AA; www.chicknsours.co.uk; @chicknsours; 10 pm, Fri & Sat 10.30 pm, Sun 9.30 pm; may need 6+ to book.

Chicken Shop £35 2 2 3
199-206 High Holborn, WC1
020 7661 3040 2–1D
274-276 Holloway Rd, N7
020 3841 7787 9–2D
79 Highgate Rd, NW5 020 3310 2020 9–1B
128 Allitsen Rd, NW8 020 3757 4849 9–3A
7a Chestnut Grove, SW12
020 8102 9300 11–2C
141 Tooting High St, SW17
020 8767 5200 11–2B
27a Mile End Rd, E1 020 3310 2010 13–2D
"Does what it says on the tin!" – these "cool-feeling" pitstops offer "tasty chicken that won't break the bank", and win praise for a formula that's "simple, delicious, fun and very reasonable". (For the odd cynic however, "Nick Jones knows exactly where the 'just-good-enough-for-the-masses' level is".) / Mon-Sun 10.30 pm ;WC1V closed Sun.

Chilli Cool WC1 £33 4 2 1
15 Leigh St 020 7383 3135 2–1D
The "best dandan noodles this side of Chengdu" and other lip-tinglingly spicy dishes make this Bloomsbury cafe a Xanadu for lovers of fiery Sichuan scoff. / WC1H 9EW; 10.15 pm; no Amex.

The Chiltern Firehouse W1 £86 1 2 3
1 Chiltern St 020 7073 7676 2–1A
"I CAN see what the fuss is about", insist fans of this "beautiful people hangout" in Marylebone, who go ape for its "relaxed cool", its "lovely" interior, "gorgeous outside area", and "inventive" menu. For far too many spoilsport critics though, it's "totally overhyped", "astronomically expensive" and "not that enjoyable" given the "nondescript and noisy" setting, and "prosaic" cuisine. / W1U 7PA; www.chilternfirehouse.com; 10.30 pm.

China Tang, Dorchester Hotel W1 £74 3 2 3
53 Park Ln 020 7629 9988 3–3A
Sir David Tang's homage to '30s Shanghai (particularly the marvellous cocktail bar) is "a weird-but-interesting basement space that feels a bit dated now", but is nevertheless "elegant beyond 99% of Chinese restaurants". "The Peking duck especially is delicious", but the food standards have long divided opinion here and prices give nothing away. / W1K 1QA; www.chinatanglondon.co.uk; @ChinaTangLondon; 11.45 pm.

Chinese Cricket Club EC4 £63 3 3 1
19 New Bridge St 020 7438 8051 10–3A
"Plate after plate of delightful, well-balanced Chinese food" emerge from the kitchen of this hotel dining room near Blackfriars Bridge. But while "the quality is up there with high-end Hong Kong", it's "a bit pricey" and "a shame it feels like an airport departure lounge". / EC4V 6DB; www.chinesecricketclub.com; @chinesecclub; 10 pm; closed Sat & Sun L.

The Chipping Forecast W11 £36
29 All Saints Road 020 7460 2745 7–1B
After trading for eight months as a stall at Soho's Berwick Street market, this fish 'n' chip shop (serving sustainably caught Cornish fish), launched its first standalone restaurant in deepest Notting Hill – early feedback says it's outstanding. / W11 1HE; www.chippingforecast.com; @CForecast; 10.30 pm, Fri & Sat 11.30 pm, Sun 10 pm; closed Mon; no bookings.

Chisou £52 4 4 2
4 Princes St, W1 020 7629 3931 3–1C
31 Beauchamp Pl, SW3 020 3155 0005 6–1D
"One of the best proper Japanese restaurants in London" – both the calm and "easily overlooked" Mayfair original and its "secret hideaway" Knightsbridge offshoot offer "excellent" sushi and sashimi backed up by a "very good range of izakaya-style dishes" and an interesting sake selection. / www.chisourestaurant.com; Mon-Sat 10.30 pm, Sun 9.30 pm.

Chiswell Street Dining Rooms EC1 £62 2 2 2
56 Chiswell St 020 7614 0177 13–2A
This reasonably "stylish" operation near the Barbican can be "very good for a business lunch", although it's "a bit expensive" and there's repeated sentiment

that "the experience is decent but should be better". / EC1Y 4SA; www.chiswellstreetdining.com; @chiswelldining; 11 pm; closed Sat & Sun.

Chor Bizarre W1 £63 324
16 Albemarle St 020 7629 9802 3–3C
"A lovely ambience created by Indian antiques" helps win fans for this bric-a-brac-infested Mayfair fixture. "OK, the food's not at the heights of the very best Indians going, but good quality across the board". / W1S 4HW; www.chorbizarre.com; @ChorBizarreUK; 11.30 pm, Sun 10.30 pm.

Chotto Matte W1 £60 435
11-13 Frith St 020 7042 7171 5–2A
"Buzzy, very hip and classy", "club-like" Soho two-year-old, which is regularly "heaving" thanks to its "fabulous cocktails" and "superb" food that's a "fantastic combination of Peruvian and Japanese cuisines". / W1D 4RB; www.chotto-matte.com; @ChottoMatteSoho; Mon-Sat 1 am, Sun 11 pm.

Chriskitch £27 443
7 Tetherdown, N10 020 8411 0051 1–1C
5 Hoxton Market, N1 020 7033 6666 13–1B
"It's opposite my house and it never disappoints!" – Chris Kitch's Muswell hill yearling in a converted front room continues to inspire love for its "fabulous salads, cakes and really good coffee"; fans "just wish it was bigger!" Owner Christian Honor's more ambitious new venture with open kitchen in hipster-central Hoxton opened too late for the survey – the cooking gets the thumbs up in the press.

Christopher's WC2 £77 323
18 Wellington St 020 7240 4222 5–3D
The "exceptional, spacious and stylish" interior is the special draw of this "wonderful" Covent Garden townhouse, where "very good but very expensive steaks" are the best feature of its American menu. Other attractions? – a good downstairs bar; and "a fabulous brunch, with a great array of choices". / WC2E 7DD; www.christophersgrill.com; @christopherswc2; 11.30 pm, Sun 10.30 pm; booking max 14 may apply.

Chuck Burger E1 £25
4 Commercial Street 020 7377 5742 13–2B
Little sister to Spitalfield's BBQ spot Hot Box, this burger bar opened in summer 2016 in a renovated 'classic East End London caff' in Whitechapel after a stint at Street Feast's Hawker House. / E1 7PT; www.chuckburgerbar.com; 10 pm.

Chucs £66 353
30b Dover St, W1 020 3763 2013 3–3C
226 Westbourne Grove, W11
020 7243 9136 7–1B
Spin-offs from the up-and-coming luxury menswear brand (inspired by Ian Fleming's look in the '50s and '60s) – this new duo of comfortable, clubbable cafés brings a hint of St Tropez (its third branch) to Mayfair and – now also – Notting Hill. Both serve "solid, classic Italian food": the former is a "tiny", "very intimate" space next to the boutique, the latter (on the ground floor below the shop, with outside terrace) is more "buzzing" and "ladies-who-lunch" in style. Notably "impeccable service" at both locations.

Churchill Arms W8 £37 335
119 Kensington Church St
020 7792 1246 7–2B
"Such a cute, little quirky place at the back of a pub" off Notting Hill, and "unbelievable value"; this "fun, butterfly-filled conservatory" ("the floral display is worth the trip alone") "never fails to deliver some of the tastiest Asian scoff this side of Thailand" and is so damn "cheap". Meanwhile "the pub itself is always cheerful with an authentic pub atmosphere" that's "popular with locals and tourists alike". / W8 7LN; www.churchillarmskensington.co.uk; @ChurchilArmsW8; 10 pm, Sun 9.30 pm.

Chutney Mary SW1 £82 434
73 St James's St 020 7629 6688 3–4D
"I needn't have been apprehensive about the move from the King's Road!" – this re-located Indian stalwart (in its new "grown-up" St James's premises for over a year now) continues to delight its large fanclub with its "exceptional, deeply flavoured and superbly textured" cuisine. / SW1A 1PH; www.chutneymary.com; @thechutneymary; 10.30 pm; closed Sat L & Sun.

Chutneys NW1 £31 322
124 Drummond St 020 7388 0604 9–4C
"Seriously good value" Keralan veggie food makes this BYO one of the stars of Euston's 'Little India'. "Quality remains consistent, with good spicing", while the lunchtime and Sunday evening buffet is one of London's top deals. / NW1 2PA; www.chutneyseuston.co.uk; 11 pm; no Amex; may need 5+ to book.

Ciao Bella WC1 £42 235
86-90 Lamb's Conduit St
020 7242 4119 2–1D
"Chaotic and charming" (like Boris Johnson, for whom apparently it's a favourite) – this "full-to-bursting", "old school Italian (like stepping back into the '70s)" in Bloomsbury is the epitome of a "cheap 'n' cheerful" trattoria. It's the "verve and enthusiasm" of the staff and "slightly manic atmosphere" that stand out though, rather than the "family-sized portions of simple classics". / WC1N 3LZ; www.ciaobellarestaurant.co.uk; @CiaobellaLondon; 11.30 pm, Sun 10.30 pm.

Cibo W14 £55 453
3 Russell Gdns 020 7371 6271 8–1D
"If you don't have time to go to Italy..." this "very

enjoyable and most-relaxed" stalwart local on a sidestreet near Olympia station will do the trick: "it really does feel the part", the "food is superb and such good value for money", and there's a "great wine list". / W14 8EZ; www.ciborestaurant.net; 10.30 pm; closed Sat L & Sun D.

Cigala WC1 **£50** 222
54 Lamb's Conduit St 020 7405 1717 2–1D
"Admirable" tapas has won a foodie reputation for this this long-serving Spanish joint, in a quaint corner of Bloomsbury. Quibbles persist, though: the food can disappoint, service can be "careless", and "I do wish they'd do something about the ambience" (although it can be "lovely outside watching the world go by"). / WC1N 3LW; www.cigala.co.uk; 10.45 pm, Sun 9.45 pm.

Cigalon WC2 **£53** 343
115 Chancery Ln 020 7242 8373 2–2D
Created originally as an auction house – the "lovely airy space" creates a "classy" but "refreshingly unstuffy atmosphere" at this favourite legal-land rendezvous (whose best seats are in the "wonderful booths"). Service is "swift", and the Provençal cooking is "exceptionally good (and never too heavy)". / WC2A 1PP; www.cigalon.co.uk; @cigalon_london; 10 pm; closed Sat & Sun.

THE CINNAMON CLUB SW1 **£74** 333
Old Westminster Library, Great Smith St
020 7222 2555 2–4C
For "inspirational Indian cuisine in a very classy setting", this "impressive", "airy" edifice that originally housed Westminster Public Library, would be many reporters' top choice in London. It can seem "a little stuffy", and even fans agree "you pay the price", but disappointments are rare. / SW1P 3BU; www.cinnamonclub.com; @cinnamonclub; 10.30 pm; no trainers; booking max 14 may apply; set weekday L £49 (FP), set Sun L £61 (FP).

Cinnamon Kitchen EC2 **£59** 323
9 Devonshire Sq 020 7626 5000 10–2D
"Inventive and subtle" dishes with "just the right amount of spice" win praise for this "high-endish Indian" – the City cousin of the famous Cinnamon Club – within a large covered atrium near Liverpool Street. Its ratings have been higher though, and critics say: "it's perfectly adequate, but it was far better than adequate once-upon-a-time". / EC2M 4YL; www.cinnamon-kitchen.com; @cinnamonkitchen; 10.45 pm; closed Sat L & Sun.

Cinnamon Soho W1 **£45** 422
5 Kingly St 020 7437 1664 4–2B
"Not like the other Cinnamons – this is a truly casual one" (the styling is "adequate"), just off Regent Street. It "breaks the stereotypes of Indian food" with dishes such as "rogan josh shepherd's pie and vindaloo ox cheek – highly recommended". / W1B 5PE; www.cinnamon-kitchen.com/soho-home; @cinnamonsoho; 11 pm, Sun 4.30 pm; closed Sun D.

City Barge W4 **£50** 334
27 Strand-on-the-Green 020 8994 2148 1–3A
A "wonderful location, right on the river" is the trump card of this refurbished boozer in Strand-on-the-Green. "Tasty food and helpful, engaging staff" complete its hand. / W4 3PH; www.citybargechiswick.com; @citybargew4; Mon-Thu 11 pm, Fri & Sat midnight, Sun 10.30 pm.

City Càphê EC2 **£18** 321
17 Ironmonger St no tel 10–2C
"Expect a queue noon–2pm" at this "authentic Vietnamese with good báhn mi and pho" near Bank – it can be "crazy busy". The "genuine" scoff mostly inspires raves, but some fear that "high demand has led to lower quality". / EC2V 8EY; www.citycapho.com; 3 pm; L only, closed Sat & Sun.

City Social EC2 **£84** 335
Tower 42 25 Old Broad St
020 7877 7703 10–2C
"Perfect with a client" – especially on a clear day when there's an "exceptional vista" – Jason Atherton's 24th floor perch, in the City's Tower 42, provides "first-rate" cuisine in "swish" surroundings. To some extent though, "you're paying for the view not the food". / EC2N 1HQ; www.citysociallondon.com; 9 pm; closed Sat & Sun.

Clarke's W8 **£64** 444
124 Kensington Church St
020 7221 9225 7–2B
"Still delivering exceptional food after all these years: amazing!" Sally Clarke's "very grown up" temple to seasonal cuisine off Notting Hill ("everything is carefully chosen by Sally herself") delivers "simple and wonderful" cooking – "very fresh" and prepared with "a gentle rarity of touch and seasoning". Old-timers may complain that "the enlarged eating area has removed the special intimacy of old" but "the packed house says she's called it right" and it's "a safe bet for business" and "romantic" too. / W8 4BH; www.sallyclarke.com; @SallyClarkeLtd; 10 pm; closed Sun; booking max 14 may apply.

Claude's Kitchen, Amuse Bouche SW6 **£51** 433
51 Parsons Green Ln 020 7371 8517 11–1B
Claude Compton's "enjoyably idiosyncratic" dining room upstairs from Amuse Bouche champagne bar (and opposite Parsons Green tube station) has a "short menu of very good food". "An unexpected treat to eat so well – and so inventively – in Fulham". / SW6 4JA; www.claudeskitchen.co.uk; @AmuseBoucheLDN; 11 pm, Sun 9.30 pm; closed weekday L.

Duende

Hoppers

Clipstone

Clipstone W1
5 Clipstone Street 020 7637 0871 2–1B
From the team behind Fitzrovia's outstanding Portland comes a new, hard-edged and minimalist venture just a few streets away. It launched in September 2016 – too late for survey feedback – but to say that press reviews have been ecstatic would be an understatement. / W1W 6BB; www.clipstonerestaurant.co.uk; @clipstonerestaurant; 11 pm; closed Sun.

Clives Midtown Diner WC1 £23 342
49 Museum Street 020 7405 3182 2–1C
"New kid on the block: hope it sticks around!" – owned by an American, this "stoic attempt at a quality diner" near the British Museum, has won instant praise for its "jolly good burgers" in particular (including a veggie option) and dishes such as "excellent chicken wings... and all the usual trimmings". / WC1A; www.clivesmidtown.co.uk; @clivesmidtown; 6 pm, Fri & Sat 9.30 pm.

CLOS MAGGIORE WC2 £74 345
33 King St 020 7379 9696 5–3C
"A man on the next table got on one knee and proposed... she said yes!" This "joyful oasis" remains London's No. 1 romantic destination thanks to its "magical" interior – in particular its "extraordinarily pretty" rear conservatory. A "well-oiled, very professional operation", "the food quality is high for Covent Garden too, but gastronomically speaking it's the enormous wine list that really sings" ("allow an hour to digest it fully!") / WC2E 8JD; www.closmaggiore.com; @closmaggiorewc2; 11 pm, Sun 10 pm.

The Clove Club EC1 £95 544
Shoreditch Town Hall, 380 Old St
020 7729 6496 13–1B
"Beyond amazing!!!!" Isaac McHale's "playful" and "exquisitely crafted" cuisine provides one of London's best trendy gastronomic experiences. Despite the hipster street cred of this "slightly sparse and echoey" chamber inside Shoreditch's fine old town hall, staff are "attentive and not overbearing", but the "pay-in-advance policy" can seem "irritating". / EC1V 9LT; www.thecloveclub.com; @thecloveclub; 9.30 pm; closed Mon L & Sun.

Club Gascon EC1 £87 432
57 West Smithfield 020 7600 6144 10–2B
"The exciting things they do with foies gras can miss, but when they hit: WOW!" – "Beautiful dishes with amazing combinations of flavour and colours", all "rooted in SW France", together with "a comprehensive range of lesser-known but delicious Gallic wines" maintain the culinary standing of this "serious" and "business-friendly" French venue, near Smithfield Market, even if the interior can seem "a bit '90s". / EC1A 9DS; www.clubgascon.com; @club_gascon; 10 pm, Fri & Sat 10.30 pm; closed Sat L & Sun.

CôBa N7 £38 433
244 York Way 0749 596 3336 9–2C
"An excellent addition to a slightly dead area in terms of food" – Damon Bui's has shifted attention from supper clubs to this new sparse pub-conversion in Barnsbury, which wins all-round praise, not least for its "tasty Vietnamese BBQ". / N7 9AG; www.cobarestaurant.co.uk; @cobafood; 10 pm; closed Sun.

Cocotte W2 £48 433
95 Westbourne Grove 020 3220 0076 7–1B
"Of course it helps if you like chicken, but this simple rôtisserie concept works a treat" – "tasty roast birds, all from the same farm in France, are served with a variety of sauces and some original and delicious salads" at this new outlet on the Notting Hill/Bayswater border. "Not for Michelin-stye gourmets, but hard to beat for a tasty, healthy and good-value family supper out". / W2 4UW; www.mycocotte.uk; @cocotte_rotisserie; 10 pm, Fri & Sat 11 pm.

Coin Laundry EC1 £48
70 Exmouth Mkt 020 7833 9000 10–1A
Despite its prime Exmouth Market location, survey feedback totally ignores this new bar/restaurant whose website boasts 'comfort food, 70's revival cocktails and a big slice of nostalgia' – despite favourable press critiques from Giles Coren and Grace Dent, it has all the hallmarks of somewhere that makes super copy but not such super food. / EC1R 4QP; www.coinlaundry.co.uk; @coinlaundryem; 11 pm, Thu-Sat 2 am; SRA-2 star.

Colbert SW1 £59 112
51 Sloane Sq 020 7730 2804 6–2D
The dud of the Corbin & King stable – a prime, Sloane Square corner-location ensures this handsome Parisian-brasserie-style haunt is "always buzzing", but "they need to get a grip": the classic fare is "so uneven" (some dishes are "a total failure") and service is too often "bored and lackadaisical". / SW1W 8AX; www.colbertchelsea.com; @ColbertChelsea; Sun 10.30 pm, Mon-Thu 11 pm, Fri & Sat 11.30 pm.

La Collina NW1 £54 333
17 Princess Rd 020 7483 0192 9–3B
"Excellent home-made pasta" gets top billing at this "obliging" local Italian on the fringes of Primrose Hill. "Top marks for ambience in the garden (but rather less indoors)", so it comes into its own in the summer. / NW1 8JR; www.lacollinarestaurant.co.uk; @LacollinaR; 10.15 pm, Mon & Tue 9.15 pm; closed Mon L.

The Collins Room SW1 **£86** 2 4 5
Wilton Place 020 3137 1302 6–1D
"A girlie afternoon not to be missed!" is to be had at this re-named Knightsbridge chamber (formerly The Caramel Room). Its "Pret-a-Portea has to be the best-looking afternoon tea in London and somehow manages not to sacrifice deliciousness at the temple of style". "Go with your mum, granny, daughter or girlfriend!" / SW1X 7RL; www.the-berkeley.co.uk; 10.45 pm, Sun 10.15 pm.

Le Colombier SW3 **£66** 3 4 3
145 Dovehouse St 020 7351 1155 6–2C
"Everyone's perfect idea of a Gallic brasserie!" – Didier Garnier's "dependable old favourite" is "tucked away on a corner of a Chelsea backstreet", and "feels like you were in France, except for so many elderly Rosbifs". The "classic French cuisine" is "always more-ish", and "service is impeccably well-mannered in the best French way". / SW3 6LB; www.le-colombier-restaurant.co.uk; 10.30 pm, Sun 10 pm.

Colony Grill Room, Beaumont Hotel W1 **£65** 3 4 4
Brown Hart Gdns 020 7499 1001 3–2A
"Utterly professional service and fabulous surroundings" help win votes for Corbin & King's "serious", "panelled" Mayfair dining room, particularly as an ideal venue "for an understated or confidential business meeting". Its "throwback menu" of "classic American dishes" fits the bill too – "proper chaps' food". / W1K 6TF; www.colonygrillroom.com; @ColonyGrillRoom; midnight, Sun 11 pm.

Como Lario SW1 **£54** 2 2 2
18-22 Holbein Pl 020 7730 2954 6–2D
Some regulars still "feel part of the family" at this age-old trattoria near Sloane Square, but there are growing signs that it's "no longer quite the place it was": "I've been going for years but after last night may not go again". / SW1W 8NL; www.comolario.co.uk; 11.30 pm, Sun 10 pm.

Comptoir Gascon EC1 **£45** 3 3 3
63 Charterhouse St 020 7608 0851 10–1A
"Interesting regional French dishes (if in slightly modest portions for the price)" inspire lots of affection for this "cute little French bistro" in Smithfield (near its parent, Club Gascon). "It's great for business lunches", but the "lovely casual Gallic ambience" is also "perfect for date night" too. Top Menu Tip – "the foie gras duck burger is worth the coronary!" / EC1M 6HJ; www.comptoirgascon.com; @ComptoirGascon; 10 pm, Thu & Fri 10.30 pm; closed Mon & Sun.

Comptoir Libanais **£34** 2 2 3
"Delicious mezze" top the bill at this "cheap, fast and tasty" Lebanese chain with "bright and quirky interiors". There is a school of thought though, which feels the food is "OK, but that's all". / www.lecomptoir.co.uk; W12 9 pm, Thu & Fri 10 pm, Sun 6 pm; W1 9.30 pm; W12 closed Sun D; no bookings.

Il Convivio SW1 **£62** 3 3 4
143 Ebury St 020 7730 4099 2–4A
A "hidden gem" in Belgravia, this "quiet" stalwart "never disappoints" its fans – the interior is "absolutely lovely" and it serves "honest, Italian-inspired food". / SW1W 9QN; www.etruscarestaurants.com/il-convivio; 10.45 pm; closed Sun.

Coopers Restaurant & Bar WC2 **£49** 2 3 3
49 Lincoln's Inn Fields 020 7831 6211 2–2D
"Very useful for the area" – this "low-key" operation in the thinly provided environs of Lincoln's Inn Fields feeds both legal types and academics from the nearby LSE. Arguably its "classic" dishes "could be more inspiring", but its performance is "sound". / WC2A 3PF; www.coopersrestaurant.co.uk; @coopers_bistro; 10.30 pm; closed Sat & Sun; no bookings.

Le Coq N1 **£42** 3 3 3
292-294 St Paul's Rd 020 7359 5055 9–2D
"The signature rôtisserie chicken is delicious" at this straightforward Islington two-year-old. Service is "efficient and friendly", while the "occasional guest-chef takeover nights are good fun, too". / N1 2LH; www.le-coq.co.uk; @LeCOQrestaurant; 10.15 pm.

Coq d'Argent EC2 **£86** 2 2 2
1 Poultry 020 7395 5000 10–2C
"Ideal for City entertaining" – D&D London's central landmark, right by Bank, boasts a wonderful rooftop location (and you can drink outside in the bar). It perennially seems "expensive for what it is" however, mixing "average food, with some good views, and silly prices". / EC2R 8EJ; www.coqdargent.co.uk; @coqdargent1; 9.45 pm; closed Sun D.

Cork & Bottle WC2 **£55** 2 3 4
44-46 Cranbourn St 020 7734 7807 5–3B
"One of the only good places to eat near Leicester Square", this age-old "cellar, bistro-style wine bar" is a venerable haven in tourist-land, "but would be great anywhere!" The "reliably good food", including more than a dozen cheeses, is simple and straightforward – top draw is the "exceptional wine list". / WC2H 7AN; www.thecorkandbottle.co.uk; @corkbottle1971; 11.30 pm, Sun 10.30 pm; no bookings at diner.

Corner Kitchen E7 **£40** 3 2 3
58 Woodgrange Road 020 8555 8068 1–1D
"A recent addition to the Forest Gate eating scene – a deli, café and shop" tipped for its "great pizza". / E7; cornerkitchen.london; @CornerKitchenE7; Mon-Thu 10 pm, Sat 10.30 pm, Sun 9 pm.

Cornish Tiger SW11 £52 3 3 3
1 Battersea Rise 020 7223 7719 11–1C
"An Asian slant on Cornish produce" has made this "lively" two-year-old "an interesting addition to the Battersea dining options". A minority is unconvinced by the fusion though ("the random addition of chilli and sometimes coriander"). / SW11 1GH; www.cornishtiger.com; @cornishtiger; 11 pm, Sun 6 pm; closed Mon.

Corrigan's Mayfair W1 £92 3 4 4
28 Upper Grosvenor St 020 7499 9943 3–3A
Richard Corrigan's "clubby" Mayfair HQ is "an opulent place with fine cuisine", but also a "manly" and business-friendly destination ("the decor shouts hunting, shooting, fishing!") "The menu reads as a homage to gutsy, comfort stalwarts, and though the food looks more delicate than you might imagine, there's nothing dainty about the flavours". "Great private dining options". / W1K 7EH; www.corrigansmayfair.com; @CorriganMayfair; 10 pm; closed Sat L & Sun D; booking max 10 may apply.

Côte £48 2 2 2
"As a useful port of call", these "safe" all-day French brasseries remain immensely popular, especially for their "bargain set lunch", and pre-theatre deals. However, even many fans would concede that the "straightforward" fare is "solid but unspectacular". / www.cote-restaurants.co.uk; 11 pm.

Counter Culture SW4 £32 4 4 4
16 The Pavement 020 8191 7960 11–2D
"New from the Dairy (next door). Tapas food... no bookings". As the name suggests the focus is on kitchen counter-style dining with just 15 seats (six right on the pass) and its "excellent" pintxos are "full of flavour"; you can even BYO. / SW4 0HY; www.countercultureclapham.co.uk; @culturesnax; 11 pm; D only, closed Mon & Sun; no bookings.

Counter Vauxhall Arches SW8 £48 2 3 3
Arch 50, South Lambeth Pl
020 3693 9600 11–1D
A "hipster" railway arch near Vauxhall tube (at 60m long, it claims to be London's longest restaurant) houses this funky yearling. It serves a versatile array of brasserie dishes, plus cocktails, with top billing going to the "American style brunch". / SW8 1SP; www.counterrestaurants.com; @eatatcounter; 12.30 am, Fri & Sat 1.30 am.

The Cow W2 £55 3 2 4
89 Westbourne Park Rd 020 7221 0021 7–1B
"A bit rough around the edges but a proper boozer" – Tom Conran's "busy" Irish pub in Bayswater makes "a refreshing change from most glammed-up pubs", and provides "simple seafood cooked well, great Guinness and a buzzing atmosphere": "I always have a whole crab and spend hours eating it!" / W2 5QH; www.thecowlondon.co.uk; @TheCowLondon; 10 pm, Sun 10 pm; no Amex.

Coya W1 £76 3 2 4
118 Piccadilly 020 7042 7118 3–4B
"Fabulous atmosphere" is the highlight of this happening haunt in Mayfair ("the main room can get noisy"). Praise too for its "amazing and beautifully presented" Peruvian dishes, even if a vocal minority feel they are "far too expensive". / W1J 7NW; www.coyarestaurant.com; @coyalondon_; Sun-Wed 10.30 pm, Thu-Sat 11 pm.

Craft London SE10 £65 4 [illegible] [illegible]
Peninsula Sq 020 8465 5910 1–3D
"Exceptional food in the culinary desert of the O2", brought to the Greenwich Peninsular by hip-crowd chef Stevie Parle in a "beautiful three-storey venue" topped by a bar. The restaurant is "a great locally sourced concept", while the "buzzing" ground-floor café scores for "rustic pizzas" and "great coffee and cardamom buns". / SE10 0SQ; www.craft-london.co.uk; @CraftLDN; café 6 pm, restaurant 10.30 pm, Sun 4 pm.

Crate Brewery & Pizzeria E9 £28 3 2 3
7, The White Building, Queens Yard
020 8533 3331 1–1D
Grungily-groovily located on the canalside looking over to the Olympic Park, this hipster craft brewery and pizzeria, in Hackney Wick's White Building, is one of the area's best-established hangouts thanks to its handy standard of pizza. / E9 5EN; www.cratebrewery.com; @cratebrewery; 10 pm, Fri & Sat 11 pm.

Crazy Bear W1 £66 2 2 4
26-28 Whitfield St 020 7631 0088 2–1C
"Quirky", swish venue hidden away off Tottenham Court Road, whose glam basement bar is the crown jewel feature. The ground floor restaurant lacks the verve it once displayed, but some still admire its "fun" style and "great Thai food". / W1T 2RG; www.crazybeargroup.co.uk; @CrazyBearGroup; 10.30 pm; closed Mon L & Sun; no shorts.

Crocker's Folly NW8 £56 2 2 3
23-24 Aberdeen Pl 020 7289 9898 9–4A
The "gorgeous interior" and "spectacular Victorian features" justify a visit to this "ornately decorated" former hotel in St John's Wood (Frank Crocker built it anticipating a railway terminus opposite, but went bust when they decided to end the line in Marylebone instead). Shame that the food – British, despite the Lebanese Maroush group ownership – is "too pricey". / NW8 8JR; www.crockersfolly.com; @Crockers_Folly; 10.30 pm.

The Crooked Well SE5 **£49** **334**
16 Grove Ln 020 7252 7798 1–3C
"Confidence and skill in the kitchen" helps inspire numerous favourable reports for this spacious, very "pleasant" gastroboozer in Camberwell. / SE5 8SY; www.thecrookedwell.com; @crookedwell; 10.30 pm; closed Mon L; no Amex.

The Cross Keys SW3 **£54** **334**
1 Lawrence St 020 7351 0686 6–3C
This "stylish dining pub" – Chelsea's oldest boozer, now revamped as a stablemate of the Sands End in Fulham – wins consistent praise for its "high-quality, reliable cooking". / SW3 5NB; www.thecrosskeyschelsea.co.uk; @CrossKeys_PH; midnight.

The Culpeper E1 **£43** **223**
40 Commercial St 020 7247 5371 13–2C
After a wizard start, this year-old Spitalfields "hipster hangout" – "a carefully curated, shabby-chic dining room over a frenetic bar" – put in a more mixed showing this year. Fans still praise its "simple", "innovative" dishes and "efficient service", but sceptics are scathing about the staff's "cavalier attitude" and food that's "really nothing to write home about given the hype". / E1 6LP; www.theculpeper.com; @TheCulpeper; Mon-Thu midnight, Fri & Sat 2 am, Sun 11 pm.

Cumberland Arms W14 **£44** **443**
29 North End Rd 020 7371 6806 8–2D
An "epic pub in the barren streetscape of Olympia" – "so reliable", with "accurate cooking of a Med-inspired menu", "(best Italian sausages and mash)", and "a great rotating selection of beers and fine wines". / W14 8SZ; www.thecumberlandarmspub.co.uk; @thecumberland; 10 pm, Sun 9.30 pm.

CURIO + TA TA E8
258 Kingsland Road 020 7254 4945 14–2A
A summer 2016 opening – ex-Viajante chefs behind street food phenomenon TA TA Eatery have teamed up with Curio Cabal coffee shop to bring their 'Chinese family style' rice fix (with a Portuguese twist to Haggerston). / E8 4DG; www.curioandtata.co.uk; @curioandTaTa; Thu 11 pm, Fri & Sat midnight; D only, closed Mon-Wed & Sun.

Cut, 45 Park Lane W1 **£118** **122**
45 Park Ln 020 7493 4545 3–4A
"Good steaks at eye-watering prices" sums up the limited appeal of US celeb-chef Wolfgang Puck's "oddly proportioned" venture, off the foyer of a boutique hotel. "It could only survive on Park Lane" – "it's one for misguided travelling businessmen": "do any Londoners actually go there?" / W1K 1PN; www.45parklane.com; @the_cut_bar; 10.30 pm.

Da Mario SW7 **£48** **234**
15 Gloucester Rd 020 7584 9078 6–1B
"Deservedly popular", this Italian stalwart near the Royal Albert Hall "may be cheesy, with its Princess Di connections", but "it's so nice to get away from chains": "they do make a really good pizza", the "pasta dishes are consistently good", and the "wine prices are sensible". / SW7 4PP; www.damario.co.uk; 11.30 pm.

Da Mario WC2 **£43** **333**
63 Endell St 020 7240 3632 5–1C
"Old-fashioned", "crowded and very noisy" neighbourhood Italian – a "star in the largely ho-hum Covent Garden gastronomic firmament". "There's always a warm welcome from the hosts", along with "plenty of daily specials" at prices that are "easy on the wallet". / WC2H 9AJ; www.da-mario.co.uk; 11.15 pm; closed Sun.

Dabbous W1 **£87** **332**
39 Whitfield St 020 7323 1544 2–1C
Ollie Dabbous's "loft-style" Fitzrovia haunt again divides reporters sharply. To advocates, it combines "precision cooking, with brilliant tastes and textures" and has an "excellent and unfussy" approach – to detractors, "portions are minuscule", dishes are "sometimes a little too wacky", and the interior's too "stark". / W1T 2SF; www.dabbous.co.uk; @dabbous; 9.30 pm (bar open until 11.30 pm); closed Sun.

The Dairy SW4 **£40** **544**
15 The Pavement 020 7622 4165 11–2D
"Like a mini-Noma on Clapham Common" – this "creative" three-year-old draws fans from across town for its "exceptional" and "clever" small plates. Service is "brisk and helpful", and most (if not quite all) reporters love its "relaxed" style. / SW4 0HY; www.the-dairy.co.uk; @thedairyclapham; 9.45 pm; closed Mon, Tue L & Sun D.

Dalloway Terrace, Bloomsbury Hotel WC1 **£56**
16-22 Great Russell St 020 7347 1221 2–1C
It's easy to feel disoriented if you stumble across this new restaurant, with lovely leafy terrace (and fully retractable roof) – how can it be so close to grungy old Centre Point! We don't yet have sufficient feedback for a rating, but one early report is all-round positive. / WC1B 3NN; www.dallowayterrace.com; @DallowayTerrace; 10.30 pm.

Daphne's SW3 **£73** **223**
112 Draycott Ave 020 7589 4257 6–2C
Thanks to its "lovely and romantic" interior, this "appealing" Chelsea old-timer has been a "special" favourite since time immemorial (it was once famously Princess Di's top spot). Its Italian cuisine has slipped notably in recent times though: "preparation could be vastly improved". / SW3 3AE;

www.daphnes-restaurant.co.uk; @DaphnesLondon; 11 pm, Sun 10 pm.

Daquise SW7 £49 222
20 Thurloe St 020 7589 6117 6–2C
This Polish veteran by South Ken tube station clocks up its 70th anniversary next year, and its overall appeal somehow exceeds the sum of its parts: "it's like meeting a friend from the distant past and discovering there's still something special". / SW7 2LT; www.daquise.co.uk; @GesslerDaquise; 11 pm; no Amex.

Darbaar EC2 £60 443
1 Snowden Street 020 7422 4100 13–2B
On the site near Liverpool Street that was formerly a svelte Japanese venture (Chrysan, RIP), this Indian newcomer is the work of Abdul Yaseen, ex-head chef of nearby Cinnamon Kitchen. It wins high ratings for its "generous dishes, delicately spiced", and "varied tasting menus giving you the opportunity of trying different options" (including "lovely 'nanza'" – naan meets pizza). / EC2A 2DQ; www.darbaarrestaurants.com; @DarbaarbyAbdul; 10.45 pm; closed Sun.

The Dartmouth Castle W6 £47 344
26 Glenthorne Rd 020 8748 3614 8–2C
"There's nothing bang-whizz about this place" – a very "solid" little gastropub bordering Hammersmith's one-way system. But "it gets the basics perfectly right" and "everything's served with a smile". / W6 0LS; www.thedartmouthcastle.co.uk; @DartmouthCastle; 10 pm, Sun 9.30 pm; closed Sat L.

Darwin Brasserie, Sky Garden EC3 £68 224
20 Fenchurch St 033 3772 0020 10–3D
"You can't beat the views over London on a beautiful day" from this large all-day operation on the top of the Walkie Talkie and although "the food's not outstanding" it's "surprisingly good" given the location. Top Tip – its "value-for-money brunch" ("but additional drinks on top of the set price are expensive"). / EC3M 3BY; skygarden.london/darwin; @SG_Darwin; 10.30 pm, Sun 8.30 pm.

Daylesford Organic £54 223
44b Pimlico Rd, SW1 020 7881 8060 6–2D
Selfridges & Co, 400 Oxford St, W1 0800 123 400 3–1A
6-8 Blandford St, W1 020 3696 6500 2–1A
208-212 Westbourne Grove, W11 020 7313 8050 7–1B
"You feel like the food's doing you good (although it probably isn't!)", at Lady Bamford's "bright" (but "crowded" and slightly "chaotic") organic-branded cafés, hailed by fans for their "fresh and healthy" dishes, including "lovely breakfasts served in quirky metal pans". / www.daylesfordorganic.com; SW1 & W11 7 pm, Sun 4 pm – W1 9 pm, Sun 6.15 pm; W11 no booking L.

Dean Street Townhouse W1 £61 235
69-71 Dean St 020 7434 1775 5–2A
Soho House Group's versatile brasserie in the heart of Soho itself, remains hugely popular. "It's the buzzy feel of the place that makes it a great hangout", although "the food's fine" and "service is attentive and friendly for such a busy place". / W1D 3SE; www.deanstreettownhouse.com; @deanstreettownhouse; 11.30 pm, Fri & Sat midnight, Sun 10.30 pm.

Defune W1 £72 431
34 George St 020 7935 8311 3–1A
"I was staggered to find it's had the same owner for 40 years!" – this "quiet" Marylebone "classic" is "just like being in Japan" (not such a boon on the ambience front...) and still delivers "outstanding" teppanyaki and "marvellously inventive" sushi. Breathe deeply when the bill arrives though – it's "pricey". / W1U 7DP; www.defune.com; 10.45 pm, Sun 10.30 pm.

Dehesa W1 £51 423
25 Ganton St 020 7494 4170 4–2B
"Lovely, little dining room and outdoor terrace" off Carnaby Street which serves "brilliant" Spanish and Italian tapas and "great wine" in a "laid-back, intimate atmosphere". / W1F 9BP; www.dehesa.co.uk; @SaltYardGroup; 10.45 pm.

THE DELAUNAY WC2 £58 234
55 Aldwych 020 7499 8558 2–2D
Like its sibling, The Wolseley, Corbin & King's "bustling and luxurious" venue on Aldwych "gives a very good impression of a middle-European café in the grand style", and makes a supremely business-friendly choice. But aside from "wonderful old-school breakfasts" and "lovely afternoon teas", the somewhat "unimaginative" cooking is "only OK for the price", and has seemed even more "ordinary" of late. Next door, 'The Counter' is "The Delaunay's little brother, serving light meals, coffee and cakes". / WC2B 4BB; www.thedelaunay.com; @TheDelaunayRest; midnight, Sun 11 pm.

Delfino W1 £49 432
121a Mount St 020 7499 1256 3–3B
"Top pizza and great value" win fans for this straightforward venue, by the Connaught – "small", hectic and "slightly squished" at peak times, but "long may it continue". / W1K 3NW; www.finos.co.uk; 10.45 pm; closed Sun.

Delhi Grill N1 £35 322
21 Chapel Mkt 020 7278 8100 9–3D
"Fast, furious, tasty, cheap!" This "buzzy" Chapel Market canteen, with its "Indian street food and

Bollywood posters" is the best bet for "simple curries in Islington". "Set lunch for just over a fiver: irresistible!" / N1 9EZ; www.delhigrill.com; @delhigrill; 10.30 pm; cash only.

La Delizia Limbara SW3 **£40** 3 2 2
63-65 Chelsea Manor St 020 7376 4111 6–3C
"Tucked away off the King's Road", this is a "locals' hangout worth searching out" for "cracking pizzas and pasta banged out with little fuss"; "always a squeeze but always worth it". / SW3 5RZ; www.ladelizia.org.uk; @ladelizia; 11 pm, Sun 10.30 pm; no Amex.

Department of Coffee & Social Affairs EC1 **£15** 3 5 4
14-16 Leather Ln 020 7419 6906 10–2A
"They're serious about their caffeine" – "some of the best and smoothest coffee in London" – at these "vibey" haunts (also offering "a small collection of delicious, simple cakes"). The site listed is the original Leather Lane branch (a converted old ironmongers) – "a cool hangout for young media start-up types which contrasts with the old-school market traders outside". / EC1N 7SU; www.departmentofcoffee.co.uk; @DeptOfCoffee; 6 pm, Sat & Sun 4 pm; L only.

The Depot SW14 **£44** 2 2 5
Tideway Yd, Mortlake High St
020 8878 9462 11–1A
"A wonderfully unspoilt location overlooking the Thames" guarantees a "magical" experience at this fixture near Barnes Bridge. "We always have a lovely time here", say regulars – even if the quality of the food "varies a bit too much". STOP PRESS – in October 2016 it was announced that the business was being purchased by Rick & Jill Stein (of Padstow fame) – no immediate changes are planned but these are likely in 2017. / SW14 8SN; www.depotbrasserie.co.uk; @TheDepotBarnes; 10 pm, Sun 9.30 pm.

Les Deux Salons WC2 **£62** 1 2 1
40-42 William IV St 020 7420 2050 5–4C
Yikes! – "Things have not improved under Sir Terence Conran's new ownership", at this large venue, just off Trafalgar Square, which nowadays combines an upstairs restaurant with ground floor 'café, bistro, épicerie and cave à vin'. OK, some reports do applaud its "very passable" Gallic fare, but the consensus is "don't bother" – it's "all a bit limited and lacking in ambience" with food that's "just factory catering". / WC2N 4DD; www.lesdeuxsalons.co.uk; @lesdeuxsalons; 10.45 pm, Sun 5.45 pm; closed Sun D.

Dickie Fitz W1 **£62** 2 2 2
48 Newman St 020 3667 1445 3–1D
Mixed reports on this Antipodean-influenced brasserie newcomer with striking yellow-leather banquettes, on the former site of The Newman Street Tavern (RIP). Its Aussie breakfasts and Pacific-inspired all-day menu do win some praise, but one or two disasters were also reported, and service can be "apathetic". / W1T 1QQ; www.dickiefitz.co.uk; @DickieFitzrovia; 10.30 pm, Sun 6 pm; closed Sun D.

Dinings W1 **£57** 4 3 1
22 Harcourt St 020 7723 0666 9–4A
"Every single bite is memorable" at this Marylebone venue where Tomonari Chiba provides some of "the best quality and most innovative Japanese food in London!" The decor – either sit at the ground floor counter or in the bunker-like basement – is decidedly "iffy" however, and critics fear it is becoming "embarrassingly expensive". / W1H 4HH; www.dinings.co.uk; @diningslondon; 10.30 pm; closed Sun.

Dinner, Mandarin Oriental SW1 **£106** 3 3 4
66 Knightsbridge 020 7201 3833 6–1D
Heston Blumenthal's "theatrical" menu "loosely based on historic British recipes" has won fame for this large, swish dining room, with "magnificent views over Hyde Park". Arguably the shtick "relies more on history-telling than cooking" however, and "now that the original hype is over" reporters divide between the majority for whom the cuisine is still plain "incredible" and a sizeable minority for whom "the original 'ooooohs' and 'aaaahs' have been superseded by 'so whats'". / SW1X 7LA; www.dinnerbyheston.com; 10.30 pm.

Dip & Flip **£25** 3 2 2
87 Battersea Rise, SW11 no tel 11–2C
115 Tooting High St, SW17 no tel 11–2C
62 The Broadway, SW19 no tel 11–2B
64-68 Atlantic Road, SW9 no tel 11–2D
This burger concept – with gravy, and a kitchen roll instead of forks – is hailed by locals as a "tremendous addition to the food scene" in southwest London, where it's grown fast (Battersea, Wimbledon, Tooting and Brixton). But not everyone is a convert: "where do the good reviews come from? Too many people are squashed into a tiny place, and the food's unexciting".

Dirty Burger **£14** 3 2 2
78 Highgate Rd, NW5 020 3310 2010 9–2B
Arch 54, 6 South Lambeth Rd, SW8
020 7074 1444 2–4D
13 Bethnal Green Rd, E1
020 7749 4525 13–1C
27a, Mile End Rd, E1 020 3727 6165 13–2D
"For a quick in/out visit when you're looking for something dirty", or "for a late night munch to soak up the alcohol", the "always impressive burgers" at these "always busy and buzzy" shacks are "how fast food should be". / www.eatdirtyburger.com; Mon-Thu 11 pm-midnight, Fri & Sat 1 am-2 am, Sun 8 pm-11 pm.

Dishoom **£40** 4 3 4
Kingly St, W1 020 7420 9322 4–2B
12 Upper St Martins Ln, WC2
020 7420 9320 5–3B
Stable St, Granary Sq, N1
020 7420 9321 9–3C
7 Boundary St, E2 020 7420 9324 13–1B
"Buzzy, bordering on frenetic" – these "wonderful replicas of Mumbai's Parsi cafés" have exceptional energy levels for a fast-expanding chain, and offer "deeply satisfying, colonially-inspired, street-food style dishes" (including "terrifically interesting breakfasts"), plus "excellent cocktails". The catch? – the limited-bookings policy leads to "massive" queues "out of all proportion to reality". Top Menu Tip – "the black dhal is a must". / www.dishoom.com; @Dishoom; 11 pm, Sun 10 pm.

Diwana Bhel-Poori House NW1 **£27** 3 2 1
121-123 Drummond St 020 7387 5556 9–4C
"An institution" of Euston's 'Little India': this "never changing" veggie canteen wouldn't win any prizes for interior design (unless the category was for authentically '60s decor). It has survived for decades on its "delicious dosas", and is known for its "excellent value buffet lunch". / NW1 2HL; www.diwanabph.com; @DiwanaBhelPoori; 11.45 pm, Sun 11 pm; no Amex; may need 10+ to book.

The Dock Kitchen, Portobello Dock W10 **£60** 3 2 3
342-344 Ladbroke Grove, Portobello Dock
020 8962 1610 1–2B
Stevie Parle serves an "eclectic", ever-changing, global menu at his Victorian dockside warehouse conversion at the north end of Ladbroke Grove, to general – but not universal – acclaim. "It's wonderful in summer and autumn, sitting outside on the deck". / W10 5BU; www.dockkitchen.co.uk/contact.php; @TheDockKitchen; 9.30 pm; closed Sun D.

Dominique Ansel Bakery London SW1
17-21 Elizabeth Street 020 7324 7705 2–4B
Famous US baker, Dominique Ansel brings some of his most famous pastries – the Cronut and the DKA (Dominique's Kouign Amann) – across the Pond as he opens his first London site in autumn 2016 (although this Belgravia site is somewhat in contrast to its relatively hip SoHo NYC roots). / SW1W 9RP; www.dominiqueansellondon.com; @DominiqueAnsel.

The Don EC4 **£66** 3 3 2
20 St Swithin's Ln 020 7626 2606 10–3C
"Tucked away in a cobbled mews, but just a stone's throw from the Bank of England", this "handily located" fixture is one of the Square Mile's top business choices. Ratings don't hit the highs they once did, but it's a "reliable" and "efficient" operation, with a smart and spacious (if perhaps slightly "sterile") interior. See also Sign of the Don. / EC4N 8AD; www.thedonrestaurant.com; @thedonlondon; 10 pm; closed Sat & Sun; no shorts.

Donna Margherita SW11 **£45** 3 3 2
183 Lavender Hill 020 7228 2660 11–2C
"Authentic Naples pizza (stone-baked too giving it a lovely crust)" wins a thumbs up for this Battersea Italian – "noisy, but that makes it fun". One minor gripe: the wine list can seem a mite "predictable". / SW11 5TE; www.donna-margherita.com; @DMargheritaUK; 10.30 pm, Fri & Sat 11 pm; Mon-Thu D only, Fri-Sun open L & D.

Donostia W1 **£49** 5 3 4
10 Seymour Pl 020 3620 1845 2–2A
"Sensational" Basque tapas (Donostia = San Sebastián) – "true to the region and featuring seasonal specials" – win ongoing acclaim for this "casual" bar, arranged around an open kitchen, whose "enthusiastic" owners also run nearby Lurra. "Sitting outside on a summer's evening feels like another world from the hectic hellhole that is Marble Arch". / W1H 7ND; www.donostia.co.uk; @DonostiaW1; 11 pm; closed Mon L.

Doppio NW1 **£6** 3 3 3
177 Kentish Town Rd 020 7267 5993 9–2B
"Brilliant, expert coffee" is to be had in a "really laid back warehouse setting (it literally is a warehouse!)" at these "trendy" concepts in Camden Town and Shoreditch; alongside brews there's "a huge range of coffee, and coffee-making equipment for sale". / NW1 8PD; www.doppiocoffee.co.uk; @doppiocoffeeltd; 6 pm.

Dorchester Grill, Dorchester Hotel W1 **£104** 3 3 3
53 Park Lane 020 7629 8888 3–3A
The bonkers former tartan-riot decor has given way to tasteful luxury at this grand chamber, nowadays overseen from afar by Alain Ducasse, with a blameless modern French menu. There's little to criticise – especially on business – but for those spending their own hard-earned lucre, little to distinguish it from so many other expensive Mayfair dining experiences. / W1K 1QA; www.thedorchester.com; @TheDorchester; 10.15 pm, Sat 10.45 pm, Sun 10.15 pm; no trainers.

Dotori N4 **£28** 4 3 2
3a Stroud Green Rd 020 7263 3562 9–1D
Packed outfit near Finsbury Park station: "go for authentic Korean and some Japanese dishes, but book in advance – it's small and sells out quickly". / N4 2DQ; www.dotorirestaurant.wix.com/dotorirestaurant; 10.30 pm; closed Mon; no Amex.

The Dove W6 £46 224
19 Upper Mall 020 8748 5405 8–2B
"It's one of the best pubs in London", "with a lovely terrace right on the Thames", but this small 18th-century tavern in a cute Hammersmith alley is "not really gastro" – "the food's OK, but you come for the beer and the atmosphere". / W6 9TA; www.fullers.co.uk; @thedovew6; 11 pm; closed Sun D; no bookings.

Dragon Castle SE17 £36 332
100 Walworth Rd 020 7277 3388 1–3C
"Excellent for an area which frankly doesn't have much, and good overall!" – a big, cavernous Cantonese near Elephant & Castle whose dim sum are "freshly prepared and very good value". What sets it apart are the "more interesting regional dishes" introduced by "a new chef who has revitalised the menu". / SE17 1JL; www.dragon-castle.com; @Dragoncastle100; Mon-Sat 11 pm, Sun 10 pm.

Dragon Palace SW5 £30 432
207 Earls Court Rd 020 7370 1461 6–2A
"More than just a neighbourhood local" – this inconspicuous modern Chinese café north of Earl's Court tube draws fans from across neighbouring postcodes for its "excellent all-day dim sum". / SW5; www.thedragonpalace.com; 11 pm.

Drakes Tabanco W1 £49 444
3 Windmill St 020 7637 9388 2–1C
"Sherry served straight from the cask" and "top-notch" tapas are the main attractions at this "easy-to-miss" Fitzrovia spot off Charlotte Street, inspired by (and named after) the sherry taverns of Andalucia. / W1T 2HY; www.drakestabanco.com; @drakestabanco; 10 pm.

The Drapers Arms N1 £50 322
44 Barnsbury St 020 7619 0348 9–3D
"Excellent pub food" ("love the pies!") lives up to the high reputation of this Islington gastro-boozer, although the "interesting, regularly changing menu" is "sometimes let down by surly service". Top tip for the summer: "there's a fabulous sun-trap garden at the back". / N1 1ER; www.thedrapersarms.com; @DrapersArms; 10.30 pm; no Amex.

The Duck & Rice W1 £59 434
90 Berwick St 020 3327 7888 4–2C
"Very impressive… and I don't even like Chinese food!" Wagamama-creator, Alan Yau maybe onto another winning format with his year-old Soho gastropub makeover, which combines "stylish decor, good-quality Chinese classics, plus dim sum and amazing bao buns". / W1F 0QB; www.theduckandrice.com; @theduckandrice; Mon -11.30 pm, midnight, Sun 10.30 pm.

Duck & Waffle EC2 £70 225
110 Bishopsgate, Heron Tower
020 3640 7310 10–2D
"You are admittedly paying for the astonishing views", at this arguably "completely over-priced", 24/7 neighbour to SushiSamba, on the 40th-floor of the Heron Tower. No one disputes the "wow factor" though, and many reports are surprisingly complimentary regarding its "chunky, meaty fashionable food and sharing plates", including "the eponymous signature dish". Top Tip – "really delicious breakfast". (Coming soon: a second branch is set to open in late 2016 in the new St James's Market development). / EC2N 4AY; www.duckandwaffle.com; @DuckandWaffle; open 24 hours.

Ducksoup W1 £55 334
41 Dean St 020 7287 4599 5–2A
A "tasty, if not overchallenging hybrid of Italian and North African" dishes along with "unusual wines" win fans for this "nicely buzzing" Soho spot. / W1D 4PY; www.ducksoupsoho.co.uk; @ducksoup; 10.30 pm; closed Sun D.

Duende WC2 £45 422
16 Maiden Ln 020 7836 5635 5–4D
"Love, love, love" the "amazing and inventive tapas", say fans of Victor Garvey's inspiring, early-2016, solo venture in Covent Garden. "Amateur service" and a "cramped" space are drawbacks though, and not everyone is wowed: "I was hoping for the same quality as his original hangout, Tapas Bravas" but "the food looked better than it tasted (even though it looked fantastic…)" / WC2E 7NJ; www.duendelondon.com; @duendelondon; 11.30 pm; D only, closed Sun.

Duke of Sussex W4 £46 334
75 South Pde 020 8742 8801 8–1A
This substantial Victorian tavern beside Acton Common Green serves an "excellent Spanish menu" of "dependable" tapas and larger plates in its grand, rear dining room. / W4 5LF; www.metropolitanpubcompany.com; @thedukew4; 10.30 pm, Sun 9.30 pm.

Duke's Brew & Que N1 £55 423
33 Downham Rd 020 3006 0795 14–2A
"Bring your appetite – you won't regret it", when you visit this "hip, crowded (with great music blasting)" Texan BBQ in Dalston. "Fred Flintstone-esque ribs (the size of your forearm), juicy, fat burgers, and spicy fries will make you salivate just thinking about them"; "fantastic beers" too. / N1 5AA; www.dukesbrewandque.com; @dukesJoint; 10 pm, Sun 9.30 pm; closed weekday L.

Dynamo SW15 £35 333
200-204 Putney Bridge Rd
020 3761 2952 11–2B
"Things seem to have taken off" at this new

"cycle-themed café in Putney": it serves "excellent sourdough pizza", and "breakfasts and brunches are really delicious, with proper barista coffee". / SW15; www.the-dynamo.co.uk; @WeAreTheDynamo; 10 pm, Thu-Sat 11 pm.

The Dysart Petersham TW10 **£69** 4 4 3
135 Petersham Rd 020 8940 8005 1–4A
"A great surprise" – Kenneth Culhane cooks "wonderful food" at this Arts & Crafts pub between Richmond Park and the Thames. If there's a gripe it is that it "could feel more lively" (especially at lunch). / TW10 7AA; www.thedysartarms.co.uk; @dysartpetersham; 9.30 pm; closed Sun D.

E&O W11 **£56** 3 3 3
14 Blenheim Cr 020 7229 5454 7–1A
"Still full and fun!" – Will Ricker's "vibrant" Notting Hill hangout may be "a bit predictable" nowadays in terms of its "well seasoned and spiced" pan-Asian tapas, but no-one very much minds, and its yummy cocktails still slip down very nicely. / W11 1NN; www.rickerrestaurants.com; 11 pm, Sun 10.30 pm; booking max 6 may apply.

The Eagle EC1 **£33** 4 3 5
159 Farringdon Rd 020 7837 1353 10–1A
"The grandfather of gastropubs" near Exmouth Market "is still showing the way after all these years". "The gastro dining experience elsewhere has become dull, but the Eagle remains true to its roots" – "loud crowd, open kitchen, stubbly chefs, short Anglo-Med menu on blackboard, good beer: brilliant!" / EC1R 3AL; www.theeaglefarringdon.co.uk; @eaglefarringdon; 10.30 pm; closed Sun D; no Amex; no bookings.

Ealing Park Tavern W5 **£52** 3 3 4
222 South Ealing Rd 020 8758 1879 1–3A
This expansive South Ealing venue – nowadays part of the ETM group – is sometimes thought "quite pricey" for a gastropub, but "they can definitely cook" and the food's "usually very good". / W5 4RL; www.ealingparktavern.com; @Ealingpark; 10 pm, Sun 9 pm.

Earl Spencer SW18 **£45** 3 2 4
260-262 Merton Rd 020 8870 9244 11–2B
"Lovely unpretentious food from a daily changing menu" in a "very friendly proper local pub" – a substantial Edwardian roadhouse in Wandsworth. "They've recently added 50 gins to their drinks menu" (which has "a good selection of local ales") – "what's not to love?" / SW18 5JL; www.theearlspencer.co.uk; @TheEarlSpencer; 11 pm; Mon-Thu D only, Fri-Sun open L & D; no booking Sun.

Eat 17 **£39** 4 4 3
28-30 Orford Rd, E17 020 8521 5279 1–1D
64-66 Brooksbys Walk, E9
020 8986 6242 1–1D
"Overlooked in 'The Stow'", but worth discovering – a British brasserie-style operation in the heart of Walthamstow Village that's part of a local food empire incorporating the award-winning SPAR in Hackney. / www.eat17.co.uk; @eat_17; –.

Eat Tokyo **£24** 4 2 2
50 Red Lion St, WC1 020 7242 3490 2–1D
15 Whitcomb St, WC2 020 7930 6117 5–4B
169 King St, W6 020 8741 7916 8–2B
18 Hillgate St, W8 020 7792 9313 7–2B
14 North End Rd, NW11
020 8209 0079 1–1B
"Hype-free, authentic Japanese cuisine", inspires "popularity amongst ex-pats" and "queues out of the door" at these "unpretentious" ("noisy" and "crowded") cafés. The menu is "voluminous", but "they understand Japanese food: tastes are fresh and genuine and come at low prices". / Mon-Sat 11.30 pm, Sun 11 pm.

Ebury Restaurant & Wine Bar SW1 **£58** 2 2 3
139 Ebury St 020 7730 5447 2–4A
This comfy, old-school wine bar near Victoria station is "a great place to meet business colleagues" in an area that doesn't offer much choice – a "fab, everyday option", if one without huge culinary pretentions. / SW1W 9QU; www.eburyrestaurant.co.uk; @EburyRestaurant; 10.15 pm.

Eco SW4 **£36** 3 3 4
162 Clapham High St 020 7978 1108 11–2D
This long-serving Clapham haunt (owned by one of the Franco Manca co-founders) is an "excellent local", even more so "since being revamped", with a new wood-burning oven and modishly stripped-to-brickwork walls: "friendly, excellent, quick, and good value for money". / SW4 7UG; www.ecorestaurants.com; @ecopizzaLDN; 11 pm, Fri & Sat 11.30 pm.

Edera W11 **£62** 3 3 3
148 Holland Park Ave 020 7221 6090 7–2A
A "high standard" of Italian cooking is to be found at this "low-key" Sardinian right on Holland Park Avenue – "not cheap" but "top rate". Top Menu Tip – "their truffle dishes are extremely good". / W11 4UE; www.edera.co.uk; 11 pm, Sun 10 pm.

Edwins SE1 **£49** 3 4 4
202-206 Borough High St
020 7403 9913 10–4B
This bistro two-year-old above a mock-Tudor pub next door to Borough tube station is a "favourite local" and consistently rated as an "all-round good option". / SE1 1JX; www.edwinsborough.co.uk; @edwinsborough; 11.30 pm, Sat midnight, Sun 4 pm; closed Sun D.

8 Hoxton Square N1 £54 444

8-9 Hoxton Sq 020 7729 4232 13–1B

A Hoxton "fave" serving "great value wines" including "unusual bottles" available to drink by the glass, carafe or half-bottle. The "short menu changes daily and the excellent cooking does justice to the quality of the ingredients used". / N1 6NU; www.8hoxtonsquare.com; @8HoxtonSquare; 10.30 pm; closed Sun D.

Eight Over Eight SW3 £56 323

392 King's Rd 020 7349 9934 6–3B

Will Ricker's "always buzzy Chelsea stalwart" has a nightclubby feel and serves "delicious small dishes reflecting a wide array of Asian cuisines", plus very gluggable cocktails. / SW3 5UZ; www.rickerrestaurants.com/eight-over-eight; 11 pm, Sun 10.30 pm.

Electric Diner W11 £51 223

191 Portobello Rd 020 7908 9696 7–1A

Rub shoulders with the Notting Hill set at this "lively, buzzy" hangout, which in particular is "great at the weekend". "But don't go just for the food – it's pretty average". / W11 2ED; www.electricdiner.com; @ElectricDiner; 11 pm, Fri & Sat midnight, Sun 10 pm.

Elliot's Café SE1 £55 323

12 Stoney St 020 7403 7436 10–4C

"Interesting tapas-style dishes" and an all-natural list of wines fit well with the vibey Borough Market location of Brett Redman's bare-brick cafe (sibling to The Richmond). / SE1 9AD; www.elliotscafe.com; @elliotscafe; 10 pm; closed Sun.

Ellory, Netil House E8 £56 243

1 Westgate St 020 3095 9455 14–2B

Divergent feedback on this yearling, set within the achingly hip environs of a set of creative studios in London Fields. Fans nominate Matthew Young's ingredient-led cuisine as their best meal of the year, others say "it's trying too hard, and needs to focus on flavour". / E8 3RL; www.ellorylondon.com; @ellorylondon; 11 pm, Sun 5 pm; closed Mon, Tue L, Wed L, Thu L & Sun D; booking max 6 may apply.

Elystan Street SW3

43 Elystan Street 020 7628 5005 6–2C

Chef Phil Howard, famous for his 25 years at the helm of The Square, Mayfair, has paired up with Rebecca Mascarenhas once again to launch a new, modern British restaurant, on the former Chelsea site of Tom Aikens Restaurant, opening in October 2016. A 'flexitarian' approach with more emphasis on vegetables is promised by comparison with the more protein-led cuisine at The Square. Stop Press – early press critiques are very upbeat. / SW3 3NT; www.elystanstreet.com; @elystanstreet.

Ember Yard W1 £51 444

60 Berwick St 020 7439 8057 3–1D

Stylish Soho sibling to Salt Yard that "seems to have moved up a notch" in recent times. Service is "really friendly and efficient" and "there's lots of interesting dishes on the menu", when it comes to the "smoky, delicate, BBQ-style small plates" from the char grill. / W1F 8SU; www.emberyard.co.uk; @emberyard; 11 pm, Thu-Sat midnight, Sun 10 pm; booking max 13 may apply.

Emile's SW15 £47 342

96-98 Felsham Rd 020 8789 3323 11–2B

"Off the beaten track in a residential street", this "hospitable" bistro is "a firm favourite" among Putney locals, not least because "the owner treats everyone as personal friends". There's always an "interesting special on the blackboard", but avoid the "quieter second room, which can be lonely". / SW15 1DQ; www.emilesrestaurant.co.uk; 11 pm; D only, closed Sun; no Amex.

The Empress E9 £46 444

130 Lauriston Rd 020 8533 5123 14–2B

"Jewel of a gastropub" beside Victoria Park, which was one of the first to gentrify in east London and which is "just what a local should be – friendly, good value and fit for all occasions". "The food's always good", from "an interesting, changing menu", and "complemented by a fun, buzzy atmosphere". / E9 7LH; www.empresse9.co.uk; @elliottlidstone; 10.15 pm, Sun 9.30 pm; closed Mon L; no Amex.

Eneko at One Aldwych, One Aldwych Hotel WC2 £76

1 Aldwych 020 7300 0300 2–2D

A partnership between One Aldwych Hotel and the owner of the Bilbao legend, Azurmendi – the basement site which was formerly Axis (RIP) re-opened in late summer 2016 as a Basque restaurant and wine bar: it's cast in a much more informal style than that which won Eneko Atxa his three Michelin stars back home. / WC2B 4BZ; www.eneko.london; @OneAldwych; Mon-Sat 11 pm, Sun 10 pm.

Engawa W1 £146 444

2 Ham Yd 020 7287 5724 4–3D

"If you don't like sushi or Kobe, don't come" to this "intimate", little shrine to Japan's highly prized Kobe beef, in the cute environs of Soho's Ham Yard – a "truly authentic experience of exceptional quality", featuring "stunning food that begs to be talked about and talked over." / W1D 7DT; www.engawa.uk; @engawaLondon; 10.45 pm, Fri & Sat 11.15 pm, Sun 10.15 pm.

Enoteca Rabezzana EC1 £49 222

62-63 Long Ln 020 7600 0266 10–2B

A "mind-expanding wine list" focussed on Italy at "reasonable mark-ups" and all available by the glass is the big draw at this City wine bar, whose owners hail from the Monferrato vineyard region in Piedmont. The "sensibly short" food selection is "fine". / EC1A 9EJ; www.rabezzana.co.uk, @RabezzanaLondon; midnight, Sat 1 am; closed Sun.

Enoteca Turi SW1 £66 454
87 Pimlico Road 020 7730 3663 6–2D
When Giuseppi and Pamela Turi lost their premises of decades' standing near Putney Bridge, who would have predicted they would undertake and pull off this "very successful move"? Still "SW15's major loss is Pimlico's gain", and their newcomer remains true to the "lovely, family-run, regional Italian" it has always been, even if the "relaxed but refined" setting is now "far superior" here. Service remains "genial" yet "dedicated", the "northern Italian menu provides regional dishes you won't find elsewhere", but the big deal remains Signor Turi's "exceptional" list of Italian wines with his own annotations – "highly educational, with superb, lesser-known vintages" and "a civilised approach to mark-ups". / SW1W 8PH; www.enotecaturi.com; @EnotecaTuri; 10.30 pm, Fri & Sat 11 pm; closed Sun; booking max 8 may apply.

The Enterprise SW3 £58 334
35 Walton St 020 7584 3148 6–2C
On a "film-set" Chelsea street, this "upmarket pub" with "book-lined windows and heavy drapes" offers a "super atmosphere and warm welcome". A "great menu of British fare" with a "slightly hip twist" completes the deal. / SW3 2HU; www.theenterprise.co.uk; 10.30 pm, Sun 10 pm; no booking, except weekday L; set weekday L £35 (FP).

L'Escargot W1 £62 344
48 Greek St 020 7439 7474 5–2A
"A long-time (and forever) favourite" (est 1927), this "romantic" Gallic classic in Soho (current owner, Brian Clivaz) retains its reputation for dependable French cuisine, "attentive" service and a "buzzy" ambience and is particularly "convenient for the theatre". / W1D 4EF; www.lescargot.co.uk; @LEscargotSoho; 11.30 pm; closed Sun D.

Escocesa N16 £45 432
67 Stoke Newington Church Street
020 7812 9189 1–1C
"A great addition to the Stoke Newington repertoire" – this "packed-to-the-rafters" tapas-newcomer ("from the founder of Crouch End's Bar Estoban") mainlines on "serving Scottish seafood with Spanish flair" ("very pure flavours and a more interesting take on familiar dishes"). It's not so comfy though, and "you can't hear yourself think". / N16 0AR; www.escocesa.co.uk; @escocesaN16; Mon-Thu 10 pm, Fri & Sat 10.30 pm, Sun 9.30 pm.

Essenza W11 £63 343
210 Kensington Park Rd 020 7792 1066 7–1A
"Reliable and very friendly Italian", which – along with its nearby siblings Mediterraneo and Osteria Basilico – is 'part of the furniture' in the heart of Notting Hill; truffles are something of a speciality. / W11 1NR; www.essenza.co.uk; 11.30 pm.

Estiatorio Milos SW1 £122 333
1 Regent St 020 7839 2080 2–3C
"Amazingly fresh fish" chosen from an icy display helps seduce devotees of this "lovely" looking new Greek fish specialist in the West End – a glamorous outpost of Costas Spiliadis's luxurious international group. Even fans note that "you could pay a small king's ransom here" however, and to cynics "it's an attempt to out-Moscow Moscow" – "stacks of dead fish on an iceberg is not decor and £15 for a teeny starter is not real life!" / SW1Y 4NR, www.milos.ca/restaurants/london; Lunch 12-3pm 11pm.

Ethos W1 £39 323
48 Eastcastle St 020 3581 1538 3–1C
"Very tasty" self-service veggie near Oxford Circus, where you pay by weight (and less for take-away). Vegan and paleo options, as well as alcohol. / W1W 8DX; www.ethosfoods.com; @ethosfoods; 10 pm, Sun 4 pm; closed Sun D; may need 6+ to book.

L'Etranger SW7 £72 332
36 Gloucester Rd 020 7584 1118 6–1B
"Elegant and poised dishes combining French technique with Asian flavours" plus an extremely impressive wine list earn a loyal following for this offbeat fixture, tucked away near the Royal Albert Hall. "Subdued decor and lighting lend romance" to this "serene room, with a slight air of the '80s about it". / SW7 4QT; www.etranger.co.uk; @letrangerSW7; 11 pm; closed Sun; credit card deposit required to book.

Everest Inn SE3 £37 433
41 Montpelier Vale 020 8852 7872 1–4D
"High-quality Gurkha dishes" and "Nepalese specialities" ("they do really tender tandoori meats") make this Blackheath favourite "a cut above your average curry house", even if "service can be a bit chaotic". / SE3 0TJ; www.everestinnblackheath.co.uk; 11.30 pm, Fri & Sat midnight; set weekday L £23 (FP).

Eyre Brothers EC2 £64 533
70 Leonard St 020 7613 5346 13–1B
"Superb food from Spain and Portugal (both as sit-down meals and light tapas at the bar)" provides ample motivation to seek out this "warm and stylish" haunt near Silicon Roundabout. There's also "the finest selection of Iberian wine", including sparklers, rosés and sherry. / EC2A 4QX; www.eyrebrothers.co.uk; @eyrebrothers2; 10.30 pm, Sun 4 pm; closed Sun D.

Faanoos £27 332

472 Chiswick High Rd, W4
020 8994 4217 8–2A
11 Bond St, W5 020 8810 0505 1–3A
481 Richmond Road, SW14
020 8878 5738 1–4A

A mini-chain serving "fab Persian-style chicken or lamb kebabs", fresh salads and flatbreads, which has built a strong following in Chiswick, Ealing and East Sheen. "The meat's good quality, the dishes tasty and the prices very reasonable". / SW14 11 pm; W4 11 pm; Fri & Sat midnight.

Fairuz W1 £48 333

3 Blandford St 020 7486 8108 2–1A

This Marylebone Lebanese stalwart wins consistent praise and solid ratings across the board for its "good Middle Eastern fare" and "attentive staff". / W1H 3DA; www.fairuz.uk.com; 11 pm, Sun 10.30 pm.

Falafel King W10 £9 322

274 Portobello Rd 020 8964 2279 7–1A

"Still the best falafel in London" claim fans of this simple Notting Hill pitstop – given the pace of service though, it's not always fast food. / W10 5TE; 7 pm.

La Famiglia SW10 £52 224

7 Langton St 020 7351 0761 6–3B

"You can always rely on this longstanding Chelsea favourite", say fans of this family-run and family-friendly "classic". Even they often admit that it's "pricey", or that the food nowadays is "not particularly good", but they treasure its "fun", "buzzy" style, and "lovely" back garden in summer. / SW10 0JL; www.lafamiglia.co.uk; @lafamiglia_sw10; 11 pm.

Farang SE1

Flat Iron Sq 07903 834 808 5–1A

Head chef of Soho's tiny Thai Smoking Goat, Seb Holmes, is to open a new Vietnamese restaurant just south of Borough Market in autumn 2016, after testing out his menus at supper clubs in Highbury's San Daniele. / SE1; www.faranglondon.co.uk; @farangLDN.

Farley Macallan E9 £34

177-179 Morning Lane 020 8510 9169 14–1B

Hot on the heels of wine-bar-cum-café, Legs, another new vino-focused venture landed in summer 2016 in Hackney's Morning Lane. There's a range of biodynamic wines by the glass and bottle alongside food from the E5 Smokehouse. Hackney's Five Points Brewery provides the beers. / E9 6LH; www.farleymacallan.com; @MeetFarley; midnight, Fri & Sat 1 am, Sun 10 pm; closed Mon, Tue, Wed L, Thu L & Fri L.

Farmacy W2 £54

74-76 Westbourne Grove
020 7221 0705 7–1B

Plant-based newcomer (inspired by founder Camilla Al Fayed's travels to California) in Bayswater offering health-conscious vegan cuisine – including its signature 'Farmacy Burger' and plant-based ice cream sundaes – and with pharmacist-inspired decor. One early-days reporter said: "Great to see a really healthy restaurant in the 'hood. We went on their first day and found interesting food showing that veggies can be satisfying!" / W2 5SH; www.farmacylondon.com; @farmacyuk; 11 pm, Sun 7 pm.

Fenchurch Restaurant, Sky Garden EC3 £82 333

20 Fenchurch St 033 3772 0020 10–3D

"The wonderful setting adds drama and panache" to this "contemporary and loungey" venue, 150m above the City below; but for somewhere with such "brilliant views" (although "oddly better on the way up") the food (from caterers, Rhubarb) is "much better than expected". / EC3M 3BY; skygarden.london/fenchurch-restaurant; @SG_Fenchurch.

FERA AT CLARIDGE'S, CLARIDGE'S HOTEL W1 £116 444

49 Brook St 020 7107 8888 3–2B

"Utterly sublime on every level" – Simon Rogan's three-year-old tenure in this "luxurious" (and "surprisingly large") Art Deco dining room has hit an even stride, providing "mindblowing food that's experimental and fun", "warm service" and a "glorious" atmosphere (although "the earthenware plates do clash a bit with the decor"). "It's not a budget option" ("prices are unjustifiable" for a few reporters) but, Top Tip – "set lunch is fantastic value". This year Rogan also added the new Aulis '6-seat development table' in a private room off the kitchen: "a magical, innovative dining experience – what makes it incredible is listening to Dan talk about the ingredients, how the team came across it, and the thinking and creative process behind each course." / W1K 4HR; www.feraatclaridges.co.uk; @FeraAtClaridges; 10 pm.

La Ferme EC1 £41 322

102-104 Farrington 020 7837 5293 10–1A

Near Exmouth Market, this new deli and restaurant's rustique styling is laid on heavily with a pitchfork (one of the items adorning the walls). The Gallic cooking is more ambitious than its small premises might imply – the odd disastrous meal is reported, but it can be very good. / EC1R 3EA; www.lafermelondon.com; @lafermelondon; 10.30 pm; closed Sun.

Fernandez & Wells £48 333
16a St Anne's Ct, W1 020 7494 4242 4–1D
43 Lexington St, W1 020 7734 1546 4–2D
73 Beak St, W1 020 7287 8124 4–2C
Somerset Hs, Strand, WC2
020 7420 9408 2–2D
"Securing a chair is like fighting for a life-jacket on the Titanic (and worth it!)", say fans of these funky cafés with "always good" coffee, plus high-quality sarnies and pastries. / www.fernandezandwells.com; Lexington St & St Anne's court 10 pm, Beak St 6 pm, Somerset House 11 pm; St Anne's Court closed Sun.

Fez Mangal W11 £26 543
104 Ladbroke Grove 020 7229 3010 7–1A
"Delicious charcoal-grilled fish and meat as well as tasty mezze" ("comparing well with Istanbul") means there are often queues at this small Notting Hill Turk. "No licence – and no corkage charged" means it's also "incredible value". / W11 1PY; www.fezmangal.com; @FezMangal; 11.30 pm; no Amex.

Ffiona's W8 £60 344
51 Kensington Church St
020 7937 4152 6–1A
Diners are made to feel welcome and special by the eponymous patronne of this "romantic" Kensington stalwart, which focuses on well-cooked traditional British dishes, and is popular for weekend brunches. / W8 4BA; www.ffionas.com; @ffionasnotes; 11 pm, Sun 10 pm; closed Mon; no Amex.

Fields SW4 £32 333
2 Rookery Rd no tel 11–2C
"The owners of hip Balham coffee shop Milk know what they're doing", and this takeover of a park café on Clapham Common delivers some "really interesting brunch options". "It can be windy, though, so take care to find the right table". / SW4 9DD; www.fieldscafe.com; @fieldscafe; 5 pm, Fri 4 pm; L only; no bookings.

Fifteen N1 £69 223
15 Westland Pl 020 3375 1515 13–1A
The project which helped Jamie Oliver establish his meeja career: this Hoxton Italian continues to divide reporters (although above all else they ignore it – for all the hype it remains well off London's 'foodie map'). Fans do applaud its "delicious dishes, buzzing atmosphere and great gin list", but as ever a significant proportion dismiss it as average-to-poor across the board. / N1 7LP; www.fifteen.net; @JamiesFifteen; 10.30 pm, Sun 9.30 pm; booking max 12 may apply.

Figlio Del Vesuvio SW17 £29 442
658 Garratt Lane 020 3609 1118 11–2B
"Never judge a book by its cover!" This "tiny, cramped" and "wholly authentic" new Neapolitan may be "lacking in location (on a roundabout in the no-mans-land between Earlsfield and Tooting Broadway) and interior aesthetics" but serves "sensational wood-fired pizzas, cooked to perfection at incredibly competitive prices". Cash only. / SW17; figlidelvesuvio.com; @figli_vesuvio; 11 pm; closed Tue.

Fischer's W1 £62 334
50 Marylebone High St 020 7466 5501 2–1A
Corbin & King's "meticulous interpretation of a classic Austrian/German restaurant" in Marylebone "captures the essence of Mitteleuropa perfectly" – "the food is a slightly stodgy, warm embrace", and the "beautiful, deeply coloured, panelled interior" creates a very "gemutlich" ambience. Top Menu Tip – "delicious schnitzel". / W1U 5HN; www.fischers.co.uk; @FischersLondon; 11 pm, Sun 10 pm.

Fish Cafe NW3 £38 223
71 Hampstead High St 020 7433 1430 9–2A
A newish venture of the Villa Bianca Group – this Hampstead two-year-old is, say fans, "a quality fish restaurant hiding behind a fish 'n' chips frontage"; the odd sceptic though accuses it of an "unimpressive" performance. / NW3; www.villabiancagroup.co.uk; 11 pm.

Fish Central EC1 £32 332
149-155 Central St 020 7253 4970 13–1A
"A favourite with cabbies for good reason" – this "socially diverse" and "friendly" Clerkenwell chippie is a "fantastic bargain". "High-quality specials are all fresh that day and cost less than at Borough Market, without the need to cook it yourself!" / EC1V 8AP; www.fishcentral.co.uk; 10.30 pm, Fri 11 pm; closed Sun.

Fish Club SW11 £40 322
189 St John's Hill 020 7978 7115 11–2C
This modern take on the classic fish 'n' chip shop in Battersea wins praise for "always fresh fish" as well as some unexpected extras: "love the sweet potato chips", and "even the Caesar salad is delicious". / SW11 1TH; www.thefishclub.com; 10 pm, Sun 10pm; closed Mon L.

Fish in a Tie SW11 £35 232
105 Falcon Rd 020 7924 1913 11–1C
"Decent food and wine at great prices" makes it worth remembering this "friendly" bistro – a handy "cheap 'n' cheerful" option north of Clapham Junction. / SW11 2PF; www.fishinatie.com; midnight, Sun 11 pm.

Fish Market EC2 £55 322
16b New St 020 3503 0790 10–2D
"The catch of the day is always a good choice" at this atmospheric converted warehouse near Bishopsgate. It's a "nice enough member of the D&D stable, though unremarkable" beyond the "well-cooked fish". / EC2M 4TR;

www.fishmarket-restaurant.co.uk; @FishMarketNS; 10.30 pm, Sun 4 pm; closed Sun D.

fish! SE1 £56 322

Cathedral St 020 7407 3803 10–4C

Glazed shed by Borough Market capable of being "an excellent fish restaurant, with plenty to choose from in a lively atmosphere". It can feel "noisy, crowded, hot and touristy" however, and given "food that's quite basic, plus occasionally indifferent service", prices can seem "OTT". / SE1 9AL; www.fishkitchen.com; @fishborough; 11 pm, Sun 10.30 pm.

Fishworks £60 322

7-9 Swallow St, W1 020 7734 5813 4–4C

89 Marylebone High St, W1

020 7935 9796 2–1A

"Simply cooked, very fresh fish" is the "straightforward formula done well" at these plain West End bistros. Aside from the fact that you walk through a fishmongers to dine, they "have no pretence to be anything other than upmarket fish 'n' chip restaurants". / www.fishworks.co.uk; 10.30 pm.

The Five Fields SW3 £89 554

8-9 Blacklands Ter 020 7838 1082 6–2D

"The epitome of fine dining, minus the stuffiness" – Taylor Bonnyman's "unflashy and grown-up" three-year-old, "tucked way in Chelsea" offers "an all-round fantastic experience". The setting is "elegant", service "genuine and unpretentious"; while the cuisine is "truly exceptional – exciting, yet accessible and (most importantly) delicious" ("expect an astonishing array of amuse bouches"). Until October 2016, this was perhaps "Michelin's most shocking omission", but finally the tyre men divvied up the requisite star. / SW3 2SP; www.fivefieldsrestaurant.com; @The5Fields; 10 pm; closed Mon L, Tue L, Wed L, Thu L, Fri L, Sat & Sun; no trainers.

Five Guys £13 322

1-3 Long Acre, WC2 020 7240 2657 5–3C

71 Upper St, N1 020 7226 7577 9–3D

"McDonald's makes more effort on the decor!", but these "amped-up fast food" joints do "great customisable burgers" ("be prepared to get messy"), "massive portions of fries", and "interesting, more-ish shakes". / @FiveGuysUK; –.

500 N19 £48 342

782 Holloway Rd 020 7272 3406 9–1C

"A haven of good food in an area not famed for gastronomy" – this "sincere, friendly and convivial" Holloway Italian provides "excellent" Sicilian food, and it's "great value" too. / N19 3JH; www.500restaurant.co.uk; @500restaurant; 10.30 pm, Sun 9.30 pm; Mon-Thu D only, Fri-Sun open L & D.

Flat Iron £22 433

17 Beak St, W1 no tel 4–2B

17 Henrietta St, WC2 no tel 5–4C

9 Denmark St, WC2 no tel 5–1A

77 Curtain Road, EC2 no tel 13–1B

"If you want simple steak, well-delivered at a bargain price, you can't go wrong" with these "consistent and effective" West End haunts (where "the unfashionable flat iron cut is elevated to first rank, and identified farms and rearing practices give credibility to the final product"). "Despite fairly basic surroundings, they feel somehow pleasant" even if "the queues are less great" ("they take your mobile number and text you when your table's ready").

Flat Three W11 £82 442

120-122 Holland Park Ave

020 7792 8987 7–2A

Limited feedback on this minimalistic Holland Park basement (originally a supper club) whose fusion cuisine blends Japanese and Scandi' influences – fans rate the food as absolutely outstanding, but some visitors feel it's a case of style over substance. / W11 4UA; www.flatthree.london; @infoflat3; Tue-Sat 9.30 pm; closed Mon & Sun.

Flesh & Buns WC2 £50 333

41 Earlham St 020 7632 9500 5–2C

"Packed to the gills with a loud and well-lubricated crowd", this "buzzing and cool" Soho basement (sibling to Bone Daddies) provides "fab" steamed buns that are "so good and fresh", plus "excellent hot stone rice dishes". / WC2H 9LX; www.bonedaddies.com/flesh-and-buns; @FleshandBuns; Mon & Tue 10.30 pm, Wed-Sat 9.30 pm, Sun 9.30 pm; booking max 8 may apply.

Flora Indica SW5

242 Old Brompton Rd 020 7370 4450 6–2A

Remember Mr Wing? Well, you're getting on a bit then! But this British/Indian fusion venture opened in summer 2016 on the two-floor Earl's Court site long known for its party potential. It's the work of former Benares chef Sameer Taneja and – with echoes of its distant predecessor – puts a big emphasis on cocktails. / SW5 0DE; www.flora-indica.com; @Flora_Indica.

Flotsam & Jetsam SW17 £17 344

4 Bellevue Parade 020 8672 7639 11–2C

"Australian coffee shop on the edge of Wandsworth Common" that's "a hit in a location that has always failed" – "eternally busy", with "helpful staff" serving up "very good breakfasts" (but "don't go if you take the King Herod view of young children!)" / SW17 7EQ; www.flotsamandjetsamcafe.co.uk; @_flotsam_jetsam; 5 pm; L only; no bookings.

FM Mangal SE5 £31 332
54 Camberwell Church St
020 7701 6677 1–4D
"A real gem in Camberwell", this Turk offers "fantastic value" for its "addictive grilled flatbread, smoky onions and toothsome grilled lamb in varying styles of preparation and spicing". "Deservedly, it's always busy". / SE5 8QZ; midnight; no Amex; no bookings.

Foley's W1
23 Foley Street 020 3137 1302 2–1B
Following a six-week pop-up (Foley's Tasting Kitchen) in Shepherd's Bush, this roaming operation has found a full-time home in Fitzrovia. The 70-cover restaurant is open all day and vaunts an open kitchen with counter dining and an alfresco coffee bar. Former Palomar chef Mitz Vora serves up an internationally-influenced menu inspired by the spice trail. / W1W 6DU; www.foleysrestaurant.co.uk; @foleyslondon.

Fortnum & Mason, The Diamond Jubilee Tea Salon W1 £66 333
181 Piccadilly 020 7734 8040 3–3D
"The best selection of teas in town" and "exceptional, endlessly refreshed platters" of sandwiches and cakes help establish this "stylish and beautiful" chamber on the third floor of the famous St James's grocery store as "a wonderful spot for a special celebration afternoon tea". / W1A 1ER; www.fortnumandmason.com; @fortnumandmason; 7 pm, Sun 6 pm.

45 Jermyn St SW1 £69 344
45 Jermyn St., St. James's London
020 7205 4545 3–3D
"Like stepping back to a much more glamorous time – the champagne, the caviar, the leather booths, even the little golden coat tickets all make an evening here very special" – F&M's successful relaunch of its all-day restaurant (formerly The Fountain, RIP) has injected more pizazz into the venue, which serves "decent if very safe food with a really good (and good-value) wine list". Top Tip – it's still "a fantastic spot for breakfast" (but doesn't do afternoon tea any more). / SW1A 6DN; www.45jermynst.com; @Fortnums; 11 pm, Sun 6 pm; closed Sun D.

40 Maltby Street SE1 £54 433
40 Maltby St 020 7237 9247 10–4D
"Carefully selected natural wines from small vineyards" are twinned with Steve Williams's "changing blackboard menu full of delights" that are "served from a tiny kitchen behind the bar" at this "truly exceptional" wine warehouse, in the well-known foodie enclave near London Bridge station. / SE1 3PA; www.40maltbystreet.com; @40maltbystreet; 9.30 pm; closed Mon, Tue, Wed L, Thu L & Sun; no Amex; no bookings.

The Four Seasons £50 411
12 Gerrard St, W1 020 7494 0870 5–3A
23 Wardour St, W1 020 7287 9995 5–3A
84 Queensway, W2 020 7229 4320 7–2C
"The famous roast duck may not be the world's best but it's extremely good" (as is the "addictive crispy pork belly") at these Chinese "classics", in Bayswater and Chinatown. "You don't go for the surroundings, and certainly not for the service!" / www.fs-restaurants.co.uk; Queensway 11 pm, Sun 10h45 pm; Gerrard St 1 am; Wardour St 1am, Fri-Sat 3.30 am.

The Fox & Hounds SW11 £50 444
66 Latchmere Rd 020 7924 5483 11–1C
This "buzzy" Battersea sibling to Earl's Court's Altas "assumes no airs and graces, but punches out its ever-changing Mediterranean-led menu at top standard, with, awesome real ales in great condition". / SW11 2JU; www.thefoxandhoundspub.co.uk; @thefoxbattersea; 10 pm; Mon-Thu D only, Fri-Sun open L & D.

The Fox & Anchor EC1 £55 334
115 Charterhouse St 020 7250 1300 10–1B
This "wonderful", "hidden-away" Victorian pub, complete with "cosy snugs", was built for meat market workers at nearby Smithfield Market – hence the 7am opening, when it's "perfect for traditional cooked breakfast and a pint". There's an "excellent range of beers on hand pump complemented by good hearty English food cooked very well with fresh ingredients". / EC1M 6AA; www.foxandanchor.com; @foxanchor; Mon-Sat 9.30 pm, Sun 6 pm.

Foxlow £51 222
11 Barley Mow Pas, W4 020 7680 2702 8–2A
71-73 Stoke Newington Ch' St, N16
020 7014 8070 1–1C
15-19 Bedford Hill, SW12
020 7680 2700 11–2C
St John St, EC1 020 7014 8070 10–2A
For a "reliable and solid" meat-fest, fans commend these Hawksmoor-lite spin-offs, also tipped for a "great brunch" and for "going the extra mile for kids". Even supporters can say they are "not exciting" though, and critics say: "I really, really, really want to love it, but I find the food and menu disappointing". / www.foxlow.co.uk; @FoxlowTweets; SRA-3 star.

Franco Manca £22 433
"Who knew a chain could do such great pizza?!" – their "slightly chewy", but thin, fresh and "so-darn-tasty" wood-fired, sourdough crusts (plus "a few simple toppings packed with flavour") help maintain surprisingly high ratings for this VC-backed brand. Branches are "chaotic and noisy" but "for such authentic quality they still offer amazing value". / www.francomanca.co.uk; SW9 10.30, Mon 5 pm;

W4 11 pm; E20 9 pm, Thu-Sat 10 pm, Sun 6 pm; no bookings.

Franco's SW1 £74 333

61 Jermyn St 020 7499 2211 3–3C

This "very old school St James's destination comes with starched linen tablecloths, courteous waiters, high quality – if unadventurous – Italian food... and astronomical prices"; ("just walking in seemingly adds £1m to your personal net worth, but while plutocratic it carries none of the blingy nonsense that passes for style in flashier quarters"). A natural for local pinstripes: "sometimes I just sit and make it my office from breakfast onwards!" / SW1Y 6LX; www.francoslondon.com; @francoslondon; 10.30 pm; closed Sun.

Franklins SE22 £55 433

157 Lordship Ln 020 8299 9598 1–4D

Well-established Dulwich neighbourhood fixture (with farm shop on the other side of the road), very consistently praised for its above-average modern British cooking (with a fair amount of game). "Sadly brunch is only on a Saturday". / SE22 8HX; www.franklinsrestaurant.com; @frankinsse22; 10.30 pm, Sun 10 pm; no Amex; set brunch £29 (FP).

Frantoio SW10 £56 234

397 King's Rd 020 7352 4146 6–3B

A "huge greeting when you arrive" from flamboyant host Bucci creates an "atmosphere more like a club", at this "bubbly and dependable" World's End trat. The cooking is generally good, "if slightly resting on its gastronomic laurels". / SW10 0LR; www.frantoio.co.uk; 11 pm.

Frederick's N1 £64 234

106 Camden Passage 020 7359 2888 9–3D

"Islington lacks upmarket restaurants", and this "well-spaced" and "attractive" old veteran – complete with "good-looking conservatory and lovely outside tables on a warm day" – has a loyal (generally silver-haired) fanclub. It's not a foodie fave rave though, with "cooking that's more akin to banqueting than to haute cuisine". / N1 8EG; www.fredericks.co.uk; @fredericks_n1; 11 pm; closed Sun; set dinner £34 (FP).

Frenchie WC2 £72 422

18 Henrietta St 020 7836 4422 5–3C

"Believe the hype!" – Grégory Marchand's "transplant direct from Paris" (where he owns a venture of the same name) is proving "a great new addition to Covent Garden", on the prominent, corner site (with basement) that was for yonks Porters (nowadays transplanted to Berkhamsted). Its appeal is his "skilled and beautiful" modern French cuisine however – service can be "slack" and the "informal", "buzzing" interior can seem too "noisy" and "cramped". / WC2E 8QH; www.frenchiecoventgarden.com; @frenchiecoventgarden; 10.30 pm.

The Frog E1

Old Truman Brewery, Hanbury St

020 3813 9832 13–2C

MasterChef finalist Adam Handling left his restaurant at St Ermin Hotel to open his own venture in Shoreditch in summer 2016 (apparently the first of many planned under 'The Frog' brand). His cuisine in Westminster sometimes seemed a tad "tortured" and "pretentious" – just right for the local hipsters? / E1 6QR; www.thefrogrestaurant.com; @TheFrogE1; closed Mon & Sun D.

La Fromagerie Café W1 £45 322

2-6 Moxon St 020 7935 0341 3–1A

"Cheese, soups, teas... the quality is good" at this superior Marylebone café attached to the acclaimed cheese store. "Fantastic breakfast" too – "even if you have toast, it's the best bread, best butter, best marmalade...!" / W1U 4EW; www.lafromagerie.co.uk; @lafromagerieuk; 7.30 pm, Sat 7 pm, Sun 6 pm; L only; no bookings.

The Frontline Club W2 £56

13 Norfolk Pl 020 7479 8960 7–1D

"In an area of fast food joints", this comfortable dining room – part of a journalists' club for war reporters – is known for its "really consistent food, with fine wine at affordable prices". It further upped the ante in summer 2016, re-launching after a major revamp adding a mezzanine, and with higher culinary ambition (so for the time being we've left it un-rated). / W2 1QJ; www.frontlineclub.com; @frontlineclub; 11 pm; closed Sat L & Sun.

Fumo WC2

37 St Martin's Lane 5–4C

An 'all-day Italian and chic cocktail bar' concept from the San Carlo group (Cicchetti, Signor Sassi), Fumo is already open in Birmingham and Manchester, and made its London debut, in Covent Garden, in September 2016. / WC2N 4JS; www.sancarlofumo.co.uk/fumo-london/.

Gaby's WC2 £33 322

30 Charing Cross Rd 020 7836 4233 5–3B

"I'm so glad it's survived!" This "iconic" and "indispensable" – if "slightly crumbling" – caff by Leicester Square tube (Jeremy Corbyn's favourite!) beat off the developers a couple of years ago, so saving its "absolutely fantastic falafel", "exemplary salt beef" and "delicious healthy salads". "The chairs and tables are vinyl and Formica covered, and service rarely involves a smile, but at least the plentiful posters signed by stars of stage and screen take your mind off the Spartan surroundings". / WC2H 0DE; midnight, Sun 10 pm; no Amex.

Gallery Mess, Saatchi Gallery SW3 £52 223
Duke of Yorks HQ, Kings Rd
020 7730 8135 6–2D
The food at Charles Saatchi's Chelsea art gallery generates little enthusiasm, but the "mess" in the former Duke of York's HQ makes a useful venue for a business lunch, and "on a sunny day the outdoor tables are quiet and classy". / SW3 4RY; www.saatchigallery.com/gallerymess; @gallerymess; 11 pm, Sun 7 pm; closed Sun D.

Galley N1 £58 434
105-106 Upper St 020 3670 0740 9–3D
"A lot of thought and care has gone into Galley – a new, firm Islington favourite". The headline attractions are the "superb seafood choices, with a mix of small and large plates" but the "very smart" interior design also gets the thumbs up. / N1 1QN; www.galleylondon.co.uk; @Galleylondon; 11 pm.

Gallipoli £35 344
102 Upper St, N1 020 7359 0630 9–3D
107 Upper St, N1 020 7226 5333 9–3D
120 Upper St, N1 020 7226 8099 9–3D
These "intimate, bazaar-style" Turkish cafés with "over-the-top" Ottoman-themed décor are just a few doors apart on Islington's main drag. From "excellent mezze to breakfast" the scoff's "serviceable and good value" (and "far better than you might expect"). / www.cafegallipoli.com; 11 pm, Fri & Sat midnight.

Galvin at the Athenaeum W1 £68
Athenaeum Hotel, 116 Piccadilly
020 7640 3557 3–4B
In July 2016 (post-survey) the Galvin brothers annexed this gracious but perennially overlooked dining room in an Art Deco hotel, facing Green Park. This is their first venture to put the emphasis more on British rather than French cuisine (and will continue to offer afternoon tea – previously one of the greater attractions here). / W1J 7BJ; www.athenaeumhotel.com; @Galvin_brothers; 11 pm.

Galvin at Windows, Park Lane London Hilton Hotel W1 £101 235
22 Park Ln 020 7208 4021 3–4A
"To wow a client", or to create an ambience "conducive to seduction", the "stunning" panorama from this 28th-floor park-side Mayfair chamber is – say fans – "unbeatable". "It's the view that makes it" though, "not the Identikit hotel decor", while the "decent" cuisine is in something of a supporting role. Top Tip – enjoy a better vista for the price of a cocktail at the adjacent bar! / W1K 1BE; www.galvinatwindows.com; @GalvinatWindows; 10 pm, Thu-Sat 10.30 pm, Sun 3 pm; closed Sat L & Sun D; no trainers; set weekday L £53 (FP), set Sun L £72 (FP).

Galvin Bistrot de Luxe W1 £69 333
66 Baker St 020 7935 4007 2–1A
"Still delivering no-nonsense, quality after more than 10 years" – the Galvin brothers' original venture, south of Baker Street tube, has built its renown on serving "consistent bistro cuisine" in a "buzzy", business-friendly setting. "It's starting to slip" though, with ratings now middling across the board. / W1U 7DJ; www.galvinbistrotdeluxe.com; @bistrotdeluxe; Mon-Wed 10.30 pm, Thu-Sat 10.45 pm, Sun 9.30 pm; set weekday L £22 (FP), set dinner & pre-theatre £24 (FP).

Galvin HOP E1 £56 443
35 Spital Sq 020 7299 0404 13–2B
On the former site of Café à Vin – to which has been added Pilsner tanks and an open kitchen – the Galvin brothers' new posh, City-fringe gastropub is the flagship of their new company (Galvin Pub de Luxe), on early reports it's the very competent, upscale boozer you'd expect. / E1 6DY; www.galvinrestaurants.com/section/62/1/galvinhop; @Galvin_brothers; 10.30 pm, Sun 9.30 pm; booking max 5 may apply.

GALVIN LA CHAPELLE E1 £82 334
35 Spital Sq 020 7299 0400 13–2B
"The breathtaking architecture of the building" – "a beautiful, cathedral-like space" created from the "clever conversion of a Victorian school chapel" – creates a "magnificent" setting for the Galvin brothers' well-known venture, near Spitalfields. At its best, this is one of London's most "memorable" all-rounders (particularly for business) combining "smooth" service and "subtle cuisine" into a "sumptuous" overall offering. Performance was less consistent this year however, with reports of "over-stretched if well-intentioned" service, and "uneven" culinary results. / E1 6DY; www.galvinlachapelle.com; @galvin_brothers; 10.30 pm, Sun 9.30 pm; no trainers; set weekday L, dinner, pre-theatre & Sun L £35 (FP).

Ganapati SE15 £43 543
38 Holly Grove 020 7277 2928 1–4C
"The true flavours of South India, with no compromises and no frills" have won a formidable foodie reputation for "what is little more than a corner shop" in Peckham; "delightful people" too. / SE15 5DF; www.ganapatirestaurant.com; 10.30 pm, Sun 10 pm; closed Mon; no Amex.

Le Garrick WC2 £52 234
10-12 Garrick St 020 7240 7649 5–3C
"Expect candles and inviting booths" in this "quirky and romantic" bistro in the heart of Covent Garden. "It's not high-end cuisine" (on occasion a bit "second rate") but it's generally "good value" and "very handy as a pre-theatre option". / WC2E 9BH; www.legarrick.co.uk; @le_garrick; 10.30 pm; closed Sun; set pre-theatre £28 (FP), set Sun L £32 (FP).

The Garrison SE1 £51 324
99-101 Bermondsey St 020 7089 9355 10–4D
"Slightly cramped but buzzy" green-tiled former pub, once at the forefront of Bermondsey's gastro-revival with its transformation into a food-led dining venue over a decade ago. It still has a "lively atmosphere", the "fish 'n' chips are brilliant" (and there's even a cinema for private viewings in the basement). / SE1 3XB; www.thegarrison.co.uk; @TheGarrisonSE1; 10 pm, Sun 9.30 pm.

Gastronhome SW11 £67 543
59 Lavender Hill, London
020 3417 5639 11–2C
"A surprising and welcome find in Lavender Hill" – Damien Fremont and Christopher Nespoux's "homely" yet "truly exceptional" French three-year-old provides an "enthusiastic" welcome, and "adds a real level of quality" to the local eating destinations. "If you can, go for the tasting menu for some really sublime dishes, and there are some brilliant accompanying wines". / SW11; www.gastronhome.co.uk; 10:15 pm; closed Mon; no jeans.

The Gate £48 433
51 Queen Caroline St, W6
020 8748 6932 8–2C
370 St John St, EC1 020 7278 5483 9–3D
"Still producing exceptional veggie dishes after 25 years" – "the best in town" – this popular duo are "a good advertisement for meat-free food, proving it can be interesting and full of flavour". The original – an intriguing "converted artists' loft" that's "hidden away" behind Hammersmith Odeon – is "splendid in an area devoid of decent restaurants", while its younger sibling is "really convenient for Sadler's Wells". / www.thegaterestaurants.com; @gaterestaurant; EC1 10.30 pm, W6 10.30, Sat 11 pm; SRA-3 star.

Gatti's £63 333
1 Finsbury Ave, EC2 020 7247 1051 13–2B
1 Ropemaker St, EC2 020 7628 8375 13–2A
"You can't fault the model" of this business-friendly City duo in Broadgate and nearby Moorgate – "Italians just like they used to be". / closed Sat & Sun.

Gaucho £74 221
"It used to be so good, what happened?" London's first upscale contemporary steak-house chain still wins praise for its "pretty fine Argentinian meat", and "wonderful" Latino wines, but its glitzy (sometimes "very loud and very dark") branches have increasingly "lost their charm". "Stratospheric" prices are the main issue, and "with so many good steak options at all levels these days, it's hard to see where Gaucho fits in". / www.gauchorestaurants.co.uk; 11 pm; EC3 & EC1 closed Sat & Sun, WC2 & EC2 closed Sat L & Sun.

GAUTHIER SOHO W1 £72 554
21 Romilly St 020 7494 3111 5–3A
"A haven in a busy part of Soho" – this "delightful" Georgian townhouse is "made all the more special by having to ring the doorbell" to enter, and once inside, its "peaceful" series of rooms "exude romance". However "it's the food that's the key element" – Alexis Gauthier's "top-league French cuisine" features "brilliant flavour combinations", and is matched by a "varied and exciting" wine list, while staff provide "wonderful hospitality from start to finish". Top Tip – "the lunchtime deal is amazing value". / W1D 5AF; www.gauthiersoho.co.uk; @GauthierSoho; Tue-Thu 9.30 pm, Fri & Sat 10.30 pm; closed Mon & Sun; booking max 7 may apply; set weekday L £46 (FP).

LE GAVROCHE W1 £132 554
43 Upper Brook St 020 7408 0881 3–2A
London's oldest temple of Gallic gastronomy narrowly missed the No. 1 slot in this year's survey, but for its legions of fans remains "the absolute pinnacle of fine dining". Established by Albert Roux nearly 50 years ago (and run by his son, Michel Roux Jr for the last 25), its hallmark style combines "richly indulgent" cuisine (overseen by head chef Rachel Humphrey) and an "astonishing, predominantly French wine list", served in a "classy" if "dated", "'70s-France" basement setting, while it follows a pleasing, "slightly anachronistic" formula ("jackets required for men, ladies' menus don't have prices"). "Ever-attentive, charming and unostentatious" staff add further to the experience, as does the "accessibility and personal attention" of the main man, who is much in evidence. The price? – best not to ask, but the set lunch is "stonking value". Top Menu Tip – soufflé Suissesse. / W1K 7QR; www.le-gavroche.co.uk; @legavroche_; 10 pm; closed Mon, Sat L & Sun; jacket required; set weekday L £63 (FP).

Gay Hussar W1 £50 234
2 Greek St 020 7437 0973 5–2A
The "ambience, history and wonderful caricatures lining the walls" are the stuff of Labour party legend at this Soho Hungarian institution. "Never mind the middling Mittel European food", it's "still reminiscent of the old days". / W1D 4NB; www.gayhussar.co.uk; @GayhussarsSoho; 10.45 pm; closed Sun.

Gaylord W1 £60 343
79-81 Mortimer St 020 7580 3615 2–1B
"Step back into the '70s (if not at '70s prices)" at this "ultimate traditional Indian" – a "favourite for authentic North Indian dishes" since it opened 50 years ago in Fitzrovia. The interior can feel "a little staid" but "wakes up in the evening", and "service is hard to surpass". / W1W 7SJ; www.gaylordlondon.com; @gaylord_london; 10.45 pm, Sun 10.30 pm; set pre theatre £38 (FP).

Gazette £39 223

79 Sherwood Ct, Chatfield Rd, SW11
020 7223 0999 11–1C
100 Balham High St, SW12
020 8772 1232 11–2C
147 Upper Richmond Rd, SW15
020 8789 6996 11–2B

"Great fun" and "traditional" (if "pretty variable") bistro cooking have won praise for this small family-friendly group with venues in Balham, Clapham and Putney. "Service is not always up to scratch, but it's local and it's French". / www.gazettebrasserie.co.uk; 11 pm.

Geales £53 122

1 Cale St, SW3 020 7965 0555 6–2C
2 Farmer St, W8 020 7727 7528 7–2B

Diehard fans still applaud this veteran (est 1939) fish 'n' chip restaurant off Notting Hill Gate (and with a much more recent Chelsea spin-off), but they disappoint far too many reporters nowadays: "they used to be great… sadly no more". / www.geales.com; @geales1; 10.30 pm, Sun 9.30 pm; Mon L.

Gelupo W1 £9 522

7 Archer St 020 7287 5555 4–3D

"Offbeat but brilliant gelateria" with branches in Soho and Cambridge Circus – "the best ice cream I have had in the UK – and I've tried a lot!" Service, though, can be a bit "Fawlty Towers". / W1D 7AU; www.gelupo.com; 11 pm, Fri & Sat midnight; no Amex; no bookings.

Gem N1 £34 343

265 Upper St 020 7359 0405 9–2D

"Bread being prepared in the window draws you in" to this "cracking" and "aptly named" Turkish-Kurdish local near Angel. "You'll be welcomed like a regular and overfed (portions are generous)" and it's "reliable", "family-friendly" and "great value for money". / N1 2UQ; www.gemrestaurant.org.uk; @Gem_restaurant; 11 pm, Sun 10 pm; no Amex.

German Gymnasium N1 £69 223

King's Boulevard 020 7287 8000 9–3C

The "jaw-dropping building" – "a high-ceilinged, former Victorian gymnasium" next to King's Cross station – provides an "amazing setting" for this D&D London yearling. Its reception has been mixed however – staff are "charming" but can be "slow"; and the German cuisine ("wurst and other classics") can seem "interesting", but is too often judged "beige", "heavy" and "not very tempting". / N1C 4BU; www.germangymnasium.com; @TheGermanGym; 11 pm, Sun 9 pm.

Giacomo's NW2 £38 332

428 Finchley Rd 020 7794 3603 1–1B

"Unpretentious rustic food" and "friendly and efficient staff" attract a "loyal local clientele" to this trad family-run Italian in Child's Hill, where "a ridiculously large pepper grinder is ceremoniously toted around in almost caricature style". / NW2 2HY; www.giacomos.co.uk; 10.30 pm; closed Mon.

Gifto's Lahore Karahi UB1 £26 322

162-164 The Broadway 020 8813 8669 1–3A

Large Pakistani canteen whose "well-priced authentic cuisine" has carved it a place as a Southall landmark; "grills are their speciality". / UB1 1NN; www.gifto.com; 11.30 pm, Sat & Sun midnight; booking weekdays only.

The Gilbert Scott, St Pancras Renaissance NW1 £74 234

Euston Rd 020 7278 3888 9–3C

"Who can resist the splendour?" of this "huge" and "iconic" dining room, not far from the Eurostar platforms? Even fans can note that Marcus Wareing's offering here is "highly priced", but ratings bounced back across the board this year for his resolutely British cuisine. / NW1 2AR; www.thegilbertscott.co.uk; @Thegilbertscott; 11 pm, Sun 9 pm; set weekday L & pre-theatre £51 (FP).

Gilgamesh NW1 £70 223

The Stables, Camden Mkt, Chalk Farm Rd
020 7428 4922 9–3B

Cecil B DeMille wouldn't have produced a more eye-catching interior than this huge and "opulent" bar/restaurant by Camden Lock, with its lavish, imported, wood-carved decoration. The pan-Asian food is "well-presented and tasty" but critics say "massively expensive". / NW1 8AH; www.gilgameshbar.com; @GilgameshBar; Sun-Thu 10 pm, Fri & Sat 11 pm.

Ginger & White £14 243

2 England's Ln, NW3 020 7722 9944 9–2A
4a-5a, Perrins Ct, NW3 020 7431 9098 9–2A

This "achingly trendy coffee shop" – "down a lane off Hampstead High Street" (there's another in Belsize Park) delivers a good caffeine fix, but won most praise this year for its "great, friendly staff"; "nice blankets to keep you warm outside on a cold day". / www.gingerandwhite.com; 5.30 pm, W1 6 pm; W1 closed Sun.

Giraffe £40 221

"I take it all back!" – "the grub seems to have gotten better of late" at these world-food diners; recently acquired by the Birmingham-based Boparan group, and scoring higher ratings across the board. "It's perfect for families", "especially those with tots… which is why no-one in their right mind would ever visit at the weekend!" / www.giraffe.net; 10.45 pm, Sun 10.30 pm; no booking, Sat & Sun 9 am-5 pm.

The Glasshouse TW9 £72 3 4 2
14 Station Pde 020 8940 6777 1–3A
Though never quite a match for its stablemate, Chez Bruce, this "sunny" ("slightly bland") dining room by Kew Gardens tube has always boasted similarly "sparkling and seasonal" modern cuisine, and "diligent and friendly" service. On most accounts it remains as "superb" as ever, but its ratings took an unexpected knock this year, due to a few reports of meals "not up to expectations" and, in particular, "tiny portions". / TW9 3PZ; www.glasshouserestaurant.co.uk; @The_Glasshouse; 10.30 pm, Sun 10 pm; booking max 8 may apply.

Gökyüzü N4 £33 4 4 4
26-27 Grand Pde, Green Lanes
020 8211 8406 1–1C
The "quality of barbecued meat is consistently high at this popular Green Lanes Turk" on Harringay's Grand Parade, with "beautiful succulent sharing platters" ("portions are enormous!"). On top of that it's fun, friendly and "good value". / N4 1LG; www.gokyuzurestaurant.co.uk; @Gokyuzulondon; midnight, Fri & Sat 1 am.

Gold Mine W2 £34 4 2 2
102 Queensway 020 7792 8331 7–2C
"When you need a Cantonese duck fix", this Bayswater café is just the job, and many fans would say it's "better than the neighbouring Four Seasons" (which is much better known). / W2 3RR; 11 pm.

Golden Dragon W1 £33 3 2 2
28-29 Gerrard St 020 7734 1073 5–3A
A Chinatown "staple" that perennially "scores for dim sum". It's "always buzzy despite the Soviet-era interior design, probably because the food quality's high". / W1 6JW; goldendragonlondon.com; 11.30 pm, Fri-Sun midnight; no bookings.

Golden Hind W1 £26 4 4 2
73 Marylebone Ln 020 7486 3644 2–1A
"Genuine", "old-style fish 'n' chip restaurant in the heart of Marylebone" that's central London's top chippy. "It's nothing fancy, but the food is excellent" – "steamed dishes or fried in batter to satisfy the most hardened northerner" – and all "served with enthusiasm" under the watchful eye of owner, Mr Christou. "BYO makes it very affordable". / W1U 2PN; 10 pm; closed Sat L & Sun.

Good Earth £58 3 2 2
233 Brompton Rd, SW3 020 7584 3658 6–2C
143-145 The Broadway, NW7
020 8959 7011 1–1B
11 Bellevue Rd, SW17 020 8682 9230 11–2C
"High-quality", family-owned Chinese venues (in Balham, Knightsbridge and Mill Hill), long known as an "expensive but good" treat. The branch near Harrods especially is seen as "not as good as it once was" though: in particular "the dated decor could use a makeover". / www.goodearthgroup.co.uk; Mon-Sat 10.30 pm, Sun 10 pm.

Goodman £88 3 3 3
24-26 Maddox St, W1 020 7499 3776 3–2C
3 South Quay, E14 020 7531 0300 12–1C
11 Old Jewry, EC2 020 7600 8220 10–2C
"For a red meat blow out" – especially "if you want a steak for a serious business lunch" – these "NYC-style", "testosterone-charged" steakhouses fully fit the bill (and outscored rivals Hawksmoor in this year's survey). "The choice of cuts – be they US, Scottish, or more 'exotic' make them a stand-out", with "a good supporting cast of sides", and "well-matched wines". Naturally "you pay for the privilege". / www.goodmanrestaurants.com; 10.30 pm; E14 & EC2 closed Sat & Sun.

Gordon Ramsay SW3 £148 2 4 3
68-69 Royal Hospital Rd
020 7352 4441 6–3D
Clare Smyth's departure – with Matt Abe taking up the reins – has stymied the recovery of GR's Chelsea flagship. Fans do still laud this "grown-up and charming" chamber as "amazing on every level", and the service in particular remains "exceptional". Ratings fell back significantly this year however, with numerous attacks on modern French cuisine that's "rather blah, fine-dining-by-numbers" and "way, way, way too expensive". The chasm between reality and Michelin's three stars has never looked greater here. / SW3 4HP; www.gordonramsay.com; @GordonRamsay; 10.15 pm; closed Sat & Sun; no jeans; booking max 8 may apply; set dinner £124 (FP), set weekday L £73 (FP).

Gordon's Wine Bar WC2 £38 1 2 5
47 Villiers St 020 7930 1408 5–4D
This "unique" wine bar (dating from 1890) by Embankment Gardens is "somewhere everyone should visit" once. Not for the food, which is barely "OK", or the "grumpy bar staff", but for the marvellously gloomy cave-like interior and huge terrace (with BBQ) in summer. / WC2N 6NE; www.gordonswinebar.com; @GordonsWineBar; 11 pm, Sun 10 pm; no bookings.

The Goring Hotel SW1 £80 3 5 4
15 Beeston Pl 020 7396 9000 2–4B
"Away from the hoi polloi, and convenient for Buck Pal'", this "splendid and unspoilt survivor" is not only "an oasis from the hustle and bustle of Victoria" but also a bastion of unchanging values: in particular its "impeccable" service "pandering to every whim". The Michelin star bestowed on the "delightful dining room" is something of a distraction – "the food is not outstandingly good, but old-fashioned and English" – perfect for business, a "traditional British breakfast par excellence", or "a masterclass in how to do afternoon tea". / SW1W 0JW; www.thegoring.com; @TheGoring; 10 pm; closed Sat

L; no jeans; booking max 8 may apply; set brunch £43 (FP), set pre-theatre £53 (FP), set weekday L £67 (FP).

Gotto Trattoria E20 £41
Here East, 27 East Bay Lane
020 3424 5035 14–1D
The owners of Soho's reliably fun Mele e Pere, Peter Hughes and Andrea Mantovani, have brought culinary life to the Olympic Park as part of the new 'Here East' development. Opened in summer 2016, press reports are of a casual Italian trattoria, with nice al fresco tables by the canal. / E20 2ST; www.gotto.co.uk; @GottoTrattoria; 10.30 pm, Sun 9.30 pm.

Gourmet Burger Kitchen £30 222
"Overtaken by funkier rivals", but this burger franchise still wins solid support from most reporters for its "good value, really good selection of options, and excellent sides". / www.gbkinfo.com; most branches close 10.30 pm; no booking.

Gourmet Goat SE1 £11 442
Borough Market 020 8050 1973 10–4C
"Great food, with a great story and people behind it!" – after two years of trading outside at Borough Market, this rising street food star has opened a new fixed indoor unit on one of the market's main byways, Rochester Walk, serving Greek/Cypriot-influenced goat dishes. / SE1 9AH; www.gourmetgoat.co.uk; @gourmet_goat; 5 pm, Fri 6 pm; closed Mon, Tue, Wed D, Thu D, Fri D, Sat D & Sun; no bookings.

The Gowlett Arms SE15 £32 434
62 Gowlett Rd 020 7635 7048 1–4D
"Blimey, it's in Peckham", but this "chilled" boozer does "the best-ever pizza" – with "tasty thin crusts", "perfectly wood-fired", and "topped with locally smoked meats" (or try the "veggie Gowlettini"). / SE15 4HY; www.thegowlett.com; @theGowlettArms; 10.30 pm, Sun 9 pm; cash only.

Goya SW1 £45 333
34 Lupus St 020 7976 5309 2–4C
"Reliable tapas" as well as "proper mains" make for a "buzzy and reasonably priced" family-run Spaniard in a part of Pimlico that has "very little choice". / SW1V 3EB; www.goyarestaurant.co.uk; midnight, Sun 11.30 pm.

Grain Store N1 £58 433
1-3 Stable St, Granary Sq
020 7324 4466 9–3C
"In the emerging new King's Cross developments", Bruno Loubet's "vast space, with attractive, big open kitchen" has "a great buzz" (it's nice outside too). His "unusual flavour combinations" with "dishes that are vegetable-led" made a return to "fabulous" form this year. / N1C 4AB; www.grainstore.com; @GrainStoreKX; Mon-Wed 11.30 pm, Thu-Sat midnight; closed Sun D; SRA-3 star.

The Grand Imperial, Guoman Grosvenor Hotel SW1 £67 433
101 Buckingham Palace Rd
020 7821 8898 2–4B
This Cantonese in a strangely grand and "spacious" hotel dining room next to Victoria station "may not be the most fashionable spot, but the food is extremely good – better than many in Chinatown". "Everything to do with duck is especially good", while "the dim sum are good value". / SW1W 0SJ; www.grandimperiallondon.com; 10.30 pm, Thu-Sat 11 pm; set weekday L £33 (FP).

Granger & Co £54 324
175 Westbourne Grove, W11
020 7229 9111 7–1B
Stanley Building, St Pancras Sq, N1
020 3058 2567 9–3C
The Buckley Building, 50 Sekforde St, EC1
020 7251 9032 10–1A
"Crazy queues are a letdown", but that's the worst gripe about Aussie star chef, Bill Granger's "chilled", "light and airy" hotspots, rammed particularly for his epic brunches – "interesting, but non-fussy combos" that are superbly "fresh and tasty". Top Menu Tip – "the legendary Granger scrambled eggs on sourdough toast". / Mon-Sat 10 pm, Sun 5pm.

The Grazing Goat W1 £56 233
6 New Quebec St 020 7724 7243 2–2A
"Handily placed near to Marble Arch", this two-floor pub is "great for Sunday lunch", and with "tasty" cooking generally. "It's nice to sit outside when there's a bit of sunshine as well!" / W1H 7RQ; www.thegrazinggoat.co.uk; @TheGrazingGoat; 10 pm, Sun 9.30 pm.

Great Nepalese NW1 £36 332
48 Eversholt St 020 7388 6737 9–3C
"Year-in year-out pushing the right buttons" – this subcontinental veteran in a grungy Euston side street is the epitome of a sweet ethnic café, and a very affordable one too. / NW1 1DA; 11.30 pm, Sun 10 pm.

Great Queen Street WC2 £53 322
32 Great Queen St 020 7242 0622 5–1D
"Sound, straightforward and earthy dishes" – "seasonal British food with fun twists" – still win praise for this "hipster-attracting" gastropub "in the tourist hellhole that is Covent Garden". There are caveats though: its "slightly dismal setting" is "very noisy when full", service is "slightly forgetful", and "standards have slipped" compared to its glory days. / WC2B 5AA; www.greatqueenstreetrestaurant.co.uk; @greatqueenstreet; 10.30 pm, Sun 3.30 pm; closed Sun D; no Amex; set weekday L £32 (FP).

The Greek Larder, Arthouse N1 £50 322

1 York Way 020 3780 2999 9–3C

"Unusual but successful food combinations" presented tapas-style, make Theodore Kyriakou's "casual and contemporary" yearling both "a lovely addition to the Greek restaurant scene", and "a top place to eat well without breaking the bank near King's Cross". / N1C 4AS; www.thegreeklarder.co.uk; @thegreeklarder; 10.30 pm, Sun 5 pm; closed Sun D.

Green Cottage NW3 £38 322

9 New College Pde 020 7722 5305 9–2A

This "long-standing and reliable local" in Swiss Cottage serves "wonderfully tasty", "superbly authentic Chinese food – and it's great value". But "don't go for service or ambience" – "if I lived closer I'd order takeaway". / NW3 5EP; 11 pm; no Amex.

The Green Room, The National Theatre SE1 £44 222

101 Upper Ground 020 7452 3630 2–3D

The NT's punningly named 'sustainable neighbourhood diner' makes good use of its garden site – and of the props and scenery recycled from productions to use as decoration. The grub's "reasonable but not cheap". / SE1 9PP; www.greenroom.london; @greenroomSE1; 10.30 pm, Sun 7 pm.

Greenberry Café NW1 £50 333

101 Regent's Park Rd 020 7483 3765 9–2B

"On a roll at the moment!" – this Primrose Hill haunt has "an excellent café atmosphere, ideal for a chat", and serves "great-value" light bites, including top breakfasts. / NW1 8UR; greenberrycafe.co.uk; @Greenberry_Cafe; 10 pm, Mon & Sun 3 pm; closed Mon D & Sun D; no Amex.

The Greenhouse W1 £130 343

27a Hays Mews 020 7499 3331 3–3B

"Absolute professionalism" characterises Marlon Abela's calm "oasis", "hidden" down a mews in a quiet part of Mayfair, particularly when it comes to chef Arnaud Bignon's "complex" cuisine, or the cellaring of its "amazing wine list" ("arrive an hour early to read it"). Prices are scary however, and although the setting can seem "romantic", it can also appear "stuffy" or "lacking atmosphere". / W1J 5NY; www.greenhouserestaurant.co.uk; 10.30 pm; closed Sat L & Sun; booking max 12 may apply; set weekday L £61 (FP).

Gremio de Brixton, St Matthew's Church SW2 £42 323

Effra Rd 020 7924 0660 11–2D

"Excellent, basic tapas plus decent and not-overpriced wine" fuels the fun ("loud!") at this atmospheric yearling, in the crypt of St Matthew's Church in Brixton. / SW2 1JF; www.gremiodebrixton.com; @gremiobrixton; 11 pm, Sat 11.30 pm, Sun 10.30 pm; D only.

Ground Coffee Society SW15 £31 333

79 Lower Richmond Rd 0845 862 9994 11–2A

"Antipodean coffee excellence" is acclaimed at this Putney outfit, which fans say serves some of the best brews in the SWs, alongside baked goodies and light bites. / SW15 1ET; www.groundcoffeesociety.com/grindcoffeebar; 6 pm; no bookings.

Guglee £33 322

7 New College Pde, NW3 020 7722 8478 9–2A

279 West End Ln, NW6 020 7317 8555 1–1B

"Hot and spicy" street-food-inspired dishes "full of fresh flavours" inspire fans of this "down-to-earth" duo in West Hampstead and Swiss Cottage, which "don't seem to follow a formula" and are "not your average locals". / www.guglee.co.uk; 11 pm.

Guildford Arms SE10 £46 333

55 Guildford Grove 020 8691 6293 1–3D

One of Greenwich's better eating options – "a great pub", with "tasty bar food", "fine dining upstairs" and a really "delightful spacious garden". / SE10 8JY; www.theguildfordarms.co.uk; Tue-Sat 11.30 pm, Sun 10.30 pm.

The Guinea Grill W1 £75 444

30 Bruton Pl 020 7409 1728 3–3B

"Steak and more steak" is the reason to visit this "old-fashioned" grill room, in a "cute" Mayfair mews: "simply cooked and fabulous". "Close your eyes when receiving the bill" though – it's "terrifyingly expensive!" (for a cheaper eat, sample one of the "legendary pies" in the well-preserved Young's pub, which forms the front of the establishment). / W1J 6NL; www.theguinea.co.uk; @guineagrill; 10.30 pm; closed Sat L & Sun; booking max 8 may apply.

The Gun E14 £62 324

27 Coldharbour 020 7515 5222 12–1C

"A magnificent view" of the Thames and O2 (which you can enjoy from the "heated outside terrace") helps make Tom and Ed Martin's "fantastic, historic gastropub" a popular destination. "It's a fine example of a pub getting the food mix right: from ambitious dishes to bar snacks". / E14 9NS; www.thegundocklands.com; @thegundocklands; 10.30 pm, Sun 9.30 pm.

Gunpowder E1 £44 444

11 Whites Row 020 7426 0542 13–2C

"Pairing Indian ingredients and East London creativity", leads to this "vibrant, if small Spitalfields newcomer", serving "indulgent" and "interesting" Indian tapas from an "ever-evolving menu". / E1 7NF; www.gunpowderlondon.com; @gunpowder_ldn; closed Sun.

Gustoso Ristorante & Enoteca SW1 £45 353
33 Willow Pl 020 7834 5778 2–4B
"A Pimlico treasure"; this newish Italian in the backstreets of Westminster has made a big impact on locals, who feel "pampered by exceptionally friendly staff", who provide "sensibly priced", "carefully prepared" traditional dishes; "take their advice on wine pairings". / SW1P 1JH; ristorantegustoso.co.uk; @GustosoRist; 10.30 pm, Fri & Sat 11 pm, Sun 9.30 pm.

GYMKHANA W1 £66 544
42 Albemarle St 020 3011 5900 3–3C
The Sethi family's "fabulous and exciting" venue, near The Ritz, is London's most talked-about posh Indian nowadays. "Downstairs is an old-style speakeasy with a superb cocktail bar", but the main action is the "gorgeous and clubby" colonial-style restaurant, where staff imbued with "impeccable, old-school manners" provide "a unique twist" on subcontinental dining, "blending regional traditions with fine-dining disciplines". Top Menu Tip – "beautifully spiced grilled meats". / W1S 4JH; www.gymkhanalondon.com; @GymkhanaLondon; 10.30 pm; closed Sun.

Habanera W12 £40 323
280 Uxbridge Rd 020 8001 4887 8–1C
"An interesting take on the Mexi-vibe" helps win fans for this year-old cantina – a bright spark in the still dross-heavy strip, facing Shepherd's Bush Green itself: "fresh and tasty" scoff, including "super taco boards". / W12 7JA; www.habanera.co.uk; @HabaneraW12; 11 pm, Fri & Sat midnight, Sun 10.30 pm; may need 6+ to book.

Haché £35 344
329-331 Fulham Rd, SW10
020 7823 3515 6–3B
24 Inverness St, NW1 020 7485 9100 9–3B
37 Bedford Hill, SW12 020 8772 9772 11–2C
153 Clapham High St, SW4
020 7738 8760 11–2D
147-149 Curtain Rd, EC2
020 7739 8396 13–1B
"What burgers at Byron hope to be when they grow up: juicy patties, awesome brioche, and fries to die for!" This excellent small group is also "not hostage to the political correctness of so many others who refuse to serve medium-rare meat". / www.hacheburgers.com; 10.30 pm, Fri-Sat 11 pm, Sun 10 pm.

Hakkasan £94 323
17 Bruton St, W1 020 7907 1888 3–2C
8 Hanway Pl, W1 020 7927 7000 5–1A
For a "classy" night out, these "noisy", "nightclub-style" operations (the seeds of what's now a global brand) have a huge reputation, with their "clever Chinese/pan-Asian" cuisine and "theatrical" Bond-lair styling. "Eye-popping" bills and "up-itself" service have always been hazards here, but accusations that they are "over-hyped and ridiculously over-priced" grew this year. / www.hakkasan.com; midnight, Sun 11 pm.

Ham Yard Restaurant, Ham Yard Hotel W1 £61 344
1 Ham Yd 020 3642 1007 4–3D
"Where better on a summer evening than the piazza tables?" at the "charming" and "chic" Firmdale hotel, whose courtyard "brings the feel of a village into central Soho". Critics do still feel its "looks are deceptive" – with "food no better than fine" and "a substantial bill" – but it has upped its game considerably since the slating it received on opening, and most accounts are of a "most enjoyable" meal. "Exceptional bar" too. Top Tip – "pound for pound, the best value afternoon tea in London". / W1D 7DT; www.firmdalehotels.com; @Ham_Yard; 11.30 pm, Sun 10.30 pm.

The Hampshire Hog W6 £53 334
227 King St 020 8748 3391 8–2B
There's "plenty of space" at this airy and unusually attractive pub (which has a sizeable garden), near Hammersmith Town Hall. Staff are "always helpful" and the food – though "not exactly cheap" – is "usually tasty". / W6 9JT; www.thehampshirehog.com; @TheHampshireHog; 10.30 pm; closed Sun D.

Hanger SW6 £49
461-465 North End Road
020 7386 9739 6–2B
Opened in summer 2106 – a hangout near Fulham Broadway dedicated to the humble hanger steak (traditionally known as the 'Butcher's Cut') from just £10 a pop. / SW6 1NZ; www.hangersteak.co.uk; @hanger_sw6; 11 pm, Wed & Thu 11.30 pm, Fri & Sat 12.30 am, Sun; closed Mon & Tue L.

The Harcourt W1 £60 434
32 Harcourt Street 020 3771 8660 7–1D
On the former site of The Harcourt Arms, this Marylebone gastropub reopened in April 2016 with a new menu and a new look. Chef Kimmo Makkonen's (Greenhouse, The Orrery) European menu nods toward Nordic and Scandi cuisine, and – though it's had the odd mixed review in the press – won instant high ratings from reporters for its "high-end restaurant quality food". / W1H 4HX; www.theharcourt.com; @the_harcourt; 11 pm, Fri & Sat 11.30 pm, Sun 10 pm.

Hard Rock Café W1 £60 224
150 Old Park Ln 020 7514 1700 3–4B
"Still rocking" is the considered verdict on the Hyde Park Corner original of what is now, 45 years later, a famous global franchise. "The atmosphere is electric, loud and proud", and it still delivers some "reliable quality" burgers, ribs and "huge nachos". / W1K

1QZ; www.hardrock.com/london; @HardRockLondon; 12.30 am, Fri & Sat 1 am, Sun 10.30 pm; may need 20+ to book.

Hardy's Brasserie W1 £49 233

53 Dorset St 020 7935 5929 2–1A

"Unpretentious" "old-style" bistro "tucked away from the tourists in Marylebone" – the cooking is dependable, and its "welcoming atmosphere" makes it very "handy in the area". / W1U 7NH; www.hardysbrasserie.com; @hardys_W1; 10 pm; closed Sun D.

Hare & Tortoise £32 333

11-13 The Brunswick, WC1
020 7278 9799 2–1D
373 Kensington High St, W14
020 7603 8887 8–1D
156 Chiswick High Rd, W4
020 8747 5966 8–2A
38 Haven Grn, W5 020 8810 7066 1–2A
296-298 Upper Richmond Rd, SW15
020 8394 7666 11–2B
90 New Bridge St, EC4 020 7651 0266 10–2A

It's "pleasantly surprising how good the chow is", at these pan-Asian fast food canteens, which are "always packed" (with "queues to contend with"). "We eat here at least twice a week and never get tired of the value-for-money sushi, noodles, etc…" / www.hareandtortoise-restaurants.co.uk; 10.45 pm, Fri & Sat 11.15 pm, EC4 10 pm; W14 no bookings.

Harry Morgan's NW8 £42 222

29-31 St John's Wood High St
020 7722 1869 9–3A

This St John's Wood institution has a loyal following for its Jewish deli classics including "excellent salt beef" and "good chicken soup". It's also "perfect for brunch during a Test match", at Lord's cricket ground nearby. / NW8 7NH; www.harryms.co.uk; @morgan_hm; 10 pm.

Harwood Arms SW6 £68 533

Walham Grove 020 7386 1847 6–3A

"Taking pub food to a new level entirely" – this "gastropub on steroids" in a quiet Fulham backwater has won fame with its "superb", "hearty" cooking, and most particularly its "interesting game" ("especially the deer"). It's a collaboration between the owners of Berkshire's Pot Kiln, and Ledbury chef, Brett Graham. Top Menu Tip – "slow-roasted venison is a must-try when in season!" / SW6 1QR; www.harwoodarms.com; 9.15 pm, Sun 9 pm; closed Mon L; credit card deposit required to book; set always available £40 (FP).

Hashi SW20 £36 443

54 Durham Rd 020 8944 1888 11–2A

This "not-so-easy-to-find Japanese" is a "real surprise to discover tucked away in Raynes Park". It's a "modest venue, but the food has always been really top notch – worthy of a more central location": "very good sushi and sashimi", and the prices are "reasonable". / SW20 0TW; www.hashi-restaurant.co.uk; 10.30 pm; closed Mon & Tue L; no Amex.

Hatchetts W1 £58

5 White Horse Street 020 7409 0567 3–4B

More life comes to picturesque Shepherd Market, with the autumn 2016 opening of this bar (ground floor) / (restaurant), serving a modern brasserie menu. / W1J 7LQ; www.hatchetts.london; @hatchettslondon; 10 pm.

The Havelock Tavern W14 £48 334

57 Masbro Rd 020 7603 5374 8–1C

This Olympia backstreet gastro-boozer isn't the stand-out it once was, but it's still an "eternally reliable" haunt – "an uncomplicated, warming experience" that's "buzzing every week night". A recent refurb "has added table reservations, and the food continues good". Top Menu Tip – "their excellent staple: bavette steak". / W14 0LS; www.havelocktavern.com; @HavelockTavern; 10 pm, Sun 9.30 pm.

The Haven N20 £52 343

1363-5 High Rd 020 8445 7419 1–1B

"An oasis in the restaurant-desert of Whetstone". The cooking is "reliable" and the staff "always welcoming and helpful" – "we've never had a bad meal here". / N20 9LN; www.haven-bistro.co.uk; 10.30 pm, Sun 10 pm; no shorts; set weekday L £29 (FP).

Hawksmoor £75 332

5a, Air St, W1 020 7406 3980 4–4C
11 Langley St, WC2 020 7420 9390 5–2C
3 Yeoman's Row, SW3 020 7590 9290 6–2C
157 Commercial St, E1 020 7426 4850 13–2B
10-12 Basinghall St, EC2
020 7397 8120 10–2C

This cult steakhouse chain (soon to hit NYC) has carved a legendary reputation for its "expert" steaks featuring "brilliant quality" British-bred beef, and "glorious cocktails", and it's also a "go-to choice for a business lunch". However, its ratings continue to slide – especially given the "noisy and unexceptional" ambience at some of the more "dull" locations – supporting those who say "Hawksmoor no longer stands out in a crowded field", while, as ever, the bloated bills can seem "just too much like taking the whatsit". All that said, the business is still on a roll and a new branch near Borough Market is to open in Spring 2017. Top Tip – "the stunning-looking Air Street branch is the best in the empire". / www.thehawksmoor.com; all branches between 10 pm & 11 pm; EC2 closed Sat & Sun; SRA-3 star.

Haz £37 2 2 2
9 Cutler St, E1 020 7929 7923 10–2D
34 Foster Ln, EC2 020 7600 4172 10–2B
112 Houndsditch, EC3 020 7623 8180 10–2D
6 Mincing Ln, EC3 020 7929 3173 10–3D
These "large" busy Turkish operations across the City provide a solid, affordable, relatively healthy offering. It's "a fuel stop not an occasion" though – the style's a bit "characterless" and the food's "OK so far as it goes, but wouldn't win any prizes". / www.hazrestaurant.co.uk; 11.30 pm; EC3 closed Sun.

Heddon Street Kitchen W1 £61 2 2 2
3-9 Heddon St 020 7592 1212 4–3B
Gordon Ramsay's "laid back" destination just off Regent Street inspires mixed feelings. That it's "very family-friendly, with kids eating free" (if they're 12 or under) earns it the parental vote, but more generally "the food is so-so, not spectacular and a little over-priced". / W1B 4BE; www.gordonramsayrestaurants.com/heddon-street-kitc; @heddonstkitchen; 11 pm, Sun 9 pm.

Hedone W4 £106 4 3 3
301-303 Chiswick High Rd
020 8747 0377 8–2A
Mikael Jonsson and his "totally committed" team create "an extraordinary culinary experience" behind a "modest" façade in outer-Chiswick (where sitting at the counter watching the preparation is a popular option). It's "one of the best restaurants in the UK", with a "total focus on sourcing the best ingredients and intensifying their flavours" via "adventurous combinations" as part of a "stunning tasting menu", and all complemented by "an exceptional wine list". On the downside, the approach can seem a little "hushed" or "over-anxious", and for a sceptical minority the whole set-up seems "monumentally over-rated and overpriced". / W4 4HH; www.hedonerestaurant.com; @HedoneLondon; 9.30 pm; closed Mon, Tue L, Wed L, Thu L & Sun; credit card deposit required to book.

Heirloom N8 £46 3 3 3
35 Park Rd 020 8348 3565 1–1C
This "fabulous restaurant in the heart of Crouch End" – supplied from its own farm in Bucks – offers "robust comfort food", and "good-value tasting menus with wine pairings". / N8 8TE; www.heirloomn8.co.uk; @HeirloomN8; 11 pm, Sun 7 pm; closed Mon & Tue.

Hélène Darroze, The Connaught Hotel W1 £130 3 4 3
Carlos Pl 020 3147 7200 3–3B
This Parisian super-chef won more consistent praise this year for her reign at this "luxurious" dining room, where "helpful and unobsequious" staff provide "brilliantly executed" modern French dishes. It's "unbelievably expensive", but then again, in Mayfair "decadence and pampering don't come cheap". / W1K 2AL; www.the-connaught.co.uk; @TheConnaught; Mon-Sat 10 pm, Sun 9 pm; no trainers; SRA-2 star.

Heliot Steak House WC2 £56 4 4 4
Cranbourn Street 020 7769 8844 5–3B
The UK's biggest casino – the current occupant of the famous London landmark above Leicester Square tube – boasts a little-known but glam', surprisingly accomplished and reasonably-priced steak house, overlooking the gambling below, from what was the circle of the original theatre. (No entry charge, nor need to wager). Top Tip – great value pre-theatre. / WC2H 7AJ; www.hippodromecasino.com; @HippodromeLDN; Mon-Fri midnight, Sat 1 am, Sun 11 pm.

Hereford Road W2 £49 4 4 3
3 Hereford Rd 020 7727 1111 7–1B
Tom Pemberton's "authentic, seasonal British food that's always interesting and sometimes unusual" maintains a very loyal following for his "professional" Bayswater venture; "thoughtful wine list" too. Top Tip – "the set lunch is a particularly good deal". / W2 4AB; www.herefordroad.org; @3HerefordRoad; 10.30 pm, Sun 10 pm.

The Heron W2 £32 5 3 1
1 Norfolk Cr 020 7706 9567 9–4A
"Cheap 'n' cheerful" Thai, in a tiny, no-frills basement beneath a grotty-looking pub built into the foot of a Bayswater block: results are regularly outstanding. / W2 2DN; 11 pm, Sun 10.30 pm.

High Road Brasserie W4 £54 2 2 3
162-166 Chiswick High Rd
020 8742 7474 8–2A
This all-day hangout (part of a Soho House club and boutique hotel) is "ever-popular" and "a good place to take someone if you're in the area" particularly for brunch on the large outside terrace. But "you can't survive on name alone – others in Chiswick are surpassing them". / W4 1PR; highroadbrasserie.co.uk; @HRBrasserie; 11 pm, Fri & Sat midnight, Sun 10 pm.

High Timber EC4 £65 3 4 3
8 High Timber 020 7248 1777 10–3B
This "very popular" 'wine-dining' spot has a fab riverside location by the Wobbly Bridge – owned by a Stellenbosch vineyard, there's a "very good cellar with the focus on South Africa, plus super French reds". It's "small inside", so – though business friendly – it's not the place for a confidential chat. The cooking: "consistently good", with some emphasis on steak. / EC4V 3PA; www.hightimber.com; @HTimber; 10 pm; closed Sat & Sun.

Hill & Szrok £42 [4][4][4]

8 East Rd, N1 020 7324 7799 13–1A
60 Broadway Mkt, E8 020 7254 8805 14–2B
Just off London Fields, this small butcher's-by-day, perched-on-stools restaurant by night has rightly carved a name for its high quality meat (although the cost of sides to accompany dishes can mount). Since January 2016, it's snapped up a grotty former boozer near Old Street, now transformed into "a lovely pub" serving "great quality steaks" which fans say "rival the likes of Hawksmoor in my eyes but are served in a fun, relaxed pub atmosphere".

Hilliard EC4 £28 [4][4][3]

26a Tudor St 020 7353 8150 10–3A
"Excellent" deli/coffee house "in the midst of legal London", serving splendid brews, cakes and light bites made from top ingredients. As one local solicitor notes – "my life changed when this wonderful place opened" (who says lawyers need to get out more...) / EC4Y 0AY; www.hilliardfood.co.uk; @hilliardcafe; 5.30 pm; L only, closed Sat & Sun; no bookings.

Hispania EC3 £54 [3][3][3]

72-74 Lombard Street 020 7621 0338 10–3D
"Busy, buzzy Spanish bar/restaurant" in the heart of the City; "as a place to eat, the bar crowd is often overpowering, which is a shame because the food and wine are both great". / EC3V 9AY; www.hispanialondon.com; Mon 9.30 pm, Tue-Fri 10 pm; closed Sat & Sun.

Hix W1 £65 [1][2][2]

66-70 Brewer St 020 7292 3518 4–3C
Mark Hix's "buzzy" Soho venture risks losing its way. It does still have fans for whom it "delivers the goods", but the food is too often judged "pretty ordinary", the ambience "flat", and prices "silly" – "I left feeling empty of soul and wallet!" / W1F 9UP; www.hixsoho.co.uk; @HixRestaurants; 11.30 pm, Sun 10.30 pm.

Hix Oyster & Chop House EC1 £58 [2][2][2]

36-37 Greenhill Rents, Cowcross St
020 7017 1930 10–1A
Fans of Mark Hix's original solo venue, near Smithfield, applaud its "solid trencherman's menu" – "one of the few places I can take Americans and not be embarrassed by the size of the steaks and chops compared with the US!" Those not on expenses though, can find the food "pricey", "only just above average", and "a little tired and redundant in a post-Hawksmoor world". / EC1M 6BN; www.hixrestaurants.co.uk/restaurant/hix-oyster-cho; @hixchophouse; 11 pm, Sun 9 pm; closed Sat L.

HKK EC2 £74 [5][4][2]

88 Worship St, Broadgate Quarter
020 3535 1888 13–2B
"Some of the best Chinese food in the UK" is to be had at this "expensive but brilliant" member of the Hakkasan clan, north of Liverpool Street, and it "attracts a broad cross-section of diners, from out-and-out foodies, via bankers to local Hoxtonians". However, reporters are "not so keen on the room" – "akin to a 4-star hotel in Bangkok", which when empty has a "ghostly quiet ambience". Top Menu Tip – "the unbelievably tender, cherry-wood smoked Peking duck is nigh-on a religious experience". / EC2A 2BE; www.hkklondon.com; @HKKlondon; 10 pm; closed Sun.

Hoi Polloi, Ace Hotel E1 £57 [2][1][2]

100 Shoreditch High St 020 8880 6100 13–1B
This trendy joint in a Shoreditch hotel can be "fantastic for breakfast (top pancakes)", but goes downhill later in the day with "overpriced", "so-so food". In particular, "atrocious service badly lets it down" – "it's not as hip as it thinks it is". / E1 6JQ; hoi-polloi.co.uk; @wearehoipolloi; Sun-Wed midnight, Thu-Sat 1 am.

Holborn Dining Room-Rosewood London WC1 £62 [3][3][4]

252 High Holborn 020 3747 8633 2–1D
The "splendid appearance" of this impressive chamber, on the fringe of the City makes it "perfect for a high-level business discussion" (fuelled perhaps by a visit to its "fantastic" adjoining Scarfes Bar). "You wouldn't maybe choose it for a gastronomic experience", but all reports agree "it won't let you down". / WC1V 7EN; www.holborndiningroom.com; @HolbornDining; 11.15 pm, Sun 10.15 pm.

Homeslice £24 [4][4][4]

52 Wells St, W1 020 3151 7488 2–1B
13 Neal's Yd, WC2 020 7836 4604 5–2C
374-378 Old St, EC1 020 3151 1121 13–1B
"Outstanding pizza" – "unusual flavours but working together really well and with a wonderful, thin dough base" – win acclaim for these "buzzy and cheery" pitstops; "have a huge pizza or just a slice" but be prepared to wait.

Honest Burgers £30 [4][4][3]

"Simple, perfect burgers... simply the best!" – the survey's top slot, certainly amongst the bigger burger brands, goes to this "cool" chain, whose "to-die-for, salty rosemary fries" help inspire addiction; expect "huge lines", but "their app allowing you to queue virtually is genius". Top Tip – the original Brixton branch remains a destination in itself. / www.honestburgers.co.uk; @honestburgers; 10 pm-11 pm; SW9 closed Mon D.

Honey & Co W1 £48 542
25a Warren St 020 7388 6175 2–1B
"Unique, modern Israeli cooking" ("incredible food that you could eat over and over again"), together with "the most fantastic welcome" leaves you "surprised and smiling" at this cute café, near Warren Street. Be prepared to "cosy up" – it's really "tiny". Top Menu Tip – leave space for the "outstanding" cakes (the cheesecake is a "must-try"). / W1T 5JZ; www.honeyandco.co.uk; @Honeyandco; Mon-Sat 10.30 pm; closed Sun; no Amex.

Hood SW2 £42 432
67 Streatham Hill 020 3601 3320 11–2D
"Fantastic local" yearling in Streatham Hill serving "on-trend brunches with some nice touches" and at other times an "excellent" (if slightly limited) seasonal menu. / SW2 4TX; www.hoodrestaurants.com; @HoodStreatham; 11 pm; closed Mon & Sun D.

Hoppers W1 £29 444
49 Frith St NONE 5–2A
"Reminds me of my childhood in South East Asia!" One of the biggest hits of late 2015, the Sethi family's Sri Lankan, street food yearling has stormed into Soho with the "incredible" and "punchy flavours" of its "curries, plus crisp dosas and hoppers (rice pancakes) for dipping". "Annoyingly this is another restaurant that doesn't take bookings", but most reporters are "happy to wait". Top Menu Tip – "the bone marrow Varuval is meaty and deep, mopped up perfectly with a roti". / W1D 4SG; www.hopperslondon.com; @HoppersLondon; 10.30 pm; closed Sun; no bookings.

The Horseshoe NW3 £48 334
28 Heath St 020 7431 7206 9–2A
This "revamped gastropub" in Hampstead "delivers on classic but tweaked dishes" and "fantastic Sunday roasts". There's a "great beer selection", too – the Camden Town Brewery was spawned in the basement before moving into bigger premises, and the whole range is available in the bar. / NW3 6TE; www.thehorseshoehampstead.com; @TheHorseShoeCTB; 10 pm, Fri & Sat 10.30pm, Sun 9.30 pm.

Hot Stuff SW8 £23 353
23 Wilcox Rd 020 7720 1480 11–1D
"Still the best curry in Vauxhall", this "lovely little Indian" BYO ("tucked away" on the "Little Portugal" stretch) "isn't the most glam place to eat, but it's usually busy and fun", providing "bright and spicy" flavours "at cheap prices" and "very friendly" service. / SW8 2XA; www.welovehotstuff.com; 10 pm, Sun 9.30 pm; closed Mon; no Amex.

The Hour Glass SW3 £52 332
279-283 Brompton Rd 020 7581 2497 6–2C
"A basic room above a pub… albeit one in SW3" hosts this new venture run by Brompton Food Market duo Luke Mackay and David Turcan. For fans its deceptively straightforward cooking and "charming service" makes it "almost the perfect neighbourhood pub", but the odd critic says "it's not as good as some have claimed". / SW3 2DY; @TheHourGlassSK; 11 pm, Sun 10.30 pm.

House of Ho £58 222
1 Percy St, W1 020 7323 9130 2–1C
57-59 Old Compton St, W1
020 7287 0770 5–3A
This high-concept 'modern Vietnamese' with Japanese influences has moved from its original Soho address to the prominent Fitzrovia site vacated by Bam-Bou (RIP), with Ian Pengelley now running the kitchen. However, food scores have declined, and while fans still applaud "flavoursome fare with some strong western crossover dishes" critics find the food "lacking" and query "why the hype?" The projected roll-out of a Ho chain has yet to happen.

House Restaurant, National Theatre SE1 £53 232
National Theatre, Belvedere Rd
020 7452 3600 2–3D
"Sensible…" "workmanlike…", "good for pre-theatre audiences with a tight turnaround" – such are the benefits of the National Theatre's in-house venue ("try to get a table with a river view"). Food quality is "variable" though. / SE1 9PX; house.nationaltheatre.org.uk; @NT_House; 11 pm; closed Sun D.

Hubbard & Bell, Hoxton Hotel WC1 £57 333
199-206 High Holborn 020 7661 3030 2–1D
Soho House's all-day diner within their hipster-inspired hotel (for all its groovy name-checking, in drab Holborn) is a useful local amenity: "good for a quick lunch" or coffee. / WC1V 7BD; www.hubbardandbell.com; @HubbardandBell; Mon-Sat midnight, Sun 11 pm.

Humble Grape EC4 £44 344
1 Saint Bride's Passage 020 7583 0688 10–2A
"A lovely venue in an old crypt of Fleet Street" (under St Bride's, the journalists' church), hosts this new bar/restaurant (which also has an older Battersea sibling). "There's good food to be had here, but it's not really the point – it's the wonderfully diverse and well-priced wine list that will keep you coming back". / EC4Y 8EJ; www.humblegrape.co.uk; @humblegrape; 11 pm, Thu-Sat midnight; closed Sun.

Hunan SW1 £80 541
51 Pimlico Rd 020 7730 5712 6–2D
"Leave all the ordering to Mr Peng Jr and you won't be disappointed" at this "packed and pedestrian-looking" Pimlico veteran – London's No. 1 Chinese. Expect "a happy adventure" of "course after delectable course" of "tastebud tingling and

multi-textured" small dishes "until you can't eat any more… and then the next three courses arrive" (all matched with "excellent, affordable wines"). The "enthusiastic" vibe set up by the "jolly" father and son team who run the place seals the experience. / SW1W 8NE; www.hunanlondon.com; 11 pm; closed Sun.

Hush £68 2 3 3
8 Lancashire Ct, W1 020 7659 1500 3–2B
95-97 High Holborn, WC1
020 7242 4580 2–1D
With a poshly located Mayfair original off Bond Street and handy branches in Holborn and St Paul's, this small group is "great for a business lunch"; there's no sign from reporters of huge excitement about the cooking, but it does the job. / www.hush.co.uk; @Hush_Restaurant; W1 10.45 pm; WC1 10.30 pm, Sun 9.30 pm; WC1 closed Sun.

Hutong, The Shard SE1 £89 3 2 5
31 St Thomas St 020 3011 1257 10–4C
"Exceptional vistas from the 33rd floor" help create a "gorgeous and very romantic" ambience at this "sister to the world-famous Hutong in HK". Seemingly "the view doubles the price" ("astronomical!") for the Chinese cuisine, although on most accounts it's "pretty good too". Less so the so-so service. / SE1 9RY; www.hutong.co.uk; @HutongShard; 11 pm; no shorts.

Ibérica £48 2 2 3
Zig Zag Building, 70 Victoria St, SW1
020 7636 8650 2–4B
195 Great Portland St, W1
020 7636 8650 2–1B
12 Cabot Sq, E14 020 7636 8650 12–1C
89 Turnmill St, EC1 020 7636 8650 10–1A
Fans of these "bustling" modern venues say "they offer a genuine taste of Spain, unrecognisable as part of a chain". And that was probably true once, but with expansion they seem more "hyped" and "impersonal" now, although they can still make "a decent fallback". / 11 pm; W1 closed Sun D.

Ichiryu WC1 £34 4 3 2
84 New Oxford St 020 3405 1254 5–1B
A new "fast food" noodle house in Bloomsbury, courtesy of Shoryu founder Tak Tokumine. Early reports are enthusiastic: "the udon noodles are the standout dish here… exceptional with a truly authentic broth: you will want to go back again and again". / WC1A 1HB; /www.ichiryuudon.com; @IchiryuUdon; 10.30 pm, Sun 9.30 pm; no bookings.

Imli Street W1 £40 2 2 2
167-169 Wardour St 020 7287 4243 4–1C
This large Soho 10-year-old "has a real buzz about it" (aided by its comprehensive cocktail menu), and its Indian street food served by the small plate is "different and enjoyable". / W1F 8WR; www.imlistreet.com; @imlistreet; 11 pm, Sun 10 pm.

Inaho W2 £44 5 3 1
4 Hereford Rd 020 7221 8495 7–1B
"You don't go for the atmosphere" to this quirky, tiny shed, in Bayswater – "the sashimi and authentic, straightforward Japanese are are as good as it gets!" / W2 4AA; 10.30 pm; closed Sat L & Sun; no Amex.

India Club, Strand Continental Hotel WC2 £29 2 2 1
143 Strand 020 7836 4880 2–2D
"You could be in Delhi circa 1960" at this "quirky" veteran near the Indian High Commission in the Strand. Service "can be frantic" and the food is arguably "unexceptional", but "it deserves mention for its great value in a central location". BYO, or grab a pint from the hotel bar. / WC2R 1JA; www.strand-continental.co.uk; 10.50 pm; cash only; booking max 6 may apply.

Indian Moment SW11 £35 3 4 3
47 Northcote Rd 020 7223 6575 11–2C
"Very civilised" Battersea Indian where the curries are "not designed to blow your head off" and there's "never a bad note". "Thalis are a great addition to a menu that is by Indian standards low fat". / SW11 1NZ; www.indianmoment.co.uk; @indianmoment; 11.30 pm, Fri & Sat midnight; closed weekday L.

Indian Ocean SW17 £35 3 3 3
214 Trinity Rd 020 8672 7740 11–2C
Long-established Indian near Wandsworth Common with a strong following for its "consistent, superior and interesting dishes". / SW17 7HP; www.indianoceanrestaurant.com; 11.30 pm.

Indian Rasoi N2 £36 4 4 3
7 Denmark Terrace 020 8883 9093 1–1B
"It's always difficult to get a table" at this "very friendly, if rather cramped" Muswell Hill Indian. In part it's "because it's a small place", but mostly it's because "it's miles better than your average curry house", with "original and delicious" dishes. / N2 9HG; www.indian-rasoi.co.uk; 10.30 pm; no Amex.

Indian Zilla SW13 £46 4 2 2
2-3 Rocks Ln 020 8878 3989 11–1A
"Distinctive and original Indian flavours" ("sometimes astounding") make this Barnes sibling to Indian Zing (across the river in Hammersmith) a "standout local curry house". The cooking is back on form after a blip noted by reporters last year. / SW13 0DB; www.indianzilla.co.uk; 11 pm; closed weekday L.

Indian Zing W6 £49 4 3 2
236 King St 020 8748 5959 8–2B
"Better than West End Indians for 2/3 the price" – Manoj Vasaikar's "fabulous, subtle yet punchy" modern cuisine has won a disproportionately huge following for his "busy" venture, especially given its nondescript location, near Ravenscourt Park. "The tables are a little too close together". / W6 0RS; www.indianzing.co.uk; @IndianZing; 11 pm, Sun 10 pm.

Ippudo £38 3 2 3
Central St Giles Piazza, WC2
020 7240 4469 5–1B
1 Crossrail Pl, E14 020 3326 9485 12–1C
"Fresh" ramen, "gorgeous miso soup", and "helpful staff" are the draws at the London outlets of this global, Japan-based noodle chain with branches near Centre Point and in Canary Wharf, although some would argue that they do suffer from "that 'chain' feel". / @IppudoLondon; –.

Isarn N1 £45 4 4 2
119 Upper St 020 7424 5153 9–3D
"Authentic, delicate, imaginative and delicious" – the "consistently good" food at this "always busy" Islington fixture, where "courteous" staff help enliven the "narrow, slightly cramped" modern interior. / N1 1QP; www.isarn.co.uk; 11 pm, Sat & Sun 10 pm.

Ishtar W1 £46 3 3 2
10-12 Crawford St 020 7224 2446 2–1A
"Typical Turkish dishes – but done very well", win fans of this Marylebone Anatolian. / W1U 6AZ; www.ishtarrestaurant.com; 11.30 pm, Sun 10.30 pm.

THE IVY WC2 £69 3 4 5
1-5 West St 020 7836 4751 5–3B
"A lesson in how to improve a legend!" – Richard Caring's "perked up" Theatreland star has staged an impressive return to form since last year's revamp: "the old menu classics – bang bang chicken, shepherd's pie, etc have been spruced up" (they needed to be!), service is "discreet and professional" and – "even without the buzz of all the c'lebs who are now upstairs in the adjoining club" – its vibe, romance and glamour have rediscovered their mojo. That said, there is a large band of refuseniks for whom it has "lost its verve and originality" – it doesn't help that with spin-offs sprouting all over town it can now "feel like a high-end franchise" rather than the unique destination of yesteryear. / WC2H 9NQ; www.the-ivy.co.uk; @TheIvyWestSt; Mon-Wed 11.30pm, Thu-Sat midnight, Sun 10.30 pm; no shorts; booking max 6 may apply.

The Ivy Brasserie, One Tower Bridge SE1
1 Tower Bridge awaiting tel 10–4D
If you don't count the Ivy Cafés, this is the fourth spin-off from Caprice Holdings' Ivy brand, this time at One Tower Bridge – a new development next to City Hall and Tower Bridge – set to serve a similar all-day menu to the Ivy Chelsea Garden. Given the, so far, remorselessly middling performance of all the spin-offs, next year we will likely treat all the properties as the single M.O.R. group which seems to be Richard Caring's aspiration. / SE1.

The Ivy Café £53 2 2 4
96 Marylebone Ln, W1 020 3301 0400 2–1A
120 St John's Wood High St, NW8 awaiting tel 9–3A
75 High St, SW19 020 3096 9333 11–2B
"Hooray, Wimbledon now has an Ivy! (in place of an old branch of Barclays)" – and Marylebone too, has a "busy and bustling" branch (on the site that was Union Café, RIP) of this spin-off chain. But whereas many fans do find them "fun" and "attractive", they are also crowded and "quite expensive", with comfort food that's arguably "not much better than at Côte" (Richard Caring's other successfully rolled out money-spinner of recent years).

The Ivy Chelsea Garden SW3 £58 2 2 5
197 King's Rd 020 3301 0300 6–3C
"The garden in summer is perhaps the finest in the capital" and the interior is "gorgeous" too, at this year-old Chelsea spin-off from the Theatreland original. Leaving aside the "magical" atmosphere however, there's less to celebrate – staff are "badly organised", "hubristic" and can indulge in "pushy table-turning", while the "boring" brasserie fare underlines the fact that "it's more a place to be seen than to eat". / SW3 5ED; www.theivychelseagarden.com; @ivychelsgarden; Mon-Thu 11 pm, Fri-Sat 11.30 pm, Sun 10.30 pm.

The Ivy Kensington Brasserie W8 £60 2 2 3
96 Kensington High St 020 3301 0500 6–1A
"What Kensington High Street has needed for many years", say fans of Richard Caring's "busy" year-old Ivy spin-off, which brings oodles of "buzz" (it's "extremely noisy") to the premises that were so dead in their previous guise (as Pavilion, RIP). But numerous sceptics feel the offer here is "truly not exciting: the food's very ordinary, takes ages to arrive, and staff seem uninterested". / W8 4SG; www.theivykensingtonbrasserie.com; @theivybrasserie; 11 pm Fri & Sat 11.30 pm, Sun 10.30 pm.

The Ivy Market Grill WC2 £58 2 2 3
1 Henrietta St 020 3301 0200 5–3D
"It's a nice-looking and handily-placed brasserie", but this recent Ivy spin-off is "really not as special as it tries to make itself out to be". Fans say its food is "very acceptable for Covent Garden" but cynics feel that "they're trading off the kudos of the brand, without putting the effort in". Top Tip – "good for a special brunch". / WC2E 8PS;

www.theivymarketgrill.com; @ivymarketgrill; midnight, Sun 11.30 pm.

Jackson & Rye £46 122

56 Wardour St, W1 020 7437 8338 4–2D
219-221 Chiswick High Rd, W4
020 8747 1156 8–2A
Hotham House, 1 Heron Sq, TW9
020 8948 6951 1–4A

These smart American-style diners do win some praise for "great breakfast and brunch", but ratings generally are so-so, particularly when it comes to "turgid efforts" at the "brilliantly located" riverside Richmond branch. / @JacksonRye; –.

Jaffna House SW17 £18 532

90 Tooting High St 020 8672 7786 11–2C

"It's bit like eating in someone's back sitting-room" (which is exactly what it is!), but this "modest" family-run outfit in Tooting provides "great flavours from some unusual Sri Lankan and South Indian specialities" and is "very good value for money". / SW17 0RN; www.jaffnahouse.co.uk; 11.30 pm.

Jago, Second Home E1 £49 322

68-80 Hanbury St 020 3818 3241 13–2C

This "curious, orange-coloured, add-on, covered balcony" adjoining a Shoreditch tech office space serves "scrumptious, healthy breakfasts", flat whites, juices and Middle East-inspired "fun tapas". Named after the area's erstwhile Victorian slums, it "should be hipster heaven, yet feels like an office canteen… which is exactly what it is, I guess". / E1 5JL; www.jagorestaurant.com; @jagorestaurant; Mon-Sat 9.30 pm; closed Sat L & Sun.

Jamavar W1

8 Mount Street 020 7499 1800 3–3B

'Jewel in the crown' of the Leela Palaces Indian hotel chain, Jamavar London will open in November 2016, under executive chef Rohit Ghai (Gymkhana, Benares). / W1K 3NF; www.jamavarrestaurants.com; @jamavarlondon.

Jamie's Italian £44 112

"Just another chain with celeb branding" – Jamie O's Italians can be "fun for the family" ("kids are very welcome") but go "only if you are desperate": "it's overly expensive for what's now very mediocre". / www.jamiesitalian.com; @JamiesItalianUK; 11.30 pm, Sun 10.30 pm; booking: min 6.

Jar Kitchen WC2 £49 333

Drury Ln 020 7405 4255 5–1C

"A cute restaurant in a very useful location" – this straightforward, year-old café on the fringes of Covent Garden delivers "unfussy, very tasty food", plus "lovely service, and an absolutely charming atmosphere". / WC2B 5QF; www.jarkitchen.com; @JarKitchen; 9 pm; closed Mon & Sun; may need 6+ to book; SRA-1 star.

Jashan N8 £32 542

19 Turnpike Ln 020 8340 9880 1–1C

"A slew of dishes not found elsewhere" make this "hard-to-find restaurant worth the trip to this grubby strip of North London" (one fan slogs up to Turnpike Lane from SW3, no less). But while the food is "properly excellent" – "in particular the lamb chops" – there's less acclaim for the "ropey" decor. / N8 0EP; www.jashan.co.uk; 10.15 pm, Fri & Sat 10.30 pm; D only, ex Sun open L & D; no Amex; may need 6+ to book.

Jikoni W1

21 Blandford Street 020 7034 1988 2–1A

Food writer Ravinder Bhogal teamed up with restaurateur Ratnesh Bagdai (previously of Corbin & King, Caprice Holdings and Brindisa) to launch her first restaurant in Marylebone in September 2016. The cuisine reflects the chef-patronne's mixed heritage with flavours from East Africa, the Middle East, Asia and Britain. / W1U 3DJ; www.jikonilondon.com; @JikoniLondon.

Jin Kichi NW3 £44 553

73 Heath St 020 7794 6158 9–1A

"Some of London's best authentic Japanese cooking" has long made a big hit of this small, "very basic" but "wonderfully reliable" Hampstead café (and fans say it's getting even better with its "recently improved interior"). "Sitting at the grill bar is the best". / NW3 6UG; www.jinkichi.com; 11 pm, Sun 10 pm; closed Mon.

Jinjuu W1 £47 333

16 Kingly St 020 8181 8887 4–2B

Korean-American Iron Chef star Judy Joo's bar (ground floor, with DJ on some nights) and restaurant (basement) off Regent Street offers a taste of "something different", with its "delicious authentic Korean fried chicken" – or some more "unusual choices" – plus cocktails and bar snacks. / W1B 5PS; www.jinjuu.com; @JinjuuLDN; Mon-Wed 11.30 pm, Thu-Sat 1 am, Sun 9.30 pm.

Joanna's SE19 £48 344

56 Westow Hill 020 8670 4052 1–4D

This "fantastic" family-owned local has become a Crystal Palace institution, providing "good and reliable" American-inspired grub and cocktails since 1978. / SE19 1RX; www.joannas.uk.com; @JoannasRest; 10.45 pm, Sun 10.15 pm.

Joe Allen WC2 £54 224

13 Exeter St 020 7836 0651 5–3D

Still-"vibrant" survivor from the '70s in a Theatreland basement – a "busy American diner" whose Covent Garden location makes it "a great spot for meeting pre-/post-show" and has long been something of a "minor celebrity hangout". That "it hasn't really changed under new ownership" (it's no longer in the same stable as its NYC namesake) is a mixed blessing – fans say "there's a time and place for it and when it's good it's really good", but critics are "not sure how it's still trading, except on a very out-of-date reputation: one friend always suggests meeting there… my heart sinks!"Top Menu Tip – "burgers can be ordered off menu for those in the know". / WC2E 7DT; joeallen.co.uk; @JoeAllenWC2; Mon-Thu 11.30 pm, Fri & Sat 12.30 am, Sun 10.30 pm.

Joe Public SW4 **£14** **423**
Former Public Convenience, The Pavement
020 7622 4676 11–1C
"Genuinely great pizza" – 20-inchers sold whole or by the slice – is the reward for trying this hip newcomer in a former loo by Clapham Common station (sibling to nearby WC, also set inside a former public lav). There's also outside seating, and a hatch for takeaway. / SW4 7AA; www.joepublicpizza.com; @JoepublicSW4; midnight; no bookings.

The Joint SW9 **£26** **533**
87 Brixton Village, Coldharbour Ln 07717 642812 11–1D
"A brilliant place in trendy Brixton market with amazing BBQ food" – "it requires a bit of a long wait, but boy is it worth it for the best pulled pork burgers" and "best ever wings". "It feels great eating in the hustle and bustle of the market" too, and "all for a very cheap price". / SW9 8PS; www.the-joint.co; @thefoodjoint; 11 pm; closed Mon.

Jolly Gardeners SW18 **£49** **323**
214 Garratt Ln 020 8870 8417 11–2B
"A cut above your neighbourhood boozer" – MasterChef winner Dhruv Baker's "excellent local" serves "interesting food with lots of flavour from a range of influences". Some Earlsfield regulars "would welcome more change on the menu". / SW18 4EA; www.thejollygardeners.com; @Jollygardensw15; 9.30 pm; closed Sun D.

Jones & Sons E8 **£55** **434**
22-27 Arcola St 020 7241 1211 1–1C
"You need to grow a beard to blend in properly", but this open kitchen operation in Dalston studios "gladdens the heart" of reporters: "steaks which rival Hawksmoor, at half the price" and other "great-tasting and reasonably priced" British fare. / E8 2DJ; www.jonesandsonsdalston.com; @JonesSons; 10 pm, Fri & Sat 11 pm.

The Jones Family Project EC2 **£51** **344**
78 Great Eastern St 020 7739 1740 13–1B
This Shoreditch basement beneath a street-level cocktail bar is a "local gem", with "friendly and efficient" staff; top culinary tips are the "delicious" steaks and "brilliant truffled macaroni cheese". / EC2A 3JL; www.jonesfamilyproject.co.uk; @JonesShoreditch; 10.30 pm, Sun 6 pm; closed Sun D.

José SE1 **£47** **545**
104 Bermondsey St 020 7403 4902 10–4D
"A bucket-list experience!" José Pizarro's "hustling and bustling" tapas bar in Bermondsey is a "must-try!" – "fun, so long as you're happy to perch", and the "Barcelona-quality" dishes are "so, so good". ("We re-located our business just so we could be next to it!") / SE1 3UB; www.josepizarro.com; @Jose_Pizarro; Mon-Sat 10.15 pm; closed Sun D; no bookings.

José Pizarro EC2 **£59** **432**
Broadgate Circle 020 7256 5333 13–2B
"The slightly impersonal location doesn't do any favours" to José P's yearling in Broadgate Circle, and service can vary too; but on the plus-side his "top-quality tapas" is "seriously good and authentic"; "arrive early to secure an outside table on sunny days". / EC2M 2QS; www.josepizarro.com/jose-pizarro-broadgate; @JP_Broadgate; 10.45 pm, Sat 9.45 pm; closed Sun.

Joy King Lau WC2 **£38** **331**
3 Leicester St 020 7437 1132 5–3A
"If you want a safe bet in Chinatown", this "old school" fixture serves "proper Cantonese" dishes over each of its busy four floors, and "reasonable prices" make it "amazing value for money" too. Just "watch out for the queues". / WC2H 7BL; www.joykinglau.com; 11.30 pm, Sun 10.30 pm.

The Jugged Hare EC1 **£66** **323**
49 Chiswell St 020 7614 0134 13–2A
"A very good selection of game" is the surprise feature of this "busy" City-fringe gastropub, which is "convenient for The Barbican", and also "serviceable for a quick business lunch". / EC1Y 4SA; www.thejuggedhare.com; @juggedhare; Mon-Wed 11 pm, Thu-Sat midnight, Sun 10.30 pm.

Julie's W11
135 Portland Rd 020 7229 8331 7–2A
Last year they said it was closed till spring 2016, this year the website says it's closed till spring 2017. Let's hope the relaunch of this famously seductive '70s warren in Holland Park does soon see the light of day… / W11 4LW; www.juliesrestaurant.com; 11 pm.

Jun Ming Xuan NW9 £42 442
28 Heritage Ave 020 8205 6987 1–1A
"A proper Hong Kong experience transplanted" to Colindale's new Beaufort Park, providing "excellent dim sum, sensibly priced and briskly served". "At 5pm, a standard Cantonese menu takes over". / NW9 5GE; junming.co.uk; @jun_ming_xuan; 11 pm.

The Junction Tavern NW5 £48 333
101 Fortess Rd 020 7485 9400 9–2B
Fans "always go home on a happy note" from this "pub with good food, rather than a restaurant disguised as a pub", on the Tufnell Park/Kentish Town borders. / NW5 1AG; www.junctiontavern.co.uk; @JunctionTavern; 11 pm, Fri & Sat midnight; Mon-Thu D only, Fri-Sun open L & D; no Amex.

K10 £38 443
20 Copthall Ave, EC2 020 7562 8510 10–2C
3 Appold St, EC2 020 7539 9209 13–2B
Minster Ct, Mincing Ln, EC3
020 3019 2510 10–3D
This "conveyor-belt sushi" chain in the City is "tasty, slick, and fun". "Always fresh and varied", with a "good selection of hot dishes too", "standards remain high" and it is "hard to find fault" – they're "buzzy even on a Friday evening". / www.k10.com; Appold 9 pm, Wed-Fri 9.30 pm.

Kaffeine £12 355
15 Eastcastle St, W1 020 7580 6755 3–1D
66 Great Titchfield St, W1
020 7580 6755 3–1C
"It feels like you're in Sydney" at this "independent Aussie/Kiwi-owned coffee shop" in Fitzrovia. "Staff are always smiling, service is fast", and "standards are exacting when it comes to making a brew"; "delicious", "deli-style breakfasts, sandwiches and salads" too. / kaffeine.co.uk; @kaffeinelondon; –.

Kai Mayfair W1 £98 322
65 South Audley St 020 7493 8988 3–3A
Bernard Yeoh's Mayfair fixture feels too "international and expensive" for some tastes (it's not everywhere you can drink a £7,500 bottle of 1990 Chateau Pétrus with your crispy duck...), but its "Chinese cuisine with a south east Asian twist" (and many other influences besides – there's a selection of Wagyu dishes for example) ranks amongst London's best. / W1K 2QU; www.kaimayfair.co.uk; @kaimayfair; 10.45 pm, Sun 10.15 pm.

Kaifeng NW4 £64 333
51 Church Rd 020 8203 7888 1–1B
"Excellent standards are maintained year after year" at this Hendon stalwart – if you want kosher Chinese cooking, this is the place! / NW4 4DU; www.kaifeng.co.uk; 10 pm; closed Fri & Sat.

Kanada-Ya £19 422
3 Panton St, SW1 020 7930 3511 5–4A
64 St Giles High St, WC2
020 7240 0232 5–1B
"Best ramen in London? Quite possibly!" These West End outposts of a Japan-based noodle chain are "nothing fancy" but boil up a "broth so meaty and delicious you have to finish the bowl, even if you feel as if you're about to pop".

Kaosarn £29 443
110 St Johns Hill, SW11
020 7223 7888 11–2C
Brixton Village, Coldharbour Ln, SW9
020 7095 8922 11–2D
"Fresh, zingy, home-cooked flavours, served quickly" ensure that these Thai cafés in Brixton and Battersea are "always packed and humming". "BYO keeps costs down", too. In SW9, it's "great in the summer when you can eat outside". / SW9 10 pm, Sun 9 pm; SW11 closed Mon L.

Kappacasein SE16 £6 522
1 Voyager Industrial Estate 07837 756852 12–2A
"Taking the cheese toastie to another level (by using three cheeses, plus onion, leek, and shallots in sourdough bread)" – this Borough Market stall is arguably "the nicest way to take in five or six hundred calories" all in one go, even if "the queuing and purchasing tedium aren't the best". / SE16 4RP; www.kappacasein.com; @kappacasein; Thu 5 pm, Fri 6 pm, Sat 5 pm; closed Mon, Tue, Wed & Sun D; cash only.

Karma W14 £40 331
44 Blythe Rd 020 7602 9333 8–1D
A highly satisfactory Indian tucked away on an Olympia corner serving "superb, authentic curries". Ambience-wise however, even its most ardent fan doesn't claim it's a wild scene. / W14 0HA; www.k-a-r-m-a.co.uk; @KarmaKensington; 11 pm; no Amex.

Kaspar's Seafood & Grill, The Savoy Hotel WC2 £83 233
100 The Strand 020 7836 4343 5–3D
"An interesting menu with hints to the orient" is a feature of the fish and seafood cooking in this "splendid" dining room, known in decades past as The Savoy's River Restaurant. Fans applaud its "breathtaking style and good cuisine" – including sushi, ceviche and laksa – but critics feel "they've ruined one of London's best rooms with poor quality, pub-like food" – "forgivable in a high-street restaurant, but not at The Savoy!" / WC2R 0EU; www.kaspars.co.uk; @KasparsLondon; 11 pm; SRA-3 star.

Kateh W9 £43 3 4 3
5 Warwick Pl 020 7289 3393 9–4A
This "deservedly busy" little spot just off the canal junction in Little Venice provides "enticing" modern Iranian dishes and "a fantastic buzz". / W9 2PX; www.katehrestaurant.co.uk; 11 pm, Sun 9.30 pm; closed weekday L.

Kazan £48 3 4 2
77 Wilton Rd, SW1 020 7233 8298 2–4B
93-94 Wilton Rd, SW1 020 7233 7100 2–4B
This "totally reliable neighbourhood Turk never misses a beat" – it's "always crowded" and "rightly so" thanks to its "friendly" style and "delicious" food. "Its younger sibling opposite offers a super selection of mezze" and both are "very good quality, considering the prices". / www.kazan-restaurant.com; 10 pm.

The Keeper's House, Royal Academy W1 £61 2 2 2
Royal Academy Of Arts, Piccadilly
020 7300 5881 3–3D
"Hidden away in the vaults under the Royal Academy", all agree there's promise in this "lovely" spot. But while some reports do find it "very enjoyable", too often "the experience doesn't match up to the prestige of the RA", delivering "mediocre" results that "miss their mark": "could (and certainly should) do better!" / W1J 0BD; www.royalacademy.org.uk/page/the-keepers-house; @KHRestaurant; 9.45 pm; closed Sun.

Ken Lo's Memories SW1 £59 3 4 2
65-69 Ebury St 020 7730 7734 2–4B
Ken Lo's "very old favourite" in Belgravia inspires devotion for its "traditional – indeed, unchanging – menu" and complete reliability: "it's easy to dismiss as old hat, but the cooking remains high quality and the service much better than at most Chinese restaurants, including some which are much more expensive". / SW1W 0NZ; www.memoriesofchina.co.uk; 11 pm, Sun 10.30 pm.

Kennington Tandoori SE11 £45 3 3 3
313 Kennington Rd 020 7735 9247 1–3C
"There's more of a buzz" at this Kennington joint "than at most local Indians" – perhaps because it's "favoured by Conservative Party politicians" from Parliament across the river. It's "much better than you might reasonably expect in the dreariness of Kennington Park Road". / SE11 4QE; www.kennigtontandoori.com; @TheKTLondon; 11 pm; closed weekday L; no Amex.

Kensington Place W8 £62 3 3 2
201-209 Kensington Church St
020 7727 3184 7–2B
"Thanks to all those windows, it's extremely bright" inside this once-famous '90s 'goldfish bowl', off Notting Hill Gate, nowadays enlarged and "re-invented as a fish restaurant to gear up on its excellent adjacent fish shop" (plus "with a popular, pop-up fish 'n' chip shop in the former private dining room"). "Don't expect to hear your dining companions", but the food's "reliable". / W8 7LX; www.kensingtonplace-restaurant.co.uk; @KPRestaurantW8; Mon-Thu 10 pm, Fri-Sat 10.30 pm; closed Mon L & Sun D.

Kensington Square Kitchen W8 £33 3 4 3
9 Kensington Sq 020 7938 2598 6–1A
"OMG I love this place for breakfast" – that's the special strength of this sweet little two-floor café, on one of Kensington's oldest squares, although "the lunches are good too". / W8 5EP; www.kensingtonsquarekitchen.co.uk; @KSKRestaurant; 4.30 pm, Sun 4 pm; L only; no Amex.

The Kensington Wine Rooms W8 £58 2 3 3
127-129 Kensington Church St
020 7727 8142 7–2B
More than 40 "very different, well-kept wines" are available by the glass at this Kensington bar (with branches in Fulham and Hammersmith). A simple food menu is designed to complement the drinks, and staff "make you feel cherished"! / W8 7LP; www.greatwinesbytheglass.com; @wine_rooms; 11.30 pm.

Brew House, Kenwood House NW3 £33 2 2 3
Hampstead Heath 020 8348 4073 9–1A
Set in the stables of the majestic mansion, this self-service café is hardly a gastronomic destination, but it has a beautiful garden for tea and a bun, and makes a good brunch stop-off after a hearty walk on Hampstead Heath. / NW3 7JR; www.english-heritage.org.uk/visit/places/ke; @EHKenwood; 6 pm (summer), 4 pm (winter); L only.

Kerbisher & Malt £25 3 3 2
53 New Broadway, W5 020 8840 4418 1–2A
164 Shepherd's Bush Rd, W6
020 3556 0228 8–1C
170 Upper Richmond Road West, SW14
020 8876 3404 1–4A
50 Abbeville Rd, SW4 020 3417 4350 11–2D
59-61 Rosebery Ave, EC1
020 7833 4434 10–1A
"Fun and trendy chippies", which are "traditional and yet modern at the same time" ("if that doesn't make sense you'll have to go and see for yourself!"). Service is "lovely" (even if it "could be slicker"), and they offer "really well-cooked, no-nonsense fish 'n' chips". / www.kerbisher.co.uk; 10 pm - 10.30 pm, Sun 9 pm - 9.30 pm; W6 closed Mon; no booking.

Khan's W2 £23 **333**
13-15 Westbourne Grove
020 7727 5420 7–1C
"It's blasted on for so many years!"This hectic and atmospheric Bayswater canteen is a "staple" of "reliable", if "basic" Indian scoff. It's 100% halal too, but there's no alcohol. / W2 4UA; www.khansrestaurant.com; @KhansRestaurant; 11 pm, Sat & Sun 11.30 pm.

Kiku W1 £56 **332**
17 Half Moon St 020 7499 4208 3–4B
A "typical old-style Japanese" veteran in Mayfair, all "minimalist and wooden décor, clean lines and quite formal", so "perfect for business lunches but maybe not a romantic meal for two". "The food is very good, if a little pricey". / W1J 7BE; www.kikurestaurant.co.uk; 10.15 pm, Sun 9.45 pm; closed Sun L.

Kikuchi W1 £74 **432**
14 Hanway St 020 7637 7720 5–1A
"Outstanding! Could have been back in Japan" – a small izakaya in the warren of streets near Tottenham Court Road. Caution: even those awarding it full marks can still find it "overpriced". / W1T 1UD; 10.30 pm, Sat 9.30 pm; closed Sun.

Kiln W1
58 Brewer Street no tel 4–3C
Ben Chapman, founder of one of London's hottest restaurants of recent times – Smoking Goat – opened a second Thai venture in September 2016. This Soho venue is described as a 'side-of-the-road-type restaurant', serving grills and a speciality daily noodle dish. / W1F 9TL.

Kintan WC1 £44 **333**
34-36 High Holborn 020 7242 8076 10–2A
This "great-fun Japanese/Korean barbecue-at-your-table outfit" near Holborn claims to be one of London's first yakiniku (grilled meat) venues. "Good for groups and excellent value at lunch". / WC1V 6AE; www.kintan.uk; @kintanuk; 10.30 pm, Sun 9.30 pm.

Kipferl N1 £46 **322**
20 Camden Passage 020 77041 555 9–3D
From the "great dumplings and schnitzel" to "authentic Viennese cakes and Austrian coffee" (and even wine), this Islington deli-café serves "a good range of dishes" showing "dedication to the Austrian style and approach". It's not a Tyrolean kitsch-fest either – in fact the interior is "rather bland". / N1 8ED; www.kipferl.co.uk; @KipferlCafe; 9.25 pm; booking weekdays only.

Kiraku W5 £35 **442**
8 Station Pde 020 8992 2848 1–3A
"When you need Japanese food without pretension, head here!" – to this simple café, near Ealing Common tube station, consistently highly rated for its straightforward but accomplished cuisine. / W5 3LD; www.kiraku.co.uk; @kirakulondon; 10 pm; closed Mon; no Amex.

Kiru SW3 £54 **433**
2 Elystan Street 020 7584 9999 6–2D
A "superb", "friendly and professional" newcomer at Chelsea Green, serving "Japanese fusion fare" ("Nobu-style, but fresher and better", featuring "very high-quality sashimi, sushi, and nigiri"), "plus smashing sake"… "albeit at a price". / SW3; www.kirurestaurant.com; @KiruRestaurant; 10 pm, Fri & Sat 10.30 pm.

Kitchen W8 W8 £71 **442**
11-13 Abingdon Road 020 7937 0120 6–1A
"A gastronomic, neighbourhood restaurant" off Kensington High Street highly lauded for its "casual and sophisticated" approach, "unusually enthusiastic" service, and "delightful", "seasonal" cuisine (overseen by Phil Howard). Ratings softened a little this year however – the atmosphere of its "intimate" interlocking dining spaces is "not electric", and "portion sizes can be a bit too haute-cuisine style". / W8 6AH; www.kitchenw8.com; @KitchenW8; 10.30 pm, Sun 9.30 pm.

Kitty Fisher's W1 £64 **444**
10 Shepherd's Mkt 020 3302 1661 3–4B
"Entirely deserving of all the hype" is the overwhelming verdict on this "small, but comfortable and cosy" yearling, by picturesque Shepherd Market. It's "a real charmer": service is "welcoming and fun", and the "highly competent cooking" is "big on simplicity and flavour". / W1J 7QF; www.kittyfishers.com; @kittyfishers; 9.30 pm; closed Sun.

Koffmann's, The Berkeley SW1 £86 **453**
The Berkeley, Wilton Pl 020 7107 8844 6–1D
"It's hard to find better French food in London" than Pierre Koffmann's "surprisingly robust" cuisine at his Belgravia basement: "un-concept plates, simply presented with perfect quality, freshness, and flavour". "The finest service" ("everything runs very smoothly") helps introduce an "intimate" ambience into the slightly "weird and sunken" location – in fact, all-in-all, it arguably "frequently outshines its better-known neighbour" Marcus nowadays. Top Menu Tip – "it's worth the trip for the pistachio soufflé, but the legendary pig's trotter is also tip top". STOP PRESS: hurry along, because the restaurant is closing in December 2016. / SW1X 7RL; www.pierrekoffmann.co.uk; @theberkeley / @pierrekoffmann; 10.30 pm; jacket & tie required.

KOJAWAN, Hilton Metropole W2 £65 234
225 Edgware Rd 020 8088 0111 7–1D
"A fabulous view over London is complemented by crazy-kitsch Asian decor", at this offbeat 23rd floor newcomer at the top of the Hilton Metropole by Edgware Road station, where two, non-Asian, Michelin-friendly chefs (Bjorn Van Der Horst – formerly of Greenhouse – and Omar Romero, a graduate of Rhodes Twenty Four) offer a fusion of KO-rean, JA-panese and Tai-WAN-ese cuisines (geddit?), complemented by a formidable list of drinks. To fans it's a "rooftop gem" – one or two critics though "like the concept, but think they just haven't got it right". / W2; www.kojawan.uk; @kojawan; 2 am; closed weekday L.

Koji SW6 £75 443
58 New King's Rd 020 7731 2520 11–1B
"Roka-quality food but at more reasonable prices (and great cocktails too!)", win all-round acclaim for Pat & Mark Barnett's "terrific" Japanese-fusion haunt in Parsons Green (which they ran for ages as Mao Tai, long RIP); its swish decor is "great if you're in a group, a bit sparse if you're à deux". / SW6 4LS; www.koji.restaurant; @koji_restaurant; 11.30 pm, Sun 10.30 pm; closed weekday L; no shorts.

Kolossi Grill EC1 £33 352
56-60 Rosebery Ave 020 7278 5758 10–1A
"You will have to travel a very long way to beat the value for money offered by this eatery off the middle of Exmouth Market" – a 50-year-old survivor that's changed little over the years. The main concern? – "where will I eat if the owner retires!" / EC1R 4RR; www.kolossigrill.com; 10.30 pm; closed Sat L & Sun; set weekday L £15 (FP).

Koya-Bar W1 £34 344
50 Frith St 020 7434 4463 5–2A
"Takes over where Koya (RIP) left off", this "cramped" but "cool" Soho Japanese is "famous for udon noodles, but their small plates and donburi rice dishes are even better". "The purity of the stocks and sauces is fantastic", so it's "well worth the queue" (you can't book). / W1D 4SQ; www.koyabar.co.uk; @KoyaBar; 10.30 pm, Thu-Sat 11 pm, Sun 10 pm; no Amex; no bookings.

Kricket £44 543
12 Denman Street, W1 awaiting tel 4–3C
Pop Brixton, 53 Brixton Station Rd, SW9 awaiting tel 11–1D
"A brilliant and totally different, fresh and wonderfully subtle fusion of southern Indian and European food" is "served up with a smile and music in a metal container in Brixton" as part of a "fun" and "funky" community project; a Soho branch is set to open in the autumn of 2016.

Kulu Kulu £32 311
76 Brewer St, W1 020 7734 7316 4–3C
51-53 Shelton St, WC2 020 7240 5687 5–2C
39 Thurloe Pl, SW7 020 7589 2225 6–2C
"The prices barely seem to have changed in the last 17 years" (similarly the drab decor) at these "grab-a-dish-from-the-belt" cafés, still popular "for a cheap, quick, sushi fix". "The key to an enjoyable meal is to go when it's busy when dishes are at their freshest and hottest". / 10 pm, SW7 10.30 pm; closed Sun; no Amex; no booking.

Kurobuta £56 522
Harvey Nichols, Knightsbridge, SW1 020 7920 6443 6–1D
312 King's Rd, SW3 020 7920 6444 6–3C
17-20 Kendal St, W2 020 7920 6444 7–1D
"Thrilling flavours" from "a wide ranging" Japanese menu again inspire rave reviews for Scott Hallsworth's "hip, modern, trendy, but unpretentious" izakaya-style haunts, which are "a real favourite for a fun night out". They're "not for the hard of hearing" though, and SW3 is "a bit trashy" and "pure Chelsea" for some tastes. / @KurobutaLondon; –.

The Ladbroke Arms W11 £53 324
54 Ladbroke Rd 020 7727 6648 7–2B
"There's always a good crowd, especially on the terrace on a sunny day" at this unusually attractive and "comfortable" pub, at the Holland Park end of Ladbroke Grove. "It's a little chaotic, always fun, bustling and friendly", with "very reliable food". / W11 3NW; www.ladbrokearms.com; @ladbrokearms; 11 pm, Sun 10.30 pm; no booking after 8 pm.

The Lady Ottoline WC1 £50 323
11a Northington St 020 7831 0008 2–1D
"Nice little pub" in Bloomsbury – a restored Victorian tavern (part of the upmarket Affinity group) whose comfort food cooking and rather civilised atmosphere are consistently well-rated by reporters. / WC1N 2JF; www.theladyottoline.com; @theladyottoline; 10 pm, Sun 8 pm.

Lahore Karahi SW17 £26 422
1 Tooting High Street, London 020 8767 2477 11–2C
"I keep coming back, week after week, year after year" – so say fans of this "top class Indian / Pakistani" BYO canteen in Tooting, extolling its "sublime food and amazing value". / SW17 0SN; www.lahorekarahirestaurant.co.uk; midnight; no Amex.

Lahore Kebab House £24 522
668 Streatham High Rd, SW16 020 8765 0771 11–2D
2-10 Umberston St, E1 020 7481 9737 12–1A
"The best Pakistani food in London!" This "Whitechapel scrum" is "a true no-nonsense star" – its lamb chops and other grills are "so delicious" but

the "curries are very good too" and it's all "so cheap, you almost don't notice paying!" (especially as you can BYO). "Consistently great for over 20 years", old timers "remember when it was just a hole in the wall – nowadays it's a multi-level factory of sorts!" (Fewer reports on the "huge" Streatham outpost, but they say it too is "brilliant" and "a nicer place to eat"). / midnight.

Lamberts SW12 **£52** 5 5 4
2 Station Pde 020 8675 2233 11–2C
"Lucky Balhamites to have it on their doorstep!" – Joe Lambert's "consistently excellent" neighbourhood favourite "nibbles at Chez Bruce's heels" in the affections of SW12 residents. Its "creative, modern and seasonal British food" is "remarkably good value" and served by "superb" staff in a "casual" setting. / SW12 9AZ; www.lambertsrestaurant.com; @lamberts_balham; 10 pm, Sun 5 pm; closed Mon & Sun L; no Amex.

The Landmark, Winter Garden NW1 **£78** 2 4 5
222 Marylebone Rd 020 7631 8000 9–4A
The "beautiful atrium, with lots of daylight" makes this Marylebone venue a "very special setting" for an "unbeatable Sunday brunch" (limitless champagne) or "traditional afternoon tea" ("great ambience with piano in the background"); it suits business lunchers too. / NW1 6JQ; www.landmarklondon.co.uk; @landmarklondon; 10.15 pm; no trainers; booking max 12 may apply.

Langan's Brasserie W1 **£68** 1 2 4
Stratton St 020 7491 8822 3–3C
"I've been going for 38 years and it still delivers...": a typical recommendation for this famous brasserie near The Ritz, whose "wonderful rooms are filled with plenty of character", and which particularly suit a business occasion. Sceptics, though, can find it even "more old school than expected" – "very masculine, with lots of boys-only tables, and comfort food" – and its harshest critics feel its "poor" catering standards put it "in dire need of a makeover/relaunch". / W1J 8LB; www.langansrestaurants.co.uk; @langanslondon; 11 pm, Fri & Sat 11.30 pm; closed Sun.

Palm Court, The Langham W1 **£72** 3 3 3
1c, Portland Place 020 7965 0195 2–1B
"I think I have done every major afternoon tea in the city and nothing beats The Langham!" – "most exquisite sweets and yummy savouries", and "really interesting sandwiches served on a platter rather than left on the table". (In fact, this "beautiful" space is a handy fall-back in general). / W1B 1JA; www.palm-court.co.uk; 10:30 pm; no trainers.

Lantana Cafe **£35** 3 3 3
13-14 Charlotte Pl, W1 020 7323 6601 2–1C
45 Middle Yd, Camden Lock Pl, NW1
020 7428 0421 9–2B
Unit 2, 1 Oliver's Yd, 55 City Rd, EC1
020 7253 5273 13–1A
An "imaginative brunch menu" has made this trio of "atmospheric" Aussie-style coffee bars worth remembering in Fitzrovia, Camden Lock and Shoreditch. Be warned, though, they are "very, very busy at times". / lantanacafe.co.uk; @lantanacafe; –.

Lardo **£40** 3 2 2
158 Sandringham Rd, E8
020 3021 0747 14–1B
197-201 Richmond Rd, E8
020 8533 8229 14–1B
"Very cool" Italian in the Arthaus building near London Fields where a hipster-heavy crowd hoover up a "fairly limited menu" from the open kitchen, majoring in charcuterie and pizza. Nearby they've opened Lardo Bebé – a shop-conversion serving "artisan pizza with original toppings".

Latium W1 **£55** 4 4 3
21 Berners St 020 7323 9123 3–1D
"Nothing's 'in yer face', at this discreet and subtle venue", "tucked away" in Fitzrovia, where new head chef Stefano Motta's seems to be maintaining its "clean and precise" cooking, "full of strong flavours and interesting combinations". Thanks to its "charming" and "unobtrusive" service and "tranquil and well-spaced" (if perhaps "not terribly inspiring") interior, it's a business favourite too. Top Menu Tip – "the ravioli can be exceptional". / W1T 3LP; www.latiumrestaurant.com; @LatiumLondon; 10.30 pm, Sat 11 pm; closed Sat L & Sun L.

Launceston Place W8 **£80** 4 5 4
1a Launceston Pl 020 7937 6912 6–1B
Raphael Francois "has maintained the excellent standards" set by Tim Allen at this "understated" townhouse in a gorgeous Kensington backwater (while "taking the menu in a welcome Gallic direction"). It's D&D London's best all-rounder nowadays: "relaxed yet opulent", with notably "charming" service and "sound, refined cooking". / W8 5RL; www.launcestonplace-restaurant.co.uk; @LauncestonPlace; 10 pm, Sun 9.30 pm; closed Mon & Tue L.

THE LEDBURY W11 **£133** 5 5 4
127 Ledbury Rd 020 7792 9090 7–1B
Brett Graham's virtuoso cuisine has established his "special yet unstuffy" Notting Hill HQ as London's No. 1 gastronomic address (topping this year's survey nominations as best meal of the year, and losing only narrowly to The Araki in achieving the highest food rating). "Absence of snob factor" is key: dishes are "sophisticated and elaborate without being pretentious"; "utterly charming" staff are

"much more easy-going than at many Michelin-starred peers"; and the "well-spaced" interior lacks grandiosity while being "calm and relaxing". / W11 2AQ; www.theledbury.com; @theledbury; 9.45 pm; closed Mon L & Tue L.

Legs E9 **£50**
120-122 Morning Lane 020 3441 8765 14–1B
A new café-cum-wine-bar (the name being a nod to wine-anorak terminology), not far from Hipster (sorry, we mean Hackney!) Central station. Beneath the restaurant is a 'makers' basement', where the team distil vermouth for the bar, cure meats, pickle veg and even mould ceramics for the tables upstairs [oh good grief, Ed]! It's the brainchild of chef Magnus Reid (founder of Shoreditch hangout CREAM) and Andy Kanter. Just one early survey report, but it's mega-enthusiastic, and some early media reviews likewise give it a big thumbs up. / E9 6LH; www.legsrestaurant.com; @legsrestaurant; Tue 5 pm, Wed-Sun 11 pm; closed Mon & Tue D; no bookings at lunch.

Lemonia NW1 **£45** 1 3 4
89 Regent's Park Rd 020 7586 7454 9–3B
"Buzzing with positive energy, seven days a week" – this "phenomenal" Primrose Hill mega-taverna remains "extraordinarily busy" and is "like home, only better" for its huge north London fanclub. Even many fans recognise that "the menu is tired and needs a complete refresh"… but it's been like that for as long as anyone can remember! / NW1 8UY; www.lemonia.co.uk; @Lemonia_Greek; 11 pm; closed Sun D; no Amex.

Leong's Legends W1 **£37** 3 2 2
3 Macclesfield St 020 7287 0288 5–3A
"Excellent Shanghai dumplings" (xiao long bao) are the big deal at this "cramped" Chinatown Taiwanese, which also serves an "abbreviated dim sum menu realised to an OK-to-good standard". / W1D 6AX; www.leongslegend.com; 11 pm, Sat 11.30 pm; no bookings.

Leyton Technical E10 **£37** 3 2 4
265b High Road 020 8558 4759 1–1D
Full marks for grandeur to this conversion of Leyton's former town hall into a prime local. It's perhaps more pub than gastro, but the scoff's consistently well rated. / E10 5QN; www.leytontechnical.com; @LeytonTechnical; 10 pm, Sun 7 pm.

The Lido Café, Brockwell Lido SE24 **£43** 2 2 4
Dulwich Rd 020 7737 8183 11–2D
No-one doubts this is a "lovely space" beside Brockwell Park's lovingly preserved Lido in Brixton – a café open from 8am through to dinner. Staff often "lack oversight" however, and – "tasty" breakfasts aside – the food can seem "expensive for what it is". / SE24 0PA; www.thelidocafe.co.uk; @thelidocafe; 4 pm; closed Sun D; no Amex.

The Light House SW19 **£54** 3 3 3
75-77 Ridgway 020 8944 6338 11–2B
Wimbledon's longest-serving contributor to modern gastronomy – a "lovely" informal fixture that has something of a name for "variable" somewhat "ill-conceived" dishes. Fans though say "it's gone up a notch in recent times: no longer does it try and put too much together on a plate or offer too much variety". / SW19 4ST; www.lighthousewimbledon.com; 10.30 pm; closed Sun D.

The Lighterman N1 **£52** 3 3 4
3 Granary Sq 020 3846 3400 9–3C
Another resident for King's Cross restaurant hub Granary Square – this new pub and dining room has "a great location on the banks of Regent's Canal", and "engaging staff" who provide "reasonably priced, tasty food". "Attractive if noisy ground floor, quieter first floor". / N1C 4BH; www.thelighterman.co.uk; @TheLightermanKX; 10.30 pm, Sun 9.30 pm.

Lima Fitzrovia **£66** 3 2 1
31 Rathbone Pl, W1 020 3002 2640 2–1C
14 Garrick St, WC2 020 7240 5778 5–3C
"Elegant renditions of tangy Latino flavours" still win praise for these modern Peruvians, in Fitzrovia and Covent Garden ('Lima Floral'). Even fans say they are "expensive" however, not helped by "rather blah" decor, and harsher critics just feel "they've lost their way". / www.limalondongroup.com; @lima_london; –.

Lime Orange SW1 **£36** 3 2 2
312 Vauxhall Bridge Rd 020 8616 0498 2–4B
"Reliable bibimbap and several other excellent dishes" score praise for this "good quality cheap 'n' cheerful Korean (with a Japanese slant)" just by Victoria station. "There's nothing wrong with the ambience, but it's not the point". / SW1V; www.limeorange.co.uk; closed Sun.

Lisboa Pâtisserie W10 **£10** 3 2 4
57 Golborne Rd 020 8968 5242 7–1A
"Pastéis de nata to die for" are a prime attraction at this lively Portuguese café – an excellent complement to a trip to nearby Portobello Market. / W10 5NR; 7 pm; L only; no bookings.

The Little Bay NW6 **£28** 2 3 4
228 Belsize Rd 020 7372 4699 1–2B
"Perfect for a cheap eat", this "very reliable" and jolly, theatre-themed bistro is "very good at catering for large groups, as well as couples in the little balconies here and there". The Farringdon branch closed this year (there is still a Croydon 'country cousin'). / NW6 4BT; www.little-bay.co.uk; 11.30 pm; cash only.

Little Georgia Café £40 333
14 Barnsbury Rd, N1 020 7278 6100 9–3D
87 Goldsmiths Row, E2 020 7739 8154 14–2B
"The best borscht in London" typifies the "truly interesting", "hearty, warming menu (particularly good in winter)" at this pair of "favourite neighbourhood" cafés in Islington and Hackney, similarly the "amazing Georgian wine". / www.littlegeorgia.co.uk; 10 pm.

Little Social W1 £76 334
5 Pollen St 020 7870 3730 3–2C
"More relaxed and better than its bigger sister" (over the road) – Jason Atherton's "home-from-home" feels "nicely hidden away like you're not in central London" and delivers a great "buzz", a menu of "classic" dishes, and a "comprehensive" wine list. Even fans can quibble though – "I feel a little mean saying it, it's very good, but just too expensive for somewhere so informal". / W1S 1NE; www.littlesocial.co.uk; @_littlesocial; 10.30 pm; closed Sun.

Little Taperia SW17 £34 441
143 Tooting High St 020 8682 3303 11–2C
"I challenge you to visit and not to spend an evening eating and drinking too much!" – "a joint project from the owners of Meza and Little Bar", this Tooting Spaniard provides "delicious tapas off a short, imaginative menu" washed down with cocktails, sherries, ports and cavas. / SW17; www.thelittletaperia.co.uk; @littletaperia; 10 pm, Fri & Sat 11 pm, Sun 9.30 pm; may need 6+ to book.

LOBOS Meat & Tapas SE1 £48 432
14 Borough High St 020 7407 5361 10–4C
"Some of the most inspiring and inspired tapas anywhere" – from a menu featuring "meat, meat, and more meat" – is waiting to be discovered in this "very squished" year-old dive in Borough Market. It's the creation of alumni from nearby Brindisa, and "brilliant". / SE1 9QG; www.lobostapas.co.uk; @LobosTapas; 11 pm, Sun 10 pm.

Lobster Pot SE11 £62 434
3 Kennington Ln 020 7582 5556 1–3C
10/10 for the very Gallic, surreal nautical decor (complete with recorded seagull cries) at this 21-year-old, family-run venture, grungily situated in deepest Kennington. At heart, it's a "fine and traditional" Breton fish and seafood restaurant. / SE11 4RG; www.lobsterpotrestaurant.co.uk; 10.30 pm; closed Mon & Sun; booking max 8 may apply.

Locanda Locatelli, Hyatt Regency W1 £81 444
8 Seymour St 020 7935 9088 2–2A
"A wonderful taste of Italy" inspires fans of Giorgio Locatelli's "dark", "classy" rather '90s Marylebone HQ. The main man has seemed more in evidence this last year – "prowling the dining room to ensure all is well" – and ratings for the "lovingly crafted food" and service (mostly "courteous", occasionally "stand-offish") were higher across the board. "Expensive, but worth it". / W1H 7JZ; www.locandalocatelli.com; 11 pm, Thu-Sat 11.30 pm, Sun 10.15 pm; booking max 8 may apply.

Locanda Ottomezzo W8 £67 323
2-4 Thackeray St 020 7937 2200 6–1B
A "backstreet Italian" near Kensington Square Garden, with "absolutely great ambience, food and wine" – service, though, can be a weak link. / W8 5ET; www.locandaottoemezzo.co.uk; 10.30 pm; closed Mon L, Sat L & Sun.

Loch Fyne £43 233
"You get what you expect" at this "sensible and reliable" chain: "reasonably priced" fish and seafood that's "basic but OK" in safe, attractive surroundings. / www.lochfyne-restaurants.com; 10 pm, WC2 10.30 pm.

London House SW11 £60 332
7-9 Battersea Sq 020 7592 8545 11–1C
Gordon Ramsay's "relaxed and friendly" two-year-old in Battersea pleases diners with its "great simple food", and a move to "less formal dining" has been well received. "The menu looks quite limited but the food was really enjoyable". / SW11 3RA; www.gordonramsay.com; @londonhouse; Tue-Fri 10 pm; closed Mon, Tue L & Wed L.

The Lord Northbrook SE12 £42 344
116 Burnt Ash Rd 020 8318 1127 1–4D
"In an area without huge amounts of choice", this Lea Green boozer provides "a good local gastropub". / SE12 8PU; www.thelordnorthbrook.co.uk; @LordNorthbrook; 9 pm, Fri & Sat 10 pm.

Lorenzo SE19 £44 333
73 Westow Hill 020 8761 7485 1–4D
This "extremely popular" Italian in Upper Norwood "is still very good value, and the cooking is generous and exemplary". Be warned, though, it's a "lunchtime favourite", so "tables get quite cramped – but it's worth it". / SE19 1TX; www.lorenzo.uk.com; 10.30 pm; no bookings.

Lotus WC2 £59 443
17 Charing Cross Rd 020 7839 8797 5–4B
This "classy" yearling off Leicester Square serves "elaborate, sophisticated Indian" dishes, "very different from all others in area". There's an "outstanding" range of game and – usefully in the heart of the West End – a "great pre-theatre menu". "I hope it survives". / WC2H 0EP; www.lotus.london; 10.30 pm.

Luce e Limoni WC1 **£57** 353
91-93 Gray's Inn Rd 020 7242 3382 10–1A
"Fabrizio is a wonderful host" and his well-appointed Bloomsbury restaurant provides "very kind and polite service" to "make you feel at home", plus "hearty Sicilian cuisine (to be enjoyed by those not accustomed to modern or light Italian food)". "It's opposite ITN so you can always get a cab!" / WC1X 8TX; www.luceelimoni.com; @Luce_e_Limoni; 10 pm, Fri - Sat 11 pm.

Luciano's SE12 **£42** 333
131 Burnt Ash Rd 020 8852 3186 1–4D
"A fantastic local Italian" in Lee ("which now also has a bar next to the main restaurant" doing "good bar snacks"). "Family owned, it serves fresh pasta and pizza from a proper wood-burning oven". / SE12; lucianoslondon.co.uk; @LucianosLondon; 10.30 pm, Sun 10 pm; closed Mon.

Lucio SW3 **£72** 332
257 Fulham Rd 020 7823 3007 6–3B
"Perfect pasta dishes" are a highlight of the "simple and tasty" cooking at this "friendly" (if "noisy") Chelsea trattoria. Top Tip – "The set lunch menu is good value and you can see why it's full most lunchtimes". / SW3 6HY; www.luciorestaurant.com; 10.45 pm.

Lucky Chip E8 **£42** 322
25 Ridley Rd 020 7686 9703 14–1A
"Might they be London's best burgers?" query fans of this new foodster-favourite: the permanent, diner-style home by Dalston's Ridley Road Market of a pop-up that's been spotted at various Hackney sites. (One or two other menu options too: steak, chicken parmigiana, and some funky, dude-ish bites). / E8 2NP; www.luckychip.co.uk/burgers-and-wine; @Lucky_Chip; 11 pm, Thu-Sat midnight, Sun 10 pm.

Lupita WC2 **£44** 322
13-15 Villiers St 020 7930 5355 5–4D
"Authentic" and "unusual" Mexican cuisine that's "good value" too can be found at this "informal" location, to the side of Charing Cross station. / WC2N 6ND; www.lupita.co.uk; @LupitaUK; 11 pm, Fri & Sat 11.30 pm, Sun 10 pm.

Lure NW5 **£40** 443
56 Chetwynd Rd 020 7267 0163 9–1B
"The new posh fish 'n' chip shop in Dartmouth Park ticks all the boxes" – "who knew a fish-and-chippy could be this elevated?". Its "very hands-on owner" also wins accolades for his "home-made pickles". / NW5 1DJ; www.lurefishkitchen.co.uk; @Lurefishkitchen; 10 pm.

Lurra W1 **£52** 433
9 Seymour Pl 020 7724 4545 2–2A
"The other Spanish food is full of flavour, but the aged Galician steak is the star" (some of London's best meat) at this year-old "Basque BBQ" near Marble Arch, a worthy sibling to the illustrious Donostia nearby. With its "lovely modern interior" and "friendly" service it's "a great night out". / W1H 5BA; www.lurra.co.uk; @LurraW1.

Lutyens EC4 **£75** 222
85 Fleet St 020 7583 8385 10–2A
A smart business-lunch venue on the edge of the City, Sir Terence Conran's brasserie provides "reliable food and service" which cause no grave complaints. There's "little adventure beyond the business lunch" however: "is this where accountants go for their Christmas meal?" / EC4Y 1AE; www.lutyens-restaurant.com; 9.45 pm; closed Sat & Sun.

Lyle's E1 **£66** 543
The Tea Building, 56 Shoreditch High St
020 3011 5911 13–1B
"James Lowe and the team continue to inspire" at this "continually excellent", "hipster-vibe" Shoreditch venue, whose menu "is designed with simplicity at heart, yet refined with complexity of flavour": "I was a bit sceptical about the set 5-course dinner but my god, was I proved wrong! Incredible cooking and great value for money!" / E1 6JJ; www.lyleslondon.com; @lyleslondon; 10 pm; closed Sat L & Sun.

M Restaurants **£75** 222
Zig Zag Building, Victoria St, SW1
020 3327 7770 2–4B
2-3 Threadneedle Walk, EC2
020 3327 7770 10–2C
"The main restaurant booths are perfect for business", as are the steak and luxurious seafood (sushi, ceviche, etc) selections, and swish bars at these big and brassy entertaining complexes in the City and Victoria. These "hangar-like" spaces can seem soulless however, and "lord above the prices", which leave any mishaps on the cooking front hard to forgive.

Ma Cuisine TW9 **£47** 323
9 Station Approach 020 8332 1923 1–3A
Retro Gallic fare ("a wonderful boudin noir starter" and "coq au vin to die for") matches the gingham tablecloths and Parisian posters of this cute bistro near Kew Gardens station. It can be "pricier than you'd expect" but "who wouldn't want it on their doorstep?" / TW9 3QB; www.macuisinebistrot.co.uk; 10 pm, Fri & Sat 10.30 pm; no Amex.

Ma Goa SW15 **£40** 442
242-244 Upper Richmond Rd
020 8780 1767 11–2B
"It's still my favourite, and I keep going back!" – this stalwart Putney south Indian has a hyper-loyal local fanclub. "You are always made to feel special (we almost feel part of the family)" and the cooking is "still authentic, still interesting, and good value for a Sunday buffet". / SW15 6TG; www.ma-goa.com;

@magoarestaurant; 10.30 pm, Fri-Sat 11 pm, Sun 10pm; closed Mon.

Mac & Wild W1 £49 443
65 Great Titchfield St 020 7637 0510 2–1B
"It's good to see this street vendor grow up into a proper restaurant" – Andy Waugh's Fitzrovia yearling offers a "successful riff on Scottish cuisine" majoring in "serious game" (from a "limited menu" focused primarily on venison steaks and burgers), much of it from his family's estate. "There's not a lot of space between tables (you can feel a bit encroached on)", but food (and whisky!) are "first rate" and "reasonably priced". A new Borough opening is planned. / W1; www.macandwild.com; 10.30 pm.

MacellaioRC £53 333
84 Old Brompton Rd, SW7
020 7589 5834 6–2B
229 Union St, SE1 07467 307 682 10–4B
38-40 Exmouth Market, EC1
020 3696 8220 10–1A
"A must for carnivores!" – These Italian grill-houses, complete with "eccentric" butcher's shop decor, attract adulatory reviews, primarily for their "fantastic range" of "superb" Piedmontese Fassone steaks (although their alternative line in Sardinian bluefin tuna dishes can also be "outstanding"), but also for their "zany" and "charming" service, "excellent, predominantly Italian wines" and "warm and inviting hubbub". And yet… they don't do it for everyone – ratings are undercut by a hardcore band of sceptics who find the whole package a disappointment. The South Kensington original was joined by an Exmouth Market branch in late 2015 (formerly Medcalf's, RIP), and a third branch opens in Southwark's Union Yard arches in autumn 2016.

Made in Italy £40 323
50 James St, W1 020 7224 0182 3–1A
249 King's Rd, SW3 020 7352 1880 6–3C
141 The Broadway, SW19
020 8540 4330 11–2A
Pizza is sold by the metre at these King's Road, Chelsea and Wimbledon venues, making "a nice change from a regular pizzeria – and the pizzas are superb". "The small space gets very crowded so it's often on the noisy side" – but that's all part of the atmosphere. / www.madeinitalygroup.co.uk; 11 pm, Sun 10 pm; SW3 closed Mon L.

Madhu's UB1 £38 543
39 South Rd 020 8574 1897 1–3A
"Excellent authentic cuisine" and a "bustling fun atmosphere", place this Southall curry legend "on the list of top Asian restaurants in Britain". Over the years it's spawned a major catering empire. / UB1 1SW; www.madhus.co.uk; 11.30 pm; closed Tue, Sat L & Sun L; no bookings.

The Magazine Restaurant, Serpentine Gallery W2 £58 234
Kensington Gdns 020 7298 7552 7–2D
Zaha Hadid's wonderful "elegant" structure in the centre of Hyde Park elicits surprisingly little feedback despite "surroundings to die for". The lunchtime menu offers 'proper' food (if in a simpler style than when it first opened) but of most interest to reporters is the "tasteful and tasty afternoon tea" (and there are also breakfast and brunch options). / W2 2AR; www.magazine-restaurant.co.uk; @TheMagazineLDN; Tue & Sun 6 pm, Wed-Sat 10.45 pm; closed Mon, Tue D & Sun D.

Magdalen SE1 £54 322
152 Tooley St 020 7403 1342 10–4D
"A welcome beacon over many years" – this "rather formal venue can offer genuine culinary fireworks for its largely business clientele, and really stands out in the poorly served London Bridge area". Its ratings are declining though, with accusations of "increasingly indifferent service", and that it's "going through the motions". / SE1 2TU; www.magdalenrestaurant.co.uk; @Magdalense1; 10 pm; closed Sat L & Sun.

Maggie Jones's W8 £56 225
6 Old Court Pl 020 7937 6462 6–1A
"Eccentric but fun", this enduring "hideaway" near Kensington Palace (named after the pseudonym Princess Margaret used to book under) is "reminiscent of a cluttered farmhouse" and ever-so romantic. "The only thing on the menu which has changed since 1976 are the prices. It's nursery comfort food for maiden aunts (and nothing wrong with that!)" / W8 4PL; www.maggie-jones.co.uk; 11 pm, Sun 10.30 pm.

Maguro W9 £48 443
5 Lanark Pl 020 7289 4353 9–4A
"Spanking-fresh sushi" and other Japanese delicacies draw a loyal following to this "useful hidden local" near Little Venice. Reporters are split between finding it "tiny and friendly" or "cramped, noisy and dark" – but either way, "the food and presentation belie the location". / W9 1BT; www.maguro-restaurant.com; 11 pm, Sun 10.30 pm; no Amex.

Maison Bertaux W1 £16 343
28 Greek St 020 7437 6007 5–2A
This "unique" Soho treasure opened over 100 years before the current tea/coffee house craze (est 1871), and "there's nothing else like it". It's "cramped and not cheap, but serves authentic French pastries and real tea" – and "the best goodies are still cooked on the premises". / W1D 5DQ; www.maisonbertaux.com; @Maison_Bertaux; 10.15 pm, Sun 8 pm.

Maison Eric Kayser W1
8 Baker St no tel 3–1A
This artisan Parisian boulanger opens its first site in London in autumn 2016, with a bakery in Marylebone. Eric Kayser already has a global empire incorporating Paris, New York, Japan and Hong Kong. / W1H 6AZ; www.maison-kayser.com/en; @Maison_EK.

Malabar W8 £42 [5][4][3]
27 Uxbridge St 020 7727 8800 7–2B
"A favourite for over 30 years", this Notting Hill Gate Indian manages to combine longevity with a perennially "fresh and quirky" approach, "superb ingredients and presentation" and "delicious, high-quality cooking". "Super-charming, intimate, stylish and lively" – "it just keeps on doing a great job!" / W8 7TQ; www.malabar-restaurant.co.uk; 11.30 pm.

Malabar Junction WC1 £41 [3][3][3]
107 Gt Russell St 020 7580 5230 2–1C
An attractive "Raj feel and low-stress ambience" help mark out this "good, long-running South Indian" near the British Museum. "Ignore the unassuming entrance and cavernous dining room which is like a business hotel lobby – the food is very tasty and well prepared!" / WC1B 3NA; www.malabarjunction.com; 11 pm.

Mamie's WC2
19 Catherine Street 020 7836 7216 5–2D
Covent Garden's new three-floor crêperie opened in summer 2016 with the added bonus of a cider bar. La Cidrothèque will serve French ciders from Normandy and Brittany, as well as other brews from Britain and beyond. / WC2B 5JS; www.mamies.co.uk; @MAMIESLondon.

Mamma Dough £28 [3][4][4]
76-78 Honor Oak Pk, SE23
020 8699 5196 1–4D
354 Coldharbour Ln, SW9
020 7095 1491 11–1D
This growing South London group (Honor Oak Park, Brixton and Peckham) serves "interesting but not too wacky" sourdough pizza in a "relaxed, cheerful atmosphere". Local craft beers and coffee roasted in Shoreditch complete the picture.

Mandarin Kitchen W2 £41 [4][1][1]
14-16 Queensway 020 7727 9012 7–2C
"Still the go-to place for lobster noodles" – this busy, crowded Bayswater operation has long been one of the capital's most notable spots for Chinese seafood. "Both service and ambience detract from the experience" however. / W2 3RX; 11.15 pm.

Mangal 1 E8 £28 [5][4][3]
10 Arcola St 020 7275 8981 14–1A
"Exceptional meat from the charcoal and fresh salads" draw fans from across town to Dalston to this "perfect Turkish grill" – "I go every week" and it "never fails to impress"! It's also cheap as chips, plus "you can BYO". / E8 2DJ; www.mangal1.com; @Mangalone; midnight, Sat & Sun 1 am; cash only.

Mangal 1.1 EC2 £30
68 Rivington Street 020 7275 8981 13–1B
It's taken them 25 years, but finally the owners of the mega popular Dalston ocakbasi have announced a second location, taking over the former site of Jubo in Shoreditch – too little feedback for a rating as yet. / EC2A 3AY; midnight; closed Sun.

Manicomio £66 [2][2][3]
85 Duke of York Sq, SW3
020 7730 3366 6–2D
6 Gutter Ln, EC2 020 7726 5010 10–2B
The Chelsea branch of this Italian duo is "such a nice spot to sit out on a sunny day", and EC2 provides "a peaceful escape from the City" – both are "pleasant", with "unfussy" cooking. / www.manicomio.co.uk; SW3 10.30 pm, Sun 10 pm; EC2 10 pm; EC2 closed Sat & Sun.

Manna NW3 £52 [3][2][2]
4 Erskine Rd 020 7722 8028 9–3B
The UK's oldest veggie has put in an up-and-down performance for the history of our guide, but reports do still mostly praise it for its "highly imaginative vegetarian cooking". / NW3 3AJ; www.mannav.com; @mannacuisine; 10 pm; closed Mon.

The Manor SW4 £58 [4][3][3]
148 Clapham Manor St
020 7720 4662 11–2D
"A food revelation!", say fans of this year-old sibling to nearby Dairy, who hail "food artistry, with novel and exciting textures and flavours that explode in the mouth". Even fans can find the place too "clinically industrial" however, not everyone likes "the tendency to slip offal into dishes, sometimes unannounced", and sceptics find the overall performance "interesting, but trying a bit too hard". / SW4 6BS; www.themanorclapham.co.uk; 10 pm, Sun 4pm.

Manuka Kitchen SW6 £48 [3][2][3]
510 Fulham Rd 020 7736 7588 6–4A
"A limited but interesting and well-prepared menu" wins ongoing praise for this "lovely" New Zealand-inspired bistro in Fulham, as does its "great gin bar downstairs". / SW6 5NJ; www.manukakitchen.com; @manukakitchen; 11 pm, Sun 5 pm.

Mar I Terra SE1 £31 [2][4][2]
14 Gambia St 020 7928 7628 10–4A
This Southwark pub-turned-tapas bar "looks a bit rough but the staff, food and wine are fantastic", making it "a real favourite". "Perfect for a pre-theatre meal" if you're heading for the Old or Young Vic, the National or Shakespeare's Globe. / SE1 0XH; www.mariterra.co.uk; 11 pm; closed Sat L & Sun.

Marcus, The Berkeley SW1 £118 323

Wilton Pl 020 7235 1200 6–1D

Reports of "stunning" cuisine, and heightened approval for the "elegant", revamped interior helped restore ratings this year for Marcus Wareing's famous Knightsbridge flagship. Not all is rosy though – the approach can still feel "over-formal", service in particular can "fall way short of expectations", and many of the worst reviews are from long-term fans who feel by comparison with its glory years, the cooking is "vastly expensive" and "not worth the bother": "Marcus, you can do better than this!" / SW1X 7RL; www.marcuswareing.com; @marcuswareing; 10.45 pm; closed Sun; no jeans; booking max 8 may apply.

Margot WC2

45 Great Queen Street 020 3409 4777 5–1D

Bar Boulud Maitre d' Paulo de Tarso leaves Knightsbridge to open this new Italian restaurant, in Covent Garden in October 2016 alongside restaurateur Nicolas Jaouën. / WC2B 5AA; www.margotrestaurant.com; @MargotLDN.

Mari Vanna SW1 £71 224

116 Knightsbridge 020 7225 3122 6–1D

"Certainly the genuine Russian experience" is to be had at this beautifully decorated Knightsbridge haunt. Unsurprisingly, it's not the greatest value-wise – "basically simple Russian cooking at top London prices" – but compensation is to be found in the huge range of vodkas. / SW1X 7PJ; www.marivanna.co.uk; @marivannalondon; 11.30 pm.

Marianne W2 £128 434

104 Chepstow Rd 020 3675 7750 7–1B

"Exceptional in so many ways" – Marianne Lumb's "tiny space for 12" is "like eating in someone's front room, but with better food", and with the "small kitchen (a vision of calm efficiency) entirely on view". "It is rare that a tasting menu is all hits: this is" and "some of her creations are breathtaking". "Truly welcoming staff" manage the confines of the space well, and it's an experience many find "romantic". / W2 5QS; www.mariannerestaurant.com; @Marianne_W2; 11 pm; closed Mon; set weekday L £95 (FP).

Market NW1 £51 342

43 Parkway 020 7267 9700 9–3B

"Always buzzing" – this "great little place" in Camden Town features "consistently good and interesting food from a subtly changing menu", prepared with "locally sourced ingredients"; "strongly recommended". / NW1 7PN; www.marketrestaurant.co.uk; @MarketCamden; 10.30 pm.

The Marksman E2 £50 323

254 Hackney Rd 020 7739 7393 14–2A

"The kitchen has a fine pedigree and has garnered excellent reviews" for this "achingly trendy" year-old, relaunched Hackney pub. Our reporters are very polarised though: to fans it's "part pub, part gastro, with absolutely brilliantly fresh, interesting as well as classic combinations, accurately cooked" – to foes it's "a case study of how the rise of East London can go really wrong – massively overpriced with bland dishes at stupid prices". / E2 7SJ; www.marksmanpub.com; @marksman_pub; midnight, Sun 11 pm.

Maroush £54 322

I) 21 Edgware Rd, W2 020 7723 0773 7–1D
II) 38 Beauchamp Pl, SW3
020 7581 5434 6–1C
V) 3-4 Vere St, W1 020 7493 5050 3–1B
VI) 68 Edgware Rd, W2 020 7224 9339 7–1D
'Garden') 1 Connaught St, W2
020 7262 0222 7–1D

"Some of the best places for Lebanese food and open all hours" – this well-known chain provides wraps and "exceptional mezze" in its café sections (part of I and II) and "well-executed" more substantial fare in its restaurants. "The decor is a bit naff, but it's all part of the charm". / www.maroush.com; most branches close between 12.30 am-5 am.

Martha Ortiz W1

InterContinental London Park Lane, Park Lane no tel 3–4A

Martha Ortiz, of Mexico City's acclaimed Dulce Patria, will open her first London venture alongside Theo Randall at The Intercontinental Park Lane. The new dining room, designed by David Collins Studio, will serve the chef's take on Mexican cuisine and is expected to open in early 2017. / W1J 7QY.

Masala Grill SW10 £58 344

535 King's Rd 020 7351 7788 6–4B

This relaunched Indian near Lot's Road – "with the same layout as Chutney Mary but a new interior" – divides regulars. Fans say "I thought I'd really miss CM, but this is just as good, with aromatic food that's not cheap, but worth it". Others are more cautious: "average food at posh prices – I like it but is it worth the money?" / SW10 0SZ; www.masalagrill.co; @masalagrill_; 10.30 pm.

Masala Zone £32 333

"Surprisingly good for a chain" – these "fun" and "fast" street-food Indians provide a "genuine, varied and healthy" pit stop, with "good value thalis" a popular bet. The handy Covent Garden branch is particularly worth remembering. / www.realindianfood.com; 11 pm, Sun 10.30 pm; no Amex; booking: min 10.

MASH Steakhouse W1 £84 [2][3][3]
77 Brewer St 020 7734 2608 4–3C
Despite its prime location (off Piccadilly Circus), "lovely" gilded interior and "great bar", this huge subterranean steakhouse (next to Brasserie Zédel) has never really made waves and – though it avoids harsh critiques and is well-rated by those who patronise it – attracts few reports. It can't be doing so badly though – its Dutch owners are said to be looking at sites in both the City and Mayfair. / W1F 9ZN; www.mashsteak.co.uk; 11.30 pm, Sun 11 pm; closed Sun L.

Massimo, Corinthia Hotel WC2 £76 [2][2][3]
10 Northumberland Ave
020 7998 0555 2–3D
Given its splendour, this Italian dining room of a luxury hotel off Trafalgar Square still inspires remarkably little feedback. All reports are positive though, and for a business meal it has evident attractions. / WC2N 5AE; www.massimo-restaurant.co.uk; @massimorest; 10.45 pm; closed Sun.

Masters Super Fish SE1 £25 [3][2][2]
191 Waterloo Rd 020 7928 6924 10–4A
"Fish and chip heaven – as generations of black cab drivers can attest" ensure that this Waterloo chippie remains "deservedly popular", even as "the bar is being raised across London". "Large portions, first-rate chips". / SE1 8UX; 10.30 pm; closed Sun; no Amex; no booking Fri D.

Matsuba TW9 £46 [3][3][2]
10 Red Lion St 020 8605 3513 1–4A
"It's not the most scenic location in Richmond", and this small Korean-run, Japanese café "lacks atmosphere". "Excellent sushi and service make up" for any deficiencies, however. / TW9 1RW; www.matsuba-restaurant.com; @matsuba; 10.30 pm; closed Sun.

Matsuri SW1 £85 [3][3][1]
15 Bury St 020 7839 1101 3–3D
"The teppanyaki hotplate grill with small sushi bar" at this low-key St James's basement "could not be more authentically Japanese". Food and service are generally praised, especially the "fixed-price lunch menu", but a sizeable minority complain that it's "overpriced for what it is". / SW1Y 6AL; www.matsuri-restaurant.com; 10.30 pm, Sun 10 pm.

Max's Sandwich Shop N4 £20 [4][3][3]
19 Crouch Hill awaiting tel 1–1C
Decidedly not for office workers: Max Halley's Crouch Hill shop sells meal-sized home-baked focaccia stuffed with hot fillings alongside beer, wine and cocktails, evenings and weekends only. "Great sarnies, great booze and great service from Max and co". / N4 4AP; @lunchluncheon; 11 pm, Sun 6 pm.

May The Fifteenth SW4 £55 [3][3][3]
47 Abbeville Rd 020 8772 1110 11–2D
Formerly Abbeville Kitchen – this "local gem" in Clapham underwent "a makeover following a part change of ownership, but chef and core team remain". The reformat seemingly "has burnished this already solid local bistro – the cooking's as good as ever, and there's a new focus on wine". / SW4 9JX; www.maythe15th.com; 11 pm, Sun 9.30 pm; closed Mon.

Mayfair Pizza Company W1 £47 [3][4][3]
4 Lancashire Ct 020 7629 2889 3–2B
A "fantastic location" in a "lovely mews" off Bond Street combines with "un-Mayfair prices" to make this pizzeria a "great standby for the area". The staff are notably "cheerful and friendly" (and "their pizza-making course is lots of fun!") / W1S 1EY; www.mayfairpizzaco.com; @mayfairpizzaco; 11 pm.

maze W1 £84 [2][2][2]
10-13 Grosvenor Sq 020 7107 0000 3–2A
A decade ago, with Jason Atherton running the kitchen, Gordon Ramsay's Mayfair outfit produced some of the most exciting meals in London. Nowadays feedback is much more limited, scores are relatively low across the board, and a significant number of reporters find the level of cooking "unacceptable". / W1K 6JP; www.gordonramsayrestaurants.com; @mazerestaurant; 11 pm.

maze Grill W1 £76 [1][2][2]
10-13 Grosvenor Sq 020 7495 2211 3–2A
"Wouldn't bother again" is a typical reaction to Gordon Ramsay's "overpriced" Mayfair grill, where even the most positive report says "there's better meat to be had elsewhere". Having once been one of the hottest tickets in town, this is a prime example of 'how have the mighty fallen'... / W1K 6JP; www.gordonramsay.com; @mazegrill; 11 pm; no shorts.

maze Grill SW10 £75 [3][3][3]
11 Park Wk 020 7255 9299 6–3B
Surprisingly little feedback on Gordon Ramsay's year-old offshoot of his maze brand on the chichi Chelsea sidestreet where he first won renown – such as there is praises its "sophisticated interior and immaculately treated meat with oodles of flavour". / SW10 0AJ; www.gordonramsay.com/mazegrill/park-walk; 11 pm.

Mazi W8 £62 [4][4][4]
12-14 Hillgate St 020 7229 3794 7–2B
"Wonderful and interesting" versions of Greek classic dishes inspire fans of this contemporary taverna, off Notting Hill Gate (which – formerly Costas, long RIP – has been the site of tavernas since the war). "Delightful garden for

summer evenings". / W8 7SR; www.mazi.co.uk; @mazinottinghill; 10.30 pm; closed Mon L & Tue L.

Meat Mission N1 £33 344
14-15 Hoxton Mkt 020 7739 8212 13–1B
"For juice-up-to-your-elbows eating" this "fun and noisy" Hoxton Square outpost of the 'Meat' franchise is just the job: melting burgers of course, plus "superb monkey fingers", "heavenly chilli cheese fries", and "excellent cocktails". / N1 6HG; www.meatmission.com; @MEATmission; midnight, Sun 10 pm.

MEATLiquor £38 334
74 Welbeck St, W1 020 7224 4239 3–1B
133b Upper St, N1 020 3711 0104 9–3D
37 Lordship Lane, SE22 020 3066 0008 1–4D
"Delicious, dirty burgers" have won fame and fortune for these "dark and loud" grunge-fests, but – given the noise, hustle, and hard chairs – "they're not a place to linger". / meatliquor.com; @MEATLiquor; –.

MEATmarket WC2 £28 422
Jubilee Market Hall, 1 Tavistock Ct
020 7836 2139 5–3D
"Sloppy and full of flavour" – the keypoints on the 'dirty' burgers at this well-known Covent Garden grungefest ("the Dead Hippie is especially great"). The rum cocktails slip down a treat too. / WC2E 8BD; www.themeatmarket.co.uk; midnight, Sun 10 pm; no Amex.

MeatUp SW18
350 Old York Road 020 8425 0017 11–2C
The name says it all about this new, summer 2016 opening – a bar/BBQ in Wandsworth Town serving up steak, burgers and rotisserie chicken (to name a few) as well as an extensive prosecco list and cocktails. / SW18 1SS; www.meatupgrill.com; @meatupuk.

Mediterraneo W11 £62 323
37 Kensington Park Rd 020 7792 3131 7–1A
"A lively traditional Italian in the heart of Notting Hill" that's been a linchpin of the area for the last quarter century. / W11 2EU; www.mediterraneo-restaurant.co.uk; 11.30 pm, Sun 10.30 pm; booking max 10 may apply.

MEDLAR SW10 £70 443
438 King's Rd 020 7349 1900 6–3B
"The location's not great" and "signage needs improving", but this "welcome refuge" near World's End – run by alumni of Chez Bruce – "exceeds expectations", and has won a huge following. "It's a comfortable, quiet space" pepped up by "professional" staff who "try extra hard", and the "masterfully executed" food is "seasonal, understated, big on flavour", and accompanied by an "outstanding" wine list. That Michelin took its star away is a screw-up on their part. Top Tip – "incredible value lunch menu". / SW10 0LJ; www.medlarrestaurant.co.uk; @MedlarChelsea; 10.30 pm, sun 9.30pm; set weekday L £28 (FP), set Sun L £35 (FP), set dinner £46 (FP).

Megan's Delicatessen SW6 £45 235
571 Kings Rd 020 7371 7837 6–4A
"Love, love, love the garden" at this "charming oasis" on the King's Road – brunch goes down particularly well, but "it's a lovely local catering to all needs". (The St John's Wood branch is no more.) / SW6 2EB; www.megansrestaurant.com; @meganscafe; Mon-Thu 10 pm, Fri & Sat 10.30 pm, Sun 5 pm; closed Sun D; no Amex.

Melange N8 £50 333
45 Topsfield Parade, Tottenham Lane
020 8341 1681 1–1C
"Just right for a local restaurant" – "a lively and cheerful bistro in Crouch End" serving an "interesting mixture of French and Italian dishes, all well-cooked with helpful service". / N8 8PT; www.melangerestaurant.co.uk; @malange_malange; 11 pm, Sat & Sun midnight.

Mele e Pere W1 £51 332
46 Brewer St 020 7096 2096 4–3C
"Accomplished Italian cooking" at "amazing prices" makes this Soho bar-trattoria a useful West End hangout. Adding "fantastic cocktails", an "interesting wine list" and even their own vermouths leaves only one drawback: "it's so noisy, you end up hoarse after a night out!" / W1F 9TF; www.meleepere.co.uk; @meleEpere; 11 pm.

Melody at St Paul's W14 £56 233
153 Hammersmith Road
020 8846 9119 8–2C
A very grand, Gothic Victorian building creates a slightly "strange" but rather "lovely" setting for this newish hotel, by a small park on the Hammersmith/Olympia borders. The dining room itself is "calm" and serves straightforward fare that's "well prepared" and "well presented". / W14 0QL; www.themelodyrestaurant.co.uk.

Menier Chocolate Factory SE1 £53 223
51-53 Southwark St 020 7234 9610 10–4B
The kitchen at this small theatre in a listed Victorian chocolate factory in Borough "does its job if you're going to a play". But "you wouldn't go out of your way to dine here" (as a standalone attraction, the fare can seem "boring, and poorly executed"). / SE1 1RU; www.menierchocolatefactory.com; @MenChocFactory; 11 pm; closed Mon & Sun D.

The Mercer EC2 £62 222
34 Threadneedle St 020 7628 0001 10–2C
Good-enough "old and modern British dishes at sensible prices" help draw a City crowd to this dining room in a converted Square Mile banking hall. It's ideal for business: "they understand that people need to be served, but not rushed, and then get back to work". / EC2R 8AY; www.themercer.co.uk; @TheMercerLondon; 9.30 pm; closed Sat & Sun.

Merchants Tavern EC2 £62 344
36 Charlotte Rd 020 7060 5335 13–1B
"Just outside the price bubble of the City", Angela Hartnett's "large pub" with open kitchen is "not just an afterthought to her flashier establishments" – the cooking "goes from strength to strength", service is "slick" and the interior feels "dark and Shoreditch-y". Tasty bar bites too. / EC2A 3PG; www.merchantstavern.co.uk; @merchantstavern; 11 pm, Sun 9 pm.

Le Mercury N1 £33 224
154-155 Upper St 020 7354 4088 9–2D
This "very cute", ancient Islington bistro has "classic" status 1) for its "efficient and consistent" provision of "good cheap French food" for as long as anyone can remember ("better than expected" at the price); and 2) the "Parisian-style, romantic candlelit atmosphere – perfect for a date". / N1 1QY; www.lemercury.co.uk; midnight, Sun 11 pm; Mon-Thu D only, Fri-Sun open L & D.

Mere W1
74 Charlotte St no tel 2–1B
Long-time right hand woman of Michel Roux Jr and 'MasterChef: The Professionals' judge, Monica Galetti, has revealed plans for her first solo venture. Incorporating a small ground-floor bar and basement restaurant, it's set to open in January 2017. / W1.

Meson don Felipe SE1 £39 234
53 The Cut 020 7928 3237 10–4A
"Olé! Why go to Spain?!" – This "plainly decorated" Hispanic veteran "just down from the Old Vic" has a "great buzz" fuelled by its "very good wine list" and sherry selection. The tapas selection is is "all the usual stuff you expect" ("simpler items are often best"), but "for a snack and a good glass of vino" this is a "top place near the South Bank". / SE1 8LF; www.mesondonfelipe.com; 11 pm; closed Sun; no Amex; no booking after 8 pm.

Mews of Mayfair W1 £68 333
10 Lancashire Ct, New Bond St
020 7518 9388 3–2B
This clubbable bistro and cocktail bar (owned by Roger Moore's son) in a super-cute yard off Bond Street knows how to keep Mayfair punters happy, with its "impressive set lunch offer" and "pleasant, busy and casual" vibe. / W1S 1EY; www.mewsofmayfair.com; @mewsofmayfair; 10.45 pm; closed Sun D; SRA-3 star.

Meza £30 443
34 Trinity Rd, SW17 0772 211 1299 11–2C
70 Mitcham Rd, SW17 020 8672 2131 11–2C
"Absolutely wonderful Lebanese/Middle Eastern dishes" – "a never-changing menu" of "very fresh bright tastes" – means this pair of "tiny" and "utilitarian" Tooting cafés tend to be "heaving"; "genuinely hospitable" and "prompt" service too. / www.mezarestaurant.co.uk; @MezaRestaurants; –.

Michael Nadra £58 442
6-8 Elliott Rd, W4 020 8742 0766 8–2A
42 Gloucester Ave, NW1
020 7722 2800 9–2B
"Top notch" modern French cuisine that "outperforms many more famous names" maintains high satisfaction with Michael Nadra's duo of local restaurants, in Chiswick (the better known original) and Camden Town ("juxtapositioned between Regents Park and Camden Town just near the canal"), even if both venues share in different ways a somewhat "difficult layout". Top Menu Tip – "always good fish" is the highlight with "an interesting twist on old favourite dishes". / www.restaurant-michaelnadra.co.uk; @michaelnadra; W4 10 pm, Fri-Sat 10.30 pm, NW1 10.30 pm, Sun 9 pm; NW1 closed Mon, W4 closed Sun.

Mien Tay £31 422
180 Lavender Hill, SW11
020 7350 0721 11–1C
122 Kingsland Rd, E2 020 7729 3074 13–1B
"The goat and galangal is one of the tastiest Asian dishes in London", at these busy Vietnamese joints in Battersea, Fulham and Shoreditch; they're "fantastically consistent" as well as "extremely good value". / 11 pm, Fri & Sat 11.30 pm, Sun 10.30 pm; cash only.

Mildreds W1 £43 333
45 Lexington St 020 7494 1634 4–2C
"Brilliant – and I don't even like veggie food!" is a typically ringing endorsement for this Soho institution that is many people's favourite for meat-free scoffing. "Shame about the wait times, as they don't take bookings". / W1F 9AN; www.mildreds.co.uk; @mildredslondon; 10.45 pm; closed Sun; no Amex; no bookings.

Milk SW12 £14 433
20 Bedford Hill 020 8772 9085 11–2C
"Hands-down the best breakfast in SW London" ("you need to get there early because this is no secret") is to be found at this kickass Antipodean joint in Balham, which (recently expanding) now has "an alcohol license and plans for evening openings". "Amazing flat whites" and other coffee too, but "avoid the yummy mummy post-school-drop-off

rush". Top Menu Tip – the Convict and Young Betty. / SW12 9RG; www.milk.london.

Min Jiang, The Royal Garden Hotel W8 **£77** **435**
2-24 Kensington High St 020 7361 1988 6–1A
"Sensational views" set the scene at this "very plush" 8th-floor dining room, bordering Kensington Gardens, which – with its "fantastically fragrant and subtle" Chinese cuisine – offers one of the capital's best all-round experiences. Top Menu Tip – "the absolutely delicious, wood-fired Beijing duck is a must!" / W8 4PT; www.minjiang.co.uk; @minjianglondon; 10 pm.

Mint Leaf **£65** **334**
Suffolk Pl, Haymarket, SW1
020 7930 9020 2–2C
Angel Ct, Lothbury, EC2
020 7600 0992 10–2C
"Delicious pimped-up Indian food" is served in a "cool and slick", "night-club-vibe" setting at this conveniently sited duo, with locations just off Trafalgar Square and Bank: "not cheap but value for money". / www.mintleafrestaurant.com; SW1 11 pm, Sun 10.30 pm – EC2 10.30 pm; SW1 closed Sat & Sun L, EC2 closed Sat & Sun.

Mirch Masala SW17 **£26** **521**
213 Upper Tooting Rd 020 8767 8638 11–2D
This "no-frills (and no licence)" Pakistani canteen in Tooting offers "fantastic flavours at amazing prices". The food is "excellent, spicy and authentic", with the "weekend slow-cooked meat specials especially good". Service is fast, but it "can be noisy and crowded". / SW17 7TG; www.mirchmasalarestaurant.co.uk; midnight; cash only.

Mister Lasagna W1 **£37**
53 Rupert Street 020 7734 0064 4–2D
A summer 2016 Soho opening serving nothing but lasagne (in no less than 21 different varieties). It's open all day, offering pastries and coffee in the mornings, communal seating and takeaway, plus Italian liqueurs in the evening. / W1D 7PG; www.misterlasagna.co.uk; @misterlasagna; 11 pm, Fri & Sat midnight, Sun 10.30 pm; no bookings.

MNKY HSE W1
10 Dover Street 020 3870 4880 3–3C
On the former site of Mayfair's long-departed Dover Street Wine Bar (RIP), this late-night dining and drinking venue is set to open in October 2016. The PR info tells us to expect 'contemporary Latin American food and drink, alongside live music and DJ performances'. No advice yet about how to pronounce the name... / W1S 4LQ; www.mnky-hse.com; @mnky_hse.

The Modern Pantry **£59** **222**
47-48 St Johns Sq, EC1 020 7553 9210 10–1A
14 Finsbury Sq, EC2 020 3696 6565 13–2A
For "an innovative brunch", many tip Aussie chef, Anna Hansen's "chilled" ("somewhat stark") ventures, in Clerkenwell, and now also in Finsbury Square too. For other meal times, fans extol her "great spin on traditional ideas" generally, but ratings are dragged down by critics of "needlessly complex" fusion "for its own sake", and "poor ambience at the new Moorgate branch". / www.themodernpantry.co.uk; –.

MOMMI SW4 **£46** **233**
44 Clapham High St 020 3814 1818 11–2D
"Buzzy Japanese/Peruvian fusion" yearling that splits opinion – to fans it's a "great addition to Clapham High Street" with "plenty of choice", but critics find it "expensive" and "disappointingly formulaic". / SW4 7UR; www.wearemommi.com; @wearemommi; 11 pm ; closed weekday L; cancellation charge for larger bookings.

Momo W1 **£69** **334**
25 Heddon St 020 7434 4040 4–3B
Mourad Mamouz's "noisy" souk-style party-Moroccan, off Regent Street maintains its dark, "romantic" allure (particularly if you kick off with a drink in the superb basement bar). Although the Moroccan cuisine is arguably incidental, it's not bad. / W1B 4BH; www.momoresto.com; @momoresto; 11.30 pm, Sun 11 pm; credit card deposit required to book; set weekday L £40 (FP).

Mon Plaisir WC2 **£59** **244**
19-21 Monmouth St 020 7836 7243 5–2B
"A firm favourite for over 20 years!" This "old-fashioned", Covent Garden 70-year-old – much-expanded over the decades – is supremely "idiosyncratic, with lots of quaint, little hidey-holes". Its "traditional Gallic staples" are "not the best in town, but you know you'll be well fed without spending crazy prices", especially if you go for the super-popular pre-theatre and lunch deals. / WC2H 9DD; www.monplaisir.co.uk; @MonPlaisir4; 11 pm; closed Sun.

Mona Lisa SW10 **£30** **332**
417 King's Rd 020 7376 5447 6–3B
"Builders for breakfast, out-of-work creatives for lunch and cheap-date couples for dinner" – that's just part of the line-up at this veteran Italian greasy spoon, near World's End, whose bargain evening 3-course deal for £10 has long epitomised its "cheap 'n' cheerful" charms. / SW10 0LR; monalisarestaurant.co.uk/new-page.html; 11 pm, Sun 5.30 pm; closed Sun D; no Amex; set weekday L £16 (FP), set dinner £17 (FP).

Monmouth Coffee Company £6 554
27 Monmouth St, WC2 020 7232 3010 5–2B
2 Park St, SE1 020 7232 3010 10–4C
"The queues can be ridiculous" for these "shrines to coffee" but "the sheer quality of their beans makes it a first choice" and "service is five-star even when they are manically busy" (i.e. mostly). The famous Borough Market shop suffers "an annoying number of hipsters outside" but otherwise "makes a wonderful place to watch the world go by", and enjoy "delicious bread and jam" too. All branches serve "a few yummy pastries". / www.monmouthcoffee.co.uk; 6 pm-6.30 pm, SE16 midnight; closed Sun; SE16 open Sat only; no Amex; no booking.

Morada Brindisa Asador W1 £48 222
18-20 Rupert St 020 7478 8758 5–3A
A "surprise find up a side street" off Shaftesbury Avenue, this ambitious Spanish yearling from the Brindisa group showcases Castilian-style asador wood-fire roasts. Fans hail both "style and substance", but there are complaints of "incompetent" staff and "high prices". / W1D 6DE; www.brindisatapaskitchens.com/morada; @Brindisa.

The Morgan Arms E3 £50 433
43 Morgan St 020 8980 6389 14–2C
"Fab Sunday roast" is typical of the "very good food" at this "pleasant (if loud)" Mile End gastropub. / E3 5AA; www.morganarmsbow.com; @TheMorganArms; 10 pm.

Morito £37 444
195 Hackney Road, E2 020 7613 0754 14–2B
32 Exmouth Mkt, EC1 020 7278 7007 10–1A
"Constantly astounding food, despite always being frenetically busy" means this Spanish/North African tapas spot in Exmouth Market is "just as good as big sister Moro next door" – some even "prefer it". Good ratings too for its new Hoxton sibling, just a stone's throw from Columbia Road Flower Market.

MORO EC1 £58 543
34-36 Exmouth Mkt 020 7833 8336 10–1A
"Gosh, it's impressive when a restaurant can stay on form in this way!" – Samuel and Samantha Clark's Exmouth Market favourite holds "many special memories" for legions of reporters. The "beautifully judged" Moorish/Iberian dishes deliver "wonderful flavours" as does the "unique selection of Iberian wines and superlative range of sherries". There is a 'but' however – ratings did ease off a smidgeon this year, with incidents of "chaotic" service and the remorseless noise-levels of this deafening, hard-edged room denting the "happy vibe". / EC1R 4QE; www.moro.co.uk; 10.30 pm; closed Sun D.

Motcombs SW1 £57 233
26 Motcomb St 020 7235 6382 6–1D
"If you want a discreet conversation", this stalwart wine bar (upstairs) and restaurant (downstairs) is something of a Belgravia "old favourite", with cooking that's "always dependable, if not exceptional". / SW1X 8JU; www.motcombs.co.uk; @Motcombs; 10 pm; closed Sun.

Mr Bao SE15 £34 322
293 Rye Ln 020 7635 0325 1–4D
"A real, new gem in the crown of Peckham's up-and-coming food scene!" – this "local Taiwanese café" may be "packed in" and "hectic", but it's also "friendly", "fun" and "affordable". "I'm not sure how authentic the food is but it's delicious!" (lots of "interesting", "snack-sized bites"). / SE15 4UA; www.mrbao.co.uk; @MrBaoUK; 11 pm; closed Mon; no bookings.

Mr Chow SW1 £87 222
151 Knightsbridge 020 7589 7347 6–1D
A Knightsbridge institution since 1968, its upscale Beijing cuisine still attracts diners; complaints too however as usual that it's "massively overpriced for what's essentially average Chinese food". / SW1X 7PA; www.mrchow.com; @mrchow; midnight; closed Mon L.

Murakami WC2 £45 333
63-66 St Martin's Ln 020 3417 6966 5–3B
Feedback remains limited on this large, glossy Japanese canteen in Covent Garden (owned by a Ukranian restaurant group) – results from its wide robata-to-sushi menu are decently rated, however. / WC2N 4JS; www.murakami-london.co.uk; @hello_murakami; 10.30 pm.

Murano W1 £99 443
20-22 Queen St 020 7495 1127 3–3B
"Not a restaurant for those who want fireworks… just very good!" Angela Hartnett's "smooth-running" Mayfair haven is low-key stylewise, but it's a "comfortable" place "exuding warmth", thanks to its "first-class" yet "unpompous" staff. Chef Pip Lacey has upped the ante, when it comes to the Italianate food – "superb" – and the flexible "build your own menu" approach is a "simple yet brilliant idea". / W1J 5PP; www.muranolondon.com; @muranolondon; 11 pm; closed Sun.

Mustard W6 £44 354
98-100 Shepherd's Bush Rd
020 3019 1175 8–1C
"A great neighbourhood newcomer" – from the same owners as Covent Garden's famous Joe Allen – on a nondescript highway north of Brook Green. It's everything the Café Rouge it replaced was not, with affordable British fare, unusually professional service and a swish refit. / W6 7PD; www.mustardrestaurants.co.uk; @mustarddining; 11 pm, Sun 10 pm.

Namaaste Kitchen NW1 £44 342
64 Parkway 020 7485 5977 9–3B
Advocates of this Camden Town cuzza hail it as a "completely unexpected delight" and would even rate it as "north London's best Indian". But this culinary ambition also prompts detractors: "not bad, but it tries to be a fine-dining restaurant with fine dining prices when it isn't one". / NW1 7AH; www.namaastekitchen.co.uk; 11 pm.

Nanban SW9 £43 432
Coldharbour Ln 020 7346 0098 11–2D
"Terrific Brixton fusion place from former MasterChef winner Tim Anderson", whose "Japanese soul food" ("blending flavours from Japan with more local staples") wins "extra points for originality" – "so unlikely this: spectacularly good Japanese carbonara of spaghetti!" "I was sceptical, but what a bangin' place!" / SW9; www.nanban.co.uk; @NanbanLondon; 11 pm, Sun 10 pm.

The Narrow E14 £56 223
44 Narrow St 020 7592 7950 12–1B
Gordon Ramsay's potentially wonderful waterfront Limehouse pub has never found its mojo, but it avoided the usual drubbing from diners this year and achieved OK ratings, despite still sometimes seeming "expensive" and "disappointing". / E14 8DP; www.gordonramsay.com; @thenarrow; 10.30 pm, Sun 8 pm.

Native WC2 £44 442
3 Neal's Yd 020 3638 8214 5–2C
"A hard working couple who care" ("the really welcoming feel from the owner made the meal") are carving a good reputation for this sweet, foraging-focused Covent Garden newcomer ("very small upstairs, larger downstairs" in the "very pleasant basement"). Even cynics who say "it doesn't really need its silly 'local food' gimmick" say "the food varies between good and excellent". / WC2H 9DP; www.eatnative.co.uk; @eatnativeuk; 10 pm; closed Mon L.

Naughty Piglets SW2 £54 553
28 Brixton Water Ln 020 7274 7796 11–2D
"You can watch the food being cooked by the husband and served by the wife" at Margaux Aubry and Joe Sharratt's "very laid back" yearling – "another fantastic addition to the Brixton scene" – which delivers "exceptional bistro food" and "awesome service"; "interesting natural wine list" too (La Patronne used to work at Terroirs). / SW2 1PE; www.naughtypiglets.co.uk; 10 pm, Sun 3 pm.

Nautilus NW6 £41 431
27-29 Fortune Green Rd
020 7435 2532 1–1B
"Still the best fish 'n' chips in North London", this "exceptional" West Hampstead chippy has been known for decades for "excellent, very fresh fish which is coated in matzo meal and then fried". Interior decor – 'nul points!' / NW6 1DU; 10 pm; closed Sun; no Amex.

Needoo E1 £28 422
87 New Rd 020 7247 0648 13–2D
"Grilled meats to die for" – not least "top lamb chops, no question" – inspire rave reviews for this East End Pakistani, which fans find "preferable to the over-hyped Tayyab's" (its much better-known near-neighbour); the ambience? – it's "dire". / E1 1HH; www.needoogrill.co.uk; @NeedooGrill; 11.30 pm.

New Mayflower W1 £42 322
68-70 Shaftesbury Ave 020 7734 9207 5–3A
"The food, especially the seafood, is good as usual" at this long-established Cantonese stalwart on the fringe of Chinatown – particularly worth discovering if you want some proper food in the wee hours. / W1D 6LY; www.newmayflowerlondon.com; 4 am; D only; no Amex; set dinner £25 (FP).

New World W1 £38 222
1 Gerrard Place 020 7734 0677 5–3A
Still a favourite for some reporters – this massive Chinatown fixture is one of the very few still to serve dim sum from circulating trolleys ("but only on weekends"). / W1D 5PA; www.newworldlondon.com; 10.30 pm; set dinner £20 (FP).

The Newman Arms W1 £46 444
23 Rathbone Street 020 3643 6205 5–1A
"Part of the Cornwall Project sourcing fresh ingredients from small producers (in Cornwall, obviously)" – Matt Chatfield's "quaint" Fitzrovia boozer inspires enthusiastic feedback on its "fantastically flavoursome and earthy dishes", "charming service and intimate style". / W1T 1NG; www.newmanarmspub.com; @NewmanArmsPub; 10 pm, Sun 6 pm; closed Sat.

The Ninth W1 £62 432
22 Charlotte St 020 3019 0880 2–1C
Jun Tanaka's Fitzrovia newcomer wins praise both for his "exceptional" cooking and some "exceedingly pleasant service". Some reporters gripe that "decor is lacking" though, or feel that "tables are too small for the sharing plates format". / W1T 2NB; www.theninthlondon.com; @theninthlondon; 10.30 pm; closed Sun.

Nirvana Kitchen W1 £66
61 Upper Berkeley Street
020 7958 3222 2–1A
A summer 2016 Indian newcomer adjoining a hotel north of Marble Arch, with a glossy interior and a menu of some ambition. / W1H 7PP; www.nirvana.restaurant; @KitchensNirvana; 10.45 pm; closed Sun.

Nissi N13 £40 333
62 Aldermans Hill 020 8882 3170 1–1C
"The ambience is modern, open and family friendly" at this refreshing Greek/Cypriot venture in Palmers Green serving "superior, fresh Greek mezze, cooked in a contemporary style". / N13; www.nissirestaurant.co.uk; @NissiRestaurant; 10.30 pm, Fri & Sat 11.30 pm, Sun 9 pm; closed Mon.

No 197 Chiswick Fire Station W4 £50 324
199 Chiswick High Road
020 3857 4669 8–2A
"Extremely buzzy and atmospheric", neighbourhood bar from chain Darwin & Wallace (in the white-walled and airy setting of a converted old fire station) that's "a great addition to the Chiswick scene" – much of the appeal is the cocktails and craft beers, but early reports say the Antipodean-influenced scoff can also be "surprisingly good". / W4 2DR; www.no197chiswickfirestation.com; @No197Chiswick; midnight, Fri & Sat 1 am, Sun 11 pm; booking max 9 may apply.

Noble Rot WC1 £58 333
51 Lamb's Conduit St 020 7242 8963 2–1D
"Paradise for wine lovers"; Mark Andrew and Daniel Keeling's Bloomsbury newcomer (they also run the cult wine mag' of the same name) offers the "unbeatably interesting" list you might hope for "with lots of intriguing vintages" (including "many mature wines") from in-the-know vineyards, "served in a wide variety by the glass in sizes as low as 75ml". Its location is the "lovely" old-school '70s wine bar premises that were formerly VATs (RIP), which provide "the perfect place to come and find your new favourite tipple". On most accounts, the "uncomplicated" cooking – with input from afar by acclaimed Sportsman chef, Stephen Harris – is "uncommonly good" too, but ratings are undercut by a minority who say it's "not as good as claimed in the newspaper reviews". / WC1N 3NB; www.noblerot.co.uk; @noblerotbar; 9.30 pm; closed Sun.

Nobu, Metropolitan Hotel W1 £99 222
19 Old Park Ln 020 7447 4747 3–4A
"The black cod is legendary" at this once path-breaking Japanese-fusion icon overlooking Park Lane, and for some long-term fans "it can never be beaten". That this erstwhile paparazzi favourite is "horrendously overpriced" and has "mediocre service" has always gone with the territory, but its culinary performance seems ever-more "tired". / W1K 1LB; www.noburestaurants.com; @NobuOldParkLane; 10.15 pm, Fri & Sat 11 pm, Sun 10 pm.

Nobu Berkeley W1 £99 322
15 Berkeley St 020 7290 9222 3–3C
"Amazingly delicate" Japanese/South American fusion fare "made with precision" and "packed with flavour" ensures Mayfair's second branch of this global franchise is "always popular and sometimes very busy". But numerous sceptics feel it "trades on its reputation and celebrity status" – "despite the work that goes into the food, and the fancy schmancy location, prices are insane", especially as "the dining room is quite rowdy, and service perfunctory". / W1J 8DY; www.noburestaurants.com; 11 pm, Thu-Sat midnight, Sun 9.45 pm; closed Sun L.

Noor Jahan £40 332
2a Bina Gdns, SW5 020 7373 6522 6–2B
26 Sussex Pl, W2 020 7402 2332 7–1D
"A consistent pleasure for over 20 years!" – this "old-fashioned Indian" in Earl's Court is "a bit crowded and expensive but reliably good" and "always attracts a well-heeled clientele" for whom it's a big old-favourite. ("Dependable" but much lesser known Bayswater spin-off too). / 11.30 pm, Sun 10 pm.

Nopi W1 £71 433
21-22 Warwick St 020 7494 9584 4–3B
"Creativity, enticing variety, vitality, sensuality and style" are combined in Yotam Ottolenghi's "very thoughtful and alternative" cuisine, and many reporters seem to leave his "guilt-free" Middle Eastern-inspired spot off Regent Street "feeling more healthy than when they arrived". Even some who rate it highly, though, say "it's not for me, given the dieter-sized portions at big prices". / W1B 5NE; www.nopi-restaurant.com; @ottolenghi; 10.30 pm, Sun 4 pm; closed Sun D; set pre-theatre £37 (FP), set dinner £47 (FP), set always available £54 (FP).

Nordic Bakery £15 343
14a Golden Sq, W1 020 3230 1077 4–3C
37b New Cavendish St, W1
020 7935 3590 2–1A
48 Dorset St, W1 020 7487 5877 2–1A
"The best coffee and cinnamon buns" make this Scandi trio in Soho and Marylebone go-to destinations for "Nordic sweet treats"; "good for people-watching, too". / Golden Square 8 pm, Sat 7 pm, Sun 7 pm, Cavendish Street & Dorset Street 6 pm.

The Norfolk Arms WC1 £44 333
28 Leigh St 020 7388 3937 9–4C
This "convivial", "efficient and reasonably priced" King's Cross gastropub doubles as a tapas bar – "all with a twist and generally very high quality" – a combination that results in a "lovely neighbourhood bar/restaurant". / WC1H 9EP; www.norfolkarms.co.uk; 11pm, Sun 10.30 pm; no Amex.

North China W3 £42 [3][3][3]
305 Uxbridge Rd 020 8992 9183 8–1A
"Consistently good and welcoming" family-run Chinese, which remains one of Acton's few contributions to London gastronomy. / W3 9QU; www.northchina.co.uk; 11 pm, Fri & Sat 11.30 pm.

North Sea Fish WC1 £38 [3][3][2]
7-8 Leigh St 020 7387 5892 9–4C
"Excellent fish, and particularly good chips" are the hallmarks of this "grand little chippie" in Bloomsbury ("with old-fashioned home-made puds if you have the stamina"). Once "so dated it was almost charming", regulars are now split over whether the recent refurb has "smartened it up" or "lost some of its former character". / WC1H 9EW; www.northseafishrestaurant.co.uk; 10.30 pm; closed Sun; no Amex.

The Northall, Corinthia Hotel WC2 £85 [3][3][4]
10a Northumberland Ave
020 7321 3100 2–3C
This "beautifully appointed venue oozes class and luxury" and not only is its "great location near Whitehall ideal for working lunches and client dinners" but is "big enough to maintain a peaceful, relaxed atmosphere, however much business is being conducted". The cooking? – it has "a fair amount of flair". / WC2N 5AE; www.thenorthall.co.uk; @CorinthiaLondon; 10.45 pm; set pre theatre £55 (FP).

Northbank EC4 £58 [2][2][3]
Millennium Bridge 020 7329 9299 10–3B
Views across the river of Tate Modern and the Shard take precedence at this bar-restaurant beside the Wobbly Bridge. But marks are wobbling across the board here – perhaps, as one critic suggests, "they need more staff". / EC4V 3QH; www.northbankrestaurant.co.uk; @NorthbankLondon; 11 pm; closed Sun; set weekday L £38 (FP).

Novikov (Asian restaurant) W1 £94 [2][1][2]
50a Berkeley St 020 7399 4330 3–3C
"It's flash, gaudy, and the crowd is very Mayfair", but "if you overlook the nightclub style" of this Russian-owned scene near Berkeley Square, "the pan-Asian food is actually exceptional – the best ingredients prepared very well… just at cripplingly expensive prices". / W1J 8HA; www.novikovrestaurant.co.uk; 11.15 pm; set weekday L £43 (FP).

Novikov (Italian restaurant) W1 £106 [1][1][2]
50a Berkeley St 020 7399 4330 3–3C
The "peaceful-at-lunch, steadily-louder-in-the-evening" Italian chamber of this Russian-owned Mayfair glam-palace is an attractive space. The food though is "nothing special, however the insane prices: OMG!! How do they get away with it? And it's rammed! I just don't get it…" / W1J 8HA; www.novikovrestaurant.co.uk; 11.15 pm, Sun 10 pm.

Numero Uno SW11 £54 [3][3][3]
139 Northcote Rd 020 7978 5837 11–2C
"Always lovely food" with "friendly service" form the recipe for a "great local" Italian on the borders of Battersea's Nappy Valley. "Not much changes: I could choose from the menu with a blindfold on, but that is the charm of this buzzy but not raucous place". / SW11 6PX; 11.30 pm; no Amex.

Nuovi Sapori SW6 £48 [3][4][2]
295 New King's Rd 020 7736 3363 11–1B
"Ultra-friendly" local near Parsons Green, which serves "consistently good" dishes. "Staff used to keep an eye on our sleeping baby when he was in his carry-cot – now they feed him proper Italian food (no nuggets or chips) and treat him like a valued guest!" / SW6 4RE; www.nuovisaporilondon.co.uk; 11 pm; closed Sun.

Oak £50 [4][3][4]
243 Goldhawk Rd, W12 020 8741 7700 8–1B
137 Westbourne Park Rd, W2
020 7221 3355 7–1B
"Perfect crispy-based pizza" – "so light that normal pizza-associated guilt is forgotten" – as usual wins high praise for this pub-conversion duo. The newish Shepherd's Bush branch is "very comfy, with a large bar", while the very "buzzy" original is a Notting Hill classic for "a fun night out". / W12 Mon-Sat 10.30 pm, Sun 9.30 pm – W2 Mon-Thu 10.30 pm, Fri-Sat 11pm, Sun 10 pm.

Obicà £52 [3][3][2]
11 Charlotte St, W1 020 7637 7153 2–1C
19-20 Poland St, W1 020 3327 7070 3–1D
96 Draycott Ave, SW3 020 7581 5208 6–2C
1 West Wintergarden, 35 Bank St, E14 awaiting Tel 12–1C
4 Limeburners Lane, 1 Ludgate Hill, EC4
020 3327 0984 10–2A
Once called Obika, these 'Mozzarella bars' – part of an international chain – are "much better than many in the pizza and pasta market", and are tipped for "grabbing a glass of wine with enjoyable small bites". / www.obica.com; 10 pm-11 pm; E14 Closed Sun.

Oblix SE1 £88 [2][1][5]
Level 32, The Shard, 31 St Thomas Street
020 7268 6700 10–4C
"The location has definite 'wow' factor" at this 32nd-floor dining lounge in the Shard – "unbeatable for romance at night time (if you can get a window table for the views)". "Rude service" is a hazard however, as is "average" food, all "at prices to match the altitude". / SE1 9RY; www.oblixrestaurant.com; @OblixRestaurant; 11 pm.

Odette's NW1 £63 444
130 Regent's Park Rd 020 7586 8569 9–3B
Bryn Williams "seems to be on top of his game" currently at his "intimate" north London old favourite in Primrose Hill, with even stronger ratings this year for his "clever" and "beautifully presented" cuisine (particularly the "astonishing tasting menu") and "exemplary" service. / NW1 8XL; www.odettesprimrosehill.com; @Odettes_rest; 10 pm, Sat 10.30 pm, Sun 9.30 pm; closed Mon & Tue L; no Amex; set weekday L £36 (FP), set Sun L £42 (FP).

Ognisko Restaurant SW7 £52 344
55 Prince's Gate, Exhibition Rd
020 7589 0101 6–1C
"The really lovely, ornate interior" – "with period features, candles and tasteful decoration" – underpins the "romantic" appeal of this quirky émigrés club dining room, near the Science Museum. Since Jan Woroniecki took it over, its "hearty" Polish fare has become more varied, and there's "a massive range of vodkas". Top Tip – at the rear there's "a wonderful, tented outside terrace". / SW7 2PN; www.ogniskorestaurant.co.uk; @OgniskoRest; 11 pm; no trainers.

Oka £47 432
Kingly Court, 1 Kingly Court, W1
020 7734 3556 4–2B
71 Regents Park Rd, NW1
020 7483 2072 9–\N
"Amazing, inventive sushi" and "Asian-fusion cooking" at "great value" prices ensure that the three small venues in this group – in Primrose Hill, Soho's Kingly Court and Chelsea – are "always packed".

Oklava EC2 £56 443
74 Luke St 020 7729 3032 13–1B
"An excellent Turkish newcomer with a modern twist" – Selin Kiazim's "ambitious flavour combinations" ("innovative" kebabs, flatbreads and mezze) inspire good vibes for this tile-and-brick Shoreditch venture with open kitchen, as does its "welcoming" attitude. / EC2A 4PY; www.oklava.co.uk; @oklava_ldn; 10.30 pm, Sun 4 pm; closed Mon & Sun D.

Oldroyd N1 £42 432
344 Upper Street 020 8617 9010 9–3D
"A really exciting addition to Upper Street in terms of innovative cooking" – Tom Oldroyd's "tiny kitchen" creates "wonderful" tapas-style dishes. Shame his Islington yearling is way "too cramped" though – "it detracts from a meal". / N1 0PD; www.oldroydlondon.com; @oldroydlondon; Mon-Thu 10.30 pm, Fri 11 pm, Sun 9 pm; set weekday L £18 (FP).

Oliver Maki W1 £69
33 Dean St 020 7734 0408 5–2A
The first London outpost of a flash Middle Eastern-owned sushi group (with branches in Kuwait and Bahrain) comes to Soho, in these two-floor premises, with former Nobu Las Vegas head chef Louis Kenji Huang heading up the kitchen. It's induced little feedback so far, however. / W1D 4PP; www.olivermaki.co.uk; @OliverMakiUK; 10.30 pm, Fri & Sat 11 pm, Sun 9.30 pm.

Oliveto SW1 £63 321
49 Elizabeth St 020 7730 0074 2–4A
"Always rammed", this Sardinian pizza and pasta specialist is "predictably good". "On weekends, it seems like all of Belgravia descends, with screaming children a-plenty" – "sometimes it's hard to tell if it's over-noisy, or jumping with energy". / SW1W 9PP; www.olivorestaurants.com; 10.30 pm, Sun 10 pm; booking max 7 may apply.

Olivo SW1 £65 332
21 Eccleston St 020 7730 2505 2–4B
This squished Belgravia Sardinian has a "fabulous menu" and its very competent cooking is very consistently highly rated; it's perennially pricey though – even fans can feel costs are "pushed up to unaffordable levels for what is in essence a neighbourhood restaurant". / SW1 9LX; www.olivorestaurants.com; 10.30 pm; closed Sat L & Sun L.

Olivocarne SW1 £61 332
61 Elizabeth St 020 7730 7997 2–4A
"Traditional cooking with a sophisticated touch", along with "the neatest of wine lists" are big draws to this slightly "oddly configured" and "very crowded" Belgravia Sardinian (stablemate to Olivo, Oliveto etc.). / SW1W 9PP; www.olivorestaurants.com; 11 pm, Sun 10.30 pm.

Olivomare SW1 £61 432
10 Lower Belgrave St 020 7730 9022 2–4B
"Low-key sophistication" is the hallmark of the "sensationally good" Sardinian seafood cooking of Mauro Sanna's well-established Belgravian. The "odd decor" ("Alice in Wonderland with an austere look") is thought "very cool" by its fans, but the consensus is that it's "soulless". / SW1W 0LJ; www.olivorestaurants.com; 11 pm, Sun 10.30 pm; booking max 10 may apply.

Olympic, Olympic Studios SW13 £52 224
117-123 Church Rd 020 8912 5161 11–1A
"Fast becoming an SW13 institution", the all-day café/brasserie at the independent Olympic Studios cinema in Barnes (formerly a recording studio) is a very agreeably "buzzy" venue. "Service can be slow" and the food's a tad complacent, but they do a "really good breakfast/brunch". / SW13 9HL;

www.olympiccinema.co.uk; @Olympic_Cinema; 11 pm, Sun 10 pm.

Olympus Fish N3 £35 452

140-144 Ballards Ln 020 8371 8666 1–1B

"Amazing charcoal-grilled fish", in addition to the more conventional deep-fried version, "is always succulent and never greasy" at this popular Finchley fixture, which is "better than the (well-known) local competition by a country mile". / N3 2PA; 11 pm; set weekday L £17 (FP).

On The Bab £36 332

39 Marylebone Ln, W1 020 7935 2000 2–1A
36 Wellington St, WC2 020 7240 8825 5–3D
305 Old St, EC1 020 7683 0361 13–1B
9 Ludgate Broadway, EC4
020 7248 8777 10–2A

"Everything is very tasty" ("the fried chicken is amazing!") at these "packed" Korean street-food joints, with their "no frills" industrial interiors, where "there's no booking, and often queueing out the door". / onthebab.co.uk; @onthebab; –.

One Canada Square E14 £58 233

1 Canada Square 020 7559 5199 12–1C

In the lobby of Canary Wharf's main 'scraper, this prominently situated establishment provides a convenient business rendezvous, but is also praised for its "amazing bottomless weekend brunch". / E14 5AB; www.onecanadasquarerestaurant.com; @OneCanadaSquare; 10.45 pm; closed Sun; set pre theatre £34 (FP).

100 Wardour Street W1 £64 223

100 Wardour St 020 7314 4000 4–2D

D&D London's latest venture on this huge Soho site that's seen their Mezzo, Meza and Floridita brands come and go (and in aeons past was The Marquee Club) inspires similarly mixed reports for its plus-ça-change formula mixing Asian/European cuisine, cocktails, live music and dancing. / W1F 0TN; /www.100wardourst.com; @100WardourSt; 2 am, Thu-Sat 3 am, Sun 5 pm; closed Mon & Sun D.

1 Lombard Street EC3 £74 222

1 Lombard St 020 7929 6611 10–3C

"Location, location and location" help explain the ongoing appeal to dealmakers of Soren Jessen's "City stalwart" in the heart of the Square Mile ("don't go for a secret meeting, as you're bound to bump into someone you know!"). The formula of this large ex-banking hall "doesn't move on" – the food's "accomplished but not an event" and "nowhere near as good as it should be for the price". / EC3V 9AA; www.1lombardstreet.com; 10 pm; closed Sat & Sun; booking max 6 may apply.

One Sixty Smokehouse £53 434

291 West End Ln, NW6 020 7794 9786 1–1B
9 Stoney Ln, E1 020 7283 8367 10–2D

"Consistently brilliant BBQ at prices that keep it friendly" – in "big portions", and with "a great selection of craft beers" – win fans for David Moore and Sean Martin's "fantastically buzzy" American-inspired operations in West Hampstead, and the City. / www.one-sixty.co.uk; @onesixtylondon; –.

One-O-One, Park Tower Knightsbridge SW1 £98 421

101 Knightsbridge 020 7290 7101 6–1D

"Pascal Proyart continues to be the 'King of Fish' in London", say fans of his Knightsbridge dining room, which despite its "totally depressing", "hotel-foyer-style" ambience, has built a formidable reputation for "stunning" seafood and fish dishes. Its ratings came off the boil this year though, with some reports of "very good, certainly inventive food, but not quite the wizardry some people have described". / SW1X 7RN; www.oneoonerestaurant.com; @OneOOneLondon; 10 pm; closed Mon & Sun; booking max 6 may apply.

Les 110 de Taillevent W1 £65 333

16 Cavendish Sq 020 3141 6016 3–1B

"110 wines by the glass with suggested matches for each dish in a range of prices" (and including 70ml options) is a "lovely, simple and tempting concept" that wins much praise for this "slightly stark and rectilinear" Parisian yearling, on the square behind Oxford Street's John Lewis. Still, "with a famous name like Taillevent, expectations are bound to be high" and while the food is "interesting", critics feel it's "not exceptional" and can seem a mite "pricey". / W1G 9DD; www.les-110-taillevent-london.com/en; @110London; D only, closed Sun.

Opera Tavern WC2 £51 443

23 Catherine St 020 7836 3680 5–3D

Some of "the capital's smartest modern tapas" are served at this "very pleasant" (if sometimes cacophonous) Dehesa sibling – a two-floor Covent Garden pub-conversion, where "results can be hit and miss, but are mostly hit". Top Menu Tip – "sinful mini Iberico pork and foie gras burgers". / WC2B 5JS; www.operatavern.co.uk; @saltyardgroup; 11.15 pm, Sun 9.45 pm.

Opso W1 £44 323

10 Paddington St 020 7487 5088 2–1A

"The food is amazing" ("my beetroot and green bean salad was to die for!") at this modern Greek two-year-old in Marylebone… "even if the set lunch is pretty expensive, and the portions teeny-tiny". / W1U 5QL; www.opso.co.uk; @OPSO_london; 10 pm, Fri & Sat 10.30 pm; closed Sun D.

The Orange SW1 £59 344
37 Pimlico Rd 020 7881 9844 6–2D
"For a fun lunch with friends", this Pimlico gastropub provides both a bar and "charming first-floor dining room" – on the menu, wood-fired pizza and other well-prepared dishes. / SW1W 8NE; www.theorange.co.uk; @theorangesw1; 10 pm, Sun 9.30 pm.

Orange Pekoe SW13 £26 344
3 White Hart Ln 020 8876 6070 11–1A
Busy Barnes tea room with pavement tables that's a "lovely place to go for a cup of something and some cake". It's "not your deluxe afternoon tea of central London hotels", but "the range of teas served is amazing" and "the kitchen turns out delicious scones and cakes" as well as breakfasts and light lunches. / SW13 0PX; www.orangepekoeteas.com; 5 pm; L only.

Orée SW10 £13 423
275-277 Fulham Rd 020 3813 9724 6–3B
'A taste of rural France' and its freshly baked viennoiserie, artisan bread and fine patisserie are promised by this new Chelsea café, also offering breakfasts and light lunches (tartines, salads, etc). Early reports applaud its "delicious food and charming staff". / SW10; www.oree.co.uk; @oreeboulangerie; 7 pm, Sun 6 pm; no bookings.

Ormer Mayfair, Flemings Mayfair Hotel W1
Half Moon St 020 7016 5601 3–4B
Star Jersey chef, Shaun Rankin, has oversight of the 85-cover dining room at this Mayfair hotel, following its recent £14m revamp – it opened in mid-summer 2016. / W1J 7BH; www.ormermayfair.com; @ormermayfair; closed Sun; no shorts.

Orrery W1 £80 333
55 Marylebone High St 020 7616 8000 2–1A
Above Marylebone's Conran Shop, this "classic" D&D London venture provides a "calm, stress-free environment" for business or romance (with "a nice al fresco terrace when the weather is fine"). "Well-drilled staff" provide modern French cuisine that's "not cheap" but "of a consistently high standard". / W1U 5RB; www.orreryrestaurant.co.uk; @orrery; 10 pm, Fri & Sat 10.30 pm, Sun 10 pm; set weekday L £47 (FP), set Sun L £50 (FP).

Orso WC2 £55 232
27 Wellington St 020 7240 5269 5–3D
"Extremely convenient for the opera or theatre" – this long-established basement in Covent Garden remains a favourite for many reporters, for its "varied Italian fare", "restrained interior" and "attentive and informal" service. However, numerous old-timers (perhaps remembering its late '80s glory days) are harsher, finding it "underwhelming" and "tired". Top Tip – "top value pre-show deal". / WC2E 7DB; www.orsorestaurant.co.uk; @Orso_Restaurant; 11.30 pm, Sun 10 pm; set weekday L £33 (FP).

Oscar Wilde Bar At Cafe Royal W1 £55 244
68 Regent Street 020 7406 3333 4–4C
"Just amazing! The theatre of the whole thing". This "most beautiful room" – dating back to 1865 and formerly known as the Café Royal Grill – nowadays operates as a bar within what, in latter years, has become an über-swanky hotel. Most of the feedback it attracts relates to the afternoon tea – "more of a full meal!" but "wonderful". / W1B; www.hotelcaferoyal.com; @HotelCafeRoyal; \N.

Oslo Court NW8 £64 454
Charlbert St, off Prince Albert Rd
020 7722 8795 9–3A
"Whether you're 70, 80 or 90 years old: the place to party!" This priceless veteran, quirkily tucked away at the foot of a Regent's Park apartment block, is "a top choice for senior citizens" across north London, "who want to take out 2-3 generations of their family for a celebratory dinner". "It's a total time warp", but "very good at what it does": "sturdy, classic '70s food" is served in "generous portions" ("you'll never leave hungry!") by "unfailing" staff of the old school, in a "wonderfully camp", "plush, pink and comfortable" (if "cramped") setting. Special marks go to the "long-serving and extremely enthusiastic dessert waiter" ("OTT but fun") who "always 'saves the last one just for you!'". Top Tip – "birthday cakes can be pre-ordered free for parties of 4+, and the singing's not bad either!" / NW8 7EN; 11 pm; closed Sun; no jeans.

Osteria, Barbican Centre EC2 £54 222
Level 2 Silk St 020 7588 3008 10–1B
Anthony Demetre (of Soho's Arbutus, and Urban Coterie in Shoreditch) has teamed up with Searcys once again, this time to jazz up the food offering at the Barbican Centre brasserie with this new Italian, which opened to mixed feedback – it's well rated in some accounts, but to sceptics merely "the usual woeful catering at the Barbican". As ever, nice views here from the window tables. / EC2Y 8DS; www.osteriabarbican.co.uk; @osterialondon; 11 pm.

Osteria 60 SW7 £77
60 Hyde Park Gate 020 7937 8886 6–1B
The new incarnation of the dining room of Kensington's luxurious Baglioni hotel – initial feedback, admittedly limited, suggests it may struggle to defy the overpriced and indifferent DNA of the site (formerly Brunello, RIP). / SW7 5BB; www.osteria60.com; @osteria_60; 10.30 pm.

Osteria Antica Bologna SW11 £43 333
23 Northcote Rd 020 7978 4771 11–2C
A "little, cheap 'n' cheerful gem" near Clapham Junction long known locally and beyond for its "good value Northern Italian cuisine, whether sitting out on the pavement on a sunny day, or tucking into wild boar stew on a wintry Sunday". / SW11 1NG; www.osteria.co.uk; @OsteriaAntica; 10.30 pm, Sun 10 pm.

Osteria Basilico W11 £58 324
29 Kensington Park Rd 020 7727 9957 7–1A
The "best authentic Italian pizza in town" plus "delicious home-made pasta and seasonal specials" ensure that this long-running Notting Hill local is "always full". / W11 2EU; www.osteriabasilico.co.uk; 11.30 pm, Sun 10.30 pm; no booking, Sat L.

Osteria Tufo N4 £47 343
67 Fonthill Rd 020 7272 2911 9–1D
"Enticing aromas hit you as you enter" this superb "find" in Finsbury Park – a "wonderfully friendly" operation, serving a "good selection of interesting Italian specialities" in "bohemian surroundings". "I had no idea it even existed, but now I'll be going back all the time!" / N4 3HZ; www.osteriatufo.co.uk; 10.30 pm, Sun 9.30 pm; closed Mon, Tue-Sat D only, Sun open L & D; no Amex.

Ostuni £49 333
1 Hampstead Lane, N6 020 7624 8035 9–1B
43-45 Lonsdale Rd, NW6
020 7624 8035 1–2B
"Authentic Puglian cuisine to an excellent standard" has won quite a following for this spacious three-year-old, in "distinctly middle-of-the-road Queen's Park". The odd sceptic fears that "it's more hit and miss than when it first opened", but they must be doing something right as June 2016 saw the opening of a Highgate sibling, similarly with an open kitchen.

Otto's WC1 £67 453
182 Grays Inn Rd 020 7713 0107 2–1D
How did this "oasis of traditional and consistently superb Gallic cooking" end up in a nondescript corner of Bloomsbury? Its overall approach is "pleasantly old-fashioned" but "not stuffy and always with a humorous twist" thanks to the "very personal" attention of "effervescent" patron Otto (who also provides "helpful advice on the impressive wine list"). Top Menu Tip – "the Canard à la Presse helped me find god!" / WC1X 8EW; www.ottos-restaurant.com; 9.45 pm; closed Sat L & Sun.

Ottolenghi £55 322
13 Motcomb St, SW1 020 7823 2707 6–1D
63 Ledbury Rd, W11 020 7727 1121 7–1B
1 Holland St, W8 020 7937 0003 6–1A
287 Upper St, N1 020 7288 1454 9–2D
50 Artillery Pas, E1 020 7247 1999 10–2D
"Zingy fresh flavours dance in the mouth", at Yotam Ottolenghi's "funky" communal cafés, known for their "inspired" salads and "scrumptious" cakes. "Cramped conditions" are a pain however, and while even fans "do wonder how a small meal can cost quite so much", critics fear they risk "disappearing up their own fundaments". / www.ottolenghi.co.uk; N1 10.15 pm, W8 & W11 8 pm, Sat 7 pm, Sun 6 pm; N1 closed Sun D; Holland St takeaway only; W11 & SW1 no booking, N1 booking for D only.

Outlaw's at The Capital SW3 £86 442
22-24 Basil St 020 7591 1202 6–1D
"Stunning" fish and seafood "presented with panache" win huge acclaim for this "hidden gem, so close to the brassiness of Harrods". The ambience of the "small" room is not to all tastes though – what is "quiet and dignified" to fans is to critics "staid" and "too formal". Top Tip – BYO with no corkage on Thursdays. / SW3 1AT; www.capitalhotel.co.uk; @OUTLAWSinLondon; 10 pm; closed Sun; set weekday L £51 (FP).

Oxo Tower, Restaurant SE1 £85 111
Barge House St 020 7803 3888 10–3A
"Urrggh!" – "Why can't they get it right?" at this South Bank landmark. It has "exceptional views over the Thames" and "feels special outside in summer", but "dreadful" standards make it the survey's perennial No. 1 disappointment. / SE1 9PH; www.harveynichols.com/restaurants; @OxoTowerWharf; 11 pm, Sun 10 pm; set weekday L & dinner £47 (FP); SRA-3 star.

Oxo Tower, Brasserie SE1 £72 112
Barge House St 020 7803 3888 10–3A
Cheaper than the adjoining restaurant, the brasserie of this South Bank landmark is likewise "one for the view rather than the food" and "should be so much better". / SE1 9PH; www.harveynichols.com/restaurants/oxo-tower-london; 11 pm, Sun 10 pm; may need 2+ to book; set weekday L & dinner £47 (FP).

P Franco E5 £35
107 Lower Clapton Road
020 8533 4660 1–1D
More reports please on this cool little wine

bar in Clapton, where you sit at a long table in the evenings and enjoy a daily-changing menu alongside superb plonk. / E5 0NP; www.pfranco.co.uk; @pfranco_e5; 9 pm, Thu 11 pm, Fri & Sat 11 pm, Sun 9pm; closed Mon, Tue-Fri D only, Sat & Sun open L & D; no Amex.

Pachamama W1 **£63** **312**
18 Thayer St 020 7935 9393 2–1A
"Peruvian fusion without the high prices" is to be found at this Marylebone two-year-old, which delivers "brilliant tapas and good Pisco cocktails" in a "fun and buzzy" – but "too noisy" – setting. Service "doesn't quite live up to the rest (lack of training, I suspect)". / W1U 3JY; www.pachamamalondon.com; @pachamama_ldn; 10.45 pm, Sun 10 pm; closed Mon L; set brunch £35 (FP).

Padella SE1 **£28** **443**
6 Southwark St no tel 10–4B
"Arrive early: the queue can be a killer", but this "simple, easy and unfussy" new Italian near Borough Market (from the team behind Trullo) is "one of the few places worth enduring them" – "amazing, freshly made pasta, and so wonderfully cheap" is the highlight of the "short menu". / SE1 1TQ; www.padella.co; @padella_pasta; 10 pm, Sun 5 pm; no bookings.

The Painted Heron SW10 **£56** **542**
112 Cheyne Walk 020 7351 5232 6–3B
"Indian food on steroids, but without being pretentious" ("familiar enough to be comforting, different enough to be exciting") wins the customary hymn of praise to this "hidden gem", off the Chelsea Embankment – "I still don't think it has the reputation it deserves!" / SW10 0DJ; www.thepaintedheron.com; @thepaintedheron; 10.30 pm; set weekday L & Sun L £15 (FP).

The Palmerston SE22 **£55** **333**
91 Lordship Ln 020 8693 1629 1–4D
"Good and sometimes exceptional cooking" with a modern British slant distinguishes this former boozer – nowadays a well-established fixture of East Dulwich. / SE22 8EP; www.thepalmerston.co.uk; @thepalmerston; 10 pm, Sun 9.30 pm; no Amex.

The Palomar W1 **£51** **554**
34 Rupert St 020 7439 8777 5–3A
"If you can't visit their original restaurant, Machneyuda in Israel" this "piece of trendy Tel Aviv in London" is "the next best thing". "Cramped, noisy and pulsating with life", you can book for the side room, but the place to be is the "buzzy, free-style" bar "rubbing elbows with your neighbours". Service is "friendly" and "as it comes", and the "adventurous Levantine food" is "ultra-fresh" and "anything but dull!" / W1D 6DN; www.thepalomar.co.uk; 11 pm, Sun 9 pm.

Pappa Ciccia **£34** **343**
105 Munster Rd, SW6 020 7384 1884 11–1B
41 Fulham High St, SW6
020 7736 0900 11–1B
This popular group cooks "by far the best pizza" in Fulham and Putney – they're even "great reheated the next day". An "exceptionally good tagliatelle nero con vongole" also wins plaudits, while the BYO policy keeps bills in check. / www.pappaciccia.com; 11 pm, Sat & Sun 11.30 pm; Munster Rd no credit cards.

Parabola W8
224-238 Kensington High Street
020 3862 5900 6–1A
Named for the shape of its roof, Parabola is Sir Terence Conran's and Peter Prescott's latest brainchild inside the re-located Design Museum, which opens by Holland Park in late November 2016. The restaurant will be open all day, then plans to host guest chefs for dinner, with private dining in a members' room. / W8 6AG; designmuseum.org.

Paradise by Way of Kensal Green W10 **£50** **335**
19 Kilburn Ln 020 8969 0098 1–2B
"An absolute gem of a restaurant" – part of a massive shabby-chic Kensal Green tavern that's long been a magnet for hip creative industry types, with gardens, roof-terraces and bars galore. / W10 4AE; www.theparadise.co.uk; @weloveparadise; 10.30 pm, Fri & Sat 11 pm, Sun 9 pm; closed weekday L; no Amex.

Paradise Garage E2 **£45** **443**
254 Paradise Row 020 7613 1502 13–1D
"The flavours and presentation are superb" at chef Robin Gill's (The Manor and Dairy in Clapham) "so-trendy" yearling under a Bethnal Green railway arch. It's "good value considering the fantastic quality of the inventive food", "although with the small plates, the cost can easily mount". / E2 9LE; www.paradise254.com; @ParadiseRow254; 10 pm; closed Mon, Tue L & Sun D; set weekday L £25 (FP).

Paradise Hampstead NW3 **£33** **454**
49 South End Rd 020 7794 6314 9–2A
A "wonderful front of house" further boosts the "highly convivial" style of this "excellent, traditional Indian" of nearly a half-century's standing, near Hampstead Heath station. It's "madly busy", "so booking is recommended" – the food's "not the most adventurous, but done exceptionally well". / NW3 2QB; www.paradisehampstead.co.uk; 10.45 pm.

El Parador NW1 **£38** **443**
245 Eversholt St 020 7387 2789 9–3C
A strong option near Mornington Crescent – this "great little Hispanic spot" offers "quality", "reasonably priced tapas". "Unstuffy", "efficient" service and a "great garden for sunny days" complete the deal, but "it gets busy and slightly

congested, so don't tell anyone…" / NW1 1BA; www.elparadorlondon.com; 11 pm, Fri & Sat 11.30 pm, Sun 9.30 pm; closed Sat L & Sun L; no Amex.

Park Chinois W1 £94 254
17 Berkeley St 020 3327 8888 3–3C
"A night out in 1920's Shanghai, with live music and dancing" is the aim at Alan Yau's barmily "opulent" Mayfair newcomer (on the site that was Automat, RIP). Service is "amazing", but the luxurious cuisine (Peking Duck, caviar, dim sum) is "bone-crunchingly expensive" yet "nothing spectacular". / W1S 4NF; www.parkchinois.com; 11 pm, Sun 10.15 pm; no jeans.

Parlour Kensal NW10 £49 444
5 Regent St 020 8969 2184 1–2B
"No ordinary gastropub" – Jesse Dunford Wood's "quirky" Kensal Rise pub conversion features a "fabulous chef's table" amongst its dining options. Top Menu Tip – the "enormous cow pie". / NW10 5LG; www.parlourkensal.com; @ParlourUK; 10 pm; closed Mon.

El Pastór SE1
7a Stoney Street awaiting tel 10–4C
Having conquered Spanish cuisine, Barrafina bros Sam & Eddie Hart are setting their sights on the Latino market with this November 2016 Mexican opening, by Borough Market. The venue will primarily be a taqueria, specialising in tacos. To drink there's to be mezcal, tequila, cocktails and Mexican beers. / SE1 9AA; @Tacos_El_Pastor.

Patara £61 344
15 Greek St, W1 020 7437 1071 5–2A
5 Berners St, W1 020 8874 6503 3–1D
7 Maddox St, W1 020 7499 6008 4–2A
181 Fulham Rd, SW3 020 7351 5692 6–2C
9 Beauchamp Pl, SW3 020 7581 8820 6–1C
"An excellent Thai chain", which "reinvents itself from time to time". "Service is amazing, and with a smile", the "always buzzing" branches are very civilised, and "the food is of a consistently high quality". / www.pataralondon.com; 10.30 pm; Greek St closed Sun L.

Paternoster Chop House EC4 £55 211
1 Warwick Court 020 7029 9400 10–2B
"With a location like this they should try harder", but D&D London's steakhouse – with its al fresco tables and magnificent pavement-side views of St Paul's – is too busy making money from its captive be-suited market: it's "overpriced and the food's not that good". / EC4M 7DX; www.paternosterchophouse.co.uk; @paternoster1; 10.30 pm; closed Sat L & Sun D.

Patio W12 £35 355
5 Goldhawk Rd 020 8743 5194 8–1C
The "delightful" and "gloriously eccentric" Polish hospitality at this family-run Shepherd's Bush veteran "never lets you down". With its "wide range of flavoured vodkas" and "old-fashioned décor", it's perfect for a "cheap 'n' cheerful" get-together. / W12 8QQ; www.patiolondon.com; 11 pm, Sat & Sun 11.30 pm; closed Sat L & Sun L.

Patogh W1 £22 433
8 Crawford Pl 020 7262 4015 7–1D
"Ignore the shabby decor, just savour the outstanding Persian food" ("grilled meat and bread is the order of the day"), at this long-established "hustling and bustling" shopfront cafe off the Edgware Road, where "waiters do their best with manic crowd control". "Don't come in a big group, there just isn't room!" (NB it's BYO, with "Waitrose round the corner for the wine"). / W1H 5NE; n/a; 11 pm; cash only; booking max may apply.

Patron NW5 £49 344
26 Fortress Road 020 7813 2540 9–2C
"Good French cooking in an intimate atmosphere" has made this cute little year old 'Cave à Manger' a "brilliant addition to the Kentish Town food scene". It's "romantic" for a date, too ("even though we ate dinner at the bar!") / NW5 2HB; www.patronlondon.com; 11 pm, Sun 10 pm; closed Mon, Tue-Thu D only, Fri-Sun open L & D.

Patty and Bun £23 432
18 Old Compton St, W1
020 7287 1818 5–2A
54 James St, W1 020 7487 3188 3–1A
36 Redchurch Street, E2
020 7613 3335 13–1B
397 Mentmore Terrace, E8
020 8510 0252 14–1B
22-23 Liverpool St, EC2
020 7621 1331 10–2D
"To-die-for", "messy" burgers – amongst "the best in London?" – are to be had at these "super hip" pitstops. "Count yourself lucky if you get a table at the James Street original!" / www.pattyandbun.co.uk; Mon - Wed 10pm, Thu - Fri 11 pm, Sat 9 pm, Sun 6 pm.

The Pear Tree W6 £44 334
14 Margravine Rd 020 7381 1787 8–2C
"A lovely romantic atmosphere" is the most distinctive feature of this "amazing", small Victorian pub hideaway, behind the Charing Cross Hospital, but its cooking is "very competent" too. / W6 8HJ; www.thepeartreefulham.com; 9.30 pm, Fri-Sun 9 pm; Mon-Thu D only, Fri-Sun open L & D.

Pear Tree Cafe SW11
Lakeside Cafe, Battersea Park no tel 6–4D
At last someone tries to do something with this gorgeously located park café, by Battersea Park's boating lake. The autumn 2016 opening by Annabel Partridge, formerly at Petersham Nurseries, and Will Burrett, previously at Spring, provides an outdoor terrace, all-day dining and weekend brunch. / SW11 4NJ; www.peartreecafe.co.uk.

Pearl Liang W2 £48 443
8 Sheldon Square 020 7289 7000 7–1C
"Always excellent dim sum" tops the list of "genuine Cantonese food" at this big basement, tucked-away in Paddington Basin. Service is "brisk but attentive", while "the room is loud enough to drown out any noise from the kids". / W2 6EZ; www.pearlliang.co.uk; 11 pm.

Peckham Bazaar SE15 £49 534
119 Consort Rd 020 7732 2525 1–4D
"Rare but smart regional food" from the Balkans via Greece to the Middle East makes for an "exciting and imaginative" eating experience at this "honest" Peckham venue. Wines, including from the Greek islands, come "at very fair mark-ups". / SE15 3RU; www.peckhambazaar.com; 10 pm, Sun 8 pm; closed Mon, Tue-Fri D only, Sat & Sun open L & D; no Amex.

Peckham Refreshment Rooms SE15 £41 322
12-16 Blenheim Grove 020 7639 1106 1–4D
Chilled, affordable Peckham hangout, again well-rated for a casual bite: "we found it hard to find (they don't seem to believe in signage), difficult to order (staff didn't seem clear what was 'on'), difficult to sit (the stools are super uncomfortable), but the food was delicious!" / SE15 4QL; www.peckhamrefreshment.com; midnight; closed Sun D.

Pedler SE15 £38 344
58 Peckham Rye 020 3030 1515 1–4D
"A kitchen with real judgement and lightness of touch" helps win praise for this trendy, packed Peckham bistro-yearling, as does its above-average weekend brunch. / SE15 4JR; www.thebeautifulpizzaboy.london; @pizzaboylondon1; 10.45 pm; closed Mon, Tue L, Wed L, Thu L, Fri L & Sun D.

Pellicano Restaurant SW3 £59 342
19-21 Elystan St 020 7589 3718 6–2C
"Reopened after redecoration, and re-relocation and back on top form". This "attentive and friendly" Chelsea old-favourite is back on its original site and maintains a loyal, small fanclub for its "limited" but "excellent menu of Sardinian specialities and wines". "The physical ambiente is a little forlorn when there isn't a full house". / SW3 3NT; www.pellicanorestaurant.co.uk; 11 pm, Sun 9.30 pm.

E Pellicci E2 £16 345
332 Bethnal Green Rd 020 7739 4873 13–1D
"Still the most fun breakfast in the East End" – this trad' caff has "been here for generations" and boasts wonderful Art Deco quarters ("you'll have seen the wood- panelled interior in many TV dramas"). A "warm welcome's guaranteed", with "fry-ups cooked to perfection" – all in "huge portions". / E2 0AG; 4 pm; L only, closed Sun; cash only.

Pentolina W14 £48 454
71 Blythe Rd 020 3010 0091 8–1C
This "smart" and "charming" Italian in the backstreets of Olympia is "just what a local restaurant should be": "a great all-round experience", with "quality at decent prices" and "interesting" cooking (although "the menu doesn't change very frequently"). / W14 0HP; www.pentolinarestaurant.co.uk; 10 pm; closed Mon & Sun; no Amex.

The Pepper Tree SW4 £33 333
19 Clapham Common South Side
020 7622 1758 11–2D
"Sharing tables makes for a fun and buzzy experience" at this "cheap 'n' cheerful", "old favourite" Thai canteen in Clapham – "great value and perfect for a bite before the movies". / SW4 7AB; www.thepeppertree.co.uk; 10.45 pm, Sun & Mon 10.15 pm; no bookings.

Percy & Founders W1 £55 432
1 Pearson Square, Fitzroy Place
020 3761 0200 2–1B
"Huge" year-old pub, dining room and bar occupying the spacious ground floor of a Fitzrovia development on the site of the old Middlesex Hospital. All reports approve its menu of grills and brasserie fare, but "it feels very new" and can seem a tad "artificial and clinical". / W1T 3BF; www.percyandfounders.co.uk; @PercyFounders; 10.30 pm; closed Sun D.

Perilla N16
1-3 Green Lanes 074 67067393 1–1C
Following their stylish pop-ups across London, Ben Marks and Matt Emmerson are set to open Perilla in a permanent Newington Green location in November, with backing from Philip Howard, among others. / N16 9BS; www.perilladining.co.uk; closed Mon, Tue L, Wed L, Thu L & Sun D.

The Perry Vale SE23 £46 343
31 Perry Vale 020 8291 0432 1–4D
From the team behind Camberwell's crowd-pleasing Crooked Well comes a simple, modern bistro/ brasserie yearling in up-and-coming Forest Hill – fans say it's proving "a wonderful addition to the SE23 scene!" / SE23 2AR; www.theperryvale.com; @theperryvale.

Petersham Hotel TW10 £65 3 3 5
Nightingale Ln 020 8939 1084 1–4A
This "beautifully situated hotel on Richmond Hill" is a little "old-fashioned" and "conservative" and generally appeals to an older crowd. It offers "magnificent views (especially at lunch)", the food is "better than you might expect from a hotel", and overall it's a "delightful experience". / TW10 6UZ; www.petershamhotel.co.uk; @thepetersham; 9.45 pm, Sun 8.45 pm.

Petersham Nurseries Cafe TW10 £69 2 1 3
Church Lane (signposted 'St Peter's Church') 020 8940 5230 1–4A
"Such a romantic venue" – "a lovely glasshouse" that's "perfect for a summer day" – along with ambitious cuisine has earnt a huge reputation for this shabby-chic garden centre café, near Richmond Park. But while it has always been "massively overpriced" ("queuing for the loo with the garden centre customers, and paying £100 per head does not feel right"), since Skye Gyngell moved on "the food is nothing like it was", and to critics it feels like "it's totally lost the plot": "laughable" to charge "elite central London prices" for "a garden shed" with "indifferent service and interspersed with a few silly antiques!" / TW10 7AG; www.petershamnurseries.com; L only, closed Mon.

Petit Pois Bistro N1 £47
9 Hoxton Square 020 7613 3689 13–1B
In a corner of hip Hoxton Square (with terrace), a new (summer 2016) French bistro serving fave raves like steak frites, moules marinière and croque madame. Its chocolate mousse has been described by Jay Rayner as 'the best three minutes you can have in London for a fiver right now'. / N1 6NU; www.petitpoisbistro.com; @petitpoisbistro; 10.30 pm, Sun 4 pm; closed Sun D.

The Petite Coree NW6 £39 4 5 2
98 West End Lane 020 7624 9209 1–1B
"A lovely and refreshing local run by a couple (husband downstairs cooking and wife serving). They deserve real support in their effort to bring French food with a Korean twist in every dish to West Hampstead!" / NW6 2LU; www.thepetitecoree.com; @thepetitecoree; Tue-Thu 10 pm, Fri & Sat 10.30 pm, Sun 10 pm; closed Mon, Tue-Thu D only, Fri-Sun open L & D; set dinner £24 (FP).

La Petite Maison W1 £83 5 4 5
54 Brook's Mews 020 7495 4774 3–2B
"The wonderful flavours of Southern Europe" ("sharing plates, that are not your typical French food: much lighter and fresher", prepared to "an incredibly high standard" and with "everything tasting of its ingredients and the sun!") – plus a "fantastic", Côte d'Azure atmosphere to match, inspire "simply outstanding" feedback on Arjun Waney's "busy and noisy" Mayfair haunt... even if "prices are flabbergasting" and "it's something of a hedge fund canteen". / W1K 4EG; www.lpmlondon.co.uk; @lpmlondon; 10.45 pm, Sun 9.45 pm.

Pétrus SW1 £111 3 3 2
1 Kinnerton St 020 7592 1609 6–1D
"It takes a week to review the wine list!" at Gordon Ramsay's plush Belgravian, whose centrepiece is a floor-to-ceiling, cylindrical, glass wine vault. On many accounts the "wonderful" cuisine lives up to it too, but enthusiasm for the "hushed" ("like a doctor's waiting room") and "spacious" interior is more muted, and even fans can feel prices are "crazy". Top Tip – "make the most of the lunch deal". / SW1X 8EA; www.gordonramsayrestaurants.com; @petrus; 10.15 pm; closed Sun; no trainers; set weekday L £42 (FP), set dinner £84 (FP).

Peyote W1 £74 3 3 2
13 Cork St 020 7409 1300 4–4A
By the yardstick of his other ventures, Arjun Waney's Mayfair Latino three-year-old has made few waves, and attracts thin feedback. Fans say the "different" cooking ('consulted on' by Mexico City legend, Eduardo Garcia) can be "surprisingly good" – certainly in comparison with the dire press reviews the place has attracted – but even they can feel that high prices and "the overt focus on the commercial side (table time limits, advance credit card guarantees) take the shine off the experience". / W1S 3NS; www.peyoterestaurant.com; Mon-Thu 1 am, Fri & Sat 2 am; closed Sat L & Sun; set weekday L & pre-theatre £27 (FP).

Peyotito W11 £53
31 Kensington Park Road
020 7043 1400 7–1A
In the heart of Notting Hill, a new Mexican serving Mezcal cocktails and sharing plates such as ceviche, moles, crudos and maza until late, as well as weekend brunch. / W11 2EU; www.peyotitorestaurant.com; @peyotitolondon; midnight, Fri & Sat 1 am.

Pham Sushi EC1 £36 5 3 1
159 Whitecross St 020 7251 6336 13–2A
Don't go for the ambience (it's "cramped and noisy"), but some of "the best-value Japanese in London" is found at this simple, "off-the-beaten-track" Barbican fixture – "consistently excellent sushi (of which crunchy tuna and flying dragon are highlights)", all "at a fraction of West End prices". / EC1Y 8JL; www.phamsushi.co.uk; @phamsushi; 10 pm; closed Sat L & Sun.

Pharmacy 2, Newport Street Gallery SE11 £54 [3][3][3]
Newport St 020 3141 9333 2–4D
As with the original Pharmacy (back in the day, on Notting Hill Gate) "there is a chalk-and-cheese clash between the sterile decor and warming food" at this new venture, "tucked away on a Lambeth backstreet". But initially at least, more people find the effect "fun" and "love it" than find it "too bright for relaxation and enjoyment". The food – "no particular stand out, but all competently done" – likewise is mostly well received, and only the odd cynic feels that "Mark Hix's cooking is as predictable as Damien Hirst's art". / SE11 6AJ; www.pharmacyrestaurant.com; @Ph2restaurant; midnight, Sun 6 pm; closed Mon & Sun D.

Pho £35 [2][3][3]
"Very fresh and genuine tastes" have driven the success of these Vietnamese street-food cafés – "great for a cheap bowl of noodles" (but nowadays "fine, but nothing more"). / www.phocafe.co.uk; EC1 10 pm, Fri & Sat 10.30 pm, W1 10.30 pm, W12 9 pm, Sat 7 pm, Sun 6 pm; EC1 closed Sat L & Sun, W1 closed Sun; no Amex; no booking.

The Phoenix SW3 £51 [2][2][4]
23 Smith St 020 7730 9182 6–2D
With its "neighbourhood feel" and "relaxed atmosphere", this Chelsea backstreet pub "exudes genuine happiness". "Great food (not just the usual pub grub)", that suits "the whole family". / SW3 4EE; www.geronimo-inns.co.uk; @ThePhoenixSW3; 10 pm.

Phoenix Palace NW1 £56 [3][2][2]
5-9 Glentworth St 020 7486 3515 2–1A
"Divine, juicy, well-stuffed, fresh mouthfuls of pure joy!" – that's the "delicious dim sum" at this "large", well-established Chinese venue, near Baker Street, "frequented by lots of Chinese". Its ratings suffered, though, from a couple of disappointing reports this year. / NW1 5PG; www.phoenixpalace.co.uk; 11.30 pm, Sun 10.30 pm.

Picture £48 [4][4][3]
110 Great Portland St, W1
020 7637 7892 2–1B
19 New Cavendish Street, W1
020 7935 0058 2–1A
"A bare dining room and small tasting plates – not everyone's idea of a satisfying formula but to my taste well prepared and interesting!" This low-key but accomplished venture near Broadcasting House can be enjoyed via its tasting menu – "a steal (and marvellous)" – or "two of their small plates is perfect for a quick light bite with friends or for business". It has a new Marylebone sibling too – one early report says it's "a really good addition north of Oxford Street".

Pidgin E8 £62 [5][5][4]
52 Wilton Way 020 7254 8311 1–2D
"A great little addition to the London dining scene" – this "small, cramped-but-magical" room with about 26 covers behind a "tiny Hackney shopfront" offers "an ever-changing, weekly set menu". "The absence of choice is abated by the spectacularly good cooking" from chef Elizabeth Allen – "truly innovative" ("we were reaching for Wikipedia to understand the ingredients") but "well thought-out", "surprising and delightful". / E8 1BG; @PidginLondon; 9.45 pm, Sun 9 pm; closed Mon, Tue-Fri D only, Sat & Sun open L & D.

Piebury Corner N7 £19 [3][4][3]
209-211 Holloway Rd 020 7700 5441 9–2D
"Pies rammed to the brim with fillings" and "fabulous gravy" draw Gunners fans and foodies to this small, "very friendly" deli near the Emirates; "good selection of craft beers" too. / N7 8DL; www.pieburycorner.com; @PieburyCorner; closed Mon, Tue, Wed & Sun; no bookings.

PIED À TERRE W1 £112 [4][4][3]
34 Charlotte St 020 7636 1178 2–1C
"In spite of another chef change, it goes from strength to strength!" – David Moore's "intimate" Fitzrovia townhouse is one of the capital's most enduring havens of gastronomy, with "very precise, fine attention to every detail". "Staff are charming from start to finish" and Andy McFadden's "assured" cuisine can be "extraordinary" ("he makes the food burst into life!") There's "one of the best cellars in London" too, presided over by the "helpful and hugely knowledgeable sommelier", Mathieu Germond. / W1T 2NH; www.pied-a-terre.co.uk; @PiedaTerreUK; 10.45 pm; closed Sat L & Sun; booking max 7 may apply.

Pig & Butcher N1 £51 [4][4][4]
80 Liverpool Road 020 7226 8304 9–3D
"Very strong all round" – this Islington hostelry provides "professional and caring" service of an "inventive and stylish, though meaty, menu" ("amazing roasts") and all reporters "have never had a poor meal". "The upstairs room is a great venue for a big party, downstairs a more traditional gastropub". / N1 0QD; www.thepigandbutcher.co.uk; @pigandbutcher; 10 pm, Sun 9 pm; Mon-Thu D only, Fri-Sun open L & D.

Pilpel £11 [4][4][2]
38 Brushfield Street, London, E1
020 7247 0146 13–2B
Old Spitalfields Mkt, E1 020 7375 2282 13–2B
146 Fleet St, EC4 020 7583 2030 10–2A
Paternoster Sq, EC4 020 7248 9281 10–2B
No wonder there are usually queues at this small Middle Eastern chain, where "great, piping-hot falafel with wonderful fresh fillings are crammed into pitta in about 45 seconds". They make a "really

Oklava
Orée
Osteria, Barbican Centre

tasty vegetarian lunch – so much better than it needs to be". / www.pilpel.co.uk; 4 pm-9 pm; some branches closed Sat & Sun.

Pique Nique SE1
32 Tanner Street awaiting tel 10–4D
What aims to be a proper, French rotisserie from the people who brought us Bermondsey's Casse-Croute – just over the road; this 40-seater café is to revolve around the AOC breed, Poulet de Bresse, and set to open in autumn 2016. / SE1 3LD; @piquenique32.

El Pirata W1 £40 344
5-6 Down St 020 7491 3810 3–4B
"If you're in Mayfair and want a low key and relatively inexpensive meal" this "hectic" little tapas spot is "perfect" (even if "the tables are so small they old hold about two dishes at once"). / W1J 7AQ; www.elpirata.co.uk; @elpirataw1; 11.30 pm; closed Sat L & Sun.

Pitt Cue Co EC2 £49 544
1 The Ave, Devonshire Sq
020 7324 7770 10–2D
"A meat Mecca and no mistake" – this epic US-style BBQ has "transitioned beautifully" from Soho to its "stunning new home" in Devonshire Square, and its dishes are "off-the-charts good", if "not for the faint hearted" ("pig's head scrumpet? Yes please!"). "Service tries hard" – "these guys clearly love their meat, treat it with respect" and "have tremendous knowledge of the breeds of animals and the cuts". "Excellent bar too". / EC2; www.pittcue.co.uk; @PittCueCo; 10.30 pm; closed Sat & Sun.

Pizarro SE1 £56 333
194 Bermondsey St 020 7256 5333 10–4D
"The bigger brother of José, nearby" – this "more traditional Spanish restaurant" in Bermondsey wins praise for its "friendly welcome", and "delicious individual or sharing plates". Some of José P's fans feel it's a turn off though – "the extraordinary just became ordinary, over-extended and over-priced". / SE1 3TQ; www.josepizarro.com; @Jose_Pizarro; 10.45 pm, Sun 9.45 pm.

Pizza East £52 334
310 Portobello Rd, W10 020 8969 4500 7–1A
79 Highgate Rd, NW5 020 3310 2000 9–1B
56 Shoreditch High St, E1
020 7729 1888 13–1B
"Channel your inner hipster, and cruise along" to these grungily-glam, industrial-style Soho House-owned haunts ("you have to be under 30 really to appreciate them fully"). They seemed a little more "over-stretched" this year, but for somewhere so "achingly trendy", service is surprisingly "amiable" and while the pizza is "inauthentic", it wins lots of praise for its "unusual toppings and fantastic, thin crispy bases". / www.pizzaeast.com; @PizzaEast; E1 Sun-Wed 11 pm, Thu 12 am, Fri-Sat 1am; W10 Mon-Thu 11.30 pm, Fri-Sat 12 am, Sun 10.30 pm.

Pizza Metro £43 322
147-149 Notting Hill Gate, W11
020 7727 8877 7–2B
64 Battersea Rise, SW11
020 7228 3812 11–2C
"Genuine pizza" – "enormous oblong offerings" – still win fans for this "noisy" Battersea stalwart (with a Notting Hill sibling) which introduced pizza-sold-by-the-metre to London. The service is "friendly" but "can be a bit hit-and-miss". / pizzametropizza.com; @pizzametropizza;

Pizza Pilgrims £33 434
102 Berwick St, W1 0778 066 7258 4–2D
11-12 Dean St, W1 020 7287 8964 4–1D
Kingly Ct, Carnaby St, W1
020 7287 2200 4–2B
23 Garrick Street, WC2 020 3019 1881 5–3C
15 Exmouth Mkt, EC1 020 7287 8964 10–1A
"Way better than the mainstream chains!" – the Elliot brothers' trendy pit-stops "do nothing fussy or exotic, just genuinely good pizza" with "just the right balance between toppings and crust". / Mon-Sat 10.30 pm, Sun 9.30 pm.

PizzaExpress £41 222
"All outlets deliver great grub and a cheery ambience" – for as long as we've produced this guide, that's been the most common view on this "amazingly consistent" 50-year-old, chain, also renowned as "a super place for kids" ("basically a crèche serving OK food!"). Is that changing since Hony Capital took over last year though? Critics have found it more "money driven" of late, and the atmosphere in particular seems far less sunny than it did. / www.pizzaexpress.co.uk; 11.30 pm-midnight; most City branches closed all or part of weekend; no booking at most branches.

Pizzeria Oregano N1 £42 343
18-19 St Albans Pl 020 7288 1123 9–3D
"Consistently good thin-crust pizza" makes it worth remembering this cute, family-friendly Italian, hidden off Upper Street. / N1 0NX; www.pizzaoregano.co.uk; @PizzeriaOregano; 11 pm, Fri & Sun 11.30 pm; closed weekday L.

Pizzeria Pappagone N4 £36 344
131 Stroud Green Rd 020 7263 2114 9–1D
"A proper, Italian, noisy trattoria" in Finsbury Park that's "a go-to family pick" for many locals, thanks to its "bustling pace with speedy service" and "exquisite pizza – we can't pass up the house special, Pizza Max no matter how hard we try!" / N4 3PX; www.pizzeriapappagone.co.uk; midnight.

Pizzeria Pellone SE24 £23 432
Herne Hill, 153a Dulwich Road
020 8001 7652 11–2D
"A cracking new pizzeria in Herne Hill": "a traditional oven turns out uncomplicated, tasty pizzas with satisfyingly chewy-yet-crispy crusts plus

a good, short list of toppings. Service is fine, staff friendly, vibe good". / SE24; www.pizzeriapellone.co.uk; @PizzeriaPellone; 11 pm, Sun 10 pm.

Pizzeria Rustica TW9 £42 332
32 The Quadrant 020 8332 6262 1–4A
"Much nicer than the chains!" – this "cheap 'n' cheerful" indie is "extremely convenient, being just by Richmond Tube" and produces "consistently excellent pizzas". / TW9 1DN; www.pizzeriarustica.co.uk; Mon-Sat 11 pm, Sun 10 pm; no Amex.

Pizzicotto W8 £40 443
267 Kensington High Street
020 7602 6777 6–1A
"An offshoot of the ever-busy Il Portico" – this "slightly downmarket, but truly excellent-value version of its parent" provides "terrific pizza", "with unusually good ingredient sourcing", and using black dough (healthier so they say). / W8 6NA; www.pizzicotto.co.uk; @pizzicottow8; 10.30 pm, Sun 9.30 pm; closed Mon.

Plateau E14 £74 223
4th Floor 020 7715 7100 12–1C
With its prime Canary Wharf perch offering splendid views of Docklands, this D&D London operation is first-and-foremost "a great place to take clients", if not an especially inspired one. After hours, look out for special evening offers. / E14 5ER; www.plateau-restaurant.co.uk; @plateaulondon; 10.30 pm; closed Sat L & Sun; set weekday L £53 (FP), set dinner £61 (FP).

The Plough SW14 £45 345
42 Christ Church Rd 020 8876 7833 11–2A
A perfect pitstop after a walk in Richmond Park, a few minutes away – this "kid and dog-friendly" pub in a quiet East Sheen lane boasts a wonderful outside terrace as well as an extremely atmospheric interior. All this plus "quality" cooking and "the nicest staff". / SW14 7AF; www.theplough.com; Mon-Thu 9.30 pm, Fri & Sat 10 pm, Sun 9 pm; no Amex.

Plum + Spilt Milk, Great Northern Hotel N1 £69 234
Great Northern Hotel 020 3388 0818 9–3C
This "beautiful dining room" has a "top location" – if you're travelling through King's Cross station anyhow – and it's a particularly handy option on business. Fans say it's "better value than its neighbour, The Gilbert Scott", although like its rival, the food can seem "lacklustre". / N1C 4TB; www.gnhlondon.com; @PlumSpiltMilk; 11 pm, Sun 10 pm.

Poco E2 £45
129a Prichards Rd, Broadway Mkt
020 7739 3042 14–2B
A new opening from a successful Bristol venture aiming to storm Hackney's Broadway Market with its eco-friendly tapas – early reports are of good food, especially for brunch, but that it's "not the most relaxing" spot at busy times. / E2 9AP; www.eatpoco.com; @eatpoco; 11 pm, Sat & Sun 10 pm; SRA-3 star.

POLLEN STREET SOCIAL W1 £101 223
8-10 Pollen St 020 7290 7600 3–2C
"Maybe a victim of its own success?" – Jason Atherton's first solo venture in Mayfair remains one of London's most popular destinations, but "seems to have lost its way a bit". To fans, the "dreamy" and "creative cuisine" is a "perfect indulgence"; and even if the "cool" decor has a challenging acoustic ("for Social, read noisy") they applaud a "refreshingly relaxed approach to fine dining" that's "not too fussy and formal". Doubters, however, have had meals here that "lack any wow-factor" and choke on prices that are now "the wrong side of excruciating". / W1S 1NQ; www.pollenstreetsocial.com; @PollenStSocial; 10.45 pm; closed Sun; set weekday L £69 (FP).

Polpetto W1 £48 233
11 Berwick St 020 7439 8627 4–2D
Fans of Russell Norman's Soho 'bacaro' say it's "so much better" than any of his other Venetian-via-New York 'cichetti' bars. Its ratings aren't that great though, because too many reporters feel it's "overpriced and boring", especially since Florence Knight gave up the stoves. / W1F 0PL; www.polpo.co.uk; 11 pm, Sun 10.30 pm; no bookings.

Polpo £40 222
Harvey Nichols, 109-125 Knightsbridge, SW1
020 7201 8625 6–1D
41 Beak St, W1 020 7734 4479 4–2B
142 Shaftesbury Ave, WC2
020 7836 3119 5–2B
6 Maiden Ln, WC2 020 7836 8448 5–3D
Duke Of York Sq, SW3 020 7730 8900 6–2D
126-128 Notting Hill Gate, W11
020 7229 3283 7–2B
2-3 Cowcross St, EC1 020 7250 0034 10–1A
"Can't see what the hype is (was) about?" Russell Norman's "frenetic", Venetian cichetti cafés are, at their best, "a fun option for a quick bite, with an appealing choice of small plates" but they are "slipping" fast – the food is "losing its edge", service is "very rushed", and "there's not enough space between tables". / www.polpo.co.uk; W1 & EC1 11 pm; WC2 11 pm, Sun 10.30 pm; W1 & EC1 closed D Sun.

Le Pont de la Tour SE1 £78 224
36d Shad Thames 020 7403 8403 10–4D
"There's something about having Tower Bridge in the background that sets the mood just right..." at this D&D London Thames-side landmark (where Tony Blair once hosted dinner with Bill Clinton). But, despite a "beautiful restoration" this year, its Gallic cuisine remains "very mediocre for the

price", and the "huge and complex wine list" likewise comes with "huge mark ups". / SE1 2YE; www.lepontdelatour.co.uk; @lepontdelatour; 10.30 pm, Sun 9.30 pm; no trainers; set weekday L £45 (FP).

Popeseye £47 322

108 Blythe Rd, W14 020 7610 4578 8–1C
36 Highgate Hill, N19 020 3601 3830 9–1B
277 Upper Richmond Rd, SW15
020 8788 7733 11–2A

"Super steaks" from 28-day-hung Aberdeen Angus served with "good chips, green salad and really good wine that's not expensive" is the raison d'être of this trio in Olympia (est 1994), Putney and Highgate; the last of these was new in 2015, and puts in "a huge effort on service in a tough location". There's the odd disappointment recorded, but fans are adamant: "for all the talk of Hawksmoor and Goodman I still prefer Popeseye, so to hell with the new boys!" / www.popeseye.com; 10.30 pm; D only, closed Sun; no credit cards.

Poppies £29 333

59 Old Compton Street, W1
020 7482 2977 5–3A
30 Hawley Cr, NW1 020 7267 0440 9–2B
6-8 Hanbury St, E1 020 7247 0892 13–2C

Fans applaud the "very good chips" and "great-tasting fresh fish" at these chippies in Spitalfields, Camden Town and now Covent Garden, all decorated with post-war memorabilia (founder Pat "Pop" Newland entered the trade aged 11 in 1952). A dissenting minority complain that they've become "overpriced tourist traps".

La Porchetta Pizzeria £34 233

33 Boswell St, WC1 020 7242 2434 2–1D
141-142 Upper St, N1 020 7288 2488 9–2D
147 Stroud Green Rd, N4
020 7281 2892 9–1D
74-77 Chalk Farm Rd, NW1
020 7267 6822 9–2B
84-86 Rosebery Ave, EC1
020 7837 6060 10–1A

"No-nonsense Italian comfort food in very generous helpings" maintains the buzz at these four family-owned north London standbys – most notably "huge, crisp, fresh pizzas". / www.laporchetta.net; Mon-Sat 11 pm, Sun 10 pm; WC1 closed Sat L & Sun; N1, EC1 & NW1 closed Mon-Fri L; N4 closed weekday L; no Amex.

La Porte des Indes W1 £79 335

32 Bryanston St 020 7224 0055 2–2A

"Travel in time and space to Pondicherry" at this exotic venue in a converted subterranean Edwardian ballroom off Marble Arch. "Inside, it's vast, like a tropical forest", and with "fine", rather unusual Franco-Indian cuisine, it adds up to "a real experience": "expensive, but understandably so". / W1H 7EG; www.laportedesindes.com; @LaPorteDesIndes; 11.30 pm, Sun 10.30 pm; no Amex; set weekday L £41 (FP), set Sun L £53 (FP).

Il Portico W8 £55 364

277 Kensington High St 020 7602 6262 8–1D

"Don't be put off by the bland exterior in an unremarkable parade of shops", say fans of this "family-owned stalwart in Kensington", which has been operated by the same family for 50 years. The dated ambience is "very warm" and they serve "wonderful northern Italian (Emilia-Romagna) cuisine, lovingly prepared". / W8 6NA; www.ilportico.co.uk; 11 pm; closed Sun.

Portland W1 £67 543

113 Great Portland St 020 7436 3261 2–1B

"Immaculately prepared", thoughtful dishes delivered "with great enthusiasm" by "youthful and charming" staff create "an air of calm contentment" at this "unassuming" Fitzrovia yearling – one of the best foodie arrivals of recent years. In looks, it's a tad "IKEA-esque". / W1W 6QQ; www.portlandrestaurant.co.uk; 9.45 pm; closed Sun.

Portobello Ristorante W11 £53 343

7 Ladbroke Rd 020 7221 1373 7–2B

"There's a great atmosphere outside when busy… which is often", at this "fun" Italian, just off Notting Hill Gate (by comparison, the indoor decor is a tad "dull"). "Charming" staff provide "reliably enjoyable" Sicilian dishes, and "great pizza". / W11 3PA; www.portobellolondon.co.uk; 10 pm, Fri-Sat 11 pm, Sun 10 pm.

The Portrait, National Portrait Gallery WC2 £65 234

St Martin's Pl 020 7312 2490 5–4B

"A new arrival is faced head-on with an amazing panorama of Nelson, Big Ben, Whitehall and Trafalgar Square", at this roof-top dining room, above the gallery. "The food is seasonal, British, tasty, and a bit unimaginative", but – even if "prices reflect the unique surroundings" – generally "better than you might expect". / WC2H 0HE; www.npg.org.uk/visit/shop-eat-drink.php; Thu-Sat 8.30 pm; closed Mon D, Tue D, Wed D & Sun D; set pre theatre £40 (FP).

Potli W6 £42 543

319-321 King St 020 8741 4328 8–2B

"Better than Indian Zing!" (nearby). This "exceptional and stylish" Hammersmith venue ("crowded and filled with artefacts from India") offers cooking that's "a great deal more accomplished than the street food it bills itself as" – "everything excites the palate, from the cocktail blending basil, cardamom and limoncello with gin, to the last scraping of the gloriously decadent mango shrikhand". / W6 9NH; www.potli.co.uk; @Potlirestaurant; 10.15 pm, Fri & Sat 10:30 pm, Sun 10 pm.

LA POULE AU POT SW1 **£63** 225

231 Ebury St 020 7730 7763 6–2D

"Romance is in the air" of this "extravagantly French" Pimlico veteran, especially "after dark in the magical candlelight" of its "secluded and dim-lit dining spots" (and also "on the pavement, under umbrellas in summer"). Foodwise, its stolid, "rustic" classics are "OK, but nothing special", and delivered – "with a Gallic shrug" – by service that's "haphazard" but generally "friendly, colourful and accommodating". / SW1W 8UT; www.pouleaupot.co.uk; 11 pm, Sun 10 pm.

Prawn On The Lawn N1 **£49** 433

220 St Paul's Rd 020 3302 8668 9–2D

"Absolutely fresh fish, beautifully cooked" is the major selling-point of this "very hipster" fishmonger and restaurant near Highbury & Islington tube. It can get "very cramped – but so what?" / N1 2LY; prawnonthelawn.com; @PrawnOnTheLawn; 11 pm; closed Mon & Sun; no Amex.

Primeur N5 **£48** 434

116 Petherton Rd 020 7226 5271 1–1C

"A great recent find", this Highbury local with communal seating serves "fantastic" sharing plates from an "ever-changing" hand-written menu, plus 'low intervention' wines – "knowledgeable staff help you pair them with the food". "Sit at the bar for the best view of the kitchen – I wanted to order everything!" / N5 2RT; www.primeurn5.co.uk; @Primeurs1; 10.30 pm, Sun 5 pm; closed Mon, Tue L, Wed L, Thu L & Sun D.

Princess of Shoreditch EC2 **£55** 333

76 Paul St 020 7729 9270 13–1B

This well-established gastropub revival of a traditional old watering hole – one of the original hip venues on the Shoreditch-City border – still pulls in a "lively and trendy clientele" with "top food" both in the bar and up the spiral stairs in a more formal dining room. / EC2A 4NE; www.theprincessofshoreditch.com; @princessofs; 10.30 pm, Sun 9 pm; no Amex.

Princess Victoria W12 **£46** 333

217 Uxbridge Rd 020 8749 5886 8–1B

"A beautiful old gin palace" on a busy highway in deepest Shepherd's Bush; the food is "variable" – at best "sensational", at worst just "fine" – but a consistent draw is the "fabulous wine list" (NB "great deal on Mondays, with wine sold at retail prices"). / W12 9DH; www.princessvictoria.co.uk; @pvwestlondon; 10.30 pm, Sun 9.30 pm; no Amex.

Princi W1 **£34** 334

135 Wardour St 020 7478 8888 4–1D

"Fast and furious" smart bakery in Soho with a "great buzz"; "cheap 'n' cheerful with plenty of choice" – "delicious Milanese pizza" wins top billing and "the cakes aren't half bad either". / W1F 0UT; www.princi.com; midnight, Sun 10 pm; no bookings.

Prix Fixe W1 **£42** 332

39 Dean St 020 7734 5976 5–2A

"Who does food at these prices in Soho these days?" "Well-executed French classics" ("the menu won't surprise you") ensure this "reliable" and "exceptional value" bistro is "always busy". It's "very handy for pre- and post-theatre dining", and – as the name suggests – "the prix fixe is not restricted to those hours". / W1D 4PU; www.prixfixe.net; @prixfixelondon; 11.30 pm.

The Promenade at The Dorchester W1 **£120** 244

The Dorchester Hotel, 53 Park Lane

020 7629 8888 3–3A

"A rare treat nowadays, but over half a century it's always been a particular pleasure!" This ultra-plush and "beautiful" lounge provides a picturebook setting for a light bite, but most particularly afternoon tea: "absolutely delicious with simply masses of yummy treats!" / W1K 1QA; 10.30 pm; no shorts.

Provender E11 **£39** 343

17 High St 020 8530 3050 1–1D

This "authentic French bistro" in Wanstead is the latest venture from seasoned restaurateur Max Renzland. It is "deservedly popular" for the "excellence" of its cuisine and a "good-value set lunch" – "the côte de boeuf for two is epic". / E11 2AA; www.provenderlondon.co.uk; @ProvenderBistro; Sun 9 pm, Mon-Thu 10 pm, Fri 10.30 pm, Sat 11.30 pm.

The Providores & Tapa Room W1 **£75** 322

109 Marylebone High St 020 7935 6175 2–1A

"Peter Gordon's genius still works its magic" at his long-established pan-Pacific HQ. The upstairs room is "small, crowded, dark and noisy", but the "fusion dishes are wondrous – simple tastes combine to make something unique and totally delicious". "Great and interesting breakfast" too. / W1U 4RX; www.theprovidores.co.uk; @theprovidores; 10 pm, Sun 9.45 pm; SRA-2 star.

Prufrock Coffee EC1 **£13** 324

23-25 Leather Ln 07852 243 470 10–2A

"Coffee just as it should be – like being back on Bondi beach!" – is found at this haven for caffeine addicts near Chancery Lane, along with "super tasty healthy and slightly different lunch options". / EC1N 7TE; www.prufrockcoffee.com; @PrufrockCoffee; L only; no Amex.

Pulia SE1 **£38** 343

36 Stoney St 020 7407 8766 10–4C

"Authentic food and interesting wine from Puglia" win approval for this invitingly chichi, "friendly and

airy" deli/café (the first outside Italy in the group), a short walk from happening Borough Market. / SE1 9AD; www.pulia.com/london; @Puliauk; 9 pm.

The Punchbowl W1 £48 4 4 4
41 Farm St 020 7493 6841 3–3A
"I went in for a bar snack and got something so much better!" – This attractive Mayfair pub (once owned by Madonna-ex, Guy Ritchie) is something of a "surprise", serving some "really inspired dishes, cooked from the heart". / W1J 5RP; www.punchbowllondon.com; @ThePunchBowlLDN; 11 pm, Sun 10.30 pm; closed Sun D.

Punjab WC2 £33 3 2 3
80 Neal St 020 7836 9787 5–2C
One of London's longest-serving Indians in a handy Covent Garden location, this traditional curry house is still managing to record some very decent food scores. / WC2H 9PA; www.punjab.co.uk; 11 pm, Sun 10.30 pm.

Pure Indian Cooking SW6 £48
67 Fulham High Street 020 7736 2521 11–1B
For a curry fix north of Putney Bridge, this straightforward contemporary Indian is worth remembering – more reports please. / SW6 3JJ; www.pureindiancooking.com; @PureCooking; closed Sat L & Sun L.

Quaglino's SW1 £72 1 1 3
16 Bury St 020 7930 6767 3–3D
Fans "love the glimmering glamour" of this big D&D-group basement in St James's – "make sure you dress up!" As it hots up though, the noise can be "overwhelming", and prices are scary for food that's so "average". / SW1Y 6AJ; www.quaglinos-restaurant.co.uk; @quaglinos; 10.30 pm, Fri & Sat 11 pm; closed Sun; no trainers; set weekday L & dinner £43 (FP).

The Quality Chop House EC1 £48 3 4 3
94 Farringdon Rd 020 7278 1452 10–1A
"Evocative", restored Victorian 'Working Class Caterer', near Exmouth Market, whose "authentic wooden booths" have infamously "uncomfortable benches". At its best currently, it's an all-round success with "enthusiastic" service and "superb quality" British-sourced fare ("meat especially") but it's not consistent – bad days feature "staff all over the place" and "unremarkable", "expensive" dishes. An "exceptionally well-chosen" wine list is the pluspoint you might expect of somewhere part-owned by Jancis Robinson's son. Top Menu Tip – "confit potato to die for". / EC1R 3EA; www.thequalitychophouse.com; @QualityChop; 10.30 pm; closed Sun; SRA-1 star.

Quantus W4 £48 4 5 4
38 Devonshire Rd 020 8994 0488 8–2A
"Fabulous service defines this place" – a "Chiswick neighbourhood gem" that serves a Latino-influenced modern European menu including "great steaks and fish". "Leo, the owner and maître d', is a great character and cements the charm". / W4 2HD; www.quantus-london.com; 10 pm; closed Mon L, Tue L & Sun.

Quattro Passi W1 £96 3 3 2
34 Dover St 020 3096 1444 3–3C
The two-year-old Mayfair outpost of Antonio Mellino's noted Amalfi venue showcases the cuisine of Campania. Ratings are solid, but the vertiginous prices – particularly when it comes to the vino – somewhat restricts appreciation to a business clientele. / W1S 4NG; www.quattropassi.co.uk; @quattropassiuk; 10.30 pm; closed Sun D.

Le Querce SE23 £39 3 4 3
66-68 Brockley Rise 020 8690 3761 1–4D
"It looks just like a café outside", but this "very friendly" family run restaurant in Brockley is known for its "superb value" Italian cooking, with the best choices from the specials board – "an impressive array" that's "particularly interesting". Its ratings have dipped however, and while reports are all upbeat, the most cautious says "it's good, but not as top notch as it used to be". Top Menu Tip – "Three scoops of a vast assortment of esoteric ice cream flavours for less than a fiver!" / SE23 1LN; www.lequerce.co.uk; 9.30 pm, Fri & Sat 9.45 pm, Sun 20.30 pm; closed Mon & Tue L.

Quilon SW1 £71 4 4 2
41 Buckingham Gate 020 7821 1899 2–4B
"Sophisticated and beautifully presented" Keralan cuisine has won much foodie acclaim for the Taj Group's luxurious Indian, near Buckingham Palace, whose plush modern decor teeters between bland and stylish. It's a practical choice too – "is this the only Michelin Star restaurant ever that understands and delivers a perfect working lunch?" / SW1E 6AF; www.quilon.co.uk; @thequilon; 11 pm, Sun 10.30 pm.

Quirinale SW1 £61 4 4 2
North Ct, 1 Gt Peter St 020 7222 7080 2–4C
"A great venue for parliamentarian-spotting – it's easy to understand why lobbyists wine and dine MPs here", when you consider the "exceptional" Italian cuisine ("consistently excellent without being overly fussy") at this "high-quality" basement near Westminster. Also, "it's a quiet room you can easily have a conversation in, and there's an extensive list of Italian wines – what more could you ask for?" / SW1P 3LL; www.quirinale.co.uk; @quirinaleresto; 10.30 pm; closed Sat & Sun.

Quo Vadis W1 **£56**
26-29 Dean St 020 7437 9585 5–2A
Just as it was hitting a "really special" stride, it's all change at the Hart Bros' Soho veteran (hence we've left it un-rated). From autumn 2016, much of the ground floor is set to become a branch of their Barrafina brand. The remainder of the ground floor, the ex-bar, will continue as Quo Vadis, while with echoes of The Ivy, chef Jeremy Lee will refocus more of his efforts on a new dining room within the Quo Vadis members' club (which occupies the floors above). / W1D 3LL; www.quovadissoho.co.uk; 11 pm; closed Sun.

Rabbit SW3 **£49** **443**
172 King's Rd 020 3750 0172 6–3C
"Finally a decent restaurant at the heart of the Kings Road!" – this offbeat "organic, farm-to-table" sibling to Notting Hill's Shed remains an unexpected hit in an area where brainless mediocrity is the prevailing norm. Despite a "cramped space" with "wonky tables and excruciatingly uncomfy seats designed to add to the rustic vibe" the style is "fun" and "there is real originality in many of the tapas-y dishes (even if they are expensive for their small size)". / SW3 4UP; www.rabbit-restaurant.com; @RabbitResto; midnight, Mon 11 pm, Sun 6 pm; closed Mon L & Sun D.

Rabot 1745 SE1 **£60** **322**
2-4 Bedale St 020 7378 8226 10–4C
This choccy-themed bar-with-dining in Borough Market, named after a 250-year-old St Lucia cocoa estate, is a "great chocolatey experience" with interesting food and drink pairings. Plus, of course, "hot chocolate to die for – seriously rich, smooth, luxurious and with deep, deep flavours". / SE1 9AL; www.rabot1745.com; @rabot1745; 9.30 pm; closed Mon.

Ragam W1 **£28** **431**
57 Cleveland St 020 7636 9098 2–1B
"Though not the greatest looker" (and that's after the refurb!) this stalwart Indian near the Telecom Tower remains "first choice for genuine Keralan food" for many reporters, with "the crowning glory being when the bill arrives – £20 a head for grub this good should be impossible!" But its ratings were hit by some unusually downbeat reports this year, saying it was "notably not as good"... "OK but no longer outstanding or destinational". / W1T 4JN; www.ragam.co.uk; 11 pm.

Rail House Café SW1
Nova, Victoria Street no tel 2–4B
From Adam White (the man behind Fitzrovia's popular brunch spot Riding House Café and trendy Village East in Bermondsey) comes a vast new café in Victoria's monumental Nova development. The 330-cover venue is spread over two floors with a raised private dining room and outdoor seating area with al-fresco bar. It's set to open just as our print guide goes to press (in September 2016). / SW1H 0HW.

Rainforest Café W1 **£61** **233**
20-24 Shaftesbury Ave 020 7434 3111 4–3D
"Eating in the Amazon rainforest! Kids love it!", "gorillas/ elephants/ thunder storms..." and all at this theatrical Piccadilly Circus experience – "it's not the greatest food, but it never fails to deliver in the entertainment stakes". / W1V 7EU; www.therainforestcafe.co.uk; @RainforestCafe; 9.30 pm, Sat 10 pm; credit card deposit required to book.

Randall & Aubin W1 **£60** **344**
14-16 Brewer St 020 7287 4447 4–2D
"There's just something about sitting on one of the stools" ("they even replaced the old uncomfortable ones!"), and "watching the world go by", at this "fun-and-frisky" Soho haven (a characterful, tiled ex butcher's shop). "Charming" and "flamboyant" staff provide "so-fresh" seafood and "excellent rôtisserie chicken". / W1F 0SG; www.randallandaubin.com; @randallandaubin; 11 pm, Fri & Sat 11.30 pm, Sun 9.30 pm; booking lunch only.

Randy's Wing Bar E15 **£30**
Here East, 28 East Bay Lane
020 8555 5971 14–1C
A summer 2016 newcomer – this chicken wing specialist at Hackney Wick's Here East development serves everything from their signature American buffalo wings to the Bombay Indian spice and Vietnamese Hanoi Tuk Tuk varieties. / E15 2GW; www.randyswingbar.co.uk; @randyswingbar; 11 pm, Thu-Sun 11.30 pm; closed Mon L.

Rani N3 **£30** **322**
7 Long Ln 020 8349 4386 1–1B
This "always dependable" Gujarati veggie veteran in Finchley is "now under new ownership but still up to scratch" – the buffet is "very good and very cheap", even if the "clean and bright" ambience "could be jollier". / N3 2PR; www.raniuk.com; 10.30 pm.

Raoul's Café **£46** **223**
105-107 Talbot Rd, W11 020 7229 2400 7–1B
13 Clifton Rd, W9 020 7289 7313 9–4A
"The best eggs Benedict in London" and "French toast to die for" make these "busy" Maida Vale ("particularly nice when you can sit outside") and Notting Hill cafés favourites for brunch. The "retro Sixties décor" goes down well, but they're "not family-friendly". / www.raoulsgourmet.com; 10.15 pm, W11 6.15 pm; booking after 5 pm only.

Rasa £38 333
6 Dering St, W1 020 7629 1346 3–2B
Holiday Inn Hotel, 1 Kings Cross, WC1
020 7833 9787 9–3D
55 Stoke Newington Church St, N16
020 7249 0344 1–1C
56 Stoke Newington Church St, N16
020 7249 1340 1–1C
"Remarkable value and delicious South Indian food" still dazzles at the Stoke Newington original of this small Keralan chain (the "decent and very convenient" branch near Oxford Circus is the next most popular). "The overall formula hasn't evolved over the years" however, and ratings generally have declined – "please Rasa, mix it up!" / www.rasarestaurants.com; 10.45 pm; WC1 & W1 closed Sun.

Rasoi SW3 £99 323
10 Lincoln St 020 7225 1881 6–2D
"A feast for the eyes is a cliché, but the dishes here are irresistible!" – Vineet Bhatia's "very quiet and peaceful" townhouse in Chelsea provides "phenomenal", "cross-over" Indian cuisine, and many reports suggest "it's on a level no other can compete with". But even fans concede "you need to get over the 'second-mortgage' prices". STOP PRESS – in summer 2016 the restaurant closed to be reformatted – not yet sure what changes are afoot. / SW3 2TS; www.rasoirestaurant.co.uk; @GujaratiRasoi; 10.30 pm, Sun 9.45 pm; closed Mon & Sat L; set weekday L £30 (FP), set dinner £66 (FP).

Ravi Shankar NW1 £32 322
132-135 Drummond St 020 7388 6458 9–4C
The "wonderful lunchtime buffet is incredible value", at this stalwart café, like many of its rivals in the Little India "just around the corner from Euston Station". / NW1 2HL; 10.30 pm.

Red Fort W1 £66 422
77 Dean St 020 7437 2525 5–2A
This "Soho classic" (which underwent a contemporary revamp some years ago) was more consistently highly rated this year for its "refined Indian cuisine" from a menu "which gets away from the normal well-trodden footpaths". Even fans though still concede that it remains "pricey". / W1D 3SH; redfort.co.uk; @redfortlondon; 10.30 pm; closed Sat L & Sun; no shorts; set weekday L & pre-theatre £42 (FP).

Red Lion & Sun N6 £52 334
25 North Road 020 8340 1780 9–1B
"A lovely location in the heights of Highgate" and "interesting" menu win all-round praise for this "perfect", "old-established" hostelry. / N6; www.theredlionandsun.com; @redlionandsun; 10 pm, Sun 9 pm.

The Red Pepper W9 £48 332
8 Formosa St 020 7266 2708 9–4A
This "cramped but surprisingly good" Italian local in Maida Vale does "great wood-fired pizza (if not much else)" – "fresh, high quality and remarkably consistent given the size of the kitchen!" / W9 1EE; www.theredpepperrestaurant.co.uk; Sat 11 pm, Sun 10 pm; Mon-Thu D only, Fri-Sun open L & D; no Amex.

Le Relais de Venise L'Entrecôte £46 322
120 Marylebone Ln, W1 020 7486 0878 2–1A
18-20 Mackenzie Walk, E14
020 3475 3331 12–1C
5 Throgmorton St, EC2
020 7638 6325 10–2C
"Addictive steak, secret sauce and fries" (and no other menu options) is the winning formula of this "busy" Gallic grill-house chain, whose "efficient but perfunctory", "bums-on-seats" approach adds little to the ambience. "Annoying no-reservations policy" – expect a queue. / www.relaisdevenise.com; W1 11 pm, Sun 10.30 pm; EC2 10 pm; EC2 closed Sat & Sun; no booking.

Le Restaurant de Paul £38 344
29-30 Bedford St, WC2 020 7836 3304 5–3C
Tower 42, Old Broad St, EC2
020 7562 5599 10–2C
Fans of the Covent Garden HQ of the well-known pâtisserie chain say that, away from the bakery counters, its civilised, traditional dining room "deserves to be taken seriously" as a Theatreland destination in its own right, for an "authentically Gallic" light bite or afternoon tea. There is also a year-old, much more contemporary-style outpost in the City's Tower 42. / @PAUL_BAKERY; –.

Restaurant Ours SW3 £68 244
264 Brompton Rd 020 7100 2200 6–2C
"Who is the target market for this strangely mixed experience?" Über-chef Tom Sellers's ambitious South Kensington newcomer – mixing "blingy, nightclub style" with funky culinary aspirations – hasn't yet found its mark. The site comes complete with indoor trees, open kitchen, and the catwalk-style, narrow, glass-floored entrance-walkway it inherited from The Collection (long RIP). However "despite the amazing interior and friendly, solicitous service, it's marred by some very clumsy and overpriced cooking", which "despite Mr Sellers at the helm, is not sharp enough for serious eaters". And "while it's attracting some tall, very thin, very well-dressed young women and their minders, that crowd gets sooo bored sooo quickly". / SW3 2AS; www.restaurant-ours.com; @restaurant_ours; 10 pm, Thu-Sat 11 pm; no bookings at lunch.

Reubens W1 £56 233

79 Baker St 020 7486 0035 2–1A

Long-established kosher deli (ground floor) / restaurant (basement) in Marylebone whose "salt beef on rye bread is still the benchmark" according to fans. Sceptics say it's "indifferent and expensive"... as they have been doing for the last 20 years. / W1U 6RG; www.reubensrestaurant.co.uk; 10 pm; closed Fri D & Sat; no Amex.

The Rib Man E1 £12 54

Brick Lane, Brick Lane Market no tel 13–2C

"A fantastic bloke with a concept and passion that others can only admire": Mark Gevaux is "one of the few pulled-pork purveyors in London to take real care over what he's doing" and sells "massive rolls piled high with meat and his trademark Holy F###k hot sauce". "Lovely piggy goodness!" / E1 6HR; www.theribman.co.uk; @theribman.

Rib Room, Jumeirah Carlton Tower Hotel SW1 £103 232

Cadogan Pl 020 7858 7250 6–1D

This luxurious Belgravia haunt has its fans – "such a special treat" – but the appeal is qualified: "the eponymous rib of beef is splendid but not really backed up by other items", and "to price it at the same level as the Ledbury and Ritz is considerably too high". / SW1X 9PY; www.theribroom.co.uk; @RibRoomSW1; 11 pm, weekends 10.30 pm; set weekday L & dinner £52 (FP).

Riccardo's SW3 £43 232

126 Fulham Rd 020 7370 6656 6–3B

"Always lively, always good", insist fans of this "popular local Italian" in Chelsea applauding its "great welcome from fantastic staff" and "options to satisfy the fussiest eater" ("spelt, wheat-free pasta, etc"). But a sizeable minority still complain that "they're content to rest on their hind legs" here, and find "the overall experience is disappointing". / SW3 6HU; www.riccardos.it; @ricardoslondon; 11.30 pm, Sun 10.30 pm.

The Richmond E8 £53 333

316 Queensbridge Rd 020 7241 1638 14–1A

"Fabulous oysters" at £1 each during happy hour set the tone at Brett Redman's "smartened up" Hackney pub conversion "with a brilliant raw bar attached". Fish dishes including "superb monkfish" also impress. / E8 3NH; www.therichmondhackney.com; @TheRichmond_; midnight, Sun 5 pm; closed Sun D.

Riding House Café W1 £57 223

43-51 Great Titchfield St

020 7927 0840 3–1C

"Quirky decoration lends an interesting and buzzy atmosphere" to this "always lively and bustling" Fitzrovia venue. It's useful for business or breakfast (or both) – for the latter "you can be healthy or sinful according to your mood". / W1W 7PQ; www.ridinghousecafe.co.uk; 10.30 pm, Sun 9.30 pm.

The Rising Sun NW7 £48 323

137 Marsh Ln, Highwood Hill

020 8959 1357 1–1B

This "lively and picturesque pub" in Mill Hill serves "the best food in the area" – a "varied menu of British and Italian dishes" now "back to its high standard" with the return of chef Paolo Mortali. / NW7 4EY; www.therisingsunmillhill.co.uk; @therisingsunpub; 9.30 pm, Sun 8.30 pm; closed Mon L.

Ristorante Frescobaldi W1 £78 332

15 New Burlington Pl 020 3693 3435 4–2A

After a year in operation, this ambitious Mayfair Italian (first UK venture of a 700-year-old Italian wine dynasty) wins praise for its "more-ish menu" and of course "great wines". However, there's a "feeling that this is a missed opportunity" – the room "looks lovely" but "doesn't quite work"; and "prices are high, even for Mayfair" yet "portions are small". / W1S 5HX; www.frescobaldirestaurants.com; @frescobaldi_uk; 11 pm; set weekday L £42 (FP).

The Ritz, Palm Court W1 £77 235

150 Piccadilly 020 7493 8181 3–4C

"The gold standard for afternoon tea" – this "splendid and iconic" room wins praise as "a quintessential English experience with melt-in-the-mouth petit fours, sandwiches and cakes" and even if it's "tooooooo expensive" most reporters feel it's "worth it" to "feel a little bit special". / W1J 9BR; www.theritzlondon.com; 7.30 pm; jacket & tie required; set always available £52 (FP); SRA-2 star.

The Ritz Restaurant, The Ritz W1 £134 345

150 Piccadilly 020 7493 8181 3–4C

"London's most beautiful dining room" (decorated in the style of Louis XVI) "never fails to work its magic" (and you can also "eat out on the terrace overlooking Green Park for a lovely treat"). Historically the "exemplary" service has tended to outshine the "traditional" British cuisine here, but most reports this year found it "exceptionally good in every way". Top Tip – "the dinner-dance on Friday and Saturday is a top experience". / W1J 9BR; www.theritzlondon.com; @theritzlondon; 10 pm; jacket & tie required; set weekday L £74 (FP); SRA-2 star.

Riva SW13 £64 442

169 Church Rd 020 8748 0434 11–1A

"The best authentic north Italian food in London" is a credible claim for Andrea Riva's intimate Barnes fixture – a long-fêted favourite of the fooderati. It is un-changing over the years: it's "a bit expensive", the "drab" decor "needs an update" and "it's rather like

a club: either you are recognised by the proprietor as a regular, or he ignores you". / SW13 9HR; 10.30 pm, Sun 9 pm; closed Sat L.

Rivea, Bulgari Hotel SW7 £71 332
171 Knightsbridge 020 7151 1025 6–1C
The second London outlet of French superchef Alain Ducasse, this "blingy" Knightsbridge basement serves up "wonderfully creative" cuisine: "small dishes of exceptionally high quality that sing of the Mediterranean". Even fans, though, can feel it's "a bit wasted on its hotel-guest clientele". / SW7 1DW; www.bulgarihotels.com; 10.30 pm.

THE RIVER CAFÉ W6 £102 324
Thames Wharf, Rainville Rd
020 7386 4200 8–2C
"So special, but also so nose-bleedingly expensive" – that's the perennial trade-off at Ruth Rogers's world-famous café, whose celebrity is totally at odds with its backstreet Hammersmith location, in a Thames-side wharf shared with hubbie Lord Richard Roger's architectural practice (till the latter moved this year). For its many advocates, it's "the holy grail of restaurants" featuring "phenomenal ingredients" (a "true definition of provenance and quality") on "an ever-changing menu" displaying both "simplicity and complexity"; and all this delivered in a "light and buzzing", "minimalist warehouse-style dining room" next to a riverside terrace that's "stunning on a sunny day". On the downside, service can be "smug", and even those sold on its virtues often leave feeling the prices make it "a glaring con": "it's good, but with this price point attached, it's such a poor representation of the heart, passion and grass roots of Italian cooking, and when you get the bill, you just feel nothing is worth this much!" (Plans for a new Mayfair branch are currently on hold.) / W6 9HA; www.rivercafe.co.uk; @RiverCafeLondon; 9 pm, Sat 9.15 pm; closed Sun D; set weekday L £51 (FP).

Rivington Grill £53 222
178 Greenwich High Rd, SE10
020 8293 9270 1–3D
28-30 Rivington St, EC2
020 7729 7053 13–1B
These "relaxed", "straightforward" grills in Shoreditch and Greenwich – owned by Richard Caring's Caprice Group – delight some reporters with their "lively buzz" and "all-round menu". They can also appear "dull" or "ordinary" however, and invite comparisons with "more edgy competition". / www.rivingtongrill.co.uk; 11 pm, Sun 10 pm; SE10 closed Mon, Tue L & Wed L.

Roast SE1 £70 223
Stoney St 0845 034 7300 10–4C
"A beautiful, light-filled interior" boosts the draw (particularly to business diners) of this "upscale" fixture over Borough Market, which specialises in the cooking of traditional British meat dishes. Aside from the "unbeatable" breakfasts however, the cuisine is no better than "pleasant", especially at prices critics feel are "scandalous". / SE1 1TL; www.roast-restaurant.com; 10.45 pm; closed Sun D.

Rocca Di Papa £37 223
73 Old Brompton Rd, SW7
020 7225 3413 6–2B
75-79 Dulwich Village, SE21
020 8299 6333 1–4D
"Good solid traditional Italian fare" helps fuel the "lively" and "extremely friendly" atmosphere at these South Kensington and Dulwich Village locals, whose "big selling point for parents is that they like children who eat properly (so anything from the main menu is approx. half price)". "Pizza is not only better than PizzaExpress across the road but cheaper" / SW7 11.30 pm; SE21 11 pm.

Rochelle Canteen E2 £51 324
Arnold Circus 020 7729 5677 13–1C
"On a sunny day you feel you have discovered the perfect escape" on the terrace of this "offbeat and vibey", "hidden-London" venue – converted bikesheds of a former school near Spitalfields. Run by Melanie Arnold and Margot Henderson (wife of St John's Fergus), it "creates great flavours from seasonal ingredients" in a "bright, airy canteen setting", and is "one of the few top-quality BYOs". / E2 7ES; www.arnoldandhenderson.com; L only, closed Sat & Sun; no Amex.

Rocket £46 333
2 Churchill Pl, E14 020 3200 2022 12–1C
201 Bishopsgate, EC2 020 7377 8863 13–2B
6 Adams Ct, EC2 020 7628 0808 10–2C
For a "decent" lunchtime or post-work pizza, salad or steak, these "cheap 'n' cheerful" cafés around the City and Canary Wharf receive a number of recommendations. / 10.30 pm, Sun 9.30 pm; W1 closed Sun; EC2 closed Sat & Sun; SW15 Mon-Wed D only, Bishopsgate closed Sun D, E14.

Rök £42 422
149 Upper Street, N1 no tel 9–3D
26 Curtain Rd, EC2 020 7377 2152 13–2B
"Outstanding smoked goods and pickled everything" inspire fans of the "brilliant Nordic-inspired food" at this white-walled Scandi-look yearling (which since mid-2016 now has an Islington sibling too). "Tables are squashed" however, and sceptics – who scent "hype" – claim "all the dishes taste the same".

Roka £80 433
30 North Audley St, W1 020 7305 5644 3–2A
37 Charlotte St, W1 020 7580 6464 2–1C
Aldwych House, 71-91 Aldwych, WC2
020 7294 7636 2–2D
Unit 4, Park Pavilion, 40 Canada Sq, E14
020 7636 5228 12–1C

"Exquisite" dishes "bursting with flavour" – be they "sumptuous sushi and sashimi" or "wonderful robata-yaki style BBQ" – are the hallmark of these "cool and vibrant" Japanese-fusion operations. The Charlotte Street original is still the best: "sit at the bar made of slabs of tree trunk and watch the chefs' delicate preparations!" / www.rokarestaurant.com; 11.15 pm, Sun 10.30 pm; booking: max 8.

Romulo Café W8 £50 333

343 Kensington High Street
020 3141 6390 6–1A

The first international branch (in Kensington) of a restaurant group from the Philippines (owned by the grandchildren of General Carlos Romulo) showcasing Filipino cuisine. Lorenzo Maderas (formerly of Latin American/Japanese fusion spot Sushisamba) oversees the kitchen – early reports say the place is "trying hard", and "worth a second visit". / W8 6NW; www.romulocafe.co.uk; @romulolondon; midnight, Sun 11.30 pm.

Rosa's £35 332

5 Gillingham Street, SW1
020 3813 6773 2–4C
23a Ganton St, W1 020 7287 9617 4–2B
48 Dean St, W1 020 7494 1638 5–3A
246 Fulham Rd, SW10 020 7583 9021 6–3B
Atlantic Road, SW9 no tel 11–2D
Westfield Stratford City, E15
020 8519 1302 14–1D
12 Hanbury St, E1 020 7247 1093 13–2C

"Does what it says on the tin!" – these "reliable" cafés are a trusty source of "tasty, unpretentious Thai food", with the "heart-of-Soho" branch by far the best known. / www.rosaslondon.com; 10.30 pm, Fri & Sat 11 pm, Ganton St Sun 10 pm; some booking restrictions apply.

Rossopomodoro £43 322

John Lewis, 300 Oxford St, W1
020 7495 8409 3–2A
50-52 Monmouth St, WC2
020 7240 9095 5–3B
214 Fulham Rd, SW10 020 7352 7677 6–3B
1 Rufus St, N1 020 7739 1899 13–1B
10 Jamestown Rd, NW1 020 7424 9900 9–3B
46 Garrett Ln, SW18 020 8877 9903 11–2B

"Surprisingly good pizza" – "really fresh and authentic" with "crispy bases" and "fresh mozzarella and other ingredients imported from Italy" – wins praise for this Naples-based chain. Service can be "disorganised" however, and depending on your tastes, the ambience is either "pleasantly frenetic" or "chaotic and noisy". / www.rossopomodoro.co.uk; 11.30 pm, WC2 Sun 11.30 pm.

Roti Chai W1 £46 434

3 Portman Mews South 020 7408 0101 3–1A

"Good Indian street food is hard to come by... even in India!", but this upbeat two-floor venue near Selfridges (no-booking ground floor, more formal basement) "brilliantly captures the charm and tastes of railway station vendors of yore" with its "varied dishes, amazing flavours, and great value for money". / W1H 6HS; www.rotichai.com; @rotichai; 10.30 pm.

Roti King, Ian Hamilton House NW1 £22 521

40 Doric Way 07966 093467 9–3C

"Boy, it gets crowded" in this "friendly but chaotic" Euston basement caff ("there's no real chance of avoiding queueing or being cheek-by-jowl at a shared table"). Why? – "the best freshly made rotis outside of Malaysia" (plus "very tasty" noodle dishes) at bargain prices. / NW1 1LH.

Rotorino E8 £48 233

434 Kingsland Rd 020 7249 9081 14–1A

Stevie Parle's low-lit, Italian-inspired kitchen in Dalston again inspired somewhat mixed feelings: most reporters applaud "interesting, yet ungimmicky" culinary creations plus "charming" staff, but to a significant minority the food seems "over-priced", and "lacks the flair associated with a big-name chef". / E8 4AA; www.rotorino.com; @Rotorino; 11 pm.

Rotunda Bar & Restaurant, Kings Place N1 £55 343

90 York Way 020 7014 2840 9–3C

"Amazing views over the canal" from the outside terrace, are a highlight of this "very relaxing" arts centre brasserie. Service is "first class" too, and the food is "very respectably cooked". / N1 9AG; www.rotundabarandrestaurant.co.uk; @rotundalondon; 10.30 pm; set weekday L £34 (FP).

Roux at Parliament Square, RICS SW1 £88 553

12 Great George St 020 7334 3737 2–3C

"Faultless cuisine" (better than MPs deserve) distinguishes the Roux family's formal Parliament Square outlet, where MasterChef winner Steve Groves thrills diners "every time". Critics say the setting is "dull" but we agree with those who find it 'stately'. / SW1P 3AD; www.rouxatparliamentsquare.co.uk; 10 pm; closed Sat & Sun; set weekday L £52 (FP).

Roux at the Landau, The Langham W1 £94 344

1c Portland Pl 020 7965 0165 2–1B

"The room will make your date swoon", at this "oasis", over the road from Broadcasting House, whose spaciousness and serenity also mark it out as being "great for a business lunch". "Classic

cuisine is beautifully presented, and immaculately served". / W1B 1JA; www.rouxatthelandau.com; @Langham_Hotel; 10.30 pm; closed Sat L & Sun; no trainers.

Rowley's SW1 **£70** 2 2 2

113 Jermyn St 020 7930 2707 4–4D

This St James's veteran occupies the original Wall's sausages and ice cream premises. Some swear by the Chateaubriand steak and "endless fries", but others say its grills are "not special" and "overpriced for what you get" ("they have to pay for that real estate somehow"). / SW1Y 6HJ; www.rowleys.co.uk; @rowleys_steak; 10.30 pm.

Rox Burger SE13 **£26** 4 3 3

82 Lee High Rd 020 3372 4631 1–4D

"Amazing burgers" mean this Lewisham joint is "so popular you can't always get a table" – in fact, "the only criticism is that it's too small!" ("although they do a takeaway service now, too"). The veggie burgers and craft beers are excellent, "and the freshly made lemonade is out of this world". / SE13 5PT; www.roxburger.com; @RoxburgerUK; 10 pm, Fri & Sat 11 pm.

Royal China **£48** 3 1 2

24-26 Baker St, W1 020 7487 4688 2–1A
805 Fulham Rd, SW6 020 7731 0081 11–1B
13 Queensway, W2 020 7221 2535 7–2C
30 Westferry Circus, E14
020 7719 0888 12–1B

Legions of fans still hail "the best dim sum outside of Hong Kong" at these "always buzzing" Cantonese stalwarts. Some reporters feel they are "starting to live on their reputation" however, but one constant is the "brusque service – like a downmarket airline!" / www.royalchinagroup.co.uk; 10.45 pm, Fri & Sat 11.15 pm, Sun 9.45 pm; no booking Sat & Sun L.

Royal China Club W1 **£75** 4 3 3

40-42 Baker St 020 7486 3898 2–1A

"Even better than Hong Kong" is the wild claim made by fans of the dim sum at this Marylebone flagship for the China Club group – it's "pricier than the rest, but a cut above, so worth it". And don't arrive late for your booking: "they limit your time to 1.5 hours because they're always packed at the weekend". / W1U 7AJ; www.royalchinagroup.co.uk; 11 pm, Sun 10.30 pm.

The Royal Exchange Grand Café, The Royal Exchange EC3 **£56** 2 2 4

The Royal Exchange Bank
020 7618 2480 10–2C

The grandeur of its majestic covered courtyard setting, and its heart-of-the-City location makes this seafood café a "constant, convenient rendezvous" for business, despite "lackadaisical service and pricey uninspired fare". / EC3V 3LR; www.royalexchange-grandcafe.co.uk; @rexlondon; 10 pm; closed Sat & Sun.

RSJ SE1 **£51** 3 3 2

33 Coin St 020 7928 4554 10–4A

"A real stalwart!" – Nigel Wilkinson's South Bank fixture, by the National Theatre, is an exemplar of "consistently solid, French-bourgeois food at fair prices". 'Nul points' for the '80s interior decor, but the wine list is "amazing" – "probably the best Loire selection in the world". / SE1 9NR; www.rsj.uk.com; @RSJWaterloo; 11 pm; closed Sat L & Sun; set weekday L & dinner £25 (FP).

Rubedo N16 **£43** 4 4 3

35 Stoke Newington Church St
020 7254 0364 1–1C

"Food from the heart!" Culinary results can be "exceptional" – and are matched with "organic, non-filtered wines from a temperature-controlled wine cellar", plus "friendly and knowledgeable" service – at this simple new bistro, on Stokie's main drag. / N16 0NX; www.rubedolondon.com; @rubedolondon; 10 pm, Fri & Sat 10.30 pm; closed Mon & Sun D.

Rucoletta EC2 **£47** 2 2 1

6 Foster Lane 020 7600 7776 10–2C

"The food's honest, not flashy", and "decent value" at this handy Italian "in the heart of the City (near St Paul's)" – "extremely popular at lunchtime" (including with business lunchers), when "the little conservatory at the back is one of the nicer places to sit in the area". / EC2V 6HH; www.rucoletta.co.uk; @RucolettaLondon; 9.30 pm, Thu-Sat 10 pm; closed Sat D & Sun; no Amex.

Rugoletta **£38** 4 3 3

308 Ballards Ln, N12 020 8445 6742 1–1B
59 Church Ln, N2 020 8815 1743 1–1B

"You feel like you're in Italy" at these traditional Barnet and East Finchley locals, which are family-run "and it shows". "It's very Lady and the Tramp, the spaghetti-sharing scene – AND the spaghetti is exceptionally good!"

Rules WC2 **£78** 4 3 5

35 Maiden Ln 020 7836 5314 5–3D

"History oozes out of the walls" of London's oldest restaurant (established 1798) – still one of its most "iconic", whose "olde-worlde, panelled interior" has a "priceless warmth and depth". Many a Londoner still considers it "a reliable old favourite" for "traditional British roasts, games, pies and oysters", but it has seemed more and more "overpriced" in recent times – any more, and it will achieve the Covent Garden tourist-trap status it's heretofore miraculously avoided. / WC2E 7LB; www.rules.co.uk; 11.30 pm, Sun 10.30 pm; no shorts.

Le Sacré-Coeur N1 £36 [4][4][4]
18 Theberton St 020 7354 2618 9–3D
"Step in from Theberton Street and you're in a little bit of France"… (in reality a veteran bistro, just north of Angel). "Good simple, rustic traditional French fare with good size portions and a well-priced wine offer". / N1 0QX; www.lesacrecoeur.co.uk; @LeSacreCoeurUK; 11 pm, Fri & Sat 11.30 pm, Sun 10.30 pm; set weekday L £22 (FP).

Sacro Cuore NW10 £36 [4][3][3]
45 Chamberlayne Rd 020 8960 8558 1–2B
"A serious contender for best pizza in London", this Kensal Rise 4-year-old has now been joined by a branch in Crouch End that's "even better". The Neapolitan-style pizza is "soft, light and airy" ("just the right internal bounce with crisp searing and delicious flavour"), and topped with "ludicrously good tomato sauce" and "super-fresh mozzarella di buffala". / NW10 3NB; www.sacrocuore.co.uk/menu.html; @SacroCuorePizza; 10.30 pm, Fri & Sat 11 pm; no Amex.

Sagar £36 [3][3][2]
17a Percy St, W1 020 7631 3319 3–2B
31 Catherine St, WC2 020 7836 6377 5–3D
157 King St, W6 020 8741 8563 8–2C
The South Indian vegetarian fare at this small chain (Covent Garden, Tottenham Court Road, Hammersmith and Harrow) "is consistently good and great value for money". "The excellent thali and dosa make up for the decor – you're here for the food". / www.sagarveg.co.uk; Sun-Thu 10.45 pm, Fri & Sat 11.30 pm.

Sagardi EC2
Cordy House, 87-95 Curtain Road awaiting tel 13–1B
A Basque-inspired international group – with operations from Barcelona to Buenos Aires – which opened its first London outpost in Shoreditch in late summer 2016. Galician (Txuleton) beef cooked on a charcoal grill is a mainstay of both menu and decor, and there's a pintxos bar serving Basque ciders, as well as wine and beer. / EC2A 3AH; @Sagardi_UK.

Sager + Wilde E2 £38 [2][4][4]
193 Hackney Rd 020 8127 7330 13–1C
"It's not about the food" at this "Brooklyn meets Hackney" haunt – "the highlight is definitely the amazing wines by the glass" ("many with real bottle age, without paying the earth"). This said, its cheese toasties ("great smell") and charcuterie are "well considered and well prepared". / E2 8JP; www.sagerandwilde.com; @snw_paradiserow; 10 pm; closed weekday L.

Sager + Wilde Restaurant E2 £56 [3][3][4]
250 Paradise Row 020 7613 0478 13–1D
"A wine-lover's haven, and the food's good as well" at this "fantastic" Bethnal Green railway arch venue, by the couple behind the popular Hackney Road wine bar of the same name. "All the staff are so helpful and knowledgeable" – "not to mention the great wines available by the glass", and "hearty, well-crafted British fare". / E2 9LE; www.sagerandwilde.com; @sagerandwilde; midnight.

Saigon Saigon W6 £39 [3][3][3]
313-317 King St 020 8748 6887 8–2B
"Authentic" Vietnamese flavours, a "friendly atmosphere" and "good prices" ensure that this long-serving local in Hammersmith is often busy – so it's worth booking. / W6 9NH; www.saigon-saigon.co.uk; @saigonsaigonuk; 11 pm, Sat & Mon 10 pm.

St John EC1 £65 [5][4][3]
26 St John St 020 7251 0848 10–1B
"A pioneer of British food" – Fergus Henderson & Trevor Gulliver's "austere" but "staunch" Smithfield ex-smokehouse remains an "amazingly consistent, ever-quirky" source of "honest" enjoyment. "Staff are so accommodating, the atmosphere is relaxed and constantly buzzing", and the focus is on the "incredible" dishes: be it "outlandish stuff (all the bits of the animal that you didn't know about that you then think you could maybe eat); or something traditional done impressively well." Top Tip – regulars go to the "atmospheric" adjacent bar, with its "simple but perfectly adequate menu". / EC1M 4AY; www.stjohngroup.uk.com; @SJRestaurant; Mon -Sun 11 pm; closed Sat L & Sun D.

St John Bread & Wine E1 £56 [5][3][2]
94-96 Commercial St 020 7251 0848 13–2C
This "stark (very St John)" white-walled canteen near Spitalfields is arguably "reminiscent of a public convenience", but it's "always a treat to go there". The often "wacky" and offal-centric British dishes are "exceptional" – "mouth-wateringly good" – and "they always seem to have a wine that you've never tried before, and it's always first class". Top Tip – breakfast comprises "bacon sandwich heaven". / E1 6LZ; www.stjohngroup.uk.com/spitalfields; @StJBW; Mon 8 pm, 10.30 pm.

St Johns N19 £46 [3][3][5]
91 Junction Rd 020 7272 1587 9–1C
A "favourite local gastropub" in Archway, where the refurb of the front bar and gorgeous old rear dining room (built as a ballroom) is now complete. Despite the gentrification, "it still has great beer" and "food that pleases everyone". / N19 5QU; www.stjohnstavern.com; @stjohnstavern; Mon 10 pm, 11 pm, Sun 9 pm; closed Mon L; no Amex; booking max 12 may apply.

Saint Luke's Kitchen, Library WC2 £56
112 Saint Martin's Lane 020 3302 7912 5–4C
Near the Coliseum, a boutique-guesthouse 'Library', which launched a new restaurant in late spring 2016, whose menu is to rotate every 6-8 weeks in accordance with a new guest chef with a forthcoming cook book launch to plug! No feedback yet on this splendid concept, but it's certainly a handsomely designed and very convenient venue. / WC2N 4BD; www.lib-rary.com/restaurant; @LibraryLondon; 1 am; closed Sun.

St Moritz W1 £54 4 3 3
161 Wardour St 020 7734 3324 4–1C
"Sharing a delicious fondue is always romantic" and where better than this "wonderful, olde worlde" chalet-style stalwart in the heart of Soho, which "feels just like you are in Switzerland!" – "not the lightest of meals" but surprisingly good. "There's nothing else like it in London" – long may it survive! / W1F 8WJ; www.stmoritz-restaurant.co.uk; Mon-Sat 11.30 pm, Sun 10.30 pm.

Sakagura W1
8 Heddon Street no tel 4–3B
From the group behind Shoryu ramen and The Japan Centre – an autumn 2016 opening in the Crown Estates development just off Regent Street. A theatrical robata grill will contribute dishes to a menu including udon, soba noodles and sushi, alongside a wide range of sake, from leading brand Gekkeikan. / W1B 4BU; www.sakaguralondon.com; @sakaguraldn.

Sake No Hana SW1 £76 3 1 2
23 St James's St 020 7925 8988 3–4C
This offbeat, potentially impressive Japanese-inspired outfit has an unusual '60s setting next to The Economist in St James's, and its "trendy" but soulless decor was the result of a refit (overseen by Alan Yau) several years ago. Its modern Asian cuisine can be "incredible", but is too often "only OK at the top-end prices" making the "patchy" service all the harder to bear. / SW1A 1HA; www.sakenohana.com; @sakenonhana; 11 pm, Fri & Sat 11.30 pm; closed Sun.

Salaam Namaste WC1 £36 3 4 3
68 Millman St 020 7405 3697 2–1D
"An Indian with a real difference", this little place "off the beaten track in Bloomsbury" serves up an "interesting menu of carefully spiced dishes" – "and it's good value for central London". / WC1N 3EF; www.salaam-namaste.co.uk; @SalaamNamasteUK; 11.30 pm, Sun 11 pm.

Sale e Pepe SW1 £68 3 4 4
9-15 Pavilion Road 020 7235 0098 6–1D
"Always very welcoming staff" ("completely nuts!") help drive the "fun" atmosphere at this "genuine" ("cramped" and "noisy") trattoria, hidden away near Harrods, which is "unchanged in over two decades" – "a fantastic all-round experience" with "a wide choice of tasty dishes". / SW1X 0HD; www.saleepepe.co.uk.

Salloos SW1 £55 4 3 2
62-64 Kinnerton St 020 7235 4444 6–1D
This age-old survivor in a Belgravia mews is known for its "very good old-fashioned Pakistani cuisine", in particular "brilliant lamb chops". Over the years however, perhaps "due to a seemingly high proportion of Gulf clientele, prices have sky-rocketed". / SW1X 8ER; www.salloos.co.uk; 11 pm; closed Sun; may need 5+ to book.

Salmontini SW1 £72 2 2 3
1 Pont St 020 7118 1999 6–1D
Mixed feedback on this Belgravia yearling some still recall [illegible] Drones (long RIP) and nowadays a plush Beirut-backed operation. Foes say it's "a good location wasted" – "all show, no substance" – but fans applaud "a great variation" on its predecessors, with very good cooking (with smoked fish and sushi the speciality). / SW1X 9EJ; www.salmontini.com; @Salmontini_Uk; 10.45 pm, Fri & Sat 11.15 pm, Sun 10.30 pm.

Salon Brixton SW9 £46 4 3 3
18 Market Row 020 7501 9152 11–2D
"A tiny upstairs restaurant in the atmospheric and hip Brixton market, whose crammed-together tables only add to the atmosphere". It serves "very good, adventurous small plates" and there's also an ever-changing, no-choice set menu. / SW9 8LD; www.salonbrixton.co.uk; @Salon_Brixton; 10 pm; closed Mon & Sun D.

Le Salon Privé TW1 £46 4 4 4
43 Crown Rd 020 8892 0602 1–4A
"You can't fault the food" at this classic French bistro, which has "hit its stride" since taking over the St Margarets site of the former Brula (RIP). "It's very good now – actually, excellent!" / TW1 3EJ; lesalonprive.net; @lesalon_tweet; 10.30 pm; closed Mon & Sun D.

Salt & Honey W2 £47 3 4 2
28 Sussex Pl 020 7706 7900 7–1D
This "tiny bistro" serving "imaginative home cooking" is a "welcome new local in the restaurant desert near Paddington station", set up by the Kiwi duo behind Fulham's Manuka Kitchen. / W2 2TH; www.saltandhoneybistro.com; @SaltHoneyBistro; 10 pm, Sun 9 pm; closed Mon; set weekday L £26 (FP).

Salt Yard W1 £49 3 3 3
54 Goodge St 020 7637 0657 2–1B
"Upmarket Italian/Spanish tapas", ("some genuinely exciting standouts") served by "knowledgeable but not over-bearing" staff in an "informal" setting

earn enduring popularity for this well-known Fitzrovia haunt (the original of Simon Mullins's small group), even if it no longer appears as cutting edge as it once did. / W1T 4NA; www.saltyard.co.uk; @SaltYardGroup; 10.45 pm, Sun 9.45 pm.

Salut N1 £50 443
412 Essex Rd 020 3441 8808 9–3D
"A gem of a place situated inauspiciously at the wrong end of Essex Road" – a new Islington opening on the site of 3 Course (RIP), whose "location can be overlooked" thanks to its "taste-bud tickling" modern European fare, with interesting Nordic and German touches. / N1 3PJ; www.salut-london.co.uk; @Salut_London; 11 pm, Sun 10 pm.

Salvation In Noodles £34 322
122 Balls Pond Rd, N1 020 7254 4534 14–1A
2 Blackstock Rd, N4 020 7254 4534 9–1D
"Still a fave for pho" – a "cheap 'n' cheerful" Dalston Vietnamese, which also has a lower-profile, year-old sibling in Finsbury Park. / www.salvationinnoodles.co.uk;

Samarkand W1
33 Charlotte Street 020 3871 4969 2–1C
Vodka has replaced sherry at this Fitzrovia basement, where the Hart Bros' tapas-spot Fino (RIP) has been usurped by this Uzbeki venture – named for the famous city on the Silk Road – which opened in late summer 2016. Plov (or pilaf) is the best-known central Asian dish. / W1T 1RR; www.samarkand.london; @SamarkandLondon.

San Carlo Cicchetti £51 334
215 Piccadilly, W1 020 7494 9435 4–4C
30 Wellington St, WC2 020 7240 6339 5–3D
"If the Tardis had been done up with a wealth of gold and mirrors" it would be akin to the "deceptively small-looking" Covent Garden branch of this northern-owned Venetian tapas chain, which is a "quieter and calmer" choice than its "really buzzy" sibling, "conveniently located a few steps from Piccadilly Circus tube". Critics accuse them of "slightly aggressive pricing", but most reports praise the "extensive, something-for-everyone menu" of "fairly authentic" small plates. / www.sancarlocicchetti.co.uk; –.

San Daniele del Friuli N5 £44 343
72 Highbury Park 020 7226 1609 9–1D
This "traditional" family-run Italian is "a good place for a quiet night out" in Highbury Park. Its kitchen sends out food that's "always good and sometimes very good". / N5 2XE; www.sandanielehighbury.co.uk; 10.30 pm; closed Mon L, Tue L, Wed L & Sun; no Amex.

The Sands End SW6 £51 233
135 Stephendale Rd 020 7731 7823 11–1B
Fans of this deepest Fulham gastroboozer still say it's "great fun", but there were a couple of reports this year over "very basic service and food issues", including the odd "shocking" dish. / SW6 2PR; www.thesandsend.co.uk; @thesandsend; 10 pm, Sun 9 pm.

Santa Maria £33 543
92-94 Waterford Road, SW6
020 7384 2844 6–4A
15 St Mary's Rd, W5 020 8579 1462 1–3A
"Superlative pizzas" – "up there with the best in Naples" – served by "warm and welcoming staff" have made the "tiny and squashed" W5 original one of the biggest things ever to happen to Ealing. Its new "well-designed" Fulham sibling is going down well too – "a great addition to SW6"… you can even book!

Santini SW1 £79 233
29 Ebury St 020 7730 4094 2–4B
This "upmarket" stalwart Belgravia Italian (an A-lister favourite in days of yore) with a "lovely terrace for summer" wins pretty solid praise for its overall appeal. "It's on the pricey side however" and its harshest critics feel "the food's not up to scratch". / SW1W 0NZ; www.santini-restaurant.com; 10 pm, Sat 11 pm.

Santore EC1 £46 433
59-61 Exmouth Mkt 020 7812 1488 10–1A
This "very genuine" Exmouth Market venue serves up "excellent" Neapolitan fare including pizza, all in notably "large portions". "A little piece of Italy in London", it's "family-friendly" and a good choice for Sunday lunch. / EC1R 4QL; www.santorerestaurant.london; @Santore_london; 11 pm; set weekday L £29 (FP).

Sapori Sardi SW6 £48 322
786 Fulham Rd 020 7731 0755 11–1B
"A home-from-home!" – fans continue to laud the "interesting, simple Sardinian food" and "friendly staff" at this "splendid place" in Fulham. / SW6 5SL; www.saporisardi.co.uk; @saporisardi; 11 pm; no Amex.

Sardine N1
15 Micawber Street 020 7490 0144 13–1A
Former Rotorino head chef Alex Jackson cooks much of the French-centric cuisine over a charcoal grill in Stevie Parle's simple, packed-in newcomer, between Angel and Old Street, which opened in September 2016. / N1 7TB; www.sardine.london; @sardinelondon.

Sardo W1 £58 322
45 Grafton Way 020 7387 2521 2–1B
This "authentic Sardinian" in Fitzrovia serves "consistently excellent food" and the "fish is always good and fresh". But it's "a little cramped", and

one former fan fears it may be "living on its past reputation" somewhat nowadays. / W1T 5DQ; www.sardo-restaurant.com; 11 pm; closed Sat L & Sun.

Sarracino NW6 £45 4 2 2
186 Broadhurst Gdns 020 7372 5889 1–1B
West Hampstead trattoria "stalwart" serving "traditional Italian dishes at a reasonable price" – "it's known for its pizzas", but "pastas and mains are equally good". / NW6 3AY; www.sarracinorestaurant.com; 11 pm; closed weekday L.

Sartoria W1 £71 2 3 3
20 Savile Row 020 7534 7000 4–3A
Fans do say D&D London's "upmarket" expense-accounter favourite in Mayfair is "much-improved" since it was re-launched in late 2015 with Francesco Mazzei at the stoves. But his arrival has done little to shake the overall consensus on this "so comfortable" but "somewhat impersonal" Italian: "unexciting and pricey". / W1S 3PR; www.sartoria-restaurant.co.uk; @SartoriaRest; 10.45 pm; closed Sun; set weekday L £37 (FP).

Satay House W2 £35 3 2 2
13 Sale Pl 020 7723 6763 7–1D
"Lip smacking" (if sometimes slightly 'rough-edged') Malaysian food continues to maintain the appeal of this "friendly" stalwart (est 1973) – a two-floor operation, in a quiet street off Edgware Road. / W2 1PX; www.satay-house.co.uk; 11 pm.

Sauterelle, Royal Exchange EC3 £62 3 3 4
Bank 020 7618 2483 10–2C
"Stunning views over the interior of the delightful Royal Exchange", a "comfortable ambience, reliable food and an excellent wine list" make this D&D London mezzanine "a great place to enjoy a decent dinner in the heart of the City". On the debit side, "you certainly pay for it". / EC3V 3LR; www.sauterelle-restaurant.co.uk; 9.30 pm; closed Sat & Sun; no trainers; set weekday L & dinner £35 (FP).

Savini at Criterion W1 £86 1 1 2
224 Piccadilly 020 7930 1459 4–4D
"Another dud" – this "extraordinary neo-Byzantine dining room" ("possibly the most jaw-dropping space in the West End") – is so "disappointing when one considers just how great it could be." With the previous incumbent going into administration, this new Milanese régime is not only "eyewateringly expensive" but too often provides "shocking food and inattentive service". / W1J 9HP; www.saviniatcriterion.co.uk; @SaviniMilano; midnight.

Savoir Faire WC1 £39 3 3 3
42 New Oxford St 020 7436 0707 5–1C
Budget, two floor Gallic bistro decorated with posters from West End productions, handy for the British Museum – "very good" classics at affordable prices. / WC1A 1EP; www.savoir.co.uk; 10.30 pm, Sun 10 pm.

The Savoy Hotel, Savoy Grill WC2 £89 2 3 3
Strand 020 7592 1600 5–3D
This "elegant" panelled grill room has for decades been a "prestigious" destination. Under Gordon Ramsay's reign, the "heftily priced" British cooking can seem a little "short of its ambitions", but most reports are upbeat, and the place remains a popular rendezvous, particularly for "a discreet business lunch". / WC2R 0EU; www.gordonramsayrestaurants.com; @savoygrill; 11 pm, Sun 10.30 pm; set weekday L & pre theatre £31 (FP).

The Savoy Hotel, Thames Foyer WC2 £79 2 3 5
The Savoy, The Strand 020 7420 2111 5–3D
"The afternoon tea of dreams" – "a wonderful range of teas" coupled with "absolutely fantastic pâtisserie" – is regularly reported in the "lavish, comfortable and enthralling" central lounge of this London landmark: service in particular "helps make for a delightful experience". / WC2R; www.fairmont.com/savoy-london; @fairmonthotels; 11 pm.

Scalini SW3 £76 3 2 3
1-3 Walton St 020 7225 2301 6–2C
"Being always full and a bit cramped only adds to the atmosphere" of this "old-fashioned" Italian on the fringes of Knightsbridge. Arguably this is "safety first" cooking and there's no doubting the "sky-high prices", but "you'll eat well" and it's "great fun". / SW3 2JD; www.scalinilondon.co.uk; 11.30 pm; no shorts.

Scandinavian Kitchen W1 £14 3 3 3
61 Great Titchfield St 020 7580 7161 2–1B
"The coffee is good and the smorgasbord offerings are excellent" – "especially the open sandwiches" – at this Nordic café/grocer in Fitzrovia. "You can also stock up on your favourite Scandi store-cupboard goodies". / W1W 7PP; www.scandikitchen.co.uk; @scanditwitchen; 7 pm, Sat 6 pm, Sun 4 pm; L only; no bookings.

SCOTT'S W1 £80 4 5 5
20 Mount St 020 7495 7309 3–3A
"Impossibly glamorous" and "oozing class" – Richard Caring's "sumptuous" Mayfair star-magnet "always creates a sense of occasion". "Effortlessly polished" service provides "impeccable" fish and seafood ("so fresh it practically swims onto your plate!") in an "understated" setting full of "old world charm". / W1K 2HE; www.scotts-restaurant.com; 10.30 pm, Sun 0 pm; booking max 6 may apply.

Sea Containers, Mondrian London SE1 £68 224
20 Upper Ground 0808 234 9523 10–3A
The "nautical-themed setting" and "splendid Thames views" of this American-owned hotel dining room on the South Bank "do justice to the former shipping-line building's heritage". Instances of food that's "nothing exciting or special" however, lead to numerous gripes about the "unwarranted price tag". / SE1 9PD; www.mondrianlondon.com; @MondrianLDN; 11 pm.

Seafresh SW1 £38 342
80-81 Wilton Rd 020 7828 0747 2–4B
This "brill fish and seafood resto" in Pimlico has for many years attracted "millionaires, MPs and taxi drivers" with its "delicious fresh fish 'n' chips" – "and the Greek salad's good, too". / SW1V 1DL; www.seafresh-dining.com; 10.30 pm; closed Sun.

The Sea Shell NW1 £44 332
49 Lisson Grove 020 7224 9000 9–4A
One of London's best-established chippies is, say fans, "still difficult to beat" and "a great stop-off for fresh fish 'n' chips". Aficionados feel that "the restaurant section lags behind its standout takeout". / NW1 6UH; www.seashellrestaurant.co.uk; @SeashellRestaur; 10.30 pm; closed Sun.

Season Kitchen N4 £42 332
53 Stroud Green Rd 020 7263 5500 9–1D
Fabulous-for-Finsbury Park local with an "uncompromising short menu" of seasonal specials: critics may find the choice "limited", but on most accounts it's "all the better for it" given the "interesting" cooking. / N4 3EF; www.seasonkitchen.co.uk; @seasonkitchen; 10.30 pm, Sun 8 pm; D only.

Señor Ceviche W1 £42 334
Kingly Ct 020 7842 8540 4–2B
The "amazing range of Peruvian street food" served at this "vibrant" hangout in Soho's Kingly Court gastro hub is "a cut above most ceviche operations", and with "decor that's very cool by the standards of this slightly lame restaurant mall". / W1B 5PW; www.senor-ceviche.com; @SenorCevicheLDN; 11.30 pm, Sun 10.15 pm; set weekday L £26 (FP).

Seven Park Place SW1 £93 444
7-8 Park Pl 020 7316 1615 3–4C
This "gorgeous", "very small, but comfortable and cosy dining room" is "so private" within a luxurious St James's hotel. It deserves to be better known thanks to its "genuinely kind, helpful and passionate" staff and – last but not least – William Drabble's "first rate cuisine". / SW1A 1LS; www.stjameshotelandclub.com; @SevenParkPlace; 10 pm; closed Mon & Sun.

Seven Stars WC2 £34 233
53 Carey St 020 7242 8521 2–2D
"This tiny, charismatic pub" behind the Royal Courts of Justice – run by landlady Roxy Beaujolais – "offers traditional ales and quirky food at very good value prices". / WC2A 2JB; 9 pm.

Fortnum & Mason, 1707 W1 £54 223
181 Piccadilly 020 7734 8040 3–3D
Named after the year Fortnum's was founded, this basement perch below the famous food halls is perfect for "trying wines from slightly off the beaten track" that you've dug up in the adjacent F&M wine department (for a £15 corkage charge). There's a "limited menu" for food, but it's "a useful stop-off for a light meal with good vino". / W1A 1ER; www.fortnumandmason.co.uk; @fortnumandmason; 7.45 pm, Sun 5 pm; closed Sun D.

Sexy Fish W1 £82 212
1-4 Berkeley Sq 020 3764 2000 3–3B
"Bling and blondes abound" at this "latest multi-million £££ venture from Richard Caring" which is "arguably better suited to Vegas than to Mayfair". A minority do swoon over the "stunning decor" and "beautifully presented" sushi, robata, and Asian seafood dishes, but for the majority of reporters it's just a "big", "brash" and "ridiculous" glitter ball, serving "uninspiring, knock-off fusion dishes" to "D-list celebs and ecstatic wannabes taking selfies"; and – given the "inattentive" service and humungous price tag – "utterly disappointing". / W1J 6BR; www.sexyfish.com; @sexyfishlondon.

Shackfuyu W1 £48 544
14a, Old Compton St 020 7734 7492 5–2B
"Power-packed", taste combinations of "wonderful Japanese-Western hybrid dishes" are served by "laid back" but "very knowledgeable" staff at this "hip" Bone Daddies sibling, near Cambridge Circus: "creative, unusual" and "amazing value for money". / W1D 4TH; www.bonedaddies.com; @shackfuyu; 11 pm, Mon & Tue 10 pm, Sun 9 pm.

Shake Shack £24 322
Nova, Buckingham Palace Rd, SW1
no tel 2–4C
80 New Oxford St, WC1
01925 555 171 5–1B
24 The Market, WC2 020 3598 1360 5–3D
The Street, Westfield Stratford, E20
awaiting tel 14–1D
"Accurately cooked, with good char", but "a bit small for the price" – such are the pros and cons of the "quality burgers (and hot dogs)" at Danny Meyer's American-style operations.

Shampers W1 £49 245
4 Kingly St 020 7437 1692 4–2B
"Like an old friend" – this "bustling", '70s-survivor wine bar in Soho is "always full of fun, as owner Simon presides over the very clubby atmosphere" ("it's seemingly perpetually full of chartered surveyors!"). "Even if the menu does seem a little trapped in time", the food is "varied, well prepared and always good value", and "the selection of wine is amazing". / W1B 5PE; www.shampers.net; @shampers_soho; 10.30 pm; closed Sun.

The Shed W8 £48 324
122 Palace Gardens Ter 020 7229 4024 7–2B
"Bigger than it first seems from the outside", this quirky, farm-to-table venture in Notting Hill "lives up to its name" decorwise, and "it's a fun place" (if with "hideously uncomfortable seats and tables that are too small"). Its "seasonal British tapas" is "interesting and different" but expect "a high bill". / W8 4RT; www.theshed-restaurant.com; @theshed_resto; 11 pm; closed Mon L & Sun; SRA-3 star.

J SHEEKEY WC2 £75 444
28-34 St Martin's Ct 020 7240 2565 5–3B
"The kind of place that makes London special!" – Richard Caring's "so-classy" institution (est 1896) is tucked away down a Dickensian alley "in the heart of Theatreland" and remains not only the survey's most talked-about destination, but also its No. 1 for fish and seafood (narrowly trumping its stablemate Scott's in nominations as London's best). Beyond the doorman and intriguing, etched-glass façade, "congenial" staff are "amazingly well-drilled", and the "warm and inviting" interior is "almost like an exclusive club, divided into small, oak-panelled areas", and decorated with "black and white stills of famous actors". Mind you, it's "noisy", and "you pack in like sardines!" Top Menu Tip – fish pie. / WC2N 4AL; www.j-sheekey.co.uk; @JSheekeyRest; 11.30 pm, Sun 10 pm; booking max 6 may apply; set weekday L £46 (FP).

J Sheekey Atlantic Bar WC2 £76 345
28-34 St Martin's Ct 020 7240 2565 5–3B
"Nothing makes me happier than sitting up at this beautiful bar, and having a range of oysters and a glass of champagne!" – This "indulgent" Theatreland rendezvous "combines a relaxed tone with a fizzing vibe" and provides "a hard-to-beat selection of shellfish". The recent rebranding and launch under a new name rightly underlines its distinctive appeal to the adjacent main restaurant. / WC2N 4AL; www.j-sheekey.co.uk; @JSheekeyRest; 11.30 pm, Sun 10.30 pm; booking max 3 may apply.

Shepherd Market Wine House W1 £54
21-23 Shepherd Market 020 7499 8555 3–4B
In the middle of super-cute Shepherd Market, a cute, old-fashioned-looking wine shop, offering quality vinos plus small plates, which opened in summer 2016 – only 18 covers but a fun perch. / W1J 7PN; www.shepherdmarketwinehouse.co.uk; @ShepMarketWine; 11 pm, Sun 10.30 pm.

Shepherd's SW1 £54 334
Marsham Ct, Marsham St
020 7834 9552 2–4C
"It's back, and doing a good job for the lobbyists!" This traditional Westminster stalwart – a well-known politico haunt – re-opened last year, and "retains its excellent ambience with booths and well-spaced tables, plus very good food and service. Top Menu Tip – The shepherd's pie (of course!) is recommended…" / SW1P 4LA; www,shepherdsrestaurant.co.uk; @shepherdsLondon; 10.30 pm; closed Mon L, Sat & Sun.

Shikumen, Dorsett Hotel W12 £39 332
58 Shepherd's Bush Grn 020 8749 9978 8–1C
Mixed feedback this year on this Chinese luminary, whose "upmarket" style in an "impressive" new hotel is slightly at odds with its location on still-grungy Shepherd's Bush Green. Fans again extol its "consistently delicious" cooking – particularly "fantastic dim sum" – but it has also seemed "unmemorable" at times this year, and the "cavernous" room strikes many as "attractive", but can also give an impression that's "subdued". / W12 5AA; www.shikumen.co.uk; @ShikumenUK; 10 pm.

Shilpa W6 £31 532
206 King St 020 8741 3127 8–2B
"From the outside it looks like an average Indian café/takeaway restaurant" but this "fantastic", if unassuming South Indian outfit "serves very good honest Keralan food at unbelievably low prices". "You don't go for the great ambience" though. / W6 0RA; www.shilparestaurant.co.uk; 11 pm, Thu-Sat midnight.

Shoryu Ramen £42 322
9 Regent St, SW1 no tel 4–3D
3 Denman St, W1 no tel 4–3C
5 Kingly Ct, W1 no tel 4–4D
Broadgate Circle, EC2 no tel 13–2B
For fans of these "crowded and cramped" Japanese, they are a "go-to, quick cheap eat with steaming bowls of ramen"; overall though, ratings were more M.O.R. this year. / Regent St 11.30 pm, Sun 10.30 pm – Soho midnight, Sun 10.30 pm; no booking (except Kingly Ct).

Shotgun W1 £50 222
26 Kingly St 020 3137 7252 4–2B
Mississippi-born Brad McDonald opened his "lively" Soho BBQ to much fanfare last year, but reporter feedback is mixed. Fans say its "combination plates make for a great evening", but sceptics "don't get the love for this place": "slowly it dawned on people that it's really not so amazing and the portions-price ratio is somewhat larcenous". / W1B 5QD; www.shotgunbbq.com; @ShotgunBBQ; 11 pm.

Shuang Shuang W1 £41 333
64 Shaftesbury Ave 020 7734 5416 5–3A
"Fun, healthy and cheap" new venture from Thai restaurateur Fah Sundravorakul, on Chinatown's northern border, seeking to differentiate itself from the competition by establishing a trend for Chinese DIY hot pot – you cook the meal yourself using implements provided, grabbing ingredients as necessary from a central conveyor belt. / W1D 6LU; www.shuangshuang.co.uk; @HotPotShuang; 11 pm, Fri & Sat 11.30 pm; may need 4+ to book.

The Sichuan EC1 £46 422
14 City Road 020 7588 5489 9–3D
"Superb", "very authentic", "spicy" Sichuan cooking has won instant acclaim for this "no-nonsense" City-fringe newcomer, near the Honourable Artillery Company, despite sometimes "perfunctory service" and "a lack of thought in the decor". / EC1Y 2AA; www.thesichuan.co.uk; 11 pm.

Sichuan Folk E1 £44 442
32 Hanbury St 020 7247 4735 12–2C
Fans say you find "probably London's best Sichuan cooking" at this small East End spot, off Brick Lane – it's "amazing value for money". / E1 6QR; www.sichuan-folk.co.uk; 10.30 pm; no Amex.

The Sign of The Don Bar & Bistro EC4 £54 234
21 St Swithin's Ln 020 7626 2606 10–3C
"In the basement of the more formal Don (next door) – a relatively relaxed venue for a business lunch" that's "quite inexpensive for the area". These converted cellars feel more "enjoyable" than their grander neighbour, with "very dependable" brasserie fare, and "a great wine list" and selection of sherries. / EC4N 8AD; www.thesignofthedon.com; @signofthedon; 10 pm; closed Sat & Sun.

Signor Sassi SW1 £69 334
14 Knightsbridge Grn 020 7584 2277 6–1D
"Lively and fun", this traditional Knightsbridge trattoria has "great Italian-family-restaurant values", making it both child-friendly and romantic: "ideal for a date, with just the right amount of fuss made of your guest to impress". / SW1X 7QL; www.signorsassi.co.uk; @SignorSassi; 11.30 pm, Sun 10.30 pm.

Silk Road SE5 £24 522
49 Camberwell Church St
020 7703 4832 1–3C
"Everyone crams in on benches at bare tables" at this "vibrant, no-frills canteen-style eatery in Camberwell". Why? – "Wonderful, spicy food from Xianjing province" that's "amazingly cheap" ("I'd happily pay double, it's so interesting"); "as a Chinese person, I can tell you this is authentic cooking at best!!" / SE5 8TR; 10.30 pm; closed weekday L; cash only.

Simpson's Tavern EC3 £40 235
38 1/2 Ball Ct, Cornhill 020 7626 9985 10–2C
This "old-school inn and chophouse" in a Dickensian City alleyway has a history that stretches back to 1757, and still serves up "top-notch grub at very sensible prices". "Fantastic staff" add to the appeal, and it's "brilliant for a breakfast meeting". / EC3V 9DR; www.simpsonstavern.co.uk; @SimpsonsTavern; 3 pm; L only, closed Sat & Sun.

Simpsons-in-the-Strand WC2 £76 111
100 Strand 020 7836 9112 5–3D
This "lovely period dining room" is renowned as a bastion of the best British cuisine (most famously Roast Beef) but its performance can seem "sad" nowadays. For "the best breakfast" it does win praise ("for business or pure indulgence") but more generally it seems "old-fashioned" and lacklustre – "a once-famous, busy and respected restaurant that's been devastated and left to a handful of tourists". / WC2R 0EW; www.simpsonsinthestrand.co.uk; 10.30 pm, Sun 9 pm; no trainers; set weekday L & dinner £53 (FP).

Singapore Garden NW6 £43 332
83a Fairfax Rd 020 7624 8233 9–2A
"Can't fault it over the years!" – this "always buzzing and noisy" north London favourite, tucked away in a parade of shops in Swiss Cottage, boasts a large and loyal fanclub thanks to its "reliable" realisation of an "eclectic" menu mixing Chinese, Malaysian and Singaporean dishes. / NW6 4DY; www.singaporegarden.co.uk; @SingaporeGarden; 11 pm, Fri & Sat 11.30 pm.

Six Portland Road W11 £53 443
6 Portland Road 020 7229 3130 7–2A
"At last we have a terrific local" – Holland Park types are cock-a-hoop with this "buzzy and busy" indie newcomer (just 40 seats) from an ex-Terroirs duo. Service is "impeccable" ("no pomposity or smugness here"), the modern British dishes are "lovely, fresh and beautifully cooked" and there's a well-selected wine list. / W11 4LA; www.sixportlandroad.com; 11 pm, Sun 5 pm; closed Mon & Sun D.

Sketch, Lecture Room W1 £134 3 3 5
9 Conduit St 020 7659 4500 4–2A
"You may feel you've taken a sip of something psychedelic!" as you take in the "fabulously camp" decor of this "spectacular" Mayfair dining room, overseen by superstar chef, Pierre Gagnaire. The idiosyncratic cuisine can be "fantastic" too, but the "complicated" combinations can also seem "too clever by half". Hallucinogens may be advisable on arrival of the bill… / W1S 2XG; www.sketch.uk.com; @sketchlondon; 10.30 pm; closed Mon, Sat L & Sun; no trainers; booking max 8 may apply.

Sketch, Gallery W1 £80 2 3 4
9 Conduit St 020 7659 4500 4–2A
"The must-visit loos" are traditionally a more consistent attraction than the perennially pricey and gimmicky cuisine at this Mayfair fashionista-favourite, given a romantic but mad, rhapsody-in-pink makeover a couple of years ago (with art from designer/director David Shrigley). It avoided harsh feedback this year however, and for afternoon tea in particular it's worth a whirl – "(over) indulgence with a lightness of touch". / W1S 2XG; www.sketch.uk.com; @sketchlondon; 1 am, Sun Midnight; booking max 10 may apply.

Skylon, South Bank Centre SE1 £76 1 1 2
Belvedere Rd 020 7654 7800 2–3D
"The bar is good and the views of the Thames unparalleled" at this vast but "anodyne" cultural-centre dining room. That's the end of the good news: "the food is nothing to write home about", "service is inconsistent" and bills can be "shocking". ("I felt extremely bad for my companions, who were visiting London and really deserved better.") See also Skylon Grill. / SE1 8XX; www.skylon-restaurant.co.uk; @skylonsouthbank; 10.30 pm; closed Sun D; no trainers; set Sun L £45 (FP), set weekday L & pre-theatre £47 (FP).

Skylon Grill SE1 £74 2 2 3
Belvedere Rd 020 7654 7800 2–3D
"The best view in London", overlooking the Thames from the "iconic Royal Festival Hall", could make this huge D&D London venue the perfect place "to impress". But while most reviews are more positive than at the adjacent restaurant, a few are similarly downbeat: "left feeling hungry and a little cheated price-wise". / SE1 8XX; www.skylon-restaurant.co.uk; @skylonsouthbank; 11 pm; closed Sun D; set weekday L & pre-theatre £39 (FP).

Smith & Wollensky WC2 £102 1 1 2
The Adelphi Building, 1- 11 John Adam St
020 7321 6007 5–4D
"Overpriced, overhyped"… and over here! This year-old outpost of the famous NYC steakhouse brand – part of the Adelphi, just off the Strand – inspires very mixed feedback. Its business appeal is evident: it's "very spacious", "very well furnished (if you like that 'prestigious' US steakhouse furnishings and decor thing)", and provides "a 500+ bin wine list featuring some esoteric US vintages". Service though is not only "American-Yank style" ("I'm your waiter this evening, etc"), but also surprisingly "hit and miss"; the interior can seem "loud and booming"; and though many reports acknowledge that this is some of the best meat in London, the price/quality trade-off is much better elsewhere. / WC2N 6HT; www.smithandwollensky.co.uk; @sandwollenskyuk; 11 pm; closed Sun D; set weekday L & pre-theatre £47 (FP).

Smith's Wapping E1 £58 4 3 4
22 Wapping High St 020 7488 3456 12–1A
"A fantastic location with brilliant views over towards Tower Bridge", isn't the only reason this Wapping venue is "always busy". Its fish and seafood is "always superb" too. Sibling to a well-established Ongar venture, it's "generally filled with Essex likely lads and their molls". / E1W 1NJ; www.smithsrestaurants.com; @smithswapping; 10 pm; closed Sun D; no trainers.

Smiths of Smithfield, Top Floor EC1 £79 2 2 2
67-77 Charterhouse St
020 7251 7950 10–1A
"Great rooftop views" over the City make this an attractive location for business entertaining, with steak the appropriate focus for the Smithfield meat market setting. The catch? – it's "expensive for what it is". / EC1M 6HJ; www.smithsofsmithfield.co.uk; @thisissmiths; 10.45 pm; closed Sat L & Sun D; booking max 10 may apply.

Smiths of Smithfield, Dining Room EC1 £56 2 2 1
67-77 Charterhouse St
020 7251 7950 10–1A
"For a run-of-the-mill brasserie, this first floor overlooking Smithfield meat market (hence the beef-heavy menu) is absolutely fine" even if the cooking is no better than "acceptable". Fans say it's "fun", but its acoustics mean it's "very noisy" to the extent it can seem "pretty unpleasant". / EC1M 6HJ; www.smithsofsmithfield.co.uk; @thisismiths; 10.45 pm; closed Sat L & Sun; booking max 12 may apply.

Smiths of Smithfield, Ground Floor EC1 £32 2 2 3
67-77 Charterhouse St
020 7251 7950 10–1A
Once one of London's ultimate brunch hotspots, this big and buzzy Smithfield hangout is "still a favourite place for breakfast" for some reporters. / EC1M 6HJ; www.smithsofsmithfield.co.uk; @thisissmiths; 5 pm; L only; no bookings.

Smoke & Salt N1 £56
The Chapel Bar, 29 Penton Street
07421 327 556 9–3D
A year-long residency in Angel's Chapel Bar (launched in May 2016), offering a set five-course dinner alongside cocktails and a small wine list, brought to us by chefs Remi Williams and Aaron Webster who met working at The Shed in Notting Hill; Sunday brunch too. / N1 9PX; www.smokeandsalt.com; @smokeandsaltldn; 10 pm; closed Mon L, Tue L, Wed L, Thu L, Fri, Sat & Sun L.

Smokehouse Chiswick W4 £50 333
12 Sutton Lane North 020 7354 1144 8–2A
"A reminder of how great pulled pork can be" – this tucked-away, year-old outpost of Smokehouse Islington has been "a good addition to W4". Other attractions? – a cute garden and an "outstanding whisky selection". / W4 4LD; www.smokehousechiswick.co.uk; 10 pm, Sun 9 pm; Mon-Thu D only, Fri-Sun open L & D.

The Smokehouse Islington N1 £54 444
63-69 Canonbury Rd 020 7354 1144 9–2D
This Canonbury gastro-boozer boasts "all the charm and hospitality of your local pub, but with extra good food". Smoked or roast meat dishes are its forte, but there are "veggie options which have lured carnivores away from the obvious choices". There's a sister pub in Chiswick. / N1 2RG; www.smokehouseislington.co.uk; @smokehouseN1; 10 pm, Sun 9 pm; closed weekday L.

Smokestak £14 53
11 Sclater Street, E1 13–C2
Dinerama, EC2 no tel –
"Once tasted no other BBQ will do!" So say fans of the results from David Carter's 4.5 tonne, custom-built smoker from Texas. Top Menu Tip – "the beef brisket is the thing of dreams!" Stop Press – now he's going permanent too with a new 75-cover Shoreditch site to open in November 2016 and centred on a 2m charcoal grill.

Smoking Goat WC2 £44 432
7 Denmark St no tel 5–1B
"Noisy hipsters; small, rickety tables and a small, dark room" set the scene at Ben Chapman's no-bookings Soho phenomenon. "Plates may be small, but they carry big, big flavours" – "deep", "well-judged", "meat-heavy" and "unusual" Thai dishes, many from the BBQ. / WC2H 8LZ; www.smokinggoatsoho.com; @smokinggoatsoho; 10 pm, Sun 8.30 pm.

Snaps & Rye W10 £40 453
93 Golborne Rd 020 8964 3004 7–1A
"Delicious, well-executed dishes with a Danish twist" and "natural, highly attentive service" (plus the house-infused Akvavit) are pluspoints of this Scandi dining room in North Kensington. "Great for brunch that's a bit out-of-the-ordinary". / W10 5NL; www.snapsandrye.com; @snapsandrye; 10 pm; closed Mon, Tue D, Wed D & Sun D.

Social Eating House W1 £73 433
58-59 Poland St 020 7993 3251 4–1C
Jason Atherton's Soho three-year-old "hits all the right buttons" for most reporters, with its "proper comfort eating", "hip" service and "lively (but not over-loud) atmosphere". "The 'Blind Pig' bar upstairs is super cool for an aperitif too". / W1F 7NR; www.socialeatinghouse.com; @socialeathouse; 10 pm; closed Sun; set weekday L £42 (FP).

Social Wine & Tapas W1 £44 323
39 James St 020 7993 3257 3–1A
With its "tempting, well thought-out and unusual wine selection", Jason Atherton's Marylebone yearling particularly wins praise for its "casual" buzz. Even fans of its "superb" tapas concede it's "not cheap" however, and critics say it's "not up to the standard of the other Socials", not helped by "blaring" music and an interior that can feel "too crowded" and "self-conscious". / W1U 1EB; www.socialwineandtapas.com; @socialwinetapas; 10.30 pm; closed Sun; credit card deposit required to book.

Soif SW11 £56 333
27 Battersea Rise 020 7223 1112 11–2C
With its "fascinating list of natural wines", this "authentically French" bistro in Battersea bears the hallmarks of its better-known sibling Terroirs – a "little gem" whose "gutsy" menu is "full of robust flavours" and "top-quality seasonal fare done nicely". So "go for the wine and fall in love with the food…" / SW11 1HG; www.soif.co; @Soif_SW11; 10 pm; closed Mon L & Sun D.

Som Saa E1 £47 523
43a Commercial St 020 7324 7790 13–2C
"The food is like good drugs!" at the new "Spitalfields forever-home" of this epic Thai ("which has perhaps lost some of its ramshackle charm in the move from Hackney railway arches"). "It's a real eye-opener for what Thai food can be" – "raw authentic flavours", "great taste combinations" and "some dishes that could blow your head off!" – "I'm addicted!" / E1 6BD; www.somsaa.com; @somsaa_london; 11.30 pm, Sat midnight, Sun 10.30 pm; D only; may need 4+ to book.

Sông Quê E2 £31 322
134 Kingsland Rd 020 7613 3222 13–1B
"It's Spartan and hurried", but this Shoreditch canteen with sharing tables does provide "delicious" Vietnamese grub: "the pho's the thing here, but other dishes are worth trying, too". / E2 8DY; www.songque.co.uk; 11 pm, Sun 10.30 pm; no Amex.

Sonny's Kitchen SW13 **£56** 2 2 3
94 Church Rd 020 8748 0393 11–1A
"Perhaps not quite as special as it used to be", this "local staple" retains the loyalty of its Barnes following despite a "pleasant but unexciting" performance in recent times. Still it's "sensibly priced", and by-and-large "what a local should be". / SW13 0DQ; www.sonnyskitchen.co.uk; @sonnyskitchen; Fri-Sat 11 pm, Sun 9.30 pm; set weekday L & dinner £35 (FP).

Sophie's Steakhouse **£58** 2 4 3
29-31 Wellington St, WC2
020 7836 8836 5–3D
311-313 Fulham Rd, SW10
020 7352 0088 6–3B
Well-established steakhouses in Covent Garden and Fulham; reports are generally of "good quality" meals, but they equally owe their popularity to their "accommodating" staff and "fun", family-friendly atmosphere. / www.sophiessteakhouse.com; SW10 11.45 pm, Sun 11.15 pm; WC2 12.45 am, Sun 11 pm; no booking.

Sosharu, Turnmill Building EC1 **£79** 2 3 2
63 Clerkenwell Rd 020 3805 2304 10–1A
So far, the wait hasn't been worth it for the opening of Jason Atherton's long-anticipated Japanese on the big Clerkenwell site that was Turnmills nightclub. Some fans do hail his "modern twist on izakaya food", but even they can find it expensive, while to critics it's "incredibly overpriced" given the "heavy-handed" cooking – "the chefs seem to have no understanding of Japanese cuisine and how to balance flavours". / EC1M 5NP; www.sosharulondon.com; @SocialCompany; 10 pm, Fri & Sat 10.30 pm; closed Sun; credit card deposit required to book.

Spring Restaurant WC2 **£88** 3 3 4
New Wing, Lancaster Pl 020 3011 0115 2–2D
"The spectacular, light-filled space" – "one of the most elegant rooms" in town, in gracious Somerset House – provides a "beautiful" ("too perfect?") setting for Skye Gyngell's "serene" two-year-old. Her "somewhat esoteric", "delicate" cuisine using "the very best seasonal ingredients" is "quietly delicious" too, but even fans concede it's "not cheap" (and critics say "it's priced only for business"). / WC2R 1LA; www.springrestaurant.co.uk; @Spring_Rest; 10.30 pm; closed Sun D; credit card deposit required to book; set weekday L & pre-theatre £51 (FP).

Spring Workshop W1 **£25**
19 Brooks Mews 020 7493 5367 3–2B
In the well-heeled environs of Mayfair, this Ikea-style café is worth knowing about it: 1) it's a modestly priced all-day option in a pricey area; and 2) it's a not-for-profit café supporting social mobility. If service lags, remember it's in a good cause… / W1 4DX; www.springworkshop.co.uk; @Spring_Workshop; 5.30 pm; closed Sat & Sun.

Spuntino W1 **£44** 3 3 3
61 Rupert St 020 7734 4479 4–2D
Russell Norman's "very cool" Italian-American bar in Soho – "27 stools and one popcorn machine" – serves "really interesting small plates". "I go again and again, but have realised that it's best to visit out of busy hours"; "after the theatre is perfect". / W1D 7PW; www.spuntino.co.uk; @Spuntino; 11.30 pm, Sun 10.30 pm; no bookings.

The Square W1 **£130**
6-10 Bruton St 020 7495 7100 3–2C
This "classy" gastronomic temple in Mayfair was sold by its creators Phil Howard and Nigel Platts-Martin in Spring 2016 (just before this year's survey). With its "very formal" ("dull"), style – underpinned by a "bible of a wine list" – it's a shoe-in for the portfolio of new owner, Marlon Abela, who seems sure to maintain its business-friendly appeal. Whether the cuisine will hold up is less certain – hence we've left it un-rated – but one early report says it's "still Fabulous with a capital F". STOP PRESS – in September 2016 Yu Sugimoto was named the new executive chef. / W1J 6PU; www.squarerestaurant.com; @square_rest; 9.45 pm, Sat 10.15 pm, Sun 9.30 pm; closed Sun L; booking max 8 may apply; set weekday L £68 (FP).

Squirrel SW7
11 Harrington Road 020 7095 0377 6–2B
From the owners of Bunga Bunga, this virtuous summer 2016 newcomer south of Gloucester Road tube is a big departure from its louche-living stablemate. A cutely decked out, simple café (acorn lights, acorn bowls, etc) – here the focus is on salads, grain bowls and porridge pots – no alcohol, so expect water infusions, matcha lattes… / SW7 3ES; www.wearesquirrel.com; @wearesquirrel.

Sree Krishna SW17 **£27** 4 3 2
192-194 Tooting High St
020 8672 4250 11–2C
"Unchanging, as ever", this "long-established South Indian" on Tooting's curry strip serves "mouth-watering" fish and chicken dishes along with "especially good Keralan starters – dosas, dahi vada, etc". "There's a lot of competition here and this is a little further from the Tube, but it's worth the walk!" / SW17 0SF; www.sreekrishna.co.uk; @SreeKrishnaUk; 10.45 pm, Thurs 12.45pm, Fri & Sat 11.30 pm.

The Stable E1 **£34** 2 2 3
16-18 Whitechapel Road
020 7377 1133 13–2D
First London outpost of a 13-site British chain, specialising in pizza, pies and featuring 80 craft ciders, which opened in Whitechapel in April 2016. All early ratings say the food's not bad, but there are

some gripes: "a 4-chilli rated pizza had ZERO heat. It didn't have balls!" / E1 1EW; www.stablepizza.com; @stablepizza; 10 pm; may need 8+ to book.

Star of India SW5 **£55** 4 2 3
154 Old Brompton Rd 020 7373 2901 6–2B
One of post-war London's original curry houses, on the Kensington edge of Earl's Court, this classic veteran still produces "interesting" cooking. The once famously camp interior "is a little tired these days, but that doesn't detract from the main event". / SW5 0BE; www.starofindia.eu; 11.45 pm, Sun 11.15 pm.

Stick & Bowl W8 **£24** 4 3 1
31 Kensington High Street
020 7937 2778 6–1A
"Been there for years, and always full" – this tiny, "everyday" High Street Ken canteen ladles out "yummy Singapore noodles, mouth-watering wonton soup, succulent pork belly and rice" as you perch on stools (defo "not a place to linger!") / W8 5NP; 10.45 pm; cash only; no bookings.

Sticks'n'Sushi **£48** 4 4 4
11 Henrietta St, WC2 020 3141 8810 5–3D
Nelson Rd, SE10 020 3141 8220 1–3D
58 Wimbledon Hill Rd, SW19
020 3141 8800 11–2B
Crossrail Pl, E14 020 3141 8230 12–1C
"A strange but pleasant mix of Denmark and Japan" – this "fun and buzzy" Danish chain puts a Scandi twist on sushi and yakitori and results from the "bewilderingly long menu" are "beautifully presented and delicious" (if "not cheap"). The original, "aircraft-hangar-sized" branch near Wimbledon Tube remains the best known. / www.sticksnsushi.com; Sun-Tue 10 pm, Wed-Sat 11 pm; SRA-1 star.

STORY SE1 **£132** 3 3 3
199 Tooley St 020 7183 2117 10–4D
The "diversity of the dishes…", "the incredible work that goes into them…", the "massively seasonal ingredients…" – Tom Sellers's "mind-blowing" multi-course epics still win huge acclaim for his "edgy, modernist, Scandi-chic temple", near Tower Bridge. But ratings dipped here palpably this year. Is it higher prices? Is it the pressure of opening Restaurant Ours? Whatever reason, a disgruntled minority found their meals "gimmicky", or "ill-conceived". / SE1 2UE; www.restaurantstory.co.uk; @Rest_Story; 9.15 pm; closed Mon & Sun.

Strut & Cluck E1 **£42**
151-153 Commercial Street
020 7078 0770 13–2B
Having popped up in Shoreditch House, this restaurant dedicated to the wonders of turkey opened in good time for Christmas in summer 2016 in Shoreditch. Dishes are often charcoal-grilled and come with a Middle Eastern twist. / E1 6BJ; www.strutandcluck.com; 10:30 pm.

Sukho Fine Thai Cuisine SW6 **£56** 5 4 3
855 Fulham Rd 020 7371 7600 11–1B
Celebrated by many as "the best Thai in London" – this "crowded" Fulham shop-conversion is "justifiably packed most nights" thanks to its "superb service" and "beautifully presented food with great depth of flavour". / SW6 5HJ; www.sukhogroups.com; 11 pm.

Suksan SW10 **£49** 4 3 2
7 Park Walk 020 7351 9881 6–3B
"Exceptionally good Thai cuisine – delicate when necessary but packing a punch when it should" – makes it worth remembering this Chelsea corner café: sibling to Fulham's esteemed 'Sukho Fine Thai Cuisine'. / SW10 0AJ; www.sukhogroups.com/suksan.html; 10.45 pm.

The Summerhouse W9 **£56** 2 3 5
60 Blomfield Rd 020 7286 6752 9–4A
The "lovely waterside location" on a Little Venice canal is the 'crown jewel' feature ("unbeatable on a summer evening… if you can get in") of this "relaxed", little outfit in Maida Vale. On most accounts the fish and seafood cooking is another strength, but the view persists in some quarters that it's merely "average". / W9 2PA; www.thesummerhouse.co; @FRGSummerhouse; 10.30 pm, Sun 10 pm; no Amex.

Sumosan W1 **£78**
26b Albemarle St 020 7495 5999 6–1D
This Russian-owned rival to Nobu is relocating after nearly 15 years – leaving Mayfair for a new Sloane Street home, where it will also (like others in their international chain) now provide Italian cuisine. Opening is planned for October 2016. / W1S 4HY; www.sumosan.com; @sumosan_; 11.30 pm, Sun 10.30 pm; closed Sat L & Sun L.

Super Tuscan E1 **£51** 4 4 3
8a, Artillery Passage 020 7247 8717 13–2B
"Very small" ("so book") and "initially tricky-to-find" Italian – in an alley on the fringe of the Square Mile: a "family-owned gem set up by brothers in 2012" offering "exceptional wines" and food "sourced direct from Italy". "The menu changes daily, and the specials are the dishes to go for". / E1 7LJ; www.supertuscan.co.uk; 10 pm.

Sushi Bar Makoto W4 **£46** 3 3 4
57 Turnham Green Terrace
020 8987 3180 8–2A
"Lovely and simple" Japanese cafe in Chiswick, newly moved to the busy strip by Turnham Green Tube from humbler premises on nearby Devonshire Road. Most reports applaud "truly excellent sushi, etc" but one or two caution that "it looks like a bargain, but is actually quite expensive". / W4 1RP; 10 pm, Sun 9 pm.

Sushi Masa NW2 **£41**
33b Walm Lane 020 8459 2971 1–1A
Sushi Say (RIP) is a very tough act to follow, and its successor attracts limited and downbeat feedback (hence no rating) – on this year's survey, it would be hard to recommend the trip to distant Willesden Green. / NW2 5SH; 10 pm.

Sushi Tetsu EC1 **£59** **554**
12 Jerusalem Pas 020 3217 0090 10–1A
"Having eaten in the fish market in Tokyo I know how authentic this restaurant is. Amazing!" – Harumi and Toru Takahashi are "charming hosts" and their "very intimate" Clerkenwell 7-seater serves "astonishing" sushi and other fare – "a mix of traditional and experimental dishes with perfect quality as the unifying factor". It invites some comparison with The Araki, although "here you can enjoy Japanese-style seasonality without splashing quite so much cash". "Booking is taken in one morning, two weeks in advance. It's a race. Follow the Twitter account for a chance to get a last-minute seat". / EC1V 4JP; www.sushitetsu.co.uk; @SushiTetsuUK; 7.45 pm, Thu-Fri 8 pm, Sat 7 pm; closed Mon, Thu L, Fri L, Sat L & Sun; booking essential.

Sushisamba **£90** **335**
The Piazza, WC2 no tel 5–3D
Heron Tower, 110 Bishopsgate, EC2
020 3640 7330 10–2D
"How can the view not create atmosphere – you're in the atmosphere!" Reached by one of Europe's fastest lifts, this "simply amazing", 39th-floor eyrie – complete with a movie-set bar, and "lovely outdoor spaces" – is hard to beat for sheer glam. The mesospheric prices "go with the height" though, and even those applauding the "beautifully tasty" Japanese/South American fusion bites "would question the price tag that goes with them!" Coming soon in 2017 – a sibling in the gorgeous, but perennially disappointing space above Covent Garden Market, overlooking the back of the Royal Opera House.

Sutton And Sons **£32** **433**
90 Stoke Newington High St, N16
020 7249 6444 1–1C
356 Essex Rd, N1 020 7359 1210 1–2C
240 Graham Road, E8 020 3643 2017 14–1B
"All chippies should be like this!" – these "upmarket" cafés have "a twist on the original look" and supply "top-quality fish 'n' chips" and also "other variants such as lobster rolls or grills for the more discerning palate". "The first branch in N16 is well worth the trip", and there's a new branch too in Hipster Central.

The Swan W4 **£49** **335**
1 Evershed Walk, 119 Acton Ln
020 8994 8262 8–1A
"A tucked-away location between Chiswick and Acton" lends a "rustic" atmosphere to this "hidden gem" of a pub, with "surprisingly sophisticated" food, plus "a good wine list, and changing list of cask beers". "It's a pub for all seasons: in the cool/freezing months, with wood panelling, open fires, and sofas… in the summer, the enormous garden and the mature trees make you feel like you're 100 miles from London". / W4 5HH; www.theswanchiswick.co.uk; @SwanPubChiswick; 10 pm, Fri & Sat 10.30 pm, Sun 10 pm; closed weekday L.

The Swan at the Globe SE1 **£60** **223**
21 New Globe Walk 020 7928 9444 10–3B
"Fabulous views of the Thames and London skyline" make this first floor venue at Shakespeare's Globe "much more than just a pre-theatre restaurant". But while fans say it's a "wonderful" all-rounder, reports of "slow service" and "ordinary food" are persistent complaints. / SE1 9DT; www.swanlondon.co.uk; @swanabout; 10.30 pm, Sun 9 pm.

Sweet Thursday N1 **£40** **323**
95 Southgate Rd 020 7226 1727 1–2C
"Very good neighbourhood pizzeria" and wine shop ("plus a good beer selection too") in "a lovely bit of De Beauvoir" – "reliable", "kid-friendly", with a "chilled-out vibe". / N1 3JS; www.sweetthursday.co.uk; @Pizza_and_Wine; 10 pm, Fri-Sat 10.30 pm, Sun 9 pm.

Sweetings EC4 **£75** **224**
39 Queen Victoria St 020 7248 3062 10–3B
"Untrammelled by fads and fashion" – this "quirky old restaurant, with its cramped tables and bar seating" has been an "unchanging staple" of City life since Victorian times. "Fun but fearsomely expensive", you get "great fish done the old-fashioned way" ("ie nothing is overly mucked around with") and alongside wines and champagnes, "Black Velvet in tankards" is another tradition. Arrive early if you want a seat. / EC4N 4SA; www.sweetingsrestaurant.co.uk; 3 pm; L only, closed Sat & Sun; no bookings.

Taberna do Mercado E1 **£44** **543**
Spitalfields Mkt 020 7375 0649 13–2B
"You can feel Nuno Medes's passion for the food" at his "casual taberna-style" yearling in Spitalfields Market, which is "equally suited to a drop in for a pastel de nata and a coffee, as for a full meal". The "unfussy" and "nostalgic" Portuguese dishes "use lots of obscure ingredients", but are "brilliantly successful", while "friendly, well-informed staff are keen to assist with selections". Top Menu Tip – "fish in a tin is the highlight". / E1 6EW; www.tabernamercado.co.uk; @tabernamercado; 9.30 pm, Sun 7.30 pm.

Taberna Etrusca EC4 £55 233
9 -11 Bow Churchyard 020 7248 5552 10–2C
This "good value" Italian is "still one of the most relaxing restaurants in the City": "well run, pleasant, efficient, helpful and upmarket", while "the al fresco patio is great in warm weather". Critics, though, feel it sells itself short: "somehow my heart never quite sings, even though nothing is missed and it's always a pleasure". / EC4M 9DQ; www.etruscarestaurants.com; 9.30 pm; closed Sat & Sun.

The Table SE1 £38 322
83 Southwark St 020 7401 2760 10–4B
A top spot for brekkie and lunch near Tate Modern, this "communal (essentially functional)" canteen offers "decent quality, simple dishes". "It gets busier every week – but it's worth tackling the pushchairs for the pancakes!" / SE1 0HX; www.thetablecafe.com; @thetablecafe; 10.30 pm; closed Mon D, Sat D & Sun D.

Tabun Kitchen W1 £37
77 Berwick Street 020 7437 8568 4–1C
A summer 2016 modern Israeli newcomer promising 'Jerusalem street food' and 'Palestinian pizza' in the heart of Soho, from breakfast on. / W1F 8TH; www.tabunkitchen.com; @TabunKitchen; midnight, Sun 11 pm.

Taiwan Village SW6 £35 453
85 Lillie Rd 020 7381 2900 6–3A
"It's all too easy to walk past" this "hidden gem" just off the North End Road, which is "as good as many of the leading Chinese restaurants in London, and much cheaper". "Pick the chef's Leave It To Us menu" and "dish after dish arrives at your table", all of them "convincing" and some "insanely good". / SW6 1UD; www.taiwanvillage.com; 11 pm, Sun 10.30 pm; D only, closed Mon; booking max 20 may apply.

Takahashi SW19 £44 533
228 Merton Rd 020 8540 3041 11–2A
"Unbelievable Japanese-European fusion food" including stellar sushi (from a "lovely ex-Nobu chef" and his wife) is a "stunning" find at this pleasant, but totally unremarkable looking, new shop-conversion in a parade near South Wimbledon tube. / SW19; www.takahashi-restaurant.co.uk; @takahashi_sw19; 10 pm, Fri & Sat 10.30 pm, Sun 9 pm; closed Mon, Tue, Wed L, Thu L & Fri L.

Talli Joe WC2 £41
152-156 Shaftesbury Avenue
020 7836 5400 5–2B
Good vibes surround this new Indian tapas/cocktails hangout in the heart of Theatreland, with the former devised by ex-Benares executive chef Sameer Taneja. It opened in late spring 2016. / WC2H 8HL; www.tallijoe.com; @tallijoe; 11.30 pm; closed Sun.

Tamarind W1 £75 542
20 Queen St 020 7629 3561 3–3B
"A class act!" This stalwart Mayfair basement put in a particularly strong showing this year, with many reports of "truly outstanding" cuisine. The location? – "pleasant but underwhelming", it's "time for a makeover". / W1J 5PR; www.tamarindrestaurant.com; @TamarindMayfair; 10.45 pm, Sun 10.30 pm; closed Sat L; no trainers; set weekday L £59 (FP), set pre-theatre £60 (FP).

Tamp Coffee W4 £40 333
1 Devonshire Road no tel 8–2A
"A great Argentinian-themed coffee stop" in Chiswick with "really good Joe" and simple fare, including "addictive empanadas". Weekend evenings, there's more substantial tapas and wine. / W4; www.tampcoffee.co.uk; @tampcoffee; 5.30 pm, Thur-Sat 10 pm, Sun 6 pm.

Tangerine Dream, Chelsea Physic Garden SW3 £30 324
66 Royal Hospital Road 020 7352 5646 6–3D
"The gardens are quite wonderful" at this very Chelsea destination, for which these airy tea rooms provide refreshments. To fans it's a "sublime secret" – "everything is home produced" and "the cakes are exceptionally good". However the "ordering system is chaotic and stressful" – "if only they could reduce the queuing time, it would indeed be nirvana". / SW3 4HS; www.chelseaphysicgarden.co.uk; Tue-Fri 5 pm, Sun 5 pm; closed Mon & Sat.

Tapas Brindisa £45 222
18-20 Rupert St, W1 020 7478 8758 5–3A
46 Broadwick St, W1 020 7534 1690 4–2B
18-20 Southwark St, SE1
020 7357 8880 10–4C
41-43 Atlantic Rd, SW9
020 7733 0634 11–2D
You're "lucky to get a table at peak times" at these "busy tapas restaurants" – especially at the Borough Market original. "Prices mount quickly" though, for the "small but densely flavoured plates", and while most reporters applaud their "excellent quality", critics – particularly those encountering "terrible service" – find them "extremely overpriced". / 10.45 pm, Sun 10 pm; W1 booking: max 10.

Taqueria W11 £35 443
141-145 Westbourne Grove
020 7229 4734 7–1B
"An authentic Mexican" – a tightly packed cantina on the Notting Hill/Bayswater borders, focused on tacos, cocktails and beer – "fresh and tasty, real street flavours, and also very friendly". / W11 2RS; www.taqueria.co.uk; @TaqueriaUK; 11 pm, Fri & Sat 11.30 pm, Sun 10.30 pm; no Amex.

Taro £36 3 3 2

10 Old Compton St, W1 020 7439 2275 5–2B
61 Brewer St, W1 020 7734 5826 4–3C

Mr Taro's "busy", "no-frills Japanese" canteens are among the "few really cheap eateries still remaining in Soho" – "food arrives quickly so it's ideal for a fast lunch or snack". "You may have to share a large table with others". / www.tarorestaurants.co.uk; 10.30 pm, Sun 9.30 pm; no Amex; Brewer St only small bookings.

Tartufo SW3 £58 3 3 2

11 Cadogan Gdns 020 7730 6383 6–2D

"Squirelled away in the basement of a lovely little hotel in a mansion block not far from Sloane Square", Alexis Gauthier's "tucked-away Italian" earnt a mixed rep this year. On most accounts, it's "a hidden gem" with "subtle and sophisticated" cooking (not least "the eponymous and hugely satisfying truffle menu") and a "romantic" ambience. Sceptics though, say it "used to be good" but feels "gloomy" nowadays, and "is not a patch on Gauthier itself". / SW3 2RJ; www.tartufolondon.co.uk; 10 pm; closed Mon & Sun D.

Tas £37 1 2 3

Its mezze-based menu is "nothing special", but – despite its low food score – these "buzzy" and "packed" Turks are still a popular "cheap 'n' cheerful" option for reporters, especially for "a quick pre- or post- theatre bite". / www.tasrestaurant.com; 11.30 pm, Sun 10.30 pm; EC4 Closed Sun.

Tas Pide SE1 £40 2 3 3

20-22 New Globe Walk
020 7928 3300 10–3B

"A very convenient location" – by Shakespeare's Globe – adds to the lustre of this "cavernous" but "nicely buzzy" branch of the "reliable Tas chain". There's a "good-value sharing menu" with "very decent mezze" and filling pide – "a Turkish take on pizza" (although "it's quite clear why it's the Italian version that's conquered the world!") / SE1 9DR; www.tasrestaurant.com/tas_pide; @TasRestaurants; 11.30 pm, Sun 10.30 pm.

Tate Britain, Whistler Restaurant SW1 £55 2 3 5

Millbank 020 7887 8825 2–4C

As well as the famous Whistler murals, "it is the wine list which steals the show" at this gracious-looking museum café – a famously "innovative world list at reasonable prices" (curated by Hamish Anderson) "with some exceptional value clarets and burgundies" thrown in. The food is "reliable" but is not the reason to detour. / SW1 4RG; www.tate.org.uk; @Tate; 3 pm, afternoon tea Sat-Sun 5 pm; L only; booking lunch only.

Tate Modern Restaurant, Switch House SE1

Level 9, Switch House, Bankside
020 7887 8888 10–3B

All the clichés about architect-designed restaurants are true at this 9th-floor dining room, where only the staff can enjoy the magnificent vistas (whose idea was it to put the windows at head height?). On early press feedback this is a re-run of the Level 6 restaurant, with admirable emphasis on British sourced food, but little culinary follow-through. At least across the way you can see the Thames. / SE1 9TG; www.tate.org.uk/visit/tate-modern/switch-ho; 6 pm, Fri & Sat 10 pm; no bookings.

Tate Modern, Restaurant, Level 6 SE1 £59 2 1 4

Bankside 020 7887 8888 10–3B

The "wonderful view" of St Paul's and the river is the most reliable attraction at this airy, rather Spartan dining room – as a showcase for British food and drink, it puts in a more mixed performance, and service is perennially so-so. / SE1 9TG; www.tate.org.uk; @TateFood; 9 pm; closed Mon D, Tue D, Wed D, Thu D & Sun D.

Taylor St Baristas £11 2 4 4

"A welcome change from monotonous high-street chains" – these "hipster-friendly" outfits provide "exceptional coffee" as well as OK cakes and salads. Staff are "dedicated" – if your order is slow it's "worth it, because it takes time to brew". / www.taylor-st.com; all branches 5 pm; Old Broad ST, Clifton St, W1, E14 closed Sat & Sun; New St closed Sat; TW9 closed Sun.

Tayyabs E1 £31 4 2 3

83 Fieldgate St 020 7247 6400 10–2D

"If you can deal with the chaos and the mayhem" (and the "enormous queue"), this "cavernous" East End Pakistani is "worth it" for its "to-die-for" tandoori lamb chops, kebabs and curries – "they're a world apart from the sorry food culture of nearby Brick Lane". / E1 1JU; www.tayyabs.co.uk; @itayyabs; 11.30 pm.

temper W1

25 Broadwick Street no tel 4–3A

Opening on Bonfire Night 2016, a new 'whole animal barbecue' concept – complete with 4.5m open fire pit – from Neil Rankin, of Pitt Cue Co and Smokehouse fame. / W1F 0DF; www.temperrestaurant.com; @temperldn.

The 10 Cases WC2 £55 2 1 3

16 Endell St 020 7836 6801 5–2C

"An innovative and really interesting wine list" underpins the "super idea and concept" ("there are only ten, ever-changing choices", hence the name) of this "great little spot" in Covent Garden, where "knowledgeable staff really help the enjoyment

of the vino". Soak it up with "simple but tasty" fare – it's not why you go, but "better than you might expect". / WC2H 9BD; www.the10cases.co.uk; @10cases; 11 pm; closed Sun.

10 Greek Street W1 £56 443
10 Greek St 020 7734 4677 5–2A
"The rough 'n' ready appearance of this small joint belies the highly competent kitchen which is open at the far end of this converted Soho shop". Yes it's "a bit cramped" and "too noisy", but staff are "laid back and friendly", and its "no-frills but faultless quality" dishes are packed with "lovely, simple flavours". "Naturally they don't accept reservations, but you can't have it all…" / W1D 4DH; www.10greekstreet.com; @10GreekStreet; 10.45 pm; closed Sun; booking lunch only.

Tendido Cero SW5 £52 233
174 Old Brompton Rd 020 7370 3685 6–2B
"You feel you are in Barcelona" at this "buzzy tapas bar" in South Kensington – except when it comes to the bill! "I love this place, but have stopped going because it's so ridiculously priced. Such a pity, they're so nice and the food is good". / SW5 0BA; www.cambiodetercio.co.uk; @CambiodTercio; 11 pm.

Tendido Cuatro SW6 £50 222
108-110 New King's Rd
020 7371 5147 11–1B
This "noisy" Parsons Green tapas bar (an offshoot of Cambio de Tercio in Earl's Court) serves "really authentic food" and Spanish wines, but at prices sceptics find "unbelievable". / SW6 4LY; www.cambiodetercio.co.uk; @CambiodTercio; 11 pm, Sun & Mon 10.30 pm.

Terroirs WC2 £49 324
5 William IV St 020 7036 0660 5–4C
"The kind of spot you'd get excited about if you chanced on it in Paris!" – this "buzzing", subterranean bistro near Charing Cross station remains a well-known pioneer both of "honestly Gallic", "rustic" dishes (with much charcuterie and cheese) and also "weird and wonderful biodynamique wines from owners Caves de Pyrene" – "organic, unfiltered, and with a heavy French accent… like the staff!" / WC2N 4DW; www.terroirswinebar.com; @TerroirsWineBar; 11 pm; closed Sun.

Texture W1 £102 433
34 Portman St 020 7224 0028 2–2A
"It somehow misses out on the acclaim it deserves", say fans of this "spacious" dining room – part of a hotel, near Selfridges. Agnar Sverrisson's "excitingly original" Icelandic cuisine is "light, clever and delicious", service is "pleasant and precise" and there's an "exceptional wine list" too. / W1H 7BY; www.texture-restaurant.co.uk; @TextureLondon; 10.30 pm; closed Mon, Tue L & Sun; set weekday L £69 (FP).

Thali SW5 £48 433
166 Old Brompton Rd 020 7373 2626 6–2B
Bollywood classic posters add character to this contemporary Indian in South Kensington – a "pleasant and reliable" option, whose "menu is made unique by following regional and family recipes of the owners". / SW5 0BA; www.thali.uk.com; @ThaliLondon; 11.30 pm, Sun 10.30 pm.

Theo Randall, W1 £91 331
1 Hamilton Pl 020 7318 8747 3–4A
"Magnifico!", say fans of this ex-River Café chef's Hyde Park Corner HQ, who hail it as "London's best Italian". Despite a major refurb in early 2016 however, its windowless quarters still feel very much "like a hotel restaurant", and more cautious reporters feel it's "better than average, but very overpriced". / W1J 7QY; www.theorandall.com; @theorandall; 11 pm; closed Sat L & Sun; set dinner £55 (FP).

Theo's SE5 £38 433
2 Grove Ln 020 3026 4224 1–3C
"A great addition to the Camberwell foodie scene" – "welcome newcomer" serving "wonderful wood-fired pizza" from "the excellent toppings to the flavoursome bases, without too much of the frippery or hype of better-known joints". / SE5; @theospizzaldn; 10.30 pm, Fri & Sat 11 pm, Sun 10 pm ; no Amex.

Theo's Simple Italian SW5 £64
34-44 Barkston Gardens
020 7370 9130 6–2A
Pasta-prodigy Theo Randall dips his toe into casual dining with an all-day cicchetti and pasta spot in a pleasant, but very anonymous west London hotel. Too little survey feedback for a rating – reading the runes online and in the press, it's a handy Earl's Court standby rather than a destination. / SW5 0EW; www.theossimpleitalian.co.uk; @TRSimpleItalian; 10.30 pm.

34 Mayfair W1 £79 222
34 Grosvenor Sq 020 3350 3434 3–3A
As "a discreet and well-spaced venue to take clients and would-be clients", Richard Caring's "upmarket steakhouse" near the old American Embassy has "the right balance of formality and a relaxed approach". Those paying their own way tend to judge it more harshly however, saying it's "very average" and "woeful value for money". / W1K 2HD; www.34-restaurant.co.uk; 11 pm, Sun 10 pm.

The Thomas Cubitt SW1 **£61** 344
44 Elizabeth St 020 7730 6060 2–4A
"Busy, exuberant and seriously popular" – this "fun" Belgravia pub become "very noisy" in its downstairs bar (where pub grub is served) but is calmer in its upstairs dining room, serving more ambitious fare. / SW1W 9PA; www.thethomascubitt.co.uk; 10 pm, Sun 9.30 pm.

3 South Place, South Place Hotel EC2 **£66** 333
3 South Pl 020 3503 0000 13–2A
For a "sound" business breakfast or lunch near Liverpool Street, D&D group's "modern and trendy" ground floor bar/restaurant provides a "solid menu and professional service". (See also Angler upstairs, for a more 'gastro' experience). / EC2M 2AF; www.southplacehotel.com; @southplacehotel; 10.30 pm.

tibits W1 **£35** 223
12-14 Heddon St 020 7758 4110 4–3B
"Unusual self-service vegan operation (where you pay by plate-weight)", which makes a handy veggie pit stop near Piccadilly Circus. The setting is "much nicer than the cafeteria style you might expect", and the "varied selection" of dishes offers "a great choice"… if "at central London prices". / W1B 4DA; www.tibits.co.uk; @tibits_uk; Sun-Wed 10 pm, Thu-Sat 10.30 pm; no Amex.

Ting, Shangri-La Hotel at the Shard SE1 **£98** 223
Level 35, 31 St Thomas St
020 7234 8000 10–4C
"What a vista (even from the gents!)" at this swanky 35th-floor chamber, which added a 'Chef's Market Table' this year to celebrate the arrival of new chef, Gareth Bowen (from the Marriott County Hall) to oversee its Asian-influenced modern British cuisine. No change yet to reporters' verdict that "you are overpaying for the view" but one bright spark: afternoon tea is widely thought to be "worth it" for the "sense of occasion". / SE1 9RY; www.ting-shangri-la.com; @ShangriLaShard; 11.30 pm; no trainers; credit card deposit required to book; set weekday L £59 (FP).

Toff's N10 **£40** 322
38 Muswell Hill Broadway
020 8883 8656 1–1B
"One of the best chippies around" – this acclaimed Muswell Hill institution inspires proper loyalty in the locality: "you get large portions of fine nosh that feels like you've had value for money". / N10 3RT; www.toffsfish.co.uk; @toffsfish; 10 pm; closed Sun.

Tokimeite W1 **£79** 443
23 Conduit St 020 3826 4411 3–2C
"Superb Japanese cuisine using the highest quality ingredients" is what you'd expect from Yoshihiro Murata's Mayfair newcomer (on the former site of Sakura, RIP) – not just because he himself has many Michelin gongs, but because his backer is Japan's largest agricultural co-operative ("you can try a true Japanese Wagyu here"). It's "expensive" naturally, but while press and food-cognoscenti reviews have been restrained, all reporters are wowed by "fabulous tastes" and "dishes that are good for breaking the ice, as they look amazing!" / W1S 2XS; www.tokimeite.com; @tokimeitelondon; 10.30 pm; closed Sun.

Tokyo Diner WC2 **£26** 343
2 Newport Place 020 7287 8777 5–3B
"Rock-bottom prices" make this stalwart Japanese café a very competitive option, even in Chinatown. Its sushi, noodles and curries are "neither fancy nor expensive, but honest, tasty, wholesome and top value". / WC2H 7JJ; www.tokyodiner.com; 11.30 pm, closed Mon; no Amex; no booking, Fri & Sat; set weekday L £16 (FP).

Tokyo Sukiyaki-Tei & Bar SW3 **£52**
85 Sloane Ave 020 3583 3797 6–2C
A Chelsea hideaway serving an eclectic range of Japanese dishes – from Wagyu beef to sushi, sashimi and shabu-shabu (hot pot); reports are still too few for a rating, but very upbeat. / SW3 3DX; www.tokyosukiyakitei.com; @TokyoSukiyakiT; online bookings only, Fri & Sat.

Tom's Kitchen **£63** 222
Somerset House, 150 Strand, WC2
020 7845 4646 2–2D
27 Cale St, SW3 020 7349 0202 6–2C
11 Westferry Circus, E14
020 3011 1555 12–1C
1 Commodity Quay, E1 020 3011 5433 10–3D
"For a serious weekend breakfast", fans do tip Tom Aikens's casual bistros (particularly the backstreet Chelsea original), but overall they give an impression that's decidedly "average". / 10 pm-10.45 pm; WC2 closed Sun D.

Tommi's Burger Joint **£20** 444
30 Thayer St, W1 020 7224 3828 3–1A
37 Berwick Street, W1 awaiting tel 3–1D
342 Kings Rd, SW3 020 7349 0691 6–3C
"Burgers are to die for, and service is slick and fast" at these "easy and effective" pitstops, where "some of it is self-service" ("you queue up for ordering and paying"). "Loud music and dim lighting" helps make them "cool and trendy" too. / 9 pm.

The Tommy Tucker SW6 **£54** 334
22 Waterford Rd 020 7736 1023 6–4A
"Forget jokes about singing for your supper – this is a very good gastropub" in Fulham, with food by Claude Compton of nearby Claude's Kitchen, and "delicious wines and ales". "Don't go when

Chelsea are playing at home". / SW6 2DR; www.thetommytucker.com; @tommytuckerpub; Mon-Sat 10 pm, Sun 9 pm.

Tomoe SW15 **£40** 4 3 2
292 Upper Richmond Road
020 3730 7884 11–2B
A new team transplanted from Marylebone have taken over this Putney site, formerly called Cho-San (RIP: that is the restaurant not the man, he's just retired!) The "small" premises retain their "very traditional", "genuine Tokyo feel" and still provide "authentic sushi" and other "excellent" fare. / SW15; closed Mon.

Tonkotsu **£32** 2 3 3
Selfridges, 400 Oxford St, W1
020 7437 0071 3–1A
63 Dean St, W1 020 7437 0071 5–2A
7 Blenheim Cr, W11 020 7221 8300 7–1B
4 Canvey St, SE1 020 7928 2228 10–4B
382 Mare St, E8 020 8533 1840 14–1B
Arch 334 1a Dunston St, E8
020 7254 2478 14–2A
"Deservedly popular for a good slurp", say fans of these "cramped and buzzy" noodle stops, who praise "broths that are things of beauty". Critics on the other hand "don't understand the hype" – they feel it's "passable when hungry" but "nothing more".

Tosa W6 **£38** 3 3 2
332 King St 020 8748 0002 8–2B
"There are always several Japanese customers (a great sign!)" at this yakitori (charcoal-grilled chicken skewers) specialist in Stamford Brook. It's "excellent value, especially the sushi and sashimi", with a "great lunch deal". / W6 0RR; www.tosauk.com; 10.30 pm.

Toto's SW3 **£88** 2 3 4
Walton Hs, Lennox Gardens Mews
020 7589 2062 6–2C
Despite a revamp a couple of years ago, this "stunning" Knightsbridge Italian (with a lovely courtyard in summer) remains resolutely of the "old school", and even fans of its "consistent, high-quality cuisine and service" concede it "can be expensive" (while foes just leave "unsatisfied and poorer"). / SW3 2JH; www.totosrestaurant.com; @TotosRestaurant; 11 pm; set weekday L £33 (FP).

Tozi SW1 **£47** 3 3 3
8 Gillingham St 020 7769 9771 2–4B
This cicchetti (Venetian small plates) specialist is a "neighbourhood go-to" near Victoria station, with "charming service, fine cooking and gentle prices". It's "attached to a hotel, although not obviously", but that doesn't prevent "a great buzz" – and it's "a brilliant place to take children". / SW1V 1HN; www.tozirestaurant.co.uk; @ToziRestaurant; 10 pm.

The Trading House EC2 **£45** 3 4 4
89-91 Gresham St 020 7600 5050 10–1A
Year-old City gastropub already making "old friends" with its "great staff", "excellent kebabs (fun too, hanging on a rack!)", and "impressive range of bottled and cask beers". "Sadly, it's not open on the weekends". / EC2V 7NQ; www.thetradinghouse.uk.com; @tradinghouse; 10 pm; closed Sat L & Sun; no Amex.

The Tramshed EC2 **£56** 2 3 4
32 Rivington St 020 7749 0478 13–1B
"Cool, dead-cow decor" (Damien Hirst's well-known formaldehyde tank artwork) adds lustre to the "sunny ambience" of Mark Hix's spacious Shoreditch shed. Sceptics feel its straightforward cooking (primarily chicken or steak-based) "has lost its mojo", but fans do applaud "simple food well done". Top Tip – "kids' deals and the special treatment they get makes it a great family lunch choice". / EC2A 3LX; www.hixrestaurants.co.uk / www.chickenandsteak.co.; @the_tramshed; Mon & Tue 11 pm, Wed-Sat midnight, Sun 9.30 pm.

Trangallan N16 **£44** 5 4 4
61 Newington Grn 020 7359 4988 1–1C
"Brilliant Galician food and a very intriguing list of Spanish wines" ensure this Stoke Newington Hispanic is a hit. "Service is attentive and staff well informed", but "some tables for two are too small". Top Menu Tip – "The chocolate ganache with sea salt and olive oil is a dish everyone should try before they die". / N16 9PX; www.trangallan.com; 10.30 pm; closed Mon; no Amex; no trainers.

Tredwell's WC2 **£61** 2 2 2
4 Upper St Martin's Ln 020 3764 0840 5–3B
Right in the heart of the West End, Marcus Wareing's casual, multi-floor diner is still struggling to make its mark with our reporters (feedback is thin for a venture by such a big name). It does have a fanbase who really dig it – they "love, love, love the very innovative dishes, and yummy cocktails, and the super-cool ambience". Many others though are "very disappointed" – they find the brasserie-with-an-haute-twist cooking "variable" and "too expensive for what it is", and are nonplussed by its styling. / WC2H 9NY; www.tredwells.com; @tredwells; 10 pm, Fri - Sat 11 pm; closed Sun D.

Tried & True SW15 **£15** 3 3 3
279 Upper Richmond Rd
020 8789 0410 11–2A
Another "great addition to the Putney breakfast/brunch scene" – an "airy", "New Zealander-run" café "a little bit off the main drag", serving "wonderfully original breakfasts (with homemade just about everything) and light lunches", plus "excellent coffee". Needless to say, "it can get a bit overrun by yummy mummies". / SW15; www.triedandtruecafe.co.uk; @tried_true_cafe; 4 pm, Sat & Sun 4.30 pm.

Trinity SW4 £71 554
4 The Polygon 020 7622 1199 11–2D
"Since the refurb last year, Adam Byatt is at the top of his game", and his "classy" Clapham ten-year-old – "so much more than a neighbourhood local!" – rivals nearby Chez Bruce as the area's top gastronomic destination. His "clever" cuisine is "exciting AND completely satisfying" and there's a "wide-ranging and superb" wine selection available by the glass, all delivered by "well-informed and un-pompous" staff. ("The addition of upstairs at Trinity is working well" too – an "interesting and appealing", but cheaper option to the ground floor – formula price £43). Mr Michelin Man – "a star must be due surely?" STOP PRESS. Michelin finally provided the much-overdue star in October 2016. / SW4 0JG; www.trinityrestaurant.co.uk; @TrinityLondon; 10 pm, Sun 9 pm.

Trishna W1 £76 533
15-17 Blandford St 020 7935 5624 2–1A
"Exciting, well-crafted, deft… balanced in terms of spicing and heat" – such are the "assured culinary delights" featuring "extremely unusual ingredients" at the Sethi family's original Marylebone venture, that made it London's No. 1 nouvelle Indian this year. When busy, it can seem "noisy" and "cramped", and service "slightly rushed". / W1U 3DG; www.trishnalondon.com; @TrishnaLondon; 10.30 pm, Sun 9.45 pm.

LA TROMPETTE W4 £75 543
5-7 Devonshire Rd 020 8747 1836 8–2A
"You can't fail to have a good meal" at this "West End-style operation" off Chiswick's main drag, whose "very accomplished cuisine" and "polished" service ("insightful wine advice" in particular) create an experience almost "on a par with Chez Bruce" (its stablemate). "Worth the schlep across town"… says a fan from E18! / W4 2EU; www.latrompette.co.uk; @LaTrompetteUK; 10.30 pm, Sun 9.30 pm.

Trullo N1 £59 433
300-302 St Paul's Rd 020 7226 2733 9–2D
"High-quality ingredients are left to speak for themselves", at this "noisy" and "crowded", "little bit of Puglia", on "the wrong side of the Highbury roundabout" – an ongoing hit, with a "stunning Italian-heavy wine list". / N1 2LH; www.trullorestaurant.com; @Trullo_LDN; 10.15 pm; closed Sun D; no Amex.

Tsunami £46 523
93 Charlotte St, W1 020 7637 0050 2–1C
5-7 Voltaire Rd, SW4 020 7978 1610 11–1D
"Sensational", Nobu-esque Japanese-fusion dishes have long made this "darkly-lit" Clapham venture an "exciting" culinary destination; in fact "both branches are good", but the Fitzrovia outlet is less well known and not quite as highly rated. / www.tsunamirestaurant.co.uk; @Tsunamirest; SW4 10.30 pm, Fri & Sat 11 pm, Sun 9.30 pm; W1 11 pm; SW4 closed Mon - Fri L, W1 closed Sat L and Sun; no Amex.

Tulse Hill Hotel SE24 £46 323
150 Norwood Rd 020 8671 7499 1–4D
"A high standard of food from a versatile menu, an amazing garden with summer BBQs, a welcome with a smile, and a great selection of real ales" have won hipster acclaim for this "hidden south London gem", between Brixton and Dulwich. / SE24 9AY; www.tulsehillhotel.com; @TulseHillHotel; 10 pm, Sun 9 pm.

28-50 £54 234
15 Maddox St, W1 020 7495 1505 4–2A
15-17 Marylebone Ln, W1
020 7486 7922 3–1A
140 Fetter Ln, EC4 020 7242 8877 10–2A
The "exceptional wine list with sensible mark-ups (available "in a wide range of glass sizes") is key to the appeal of this very popular bar/bistro chain – supporting features are the "very pleasant staff" ("happy to discuss without being in your face"), and "simple", "reliable" cooking. / www.2850.co.uk; EC4 9.30 pm, W1 Mon-Wed 10 pm, Thu-Sat 10.30 pm, Sun 9.30 pm; EC4 closed Sat & Sun.

Twist W1 £59 444
42 Crawford St 020 7723 3377 2–1A
"There's so much passion and creativity" in Eduardo Tuccillo's "enjoyable and brilliantly cooked" Italo-Spanish tapas, at this Marylebone yearling, which fans say is "something special". / W1H 1JW; www.twistkitchen.co.uk; @twistkitchen; 11 pm, Fri & Sat 11.30 pm; closed Sun.

Two Brothers N3 £33 322
297-303 Regent's Park Rd
020 8346 0469 1–1B
"Really authentic, old-fashioned fish 'n' chips" have long been the raison d'être of this Finsbury "old favourite". There's a wide range of dishes, portions are "huge, fresh and hot" – and "even the fried chicken is good". / N3 1DP; www.twobrothers.co.uk; 10 pm; closed Mon; set weekday L £20 (FP).

2 Veneti W1 £52 343
10 Wigmore St 020 7637 0789 3–1B
This "friendly" outfit close to the Wigmore Hall serves an "authentic, high-quality Venetian menu" – "not the standard Italian dishes" – and shows "depth in the list of Italian wines and grappas". / W1U 2RD; www.2veneti.com; @2Veneti; 10.30 pm, Sat 11 pm; closed Sat L & Sun.

Typing Room, Town Hall Hotel E2 £86 453
Patriot Square 020 7871 0461 14–2B
A minority find it "over-fussy", but Lee Westcott's "brilliantly executed" cuisine wins ecstatic reviews

from most reporters, who say its "flair and creativity" are "well worth the trip to deepest Bethnal Green" (and that "it's crazy it doesn't have a Michelin Star!"). An open kitchen adds life to the "clean and elegant" dining room – the corner of "a boutique hotel created from the old town hall" – as does the "terrific" service. / E2 9NF; www.typingroom.com; @TypingRoom; 10 pm; closed Mon & Tue L; set weekday L £50 (FP).

Uli W11
5 Ladbroke Road 020 3141 5878 7–2B
Previously tucked away in nearby All Saints Road, this neighbourhood pan-Asian restaurant – formerly one of the west London's better local hideaways – was resurrected, after a couple of years' closure, in summer 2016 in a new location on Ladbroke Road. The ebullient Michael is back too – looking forward to next year's survey reports. / W11 3PA; www.ulilondon.com; 10.30 pm; D only, closed Sun; no Amex.

Umu W1 **£118** 332
14-16 Bruton Pl 020 7499 8881 3–2C
If you can get over the "insane prices", Marlon Abela's Kyoto-style fixture in a cute Mayfair mews provides "superb and beautifully presented Kaiseki-cuisine" – even those griping about the "dizzying expense" say "it's worth it for the sensational sushi" and other fare from chef Yoshinori Ishii. / W1J 6LX; www.umurestaurant.com; 10.30 pm; closed Sat L & Sun; no trainers; booking max 14 may apply.

Union Street Café SE1 **£58** 232
47-51 Great Suffolk St 020 7592 7977 10–4B
Gordon Ramsay's bare-walled casual Italian, with ingredients from nearby Borough Market, inspires some praise for its "relaxed" style, "fabulous" wines and dependable food. Overall however, the verdict is "nice but uninspiring" (and "not cheap"). / SE1 0BS; www.gordonramsayrestaurants.com/union-street-cafe; @unionstreetcafe; Mon-Sat 10.45 pm; closed Sun D.

Upstairs at John the Unicorn SE15 **£39**
Rye Lane 020 7732 8483 1–4D
Yet-to-be-rated small-plates-focused dining room above a newly opened Antic pub near Peckham Rye station. Ex-Opera Tavern chef Ben Mulock heads up the kitchen. / SE15 4TL; www.johntheunicorn.com; @JohnTUnicorn; 10 pm, Sun 5 pm; closed Mon, Tue L, Wed L, Thu L, Fri L & Sun D.

Urban Coterie, M By Montcalm EC1 **£61**
17th-floor, 151-157 City Rd
020 3837 3000 13–1A
You get some "great views" from the 17th-floor dining room of this eye-catchingly angular building, just north of Old Street roundabout. A collaboration between Searcys, chef Anthony Demetre, and the hotel – limited feedback as yet, but very positive. / EC1V 1JH; www.mbymontcalm.co.uk/urban-coterie-at-m-by-montca; @UrbanCoterie; 10 pm, Fri & Sat 10.30 pm; closed Mon; no trainers.

Le Vacherin W4 **£63** 322
76-77 South Pde 020 8742 2121 8–1A
Malcolm John's authentically Gallic bistro beside Acton Green has become a well-known local fixture thanks to its "reliable" traditional French cuisine. Top Tip – particularly "good-value deals at lunchtime". / W4 5LF; www.levacherin.co.uk; @Le_Vacherin; 9.45 pm, Fri & Sat 10.15 pm, Sun 8.30 pm; closed Mon L.

Vanilla Black EC4 **£61** 422
17-18 Tooks Ct 020 7242 2622 10–2A
"Seductive and tasty vegetarian food" from an "impressive and expansive menu" at this modern Chancery Lane establishment make it "great, even if you aren't a veggie": "I went with a meat-eater, and it's one of their favourite places!" / EC4A 1LB; www.vanillablack.co.uk; @vanillablack1; 10 pm; closed Sun; no Amex.

Vapiano **£30** 323
19-21 Great Portland St, W1
020 7268 0080 3–1C
90b Southwark St, SE1 020 7593 2010 10–4B
"Love the concept but it can be a scrum at the counters!" This global Italian fast-food franchise, (founded in Hamburg, with UK branches in Soho, Southwark and Fitzrovia) offers a food court format with salads, pizza or pasta prepared in front of you. It can be a bit of a bun-fight, but it's cheap, and "the food quality is generally good". / www.vapiano.co.uk; Mon-Thu 11 pm, SE1 Fri & Sat 10.30 pm, W1 Fri & Sat 11.30 pm.

Vasco & Piero's Pavilion W1 **£60** 343
15 Poland St 020 7437 8774 4–1C
This "old-style" Soho veteran is easily overlooked but worth discovering, in particular for its "attentive, funny and charming service" ("father and son have been together for over 40 years and they're training the grandson too"). The "traditional" cooking can seem "fairly standard" – go for the Umbrian specialities. / W1F 8QE; www.vascosfood.com; @Vasco_and_Piero; 9.30 pm; closed Sat L & Sun; set dinner £39 (FP).

Veeraswamy W1 **£77** 333
Victory Hs, 99-101 Regent St
020 7734 1401 4–4B
"A veteran that's still delivering the goods!" – London's oldest Indian (est 1926), near Piccadilly Circus remains "a favourite upscale subcontinental", with "up-to-date" contemporary decor, "attentive" staff, and "very special, interesting and delicate cooking"; predictably, it's not especially cheap. / W1B

4RS; www.veeraswamy.com; @theveeraswamy; 10.30 pm, Sun 10 pm; booking max 12 may apply.

Veneta SW1
St James's Market no tel 4–3D
From the Salt Yard Group (Opera Tavern, Salt Yard, Dehesa, Ember Yard) a new autumn-2016 Venetian-inspired restaurant in Haymarket's St James's Market development. (It will open alongside a second Duck & Waffle outpost and the London version of Aquavit). / SW1Y 4SB; www.veneta-stjames.co.uk; midnight.

Verdi's E1 £44 333
237 Mile End Rd 020 7423 9563 14–2B
"A very welcome change from the chicken shops of Whitechapel" – this East End trattoria specialises in the regional cuisine of Emilia-Romagna. Scores have dropped a little since it opened last year, but most reporters still rate it as very good. / E1 4AA; www.verdi.uk; @verdislondon.

El Vergel SE1 £30 434
132 Webber St 020 7401 2308 10–4B
"A great South American place", near Borough tube – this "cheap 'n' cheerful", lively canteen serves a wide range of zesty Latino fare, including empanadas and steak sarnies; recommended for brunch. / SE1 0QL; www.elvergel.co.uk; @ElVergel_London; 3 pm Mon-Fri, Sat-Sun 4 pm; L only; no Amex.

Vico WC2 £58 221
140a Shaftesbury Ave 020 7379 0303 5–2B
"No wow factor" on any front came as a surprise at the Bocca di Lupo team's Italian street food and gelati yearling, right on Cambridge Circus. A mid-year shake-up seems to be working though: "how this has improved now they have changed the furniture and have some front-of-house staff. I'm a Bocco di Lupo fan and was so disappointed on my first visit last year – only went back by chance and had a so much better experience: a very good lunch at reasonable price". / WC2H 8PA; www.eatvico.com; @eatvico.

Il Vicolo SW1 £49 333
3-4 Crown Passage 020 7839 3960 3–4D
"Tucked away" in a St James's passage, this "good-value family-run Italian" comes as a nice surprise in what can be a forbiddingly expensive district. "The owner and staff are engaging" and it scores well for its daily specials. / SW1Y 6PP; 10 pm; closed Sat L & Sun.

The Victoria SW14 £51 234
10 West Temple Sheen 020 8876 4238 11–2A
A short walk from Richmond Park, Paul Merrett's "super local gastropub" deep in residential Sheen is unusually stylish, and boasts a huge dining conservatory plus "a garden with a play area for children" ("sometimes it feels a bit too family-friendly, a bit like dining in a crèche"). Foodwise "perhaps it doesn't have the culinary flair it once did", but most reporters still find the menu has "something for everyone". / SW14 7RT; www.thevictoria.net; @TheVictoria_Pub; 10 pm, Sun 9 pm; no Amex.

Viet Food W1 £31 333
34-36 Wardour St 020 7494 4555 5–3A
"Very good Vietnamese food" – with "tasty, clean flavours" and at "excellent prices" ("especially for Chinatown") is building a following for Jeff Tan's consistent newcomer – "a bit of a clattery place", but with attractive (if slightly "rustic") styling. / W1D 6QT; www.vietnamfood.co.uk; 10.30 pm, Fri & Sat 11 pm.

Viet Grill E2 £44 3[illegible][illegible]
58 Kingsland Rd 020 7739 6686 13–1B
Critics diss it as "poor, dismal and studenty", but most reports acclaim this cafe on Kingsland Road, Shoreditch – aka "pho mile" – lauding "terrific fresh food, consistent quality and excellent customer service", and say it's "a great introduction to Vietnamese food". / E2 8DP; www.vietnamesekitchen.co.uk; @CayTreVietGrill; 11 pm, Fri & Sat 11.30 pm, Sun 10.30 pm.

View 94 SW18
Prospect Quay, 94 Point Pleasant
020 8425 9870 11–2B
A fine position – with a Thames-side terrace – is a highpoint at this bar/restaurant near Wandsworth Park: too limited feedback yet on its ambitious modern European cooking for a rating. / SW18 1PP; view94.com; @view94_sw18; closed Sat L & Sun; no shorts.

Vijay NW6 £33 321
49 Willesden Ln 020 7328 1087 1–1B
"Unfussy, unfussed, unhurried and happily obscure" – this long-running (since 1964), slightly decrepit South Indian fixture in Kilburn can be "excellent, including for vegetarians". / NW6 7RF; www.vijayrestaurant.co.uk; 10.45 pm, Fri & Sat 11.45 pm; no bookings.

Villa Bianca NW3 £58 222
1 Perrins Ct 020 7435 3131 9–2A
"This Hampstead veteran continues to churn out classic Italian fare" – "great pasta, fish and steaks/veal" – in a "proper, unpretentious setting" replete with "1970s Capri-style elegance". Even fans, though, can find the cooking a tad "uninspired" ("tasty, but the usual Italian panache is absent"). / NW3 1QS; www.villabiancanw3.com; @VillaBiancaNW3; 11.30 pm, Sun 10.30 pm.

Villa Di Geggiano W4 £64 222
66-68 Chiswick High Rd 020 3384 9442 8–2B
The "high-end"Tuscan cuisine and "wine from their own vineyard" at this Chiswick-fringe establishment do inspire some rave reviews. Its "high prices" are a major sticking point however, and for its harshest critics it's "noisy, unappealing and rather gaudy". / W4 1SY; www.villadigeggiano.co.uk; @villadigeggiano; 10 pm; closed Mon.

Village East SE1 £58 223
171-173 Bermondsey St
020 7357 6082 10–4D
The food – brunch and European brasserie fare – and cocktails are "always great, and there's a brilliant atmosphere" at this Bermondsey joint. On the downside, it can be so busy that "you feel squashed in" and "service gets a bit hit-and-miss". / SE1 3UW; www.villageeast.co.uk; @VillageEastSE1; 10 pm, Sun 9.30 pm.

Villandry £56 112
11-12 Waterloo Pl, SW1
020 7930 3305 3–3D
170 Gt Portland St, W1 020 7631 3131 2–1B
These "elegant and rather peaceful" cafes with smart St James's and Marylebone addresses are potentially "useful", "versatile" rendezvous, but "sadly, the cooking lets them down"; breakfast though is "good value". / www.villandry.com; –.

The Vincent Rooms, Westminster Kingsway College SW1 £38 333
76 Vincent Sq 020 7802 8391 2–4C
This training-ground for young chefs – part of a catering college in a tranquil and leafy corner of Westminster – is worth a try: you get "large portions" and "excellent value for money". "Serving staff can be erratic, but they're learning!" / SW1P 2PD; www.westking.ac.uk; @thevincentrooms; 7 pm; closed Mon D, Tue D, Fri D, Sat & Sun; no Amex.

Vinoteca £51 223
15 Seymour Pl, W1 020 7724 7288 2–2A
55 Beak St, W1 020 3544 7411 4–2B
18 Devonshire Rd, W4 020 3701 8822 8–2A
One Pancras Sq, N1 020 3793 7210 9–3C
7 St John St, EC1 020 7253 8786 10–1B
"One of the best and most unusual wine selections in London" underpins the high popularity of these "appealing" modern haunts (whose "smart" King's Cross branch attracts most mention). The "unfussy" food? – "nothing too thrilling, but competent". / www.vinoteca.co.uk.

Vintage Salt £44 343
189 Upper St, N1 020 3227 0979 9–2D
69 Old Broad St, EC2 020 7920 9103 10–2C
"Marvellous" fish 'n' chips (plain or grilled if you prefer) are on the menu at this Islington prototype and Liverpool Street spin-off for a planned chain of "posh", "modern chippie/diners". (Old-timers see echoes of former concepts that have come and gone nearby: "If Alan and Olga – of the original Upper Street Fish Shop – were still around, I think they would approve!") / @vintagesaltldn; –.

Vivat Bacchus £53 333
4 Hay's Ln, SE1 020 7234 0891 10–4C
47 Farringdon St, EC4 020 7353 2648 10–2A
"An all-round winner" – this busy operation in Farringdon (there's a second venue in Bankside) majors on South African wines, steaks and cheeses. "They take real care of their customers" – "and I loved the cheese room" (you can visit to make your choice). / www.vivatbacchus.co.uk; 10.30 pm; EC4 closed Sat & Sun, SE1 closed Sat L & Sun.

VQ £46 243
St Giles Hotel, Great Russell St, WC1
020 7636 5888 5–1A
325 Fulham Rd, SW10 020 7376 7224 6–3B
24 Pembridge Road, W11
020 3745 7224 7–2B
"Smoked salmon and scrambled eggs"... "great veggie fry-ups" – that's the kind of all-day breakfast food that's "always reliable" at these 24/7 diners. The ancient SW10 branch is the best known, while the new Notting Hill branch isn't actually open the whole 24 hours (but is still handy if you fancy a full English in W11 at 2am). / www.vingtquatre.co.uk; open 24 hours.

Vrisaki N22 £37 332
73 Middleton Rd 020 8889 8760 1–1C
Last year this ancient Bounds Green Greek "underwent a modern refit and a big change from its traditional taverna-style setting". But even those who feel the "atmosphere is now depleted" say the "food is still OK" – including the massive mezze special, which it has been a challenge to finish since time immemorial. / N22 8LZ; www.vrisaki.uk.com; @vrisakiuk; 11.30 pm, Sun 9 pm; closed Mon; no Amex.

Wagamama £39 243
"The UK's rising standard of Asian cuisine has outpaced these well-established noodle canteens", but – for a "fresh and reasonably healthy" bite, with "generous portions and reasonable prices" – armies of fans still say it's "a great format", and "a staple with kids". / www.wagamama.com; 10 pm-11 pm; EC4 & EC2 closed Sat & Sun; no booking.

Wahaca £33 333
"Bustling and so fun!"; Thomasina Miers's "easygoing" Mexican chain offers a "constantly refreshed" menu of zesty dishes, which – "even if consistency can vary – are usually good, filling and amazing value". Service is "accommodating too", but "that branches get so rammed can impact wait times", and queues to enter "are a pain" too. / www.wahaca.com; 10 pm-11 pm; no booking; SRA-3 star.

The Wallace, The Wallace Collection W1 £55 2 1 5
Hertford Hs, Manchester Sq
020 7563 9505 3–1A
"A beautiful glass-ceilinged atrium" creates a "wonderful bright and open" atmosphere at this café adjoining the famous 18th-century palazzo and gallery. In other respects this Peyton & Byrne operation is a mixed bag – the food's just about OK (stick to coffee and simpler items), while service is "a bit crap". / W1U 3BN; www.peytonandbyrne.co.uk; Fri & Sat 9.30 pm; closed Mon D, Tue D, Wed D, Thu D & Sun D; no Amex.

Walter & Monty EC3 £26
6 Bury Street 020 7283 6666 10–2D
Yet another street food trader puts down permanent roots – this time in the City with this small, carnivorous café/takeaway by the Gherkin, majoring in charcoal-grilled meats. / EC3A 7BA; www.walterandmonty.com; @walterandmonty; 2.30 pm, L only, closed Sat & Sun; no bookings.

Waterloo Bar & Kitchen SE1 £51 2 1 2
131 Waterloo Rd 020 7928 5086 10–4A
This "great-value brasserie" near Waterloo is often packed, perhaps because it's "the perfect place to eat when going to the Old Vic". / SE1 8UR; www.barandkitchen.co.uk; @BarKitchen; 10.30 pm.

The Waterway W9 £53 2 2 4
54 Formosa St 020 7266 3557 9–4A
Well-named canal-side bar/restaurant on the fringe of Little Venice – sibling to the nearby Summerhouse – lovely in summer and serving "a reasonable menu". / W9 2JU; www.thewaterway.co.uk; @thewaterway_; 11 pm, Sun 10.30 pm.

Wazen WC1 £55 4 4 2
2 Acton St 020 3632 1069 9–3D
South of King's Cross, this "rather sparse" Japanese newcomer occupies a tough site (once home to Konstam at The Prince Albert, long RIP). "It needs your help" and will repay it with "charming service", and "exceptional quality sushi and sashimi" and other "innovative fare without the pomp", prepared by an ex-Matsuri head chef. / WC1X 9NA; www.wazen-restaurant.co.uk; @wazenlondon; 11 pm; closed Mon & Sun.

The Wells NW3 £51 2 2 3
30 Well Walk 020 7794 3785 9–1A
"The dog comes too", with many regulars at Hampstead's most popular pub, about 100m from the Heath: a top choice for a Sunday roast, either in the bar, or the "light and airy upstairs room". The food – "classics and also some grills, such as steak" – is "variable, but usually pretty dependable". / NW3 1BX; www.thewellshampstead.co.uk; @WellsHampstead; 10 pm, Sun 9.30 pm.

West Thirty Six W10 £60 2 2 3
36 Golborne Rd 020 3752 0530 7–1A
Very mixed reports on this ambitious three-story yearling (with grill, lounge, bar, terrace and BBQ) in the shadow of north Kensington's Trellick Tower. Fans applaud "the best burger in a while" and a "cosy upstairs" – critics say that "hype doesn't match reality" with "variable food and high prices". / W10 5PR; www.westthirtysix.co.uk; @westthirtysix; 10 pm.

The Wet Fish Café NW6 £50 3 2 3
242 West End Ln 020 7443 9222 1–1B
This all-day café in West Hampstead is named after the "original fish shop, whose (Art Deco) wall tiles make the whole experience something special". An "inventive menu which always delivers" combines with "friendly service" to make it a "dream local" (especially for brunch). / NW6 1LG; www.thewetfishcafe.co.uk; @thewetfishcafe; 10 pm; no Amex; booking evening only.

The White Onion SW19 £60 3 2 2
67 High St 020 8947 8278 11–2B
"This really could be it for Wimbledon finally cracking fine dining!" – Eric and Sarah Guignard's ambitious yearling is, say fans, "just as good as its Surbiton sibling" (the well-known French Table) and brings "classic French cuisine plus a few surprise choices" to this perennially underserved 'burb. On the downside, "service is friendly but can be unfocused, the place can lack a little buzz" and the cooking strikes sceptics as "OK, but too fussy and overcomplicated". Top Tip – "impressive set lunch". / SW19 5EE; www.thewhiteonion.co.uk; @thewhiteonionSW; 10.30 pm; closed Mon, Tue-Thu D only, Fri-Sun open L & D.

The White Swan EC4 £62 3 3 2
108 Fetter Ln 020 7242 9696 10–2A
Look out for the "frequent 50% discount offer" if you want "value for money" in the "thankfully quiet" dining room on the top floor of this "loud" pub off Fleet Street, where the cooking can be surprisingly ambitious. / EC4A 1ES; www.thewhiteswanlondon.com; @thewhiteswanEC4; 10 pm; closed Sat & Sun.

Wild Honey W1 £79 3 3 3
12 St George St 020 7758 9160 3–2C
Back on form this year: Will Smith and Anthony Demetre's club-like (and business-friendly) fixture provides meaty fare and an "excellent array of wines by the glass", and "understated and professional service". It's "well-priced" for Mayfair too ("I often go for the fixed-price lunch, but happily pay my bill when I go à la carte"). / W1S 2FB; www.wildhoneyrestaurant.co.uk; @whrestaurant; 10.30 pm; closed Sun.

Wiltons SW1 £95 3 4 4
55 Jermyn St 020 7629 9955 3–3C
"The equivalent of the best of St James's clubs"; this

"bastion of traditional British cuisine" (est 1742, here since 1984) offers a "truly magnificent", "old-school" experience majoring in "wonderful fish" ("the best-ever sole meunière") and "great game" ("it's the only place I've ever had the chance to eat snipe, then woodcock!"). "Long may it survive, even if prices are crazy!" / SW1Y 6LX; www.wiltons.co.uk; @wiltons1742; 10.15 pm; closed Sat L & Sun; jacket required.

The Windmill W1 £48 322
6-8 Mill St 020 7491 8050 4–2A
"Excellent pies!" – steak 'n' kidney particularly recommended – put this Mayfair boozer in a class of its own. "What a joy to go to a real pub as against a tarted-up wine bar, with more people drinking beer than lager". / W1S 2AZ; www.windmillmayfair.co.uk; @tweetiepie_w1; 10 pm, Sat 5 pm.

The Wine Library EC3 £34 135
43 Trinity Sq 020 7481 0415 10–3D
"Many a happy afternoon can be lost" at this extremely atmospheric, ancient cellar near Tower Hill – a "fabulous selection of bottles" are available at shop prices plus corkage, accompanied by a "cold smorgasbord" of nibbles ("love the rillettes"). / EC3N 4DJ; www.winelibrary.co.uk; Mon 6 pm, 7.30 pm; closed Mon D, Sat & Sun.

Wolfe's Bar & Grill WC2 £49 322
30 Gt Queen St 020 7831 4442 5–1D
An early-wave surfer of the burger craze – the one in the 1970s that is (when it was on Park Lane) – this Covent Garden family diner still serves "consistently good" burgers, plus other decent, retro-ish fare. / WC2B 5BB; www.wolfes-grill.net; @wolfesbargrill; 9.30 pm, Fri & Sat 10.30 pm; no bookings.

THE WOLSELEY W1 £62 235
160 Piccadilly 020 7499 6996 3–3C
From "the perfect power breakfast" ("like a Who's Who of the FTSE100!") to "celeb-spotting" over lunch or dinner, Corbin & King's "cosmopolitan and Continental feeling" Grand Café by The Ritz is "always full of fizz", even if the "bistro-style" Mittel-European fare has always been decidedly "formulaic". A few accuse it of laurel-resting though? – in particular service (typically "very professional") was patchier this year. Top Tip – "one of the few grand afternoon teas in central London that isn't a total rip-off". / W1J 9EB; www.thewolseley.com; @TheWolseleyRest; midnight, Sun 11 pm.

Wong Kei W1 £33 222
41-43 Wardour St 020 7437 8408 5–3A
For a "cheap if not so cheerful" chow in Chinatown, this "solid and consistent" multi-storey canteen of decades standing "is the daddy of them all". But while it's known for its "famously abrupt" staff, reporters feel they've lightened up under the new management of the last couple of years. / W1D 6PY; www.wongkeilondon.com; Mon-Sat 11.15 pm, Sun 10.30 pm; cash only.

The Woodford E18 £77 344
159 High Rd 020 8504 5952 1–1D
"A star on the outskirts of London" – Pierre Koffmann protégé (and former Young Chef of the Year) Ben Murphy – just 25 – was backed by Essex restaurateur Steve Andrews to open this "ambitious" (one or two critics would say "over-ambitious") and very plushly "comfortable" new 100-cover restaurant in South Woodford (complete with Churchill Lounge bar). It's "a fabulous addition to an area which surprisingly lacks an upmarket establishment" and "shows great promise", even if some of the classic cuisine is "still finding its feet". / E18 2PA; www.thewoodford.co.uk; @TheWoodford_; 9.30 pm, Sun 6 pm; closed Mon & Tue.

Workshop Coffee £45 334
80a Mortimer St, W1 020 7253 5754 10–1A
St Christopher's Place, W1
020 7253 5754 3–1A
27 Clerkenwell Rd, EC1
020 7253 5754 10–1A
60a Holborn Viaduct, EC1 no tel 10–2A
'Source, Roast, Brew' is the motto of this "casual" chain, nominated by its many fans for its brilliant, in-house-roasted brews (it opened a new Bethnal Green roastery this year). The five-year-old Clerkenwell original has the only significant food operation, and is particularly tipped for "great breakfast options". / workshopcoffee.com; @workshopcoffee; –.

Wormwood W11 £65 432
16 All Saints Rd 020 7854 1808 7–1B
"Successful experimentation" in combining North African and Mediterranean flavours to produce shared plates win praise for this "boho hangout" in deepest Notting Hill – "beautifully presented and they taste delicious!" / W11 1HH; www.wormwoodnottinghill.com; 9.30 pm, Fri & Sat 10 pm; closed Mon, Tue, Wed L, Thu L, Fri L, Sat L & Sun L.

Wright Brothers £63 433
13 Kingly St, W1 020 7434 3611 4–2B
56 Old Brompton Rd, SW7
020 7581 0131 6–2B
11 Stoney St, SE1 020 7403 9554 10–4C
8 Lamb St, E1 020 7377 8706 10–2D
"A terrific oyster selection"... "fabulous dressed crab"... "superb mussels" – such are the "fuss-free" delicacies at these extremely popular, "friendly" and "always buzzing" seafood specialists. / 10.30 pm, Sun 9 pm; booking: max 8.

Xi'an Impression N7 £21 442
117 Benwell Rd 020 3441 0191 9–2D
"A little gem, tucked away in the shadows of the Emirates stadium", whose "incredible, homemade noodles are a thing of wonder". "With its slick service and top street-food, you forget the basic chairs and Formica tables". / N7; www.xianimpression.co.uk; @xianimpression; 10 pm.

Yalla Yalla £39 323
1 Green's Ct, W1 020 7287 7663 4–2D
12 Winsley St, W1 020 7637 4748 3–1C
Greenwich Peninsula Sq, SE10 0772 584 1372 9–3C
"Cheap, cheerful, plentiful and so very tasty" – the "zingy" mezze at these "down-to-earth" ("tiny and cramped") Lebanese cafés, where "it's easy to get carried away and order too much". Top Menu Tip – "never go without having the chicken livers". / www.yalla-yalla.co.uk; Green's Court 11 pm, Sun 10 pm – Winsley Street 11.30 pm, Sat 11 pm, W1 Sun.

Yama Momo SE22 £56 423
72 Lordship Ln 020 8299 1007 1–4D
"There's superb sushi and sashimi, but also a Pacific-fusion element to the main dishes" at this outpost of Clapham's long-running Tsunami which has "come to Lordship Lane and conquered!", despite service that can be "a bit slapdash". "Tasty cocktails" help fuel "something of a nightclub atmosphere": "it's buzzy for the suburbs on a weekday night!" / SE22 8HF; www.yamamomo.co.uk; @YamamomoRest; 10 pm, Fri & Sat 10.30 pm, Sun 9.30 pm; closed weekday L.

Yard Sale Pizza £30 432
54 Blackstock Road, N4 020 7226 2651 9–1D
105 Lower Clapton Rd, E5
020 3602 9090 14–1B
"Inventive pizza in hipster-land" is the promise at this "too-cool-for-school" Clapton haunt, which now also has a trendy outpost in Finsbury Park too.

Yashin W8 £79 322
1a Argyll Rd 020 7938 1536 6–1A
This pioneering modern Japanese haunt in Kensington ranks "among the best sushi in London", but scores have taken a tumble in the past year. For some critics, "delicious food" is balanced by "diabolical service: incompetent and snooty". Others complain that it is "overpriced" and "overrated". (Very limited feedback on its lesser-known 'Ocean' branch, on the Old Brompton Road). / W8 7DB; www.yashinsushi.com; @Yashinsushi; 10 pm.

Yauatcha £77 433
Broadwick Hs, 15-17 Broadwick St, W1
020 7494 8888 4–1C
Broadgate Circle, EC2 020 3817 9888 13–2B
"A happy combo of exquisite dim sum and glamorous settings" creates massive popularity for these "staple" but still "on-trend" pan-Asians. Fans of the Soho original dispute the virtues of the basement ("dark" and "clubby") and the ground floor ("lovely openness"), while the "bright and light branch above Broadgate Circle" is proving "a great addition to the CIty".

The Yellow House SE16 £45 332
126 Lower Rd 020 7231 8777 12–2A
A neighbourhood bar/restaurant right next to Surrey Quays station – pizza is the most popular culinary pick but more substantial fare is also available. / SE16 2UE; www.theyellowhouse.eu; @theyellowhousejazz; 10 pm, Sun 8 pm; closed Mon, Tue-Sat D only, Sun open L & D.

Yi-Ban E16 £45 333
London Regatta Centre, Dockside Rd, Royal Albert Dock 020 7473 6699 12–1D
"An interesting waterside location near City Airport helps justify the trek to this obscure Chinese in deepest Docklands", where "watching the planes take off opposite" provides a moving backdrop to a meal. A "spacious and convivial" venue, it offers "solidly good (without being quite top-drawer and fusion-y) dim sum" at "very reasonable prices". / E16 2QT; www.yi-ban.co.uk; 11 pm, Sun 10.30 pm.

Yipin China N1 £43 321
70-72 Liverpool Rd 020 7354 3388 9–3D
"It's not for the faint-hearted" ("heavy use of chilli", and "a heavy hand on the oil"), but for an "authentic taste" of "China in N1", this "brusque" and "basic" Hunanese/Sichuan operation has a certain "utilitarian" charm, and the best results are "sensational". / N1 0QD; www.yipinchina.co.uk; 11 pm.

Yming W1 £42 343
35-36 Greek St 020 7734 2721 5–2A
"So different from Chinatown a hundred yards south!" – this "unpretentious" but "welcoming" Soho "refuge" maintains a big following thanks to its "smiling staff" (overseen by "convivial host, William") and food that's been "steadfastly good" over many years (if a tad "predictable"). / W1D 5DL; www.yminglondon.com; 11.45 pm; closed Sun.

York & Albany NW1 £59 222
127-129 Parkway 020 7592 1227 9–3B
Gordon Ramsay's "roomy" and rambling old tavern on the edge of Regent's Park is a "pleasant old building". No great culinary fireworks though – more upbeat reports say it's "good, plain food". / NW1 7PS; www.gordonramsayrestaurants.com/york-and-a; @yorkandalbany; 11 pm, Sun 9 pm.

Yoshi Sushi W6 £39 342
210 King St 020 8748 5058 8–2B
"Fine Japanese/Korean food at very reasonable prices plus super-friendly staff" maintain the appeal of this traditional stalwart, in a nondescript run of cafés near Ravenscourt Park tube. It's a favourite of

many food-writers, including Toby Young and Simon Parker Bowles. / W6 0RA; 11 pm, Sun 10.30 pm; closed Sun L.

Yoshino W1 £44 443
3 Piccadilly Pl 020 7287 6622 4–4C
"Tucked away in an alley off Piccadilly", this quirky café-style venue is "as near as you can get to genuine Japanese food" in London. Opinions differ on whether it is nicer downstairs or in the small upstairs area, but "sitting at the counter is a great option for the solo diner". / W1J 0DB; www.yoshino.net; @Yoshino_London; 10 pm; closed Sun.

Yum Bun EC2 £14 53
Dinerama, 19 Great Eastern St
07919 408 221 13–1A
Lisa Meyer's Taiwanese-style steamed buns are "great fun street food that pack flavour and texture", and "deserve the respect of being eaten slowly". You can find stalls at various food events in East London. / EC2A 3EJ; www.yumbun.co.uk; @yum_bun; 10 pm; closed Mon D, Tue D, Wed D, Sat L & Sun.

Yum Yum N16 £43 322
187 Stoke Newington High St
020 7254 6751 1–1D
"It looks wonderful from the outside" – a Georgian building "with fairy lights galore and Thai statues" – once inside this Stoke Newington stalwart the "absolutely massive" space feels a tad "barn-like", but the affordable cooking remains good value. / N16 0LH; www.yumyum.co.uk; @yumyum; 11 pm, Fri & Sat midnight; set weekday L £17 (FP).

Yumi Izakaya W1 £40
The Piccadilly West End hotel, 67 Shaftesbury Ave no tel 5–3A
A collaboration between Tom & Ed Martin of the ETM Group (The Gun, The Botanist et al) and Caspar von Hofmannsthal (ex-Quo Vadis and Rotorino) has brought this izakaya to a Theatreland hotel. An early report is upbeat: "a very friendly spot with wonderful skewers and other Japanese classics – the smoky interior adds to the experience". / W1D 6EX; www.yumirestaurants.com; @yumi_izakaya; 12.30 am; no bookings.

Zafferano SW1 £81 222
15 Lowndes St 020 7235 5800 6–1D
"Having once been amongst the best Italian restaurants in London the cuisine has become more ordinary" at this well-known Belgravian, which is widely seen as "resting on its laurels", and to its harshest critics is "awful". It's not without support though: even some who feel it's "overpriced, staid and could do better" say "it's still worth a visit for the bible-like wine list and classic cooking". / SW1X 9EY; www.zafferanorestaurant.com; 11.30 pm, Sun 11 pm; set weekday L £42 (FP).

Zaffrani N1 £46 322
47 Cross St 020 7226 5522 9–3D
"Upmarket" Indian off Islington's main drag, with "a menu that's markedly different from the average"; to the odd reporter results are "nothing special", but on most accounts a meal here is "seriously good". / N1 2BB; www.zaffrani.co.uk; 10.30 pm.

Zaibatsu SE10 £35 452
96 Trafalgar Rd 020 8858 9317 1–3D
Both staff and prices are "very friendly" at this tiny Japanese BYO café in Greenwich, serving "really fresh sushi and sashimi". "The decor's basic but that's part of the charm". / SE10 9UW; www.zaibatsufusion.co.uk; @ong_teck; 11 pm; closed Mon.

Zaika, Tamarind Collection W8 £68 444
1 Kensington High St 020 7795 6533 6–1A
"Stunning Indian food" wins consistent high ratings for this impressive venue, opposite Kensington Gardens. Some feel that "the high ceilings (it was formerly a bank) detract from the ambience", but most reports say it's "all-round great". / W8 5NP; www.zaikaofkensington.com; @ZaikaLondon; 10.45 pm, Sun 9.45 pm; closed Mon L; credit card deposit required to book; set weekday L £38 (FP), set pre-theatre £44 (FP).

Zayane W10 £46 444
91 Golborne Road 020 8960 1371 7–1A
A modern North African restaurant, in the northerly reaches of Portobello. Heading up the kitchen is Chris Bower (ex-head chef of Tunbridge Wells's lovely Thackeray's) – one or two early reports hail his "terrific European-influenced Moroccan cooking". / W10 5NL; www.zayanerestaurant.com; 10 pm.

Zelman Meats £58 544
Harvey Nichols, Fifth Floor, 109-125 Knightsbridge, SW1 020 7201 8625 6–1D
2 St Anne's Ct, W1 020 7437 0566 5–2A
"Goodman's cool and interesting little sibling...." – this "trendy industrial-style" steakhouse (on the cutely tucked-away site that was briefly Rex & Mariano, RIP) is proving "a brilliant addition to Soho": a "simple, but perfectly executed concept" combining "wonderful, well-cooked meat", plus service that's "knowledgeable, enthusiastic and friendly", all at a price that's "relatively affordable".

Zest, JW3 NW3 £49 333
341-351 Finchley Rd 020 7433 8955 1–1B
"Creative Middle Eastern cuisine" and cool contemporary styling win fans for this subterranean modern Israeli in West Hampstead. On Sunday they run a "bottomless brunch": not just the "pomegranate mimosa and fresh carrot juice" but food too! / NW3 6ET; Sat-Thu 9.45 pm; closed Fri & Sat L.

Zia Lucia N7 **£31**
157 Holloway Road 020 7700 3708 9–2D
A new spot on Holloway Road, featuring (apparently) a unique-for-London selection of 48-hour, slow-fermented Italian pizza doughs. It opened too late for survey feedback, but the early word-on-the-street says it's cracking. / N7 8LX; www.zialucia.com; @zialuciapizza; closed Mon.

Ziani's SW3 **£57** **232**
45 Radnor Walk 020 7351 5297 6–3C
"Ever-buzzy", "squashed" trattoria just off the King's Road, with a "friendly padrone", and "acceptable food" from "the smallest kitchen ever seen". "Reservations can be unreliable at peak times (which are many), but it's where the locals eat or entertain". / SW3 4BP; www.ziani.co.uk; 11 pm, Sun 10 pm.

Zima W1 **£29**
45 Frith Street 020 7494 9111 3–2A
Next door to Soho's legendary Ronnie Scott's jazz club – a new venture from Russian chef Alexei Zimin that combines Russian street food and drink in a kitsch speakeasy-style atmosphere. / W1D 4SD; www.zima.bar; @ZimaLondon; 1 am; closed Mon & Sun; no bookings.

Zoilo W1 **£56** **423**
9 Duke St 020 7486 9699 3–1A
"Innovative sharing-dishes at affordable prices" win rave write-ups from fans of this "small tapas-style Argentinian restaurant", which is tucked-away near Selfridges. The top perches are in the downstairs bar, with views of the chefs at work. / W1U 3EG; www.zoilo.co.uk; @Zoilo_London; 10.30 pm; closed Sun.

Zuma SW7 **£80** **434**
5 Raphael St 020 7584 1010 6–1C
"The big wristwatch brigade" are out in force, especially at the "very cool bar" of this swish haunt, which is "always buzzing with the Knightsbridge set". Its Japanese-fusion morsels are "truly sensational" too, but service has seemed more "inattentive" of late, and "the bill can leave you feeling flat". / SW7 1DL; www.zumarestaurant.com; 10.45 pm, Sun 10.15 pm; booking max 8 may apply.

LONDON INDEXES

BRUNCH MENUS

Central

Aurora
Balthazar
Barnyard
Bob Bob Ricard
Bodean's: *all branches*
Boisdale
Boulestin
Le Caprice
Cecconi's
Christopher's
Daylesford Organic: *all branches*
Dean Street Townhouse
The Delaunay
Dickie Fitz
Dishoom: *all branches*
45 Jermyn St
Franco's
La Fromagerie Café
Galvin at Windows
The Goring Hotel
Hawksmoor: *all branches*
Hélène Darroze
Hubbard & Bell
Hush: *W1*
The Ivy
The Ivy Market Grill
Jackson & Rye: *all branches*
Joe Allen
Kaffeine: *all branches*
Lantana Café: *all branches*
Nordic Bakery: *Golden SqW1*
Ottolenghi: *all branches*
La Porte des Indes
Providores
Rail House Café
Riding House Café
Scandinavian Kitchen
Simpsons-in-the-Strand
Sophie's Steakhouse: *all branches*
Tabun Kitchen
Tom's Kitchen: *all branches*
Villandry St James's: *all branches*
VQ: *all branches*
The Wolseley
Workshop Coffee: *all branches*

West

The Abingdon
Annie's: *all branches*
Bluebird
Bodean's: *all branches*
La Brasserie
The Builders Arms
Bumpkin: *SW7*
Cheneston's Restaurant
Cheyne Walk Brasserie
The Cross Keys
Daylesford Organic: *all branches*
Electric Diner
The Enterprise
Ffiona's
Foxlow: *all branches*
The Frontline Club
Granger & Co: *all branches*
Hawksmoor: *all branches*
High Road Brasserie
Jackson & Rye Chiswick: *all branches*
Kensington Sq Kitchen
Magazine
Manuka Kitchen
Megan's Delicatessen
Mona Lisa
The Oak: *W2*
Orée
Ottolenghi: *all branches*
Peyotito
Raoul's Café & Deli: *all branches*
The Sands End
The Shed
Snaps & Rye
Sophie's Steakhouse: *all branches*
Taqueria
Tom's Kitchen: *all branches*
VQ: *all branches*

North

Banners
Bodean's: *all branches*
The Booking Office
Caravan King's Cross: *all branches*
Dishoom: *all branches*
Foxlow: *all branches*
Gallipoli: *all branches*
Ginger & White: *all branches*
Granger & Co: *all branches*
Greenberry Café
Harry Morgan's
Brew House
Kipferl
The Landmark
Lantana Cafe: *all branches*
Ottolenghi: *all branches*
Smoke & Salt
The Wet Fish Café
Zest

South

Albion: *SE1*
Annie's: *all branches*
Bodean's: *all branches*
Butlers Wharf Chop House
Caravan Bankside: *all branches*
Chapters
Counter
Dynamo
Fields
Flotsam & Jetsam
Foxlow: *all branches*
Franklins
The Garrison
Ground Coffee Society
Hood
Jackson & Rye Richmond: *all branches*
Joanna's
Lamberts
The Lido Café
Milk
Olympic
Orange Pekoe
Pear Tree Cafe
Pedler
Petersham Hotel
Rivington Grill: *all branches*
Roast
Sonny's Kitchen
The Table
Tried & True
El Vergel
Village East

East

Albion: *E2*
Bistrotheque
Blixen
Bodean's: *all branches*
Bread Street Kitchen
Caravan: *all branches*
Darwin Brasserie
Dishoom: *all branches*
Duck & Waffle
The Fox & Anchor
Foxlow: *all branches*
Granger & Co: *all branches*
Hawksmoor: *all branches*
Hoi Polloi
Jago
Lantana Café: *all branches*
The Modern Pantry: *all branches*
One Canada Square
Ottolenghi: *all branches*
E Pellicci
Poco
Rivington Grill: *all branches*
St John Bread & Wine
Simpson's Tavern
Smiths of Smithfield
3 South Place
Tom's Kitchen: *all branches*
Workshop Coffee: *all branches*

BUSINESS

Central

Al Duca
Alain Ducasse
Alyn Williams
Amaya
The Araki
The Avenue
The Balcon
Bar Boulud
Bbar
Bellamy's
Benares
Bentley's
Bob Bob Ricard
Boisdale
Bonhams Restaurant
The Botanist: *SW1*
Boudin Blanc
Boulestin
Bronte
Brown's Hotel
Le Caprice

1 Lombard Street
Paternoster Chop House
Plateau
Restaurant de Paul: *all branches*
Rocket Canary Wharf: *E14*
Roka: *E14*
Royal Exch Grand Café
St John
Sauterelle
Sign of the Don
Smith's Wapping
Smiths of Smithfield
Smiths of Smithfield
Sushisamba: *EC2*
Sweetings
Taberna Etrusca
3 South Place
The Trading House
The Tramshed
28-50: *all branches*
Vivat Bacchus: *all branches*
The White Swan

BYO

(Bring your own wine at no or low – less than £3 – corkage. Note for £5-£15 per bottle, you can normally negotiate to take your own wine to many, if not most, places.)

Central

Golden Hind
India Club
Patogh

West

Adams Café
Alounak: *all branches*
Best Mangal: *North End RdW14*
Fez Mangal
The Gate: *W6*
Outlaw's at The Capital
Pappa Ciccia: *all branches*

North

Ali Baba
Anima e Cuore
Ariana II
Chutneys
Diwana Bhel-Pouri Hs
Nautilus
Toff's
Vijay
Vintage Salt: *N1*

South

Bistro Union
Cah-Chi: *all branches*
Counter Culture
Fish Club
Hashi
Hot Stuff
Kaosarn: *all branches*
Lahore Karahi
Lahore Kebab House: *all branches*
Mirch Masala
Zaibatsu

East

Caboose
Café Below
Jones Family Project
Lahore Kebab House: *all branches*
Mangal 1
Rochelle Canteen
Tayyabs

LATE

(open till midnight or later as shown; may be earlier Sunday)

Central

Asia de Cuba *(Fri & Sat midnight)*
Assunta Madre
Atelier de Joel Robuchon
Balthazar
Bar Italia *(open 24 hours, Sun 4 am)*
Bar Termini *(Fri & Sat 1 am)*
Bob Bob Ricard *(Sat only)*
La Bodega Negra *(1 am, not Sun)*
Boisdale
Bone Daddies: *Peter StW1 (Thu-Sat midnight)*
Café Monico *(midnight, Fri & Sat 1 am)*
Cantina Laredo *(Fri & Sat midnight)*
Chotto Matte *(Mon-Sat 1 am)*
Chucs: *W1 (Sat only)*
Colony Grill Room
Dean Street Townhouse *(Fri & Sat midnight)*
The Delaunay
Dishoom: *WC2 (Fri & Sat midnight)*
Ember Yard *(Thu-Sat midnight)*
Five Guys: *all branches (Fri & Sat midnight)*
Flat Iron: *all central branches*
The Four Seasons: *Gerrard StW1 (1 am); Wardour StW1 (1 am, Fri & Sat 3.30 am)*
Gaby's
Gelupo *(Fri & Sat midnight)*
Golden Dragon
Goya
Hakkasan Mayfair: *Bruton StW1 (12.30 am); Hanway PlW1 (Thu-Sat midnight)*
Hard Rock Café *(12.30 am, Fri & Sat 1 am, not Sun)*
Heliot Steak House *(1 am)*
Hubbard & Bell
The Ivy *(Thu-Sat midnight)*
The Ivy Market Grill
Jinjuu *(Thu-Sat 1 am)*
Joe Allen *(Fri & Sat 12.45 am)*
M Restaurant: *all branches*
Maroush: *W1 (12.30 am)*
MEATLiquor: *W1 (midnight, Fri & Sat 2 am)*
MEATmarket
Mister Lasagna *(Fri & Sat midnight)*
Mr Chow
New Mayflower *(4 am)*
Nobu Berkeley *(Thu-Sat midnight)*
100 Wardour Street *(2 am, Thu-Sat 3 am, Sun 5 pm)*
Peyote *(Mon-Thu 1 am, Fri & Sat 2 am)*
Poppies: *W1*
La Porchetta Pizzeria: *WC1 (Fri & Sat midnight)*
Princi
Rossopomodoro: *WC2*
Saint Luke's Kitchen *(1 am)*
Savini at Criterion
Shoryu Ramen: *Denman StW1*
Sketch *(1 am, Sun Midnight)*
Sophie's Steakhouse: *all branches (12.45 am, not Sun)*
Tabun Kitchen
Veneta
VQ: *WC1 (24 hours)*
The Wolseley
Yumi Izakaya *(12.30 am)*
Zelman Meats: *SW1 (Thu midnight, Fri & Sat 1 am)*
Zima *(1 am)*

West

Albertine *(Thu-Sat midnight)*
Anarkali
Best Mangal: *SW6; North End RdW14 (midnight, Sat 1 am)*
Buona Sera: *all branches*
Casa Cruz *(12.30 am)*
City Barge *(Fri & Sat midnight)*
The Cross Keys
Electric Diner *(Fri & Sat midnight)*
Gifto's Lahore Karahi *(Sat & Sun midnight)*
Habanera *(Fri & Sat midnight)*
Hanger *(Fri & Sat 12.30 am)*
High Road Brasserie *(Fri & Sat midnight)*
Kojawan *(2 am)*
Maroush: *I) 21 Edgware RdW2 (1.45 am); VI) 68 Edgware RdW2 (12.30 am); SW3 (3.30 am)*
No 197 Chiswick Fire
Stn *(midnight, Fri & Sat 1 am)*
Peyotito *(midnight, Fri & Sat 1 am)*
Pizza East Portobello: *W10 (Fri & Sat midnight)*
Pizza Metro: *all branches (Fri & Sat midnight)*
Rabbit
Romulo Café
Rossopomodoro: *SW10*
Shilpa *(Thu-Sat midnight)*
Sophie's Steakhouse: *all branches (12.45 am, not Sun)*
VQ: *SW10 (24 hours); W11 (Mon-Wed 1am, Thu-Sat 3 am, Sun midnight)*

North

Ali Baba
Ariana II
Banners *(Sat only)*
Dirty Burger: *NW5 (midnight, Fri &*

South

East

ROMANTIC

Central

West

ROOMS WITH A VIEW

NOTABLE WINE LISTS

Sartoria
Savoy Grill
Seven Park Place
Shampers
Shepherd Mkt Wine Hs
Smith &Wollensky
Social Eating House
Social Wine & Tapas
The Square
Tapas Brindisa Soho: *Broadwick StW1*
Tate Britain
The 10 Cases
10 Greek Street
Terroirs
Texture
28-50: *all branches*
Vinoteca Seymour Place: *all branches*
Wild Honey
Zafferano

West

Albertine
L'Amorosa
Angelus
Bibendum
Brinkley's
Cambio de Tercio
Capote Y Toros
Cheneston's Restaurant
Cibo
Clarke's
Le Colombier
L'Etranger
The Five Fields
The Frontline Club
Gordon Ramsay
Hedone
Hereford Road
Kensington Wine Rms
The Ledbury
Locanda Ottomezzo
Medlar
Osteria 60
Popeseye: *W14*
Princess Victoria
The River Café
Tendido Cero
Tendido Cuatro
The Tommy Tucker
La Trompette
Villa Di Geggiano
Vinoteca: *all branches*

North

La Collina
8 Hoxton Square
Prawn On The Lawn
Primeur
Rubedo
St Johns
Sweet Thursday
Trangallan
Trullo
Vinoteca: *all branches*

South

A Cena
Antico
Chez Bruce
Counter
Emile's
40 Maltby Street
The Glasshouse
José
Magdalen
Meson don Felipe
MOMMI
Naughty Piglets
Peckham Bazaar
Pizarro
Le Pont de la Tour
Popeseye: *SW15*
Riva
RSJ
Le Salon Privé
Soif
Ting
Trinity
Vivat Bacchus: *all branches*

East

Bleeding Heart
Bob Bob Exchange
Brawn
Cellar Gascon
Club Gascon
Comptoir Gascon
Coq d'Argent
The Don
Enoteca Rabezzana
Eyre Brothers
Farley Macallan
Goodman: *all branches*
High Timber
Humble Grape
The Jugged Hare
Legs
Moro
P Franco
The Quality Chop House
Restaurant de Paul: *all branches*
Rocket Canary Wharf: *E14*
Sager + Wilde
St John Bread & Wine
Sauterelle
Sign of the Don
Smiths of Smithfield
Sông Quê
Super Tuscan
28-50: *all branches*
Typing Room
Vinoteca: *all branches*
Vivat Bacchus: *all branches*
The Wine Library

Pharmacy 2
The Cafe, Hotel Cafe Royal
The Ivy Cafe

LONDON CUISINES

AMERICAN

Central
The Avenue *(SW1)*
Big Easy *(WC2)*
Bodean's *(W1,WC2)*
Breakfast Club *(W1)*
The Chiltern Firehouse *(W1)*
Christopher's *(WC2)*
Hard Rock Café *(W1)*
Hubbard & Bell *(WC1)*
Jackson & Rye *(W1)*
Joe Allen *(WC2)*
Rainforest Café *(W1)*
Shake Shack *(WC1,WC2)*
Shotgun *(W1)*
Spuntino *(W1)*
temper *(W1)*
Wolfe's Bar & Grill *(WC2)*
Breakfast Club Angel *(N1)*

West
Big Easy *(SW3)*
Bodean's *(SW6)*
Electric Diner *(W11)*
Jackson & Rye Chiswick *(W4)*

North
Bodean's *(N10)*
One Sixty Smokehouse *(NW6)**

South
Bodean's *(SW17, SW4)*
Counter *(SW8)*
Jackson & Rye Richmond *(TW9)*
The Joint *(SW9)**
MeatUp *(SW18)*

East
Big Easy *(E14)*
Bodean's *(EC1, EC3)*
Boondocks *(EC1)*
Breakfast Club *(E1)*
One Sixty Smokehouse *(E1)**
Pitt Cue Co *(EC2)**
Shake Shack *(E20)*
Smokestak *(E1, EC2)**
Walter & Monty *(EC3)*

AUSTRALIAN

Central
Bronte *(WC2)*
Dickie Fitz *(W1)*
Lantana Café *(W1)*

West
Granger & Co *(W11)*
No 197 Chiswick Fire Stn *(W4)*

North
Granger & Co *(N1)*
Lantana Cafe *(NW1)*

South
Flotsam & Jetsam *(SW17)*

East
Granger & Co *(EC1)*
Lantana Café *(EC1)*

BRITISH, MODERN

Central
Alyn Williams *(W1)**
Andrew Edmunds *(W1)*
Aurora *(W1)*
Balthazar *(WC2)*
Barnyard *(W1)*
Bellamy's *(W1)*
The Berners Tavern *(W1)*
Blacklock *(W1)**
Bob Bob Ricard *(W1)*
Bonhams Restaurant *(W1)**
The Botanist *(SW1)*
Le Caprice *(SW1)*
The Cavendish *(W1)*
Caxton Grill *(SW1)*
Clipstone *(W1)*
The Collins Room *(SW1)*
Coopers *(WC2)*
Daylesford Organic *(SW1,W1)*
Dean Street Townhouse *(W1)*
Dorchester Grill *(W1)*
Ducksoup *(W1)*
Ebury *(SW1)*
Fera at Claridge's *(W1)**
45 Jermyn St *(SW1)*
Galvin,Athenaeum *(W1)*
Gordon's Wine Bar *(WC2)*
The Goring Hotel *(SW1)*
The Grazing Goat *(W1)*
Ham Yard Restaurant *(W1)*
Hardy's Brasserie *(W1)*
Hatchetts *(W1)*
Heddon Street Kitchen *(W1)*
Hix *(W1)*
Hush *(W1,WC1)*
The Ivy *(WC2)*
The Ivy Café *(W1)*
The Ivy Market Grill *(WC2)*
Jar Kitchen *(WC2)*
Kitty Fisher's *(W1)**
Langan's Brasserie *(W1)*
Little Social *(W1)*
Mere *(W1)*
Mews of Mayfair *(W1)*
Native *(WC2)**
The Newman Arms *(W1)**
Noble Rot *(WC1)*
The Norfolk Arms *(WC1)*
The Northall *(WC2)*
The Orange *(SW1)*
Ormer Mayfair *(W1)*
Percy & Founders *(W1)**
Picture Marylebone *(W1)**
Pollen Street Social *(W1)*
Polpo at Ape & Bird *(WC2)*
Portland *(W1)**
The Portrait *(WC2)*
The Punchbowl *(W1)**
Quaglino's *(SW1)*
Quo Vadis *(W1)*
Rail House Café *(SW1)*
Roux Parliament Sq *(SW1)**
Roux at the Landau *(W1)*
Saint Luke's Kitchen *(WC2)*
Seven Park Place *(SW1)**
Seven Stars *(WC2)*
Fortnum & Mason *(W1)*
Shampers *(W1)*
Social Eating House *(W1)**
Spring Restaurant *(WC2)*
Tate Britain *(SW1)*
10 Greek Street *(W1)**
The Thomas Cubitt *(SW1)*
Tom's Kitchen *(WC2)*
Tredwell's *(WC2)*
Villandry *(W1)*
The Vincent Rooms *(SW1)*
Vinoteca Seymour Place *(W1)*
VQ *(WC1)*
Wild Honey *(W1)*
The Wolseley *(W1)*

West
The Abingdon *(W8)*
The Anglesea Arms *(W6)*
Babylon *(W8)*
Belvedere *(W8)*
Bluebird *(SW3)*
The Brackenbury *(W6)*
Brinkley's *(SW10)*
The Builders Arms *(SW3)*
Charlotte's Place *(W5)*
Charlotte'sW4 *(W4)*
Charlotte's W5 *(W5)*
City Barge *(W4)*
Clarke's *(W8)**
Claude's Kitchen *(SW6)**
The Dartmouth Castle *(W6)*
Daylesford Organic *(W11)*
The Dock Kitchen *(W10)*
The Dove *(W6)*
Duke of Sussex *(W4)*
Ealing Park Tavern *(W5)*
Elystan Street *(SW3)*
The Enterprise *(SW3)*
The Five Fields *(SW3)**
The Frontline Club *(W2)*
Harwood Arms *(SW6)**
The Havelock Tavern *(W14)*
Hedone *(W4)**
High Road Brasserie *(W4)*
The Hour Glass *(SW3)*
The Ivy Chelsea Garden *(SW3)*
Ivy Kensington Brasserie *(W8)*
Julie's *(W11)*
Kensington Place *(W8)*
Kensington Sq Kitchen *(W8)*
Kitchen W8 *(W8)**
The Ladbroke Arms *(W11)*
Launceston Place *(W8)**
The Ledbury *(W11)**
Magazine *(W2)*
Manuka Kitchen *(SW6)*
Marianne *(W2)**
maze Grill *(SW10)*
Medlar *(SW10)**

Megan's Delicatessen *(SW6)*
Mustard *(W6)*
Parabola *(W8)*
Paradise by Way of KG *(W10)*
The Pear Tree *(W6)*
The Phoenix *(SW3)*
Princess Victoria *(W12)*
Rabbit *(SW3)**
Restaurant Ours *(SW3)*
Salt & Honey *(W2)*
The Sands End *(SW6)*
The Shed *(W8)*
Six Portland Road *(W11)**
Tangerine Dream *(SW3)*
Tom's Kitchen *(SW3)*
The Tommy Tucker *(SW6)*
Vinoteca *(W4)*
VQ *(SW10,W11)*
The Waterway *(W9)*

North

The Albion *(N1)*
The Booking Office *(NW1)*
Bradley's *(NW3)*
The Bull *(N6)*
Caravan King's Cross *(N1)*
Chriskitch *(N1, N10)**
Crocker's Folly *(NW8)*
The Drapers Arms *(N1)*
Fifteen *(N1)*
Frederick's *(N1)*
Grain Store *(N1)**
The Haven *(N20)*
Heirloom *(N8)*
Hill & Szrok *(N1)**
The Horseshoe *(NW3)*
The Ivy Café *(NW8)*
The Junction Tavern *(NW5)*
The Landmark *(NW1)*
The Lighterman *(N1)*
Market *(NW1)*
Odette's *(NW1)**
Oldroyd *(N1)**
Parlour Kensal *(NW10)**
Perilla *(N16)*
Pig & Butcher *(N1)**
Plum + Spilt Milk *(N1)*
Red Lion & Sun *(N6)*
Rotunda *(N1)*
Season Kitchen *(N4)*
Smoke & Salt *(N1)*
The Wells *(NW3)*
The Wet Fish Café *(NW6)*

South

Albion *(SE1)*
Aqua Shard *(SE1)*
The Bingham *(TW10)*
Bistro Union *(SW4)*
Blueprint Café *(SE1)*
The Brown Dog *(SW13)*
Brunswick House Café *(SW8)*
The Camberwell Arms *(SE5)**
Cannizaro House *(SW19)*
Chapters *(SE3)*
Chez Bruce *(SW17)**
Counter Culture *(SW4)**
Craft London *(SE10)**
The Crooked Well *(SE5)*
The Dairy *(SW4)**
The Depot *(SW14)*
The Dysart Petersham *(TW10)**
Earl Spencer *(SW18)*
Edwins *(SE1)*
Elliot's Café *(SE1)*
Emile's *(SW15)*
Fields *(SW4)*
40 Maltby Street *(SE1)**
Franklins *(SE22)**
The Garrison *(SE1)*
The Glasshouse *(TW9)*
The Green Room *(SE1)*
Guildford Arms *(SE10)*
Hood *(SW2)**
House Restaurant *(SE1)*
The Ivy Brasserie *(SE1)*
The Ivy Café *(SW19)*
Lamberts *(SW12)**
The Lido Café *(SE24)*
The Light House *(SW19)*
Magdalen *(SE1)*
The Manor *(SW4)**
May The Fifteenth *(SW4)*
Menier Chocolate Factory *(SE1)*
Oblix *(SE1)*
Olympic *(SW13)*
Oxo Tower *(SE1)*
Oxo Tower *(SE1)*
The Palmerston *(SE22)*
Pear Tree Cafe *(SW11)*
Peckham Ref' Rooms *(SE15)*
The Perry Vale *(SE23)*
Petersham Hotel *(TW10)*
Petersham Nurseries *(TW10)*
Pharmacy 2 *(SE11)*
Le Pont de la Tour *(SE1)*
Rivington Grill *(SE10)*
RSJ *(SE1)*
Salon Brixton *(SW9)**
Sea Containers *(SE1)*
Skylon *(SE1)*
Skylon Grill *(SE1)*
Soif *(SW11)*
Sonny's Kitchen *(SW13)*
Story *(SE1)*
The Swan at the Globe *(SE1)*
The Table *(SE1)*
Tate Modern Restaurant *(SE1)*
Tate Modern *(SE1)*
Tried & True *(SW15)*
Trinity *(SW4)**
Tulse Hill Hotel *(SE24)*
Union Street Café *(SE1)*
Upstairs at John The Un' *(SE15)*
The Victoria *(SW14)*
View 94 *(SW18)*
Waterloo Bar & Kitchen *(SE1)*

East

Anglo *(EC1)**
The Anthologist *(EC2)*
Bird of Smithfield *(EC1)*
Bistrotheque *(E2)*
Bob Bob Exchange *(EC3)*
The Botanist *(EC2)*
The Boundary *(E2)*
Bread Street Kitchen *(EC4)*
Café Below *(EC2)*
Caravan *(EC1)*
The Chancery *(EC4)**
Chiswell St Dining Rms *(EC1)*
City Social *(EC2)*
The Clove Club *(EC1)**
The Culpeper *(E1)*
Darwin Brasserie *(EC3)*
The Don *(EC4)*
Duck & Waffle *(EC2)*
Eat 17 *(E17)**
Ellory *(E8)*
The Empress *(E9)**
Farley Macallan *(E9)*
Fenchurch Restaurant *(EC3)*
The Frog *(E1)*
Galvin HOP *(E1)**
The Gun *(E14)*
High Timber *(EC4)*
Hilliard *(EC4)**
Hoi Polloi *(E1)*
Humble Grape *(EC4)*
Hush *(EC4)*
Jones & Sons *(E8)**
The Jugged Hare *(EC1)*
Legs *(E9)*
Leyton Technical *(E10)*
Lyle's *(E1)**
The Mercer *(EC2)*
Merchants Tavern *(EC2)*
The Morgan Arms *(E3)**
The Narrow *(E14)*
Northbank *(EC4)*
One Canada Square *(E14)*
1 Lombard Street *(EC3)*
P Franco *(E5)*
Paradise Garage *(E2)**
Pidgin *(E8)**
Poco *(E2)*
Princess of Shoreditch *(EC2)*
The Richmond *(E8)*
Rivington Grill *(EC2)*
Rochelle Canteen *(E2)*
Rök *(EC2)**
Sager + Wilde *(E2)*
St John Bread & Wine *(E1)**
Sign of the Don *(EC4)*
Smith's Wapping *(E1)**
Smiths of Smithfield *(EC1)*
Smiths of Smithfield *(EC1)*
3 South Place *(EC2)*
Tom's Kitchen *(E1, E14)*
The Trading House *(EC2)*
Urban Coterie *(EC1)*
Vinoteca *(EC1)*
The White Swan *(EC4)*
The Woodford *(E18)*

BRITISH, TRADITIONAL

Central

Brown's Hotel *(W1)*

Brown's Hotel *(W1)*
Butler's Restaurant *(W1)*
Corrigan's Mayfair *(W1)*
Dinner *(SW1)*
Great Queen Street *(WC2)*
The Guinea Grill *(W1)**
Hardy's Brasserie *(W1)*
Holborn Dining Room *(WC1)*
The Keeper's House *(W1)*
The Lady Ottoline *(WC1)*
Randall & Aubin *(W1)*
Rib Room *(SW1)*
Rules *(WC2)**
Savoy Grill *(WC2)*
Scott's *(W1)**
Shepherd's *(SW1)*
Simpsons-in-the-Strand *(WC2)*
Tate Britain *(SW1)*
Wiltons *(SW1)*
The Windmill *(W1)*

West

Bumpkin *(SW3, SW7)*
Cheneston's Restaurant *(W8)*
Churchill Arms *(W8)*
Ffiona's *(W8)*
The Hampshire Hog *(W6)*
Hereford Road *(W2)**
Maggie Jones's *(W8)*
The Swan *(W4)*

North

The Gilbert Scott *(NW1)*
Piebury Corner *(N7)*
St Johns *(N19)*
York & Albany *(NW1)*

South

The Anchor & Hope *(SE1)**
Butlers Wharf Chop House *(SE1)*
Canton Arms *(SW8)**
Jolly Gardeners *(SW18)*
The Lord Northbrook *(SE12)*
Oxo Tower *(SE1)*
Oxo Tower *(SE1)*
The Plough *(SW14)*
Roast *(SE1)*
The Swan at the Globe *(SE1)*

East

Albion *(E2)*
Albion Clerkenwell *(EC1)*
Bumpkin *(E20)*
Coin Laundry *(EC1)*
The Fox & Anchor *(EC1)*
Hix Oyster & Ch' Hs *(EC1)*
The Marksman *(E2)*
Paternoster Chop House *(EC4)*
E Pellicci *(E2)*
The Quality Chop House *(EC1)*
St John *(EC1)**
St John Bread & Wine *(E1)**
Simpson's Tavern *(EC3)*
Sweetings *(EC4)*

DANISH

Central

Sticks'n'Sushi *(WC2)**

West

Snaps & Rye *(W10)**

South

Sticks'n'Sushi *(SE10, SW19)**

East

Sticks'n'Sushi *(E14)**

EAST & CENT. EUROPEAN

Central

The Delaunay *(WC2)*
Fischer's *(W1)*
Gay Hussar *(W1)*
Sketch *(W1)*
Texture *(W1)**
The Wolseley *(W1)*

North

Bellanger *(N1)*
Black Axe Mangal *(N1)**
German Gymnasium *(N1)*
Kipferl *(N1)*
St Johns *(N19)*

East

The Trading House *(EC2)*

FISH & SEAFOOD

Central

Bellamy's *(W1)*
Bentley's *(W1)*
Bonnie Gull *(W1)**
Burger & Lobster *(SW1,W1)*
Fishworks *(W1)*
Kaspar's *(WC2)*
Olivomare *(SW1)**
One-O-One *(SW1)**
Quaglino's *(SW1)*
Randall & Aubin *(W1)*
Rib Room *(SW1)*
Royal China Club *(W1)**
Salmontini *(SW1)*
Scott's *(W1)**
Sexy Fish *(W1)*
J Sheekey *(WC2)**
J Sheekey Atlantic Bar *(WC2)*
Smith & Wollensky *(WC2)*
Wiltons *(SW1)*
Wright Brothers *(W1)**

West

Bibendum Oyster Bar *(SW3)**
Big Easy *(SW3)*
The Cow *(W2)*
Geales *(W8)*
Kensington Place *(W8)*
Mandarin Kitchen *(W2)**
Outlaw's at The Capital *(SW3)**
The Summerhouse *(W9)*
Wright Brothers *(SW7)**

North

Bradley's *(NW3)*
Carob Tree *(NW5)*
Fish Cafe *(NW3)*
Galley *(N1)**
Lure *(NW5)**
Olympus Fish *(N3)**
Prawn On The Lawn *(N1)**
Toff's *(N10)*

South

Applebee's Café *(SE1)**
Cornish Tiger *(SW11)*
fish! *(SE1)*
Lobster Pot *(SE11)**
Le Querce *(SE23)*
Wright Brothers *(SE1)**

East

Angler *(EC2)*
Burger & Lobster *(EC1, EC4)*
Chamberlain's *(EC3)*
Fish Central *(EC1)*
Fish Market *(EC2)*
Hix Oyster & Ch' Hs *(EC1)*
Royal Exch Grand Café *(EC3)*
Smith's Wapping *(E1)**
Sweetings *(EC4)*
Wright Brothers *(E1)**

FRENCH

Central

Alain Ducasse *(W1)*
Antidote *(W1)*
L'Artiste Musclé *(W1)*
Atelier de Joel Robuchon *(WC2)*
L'Autre Pied *(W1)**
The Balcon *(SW1)*
Bao Fitzrovia *(W1)**
Bar Boulud *(SW1)*
Bellamy's *(W1)*
Blanchette *(W1)**
Boudin Blanc *(W1)*
Boulestin *(SW1)*
Brasserie Zédel *(W1)*
Café Monico *(W1)*
Céleste *(SW1)*
Cigalon *(WC2)*
Clos Maggiore *(WC2)*
Colbert *(SW1)*
Les Deux Salons *(WC2)*
L'Escargot *(W1)*
Frenchie *(WC2)**
Galvin at Windows *(W1)*
Galvin Bistrot de Luxe *(W1)*
Le Garrick *(WC2)*
Gauthier Soho *(W1)**
Le Gavroche *(W1)**
The Greenhouse *(W1)*
Hélène Darroze *(W1)*
Koffmann's *(SW1)**
Marcus *(SW1)*
Margot *(WC2)*
maze *(W1)*
Mon Plaisir *(WC2)*

Les 110 de Taillevent *(W1)*
Orrery *(W1)*
Otto's *(WC1)**
Park Chinois *(W1)*
La Petite Maison *(W1)**
Pétrus *(SW1)*
Pied à Terre *(W1)**
La Poule au Pot *(SW1)*
Prix Fixe *(W1)*
Relais de Venise *(W1)*
Le Restaurant de PAUL *(WC2)*
The Ritz Restaurant *(W1)*
Savoir Faire *(WC1)*
Savoy Grill *(WC2)*
Savoy, Thames Foyer *(WC2)*
Seven Park Place *(SW1)**
Sketch *(W1)*
Sketch *(W1)*
The Square *(W1)*
Terroirs *(WC2)*
28-50 *(W1)*
Villandry *(W1)*
Villandry St James's *(SW1)*
The Wallace *(W1)*

West

Albertine *(W12)*
Angelus *(W2)*
Bandol *(SW10)*
Bel Canto *(W2)*
Belvedere *(W8)*
Bibendum *(SW3)*
La Brasserie *(SW3)*
Brasserie Gustave *(SW3)*
Cheyne Walk Brasserie *(SW3)*
Le Colombier *(SW3)*
L'Etranger *(SW7)*
Gordon Ramsay *(SW3)*
Michael Nadra *(W4)**
Orée *(SW10)**
Quantus *(W4)**
La Trompette *(W4)**
Le Vacherin *(W4)*

North

L'Absinthe *(NW1)*
Almeida *(N1)*
L'Aventure *(NW8)*
Bistro Aix *(N8)**
Bradley's *(NW3)*
La Cage Imaginaire *(NW3)*
Le Mercury *(N1)*
Michael Nadra *(NW1)**
Oslo Court *(NW8)**
Patron *(NW5)*
Petit Pois Bistro *(N1)*
Le Sacré-Coeur *(N1)**
The Wells *(NW3)*

South

Augustine Kitchen *(SW11)*
Boro Bistro *(SE1)*
Brasserie Toulouse-Lautrec *(SE11)*
La Buvette *(TW9)*
Casse-Croute *(SE1)**
Counter *(SW8)*
Gastronhome *(SW11)**
Gazette *(SW11, SW12, SW15)*
Lobster Pot *(SE11)**
Ma Cuisine *(TW9)*
Le Salon Privé *(TW1)**
Soif *(SW11)*
The White Onion *(SW19)*

East

Blanchette East *(E1)**
Bleeding Heart *(EC1)*
Brawn *(E2)**
Café du Marché *(EC1)*
Café Pistou *(EC1)*
Cellar Gascon *(EC1)*
Club Gascon *(EC1)**
Comptoir Gascon *(EC1)*
Coq d'Argent *(EC2)*
The Don *(EC4)*
La Ferme *(EC1)*
Galvin La Chapelle *(E1)*
Lutyens *(EC4)*
Plateau *(E14)*
Provender *(E11)*
Relais de Venise *(E14, EC2)*
Restaurant de Paul *(EC2)*
Royal Exch Grand Café *(EC3)*
Sauterelle *(EC3)*
The Trading House *(EC2)*
28-50 *(EC4)*

FUSION

Central

Asia de Cuba *(WC2)*
Bronte *(WC2)*
Bubbledogs *(W1)**
Carousel *(W1)**
Dabbous *(W1)*
Jikoni *(W1)*
La Porte des Indes *(W1)*
Providores *(W1)*
Twist *(W1)**

West

E&O *(W11)*
Eight Over Eight *(SW3)*
L'Etranger *(SW7)*

North

Caravan King's Cross *(N1)*
The Petite Coree *(NW6)**

South

Caravan Bankside *(SE1)*
Champor-Champor *(SE1)**
Ting *(SE1)*
Tsunami *(SW4)**
Village East *(SE1)*

East

Caravan *(EC1)*
CURIO + TA TA *(E8)*
Jago *(E1)*
The Modern Pantry *(EC1, EC2)*
Typing Room *(E2)**

GAME

Central

Bocca Di Lupo *(W1)**
Boisdale *(SW1)*
Rules *(WC2)**
Wiltons *(SW1)*

West

Harwood Arms *(SW6)**

North

San Daniele del Friuli *(N5)*

South

The Anchor & Hope *(SE1)**

East

Boisdale of Bishopsgate *(EC2)*
Boisdale of Canary Wharf *(E14)*
The Jugged Hare *(EC1)*

GREEK

Central

Estiatorio Milos *(SW1)*
Opso *(W1)*

West

Mazi *(W8)**

North

Carob Tree *(NW5)*
The Greek Larder *(N1)*
Lemonia *(NW1)*
Nissi *(N13)*
Vrisaki *(N22)*

South

Peckham Bazaar *(SE15)**

East

Kolossi Grill *(EC1)*

HUNGARIAN

Central

Gay Hussar *(W1)*

INTERNATIONAL

Central

Café in the Crypt *(WC2)*
Canvas *(SW1)*
Colony Grill Room *(W1)*
Cork & Bottle *(WC2)*
Foley's *(W1)*
Gordon's Wine Bar *(WC2)*
Motcombs *(SW1)*
The 10 Cases *(WC2)*

West

The Admiral Codrington *(SW3)*
The Andover Arms *(W6)*
Annie's *(W4)*
Gallery Mess *(SW3)*
Kensington Wine Rms *(W8)*
Melody at St Paul's *(W14)*
Mona Lisa *(SW10)*
Rivea *(SW7)*

North

Banners (N8)
Bull & Last (NW5)
8 Hoxton Square (N1)*
The Haven (N20)
Primeur (N5)*
Salut (N1)*

South

Annie's (SW13)
Joanna's (SE19)
London House (SW11)
Pedler (SE15)
The Plough (SW14)
Rabot 1745 (SE1)
Tulse Hill Hotel (SE24)
Vivat Bacchus (SE1)
The Yellow House (SE16)

East

Blixen (E1)
Eat 17 (E9)*
Sager + Wilde (E2)
Vivat Bacchus (EC4)
The Wine Library (EC3)

IRISH

West

The Cow (W2)

ITALIAN

Central

Al Duca (SW1)
Assunta Madre (W1)
Bar Italia (W1)
Bar Termini (W1)
Il Baretto (W1)
Bernardi's (W1)
Bocca Di Lupo (W1)*
Bocconcino (W1)
Briciole (W1)
C London (W1)
Cacio & Pepe (SW1)*
Café Murano (SW1,WC2)
Caffè Caldesi (W1)
Caraffini (SW1)
Cecconi's (W1)
Chucs (W1)
Ciao Bella (WC1)
Como Lario (SW1)
Il Convivio (SW1)
Da Mario (WC2)
Dehesa (W1)*
Delfino (W1)*
Enoteca Turi (SW1)*
Franco's (SW1)
Fumo (WC2)
Gustoso (SW1)
Latium (W1)*
Locanda Locatelli (W1)*
Luce e Limoni (WC1)
Made in Italy James St (W1)
Mele e Pere (W1)
Mister Lasagna (W1)
Murano (W1)*
Novikov (W1)
Obicà (W1)
Oliveto (SW1)
Olivo (SW1)
Olivocarne (SW1)
Olivomare (SW1)*
Opera Tavern (WC2)*
Orso (WC2)
Ottolenghi (SW1)
Park Chinois (W1)
Polpetto (W1)
Polpo (SW1,W1,WC2)
La Porchetta Pizzeria (WC1)
Princi (W1)
Quattro Passi (W1)
Quirinale (SW1)*
Ristorante Frescobaldi (W1)
Rossopomodoro (W1,WC2)
Sale e Pepe (SW1)
Salt Yard (W1)
San Carlo Cicchetti (W1,WC2)
Santini (SW1)
Sardo (W1)
Sartoria (W1)
Savini at Criterion (W1)
Signor Sassi (SW1)
Theo Randall (W1)
Tozi (SW1)
2 Veneti (W1)
Vapiano (W1)
Vasco & Piero's (W1)
Veneta (SW1)
Vico (WC2)
Il Vicolo (SW1)
Zafferano (SW1)

West

Aglio e Olio (SW10)*
L'Amorosa (W6)*
Assaggi (W2)*
Bird in Hand (W14)
Buona Sera (SW3)
Buoni Amici (W12)
Chucs (W11)
Cibo (W14)*
Clarke's (W8)*
Da Mario (SW7)
Daphne's (SW3)
La Delizia Limbara (SW3)
Edera (W11)
Essenza (W11)
La Famiglia (SW10)
Frantoio (SW10)
Locanda Ottomezzo (W8)
Lucio (SW3)
Made in Italy (SW3)
Manicomio (SW3)
Mediterraneo (W11)
Mona Lisa (SW10)
Nuovi Sapori (SW6)
The Oak W12 (W12,W2)*
Obicà (SW3)
Osteria 60 (SW7)
Osteria Basilico (W11)
Ottolenghi (W11,W8)
Pappa Ciccia (SW6)
Pellicano Restaurant (SW3)
Pentolina (W14)*
Polpo (SW3,W11)
Il Portico (W8)
Portobello Ristorante (W11)
The Red Pepper (W9)
Riccardo's (SW3)
The River Café (W6)
Rossopomodoro (SW10)
Sapori Sardi (SW6)
Scalini (SW3)
Tartufo (SW3)
Theo's Simple Italian (SW5)
Toto's (SW3)
Villa Di Geggiano (W4)
Ziani's (SW3)

North

Anima e Cuore (NW1)*
Artigiano (NW3)
L'Artista (NW11)
La Collina (NW1)
500 (N19)
Giacomo's (NW2)
Melange (N8)
Osteria Tufo (N4)
Ostuni (N6, NW6)
Ottolenghi (N1)
Pizzeria Oregano (N1)
Pizzeria Pappagone (N4)
La Porchetta Pizzeria (N1, N4, NW1)
The Rising Sun (NW7)
Rugoletta (N12, N2)*
San Daniele del Friuli (N5)
Sarracino (NW6)*
Trullo (N1)*
Villa Bianca (NW3)

South

A Cena (TW1)
Al Forno (SW15, SW19)
Antico (SE1)
Artusi (SE15)
Bacco (TW9)
La Barca (SE1)
Bibo (SW15)
Al Boccon di'vino (TW9)*
Buona Sera (SW11)
Canada Water Cafe (SE16)
Donna Margherita (SW11)
Figlio Del Vesuvio (SW17)*
Lorenzo (SE19)
Luciano's (SE12)
MacellaioRC (SE1)
Made in Italy (SW19)
Numero Uno (SW11)
Osteria Antica Bologna (SW11)
Padella (SE1)*
Pizza Metro (SW11)
Pizzeria Rustica (TW9)
Pulia (SE1)
Le Querce (SE23)
Riva (SW13)*

The Table *(SE1)*
Vapiano *(SE1)*

East
L'Anima *(EC2)*
L'Anima Café *(EC2)*
Apulia *(EC1)*
Bombetta *(E11)*
Il Bordello *(E1)*
Canto Corvino *(E1)**
Caravaggio *(EC3)*
Enoteca Rabezzana *(EC1)*
Gatti's City Point *(EC2)*
Gotto Trattoria *(E20)*
Lardo Bebè *(E8)*
MacellaioRC *(EC1)*
Manicomio *(EC2)*
Obicà *(E14, EC4)*
Osteria *(EC2)*
E Pellicci *(E2)*
Polpo *(EC1)*
La Porchetta Pizzeria *(EC1)*
Rotorino *(E8)*
Rucoletta *(EC2)*
Santore *(EC1)**
Super Tuscan *(E1)**
Taberna Etrusca *(EC4)*
Verdi's *(E1)*

MEDITERRANEAN

Central
Blandford Comptoir *(W1)**
Massimo *(WC2)*
The Ninth *(W1)**
Nopi *(W1)**
The Norfolk Arms *(WC1)*
100 Wardour Street *(W1)*
Riding House Café *(W1)*
Shepherd Mkt Wine Hs *(W1)*

West
Adams Café *(W12)*
The Atlas *(SW6)**
The Cross Keys *(SW3)*
Cumberland Arms *(W14)**
Locanda Ottomezzo *(W8)*
Made in Italy *(SW3)*
Mediterraneo *(W11)*
Raoul's Café *(W9)*
Raoul's Café & Deli *(W11)*
The Swan *(W4)*
Wormwood *(W11)**

North
The Little Bay *(NW6)*
Rubedo *(N16)**
Sardine *(N1)*
Vinoteca *(N1)*

South
The Bobbin *(SW4)*
Fish in a Tie *(SW11)*
The Fox & Hounds *(SW11)**
Gourmet Goat *(SE1)**
Peckham Bazaar *(SE15)**
El Vergel *(SE1)**

East
The Eagle *(EC1)**
Morito *(EC1)**
Rocket Bishopgate *(EC2)*
Rocket Canary Wharf *(E14)*
Vinoteca *(EC1)*

ORGANIC

Central
Daylesford Organic *(SW1,W1)*

West
Daylesford Organic *(W11)*
Squirrel *(SW7)*

East
Smiths of Smithfield *(EC1)*

POLISH

West
Daquise *(SW7)*
Ognisko Restaurant *(SW7)*
Patio *(W12)*

South
Baltic *(SE1)*

PORTUGUESE

West
Lisboa Pâtisserie *(W10)*

East
Eyre Brothers *(EC2)**
The Gun *(E14)*
Taberna do Mercado *(E1)**

RUSSIAN

Central
Bob Bob Ricard *(W1)*
Mari Vanna *(SW1)*
Zima *(W1)*

SCANDINAVIAN

Central
Aquavit *(SW1)*
Bageriet *(WC2)*
The Harcourt *(W1)**
Nordic Bakery *(W1)*
Scandinavian Kitchen *(W1)*
Texture *(W1)**

West
Flat Three *(W11)**

North
Rök *(N1)**

SCOTTISH

Central
Boisdale *(SW1)*
Mac & Wild *(W1)**

East
Boisdale of Bishopsgate *(EC2)*
Boisdale of Canary Wharf *(E14)*

SPANISH

Central
About Thyme *(SW1)*
Ametsa *(SW1)**
aqua nueva *(W1)*
Barrafina *(W1)**
Barrafina Drury Lane *(WC2)**
Barrica *(W1)*
Cigala *(WC1)*
Dehesa *(W1)**
Donostia *(W1)**
Drakes Tabanco *(W1)**
Duende *(WC2)**
Ember Yard *(W1)**
Eneko at One Aldwych *(WC2)*
Goya *(SW1)*
Ibérica *(SW1,W1)*
Lurra *(W1)**
Morada Brindisa Asador *(W1)*
Opera Tavern *(WC2)**
El Pirata *(W1)*
Salt Yard *(W1)*
Social Wine & Tapas *(W1)*

West
Cambio de Tercio *(SW5)*
Capote Y Toros *(SW5)*
Casa Brindisa *(SW7)*
Duke of Sussex *(W4)*
Tamp Coffee *(W4)*
Tendido Cero *(SW5)*
Tendido Cuatro *(SW6)*

North
Bar Esteban *(N8)**
Café del Parc *(N19)**
Camino King's Cross *(N1)*
Escocesa *(N16)**
El Parador *(NW1)**
Trangallan *(N16)**

South
Alquimia *(SW15)*
Boqueria *(SW2)*
Brindisa Food Rooms *(SW9)*
Camino Bankside *(SE1)*
Gremio de Brixton *(SW2)*
José *(SE1)**
Little Taperia *(SW17)**
LOBOS Meat & Tapas *(SE1)**
Mar I Terra *(SE1)*
Meson don Felipe *(SE1)*
Pizarro *(SE1)*
Tapas Brindisa *(SE1)*

East
Bravas *(E1)*
Camino Blackfriars *(EC4)*
Camino Monument *(EC3)*
Eyre Brothers *(EC2)**
Hispania *(EC3)*
Ibérica *(E14, EC1)*
José Pizarro *(EC2)**
Morito *(E2, EC1)**

Moro *(EC1)**
Sagardi *(EC2)*

STEAKS & GRILLS

Central

Barbecoa *(SW1)*
Barbecoa Piccadilly *(W1)*
Beast *(W1)*
Bentley's *(W1)*
Bodean's *(W1)*
Boisdale *(SW1)*
Bukowski Grill *(W1)**
Christopher's *(WC2)*
Cut *(W1)*
Flat Iron *(W1,WC2)**
Goodman *(W1)*
The Guinea Grill *(W1)**
Hawksmoor *(W1,WC2)*
Heliot Steak House *(WC2)**
M Restaurant *(SW1)*
MASH Steakhouse *(W1)*
maze Grill *(W1)*
Relais de Venise *(W1)*
Rib Room *(SW1)*
Rowley's *(SW1)*
Smith & Wollensky *(WC2)*
Sophie's Steakhouse *(WC2)*
34 Mayfair *(W1)*
Wolfe's Bar & Grill *(WC2)*
Zelman Meats *(SW1,W1)**
Zoilo *(W1)**

West

Bodean's *(SW6)*
Casa Malevo *(W2)*
Foxlow *(W4)*
Haché *(SW10)*
Hanger *(SW6)*
Hawksmoor *(SW3)*
MacellaioRC *(SW7)*
Megan's Delicatessen *(SW6)*
Popeseye *(W14)*
Smokehouse Chiswick *(W4)*
Sophie's Steakhouse *(SW10)*
West Thirty Six *(W10)*

North

Foxlow *(N16)*
Haché *(NW1)*
Popeseye *(N19)*
Smokehouse Islington *(N1)**
The Wells *(NW3)*

South

Bodean's *(SW4)*
Bukowski Grill *(SW9)**
Cau *(SE3, SW19)*
Cornish Tiger *(SW11)*
Counter *(SW8)*
Foxlow *(SW12)*
MeatUp *(SW18)*
Naughty Piglets *(SW2)**
Oblix *(SE1)*
Popeseye *(SW15)*
El Vergel *(SE1)**

East

Barbecoa *(EC4)*
Bodean's *(EC1, EC3)*
Boisdale of Bishopsgate *(EC2)*
Boisdale of Canary Wharf *(E14)*
Buen Ayre *(E8)**
Bukowski Grill *(E1)**
Cau *(E1)*
Flat Iron *(EC2)**
Foxlow *(EC1)*
Goodman *(E14)*
Goodman City *(EC2)*
Hawksmoor *(E1, EC2)*
High Timber *(EC4)*
Hill & Szrok *(E8)**
Hix Oyster & Ch' Hs *(EC1)*
Jones & Sons *(E8)**
Jones Family Project *(EC2)*
M Restaurant *(EC2)*
Paternoster Chop House *(EC4)*
Relais de Venise *(E14, EC2)*
Rocket Canary Wharf *(E14)*
Simpson's Tavern *(EC3)*
Smith's Wapping *(E1)**
Smiths of Smithfield *(EC1)*
Smiths of Smithfield *(EC1)*
Smiths of Smithfield *(EC1)*
The Tramshed *(EC2)*

SWISS

Central

St Moritz *(W1)**

VEGETARIAN

Central

Chettinad *(W1)**
Ethos *(W1)*
Malabar Junction *(WC1)*
Mildreds *(W1)*
Ormer Mayfair *(W1)*
Ragam *(W1)**
Rasa *(W1)*
Rasa Maricham *(WC1)*
Sagar *(W1)*
The Square *(W1)*
Texture *(W1)**
tibits *(W1)*

West

Farmacy *(W2)*
The Gate *(W6)**
Sagar *(W6)*

North

Chutneys *(NW1)*
Diwana Bhel-Pouri Hs *(NW1)*
Jashan *(N8)**
Manna *(NW3)*
Rani *(N3)*
Rasa Travancore *(N16)*
Vijay *(NW6)*

South

Ganapati *(SE15)**
Le Pont de la Tour *(SE1)*
Skylon *(SE1)*
Sree Krishna *(SW17)**
Tas Pide *(SE1)*

East

The Gate *(EC1)**
Vanilla Black *(EC4)**

AFTERNOON TEA

Central

Bea's Cake Boutique *(WC1)*
Brown's Hotel *(W1)*
The Collins Room *(SW1)*
Dalloway Terrace *(WC1)*
The Delaunay *(WC2)*
F&M, Diamond Tea Rm *(W1)*
La Fromagerie Café *(W1)*
Galvin, Athenaeum *(W1)*
The Goring Hotel *(SW1)*
Ham Yard Restaurant *(W1)*
Palm Court *(W1)*
Maison Bertaux *(W1)*
Oscar Wilde Bar *(W1)*
Promenade *(W1)*
Le Restaurant de PAUL *(WC2)*
The Ritz *(W1)*
Savoy, Thames Foyer *(WC2)*
Sketch *(W1)*
Villandry *(W1)*
Villandry St James's *(SW1)*
The Wallace *(W1)*
The Wolseley *(W1)*
Yauatcha *(W1)**

West

Cheneston's Restaurant *(W8)*
Magazine *(W2)*

North

Brew House *(NW3)*
The Landmark *(NW1)*

South

The Bingham *(TW10)*
Cannizaro House *(SW19)*
Orange Pekoe *(SW13)*
Oxo Tower *(SE1)*
Petersham Nurseries *(TW10)*
Ting *(SE1)*

East

Restaurant de Paul *(EC2)*

BURGERS, ETC

Central

Bar Boulud *(SW1)*
Bbar *(SW1)*
Bobo Social *(W1)**
Bodean's *(W1)*
Burger & Lobster *(SW1,W1,WC1)*
Clives Midtown Diner *(WC1)*
Five Guys *(WC2)*
Goodman *(W1)*
Hard Rock Café *(W1)*
Hawksmoor *(W1,WC2)*
Joe Allen *(WC2)*
Mac & Wild *(W1)**

MEATLiquor *(W1)*
MEATmarket *(WC2)**
Opera Tavern *(WC2)**
Patty & Bun *(W1)**
Rainforest Café *(W1)*
Shake Shack *(SW1,WC1,WC2)*
Tommi's Burger Joint *(W1)**
Zoilo *(W1)**

West

The Admiral Codrington *(SW3)*
Big Easy *(SW3)*
Bodean's *(SW6)*
Electric Diner *(W11)*
Haché *(SW10)*
Tommi's Burger Joint *(SW3)**
West Thirty Six *(W10)*

North

Bill or Beak *(NW1)**
Dirty Burger *(NW5)*
Duke's Brew & Que *(N1)**
Five Guys Islington *(N1)*
Haché *(NW1)*
Harry Morgan's *(NW8)*
Meat Mission *(N1)*
MEATLiquor *(N1)*
One Sixty Smokehouse *(NW6)**

South

Bodean's *(SW4)*
Dip & Flip *(SW11, SW17, SW19, SW9)*
Dirty Burger *(SW8)*
Haché *(SW12, SW4)*
MEATLiquor *(SE22)*
Rivington Grill *(SE10)*
Rox Burger *(SE13)**
Sonny's Kitchen *(SW13)*
Village East *(SE1)*

East

Bleecker Street Burger *(E1)**
Bodean's *(EC1, EC3)*
Burger & Lobster *(EC1, EC4)*
Caboose *(E1)*
Chicken Shop & Dirty Burger *(E1)*
Chuck Burger *(E1)*
Comptoir Gascon *(EC1)*
Dirty Burger *(E1)*
Goodman *(E14)*
Goodman City *(EC2)*
Haché *(EC2)*
Hawksmoor *(E1, EC2)*
Lucky Chip *(E8)*
One Sixty Smokehouse *(E1)**
Patty & Bun *(E2, E8, EC2)**
The Rib Man *(E1)**
Rivington Grill *(EC2)*
Shake Shack *(E20)*
Smiths of Smithfield *(EC1)*

CRÊPES

Central

Mamie's *(WC2)*

FISH & CHIPS

Central

Golden Hind *(W1)**
North Sea Fish *(WC1)*
Poppies *(W1)*
Seafresh *(SW1)*

West

The Chipping Forecast *(W11)*
Geales *(W8)*
Geales Chelsea Green *(SW3)*
Kensington Place *(W8)*
Kerbisher & Malt *(W5,W6)*

North

Nautilus *(NW6)**
Olympus Fish *(N3)**
Poppies Camden *(NW1)*
The Sea Shell *(NW1)*
Sutton & Sons *(N1, N16)**
Toff's *(N10)*
Two Brothers *(N3)*
Vintage Salt *(N1)*

South

Brady's *(SW18)*
Fish Club *(SW11)*
fish! *(SE1)*
Kerbisher & Malt *(SW14, SW4)*
Masters Super Fish *(SE1)*

East

Ark Fish *(E18)**
Kerbisher & Malt *(EC1)*
Poppies *(E1)*
Sutton & Sons *(E8)**
Vintage Salt *(EC2)*

ICE CREAM

Central

Gelupo *(W1)**

PIZZA

Central

Il Baretto *(W1)*
Bocconcino *(W1)*
Delfino *(W1)**
Homeslice *(W1,WC2)**
Made in Italy James St *(W1)*
Mayfair Pizza Company *(W1)*
Oliveto *(SW1)*
The Orange *(SW1)*
Pizza Pilgrims *(W1,WC2)**
La Porchetta Pizzeria *(WC1)*
Princi *(W1)*
Rossopomodoro *(W1,WC2)*

West

Bird in Hand *(W14)*
Buona Sera *(SW3)*
Da Mario *(SW7)*
La Delizia Limbara *(SW3)*
Made in Italy *(SW3)*
The Oak W12 *(W12,W2)**
Osteria Basilico *(W11)*
Pappa Ciccia *(SW6)*
Pizza East Portobello *(W10)*
Pizza Metro *(W11)*
Pizzicotto *(W8)**
Portobello Ristorante *(W11)*
The Red Pepper *(W9)*
Rocca Di Papa *(SW7)*
Rossopomodoro *(SW10)*
Santa Maria *(SW6,W5)**

North

L' Antica Pizzeria *(NW3)**
L'Artista *(NW11)*
Pizza East *(NW5)*
Pizzeria Oregano *(N1)*
Pizzeria Pappagone *(N4)*
La Porchetta Pizzeria *(N1, N4, NW1)*
Rossopomodoro *(N1, NW1)*
Sacro Cuore *(NW10)**
Sarracino *(NW6)**
Sweet Thursday *(N1)*
Yard Sale Pizza *(N4)**
Zia Lucia *(N7)*

South

Al Forno *(SW15, SW19)*
Buona Sera *(SW11)*
Canada Water Cafe *(SE16)*
Craft London *(SE10)**
Donna Margherita *(SW11)*
Dynamo *(SW15)*
Eco *(SW4)*
Figlio Del Vesuvio *(SW17)**
The Gowlett Arms *(SE15)**
Joe Public *(SW4)**
Lorenzo *(SE19)*
Made in Italy *(SW19)*
Mamma Dough *(SE23, SW9)*
Numero Uno *(SW11)*
Pedler *(SE15)*
Pizza Metro *(SW11)*
Pizzeria Pellone *(SE24)**
Pizzeria Rustica *(TW9)*
Rocca Di Papa *(SE21)*
Rossopomodoro *(SW18)*
Theo's *(SE5)**
The Yellow House *(SE16)*

East

Il Bordello *(E1)*
Corner Kitchen *(E7)*
Crate *(E9)*
Homeslice *(EC1)**
Lardo Bebè *(E8)*
Pizza East *(E1)*
Pizza Pilgrims *(EC1)**
La Porchetta Pizzeria *(EC1)*
Rocket Bishopgate *(EC2)*
Rocket Canary Wharf *(E14)*
Santore *(EC1)**
The Stable *(E1)*
Yard Sale Pizza *(E5)**

SANDWICHES, CAKES, ETC

Central
Bageriet *(WC2)*
Bea's Cake Boutique *(WC1)*
Daylesford Organic *(W1)*
Dominique Ansel *(SW1)*
Fernandez & Wells *(W1,WC2)*
La Fromagerie Café *(W1)*
Kaffeine *(W1)*
Maison Bertaux *(W1)*
Maison Eric Kayser *(W1)*
Monmouth Coffee Company *(WC2)**
Nordic Bakery *(W1)*
Scandinavian Kitchen *(W1)*
Spring Workshop *(W1)*
Workshop Coffee *(W1)*

West
Lisboa Pâtisserie *(W10)*

North
Doppio *(NW1)*
Ginger & White *(NW3)*
Greenberry Café *(NW1)*
Brew House *(NW3)*
Max's Sandwich Shop *(N4)**

South
Ground Coffee Society *(SW15)*
Kappacasein *(SE16)**
Milk *(SW12)**
Monmouth Coffee Company *(SE1)**
Orange Pekoe *(SW13)*

East
Brick Lane Beigel Bake *(E1)**
Dept of Coffee *(EC1)*
Prufrock Coffee *(EC1)*
Workshop Coffee *(EC1)*

SALADS

Central
Kaffeine *(W1)*

CHICKEN

Central
Bao *(W1)**
Billy & The Chicks *(W1)*
Chicken Shop *(WC1)*
Clives Midtown Diner *(WC1)*
On The Bab *(WC2)*
On The Bab Express *(W1)*
Randall & Aubin *(W1)*

West
Cocotte *(W2)**

North
Bird Camden *(NW1)*
Bird Islington *(N7)*
Chicken Shop *(N7, NW5, NW8)*
Le Coq *(N1)*

South
Chicken Shop *(SW17)*
Chicken Shop & Dirty Burger *(SW12)*
MeatUp *(SW18)*
Pique Nique *(SE1)*

East
Bird *(E2)*
Bird Stratford *(E20)*
Chick 'n' Sours *(E8)*
Chicken Shop & Dirty Burger *(E1)*
On The Bab *(EC1, EC4)*
Randy's Wing Bar *(E15)*
The Tramshed *(EC2)*

ARGENTINIAN

Central
Zoilo *(W1)**

West
Casa Malevo *(W2)*
Quantus *(W4)**

East
Buen Ayre *(E8)**

BRAZILIAN

East
Sushisamba *(EC2)*

MEXICAN/TEXMEX

Central
La Bodega Negra *(W1)*
Cantina Laredo *(WC2)*
Lupita *(WC2)*
Martha Ortiz *(W1)*
Peyote *(W1)*

West
Habanera *(W12)*
Peyotito *(W11)*
Taqueria *(W11)**

South
El Pastór *(SE1)*

PERUVIAN

Central
Casita Andina *(W1)*
Ceviche Soho *(W1)*
Coya *(W1)*
Lima *(W1)*
Lima Floral *(WC2)*
Pachamama *(W1)*
Señor Ceviche *(W1)*

West
Chicama *(SW10)*

South
MOMMI *(SW4)*

East
Andina *(E2)**
Ceviche Old St *(EC1)*
Sushisamba *(EC2)*

SOUTH AMERICAN

Central
MNKY HSE *(W1)*

West
Casa Cruz *(W11)*
Quantus *(W4)**

South
MOMMI *(SW4)*
El Vergel *(SE1)**

MOROCCAN

West
Adams Café *(W12)*
Zayane *(W10)**

NORTH AFRICAN

Central
The Barbary *(WC2)*
Momo *(W1)*

SOUTH AFRICAN

Central
Bbar *(SW1)*

East
High Timber *(EC4)*

TUNISIAN

West
Adams Café *(W12)*

EGYPTIAN

North
Ali Baba *(NW1)*

ISRAELI

Central
Gaby's *(WC2)*
The Palomar *(W1)**

East
Ottolenghi *(E1)*

KOSHER

Central
Reubens *(W1)*

North
Kaifeng *(NW4)*
Zest *(NW3)*

East
Brick Lane Beigel Bake *(E1)**

LEBANESE

Central
Fairuz *(W1)*
Maroush *(W1)*
Yalla Yalla *(W1)*

West
Chez Abir *(W14)*
Maroush *(SW3)*
Maroush Gardens *(W2)*

South
Arabica Bar & Kitchen *(SE1)*
Meza Trinity Road *(SW17)**
Yalla Yalla *(SE10)*

MIDDLE EASTERN

Central
The Barbary *(WC2)*
Honey & Co *(W1)**
Patogh *(W1)**
Samarkand *(W1)*
Tabun Kitchen *(W1)*

West
Falafel King *(W10)*

East
Berber & Q *(E8)**
Berber & Q Sh' Bar *(EC1)*
Morito *(EC1)**
Pilpel *(E1, EC4)**
Strut & Cluck *(E1)*

PERSIAN

Central
Patogh *(W1)**

West
Alounak *(W14,W2)*
Faanoos *(W4,W5)*
Kateh *(W9)*

South
Faanoos *(SW14)*

SYRIAN

West
Abu Zaad *(W12)*

TURKISH

Central
Le Bab *(W1)**
Babaji Pide *(W1)*
Ishtar *(W1)*
Kazan (Café) *(SW1)*

West
Best Mangal *(SW6,W14)**
Fez Mangal *(W11)**

North
Gallipoli *(N1)*
Gem *(N1)*
GoÅNkyüzü *(N4)**

South
FM Mangal *(SE5)*
Tas Pide *(SE1)*

East
Haz *(E1, EC2, EC3)*
Mangal 1 *(E8)**
Mangal 1.1 *(EC2)*
Oklava *(EC2)**

AFGHANI

North
Afghan Kitchen *(N1)*
Ariana II *(NW6)*

CHINESE

Central
A Wong *(SW1)**
Baozi Inn *(WC2)**
Barshu *(W1)**
The Bright Courtyard *(W1)**
Chilli Cool *(WC1)**
China Tang *(W1)*
The Duck & Rice *(W1)**
Four Seasons *(W1)**
Golden Dragon *(W1)*
The Grand Imperial *(SW1)**
Hakkasan Mayfair *(W1)*
Hunan *(SW1)**
Joy King Lau *(WC2)*
Kai Mayfair *(W1)*
Ken Lo's Memories *(SW1)*
Leong's Legends *(W1)*
Mr Chow *(SW1)*
New Mayflower *(W1)*
New World *(W1)*
Park Chinois *(W1)*
Royal China *(W1)*
Royal China Club *(W1)**
Shuang Shuang *(W1)*
Wong Kei *(W1)*
Yauatcha *(W1)**
Yming *(W1)*

West
Dragon Palace *(SW5)**
The Four Seasons *(W2)**
Gold Mine *(W2)**
Good Earth *(SW3)*
Mandarin Kitchen *(W2)**
Min Jiang *(W8)**
North China *(W3)*
Pearl Liang *(W2)**
Royal China *(SW6,W2)*
Shikumen *(W12)*
Stick & Bowl *(W8)**
Taiwan Village *(SW6)**

North
Good Earth *(NW7)*
Green Cottage *(NW3)*
Kaifeng *(NW4)*
Phoenix Palace *(NW1)*
Singapore Garden *(NW6)*
Xi'an Impression *(N7)**
Yipin China *(N1)*

South
Dragon Castle *(SE17)*
Good Earth *(SW17)*
Hutong *(SE1)*
Silk Road *(SE5)**

East
Chinese Cricket Club *(EC4)*
HKK *(EC2)**
Royal China *(E14)*
The Sichuan *(EC1)**
Sichuan Folk *(E1)**
Yauatcha City *(EC2)**
Yi-Ban *(E16)*

CHINESE, DIM SUM

Central
The Bright Courtyard *(W1)**
Golden Dragon *(W1)*
The Grand Imperial *(SW1)**
Hakkasan Mayfair *(W1)*
Joy King Lau *(WC2)*
New Mayflower *(W1)*
New World *(W1)*
Novikov *(W1)*
Royal China *(W1)*
Royal China Club *(W1)**
Yauatcha *(W1)**

West
Min Jiang *(W8)**
Pearl Liang *(W2)**
Royal China *(SW6,W2)*
Shikumen *(W12)*

North
Jun Ming Xuan *(NW9)**
Phoenix Palace *(NW1)*

South
Dragon Castle *(SE17)*

East
Royal China *(E14)*
Yauatcha City *(EC2)**
Yi-Ban *(E16)*

FILIPINO

West
Romulo Café *(W8)*

GEORGIAN

North
Little Georgia Café *(N1)*

East
Little Georgia Café *(E2)*

HAWAIIAN

Central
Ahi Poké *(W1)*

INDIAN

Central

Amaya *(SW1)**
Benares *(W1)*
Chettinad *(W1)**
Chor Bizarre *(W1)*
Chutney Mary *(SW1)**
The Cinnamon Club *(SW1)*
Cinnamon Soho *(W1)**
Dishoom *(W1,WC2)**
Gaylord *(W1)*
Gymkhana *(W1)**
Imli Street *(W1)*
India Club *(WC2)*
Jamavar *(W1)*
Kricket *(W1)**
Lotus *(WC2)**
Malabar Junction *(WC1)*
Mint Leaf *(SW1)*
Nirvana Kitchen *(W1)*
La Porte des Indes *(W1)*
Punjab *(WC2)*
Ragam *(W1)**
Red Fort *(W1)**
Roti Chai *(W1)**
Sagar *(W1,WC2)*
Salaam Namaste *(WC1)*
Salloos *(SW1)**
Talli Joe *(WC2)*
Tamarind *(W1)**
Trishna *(W1)**
Veeraswamy *(W1)*

West

Anarkali *(W6)*
Bombay Brasserie *(SW7)*
Bombay Palace *(W2)*
Brilliant *(UB2)*
Chakra *(W8)**
Flora Indica *(SW5)*
Gifto's Lahore Karahi *(UB1)*
Indian Zing *(W6)**
Karma *(W14)*
Khan's *(W2)*
Madhu's *(UB1)**
Malabar *(W8)**
Masala Grill *(SW10)*
Noor Jahan *(SW5,W2)*
The Painted Heron *(SW10)**
Potli *(W6)**
Pure Indian Cooking *(SW6)*
Rasoi *(SW3)*
Sagar *(W6)*
Star of India *(SW5)**
Thali *(SW5)**
Zaika *(W8)**

North

Chutneys *(NW1)*
Delhi Grill *(N1)*
Dishoom *(N1)**
Diwana Bhel-Pouri Hs *(NW1)*
Great Nepalese *(NW1)*
Guglee *(NW3, NW6)*
Indian Rasoi *(N2)**
Jashan *(N8)**
Namaaste Kitchen *(NW1)*
Paradise Hampstead *(NW3)**
Rani *(N3)*
Ravi Shankar *(NW1)*
Vijay *(NW6)*
Zaffrani *(N1)*

South

Babur *(SE23)**
Everest Inn *(SE3)**
Ganapati *(SE15)**
Hot Stuff *(SW8)*
Indian Moment *(SW11)*
Indian Ocean *(SW17)*
Indian Zilla *(SW13)**
Kennington Tandoori *(SE11)*
Kricket *(SW9)**
Lahore Karahi *(SW17)**
Lahore Kebab House *(SW16)**
Ma Goa *(SW15)**
Mirch Masala *(SW17)**
Sree Krishna *(SW17)**

East

Café Spice Namaste *(E1)**
Cinnamon Kitchen *(EC2)*
Darbaar *(EC2)**
Dishoom *(E2)**
Gunpowder *(E1)**
Lahore Kebab House *(E1)**
Mint Leaf Lounge *(EC2)*
Needoo *(E1)**
Tayyabs *(E1)**

INDIAN, SOUTHERN

Central

Hoppers *(W1)**
India Club *(WC2)*
Malabar Junction *(WC1)*
Quilon *(SW1)**
Ragam *(W1)**
Rasa *(W1)*
Rasa Maricham *(WC1)*
Sagar *(W1,WC2)*

West

Sagar *(W6)*
Shilpa *(W6)**

North

Chutneys *(NW1)*
Rani *(N3)*
Rasa Travancore *(N16)*
Vijay *(NW6)*

South

Ganapati *(SE15)**
Jaffna House *(SW17)**
Sree Krishna *(SW17)**

JAPANESE

Central

Anzu *(SW1)*
The Araki *(W1)**
Atari-Ya *(W1)**
Bone Daddies *(SW1,W1)**
Chisou *(W1)**
Chotto Matte *(W1)**
Defune *(W1)**
Dinings *(W1)**
Eat Tokyo *(WC1,WC2)**
Engawa *(W1)**
Flesh & Buns *(WC2)*
Ichiryu *(WC1)**
Ippudo London *(WC2)*
Kanada-Ya *(SW1,WC2)**
Kiku *(W1)*
Kikuchi *(W1)**
Kintan *(WC1)*
Koya-Bar *(W1)*
Kulu Kulu *(W1,WC2)*
Kurobuta Harvey Nics *(SW1)**
Matsuri *(SW1)*
Murakami *(WC2)*
Nobu *(W1)*
Nobu Berkeley *(W1)*
Oka *(W1)**
Oliver Maki *(W1)*
Roka *(W1,WC2)**
Sakagura *(W1)*
Sake No Hana *(SW1)*
Salmontini *(SW1)*
Shoryu Ramen *(SW1,W1)*
Sticks'n'Sushi *(WC2)**
Sumosan *(W1)*
Sushisamba *(WC2)*
Taro *(W1)*
Tokimeite *(W1)**
Tokyo Diner *(WC2)*
Tonkotsu *(W1)*
Tsunami *(W1)**
Umu *(W1)*
Wazen *(WC1)**
Yoshino *(W1)**
Yumi Izakaya *(W1)*

West

Atari-Ya *(W3,W5)**
Bone Daddies *(W8)**
Chisou *(SW3)**
Eat Tokyo *(W6,W8)**
Flat Three *(W11)**
Inaho *(W2)**
Kiraku *(W5)**
Kiru *(SW3)**
Kojawan *(W2)*
Kulu Kulu *(SW7)*
Kurobuta *(SW3,W2)**
Maguro *(W9)**
Sushi Bar Makoto *(W4)*
Tokyo Sukiyaki-Tei *(SW3)*
Tonkotsu *(W11)*
Tosa *(W6)*
Yashin *(W8)*
Yoshi Sushi *(W6)*
Zuma *(SW7)**

North
Asakusa (NW1)*
Atari-Ya (N12, NW4, NW6)*
Dotori (N4)*
Eat Tokyo (NW11)*
Jin Kichi (NW3)*
Oka (NW1)*
Sushi Masa (NW2)

South
Hashi (SW20)*
Matsuba (TW9)
MOMMI (SW4)
Nanban (SW9)*
Sticks'n'Sushi (SE10, SW19)*
Takahashi (SW19)*
Tomoe (SW15)*
Tonkotsu Bankside (SE1)
Tsunami (SW4)*
Yama Momo (SE22)*
Zaibatsu (SE10)*

East
Beer & Buns (EC2)
Bone Daddies (EC1)*
Ippudo London (E14)
K10 (EC2, EC3)*
Pham Sushi (EC1)*
Roka (E14)*
Shoryu Ramen (EC2)
Sosharu (EC1)
Sticks'n'Sushi (E14)*
Sushisamba (EC2)
Sushi Tetsu (EC1)*
Tonkotsu East (E8)
Yum Bun (EC2)*

KOREAN

Central
Bibimbap (W1)
Jinjuu (W1)
Kintan (WC1)
Lime Orange (SW1)
On The Bab (WC2)
On The Bab Express (W1)

West
Kojawan (W2)
Yoshi Sushi (W6)

North
Dotori (N4)*
The Petite Coree (NW6)*

South
Cah-Chi (SW18, SW20)
Matsuba (TW9)

East
Bibimbap (EC3)
Chick 'n' Sours (E8)
On The Bab (EC1, EC4)

MALAYSIAN

Central
C&R Café (W1)*

West
C&R Café (W2)*
Satay House (W2)

North
Roti King (NW1)*
Singapore Garden (NW6)

South
Champor-Champor (SE1)*

PAKISTANI

Central
Salloos (SW1)*

South
Lahore Karahi (SW17)*
Lahore Kebab House (SW16)*
Mirch Masala (SW17)*

East
Lahore Kebab House (E1)*
Needoo (E1)*
Tayyabs (E1)*

PAN-ASIAN

Central
Black Roe (W1)
Buddha-Bar London (SW1)
Hare & Tortoise (WC1)
Nopi (W1)*
Novikov (W1)

West
E&O (W11)
Eight Over Eight (SW3)
Hare & Tortoise (W14,W4,W5)
Kojawan (W2)
Koji (SW6)*
Uli (W11)

North
Gilgamesh (NW1)

South
Hare & Tortoise (SW15)

East
Hare & Tortoise (EC4)

THAI

Central
Crazy Bear (W1)
Kiln (W1)
Patara Fitzrovia (W1)
Rosa's (SW1)
Rosa's Soho (W1)
Smoking Goat (WC2)*

West
Addie's Thai Café (SW5)*
The Heron (W2)*
Patara (SW3)
Rosa's Fulham (SW10)
Sukho Thai Cuisine (SW6)*
Suksan (SW10)*

North
Isarn (N1)*
Yum Yum (N16)

South
Awesome Thai (SW13)
The Begging Bowl (SE15)*
Farang (SE1)
Kaosarn (SW11, SW9)*
The Pepper Tree (SW4)
Rosa's (SW9)

East
Rosa's (E1)
Rosa's (E15)
Som Saa (E1)*

VIETNAMESE

Central
Cây Tre (W1)*
Ho (W1)
Viet Food (W1)

West
Saigon Saigon (W6)

North
CôBa (N7)*
Salvation In Noodles (N1, N4)
Singapore Garden (NW6)

South
Bánh Bánh (SE15)*
Café East (SE16)*
Mien Tay (SW11)*

East
Cây Tre (EC1)*
City Càphê (EC2)
Mien Tay (E2)*
Sông Quê (E2)
Viet Grill (E2)

TAIWANESE

Central
Bao (W1)*
Leong's Legends (W1)

West
Taiwan Village (SW6)*

South
Mr Bao (SE15)

LONDON AREA OVERVIEWS

CENTRAL

Soho, Covent Garden & Bloomsbury (Parts of W1, all WC2 and WC1)

£140+	Engawa	*Japanese*	444
£110+	Atelier de Joel Robuchon	*French*	223
£100+	Smith & Wollensky	*Steaks & grills*	112
£90+	Sushisamba	*Japanese*	335
£80+	The Northall	*British, Modern*	334
	Spring Restaurant	*"*	334
	Savoy Grill	*British, Traditional*	233
	Kaspar's	*Fish & seafood*	233
	Asia de Cuba	*Fusion*	122
	MASH Steakhouse	*Steaks & grills*	233
	Roka	*Japanese*	433
£70+	Christopher's	*American*	323
	Social Eating House	*British, Modern*	433
	Rules	*British, Traditional*	435
	Simpsons-in-the-Strand	*"*	111
	J Sheekey	*Fish & seafood*	444
	J Sheekey Atlantic Bar	*"*	345
	Clos Maggiore	*French*	345
	Frenchie	*"*	422
	Gauthier Soho	*"*	554
	Massimo	*Mediterranean*	223
	Nopi	*"*	433
	Eneko at One Aldwych	*Spanish*	– – –
	Hawksmoor	*Steaks & grills*	332
	Savoy, Thames Foyer	*Afternoon tea*	235
	Yauatcha	*Chinese*	433
£60+	Balthazar	*British, Modern*	113
	Bob Bob Ricard	*"*	345
	Dean Street Townhouse	*"*	235
	Ham Yard Restaurant	*"*	344
	Hix	*"*	122
	Hush	*"*	233
	The Ivy	*"*	345
	The Portrait	*"*	234
	Tom's Kitchen	*"*	222
	Tredwell's	*"*	222
	Holborn Dining Room	*British, Traditional*	334
	Randall & Aubin	*Fish & seafood*	344
	Wright Brothers	*"*	433

	Antidote	*French*	222
	Café Monico	*"*	234
	Les Deux Salons	*"*	121
	L'Escargot	*"*	344
	Otto's	*"*	453
	Vasco & Piero's	*Italian*	343
	100 Wardour Street	*Mediterranean*	223
	aqua nueva	*Spanish*	122
	Rainforest Café	*Burgers, etc*	233
	Lima Floral	*Peruvian*	321
	Red Fort	*Indian*	422
	Chotto Matte	*Japanese*	435
	Oliver Maki	*"*	– – –
	Patara Soho	*Thai*	344
£50+	Big Easy	*American*	223
	Hubbard & Bell	*"*	333
	Joe Allen	*"*	224
	Shotgun	*"*	222
	Andrew Edmunds	*British, Modern*	345
	Aurora	*"*	344
	Ducksoup	*"*	334
	The Ivy Market Grill	*"*	223
	Noble Rot	*"*	333
	Quo Vadis	*"*	– – –
	Saint Luke's Kitchen	*"*	– – –
	10 Greek Street	*"*	442
	Vinoteca	*"*	223
	Great Queen Street	*British, Traditional*	322
	The Lady Ottoline	*"*	323
	The Delaunay	*Cent. European*	234
	Cigalon	*French*	343
	Le Garrick	*"*	234
	Mon Plaisir	*"*	244
	Gay Hussar	*Hungarian*	234
	Cork & Bottle	*International*	234
	The 10 Cases	*"*	213
	Bocca Di Lupo	*Italian*	544
	Café Murano	*"*	333
	Dehesa	*"*	423
	Luce e Limoni	*"*	353
	Mele e Pere	*"*	332
	Obicà	*"*	332
	Orso	*"*	232
	San Carlo Cicchetti	*"*	334
	Vico	*"*	221
	Cigala	*Spanish*	222
	Ember Yard	*"*	444
	Opera Tavern	*"*	442
	Heliot Steak House	*Steaks & grills*	444

	Sophie's Steakhouse	"	243
	Zelman Meats	"	544
	St Moritz	*Swiss*	433
	Dalloway Terrace	*Afternoon tea*	– – –
	Oscar Wilde Bar	"	244
	La Bodega Negra	*Mexican/TexMex*	334
	Cantina Laredo	"	323
	The Palomar	*Israeli*	554
	Barshu	*Chinese*	422
	The Duck & Rice	"	434
	Four Seasons	"	411
	Lotus	*Indian*	442
	Flesh & Buns	*Japanese*	333
	Wazen	"	442
	Ho	*Vietnamese*	222

£40+	Bodean's	*American*	222
	Jackson & Rye	"	122
	Spuntino	"	333
	Wolfe's Bar & Grill	"	322
	Coopers	*British, Modern*	233
	Jar Kitchen	"	333
	Native	"	442
	The Norfolk Arms	"	333
	Polpo at Ape & Bird	"	222
	Shampers	"	245
	VQ	"	243
	Brasserie Zédel	*French*	135
	Prix Fixe	"	332
	Terroirs	"	324
	Ciao Bella	*Italian*	235
	Da Mario	"	333
	Polpetto	"	233
	Polpo	"	222
	Barrafina Drury Lane	*Spanish*	555
	Duende	"	422
	Morada Brindisa Asador	"	222
	Mildreds	*Vegetarian*	333
	Burger & Lobster	*Burgers, etc*	333
	Rossopomodoro	*Pizza*	322
	Fernandez & Wells	*Sandwiches, cakes, etc*	333
	Lupita	*Mexican/TexMex*	322
	Ceviche Soho	*Peruvian*	333
	Señor Ceviche	"	334
	The Barbary	*North African*	– – –
	Le Bab	*Turkish*	543
	New Mayflower	*Chinese*	322
	Shuang Shuang	"	333
	Yming	"	343
	Cinnamon Soho	*Indian*	422

	Dishoom	"	434
	Imli Street	"	222
	Kricket	"	543
	Malabar Junction	"	333
	Talli Joe	"	– – –
	Kintan	*Japanese*	333
	Murakami	"	333
	Oka	"	432
	Shoryu Ramen	"	322
	Sticks'n'Sushi	"	444
	Yumi Izakaya	"	– – –
	Jinjuu	*Korean*	333
	Smoking Goat	*Thai*	432
£35+	Blacklock	*British, Modern*	544
	Blanchette	*French*	445
	Le Restaurant de PAUL	"	344
	Savoir Faire	"	333
	Gordon's Wine Bar	*International*	125
	Bar Termini	*Italian*	345
	Mister Lasagna	"	– – –
	Bukowski Grill	*Steaks & grills*	432
	North Sea Fish	*Fish & chips*	332
	Bea's Cake Boutique	*Sandwiches, cakes, etc*	323
	Chicken Shop	*Chicken*	223
	Yalla Yalla	*Lebanese*	323
	Tabun Kitchen	*Middle Eastern*	– – –
	Joy King Lau	*Chinese*	331
	NewWorld	"	222
	Sagar	*Indian*	332
	Salaam Namaste	"	343
	Rasa Maricham	*Indian, Southern*	333
	Ippudo London	*Japanese*	323
	Taro	"	332
	On The Bab	*Korean*	332
	C&R Café	*Malaysian*	422
	Rosa's Soho	*Thai*	332
	Cây Tre	*Vietnamese*	433
	Leong's Legends	*Taiwanese*	322
£30+	Seven Stars	*British, Modern*	233
	Café in the Crypt	*International*	224
	Bar Italia	*Italian*	235
	La Porchetta Pizzeria	"	233
	Princi	"	334
	Pizza Pilgrims	*Pizza*	434
	Gaby's	*Israeli*	322
	Chilli Cool	*Chinese*	421
	Golden Dragon	"	322
	Wong Kei	"	222

	Punjab	*Indian*	323
	Bone Daddies	*Japanese*	444
	Ichiryu	"	432
	Koya-Bar	"	344
	Kulu Kulu	"	311
	Tonkotsu	"	233
	Hare & Tortoise	*Pan-Asian*	333
	Viet Food	*Vietnamese*	333
£25+	Breakfast Club	*American*	332
	Zima	*Russian*	– – –
	MEATmarket	*Burgers, etc*	422
	Poppies	*Fish & chips*	333
	Billy & The Chicks	*Chicken*	332
	India Club	*Indian*	221
	Hoppers	*Indian, Southern*	444
	Tokyo Diner	*Japanese*	343
	Bibimbap	*Korean*	222
	Bao	*Taiwanese*	422
£20+	Flat Iron	*Steaks & grills*	433
	Clives Midtown Diner	*Burgers, etc*	342
	Patty & Bun	"	432
	Shake Shack	"	322
	Tommi's Burger Joint	"	444
	Homeslice	*Pizza*	444
	Baozi Inn	*Chinese*	422
	Eat Tokyo	*Japanese*	422
£15+	Nordic Bakery	*Scandinavian*	343
	Maison Bertaux	*Afternoon tea*	343
	Kanada-Ya	*Japanese*	422
£10+	Five Guys	*Burgers, etc*	322
	Bageriet	*Sandwiches, cakes, etc*	343
£5+	Gelupo	*Ice cream*	522
	Monmouth Coffee Company	*Sandwiches, cakes, etc*	554

Mayfair & St James's (Parts of W1 and SW1)

£380+	The Araki	*Japanese*	554
£130+	Le Gavroche	*French*	554
	The Greenhouse	"	343
	Hélène Darroze	"	343
	The Ritz Restaurant	"	345
	Sketch	"	335
	The Square	"	– – –

Price	Restaurant	Cuisine	Ratings
£120+	Alain Ducasse	*French*	243
	Estiatorio Milos	*Greek*	333
	Promenade	*Afternoon tea*	244
£110+	Fera at Claridge's	*British, Modern*	444
	Cut	*Steaks & grills*	122
	Umu	*Japanese*	332
£100+	Dorchester Grill	*British, Modern*	333
	Pollen Street Social	"	223
	Galvin at Windows	*French*	235
	Assunta Madre	*Italian*	222
	C London	"	113
	Novikov	"	112
£90+	Alyn Williams	*British, Modern*	453
	Corrigan's Mayfair	*British, Traditional*	344
	Wiltons	"	344
	Seven Park Place	*French*	444
	Murano	*Italian*	442
	Quattro Passi	"	332
	Theo Randall	"	331
	Hakkasan Mayfair	*Chinese*	323
	Kai Mayfair	"	322
	Park Chinois	"	254
	Benares	*Indian*	112
	Nobu	*Japanese*	222
	Nobu Berkeley	"	322
	Novikov	*Pan-Asian*	212
£80+	Butler's Restaurant	*British, Traditional*	343
	Bentley's	*Fish & seafood*	344
	Scott's	"	455
	Sexy Fish	"	212
	maze	*French*	222
	La Petite Maison	"	545
	Sketch	"	234
	Savini at Criterion	*Italian*	112
	Goodman	*Steaks & grills*	333
	Chutney Mary	*Indian*	434
	Matsuri	*Japanese*	331
	Roka	"	433
£70+	The Berners Tavern	*British, Modern*	224
	Le Caprice	"	344
	Little Social	"	334
	Quaglino's	"	113
	Wild Honey	"	333
	Brown's Hotel	*British, Traditional*	344
	Brown's Hotel	"	233

	Boulestin	*French*	2 2 2
	Cecconi's	*Italian*	2 2 3
	Franco's	"	3 3 3
	Ristorante Frescobaldi	"	3 3 2
	Sartoria	"	2 3 3
	The Guinea Grill	*Steaks & grills*	4 4 4
	Hawksmoor	"	3 3 2
	maze Grill	"	1 2 2
	Rowley's	"	2 2 2
	34 Mayfair	"	2 2 2
	The Ritz	*Afternoon tea*	2 3 5
	Bocconcino	*Pizza*	3 3 3
	Peyote	*Mexican/TexMex*	3 3 2
	Coya	*Peruvian*	3 2 4
	China Tang	*Chinese*	3 2 3
	Tamarind	*Indian*	[illegible]
	Veeraswamy	"	3 3 3
	Sake No Hana	*Japanese*	3 1 2
	Sumosan	"	– – –
	Tokimeite	"	4 4 2
£60+	The Avenue	*American*	1 2 2
	Hard Rock Café	"	2 2 4
	Bellamy's	*British, Modern*	3 4 3
	Bonhams Restaurant	"	4 5 3
	Galvin, Athenaeum	"	– – –
	Heddon Street Kitchen	"	2 2 2
	Hush	"	2 3 3
	Kitty Fisher's	"	4 4 4
	Langan's Brasserie	"	1 2 4
	Mews of Mayfair	"	3 3 3
	The Wolseley	"	2 3 5
	The Keeper's House	*British, Traditional*	2 2 2
	Fishworks	*Fish & seafood*	3 2 2
	The Balcon	*French*	2 2 2
	Colony Grill Room	*International*	3 4 4
	Chucs	*Italian*	3 5 3
	Barbecoa Piccadilly	*Steaks & grills*	2 2 2
	F&M, Diamond Tea Rm	*Afternoon tea*	3 3 3
	Momo	*North African*	3 3 4
	Chor Bizarre	*Indian*	3 2 4
	Gymkhana	"	5 4 4
	Mint Leaf	"	3 3 4
	Nirvana Kitchen	"	– – –
	Black Roe	*Pan-Asian*	3 3 3
	Patara Mayfair	*Thai*	3 4 4
£50+	Hatchetts	*British, Modern*	– – –
	Fortnum & Mason	"	2 2 3
	Boudin Blanc	*French*	2 3 4

	28-50	"	234
	Villandry St James's	"	112
	Café Murano	*Italian*	333
	Shepherd Mkt Wine Hs	*Mediterranean*	– – –
	Chisou	*Japanese*	442
	Kiku	"	332
£40+	The Punchbowl	*British, Modern*	444
	The Windmill	*British, Traditional*	323
	L'Artiste Musclé	*French*	225
	Al Duca	*Italian*	343
	Il Vicolo	"	333
	El Pirata	*Spanish*	344
	Burger & Lobster	*Burgers, etc*	333
	Delfino	*Pizza*	432
	Mayfair Pizza Company	"	343
	Shoryu Ramen	*Japanese*	322
	Yoshino	"	442
£35+	tibits	*Vegetarian*	223
	Rasa	*Indian, Southern*	333
£25+	Spring Workshop	*Sandwiches, cakes, etc*	– – –
£15+	Kanada-Ya	*Japanese*	422

Fitzrovia & Marylebone (Part of W1)

£110+	Pied à Terre	*French*	442
	Beast	*Steaks & grills*	222
£100+	Bubbledogs	*Fusion*	543
	Texture	*Scandinavian*	433
£90+	Roux at the Landau	*British, Modern*	344
	Hakkasan	*Chinese*	323
£80+	The Chiltern Firehouse	*American*	123
	L'Autre Pied	*French*	442
	Orrery	"	333
	Dabbous	*Fusion*	332
	Locanda Locatelli	*Italian*	444
	Roka	*Japanese*	433
£70+	Providores	*Fusion*	322
	Il Baretto	*Italian*	222
	Palm Court	*Afternoon tea*	333
	Royal China Club	*Chinese*	433
	La Porte des Indes	*Indian*	335

Price	Restaurant	Cuisine	Rating
	Trishna	"	533
	Defune	*Japanese*	431
	Kikuchi	"	432
£60+	Dickie Fitz	*Australian*	222
	The Cavendish	*British, Modern*	333
	Portland	"	543
	Fischer's	*Cent. European*	334
	Fishworks	*Fish & seafood*	322
	Galvin Bistrot de Luxe	*French*	333
	Les 110 de Taillevent	"	333
	Bernardi's	*Italian*	343
	Caffè Caldesi	"	333
	The Ninth	*Mediterranean*	432
	The Harcourt	*Scandinavian*	434
	Lima	*Peruvian*	321
	Pachamama	"	312
	The Bright Courtyard	*Chinese*	532
	Gaylord	*Indian*	343
	Crazy Bear	*Thai*	224
	Patara Fitzrovia	"	344
£50+	Daylesford Organic	*British, Modern*	223
	The Grazing Goat	"	233
	The Ivy Café	"	224
	Percy & Founders	"	432
	Vinoteca Seymour Place	"	223
	Bonnie Gull	*Fish & seafood*	442
	28-50	*French*	234
	Villandry	"	112
	The Wallace	"	215
	Carousel	*Fusion*	454
	Twist	"	444
	Latium	*Italian*	442
	Obicà	"	332
	Sardo	"	322
	2 Veneti	"	343
	Blandford Comptoir	*Mediterranean*	444
	Riding House Café	"	223
	Barrica	*Spanish*	333
	Lurra	"	433
	Daylesford Organic	*Sandwiches, cakes, etc*	223
	Zoilo	*Argentinian*	423
	Reubens	*Kosher*	233
	Maroush	*Lebanese*	322
	Dinings	*Japanese*	431
	House of Ho	*Vietnamese*	222
£40+	Barnyard	*British, Modern*	233
	Hardy's Brasserie	"	233

	The Newman Arms	"	444
	Picture Marylebone	"	442
	Opso	*Greek*	323
	Briciole	*Italian*	333
	Made in Italy James St	"	323
	Rossopomodoro	"	322
	Mac & Wild	*Scottish*	442
	Donostia	*Spanish*	534
	Drakes Tabanco	"	444
	Ibérica	"	223
	Salt Yard	"	333
	Social Wine & Tapas	"	323
	Relais de Venise	*Steaks & grills*	322
	Bobo Social	*Burgers, etc*	442
	Burger & Lobster	"	333
	La Fromagerie Café	*Sandwiches, cakes, etc*	322
	Workshop Coffee	"	334
	Fairuz	*Lebanese*	333
	Honey & Co	*Middle Eastern*	542
	Ishtar	*Turkish*	332
	Royal China	*Chinese*	312
	Roti Chai	*Indian*	434
	Tsunami	*Japanese*	523
£35+	Lantana Café	*Australian*	333
	Ethos	*Vegetarian*	323
	MEATLiquor	*Burgers, etc*	334
	Yalla Yalla	*Lebanese*	323
	Babaji Pide	*Turkish*	223
	Chettinad	*Indian*	423
	Sagar	"	332
	On The Bab Express	*Korean*	332
£30+	Vapiano	*Italian*	323
	Atari-Ya	*Japanese*	422
	Tonkotsu	"	233
£25+	Bao Fitzrovia	*French*	422
	Golden Hind	*Fish & chips*	442
	Ragam	*Indian*	431
	Bibimbap	*Korean*	222
£20+	Patty & Bun	*Burgers, etc*	432
	Tommi's Burger Joint	"	444
	Homeslice	*Pizza*	444
	Patogh	*Middle Eastern*	433
£15+	Nordic Bakery	*Scandinavian*	343

£10+	Ahi Poké	*Hawaiian*	– – –
	Scandinavian Kitchen	*Scandinavian*	3 3 3
	Kaffeine	*Sandwiches, cakes, etc*	3 5 5

Belgravia, Pimlico, Victoria & Westminster (SW1, except St James's)

£110+	Marcus	*French*	3 2 3
	Pétrus	"	3 3 2
£100+	Dinner	*British, Traditional*	3 3 4
	Céleste	*French*	2 3 2
	Rib Room	*Steaks & grills*	2 3 2
£90+	One-O-One	*Fish & seafood*	4 2 1
	Ametsa	*Spanish*	4 3 2
£80+	The Collins Room	*British, Modern*	2 4 5
	The Goring Hotel	"	3 5 4
	Roux Parliament Sq	"	5 5 3
	Koffmann's	*French*	4 5 3
	Zafferano	*Italian*	2 2 2
	Hunan	*Chinese*	5 4 1
	Mr Chow	"	2 2 2
£70+	Caxton Grill	*British, Modern*	– – –
	Salmontini	*Fish & seafood*	2 2 3
	Bar Boulud	*French*	2 3 3
	Canvas	*International*	2 3 2
	Santini	*Italian*	2 3 3
	Mari Vanna	*Russian*	2 2 4
	M Restaurant	*Steaks & grills*	2 2 2
	Amaya	*Indian*	5 3 3
	The Cinnamon Club	"	3 3 3
	Quilon	*Indian, Southern*	4 4 2
	Buddha-Bar London	*Pan-Asian*	2 2 3
£60+	The Botanist	*British, Modern*	2 1 2
	45 Jermyn St	"	3 4 4
	The Thomas Cubitt	"	3 4 4
	Olivomare	*Fish & seafood*	4 3 2
	La Poule au Pot	*French*	2 2 5
	Il Convivio	*Italian*	3 3 4
	Enoteca Turi	"	4 5 4
	Olivo	"	3 3 2
	Olivocarne	"	3 3 2
	Quirinale	"	4 4 2
	Sale e Pepe	"	3 4 4
	Signor Sassi	"	3 3 4
	Boisdale	*Scottish*	2 2 3

	Barbecoa	*Steaks & grills*	222
	Oliveto	*Pizza*	321
	The Grand Imperial	*Chinese*	433
£50+	Daylesford Organic	*British, Modern*	223
	Ebury	"	223
	The Orange	"	344
	Tate Britain	"	235
	Shepherd's	*British, Traditional*	334
	Colbert	*French*	112
	Motcombs	*International*	233
	Cacio & Pepe	*Italian*	444
	Caraffini	"	354
	Como Lario	"	222
	Ottolenghi	"	322
	About Thyme	*Spanish*	333
	Zelman Meats	*Steaks & grills*	544
	Bbar	*South African*	343
	Ken Lo's Memories	*Chinese*	342
	Kurobuta Harvey Nics	*Japanese*	522
	Salloos	*Pakistani*	432
£40+	Gustoso	*Italian*	353
	Polpo	"	222
	Tozi	"	333
	Goya	*Spanish*	333
	Ibérica	"	223
	Burger & Lobster	*Burgers, etc*	333
	Kazan (Café)	*Turkish*	342
£35+	The Vincent Rooms	*British, Modern*	333
	Seafresh	*Fish & chips*	342
	AWong	*Chinese*	554
	Lime Orange	*Korean*	322
	Rosa's	*Thai*	332
£30+	Bone Daddies	*Japanese*	444
£20+	Shake Shack	*Burgers, etc*	322

WEST

Chelsea, South Kensington, Kensington, Earl's Court & Fulham (SW3, SW5, SW6, SW7, SW10 & W8)

Price	Restaurant	Cuisine	Rating
£140+	Gordon Ramsay	*French*	243
£90+	Vineet Bhatia	*Indian*	323
£80+	The Five Fields	*British, Modern*	554
	Launceston Place	"	454
	Cheneston's Restaurant	*British, Traditional*	234
	Outlaw's at The Capital	*Fish & seafood*	442
	Toto's	*Italian*	234
	Zuma	*Japanese*	434
£70+	Babylon	*British, Modern*	223
	Kitchen W8	"	442
	maze Grill	"	333
	Medlar	"	442
	Bibendum	*French*	– – –
	L'Etranger	"	332
	Rivea	*International*	332
	Daphne's	*Italian*	223
	Lucio	"	332
	Osteria 60	"	– – –
	Scalini	"	323
	Cambio de Tercio	*Spanish*	343
	Hawksmoor	*Steaks & grills*	332
	Min Jiang	*Chinese*	435
	Yashin	*Japanese*	322
	Koji	*Pan-Asian*	442
£60+	The Abingdon	*British, Modern*	333
	Bluebird	"	– – –
	Clarke's	"	444
	Harwood Arms	"	533
	Ivy Kensington Brasserie	"	223
	Kensington Place	"	332
	Restaurant Ours	"	244
	Tom's Kitchen	"	222
	Ffiona's	*British, Traditional*	344
	Wright Brothers	*Fish & seafood*	433
	Bandol	*French*	332
	Belvedere	"	224
	Brasserie Gustave	"	343
	Cheyne Walk Brasserie	"	333
	Le Colombier	"	343
	Mazi	*Greek*	444
	Manicomio	*Italian*	223

	Theo's Simple Italian	"	– – –
	Locanda Ottomezzo	*Mediterranean*	3 2 3
	Bombay Brasserie	*Indian*	3 3 3
	Zaika	"	4 4 4
	Patara	*Thai*	3 4 4
£50+	Big Easy	*American*	2 2 3
	Brinkley's	*British, Modern*	1 2 3
	Claude's Kitchen	"	4 3 3
	The Enterprise	"	3 3 4
	The Hour Glass	"	3 3 2
	The Ivy Chelsea Garden	"	2 2 5
	The Phoenix	"	2 2 4
	The Sands End	"	2 3 3
	The Tommy Tucker	"	3 3 4
	Bumpkin	*British, Traditional*	2 2 2
	Maggie Jones's	"	2 2 5
	Bibendum Oyster Bar	*Fish & seafood*	4 2 4
	La Brasserie	*French*	2 2 4
	The Admiral Codrington	*International*	1 2 3
	Gallery Mess	"	2 2 3
	Kensington Wine Rms	"	2 3 3
	La Famiglia	*Italian*	2 2 4
	Frantoio	"	2 3 4
	Obicà	"	3 3 2
	Ottolenghi	"	3 2 2
	Pellicano Restaurant	"	3 4 2
	Il Portico	"	3 5 4
	Tartufo	"	3 3 2
	Ziani's	"	2 3 2
	The Cross Keys	*Mediterranean*	3 3 4
	Ognisko Restaurant	*Polish*	3 4 4
	Tendido Cero	*Spanish*	2 3 3
	Tendido Cuatro	"	2 2 2
	MacellaioRC	*Steaks & grills*	3 3 3
	Sophie's Steakhouse	"	2 4 3
	Geales Chelsea Green	*Fish & chips*	1 2 2
	Maroush	*Lebanese*	3 2 2
	Good Earth	*Chinese*	3 2 2
	Romulo Café	*Filipino*	3 3 3
	Chakra	*Indian*	4 2 3
	Masala Grill	"	3 4 4
	The Painted Heron	"	5 4 2
	Star of India	"	4 2 3
	Chisou	*Japanese*	4 4 2
	Kiru	"	4 3 3
	Kurobuta	"	5 2 2
	Tokyo Sukiyaki-Tei	"	– – –
	Eight Over Eight	*Pan-Asian*	3 2 3
	Sukho Thai Cuisine	*Thai*	5 4 3

Price	Restaurant	Cuisine	Rating
£40+	Bodean's	American	222
	The Builders Arms	British, Modern	224
	Manuka Kitchen	"	323
	Megan's Delicatessen	"	235
	Rabbit	"	442
	The Shed	"	324
	VQ	"	243
	Aglio e Olio	Italian	432
	Buona Sera	"	333
	Da Mario	"	234
	Made in Italy	"	323
	Nuovi Sapori	"	342
	Polpo	"	222
	Riccardo's	"	232
	Sapori Sardi	"	322
	The Atlas	Mediterranean	444
	Daquise	Polish	222
	Capote Y Toros	Spanish	344
	Casa Brindisa	"	222
	Hanger	Steaks & grills	– – –
	La Delizia Limbara	Pizza	322
	Pizzicotto	"	442
	Rossopomodoro	"	322
	Royal China	Chinese	312
	Malabar	Indian	543
	Noor Jahan	"	332
	Pure Indian Cooking	"	– – –
	Thali	"	433
	Suksan	Thai	432
£35+	Churchill Arms	British, Traditional	335
	Haché	Steaks & grills	344
	Rocca Di Papa	Pizza	223
	Best Mangal	Turkish	432
	Rosa's Fulham	Thai	332
	Taiwan Village	Taiwanese	453
£30+	Kensington Sq Kitchen	British, Modern	343
	Tangerine Dream	"	324
	Mona Lisa	International	332
	Pappa Ciccia	Italian	343
	Santa Maria	Pizza	543
	Dragon Palace	Chinese	432
	Bone Daddies	Japanese	444
	Kulu Kulu	"	311
	Addie's Thai Café	Thai	442
£20+	Tommi's Burger Joint	Burgers, etc	444
	Stick & Bowl	Chinese	431
	Eat Tokyo	Japanese	422
£10+	Orée	French	423

Notting Hill, Holland Park, Bayswater, North Kensington & Maida Vale (W2,W9,W10,W11)

£130+	The Ledbury	*British, Modern*	554
£120+	Marianne	*British, Modern*	434
£80+	Flat Three	*Japanese*	442
£70+	Assaggi	*Italian*	442
£60+	The Dock Kitchen	*British, Modern*	323
	Angelus	*French*	343
	Chucs	*Italian*	353
	Edera	"	333
	Essenza	"	343
	Mediterraneo	"	323
	Wormwood	*Mediterranean*	432
	West Thirty Six	*Steaks & grills*	223
	Kojawan	*Pan-Asian*	234
£50+	Electric Diner	*American*	223
	Granger & Co	*Australian*	324
	Daylesford Organic	*British, Modern*	223
	The Frontline Club	"	– – –
	The Ladbroke Arms	"	324
	Magazine	"	234
	Paradise by Way of KG	"	335
	Six Portland Road	"	442
	The Waterway	"	224
	The Summerhouse	*Fish & seafood*	235
	Bel Canto	*French*	234
	The Cow	*Irish*	324
	The Oak	*Italian*	434
	Osteria Basilico	"	324
	Ottolenghi	"	322
	Portobello Ristorante	"	343
	Farmacy	*Vegetarian*	– – –
	Pizza East Portobello	*Pizza*	334
	Casa Malevo	*Argentinian*	342
	Peyotito	*Mexican/TexMex*	– – –
	Maroush Gardens	*Lebanese*	322
	The Four Seasons	*Chinese*	411
	Kurobuta	*Japanese*	522
	E&O	*Pan-Asian*	333
£40+	Salt & Honey	*British, Modern*	342
	VQ	"	243
	Hereford Road	*British, Traditional*	442

Price	Restaurant	Cuisine	Rating
	Snaps & Rye	*Danish*	4 5 3
	Polpo	*Italian*	2 2 2
	Raoul's Café	*Mediterranean*	2 2 3
	Pizza Metro	*Pizza*	3 2 2
	The Red Pepper	"	3 3 2
	Cocotte	*Chicken*	4 3 3
	Casa Cruz	*South American*	2 4 4
	Zayane	*Moroccan*	4 4 4
	Kateh	*Persian*	3 4 3
	Mandarin Kitchen	*Chinese*	4 1 1
	Pearl Liang	"	4 4 2
	Royal China	"	3 1 2
	Bombay Palace	*Indian*	– – –
	Noor Jahan	"	3 3 2
	Inaho	*Japanese*	5 3 1
	Maguro	"	4 4 2
£35+	The Chipping Forecast	*Fish & chips*	– – –
	Taqueria	*Mexican/TexMex*	4 4 2
	C&R Café	*Malaysian*	4 2 2
	Satay House	"	3 2 2
£30+	Alounak	*Persian*	3 2 4
	Gold Mine	*Chinese*	4 2 2
	Tonkotsu	*Japanese*	2 3 3
	The Heron	*Thai*	5 3 1
£25+	Fez Mangal	*Turkish*	5 4 3
£20+	Khan's	*Indian*	3 3 3
£10+	Lisboa Pâtisserie	*Sandwiches, cakes, etc*	3 2 4
£5+	Falafel King	*Middle Eastern*	3 2 2

Hammersmith, Shepherd's Bush, Olympia, Chiswick, Brentford & Ealing (W4,W5,W6,W12,W13,W14,TW8)

Price	Restaurant	Cuisine	Rating
£100+	Hedone	*British, Modern*	4 3 3
	The River Café	*Italian*	3 2 4
£70+	La Trompette	*French*	5 4 3
£60+	Le Vacherin	*French*	3 2 2
	Villa Di Geggiano	*Italian*	2 2 2
£50+	No 197 Chiswick Fire Stn	*Australian*	3 2 4
	The Anglesea Arms	*British, Modern*	3 4 4

Price	Restaurant	Cuisine	Rating
	The Brackenbury	"	343
	Charlotte's Place	"	333
	Charlotte's W5	"	353
	City Barge	"	334
	Ealing Park Tavern	"	334
	High Road Brasserie	"	223
	Vinoteca	"	223
	The Hampshire Hog	*British, Traditional*	334
	Michael Nadra	*French*	442
	Melody at St Paul's	*International*	233
	Cibo	*Italian*	453
	The Oak W12	"	434
	Foxlow	*Steaks & grills*	222
	Smokehouse Chiswick	"	333
£40+	Jackson & Rye Chiswick	*American*	122
	The Dartmouth Castle	*British, Modern*	344
	The Dove	"	224
	Duke of Sussex	"	334
	The Havelock Tavern	"	334
	Mustard	"	354
	The Pear Tree	"	334
	Princess Victoria	"	333
	The Andover Arms	*International*	355
	Annie's	"	234
	L'Amorosa	*Italian*	442
	Buoni Amici	"	333
	Pentolina	"	454
	Cumberland Arms	*Mediterranean*	442
	The Swan	"	335
	Tamp Coffee	*Spanish*	333
	Popeseye	*Steaks & grills*	322
	The Gate	*Vegetarian*	433
	Bird in Hand	*Pizza*	334
	Habanera	*Mexican/TexMex*	323
	Quantus	*South American*	454
	North China	*Chinese*	333
	Indian Zing	*Indian*	432
	Karma	"	331
	Potli	"	543
	Sushi Bar Makoto	*Japanese*	334
£35+	Albertine	*French*	244
	Patio	*Polish*	355
	Chez Abir	*Lebanese*	323
	Best Mangal	*Turkish*	432
	Shikumen	*Chinese*	332
	Anarkali	*Indian*	343
	Brilliant	"	343
	Madhu's	"	543

	Sagar	"	332
	Kiraku	*Japanese*	442
	Tosa	"	332
	Yoshi Sushi	"	342
	Saigon Saigon	*Vietnamese*	333
£30+	Santa Maria	*Pizza*	543
	Adams Café	*Moroccan*	353
	Alounak	*Persian*	324
	Shilpa	*Indian, Southern*	532
	Atari-Ya	*Japanese*	422
	Hare & Tortoise	*Pan-Asian*	333
£25+	Kerbisher & Malt	*Fish & chips*	332
	Faanoos	*Persian*	332
	Gifto's Lahore Karahi	*Indian*	322
£20+	Abu Zaad	*Syrian*	332
	Eat Tokyo	*Japanese*	422

NORTH

Hampstead, West Hampstead, St John's Wood, Regent's Park, Kilburn & Camden Town (NW postcodes)

Price	Restaurant	Cuisine	Ratings
£70+	The Landmark	*British, Modern*	245
	The Gilbert Scott	*British, Traditional*	234
	Gilgamesh	*Pan-Asian*	223
£60+	The Booking Office	*British, Modern*	224
	Bradley's	"	322
	Odette's	"	444
	L'Aventure	*French*	335
	Oslo Court	"	454
	Bull & Last	*International*	323
	Kaifeng	*Chinese*	333
£50+	One Sixty Smokehouse	*American*	434
	Crocker's Folly	*British, Modern*	223
	The Ivy Café	"	224
	Market	"	342
	The Wells	"	223
	The Wet Fish Café	"	323
	York & Albany	*British, Traditional*	222
	Michael Nadra	*French*	442
	La Collina	*Italian*	333
	Villa Bianca	"	222
	Manna	*Vegetarian*	322
	Pizza East	*Pizza*	334
	Greenberry Café	*Sandwiches, cakes, etc*	333
	Good Earth	*Chinese*	322
	Phoenix Palace	"	322
£40+	The Horseshoe	*British, Modern*	334
	The Junction Tavern	"	333
	Parlour Kensal	"	444
	Lure	*Fish & seafood*	442
	L'Absinthe	*French*	232
	La Cage Imaginaire	"	223
	Patron	"	344
	Lemonia	*Greek*	134
	Anima e Cuore	*Italian*	421
	Artigiano	"	233
	Ostuni	"	333
	The Rising Sun	"	323
	Sarracino	"	422
	Harry Morgan's	*Burgers, etc*	222
	Nautilus	*Fish & chips*	431
	The Sea Shell	"	332
	Rossopomodoro	*Pizza*	322

	Zest	*Kosher*	333
	Jun Ming Xuan	*Chinese, Dim sum*	442
	Namaaste Kitchen	*Indian*	342
	Jin Kichi	*Japanese*	553
	Oka	*"*	432
	Sushi Masa	*"*	– – –
	Singapore Garden	*Malaysian*	332
£35+	Lantana Cafe	*Australian*	333
	Fish Cafe	*Fish & seafood*	223
	Carob Tree	*Greek*	353
	L'Artista	*Italian*	244
	Giacomo's	*"*	332
	El Parador	*Spanish*	442
	Haché	*Steaks & grills*	344
	L' Antica Pizzeria	*Pizza*	433
	Sacro Cuore	*"*	433
	Bird Camden	*Chicken*	322
	Chicken Shop	*"*	223
	Green Cottage	*Chinese*	322
	Great Nepalese	*Indian*	332
	Asakusa	*Japanese*	532
	The Petite Coree	*Korean*	452
£30+	La Porchetta Pizzeria	*Italian*	233
	Brew House	*Sandwiches, cakes, etc*	223
	Ariana II	*Afghani*	322
	Chutneys	*Indian*	322
	Guglee	*"*	322
	Paradise Hampstead	*"*	454
	Ravi Shankar	*"*	322
	Vijay	*"*	321
	Atari-Ya	*Japanese*	422
£25+	The Little Bay	*Mediterranean*	234
	Poppies Camden	*Fish & chips*	333
	Ali Baba	*Egyptian*	324
	Diwana Bhel-Pouri Hs	*Indian*	321
£20+	Eat Tokyo	*Japanese*	422
	Roti King	*Malaysian*	521
£10+	Bill or Beak	*Burgers, etc*	44 –
	Dirty Burger	*"*	322
	Ginger & White	*Sandwiches, cakes, etc*	243
£5+	Doppio	*Sandwiches, cakes, etc*	333

Hoxton, Islington, Highgate, Crouch End, Stoke Newington, Finsbury Park, Muswell Hill & Finchley (N postcodes)

£60+	Fifteen	*British, Modern*	223
	Frederick's	"	234
	Plum + Spilt Milk	"	234
	German Gymnasium	*Cent. European*	223
	Almeida	*French*	322
£50+	Granger & Co	*Australian*	324
	The Drapers Arms	*British, Modern*	322
	Grain Store	"	433
	The Haven	"	343
	The Lighterman	"	334
	Pig & Butcher	"	444
	Red Lion & Sun	"	334
	Rotunda	"	343
	Smoke & Salt	"	– – –
	Bellanger	*Cent. European*	223
	Black Axe Mangal	"	532
	Galley	*Fish & seafood*	434
	Bistro Aix	*French*	433
	Caravan King's Cross	*Fusion*	323
	The Greek Larder	*Greek*	322
	8 Hoxton Square	*International*	444
	Salut	"	442
	Melange	*Italian*	333
	Ottolenghi	"	322
	Trullo	"	433
	Vinoteca	*Mediterranean*	223
	Foxlow	*Steaks & grills*	222
	Smokehouse Islington	"	444
	Duke's Brew & Que	*Burgers, etc*	423
£40+	Bodean's	*American*	222
	The Albion	*British, Modern*	213
	The Bull	"	234
	Heirloom	"	333
	Hill & Szrok	"	444
	Oldroyd	"	432
	Season Kitchen	"	332
	St Johns	*British, Traditional*	335
	Kipferl	*Cent. European*	322
	Prawn On The Lawn	*Fish & seafood*	433
	Petit Pois Bistro	*French*	– – –
	Nissi	*Greek*	333
	Banners	*International*	345
	Primeur	"	434
	500	*Italian*	342
	Osteria Tufo	"	343

	Ostuni	"	333
	Pizzeria Oregano	"	343
	San Daniele del Friuli	"	343
	Rubedo	*Mediterranean*	442
	Rök	*Scandinavian*	422
	Café del Parc	*Spanish*	554
	Camino King's Cross	"	333
	Escocesa	"	432
	Trangallan	"	544
	Popeseye	*Steaks & grills*	322
	Toff's	*Fish & chips*	322
	Vintage Salt	"	343
	Rossopomodoro	*Pizza*	322
	Sweet Thursday	"	323
	Le Coq	*Chicken*	333
	Yipin China	*Chinese*	321
	Little Georgia Café	*Georgian*	333
	Dishoom	*Indian*	434
	Zaffrani	"	322
	Isarn	*Thai*	442
	Yum Yum	"	322
£35+	Le Sacré-Coeur	*French*	444
	Vrisaki	*Greek*	332
	Pizzeria Pappagone	*Italian*	344
	Rugoletta	"	433
	Bar Esteban	*Spanish*	444
	MEATLiquor	*Burgers, etc*	334
	Olympus Fish	*Fish & chips*	452
	Bird Islington	*Chicken*	322
	Chicken Shop	"	223
	Gallipoli	*Turkish*	344
	Delhi Grill	*Indian*	322
	Indian Rasoi	"	442
	Rasa Travancore	*Indian, Southern*	333
	CôBa	*Vietnamese*	433
£30+	Le Mercury	*French*	224
	La Porchetta Pizzeria	*Italian*	233
	Meat Mission	*Burgers, etc*	334
	Sutton & Sons	*Fish & chips*	433
	Two Brothers	"	322
	Yard Sale Pizza	*Pizza*	432
	Zia Lucia	"	– – –
	Gem	*Turkish*	343
	GoÅNkyüzü	"	444
	Jashan	*Indian*	542
	Rani	"	322
	Atari-Ya	*Japanese*	422
	Salvation In Noodles	*Vietnamese*	322

£25+	Breakfast Club Angel	*American*	332
	Chriskitch	*British, Modern*	442
	Afghan Kitchen	*Afghani*	322
	Dotori	*Korean*	432
£20+	Max's Sandwich Shop	*Sandwiches, cakes, etc*	433
	Xi'an Impression	*Chinese*	442
£15+	Piebury Corner	*British, Traditional*	343
£10+	Five Guys Islington	*Burgers, etc*	322

SOUTH

South Bank (SE1)

£130+	Story	*British, Modern*	333
£90+	Aqua Shard	*British, Modern*	113
	Ting	*Fusion*	223
£80+	Oblix	*British, Modern*	215
	Oxo Tower	"	111
	Hutong	*Chinese*	325
£70+	Oxo Tower	*British, Modern*	112
	Le Pont de la Tour	"	224
	Skylon	"	112
	Skylon Grill	"	223
	Roast	*British, Traditional*	223
	La Barca	*Italian*	222
£60+	Sea Containers	*British, Modern*	224
	The Swan at the Globe	"	223
	Butlers Wharf Chop House	*British, Traditional*	222
	Wright Brothers	*Fish & seafood*	433
	Rabot 1745	*International*	322
£50+	Albion	*British, Modern*	222
	Blueprint Café	"	225
	Elliot's Café	"	323
	40 Maltby Street	"	433
	The Garrison	"	324
	House Restaurant	"	232
	Magdalen	"	322
	Menier Chocolate Factory	"	223
	RSJ	"	332
	Tate Modern	"	214
	Union Street Café	"	232
	Waterloo Bar & Kitchen	"	212
	The Anchor & Hope	*British, Traditional*	433
	Applebee's Café	*Fish & seafood*	442
	fish!	"	322
	Caravan Bankside	*Fusion*	323
	Champor-Champor	"	445
	Village East	"	223
	Vivat Bacchus	*International*	333
	MacellaioRC	*Italian*	333
	Baltic	*Polish*	344
	Pizarro	*Spanish*	333

£40+	Edwins	*British, Modern*	344
	The Green Room	"	222
	Boro Bistro	*French*	333
	Casse-Croute	"	434
	Antico	*Italian*	343
	Camino Bankside	*Spanish*	333
	José	"	545
	LOBOS Meat & Tapas	"	432
	Tapas Brindisa	"	222
	Arabica Bar & Kitchen	*Lebanese*	333
	Tas Pide	*Turkish*	233
£35+	The Table	*British, Modern*	322
	Pulia	*Italian*	343
	Meson don Felipe	*Spanish*	234
£30+	Vapiano	*Italian*	323
	Mar I Terra	*Spanish*	242
	El Vergel *South*	*American*	434
	Tonkotsu Bankside	*Japanese*	233
£25+	Padella	*Italian*	442
	Masters Super Fish	*Fish & chips*	322
£10+	Gourmet Goat	*Mediterranean*	442
£5+	Monmouth Coffee Company	*Sandwiches, cakes, etc*	554

Greenwich, Lewisham, Dulwich & Blackheath (All SE postcodes, except SE1)

£60+	Lobster Pot	*Fish & seafood*	434
	Craft London	*Pizza*	433
£50+	The Camberwell Arms	*British, Modern*	433
	Chapters	"	222
	Franklins	"	433
	The Palmerston	"	333
	Pharmacy 2	"	333
	Rivington Grill	"	222
	Babur	*Indian*	554
	Yama Momo	*Japanese*	423
£40+	The Crooked Well	*British, Modern*	334
	Guildford Arms	"	333
	The Lido Café	"	224
	Peckham Ref' Rooms	"	322
	The Perry Vale	"	343
	The Lord Northbrook	*British, Traditional*	344

	Brasserie Toulouse-Lautrec	*French*	333
	Peckham Bazaar	*Greek*	534
	Joanna's	*International*	344
	Tulse Hill Hotel	*"*	323
	The Yellow House	*"*	332
	Artusi	*Italian*	333
	Lorenzo	*"*	333
	Luciano's	*"*	333
	Cau	*Steaks & grills*	122
	Ganapati	*Indian*	543
	Kennington Tandoori	*"*	333
	Sticks'n'Sushi	*Japanese*	444
£35+	Upstairs at John The Un'	*British, Modern*	– – –
	Canada Water Cafe	*Italian*	343
	Le Querce	*"*	343
	MEAT Liquor	*Burgers, etc*	334
	Pedler	*Pizza*	344
	Rocca Di Papa	*"*	223
	Theo's	*"*	433
	Yalla Yalla	*Lebanese*	323
	Dragon Castle	*Chinese*	332
	Everest Inn	*Indian*	433
	Zaibatsu	*Japanese*	452
	The Begging Bowl	*Thai*	543
£30+	The Gowlett Arms	*Pizza*	434
	FM Mangal	*Turkish*	332
	Bánh Bánh	*Vietnamese*	453
	Mr Bao	*Taiwanese*	322
£25+	Rox Burger	*Burgers, etc*	433
	Mamma Dough	*Pizza*	344
£20+	Pizzeria Pellone	*Pizza*	432
	Silk Road	*Chinese*	522
	Café East	*Vietnamese*	422
£5+	Kappacasein	*Sandwiches, cakes, etc*	522

Battersea, Brixton, Clapham, Wandsworth
Barnes, Putney & Wimbledon
(All SW postcodes south of the river)

£70+	Chez Bruce	*British, Modern*	554
	Trinity	*"*	554
£60+	Gastronhome	*French*	543
	The White Onion	*"*	322

	London House	*International*	332
	Riva	*Italian*	442
£50+	The Brown Dog	*British, Modern*	323
	Cannizaro House	"	233
	The Ivy Café	"	224
	Lamberts	"	554
	The Light House	"	333
	The Manor	"	433
	May The Fifteenth	"	333
	Olympic	"	224
	Sonny's Kitchen	"	223
	The Victoria	"	234
	Soif	*French*	333
	Bibo	*Italian*	333
	Numero Uno	"	333
	The Fox & Hounds	*Mediterranean*	444
	Alquimia	*Spanish*	332
	Cornish Tiger	*Steaks & grills*	333
	Foxlow	"	222
	Naughty Piglets	"	553
	Good Earth	*Chinese*	322
£40+	Bodean's	*American*	222
	Counter	"	233
	Bistro Union	*British, Modern*	333
	Brunswick House Café	"	235
	The Dairy	"	544
	The Depot	"	225
	Earl Spencer	"	324
	Emile's	"	342
	Hood	"	432
	Salon Brixton	"	433
	Canton Arms	*British, Traditional*	434
	Jolly Gardeners	"	323
	The Plough	"	345
	Augustine Kitchen	*French*	342
	Annie's	*International*	234
	Buona Sera	*Italian*	333
	Donna Margherita	"	332
	Made in Italy	"	323
	Osteria Antica Bologna	"	333
	Pizza Metro	"	322
	The Bobbin	*Mediterranean*	344
	Brindisa Food Rooms	*Spanish*	222
	Gremio de Brixton	"	323
	Cau	*Steaks & grills*	122
	Popeseye	"	322
	Fish Club	*Fish & chips*	322
	Rossopomodoro	*Pizza*	322

	MOMMI	*Peruvian*	233
	Indian Zilla	*Indian*	422
	Kricket	*"*	543
	Ma Goa	*"*	442
	Nanban	*Japanese*	432
	Sticks'n'Sushi	*"*	444
	Takahashi	*"*	533
	Tomoe	*"*	432
	Tsunami	*"*	523
£35+	Gazette	*French*	223
	Fish in a Tie	*Mediterranean*	232
	Bukowski Grill	*Steaks & grills*	432
	Haché	*Burgers, etc*	344
	Dynamo	*Pizza*	333
	Eco	*"*	334
	Chicken Shop & Dirty Burger	*Chicken*	223
	Indian Moment	*Indian*	[illegible]
	Indian Ocean	*"*	333
	Hashi	*Japanese*	442
	Cah-Chi	*Korean*	342
	Rosa's	*Thai*	332
£30+	Counter Culture	*British, Modern*	444
	Fields	*"*	333
	Boqueria	*Spanish*	344
	Little Taperia	*"*	441
	Brady's	*Fish & chips*	333
	Al Forno	*Pizza*	244
	Ground Coffee Society	*Sandwiches, cakes, etc*	333
	Meza Trinity Road	*Lebanese*	442
	Hare & Tortoise	*Pan-Asian*	333
	The Pepper Tree	*Thai*	333
	Mien Tay	*Vietnamese*	422
£25+	The Joint	*American*	533
	Figlio Del Vesuvio	*Italian*	442
	Dip & Flip	*Burgers, etc*	322
	Kerbisher & Malt	*Fish & chips*	332
	Mamma Dough	*Pizza*	344
	Orange Pekoe	*Sandwiches, cakes, etc*	344
	Faanoos	*Persian*	332
	Sree Krishna	*Indian*	432
	Lahore Karahi	*Pakistani*	422
	Mirch Masala	*"*	521
	Awesome Thai	*Thai*	343
	Kaosarn	*"*	442
£20+	Hot Stuff	*Indian*	353
	Lahore Kebab House	*Pakistani*	522

£15+	Flotsam & Jetsam	*Australian*	344
	Tried & True	*British, Modern*	333
	Jaffna House	*Indian, Southern*	532
£10+	Dirty Burger	*Burgers, etc*	322
	Joe Public	*Pizza*	423
	Milk	*Sandwiches, cakes, etc*	433

Outer western suburbs
Kew, Richmond,Twickenham,Teddington

£70+	The Glasshouse	*British, Modern*	342
£60+	The Bingham	*British, Modern*	344
	The Dysart Petersham	"	442
	Petersham Hotel	"	335
	Petersham Nurseries	"	213
	Al Boccon di'vino	*Italian*	445
£50+	A Cena	*Italian*	333
£40+	Jackson & Rye Richmond	*American*	122
	La Buvette	*French*	333
	Ma Cuisine	"	323
	Le Salon Privé	"	444
	Bacco	*Italian*	333
	Pizzeria Rustica	*Pizza*	332
	Matsuba	*Japanese*	332

EAST

Smithfield & Farringdon (EC1)

£90+	The Clove Club	*British, Modern*	544
£80+	Club Gascon	*French*	432
£70+	Smiths of Smithfield	*Steaks & grills*	222
	Sosharu	*Japanese*	232
£60+	Anglo	*British, Modern*	432
	Bird of Smithfield	"	222
	Chiswell St Dining Rms	"	222
	The Jugged Hare	"	323
	Urban Coterie	"	– – –
	St John	*British, Traditional*	543
	Bleeding Heart	*French*	335
£50+	Granger & Co	*Australian*	324
	Vinoteca	*British, Modern*	223
	Albion Clerkenwell	*British, Traditional*	222
	The Fox & Anchor	"	334
	Café du Marché	*French*	334
	Caravan	*Fusion*	323
	The Modern Pantry	"	222
	MacellaioRC	*Italian*	333
	Moro	*Spanish*	543
	Foxlow	*Steaks & grills*	222
	Hix Oyster & Ch' Hs	"	222
	Smiths of Smithfield	"	221
	Sushi Tetsu	*Japanese*	554
£40+	Bodean's	*American*	222
	Coin Laundry	*British, Traditional*	– – –
	The Quality Chop House	"	343
	Café Pistou	*French*	322
	Comptoir Gascon	"	333
	La Ferme	"	322
	Enoteca Rabezzana	*Italian*	222
	Polpo	"	222
	Santore	"	433
	Ibérica	*Spanish*	223
	The Gate	*Vegetarian*	433
	Burger & Lobster	*Burgers, etc*	333
	Workshop Coffee	*Sandwiches, cakes, etc*	334
	Ceviche Old St	*Peruvian*	333
	The Sichuan	*Chinese*	422
£35+	Lantana Café	*Australian*	333

	Apulia	*Italian*	333
	Morito	*Spanish*	444
	Pham Sushi	*Japanese*	531
	On The Bab	*Korean*	332
	Cây Tre	*Vietnamese*	433
£30+	Smiths of Smithfield	*British, Modern*	223
	Fish Central	*Fish & seafood*	332
	Cellar Gascon	*French*	333
	Kolossi Grill	*Greek*	352
	La Porchetta Pizzeria	*Italian*	233
	The Eagle	*Mediterranean*	435
	Pizza Pilgrims	*Pizza*	434
	Berber & Q Sh' Bar	*Middle Eastern*	– – –
	Bone Daddies	*Japanese*	444
£25+	Kerbisher & Malt	*Fish & chips*	332
£20+	Homeslice	*Pizza*	444
£15+	Dept of Coffee	*Sandwiches, cakes, etc*	354
£10+	Prufrock Coffee	*Sandwiches, cakes, etc*	324

The City (EC2, EC3, EC4)

£90+	Sushisamba	*Japanese*	335
£80+	City Social	*British, Modern*	335
	Fenchurch Restaurant	"	333
	Angler	*Fish & seafood*	333
	Coq d'Argent	*French*	222
	Goodman City	*Steaks & grills*	333
£70+	Duck & Waffle	*British, Modern*	225
	I Lombard Street	"	222
	Sweetings	*Fish & seafood*	224
	Lutyens	*French*	222
	L'Anima	*Italian*	333
	Hawksmoor	*Steaks & grills*	332
	M Restaurant	"	222
	HKK	*Chinese*	542
	Yauatcha City	"	433
£60+	The Botanist	*British, Modern*	212
	Bread Street Kitchen	"	223
	The Chancery	"	442
	Darwin Brasserie	"	224
	The Don	"	332
	High Timber	"	343
	Hush	"	233
	The Mercer	"	222

	Merchants Tavern	"	344
	3 South Place	"	333
	The White Swan	"	332
	Chamberlain's	*Fish & seafood*	232
	Sauterelle	*French*	334
	Caravaggio	*Italian*	233
	Gatti's City Point	"	333
	Manicomio	"	223
	Boisdale of Bishopsgate	*Scottish*	222
	Eyre Brothers	*Spanish*	533
	Barbecoa	*Steaks & grills*	222
	Vanilla Black	*Vegetarian*	422
	Chinese Cricket Club	*Chinese*	331
	Darbaar	*Indian*	442
	Mint Leaf Lounge	"	334
£50+	Northbank	*British, Modern*	223
	Princess of Shoreditch	"	333
	Rivington Grill	"	222
	Sign of the Don	"	234
	Paternoster Chop House	*British, Traditional*	211
	Fish Market	*Fish & seafood*	322
	Royal Exch Grand Café	*French*	224
	28-50	"	234
	The Modern Pantry	*Fusion*	222
	Vivat Bacchus	*International*	333
	L'Anima Café	*Italian*	323
	Obicà	"	332
	Osteria	"	222
	Taberna Etrusca	"	233
	Hispania	*Spanish*	333
	José Pizarro	"	432
	Jones Family Project	*Steaks & grills*	344
	The Tramshed	"	234
	Oklava	*Turkish*	442
	Cinnamon Kitchen	*Indian*	323
£40+	Bodean's	*American*	222
	Pitt Cue Co	"	544
	The Anthologist	*British, Modern*	223
	Café Below	"	223
	Humble Grape	"	344
	Rök	"	422
	The Trading House	"	344
	Simpson's Tavern	*British, Traditional*	235
	Rucoletta	*Italian*	221
	Rocket Bishopgate	*Mediterranean*	333
	Camino Blackfriars	*Spanish*	333
	Relais de Venise	*Steaks & grills*	322
	Burger & Lobster	*Burgers, etc*	333
	Vintage Salt	*Fish & chips*	343

	Shoryu Ramen	*Japanese*	322
£35+	Restaurant de Paul	*French*	344
	Haché	*Burgers, etc*	344
	Haz	*Turkish*	222
	Beer & Buns	*Japanese*	334
	K10	"	442
	On The Bab	*Korean*	332
£30+	The Wine Library	*International*	135
	Mangal 1.1	*Turkish*	– – –
	Hare & Tortoise	*Pan-Asian*	333
£25+	Walter & Monty	*American*	– – –
	Hilliard	*British, Modern*	442
	Bibimbap	*Korean*	222
£20+	Flat Iron	*Steaks & grills*	433
	Patty & Bun	*Burgers, etc*	432
£15+	City Càphê	*Vietnamese*	321
£10+	Smokestak	*American*	53 –
	Pilpel	*Middle Eastern*	442
	Yum Bun	*Japanese*	53 –

East End & Docklands (All E postcodes)

£80+	Galvin La Chapelle	*French*	334
	Typing Room	*Fusion*	453
	Goodman	*Steaks & grills*	333
	Roka	*Japanese*	433
£70+	The Woodford	*British, Modern*	344
	Plateau	*French*	223
	Hawksmoor	*Steaks & grills*	332
£60+	The Boundary	*British, Modern*	113
	The Gun	"	324
	Lyle's	"	543
	Pidgin	"	554
	Tom's Kitchen	"	222
	Wright Brothers	*Fish & seafood*	433
	Canto Corvino	*Italian*	444
	Boisdale of Canary Wharf	*Scottish*	223
£50+	Big Easy	*American*	223
	One Sixty Smokehouse	"	434
	Bistrotheque	*British, Modern*	334
	Ellory	"	243
	Galvin HOP	"	442

	Hoi Polloi	"	212
	Jones & Sons	"	434
	Legs	"	– – –
	The Morgan Arms	"	433
	The Narrow	"	223
	One Canada Square	"	233
	The Richmond	"	333
	Rochelle Canteen	"	324
	Smith's Wapping	"	434
	Albion	*British, Traditional*	222
	Bumpkin	"	222
	The Marksman	"	323
	St John Bread & Wine	"	532
	Brawn	*French*	544
	Blixen	*International*	344
	Sager + Wilde	"	334
	Il Bordello	*Italian*	345
	Obicà	"	332
	Super Tuscan	"	442
	Pizza East	*Pizza*	334
	Buen Ayre	*Argentinian*	422
	Ottolenghi	*Israeli*	322
	Café Spice Namaste	*Indian*	554

£40+	The Culpeper	*British, Modern*	223
	The Empress	"	444
	Paradise Garage	"	442
	Poco	"	– – –
	Jago	*Fusion*	322
	Gotto Trattoria	*Italian*	– – –
	Lardo Bebè	"	322
	Rotorino	"	233
	Verdi's	"	333
	Rocket Canary Wharf	*Mediterranean*	333
	Taberna do Mercado	*Portuguese*	543
	Bravas	*Spanish*	332
	Ibérica	"	223
	Cau	*Steaks & grills*	122
	Hill & Szrok	"	444
	Relais de Venise	"	322
	Lucky Chip	*Burgers, etc*	322
	Ark Fish	*Fish & chips*	442
	Corner Kitchen	*Pizza*	323
	Andina	*Peruvian*	434
	Berber & Q	*Middle Eastern*	435
	Strut & Cluck	"	– – –
	Royal China	*Chinese*	312
	Sichuan Folk	"	442
	Yi-Ban	"	333
	Little Georgia Café	*Georgian*	333
	Dishoom	*Indian*	434

Price	Restaurant	Cuisine	Rating
	Gunpowder	"	444
	Sticks'n'Sushi	*Japanese*	444
	Som Saa	*Thai*	523
	Viet Grill	*Vietnamese*	322
£35+	Eat 17	*British, Modern*	442
	Leyton Technical	"	324
	P Franco	"	– – –
	Sager + Wilde	"	244
	Blanchette East	*French*	445
	Provender	"	343
	Eat 17	*International*	442
	Morito	*Spanish*	444
	Bukowski Grill	*Steaks & grills*	432
	Bird Stratford	*Chicken*	322
	Chicken Shop & Dirty Burger	"	223
	Haz	*Turkish*	222
	Ippudo London	*Japanese*	323
	Rosa's	*Thai*	332
£30+	Farley Macallan	*British, Modern*	– – –
	Caboose	*Burgers, etc*	234
	Sutton & Sons	*Fish & chips*	433
	The Stable	*Pizza*	223
	Yard Sale Pizza	"	432
	Chick 'n' Sours	*Chicken*	323
	Randy's Wing Bar	"	– – –
	Tonkotsu East	*Japanese*	233
	Tayyabs	*Pakistani*	423
	Mien Tay	*Vietnamese*	422
	Sông Quê	"	322
£25+	Breakfast Club	*American*	332
	Chuck Burger	*Burgers, etc*	– – –
	Poppies	*Fish & chips*	333
	Crate	*Pizza*	323
	Mangal 1	*Turkish*	543
	Needoo	*Pakistani*	422
£20+	Patty & Bun	*Burgers, etc*	432
	Shake Shack	"	322
	Lahore Kebab House	*Pakistani*	522
£15+	E Pellicci	*Italian*	345
	Bleecker Street Burger	*Burgers, etc*	522
£10+	Smokestak	*American*	53–
	Dirty Burger	*Burgers, etc*	322
	The Rib Man	"	54–
	Pilpel	*Middle Eastern*	442
£5+	Brick Lane Beigel Bake	*Sandwiches, cakes, etc*	411

Frenchie

Randy's Wing Bar

Saint Luke's Kitchen, Library

LONDON MAPS

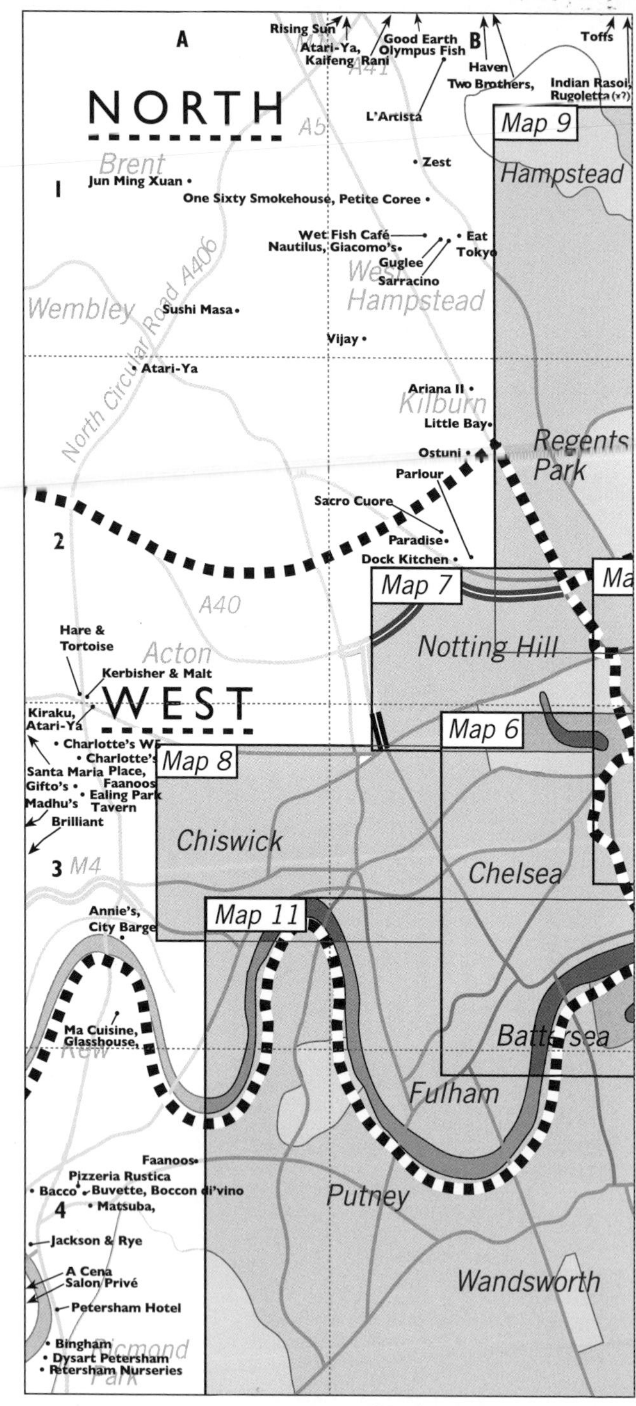
A
B
1
2
3
4
NORTH
WEST
Rising Sun
Atari-Ya,
Kaifeng
Rani
Good Earth
Olympus Fish
Haven
Two Brothers,
Toffs
Indian Rasoi,
Rugoletta (x2)
L'Artista
Map 9
Hampstead
Brent
Zest
Jun Ming Xuan
One Sixty Smokehouse, Petite Coree
Wet Fish Café
Nautilus, Giacomo's
Eat Tokyo
Guglee
Sarracino
West Hampstead
Wembley
Sushi Masa
North Circular Road A406
Vijay
Atari-Ya
Ariana II
Kilburn
Little Bay
Ostuni
Regents Park
Parlour
Sacro Cuore
Paradise
Dock Kitchen
A5
A41
A40
Map 7
Notting Hill
Hare & Tortoise
Acton
Kerbisher & Malt
Kiraku,
Atari-Ya
Charlotte's W5
Charlotte's Place,
Faanoos
Santa Maria
Gifto's
Ealing Park Tavern
Madhu's
Brilliant
Map 6
Map 8
Chiswick
Chelsea
M4
Annie's,
City Barge
Map 11
Ma Cuisine,
Glasshouse
Kew
Battersea
Fulham
Faanoos
Pizzeria Rustica
Bacco
Buvette, Boccon di'vino
Matsuba,
Putney
Jackson & Rye
A Cena
Salon Privé
Petersham Hotel
Wandsworth
Bingham
Dysart Petersham
Petersham Nurseries
Richmond Park

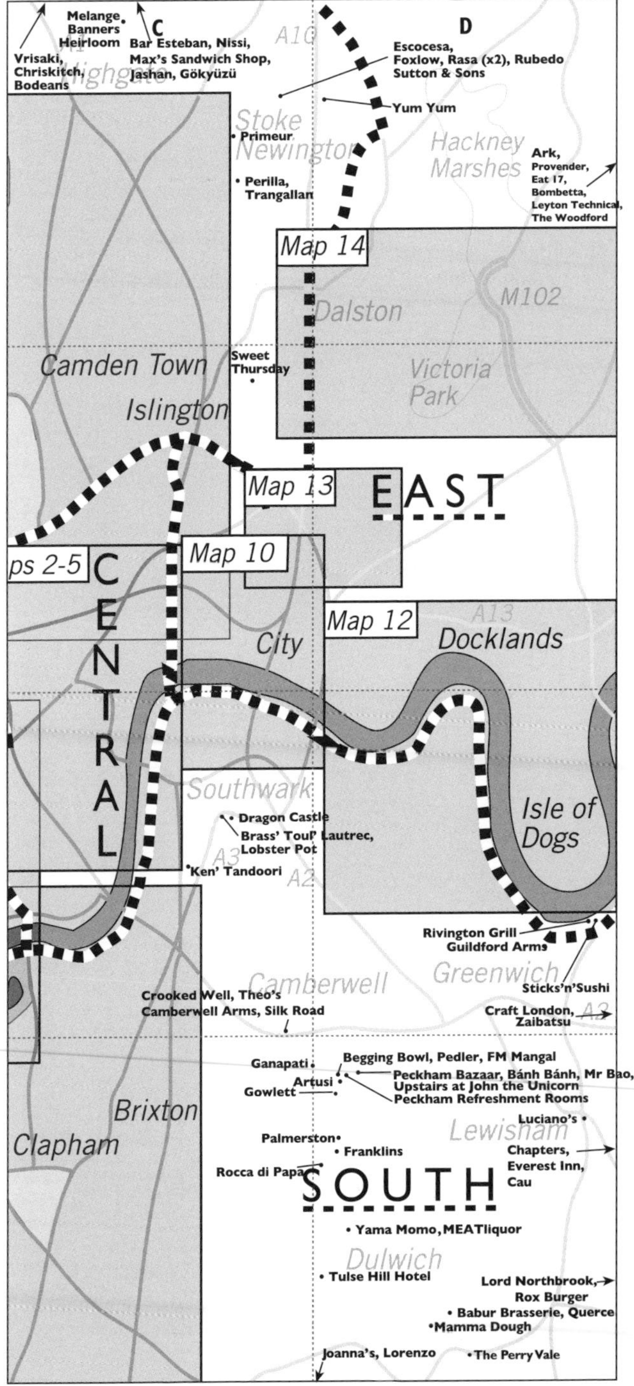
C
D
Melange,
Banners
Heirloom
Vrisaki,
Chriskitch,
Bodeans
Bar Esteban, Nissi,
Max's Sandwich Shop,
Jashan, Gökyüzü
A10
Highgate
Escocesa,
Foxlow, Rasa (x2), Rubedo
Sutton & Sons
Yum Yum
Stoke
Newington
Primeur
Perilla,
Trangallan
Hackney
Marshes
Ark,
Provender,
Eat 17,
Bombetta,
Leyton Technical,
The Woodford
Map 14
Dalston
M102
Camden Town
Sweet
Thursday
Victoria
Park
Islington
Map 13
EAST
ps 2-5
Map 10
CENTRAL
Map 12
A13
City
Docklands
Southwark
Dragon Castle
Brass' Toul' Lautrec,
Lobster Pot
A3
Ken' Tandoori
A2
Isle of
Dogs
Rivington Grill
Guildford Arms
Greenwich
Sticks'n'Sushi
Camberwell
Crooked Well, Theo's
Camberwell Arms, Silk Road
Craft London,
Zaibatsu
A2
Ganapati
Begging Bowl, Pedler, FM Mangal
Artusi
Peckham Bazaar, Bánh Bánh, Mr Bao,
Upstairs at John the Unicorn
Gowlett
Peckham Refreshment Rooms
Brixton
Luciano's
Lewisham
Clapham
Palmerston
Franklins
Chapters,
Everest Inn,
Cau
Rocca di Papa
SOUTH
Yama Momo, MEATliquor
Dulwich
Tulse Hill Hotel
Lord Northbrook,
Rox Burger
Babur Brasserie, Querce
Mamma Dough
Joanna's, Lorenzo
The Perry Vale

MAP 2 – WEST END OVERVIEW

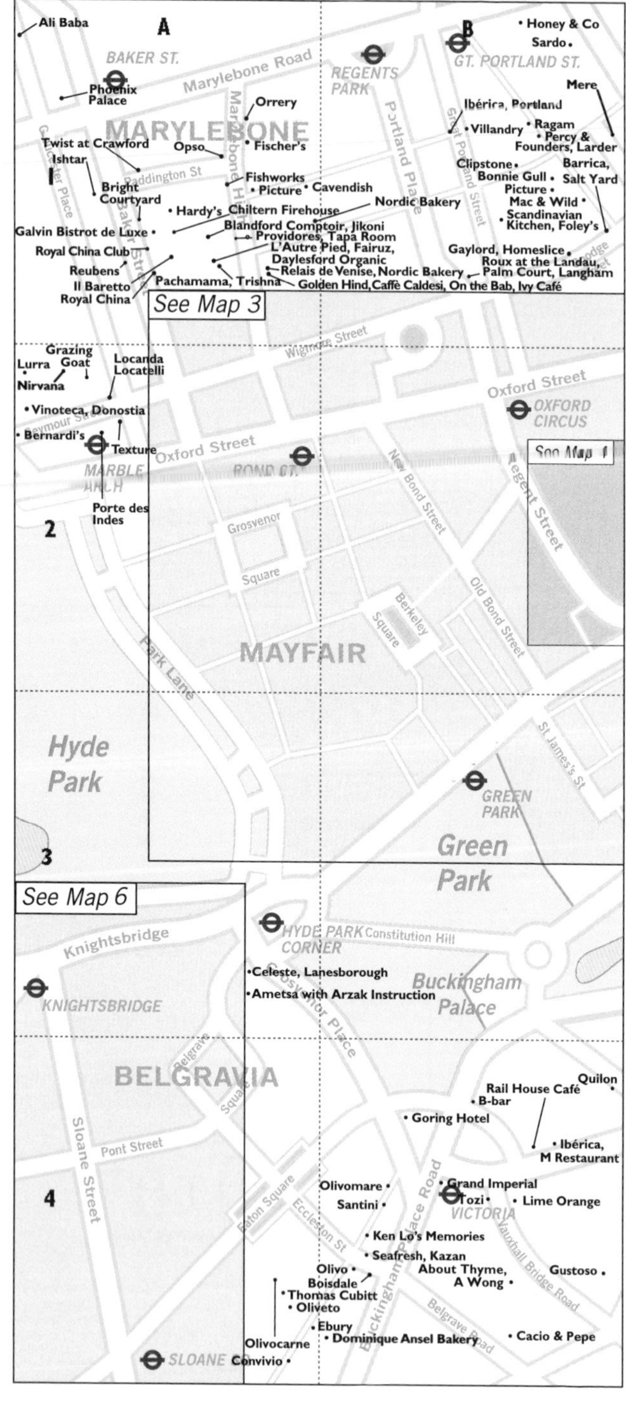

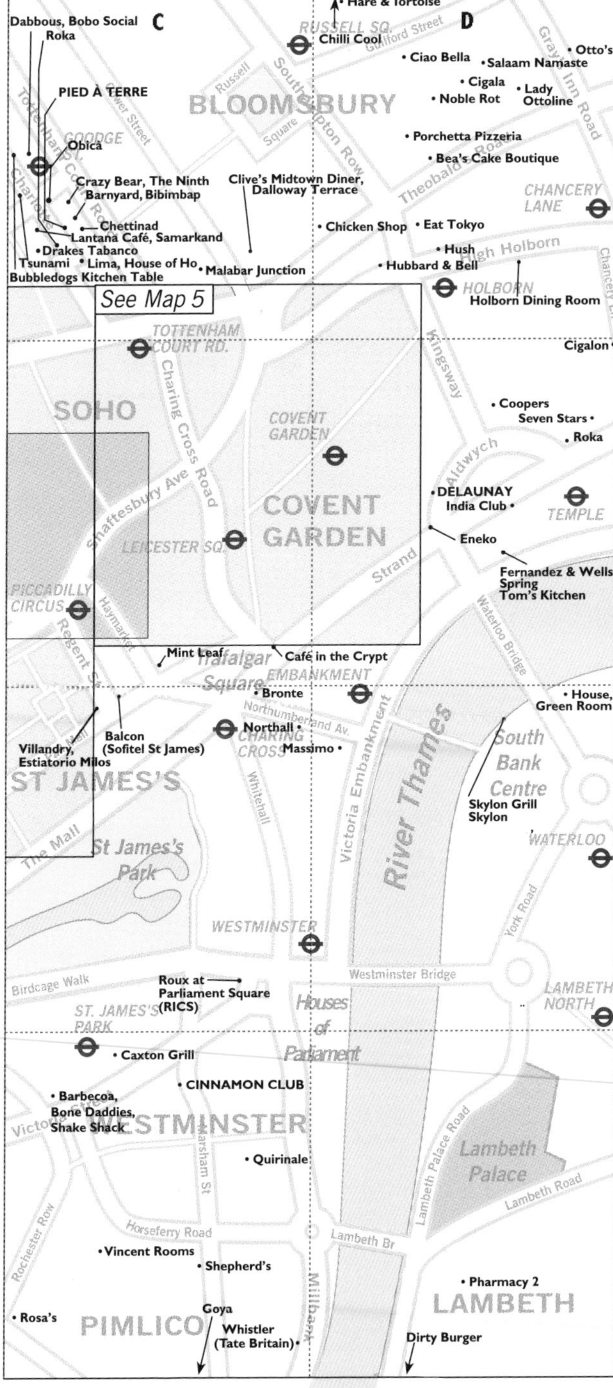

Hare & Tortoise
Dabbous, Bobo Social
Roka
C
D
RUSSELL SQ.
Chilli Cool
Guilford Street
Ciao Bella
Salaam Namaste
Otto's
Cigala
Noble Rot
Lady Ottoline
PIED À TERRE
BLOOMSBURY
Russell Square
Southampton Row
Gray's Inn Road
GOODGE
Gower Street
Tottenham Ct Road
Obicà
Porchetta Pizzeria
Bea's Cake Boutique
Theobald's Road
Crazy Bear, The Ninth
Barnyard, Bibimbap
Clive's Midtown Diner, Dalloway Terrace
CHANCERY LANE
Chettinad
Lantana Café, Samarkand
Drakes Tabanco
Tsunami
Lima, House of Ho
Bubbledogs Kitchen Table
Malabar Junction
Chicken Shop
Eat Tokyo
Hush
High Holborn
Hubbard & Bell
HOLBORN
Holborn Dining Room
Chancery Ln
See Map 5
TOTTENHAM COURT RD.
Cigalon
Kingsway
SOHO
Charing Cross Road
COVENT GARDEN
Coopers
Seven Stars
Roka
Aldwych
Shaftesbury Ave
DELAUNAY
India Club
TEMPLE
COVENT GARDEN
LEICESTER SQ.
Eneko
Strand
Fernandez & Wells
Spring
Tom's Kitchen
PICCADILLY CIRCUS
Haymarket
Regent St
Waterloo Bridge
Mint Leaf
Café in the Crypt
Trafalgar Square
EMBANKMENT
Bronte
House, Green Room
Northumberland Av.
Northall
Balcon (Sofitel St James)
Villandry, Estiatorio Milos
CHARING CROSS
Massimo
Victoria Embankment
River Thames
South Bank Centre
ST JAMES'S
Whitehall
Skylon Grill
Skylon
The Mall
St James's Park
WATERLOO
York Road
WESTMINSTER
Birdcage Walk
Roux at Parliament Square (RICS)
Westminster Bridge
Houses of Parliament
LAMBETH NORTH
ST. JAMES'S PARK
Caxton Grill
CINNAMON CLUB
Barbecoa, Bone Daddies, Shake Shack
Victoria Street
WESTMINSTER
Marsham St
Quirinale
Lambeth Palace Road
Lambeth Palace
Lambeth Road
Rochester Row
Horseferry Road
Lambeth Br
Vincent Rooms
Shepherd's
Pharmacy 2
Millbank
LAMBETH
Rosa's
PIMLICO
Goya
Whistler (Tate Britain)
Dirty Burger

MAP 3 – MAYFAIR, ST. JAMES'S & WEST SOHO

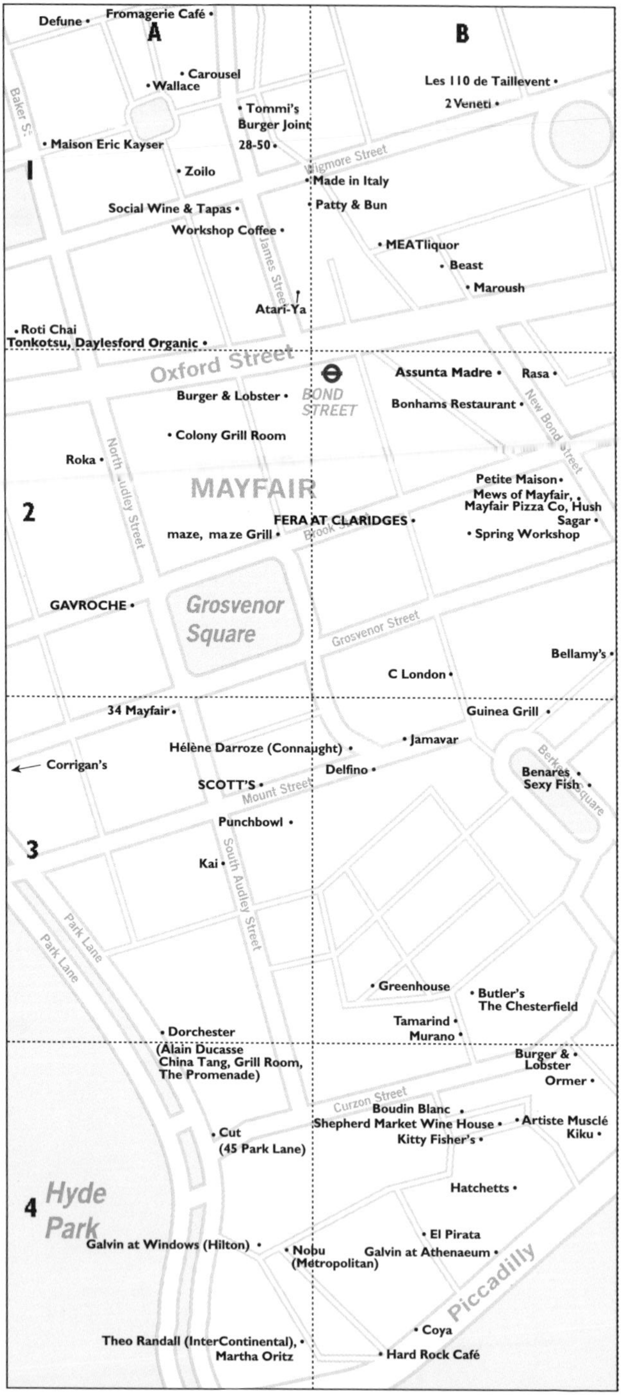

A
B
1
2
3
4

Defune
Fromagerie Café
Carousel
Wallace
Tommi's Burger Joint
28-50
Maison Eric Kayser
Zoilo
Social Wine & Tapas
Workshop Coffee
Atari-Ya
Roti Chai
Tonkotsu, Daylesford Organic
Les 110 de Taillevent
2 Veneti
Made in Italy
Patty & Bun
MEATliquor
Beast
Maroush
Baker St.
Wigmore Street
James Street

Oxford Street
BOND STREET
Burger & Lobster
Colony Grill Room
Roka
North Audley Street
MAYFAIR
maze, maze Grill
FERA AT CLARIDGES
Brook St.
GAVROCHE
Grosvenor Square
Grosvenor Street
Assunta Madre
Rasa
Bonhams Restaurant
New Bond Street
Petite Maison
Mews of Mayfair, Mayfair Pizza Co, Hush
Sagar
Spring Workshop
C London
Bellamy's

34 Mayfair
Hélène Darroze (Connaught)
Corrigan's
SCOTT'S
Mount Street
Punchbowl
Kai
South Audley Street
Park Lane
Park Lane
Guinea Grill
Jamavar
Delfino
Benares
Sexy Fish
Berkeley Square
Greenhouse
Butler's
The Chesterfield
Tamarind
Murano
Dorchester
(Alain Ducasse
China Tang, Grill Room,
The Promenade)

Burger & Lobster
Ormer
Curzon Street
Boudin Blanc
Shepherd Market Wine House
Artiste Musclé
Kiku
Kitty Fisher's
Cut
(45 Park Lane)
Hatchetts
Hyde Park
El Pirata
Galvin at Windows (Hilton)
Nobu
(Metropolitan)
Galvin at Athenaeum
Piccadilly
Coya
Theo Randall (InterContinental),
Martha Oritz
Hard Rock Café

MAP 3 – MAYFAIR, ST. JAMES'S & WEST SOHO

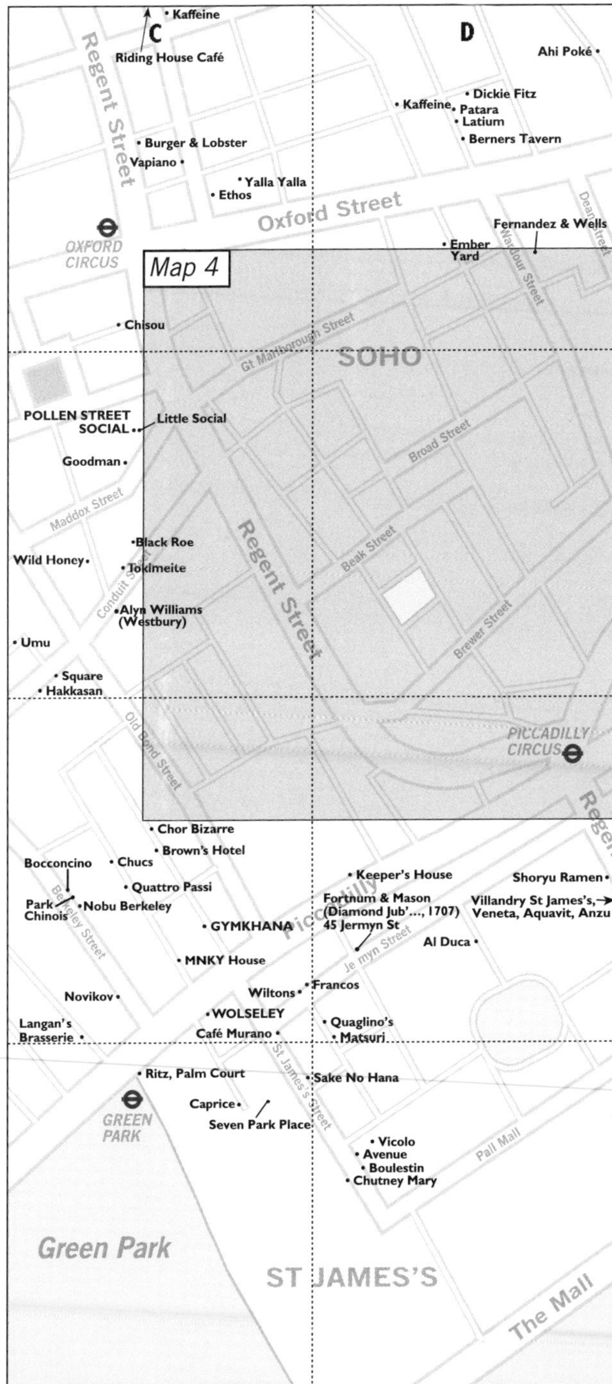

MAP 4 – WEST SOHO & PICCADILLY

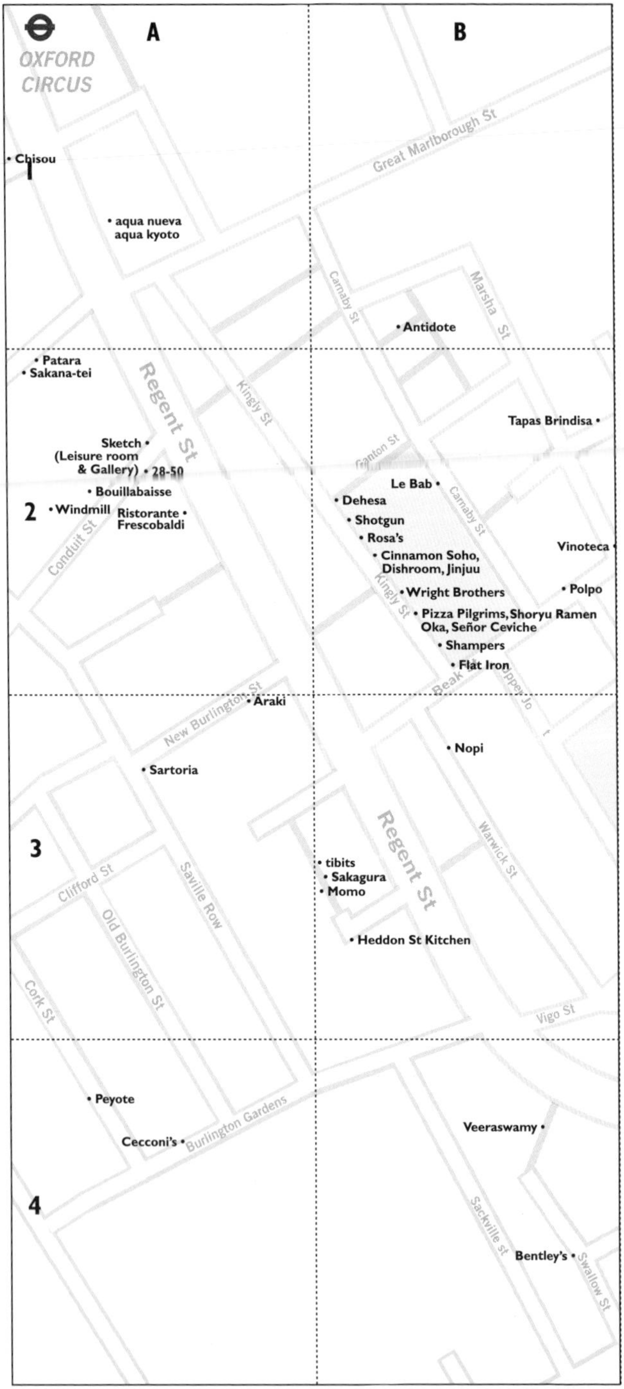

A B

OXFORD CIRCUS

1

Chisou
aqua nueva
aqua kyoto
Great Marlborough St
Carnaby St
Marshall St
Antidote

2

Patara
Sakana-tei
Regent St
Kingly St
Sketch (Leisure room & Gallery)
28-50
Bouillabaisse
Windmill
Ristorante Frescobaldi
Conduit St
Tapas Brindisa
Ganton St
Le Bab
Dehesa
Shotgun
Rosa's
Cinnamon Soho, Dishroom, Jinjuu
Vinoteca
Wright Brothers
Polpo
Pizza Pilgrims, Shoryu Ramen
Oka, Señor Ceviche
Shampers
Flat Iron
Beak St
Upper John St

3

New Burlington St
Araki
Sartoria
Nopi
Clifford St
Savile Row
Old Burlington St
Cork St
tibits
Sakagura
Momo
Regent St
Warwick St
Heddon St Kitchen
Vigo St

4

Peyote
Cecconi's
Burlington Gardens
Veeraswamy
Sackville St
Bentley's
Swallow St

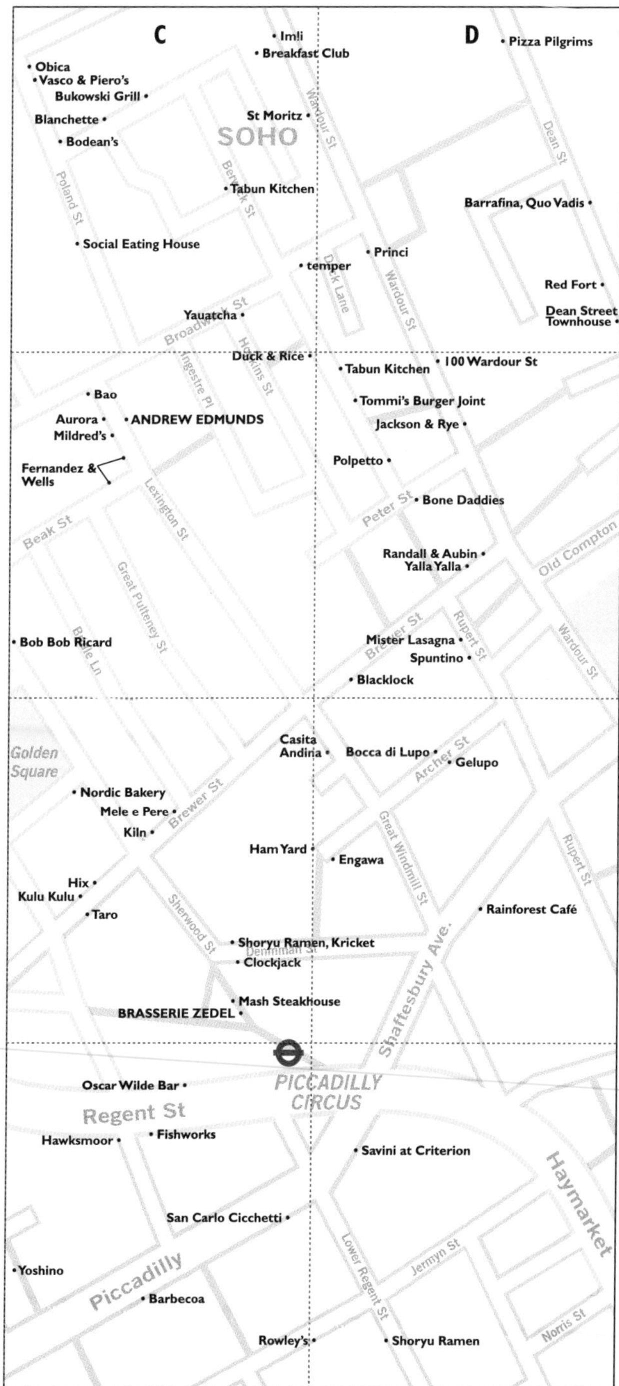
C
D
Imli
Breakfast Club
Pizza Pilgrims
Obica
Vasco & Piero's
Bukowski Grill
Blanchette
St Moritz
SOHO
Bodean's
Tabun Kitchen
Barrafina, Quo Vadis
Social Eating House
Princi
temper
Red Fort
Yauatcha
Dean Street Townhouse
Duck & Rice
Tabun Kitchen
100 Wardour St
Bao
Tommi's Burger Joint
Aurora
ANDREW EDMUNDS
Jackson & Rye
Mildred's
Polpetto
Fernandez & Wells
Bone Daddies
Randall & Aubin
Yalla Yalla
Bob Bob Ricard
Mister Lasagna
Spuntino
Blacklock
Casita Andina
Bocca di Lupo
Gelupo
Golden Square
Nordic Bakery
Mele e Pere
Kiln
Ham Yard
Engawa
Hix
Kulu Kulu
Taro
Rainforest Café
Shoryu Ramen, Kricket
Clockjack
Mash Steakhouse
BRASSERIE ZEDEL
Oscar Wilde Bar
PICCADILLY CIRCUS
Regent St
Hawksmoor
Fishworks
Savini at Criterion
Haymarket
San Carlo Cicchetti
Yoshino
Piccadilly
Barbecoa
Rowley's
Shoryu Ramen
Wardour St
Dean St
Poland St
Berwick St
Dick Lane
Broadwick St
Hopkins St
Ingestre Pl
Lexington St
Peter St
Beak St
Great Pulteney St
Old Compton
Brewer St
Rupert St
Archer St
Great Windmill St
Sherwood St
Denman St
Shaftesbury Ave.
Lower Regent St
Jermyn St
Norris St

MAP 5 – EAST SOHO, CHINATOWN & COVENT GARDEN

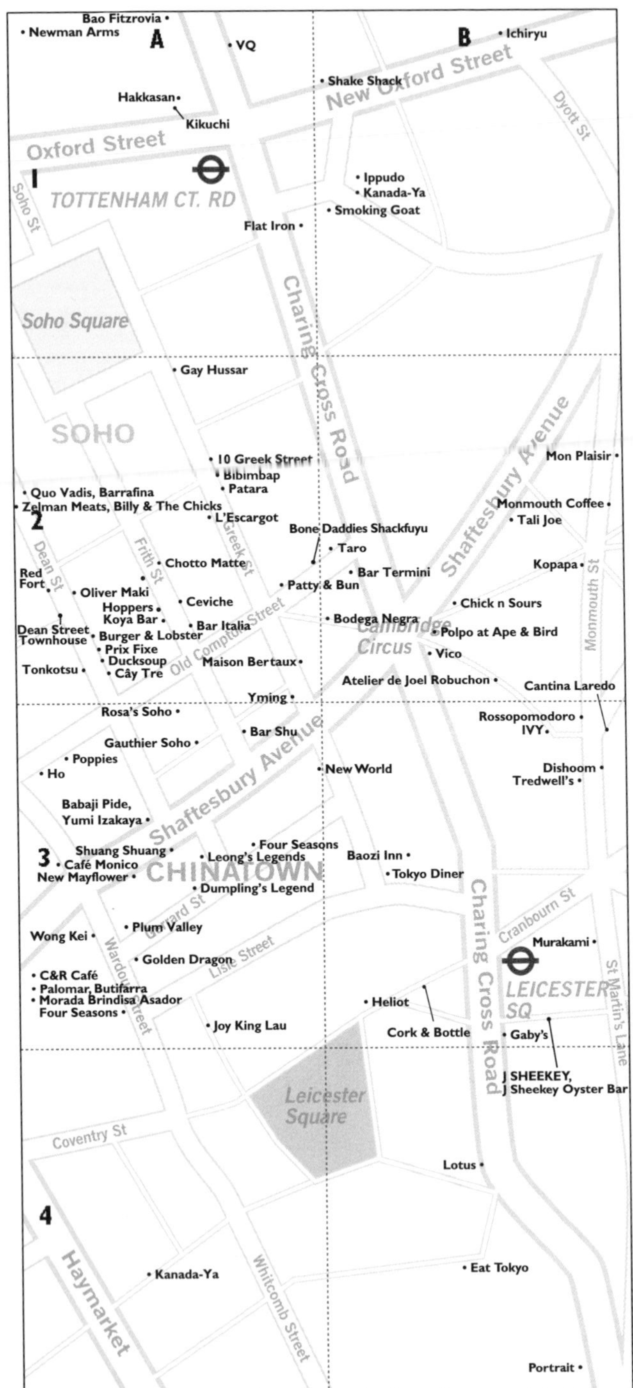

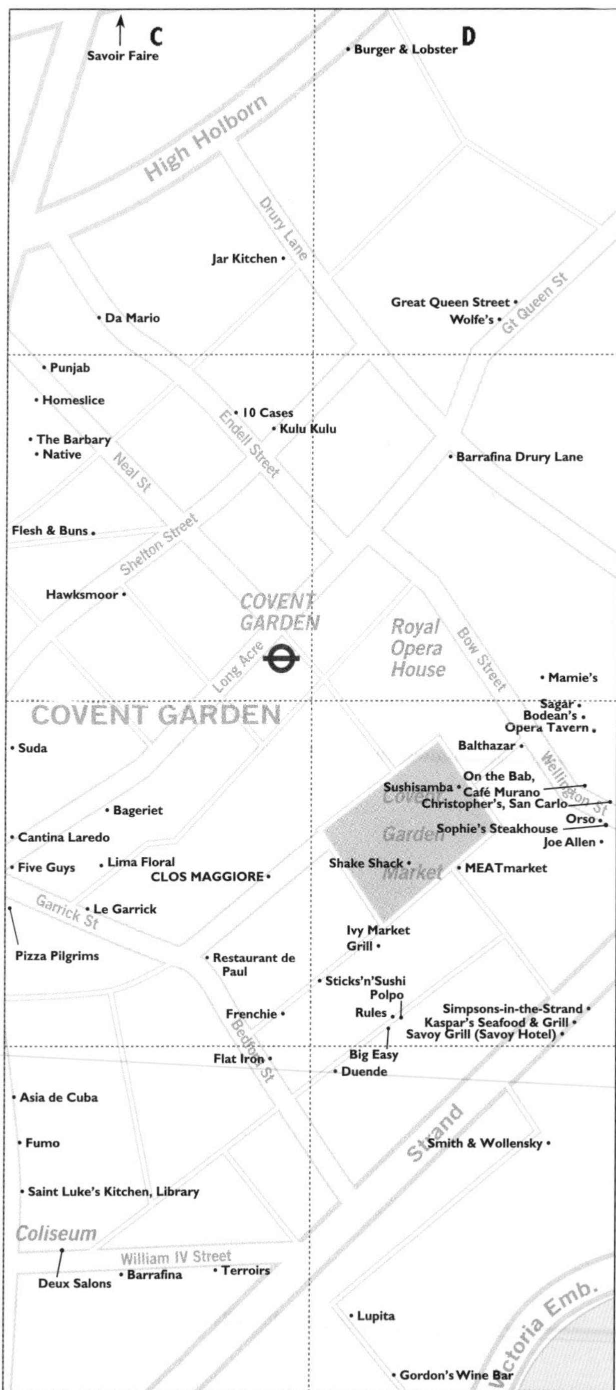
C
D
Savoir Faire
Burger & Lobster
High Holborn
Drury Lane
Jar Kitchen
Great Queen Street
Wolfe's
Gt Queen St
Da Mario
Punjab
Homeslice
10 Cases
Kulu Kulu
The Barbary
Native
Endell Street
Neal St
Barrafina Drury Lane
Flesh & Buns
Shelton Street
Hawksmoor
COVENT GARDEN
Royal Opera House
Long Acre
Bow Street
Mamie's
COVENT GARDEN
Sagar
Bodean's
Opera Tavern
Suda
Balthazar
Wellington St
On the Bab, Café Murano
Sushisamba
Covent Garden Market
Christopher's, San Carlo
Bageriet
Orso
Sophie's Steakhouse
Cantina Laredo
Joe Allen
Five Guys
Lima Floral
Shake Shack
MEATmarket
CLOS MAGGIORE
Garrick St
Le Garrick
Ivy Market Grill
Pizza Pilgrims
Restaurant de Paul
Sticks'n'Sushi
Polpo
Simpsons-in-the-Strand
Frenchie
Rules
Kaspar's Seafood & Grill
Savoy Grill (Savoy Hotel)
Bedford St
Big Easy
Flat Iron
Duende
Asia de Cuba
Strand
Fumo
Smith & Wollensky
Saint Luke's Kitchen, Library
Coliseum
William IV Street
Deux Salons
Barrafina
Terroirs
Victoria Emb.
Lupita
Gordon's Wine Bar

MAP 6 – KNIGHTSBRIDGE, CHELSEA & SOUTH KENSINGTON

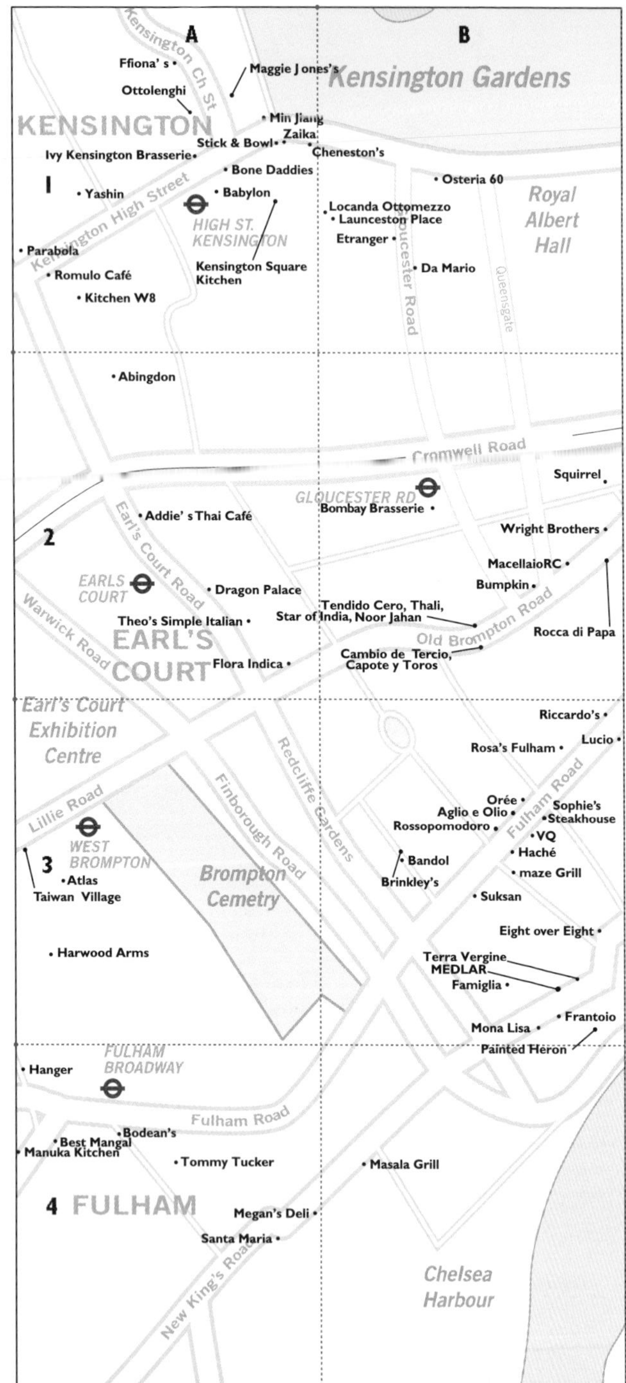

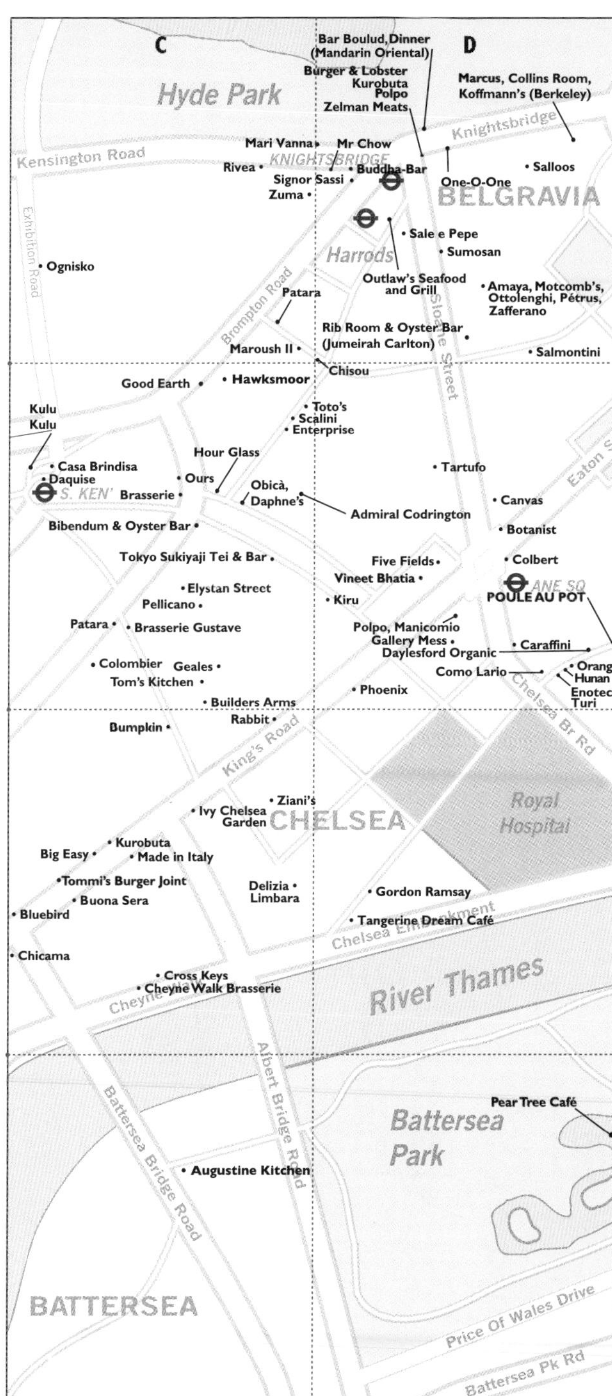
C
D
Hyde Park
Bar Boulud, Dinner (Mandarin Oriental)
Burger & Lobster
Kurobuta
Polpo
Zelman Meats
Marcus, Collins Room, Koffmann's (Berkeley)
Knightsbridge
Kensington Road
Mari Vanna
Mr Chow
KNIGHTSBRIDGE
Rivea
Buddha-Bar
Signor Sassi
Zuma
One-O-One
Salloos
BELGRAVIA
Exhibition Road
Sale e Pepe
Sumosan
Ognisko
Harrods
Outlaw's Seafood and Grill
Amaya, Motcomb's, Ottolenghi, Pétrus, Zafferano
Brompton Road
Patara
Sloane Street
Rib Room & Oyster Bar (Jumeirah Carlton)
Maroush II
Salmontini
Chisou
Good Earth
Hawksmoor
Toto's
Scalini
Enterprise
Kulu Kulu
Hour Glass
Tartufo
Eaton Sq
Casa Brindisa
Daquise
Ours
S. KEN'
Brasserie
Obicà, Daphne's
Admiral Codrington
Canvas
Bibendum & Oyster Bar
Botanist
Tokyo Sukiyaji Tei & Bar
Five Fields
Colbert
Vineet Bhatia
Elystan Street
SLOANE SQ
Pellicano
Kiru
POULE AU POT
Patara
Brasserie Gustave
Polpo, Manicomio
Gallery Mess
Caraffini
Daylesford Organic
Colombier
Geales
Orange
Como Lario
Hunan
Tom's Kitchen
Enoteca Turi
Phoenix
Chelsea Br Rd
Builders Arms
Rabbit
Bumpkin
King's Road
Ziani's
Royal Hospital
Ivy Chelsea Garden
CHELSEA
Kurobuta
Big Easy
Made in Italy
Tommi's Burger Joint
Delizia Limbara
Gordon Ramsay
Buona Sera
Bluebird
Tangerine Dream Café
Chelsea Embankment
Chicama
River Thames
Cross Keys
Cheyne Walk Brasserie
Cheyne Walk
Albert Bridge Road
Battersea Bridge Road
Pear Tree Café
Battersea Park
Augustine Kitchen
BATTERSEA
Price Of Wales Drive
Battersea Pk Rd

MAP 7 – NOTTING HILL & BAYSWATER

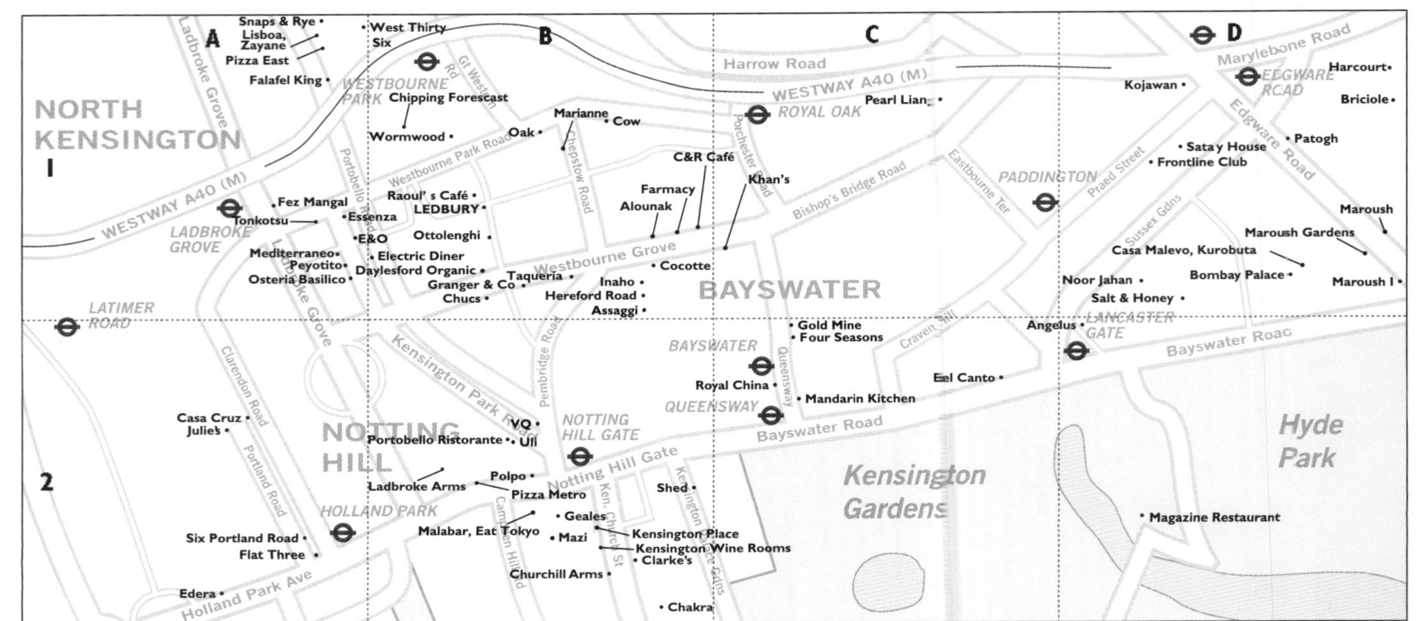

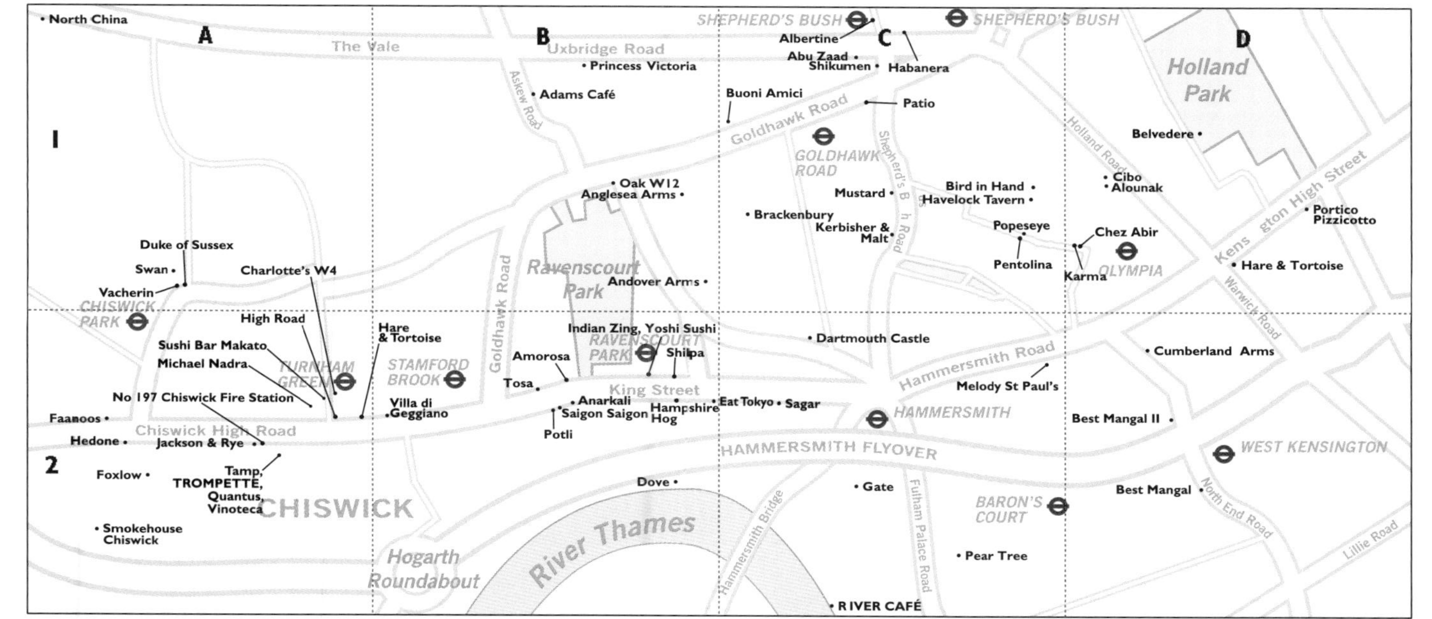

MAP 8 – HAMMERSMITH & CHISWICK

MAP 9 – HAMPSTEAD, CAMDEN TOWN & ISLINGTON

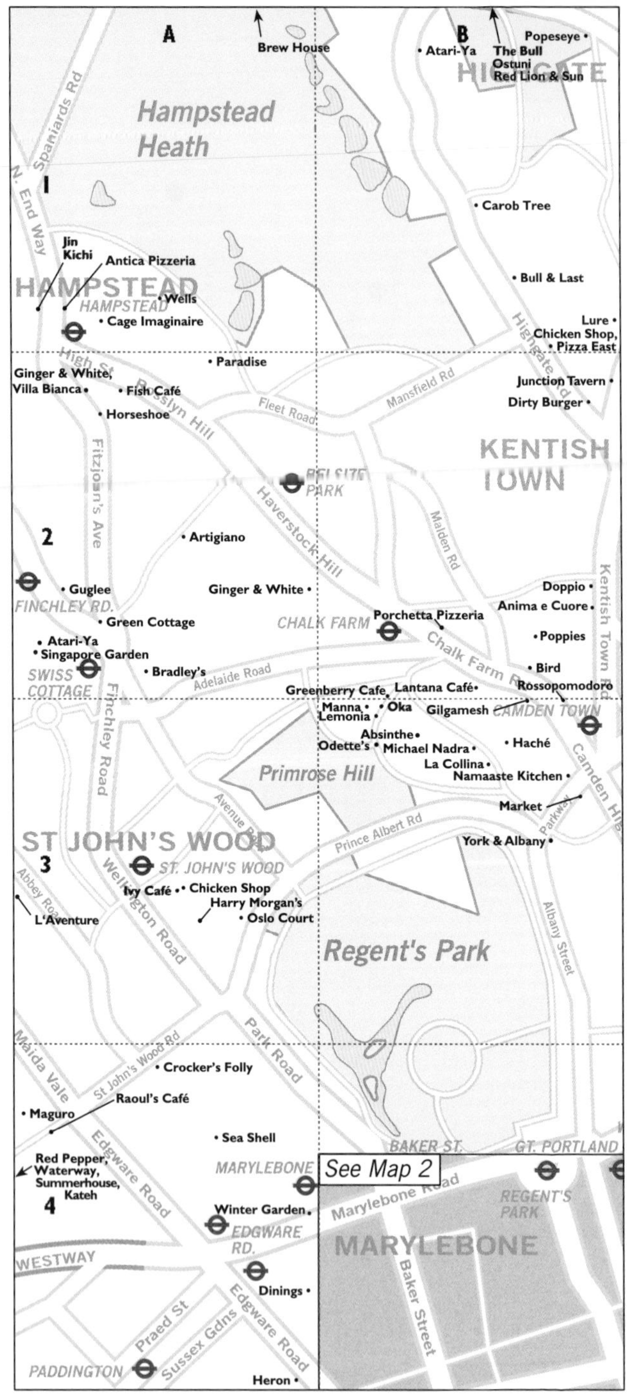

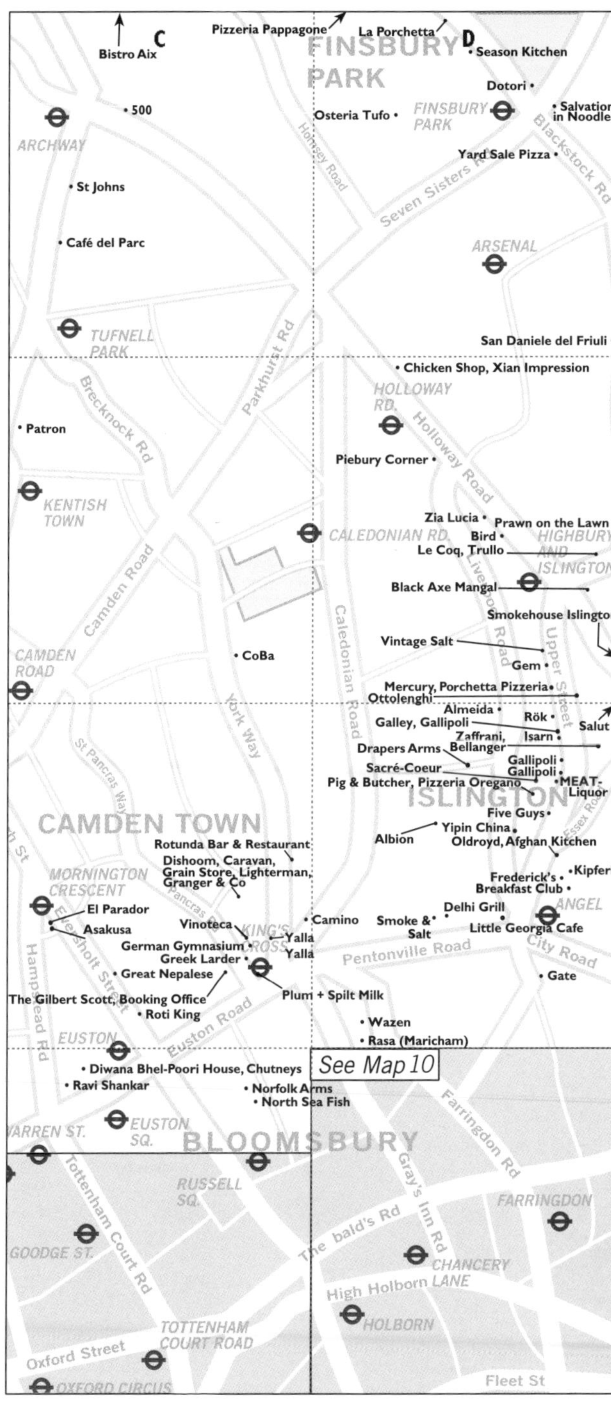
Bistro Aix
C
Pizzeria Pappagone
La Porchetta
D
FINSBURY PARK
Season Kitchen
Dotori
500
Osteria Tufo
FINSBURY PARK
Salvation in Noodles
ARCHWAY
Hornsey Road
Blackstock Rd
Yard Sale Pizza
St Johns
Seven Sisters R
Café del Parc
ARSENAL
TUFNELL PARK
Parkhurst Rd
San Daniele del Friuli
Chicken Shop, Xian Impression
HOLLOWAY RD.
Brecknock Rd
Patron
Holloway Road
Piebury Corner
KENTISH TOWN
Zia Lucia
Prawn on the Lawn
CALEDONIAN RD.
Bird
HIGHBURY AND ISLINGTON
Le Coq, Trullo
Camden Road
Black Axe Mangal
Liverpool Road
Smokehouse Islington
Caledonian Road
Vintage Salt
Upper Street
CAMDEN ROAD
CoBa
Gem
Mercury, Porchetta Pizzeria
Ottolenghi
York Way
Almeida
Rök
Galley, Gallipoli
Salut
Zaffrani, Bellanger
Isarn
St Pancras Way
Drapers Arms
Gallipoli
Sacré-Coeur
Gallipoli
Pig & Butcher, Pizzeria Oregano
MEAT-Liquor
ISLINGTON
Essex Rd
CAMDEN TOWN
Five Guys
Yipin China
Albion
Oldroyd, Afghan Kitchen
Rotunda Bar & Restaurant
Dishoom, Caravan, Grain Store, Lighterman, Granger & Co
MORNINGTON CRESCENT
Frederick's
Kipferl
Breakfast Club
El Parador
Delhi Grill
ANGEL
Camino
Smoke & Salt
Asakusa
Vinoteca
KING'S CROSS
Little Georgia Cafe
Yalla Yalla
City Road
German Gymnasium
Pentonville Road
Greek Larder
Eversholt Street
Great Nepalese
Gate
Hampstead Rd
The Gilbert Scott, Booking Office
Plum + Spilt Milk
Roti King
Euston Road
Wazen
EUSTON
Rasa (Maricham)
See Map 10
Diwana Bhel-Poori House, Chutneys
Ravi Shankar
Norfolk Arms
North Sea Fish
Farringdon Rd
WARREN ST.
EUSTON SQ.
BLOOMSBURY
Gray's Inn Rd
Tottenham Court Rd
RUSSELL SQ.
FARRINGDON
GOODGE ST.
The bald's Rd
CHANCERY LANE
High Holborn
HOLBORN
TOTTENHAM COURT ROAD
Oxford Street
Fleet St
OXFORD CIRCUS

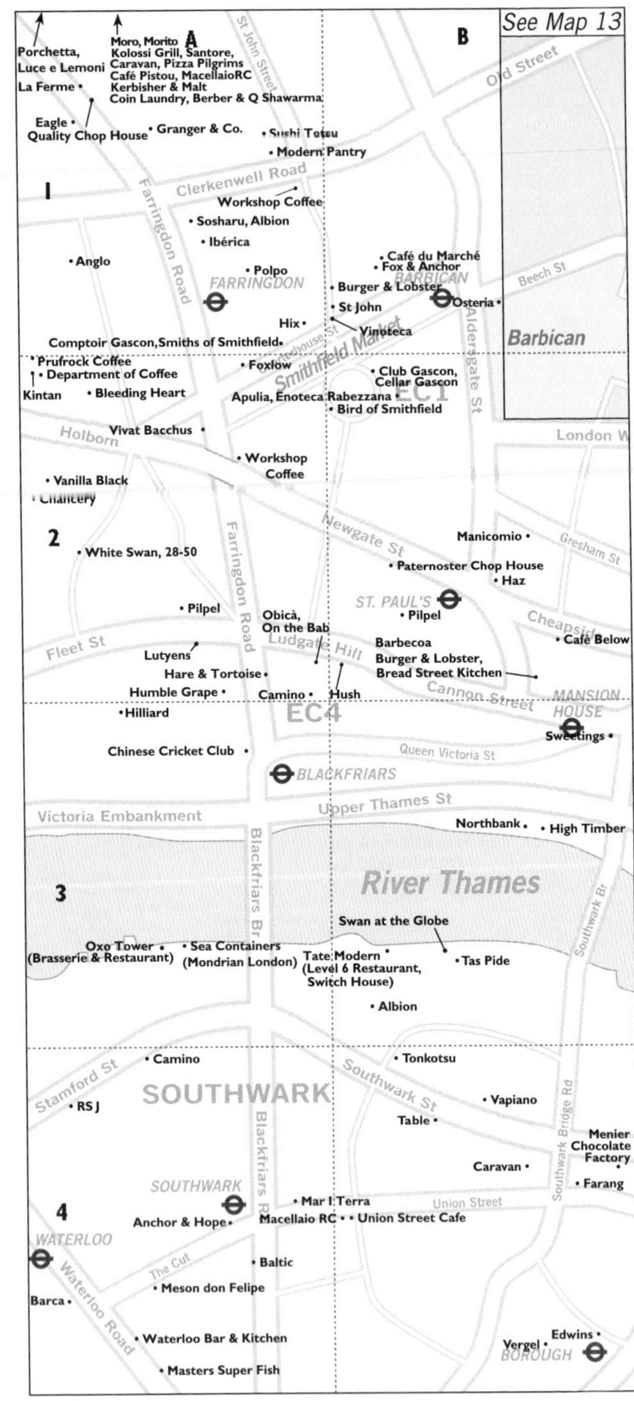
See Map 13
A
B
1
2
3
4
Porchetta,
Luce e Lemoni
La Ferme
Moro, Morito
Kolossi Grill, Santore,
Caravan, Pizza Pilgrims
Café Pistou, MacellaioRC
Kerbisher & Malt
Coin Laundry, Berber & Q Shawarma
Eagle
Quality Chop House
Granger & Co.
Sushi Tetsu
Modern Pantry
St John Street
Old Street
Clerkenwell Road
Workshop Coffee
Sosharu, Albion
Ibérica
Anglo
Polpo
Farringdon Road
FARRINGDON
Café du Marché
Fox & Anchor
BARBICAN
Burger & Lobster
Osteria
St John
Beech St
Barbican
Hix
Vinoteca
Charterhouse St
Smithfield Market
Aldersgate St
Comptoir Gascon, Smiths of Smithfield
Prufrock Coffee
Department of Coffee
Kintan
Bleeding Heart
Foxlow
Club Gascon,
Cellar Gascon
EC1
Apulia, Enoteca Rabezzana
Bird of Smithfield
Holborn
Vivat Bacchus
Workshop
Coffee
London W
Vanilla Black
Chancery
Newgate St
Manicomio
Gresham St
White Swan, 28-50
Paternoster Chop House
Haz
ST. PAUL'S
Pilpel
Pilpel
Obicà,
On the Bab
Cheapside
Café Below
Fleet St
Ludgate Hill
Barbecoa
Burger & Lobster,
Bread Street Kitchen
Lutyens
Hare & Tortoise
Humble Grape
Camino
Hush
Cannon Street
MANSION HOUSE
Hilliard
EC4
Sweetings
Chinese Cricket Club
Queen Victoria St
BLACKFRIARS
Upper Thames St
Victoria Embankment
Northbank
High Timber
Blackfriars Br
River Thames
Southwark Br
Swan at the Globe
Oxo Tower
(Brasserie & Restaurant)
Sea Containers
(Mondrian London)
Tate Modern
(Level 6 Restaurant,
Switch House)
Tas Pide
Albion
Camino
Tonkotsu
Stamford St
SOUTHWARK
Southwark St
RSJ
Vapiano
Table
Menier
Chocolate
Factory
Southwark Bridge Rd
Caravan
Farang
SOUTHWARK
Mar I Terra
Union Street
Anchor & Hope
Macellaio RC
Union Street Cafe
WATERLOO
Baltic
The Cut
Waterloo Road
Meson don Felipe
Barca
Waterloo Bar & Kitchen
Edwins
Vergel
BOROUGH
Masters Super Fish

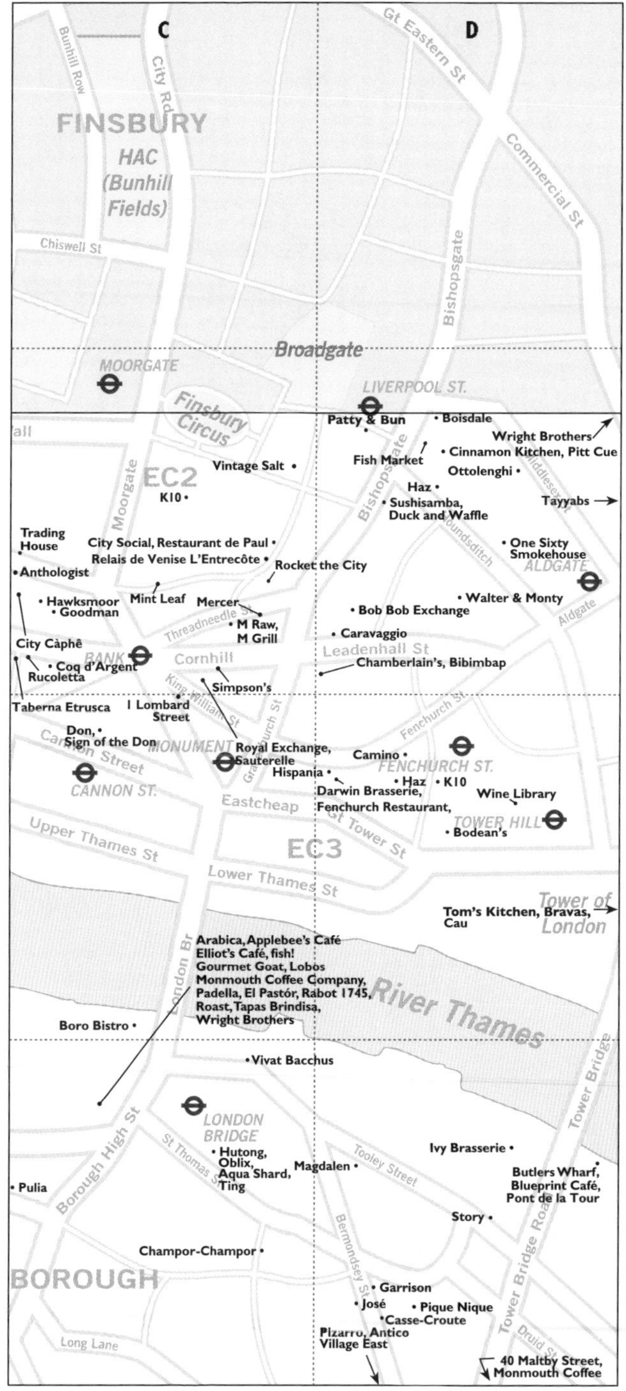
C
D
FINSBURY
HAC (Bunhill Fields)
Bunhill Row
City Rd
Gt Eastern St
Commercial St
Chiswell St
Bishopsgate
Broadgate
MOORGATE
LIVERPOOL ST.
Finsbury Circus
EC2
Moorgate
Patty & Bun
Boisdale
Wright Brothers
Fish Market
Cinnamon Kitchen, Pitt Cue
Vintage Salt
Ottolenghi
Haz
K10
Sushisamba, Duck and Waffle
Tayyabs
Trading House
City Social, Restaurant de Paul
Relais de Venise L'Entrecôte
Rocket the City
One Sixty Smokehouse
ALDGATE
Anthologist
Mint Leaf
Walter & Monty
Hawksmoor
Goodman
Mercer
Bob Bob Exchange
Aldgate
M Raw, M Grill
Threadneedle St
City Càphê
Caravaggio
Leadenhall St
BANK
Cornhill
Chamberlain's, Bibimbap
Coq d'Argent
Rucoletta
Simpson's
Taberna Etrusca
1 Lombard Street
King William St
Fenchurch St
Don, Sign of the Don
Cannon Street
MONUMENT
Royal Exchange, Sauterelle
Camino
FENCHURCH ST.
Hispania
CANNON ST.
Haz
K10
Darwin Brasserie, Fenchurch Restaurant,
Wine Library
Eastcheap
Gt Tower St
TOWER HILL
Bodean's
Upper Thames St
EC3
Lower Thames St
Tower of London
Tom's Kitchen, Bravas, Cau
Arabica, Applebee's Café
Elliot's Café, fish!
Gourmet Goat, Lobos
Monmouth Coffee Company,
Padella, El Pastór, Rabot 1745,
Roast, Tapas Brindisa,
Wright Brothers
London Br
River Thames
Boro Bistro
Vivat Bacchus
Tower Bridge
LONDON BRIDGE
Ivy Brasserie
Hutong, Oblix, Aqua Shard, Ting
Magdalen
Tooley Street
St Thomas St
Butlers Wharf, Blueprint Café, Pont de la Tour
Pulia
Borough High St
Story
Bermondsey St
Tower Bridge Road
Champor-Champor
BOROUGH
Garrison
José
Pique Nique
Casse-Croute
Pizarro, Antico
Village East
Druid St
Long Lane
40 Maltby Street, Monmouth Coffee

MAP 11 – SOUTH LONDON (& FULHAM)

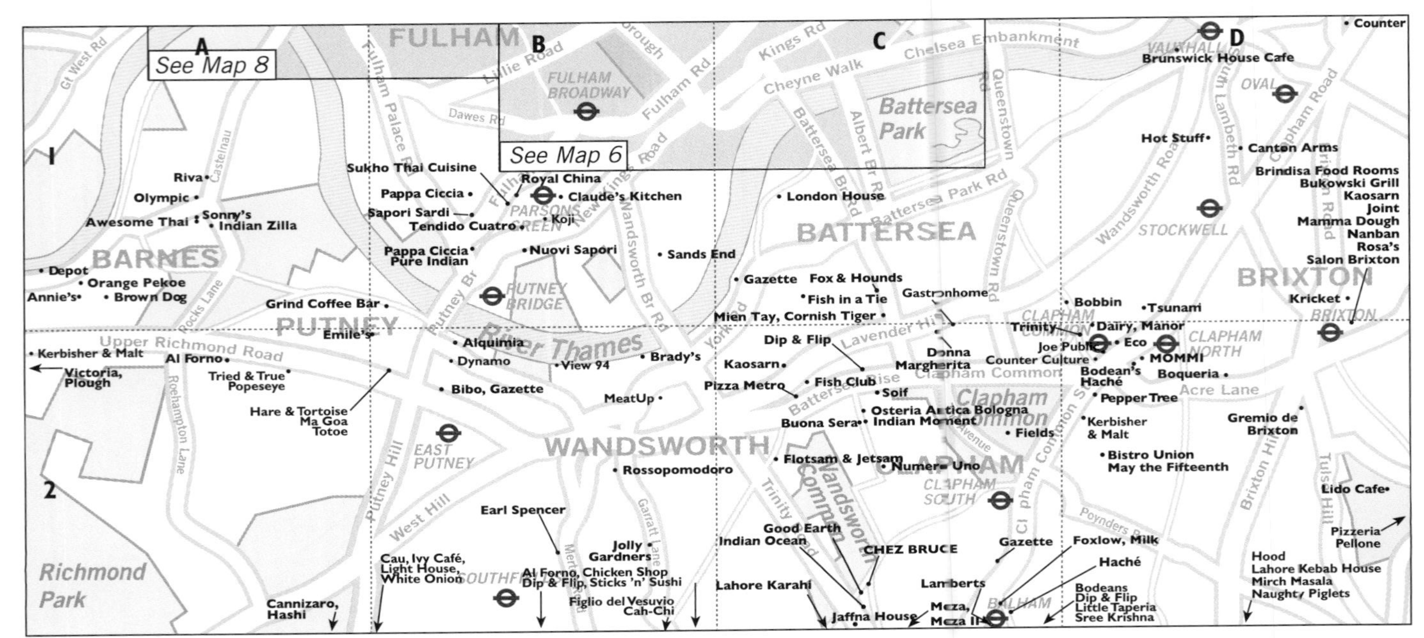

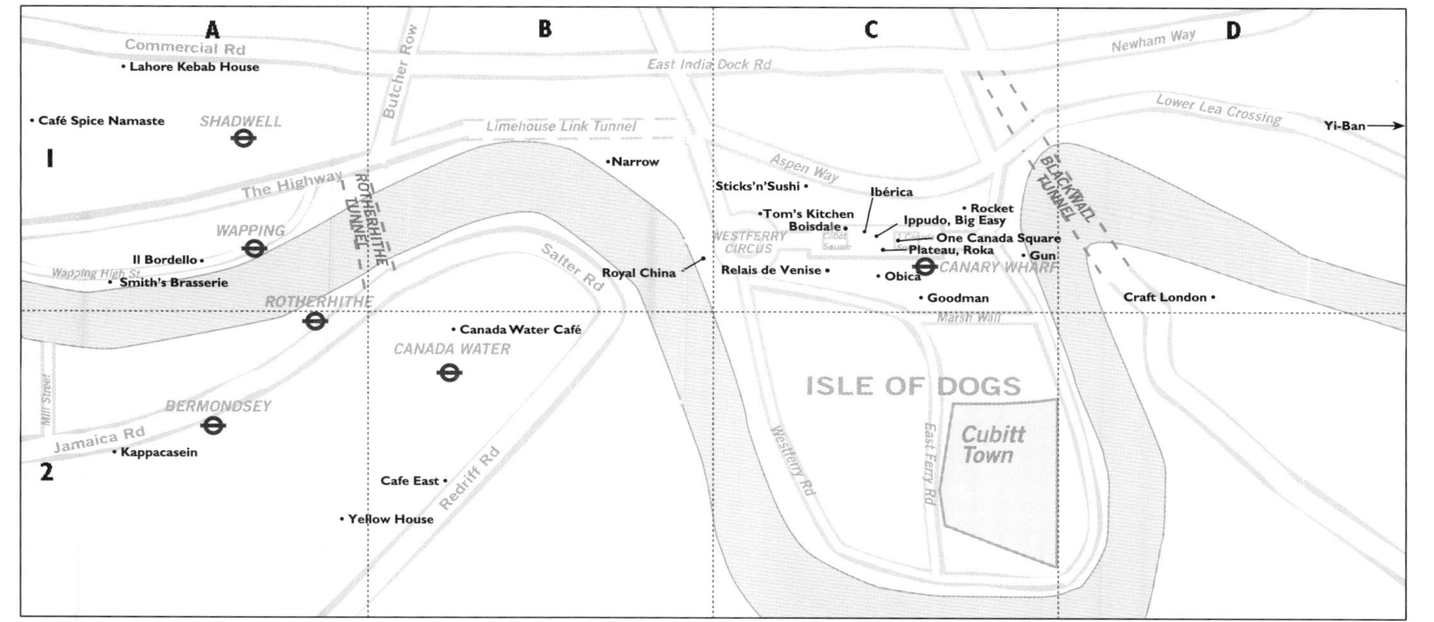

MAP 12 – EAST END & DOCKLANDS

MAP 13 – SHOREDITCH & BETHNAL GREEN

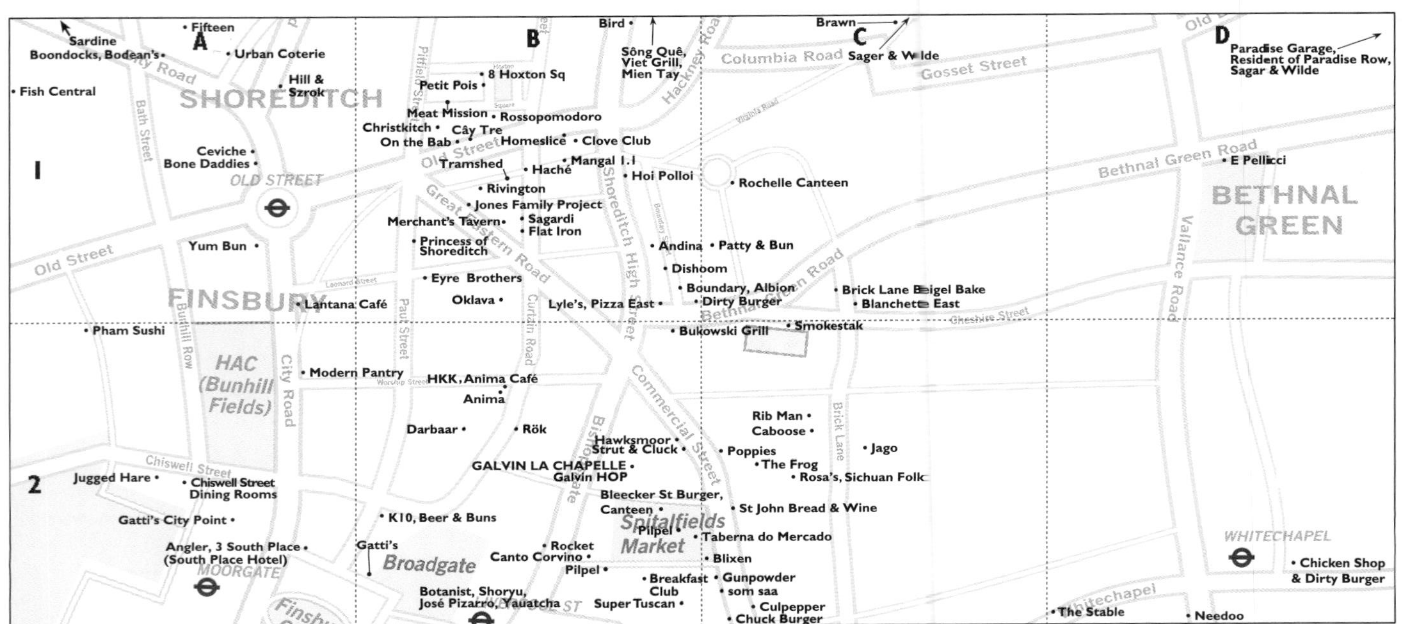

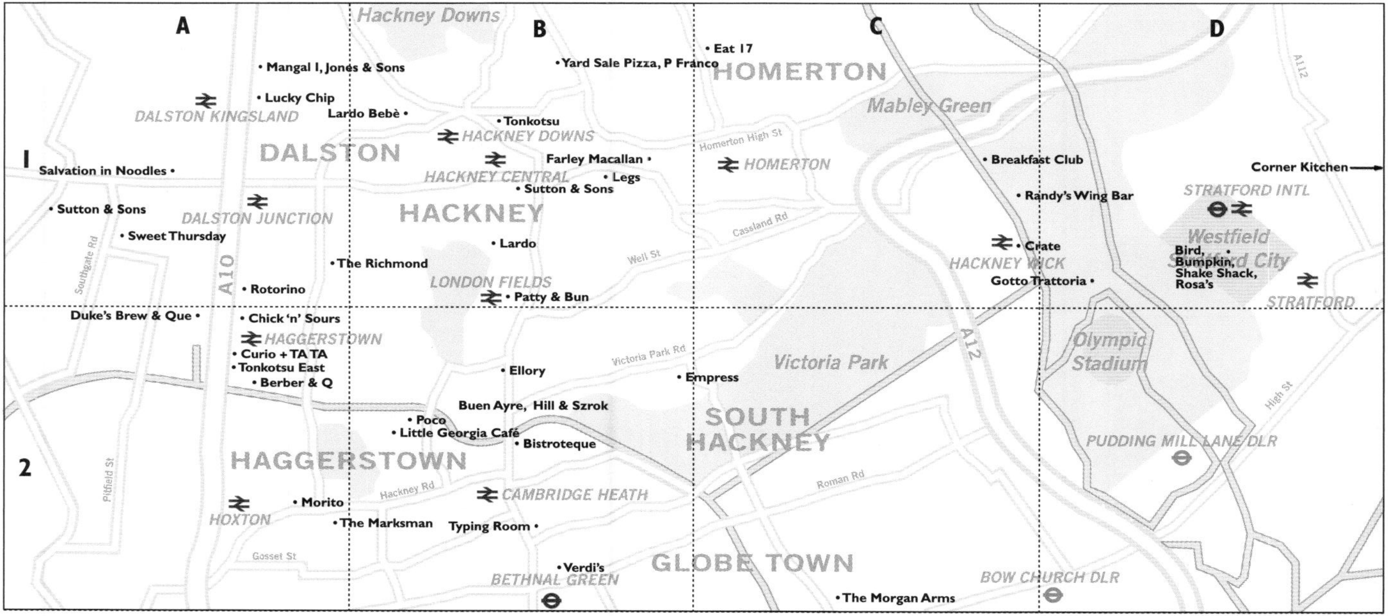

MAP 14 – EAST LONDON

Heliot Steak House

Le Gavroche

The Lighterman

UK SURVEY RESULTS & TOP SCORERS

PLACES PEOPLE TALK ABOUT

These are the restaurants outside London that were mentioned most frequently by reporters (last year's position is shown in brackets). For a list of London's most mentioned restaurants, see page 12.

1 **Manoir aux Quat' Saisons** (1)
Great Milton, Oxon
2 **Waterside Inn** (2)
Bray, Berks
3 **Seafood Restaurant** (9)
Padstow, Cornwall
4 **L'Enclume** (3)
Cartmel, Cumbria
5 **Sportsman** (5)
Whitstable, Kent

L'Enclume

6 **Midsummer House** (6)
Cambridge, Cambs
7 **Artichoke** (8)
Amersham, Bucks
8 **Hand & Flowers** (4)
Marlow, Bucks
9 **Restaurant Nathan Outlaw** (16=)
Port Isaac, Cornwall
10 **Gidleigh Park** (10)
Chagford, Devon

Hand & Flowers

11 **Fat Duck** (12)
Bray, Berks
12 **Restaurant Sat Bains** (15)
Nottingham, Notts
13 **Northcote** (7)
Langho, Lancs
14 **Hambleton Hall** (18=)
Hambleton, Rutland
15= **Sir Charles Napier** (-)
Chinnor, Oxon

Sir Charles Napier

15= **Adams** (-)
Birmingham, West Midlands
17= **Hind's Head** (14)
Bray, Berks
17= **Chapter One** (13)
Locksbottom, Kent
17= **Magpie** (20)
Whitby, N Yorks
20 **Walnut Tree** (-)
Llandewi Skirrid, Monmouthshire

Magpie

All restaurants whose food rating is **5** *plus restaurants whose price is £60+ with a food rating of* **4**

£320+	The Fat Duck *(Bray)*	442
£230+	Waterside Inn *(Bray)*	455
£190+	Le Manoir aux Quat' Saisons *(Great Milton)*	555
£170+	L'Enclume *(Cartmel)*	554
£150+	Gidleigh Park *(Chagford)*	555
£140+	Restaurant Nathan Outlaw *(Port Isaac)*	545
	Midsummer House *(Cambridge)*	544
	The Dining Room, Whatley Manor *(Easton Grey)*	433
£130+	Andrew Fairlie, Gleneagles Hotel *(Auchterarder)*	544
£120+	Restaurant Sat Bains *(Nottingham)*	533
£110+	Casamia, The General *(Bristol)*	545
£100+	Fraiche *(Oxton)*	554
	Raby Hunt *(Summerhouse)*	554
	Winteringham Fields *(Winteringham)*	554
	Lucknam Park, Lucknam Park Hotel *(Colerne)*	544
	Restaurant Coworth Park *(Ascot)*	445
	Bybrook Restaurant, Manor House Hotel *(Castle Combe)*	444
	Martin Wishart, Cameron House *(Loch Lomond)*	444
	The Pass Restaurant, South Lodge Hotel *(Lower Beeding)*	443
£90+	Hambleton Hall *(Hambleton)*	554
	Northcote *(Langho)*	554
	Number One, Balmoral Hotel *(Edinburgh)*	544
	Yorke Arms *(Ramsgill-in-Nidderdale)*	544
	The Man Behind The Curtain *(Leeds)*	543
	Sharrow Bay *(Ullswater)*	435
	Fischers at Baslow Hall *(Baslow)*	444
	Morston Hall *(Morston)*	444
	The Samling *(Windermere)*	444
	Kinloch Lodge *(Sleat)*	434
	Manchester House *(Manchester)*	434

The Kitchin *(Edinburgh)* 4 3 4
21212 *(Edinburgh)* 4 4 3
Restaurant Martin Wishart *(Edinburgh)* 4 4 3
The Slaughters Manor House *(Lower Slaughter)* 4 3 3

£80+ Adam's *(Birmingham)* 5 5 5
Tyddyn Llan *(Llandrillo)* 5 4 5
Black Swan *(Oldstead)* 5 5 4
Bohemia, The Club Hotel & Spa *(Jersey)* 5 4 4
Paul Ainsworth at Number 6 *(Padstow)* 5 4 4
The Feathered Nest Inn *(Nether Westcote)* 5 4 4
The Three Chimneys *(Dunvegan)* 5 4 4
Lake Road Kitchen *(Ambleside)* 5 5 3
Le Champignon Sauvage *(Cheltenham)* 5 5 3
Cotto *(Cambridge)* 5 4 3
Samuel's, Swinton Park Hotel & Spa *(Masham)* 4 4 5
Lumière *(Cheltenham)* 4 5 4
Longueville Manor *(Jersey)* 4 4 4
Airds Hotel *(Port Appin)* 4 4 3
The Castle Terrace *(Edinburgh)* 4 4 3
The Whitebrook, Restaurant with Rooms *(Whitebrook)* 4 4 3
Gilpin Hotel *(Windermere)* 4 3 3
Hand & Flowers *(Marlow)* 4 3 3

£70+ The Forest Side *(Grasmere)* 5 5 5
Summer Lodge Country House Hotel *(Evershot)* 5 4 5
The Box Tree *(Ilkley)* 5 4 5
Artichoke *(Amersham)* 5 5 4
Gareth Ward at Ynyshir *(Eglwys Fach)* 5 5 4
Little Barwick House *(Barwick)* 5 5 4
The Harrow at Little Bedwyn *(Marlborough)* 5 5 4
The Neptune *(Old Hunstanton)* 5 5 4
The Grove - Narberth *(Dyfed)* 5 4 4
The Peat Inn *(Cupar)* 5 4 4
Timberyard *(Edinburgh)* 5 4 4
Monachyle Mhor *(Balquhidder)* 5 3 4
Checkers *(Montgomery)* 5 4 3
House of Tides *(Newcastle upon Tyne)* 5 4 3
Little Fish Market *(Brighton)* 5 4 3
Whites *(Beverley)* 5 4 3
Menu Gordon Jones *(Bath)* 5 4 2
Wilks *(Bristol)* 5 4 2
The Cross at Kenilworth *(Kenilworth)* 5 3 2
Seafood Restaurant *(St Andrews)* 4 3 5

	Caldesi in Campagna *(Bray)*	444
	Driftwood Hotel *(Rosevine)*	444
	Hipping Hall *(Kirkby Lonsdale)*	444
	The Alderley, Alderley Edge Hotel *(Alderley Edge)*	444
	The Cellar *(Anstruther)*	444
	The Old Inn *(Drewsteignton)*	453
	Carters of Moseley *(Birmingham)*	443
	Cheal's of Henley *(Henley in Arden)*	443
	The Peacock at Rowsley *(Rowsley)*	443
	Clock Tower, Rudding Park *(Harrogate)*	433
	Restaurant James Sommerin *(Penarth)*	433
	Thackeray's *(Tunbridge Wells)*	433
	Restaurant Mark Greenaway *(Edinburgh)*	432
	JSW *(Petersfield)*	422
£60+	The Sir Charles Napier *(Chinnor)*	535
	Braidwoods *(Dalry)*	554
	Freemasons at Wiswell *(Wiswell)*	554
	Great House *(Lavenham)*	554
	Aizle *(Edinburgh)*	544
	Askham Hall *(Askham)*	544
	Roger Hickman's *(Norwich)*	544
	Sosban And The Old Butchers *(Menai Bridge)*	544
	Stovell's *(Chobham)*	544
	The Albannach *(Lochinver)*	544
	The Coach House *(Kentisbury)*	544
	Woodspeen *(Newbury)*	544
	The Seahorse *(Dartmouth)*	534
	5 North Street *(Winchcombe)*	543
	Ode *(Shaldon)*	543
	Orwells *(Shiplake)*	543
	Restaurant Tristan *(Horsham)*	543
	St Enodoc Restaurant *(Rock)*	543
	The Old Passage Inn *(Arlingham)*	543
	The Vanilla Pod *(Marlow)*	543
	The West House *(Biddenden)*	543
	Thompsons *(Newport)*	543
	The Mason's Arms *(Knowstone)*	533
	The Olive Tree, Queensberry Hotel *(Bath)*	533
	The Walnut Tree *(Llandewi Skirrid)*	533
	Verveine Fishmarket Restaurant *(Milford-on-Sea)*	533
	Coast *(Saundersfoot)*	445
	Crab & Lobster *(Asenby)*	445
	Fairyhill *(Reynoldston)*	445

	Plas Bodegroes *(Pwllheli)*	445
	Silver Darling *(Aberdeen)*	435
	Killiecrankie House Hotel *(Killiecrankie)*	454
	Rafters *(Sheffield)*	454
	Stock Hill Country House Hotel & Restaurant *(Gillingham)*	454
	Mortimers *(Ludlow)*	444
	Shaun Dickens at The Boathouse *(Henley-on-Thames)*	444
	The Hind's Head *(Bray)*	444
	The Kingham Plough *(Kingham)*	444
	The Lawn, Thornton Hall Hotel & Spa *(Thornton Hough)*	444
	The Pheasant Hotel *(Harome)*	444
	The Sundial *(Herstmonceux)*	444
	Toi Et Moi *(Abbey Dore)*	444
	Barley Bree *(Muthill)*	434
	Brockencote Hall *(Chaddesley Corbett)*	434
	Eriska Hotel *(Benderloch)*	434
	The Nut Tree Inn *(Murcott)*	434
	Whitstable Oyster Fishery Co. *(Whitstable)*	434
	Sebastian's *(Oswestry)*	453
	Vero Gusto *(Sheffield)*	453
	Gamba *(Glasgow)*	443
	John's House *(Mountsorrel)*	443
	La Rock *(Sandiacre)*	443
	Rick Stein *(Sandbanks)*	443
	Sienna *(Dorchester)*	443
	The Butcher's Arms *(Eldersfield)*	443
	The Chef's Dozen *(Chipping Campden)*	443
	The Star Inn *(Harome)*	443
	ABode Restaurant, ABode Hotels *(Chester)*	433
	Black Swan *(Helmsley)*	433
	Forbury's *(Reading)*	433
	Hawksmoor *(Manchester)*	433
	Sindhu *(Marlow)*	433
	The Magic Mushroom *(Billericay)*	433
	The Pony & Trap *(Chew Magna)*	433
	The Bildeston Crown *(Bildeston)*	423
	The Flitch of Bacon *(Dunmow)*	423
	Haywards Restaurant *(Epping)*	452
	Chapter One *(Locksbottom)*	432
	Dining Room *(Rock)*	432
£50+	The Sportsman *(Whitstable)*	555
	The Jetty *(Christchurch)*	545
	Bell's Diner And Bar Rooms *(Bristol)*	554

	Fat Olives *(Emsworth)*	554
	Gingerman *(Brighton)*	554
	Les Mirabelles *(Nomansland)*	554
	Pea Porridge *(Bury St Edmunds)*	554
	Riverside *(Bridport)*	554
	Yalbury Cottage *(Lower Bockhampton)*	554
	Castle Dairy *(Kendal)*	544
	Kilberry Inn *(Argyll)*	544
	Le Cochon Aveugle *(York)*	544
	Loch Bay *(Waternish)*	544
	Maison Bleue *(Bury St Edmunds)*	544
	Yu And You *(Copster Green)*	544
	Pierhouse Hotel *(Port Appin)*	534
	Lanterna *(Scarborough)*	553
	Bhoomi *(Cheltenham)*	543
	Bosquet *(Kenilworth)*	543
	Elephant Restaurant & Brasserie *(Torquay)*	543
	Lord Clyde *(Bollington)*	543
	No 7 Fish Bistro *(Torquay)*	543
	Old Stamp House *(Ambleside)*	543
	Terre à Terre *(Brighton)*	543
	The Ambrette *(Margate)*	543
	The Boat House *(Bangor)*	543
	Treby Arms *(Sparkwell)*	543
	Crabshakk *(Glasgow)*	533
	Tailors *(Warwick)*	533
	The Wildebeest Arms *(Stoke Holy Cross)*	533
	Lasan *(Birmingham)*	542
£40+	Wheelers Oyster Bar *(Whitstable)*	555
	Hare Inn *(Scawton)*	554
	Orchid *(Harrogate)*	554
	The Parkers Arms *(Newton-in-Bowland)*	554
	Crab Shack *(Teignmouth)*	544
	Food by Breda Murphy *(Whalley)*	544
	Inver *(Strachur)*	544
	Ox *(Belfast)*	544
	Shillingfords *(Sudbury)*	544
	Maliks *(Cookham)*	534
	Mourne Seafood Bar *(Belfast)*	534
	Prithvi *(Cheltenham)*	553
	Sukhothai *(Leeds)*	553
	1921 *(Bury St Edmunds)*	543
	Ben's Cornish Kitchen *(Marazion)*	543

	Restaurant	Score
	Indian Zest *(Sunbury on Thames)*	543
	The Gannet *(Glasgow)*	543
	White Swan at Fence *(Fence)*	543
	King And Thai *(Broseley)*	533
	My Sichuan *(Oxford)*	533
	The Chilli Pickle *(Brighton)*	533
	The Marram Grass *(Newborough)*	533
	Acorn Vegetarian Kitchen *(Bath)*	542
	Hooked *(Windermere)*	542
	Ebi Sushi *(Derby)*	532
	Magpie Café *(Whitby)*	532
	Novello *(Lytham St Annes)*	532
	Sojo *(Oxford)*	532
	Yuzu *(Manchester)*	532
£30+	Riley's Fish Shack *(Tynemouth)*	535
	Green Café, Ludlow Mill On The Green *(Ludlow)*	554
	JoJo *(Whitstable)*	554
	Oli's Thai *(Oxford)*	554
	Colmans *(South Shields)*	544
	Levanter *(Ramsbottom)*	544
	Sole Bay Fish Company *(Southwold)*	534
	Butley Orford Oysterage *(Orford)*	543
	Kanpai *(Edinburgh)*	543
	Mother India's Cafe *(Edinburgh)*	543
	Tharavadu *(Leeds)*	543
	Xian *(Orpington)*	543
	Akbar's *(Manchester)*	523
	The Company Shed *(West Mersea)*	523
	Hansa's *(Leeds)*	542
	Shanghai Shanghai *(Nottingham)*	532
£25+	Anstruther Fish Bar *(Anstruther)*	543
	Original Patty Men *(Birmingham)*	533
	Fuji Hiro *(Leeds)*	542
	Cods Scallops *(Wollaton)*	532
	McDermotts Fish & Chips *(Croydon)*	532
£10+	Burger Brothers *(Brighton)*	542
	This & That *(Manchester)*	522

UK DIRECTORY

ABBEY DORE, HEREFORDSHIRE 2–1A

Toi Et Moi £63 444

Holling Grange HR2 0JJ (01981) 240244

"Classic, simple French cooking at its best, combined with genuine caring service" is a winning combination at Cédric Lherbier's modern bistro "on the side of a hill, in the middle of nowhere", and with striking views over Herefordshire's Golden Valley. / **Details:** *www.toietmoi.co.uk; 1.30 pm lunch, 9 pm.*

ABERAERON, CEREDIGION 4–3C

Harbourmaster £45 323

2 Quay Pde SA46 0BT (01545) 570755

For "stonking" seafood "fresh from the sea", it's "really worth a detour" to this harbourside hotel; the "bar food in the bistro is probably better than in the attached, but also very good, restaurant". / **Details:** *www.harbour-master.com; 9 pm; no Amex* / **Accommodation:** *13 rooms, from £110*

ABERDEEN, ABERDEENSHIRE 9–2D

IX, Chester Hotel £75 322

59-63 Queen's Rd AB15 4YP (01224) 327 777

"Clearly aiming for culinary awards", this contemporary two-year-old ("lots of black and chrome") inspires slightly uneven reports, but the products from its Josper grill – you choose the cut from the fresh fish or meat counters – are consistently well rated. / **Details:** *www.chester-hotel.com.*

Silver Darling £64 435

43 Pocra Quay, North Pier AB11 5DQ (01224) 576229

"Fabulous fish dishes" have long been the hallmark of this "very professional and enjoyable" glass-walled fixture, in a former harbour control building; given the location – "as close to the briny as it's possible to be without getting one's feet wet" – it also boasts "great" views. / **Details:** *www.thesilverdarling.co.uk; Mon - Sat 9.30 pm, Sun closed; closed Sat L & Sun; children: 16+ after 8 pm.*

ABERDOUR, FIFE 9–4C

Room With A View £47 445

Hawkcraig Point KY3 0TZ (01383) 860402

"Situated at the water's edge", and offering prime views across the Forth estuary to Edinburgh, this "exceptional restaurant run by a husband-and-wife-team" turns out fish and seafood that's "expertly cooked and served at reasonable prices" too. / **Details:** *www.roomwithaviewrestaurant.co.uk; Mon & Tue closed, Wed - Sat 9 pm, Sun 2 pm; closed Mon, Tue & Sun D.*

ABERGAVENNY, MONMOUTHSHIRE 2–1A

The Angel Hotel £52 323

15 Cross St NP7 5EN (01873) 857121

A gastroboozer and country hotel with an art lined-dining room and (preferred by reporters) a cosy bar/lounge. Top Tips are the "enormous" seafood platters and "superb" scones – "no wonder it regularly wins awards" (mostly from the UK Tea Guild). On the downside, it's "very busy" at lunchtimes. / **Details:** *www.angelhotelabergavenny.com; 10 pm.* / **Accommodation:** *35 rooms, from £101*

The Hardwick £59 333

Old Raglan Rd NP7 9AA (01873) 854220

Stephen Terry's rural gastropub-with-rooms remains one of Wales's best-known destinations. The feedback it inspires remains a tad uneven (one or two report "distinctly underwhelming" meals), but the majority laud "consistently fantastic food from local ingredients", and claim that they "were made to feel special even though the restaurant was busy". / **Details:** *www.thehardwick.co.uk; 10 pm, Sun 9 pm; no Amex.* / **Accommodation:** *8 rooms, from £150*

ABERYSTWYTH, CEREDIGION 4–3C

Pysgoty £48 434

South Marine Ter SY23 1JY (01970) 624611

"By the fish docks and facing out to sea across the prom" – "a fish restaurant with (you guessed it) mega-fresh fish!"; despite its unsavoury past (it's "located in former public toilets!"), this "stylish" place is now a "charming and quirky" destination, with "outstanding sea views", plus "enthusiastic staff". NB "It's tiny so you'll have to book – the only downside!" / **Details:** *www.pysgoty.co.uk.*

Ultracomida £34 443

31 Pier St SY23 2LN (01970) 630686

"Fabulous tapas and wines" await at this "casual" Spanish haunt, where diners "sit on tall stools, or share a large round table" at the rear of the deli; one sceptic of the communal seating confesses that they nonetheless "always go back because of the very high standards...and the great (Iberian) wine list". (Fans can plan a trip to Cardiff too, with the opening of their new Curado Bar in late 2016.) / **Details:** *www.ultracomida.com; 9 pm; Mon-Thu & Sat L only, Fri open L & D, closed Sun.*

ALBOURNE, WEST SUSSEX 3–4B

The Ginger Fox £50 344

Muddleswood Road BN6 9EA (01273) 857 888

Rural outpost of the Brighton-based Gingerman

Group – a "pleasant thatched pub on the edge of the South Downs, with a garden for the summer", which makes "an excellent place, close to the A23" offering "local cooking that's always good". / ***Details:*** *www.thegingerfox.com; Fri & Sat 10 pm, Sun - Mon 9 pm.*

ALDEBURGH, SUFFOLK 3–1D

Aldeburgh Fish And Chips £15 432

226 High St IP15 5DB (01728) 454685

"The reason I go to Aldeburgh – you will not get better fish 'n' chips anywhere" ("the batter is so light" and "the chips are perfection"). Queues are par for the course, but "the people in line smile as they know what a treat they have in store". / ***Details:*** *www.aldeburghfishandchips.co.uk; 8 pm, Fri 9 pm; closed Mon, Tue D, Wed D & Sun D; Cash only.*

The Lighthouse £44 343

77 High Street IP15 5AU (01728) 453377

"The newish owners have kept up the standard and the welcome (no surprise as Sam is still front of house)" at this favourite local destination – the most commented-on place in town, which serves "simple and good-value" (mostly fish-based) cuisine. / ***Details:*** *www.lighthouserestaurant.co.uk; 10 pm.*

Regatta £44 322

171 High Street IP15 5AN (01728) 452011

"A longstanding, friendly, attractive spot" which is "a good place for reasonably priced fish". / ***Details:*** *www.regattaaldeburgh.com; 10 pm.*

ALDERLEY EDGE, CHESHIRE 5–2B

The Alderley, Alderley Edge Hotel £77 444

Macclesfield Rd SK9 7BJ (01625) 583033

Chris Holland's pricey fine dining outpost – a magnet for local footballers and their WAGs – continues to score raves for "superb food and great service in a formal setting". / ***Details:*** *www.alderleyedgehotel.com; 9.45 pm; closed Sun.*

ALDFORD, CHESHIRE 5–3A

The Grosvenor Arms £41 344

Chester Rd CH3 6HJ (01244) 620228

"Although part of a rapidly growing chain" (Brunning & Price), this "friendly" and "old-fashioned" pub, nestled "at the gates of the Duke of Westminster's estate", continues to serve "great food" in "very characterful surroundings"; big garden, too. / ***Details:*** *www.grosvenorarms-aldford.co.uk; 6m S of Chester on B5130; 10 pm, Sun 9 pm.*

ALKHAM, KENT 3–3D

The Marquis £59 433

Alkham Valley Rd CT15 7DF (01304) 873410

"Very handy for the port and Channel Tunnel", a "quaint" pub-with-rooms (or boutique hotel, depending on your terminology) whose dining room provides an "interesting" and "reasonably priced menu". / ***Details:*** *www.themarquisatalkham.co.uk; 9.30 pm, Sun 8.30 pm; children: 8+ at D.* / ***Accommodation:*** *10 rooms, from £95*

ALNWICK, NORTHUMBERLAND 8–1B

Treehouse, Alnwick Castle £45 335

The Alnwick Garden NE66 1YU (01665) 511350

A "stunning, romantic setting up in the trees" lends magic to this quirky treehouse venture, set next to the castle's gardens; the odd sceptic finds the food "disappointing" ("by far the best feature is the tree itself!"), but fans say it's "consistently outstanding". / ***Details:*** *www.alnwickgarden.com; Mon - Wed 3 pm, Thur - Sun 9.15 pm; closed Mon D, Tue D & Wed D.*

ALRESFORD, HAMPSHIRE 2–3D

Caracoli £20 443

15 Broad St SO24 9AR (01962) 738730

The "best coffee anywhere" is one of the draws to this posh and rather "cramped" café-deli tied to a city-centre branch of a local cookware chain – "but if you can get in, everything is top notch" (with the menu ranging from cakes and muffins to savoury bakes). / ***Details:*** *www.caracoli.co.uk; 3 pm; L only; no Amex; No bookings.*

Pulpo Negro £39 443

28 Broad St SO24 9AQ (01962) 732262

The brainchild of Andres & Marie-Lou Alemany, owners of nearby hit the Purefoy Arms, this "pleasant but no-frills" two-year-old continues to win praise for its "excellent and authentic tapas" (and "at reasonable prices" too). / ***Details:*** *www.pulponegro.co.uk; 10.30 pm; closed Mon & Sun.*

ALSTONEFIELD, DERBYSHIRE 5–3C

The George £48 333

DE6 2FX (01335) 310205

In a pretty Peak District setting, a "very friendly and accommodating village pub", where the "food, wine and beer are all to be recommended". / ***Details:*** *www.thegeorgeatalstonefield.com; Mon - Sat 11 pm, Sun 9.30 pm.*

ALTRINCHAM, CHESHIRE 5–2B

Honest Crust [4][3][4]
26 Market St WA14 1SA awaiting tel
"Crowning glory" of the "wonderfully revitalised Alti market hall which has transformed Altrincham" – this "superb" outpost of the acclaimed local wood-fired pizza purveyors serves "brilliant" sourdough pizza ("excellent bases and imaginative toppings") for an "unbeatable price". Stop Press – Manchester's Mackie Mayor market is to receive the same kind of treatment, and Honest Crust will feature there too. / **Details:** *www.honestcrustwoodfiredpizza.com.*

Sugo [5][3][4]
22 Shaw's Rd WA14 1QU (0161) 929 77069
Opened in summer 2015, this "tiny, tiny", "hustling and bustling" Italian, handy for Altrincham Market, is already "rammed, as it should be" given "the best pasta this side of Milan"; a takeaway sandwich shop and deli, Sugo Shop & Panino, launched next door but one in March 2016. / **Details:** *www.sugopastakitchen.co.uk.*

ALVESTON, WARWICKSHIRE 2–1C

Baraset Barn £47 [3][3][3]
Pimlico Lane CV37 7RJ (01789) 295510
Buzzing gastroboozer in an attractively converted barn, most recommended as a lunch spot; its food is "well served, tasty and different". / **Details:** *www.barasetbarn.co.uk; children: Highchair, Portions, .*

AMBERLEY, WEST SUSSEX 3–4A

Amberley Castle £93 [3][3][5]
BN18 9LT (01798) 831992
"Dine in a real castle" – that's the promise at this "historic" venue (complete with peacocks and working portcullis!). Following a change of chef in early 2016, its food ratings slipped this year, but there were no grievous complaints, and most reports remain of somewhere that's "a little pricey, perhaps", but "a magical romantic destination for a special occasion, with excellent food". / **Details:** *www.amberleycastle.co.uk; N of Arundel on B2139; 9 pm; No jeans; Booking max 6 may apply; children: 12+. /* **Accommodation:** *19 rooms, from £265*

AMBLE, NORTHUMBERLAND 8–1B

The Old Boat House £48 [4][4][3]
Leazes Street NE65 0AA (01665) 711 232
"Right on the harbour, with lovely views", this "bustling" operation – manned by "personable and confident" staff – serves an "exceptional choice of fresh fish and seafood". / **Details:** *boathousefoodgroup.co.uk/theoldboathouse-amble.htm; Mon - Thur 9 pm, Fri & Sat 9.30 pm, Sun 9 pm.*

AMBLESIDE, CUMBRIA 7–3D

Drunken Duck £58 [4][4][5]
Barngates LA22 0NG (01539) 436347
"Remote" Lakes pub and microbrewery with a "dark, rustic and romantic interior", and splendid views; its "varied" menu is based on "absolutely top-quality ingredients" – add in fine local ales, and it "never fails to please". / **Details:** *www.drunkenduckinn.co.uk; 3m from Ambleside, towards Hawkshead; 9 pm; no Amex; Booking max 10 may apply. /* **Accommodation:** *17 rooms, from £105*

Fellini's £41 [4][3][3]
Church St LA22 0BT (01539) 432487
"All vegetarian, but you wouldn't really notice", as the "Mediterranean (usually Italian)" food is "always tasty" at this popular operation; "it works well with the adjacent cinema – a delicious meal followed by a film…perfect!" / **Details:** *www.fellinisambleside.com; 10 pm; D only; no Amex.*

Lake Road Kitchen £83 [5][5][3]
Lake Rd LA22 0AD (015394) 22012
"A worth rival to L'Enclume?" – "lots of foraged ingredients, lots of fermented things and pickled stuff, all clearly done with earnest passion" help inspire utter rave reviews for ex-Noma chef James Cross's "strongly Scandi-influenced" two-year-old, in "stripped-back premises, warmly decorated with wood, muted taupes and browns", and with a "semi-open kitchen". That "service feels very natural and unscripted" is a major part of its charm – "the cuisine's amazing, yet the approach is all so casual and friendly", and "without any pretension". "What really underpins the experience, though, is some of the most brightly flavoured, unusual and downright delicious food I've eaten in a long while." / **Details:** *www.lakeroadkitchen.co.uk; Mon & Tues closed, Wed - Sun 9.30 pm; closed Mon & Tue.*

Old Stamp House £57 [5][4][3]
Church St LA22 0BU (015394) 32775
"Hidden away in Ambleside", this pared-down two-year-old basement-venture, run by talented young chef Ryan Blackburn (ex-Martin Wishart), continues to elicit real raves. The food is "truly exceptional", with a choice of two tasting menus and an à la carte option at dinner. / **Details:** *www.oldstamphouse.com; Mon closed, Tue - Sat 9 pm , Sun closed; closed Mon & Sun.*

Zeffirelli's £35 [3][3][4]
Compston Rd LA22 9AD (01539) 433845
Nigh on the "only decent pizza in Cumbria" is just one of the draws to this "fun" combined cinema,

concert hall and veggie outfit (the older, more casual sibling to Fellini's); the "'meal plus film' offers are always superb value too". / **Details:** *www.zeffirellis.com; 10 pm; no Amex.*

AMERSHAM, BUCKINGHAMSHIRE 3–2A

Artichoke £75 554
9 Market Sq HP7 0DF (01494) 726611
"I cannot understand why this simply sublime restaurant has yet to achieve a Michelin star!" – inexplicably, Laurie Gear's "classy" operation in Old Amersham continues to fly under the tyre men's radar. "Chef Laurie always seems to be in the kitchen, and the entire team provide a genuinely warm welcome combined with professional service" in a setting that's "very pretty and cosy". "Fabulous tasting menus deliver so many flavours and textures"... "some dishes are so memorable, and all are delightful", and it's good value too – "at the high end of fine dining and the lower end of the haute-type price bracket!" / **Details:** *www.theartichokerestaurant.co.uk; 9.15 pm, Fri & Sat 9.30 pm; closed Mon & Sun; No shorts.*

Gilbey's £51 344
1 Market Sq HP7 0DF (01494) 727242
This stalwart wine bar run by the eponymous gin empire is a "good all-rounder that never disappoints" – even if, paradoxically, the food is "not totally consistent"; "great wine list" from the owners' vineyards. / **Details:** *www.gilbeygroup.com/restaurants/gilbeys-old; 9.30 pm, Sat 9.45 pm, Sun 8.45 pm.*

The Grocer At 15 344
15 The Broadway HP7 0HL (01494) 72458
One of two branches of this appealing independent coffee shop, set "within half a mile of one another in the old town", and offering a range of "great cakes", salads, open sandwiches and freshly squeezed juices; "the fact that they are both always packed tells its own story". / **Details:** *www.thegrocerat91.co.uk.*

ANSTRUTHER, FIFE 9–4D

Anstruther Fish Bar £26 543
42-44 Shore St KY10 3AQ (01333) 310518
"A great establishment" combining the "freshest fish possible" with "perfect chips" and "amazing (non-greasy) batter". You can eat in the 1950s-style dining room, but the spoils are arguably "best taken away and enjoyed by the harbour across the road". / **Details:** *www.anstrutherfishbar.co.uk; 9.30 pm; no Amex; No bookings.*

The Cellar £70 444
24 East Green KY10 3AA (01333) 310378
This well-known culinary address has been in the hands of Billy Boyter since April 2014, and aims to put a cutting-edge spin on quality Scottish ingredients. Notwithstanding an August 2016 pasting for over-complexity from ace press critic Joanna Blythman, our reporters award very high praise, particularly for its "beautiful" preparation of fish. / **Details:** *www.thecellaranstruther.co.uk; in the harbour area; Wed - Sun 9.00 pm; closed Mon, Tue & Wed L; no Amex.*

APPLECROSS, HIGHLAND 9–2B

Applecross Inn £41 444
Shore St IV54 8LR (01520) 744262
"The restaurant (with rooms) at the end of the universe" – or at least a remote Highlands peninsula; notwithstanding this, it's "always worth the intergalactic journey" ("along alpine roads") to get there, due to its "wonderful fresh fish" and "amazing views". / **Details:** *www.applecross.uk.com/inn; off A896, S of Shieldaig; 9 pm; no Amex; May need 6+ to book. /* **Accommodation:** *7 rooms, from £90*

APPLEDORE, DEVON 1–2C

The Coffee Cabin £15 444
22 The Quay EX39 1QS (01237) 475843
"Ambience by the bucketload" is to be found at this "little treasure" – a two-year-old café with uplifting estuary views, and "probably the world's best crab sandwich!". It makes "a great place to watch the world go by". / **Details:** *5 pm; L only.*

ARGYLL, ARGYLL AND BUTE 9–3B

Kilberry Inn £55 544
Kilberry PA29 6YD (01880) 770223
"If only all little restaurants-with-rooms could meet the standards set at Kilberry" – a "small but beautiful" family-run venture, complete with "large open fires", and "set down a single-track road amidst stunning scenery". It offers "some of the best simple, local food in Scotland" – and "just to see the islands of Gigha, Jura and Islay set in a blue sea was a joy". / **Details:** *www.kilberryinn.com; Mon closed, Tue - Sun 9 pm; closed Mon, Tue L & Wed L; no Amex. /* **Accommodation:** *5 rooms, from £210*

ARLINGHAM, GLOUCESTERSHIRE 2–2B

The Old Passage Inn £67 543
Passage Road GL2 7JR (01452) 740547
Overlooking the River Severn, this "attractive" restaurant-with-rooms "takes some beating" owing to its "delightful staff", and food with a real "density of flavour" (including fish and shellfish

*which are "top class"); according to one of its fans, it's "always excellent", but "particularly so" of late. / **Details:** www.theoldpassage.com; Mon closed, Tue - Sat 9 pm, Sun 2.30 pm; closed Mon & Sun D. /* **Accommodation:** *2 rooms, from £80*

ARUNDEL, WEST SUSSEX 3–4A

The Town House £48 444
65 High Street BN18 9AJ (01903) 883 847
*A "quite small but beautifully decorated restaurant-with-rooms, with a spectacularly ornate ceiling"; it's lauded for its "unstuffy service" and "fabulous food". / **Details:** www.thetownhouse.co.uk; Mon closed, Tue - Sat 9.30 pm, Sun closed; closed Mon & Sun. /* **Accommodation:** *4 rooms, from £95*

ASCOT, BERKSHIRE 3–3A

Restaurant Coworth Park £100 445
Coworth Park SL5 7SE (01344) 876 600
*Another year, another chef – the merry-go-round shows no sign of slowing down at the Dorchester Collection's "breathtaking" country house hotel, where former Roux Scholar Adam Smith was set to replace Simon Whiteley in summer 2016; ratings shown assume a continuation in standards. / **Details:** www.coworthpark.com; Mon & Tue closed, Wed - Fri 9.30 pm, Sat 10 pm, Su; closed Mon & Sun D.*

ASENBY, NORTH YORKSHIRE 8–4C

Crab & Lobster £66 445
Dishforth Rd YO7 3QL (01845) 577286
*"An eccentric place serving wonderful food" – off the A1, a "quirky" thatched inn whose interior is packed with bric-à-brac, and which is one of the best-known pubs in the country, never mind the county. Foodwise, the speciality is fish: "exceptionally fresh fare, delivered with genuinely warm hospitality and professional service". / **Details:** www.crabandlobster.co.uk; at junction of Asenby Rd & Topcliffe Rd; 9 pm, Sat 9.30 pm. /* **Accommodation:** *17 rooms, from £160*

ASKHAM, CUMBRIA 7–3D

Askham Hall £67 544
CA10 2PF (01931) 712350
*"A new star in Cumbria of outstanding quality". This three-year-old hotel, occupying a handsome old manor in a very pretty village, wins all-round praise as a "wonderful country house restaurant"; chef Richard Swale follows a foraging/local sourcing ethos to excellent effect. / **Details:** www.askhamhall.co.uk; Yes; children: 10.*

AUCHTERARDER, PERTH AND KINROSS 9–3C

Andrew Fairlie, Gleneagles Hotel £133 544
PH3 1NF (01764) 694267
*Andrew Fairlie's "romantic" dining room in this famous Scottish bastion won particularly strong ratings this year, with top billing going to his "pretty much perfect" cuisine. "Sumptuous dishes" feature on a "perfectly balanced tasting menu which flows splendidly, and lets the amazing ingredients sing", and come with "an accompanying wine flight that's impeccably matched and presented with great aplomb by the sommelier". It's a windowless space, but fans "like that it's closed off" – it's "like stepping through a door into another world…." / **Details:** www.andrewfairlie.co.uk; 10 pm; L only, closed Sun; children: 12+.*

Strathearn Restaurant, Gleneagles Hotel £88 343
PH3 1NF (0800) 731 9219
*An "absolutely wonderful Art Deco-style dining room" offering "lovely views over Glen Devon"; it's particularly of note for its "massive buffet", but the "exceptional" breakfast and "daily specials from the trolley" can also forge a "lifetime memory" – just "never mind the price!" / **Details:** www.gleneagles.com; 10 pm; D only, ex Sun open L & D.*

AUGHTON, LANCASHIRE 5–1A

Moor Hall
Prescot Rd L39 6RT awaiting tel
*Simon Rogan's one-time righthand man Mark Birchall (former exec chef at L'Enclume) sets out to open his own restaurant-with-rooms at this Grade II-listed Lancastrian gentry house. An opening date of 1 February, 2017 has been set for his 50-seater, glass-walled dining room (with adjacent cheese and wine rooms) and a more informal eatery in a nearby barn is pencilled in for later in the year. / **Details:** www.moor-hall.co.uk.*

AXMINSTER, DEVON 2–4A

River Cottage Canteen £49 333
Trinity Sq EX13 5AN (01297) 630 300
*HFW's "busy" communal canteen – an airy, attractively converted space – avoided the critiques of last year, with praise for its "timely" service and healthy, "very tasty" dishes. / **Details:** www.rivercottage.net; 8.30 pm; closed Mon D & Sun D.*

AYLESBURY, BUCKINGHAMSHIRE 3–2A

Hartwell House, Dining Room £71 344

Oxford Rd HP17 8NR (01296) 747444

*"For a hotel dining room the food is consistently good" at this "imposing and superior" Relais & Châteaux establishment – and it certainly "has the wow factor!"; it's especially commended as an "amazing venue for a special tea" – best taken in the main building's "historic lounges" (once host to Louis XVIII). / **Details:** www.hartwell-house.com/wine-and-dine; 2m W of Aylesbury on A418; 9.45 pm; No jeans; children: 4+. / **Accommodation:** 50 rooms, from £290*

BAGSHOT, SURREY 3–3A

The Latymer, Pennyhill Park Hotel £135 333

London Road GU19 5EU (01276) 486150

*Under ex-chef Michael Wignall (now of Gidleigh Park), this celebrated country house hotel dining room "was ascending the culinary league", but feedback and ratings have become unsettled since his departure, with its harsher critics bemoaning a "dull, corporate money-laundering experience from a former favourite". Fans of the panelled, olde-worlde dining room are still in the majority, though, and insist it's "amazing what (new replacement) Matt Worswick has accomplished" with his "sensational" cuisine. / **Details:** www.exclusive.co.uk; Mon & Tue closed, Wed - Sat 9 pm, Sun closed; closed Mon, Tue L, Sat L & Sun; Booking max 8 may apply; children: 12+. / **Accommodation:** 123 rooms, from £315*

BAKEWELL, DERBYSHIRE 5–2C

Piedaniels £50 343

Bath St DE45 1BX (01629) 812687

*"What a brilliant find!"; while "some might feel the white leather sofas by the entrance are a little overpowering, stick with it – this is a serious husband-and-wife operation cooking good French food at outstanding prices" ("particularly midweek and lunch"). / **Details:** www.piedaniels-restaurant.com; 10.30 pm, open on Sun only 2 weekends per month; closed Mon & Sun D.*

BALQUHIDDER, PERTH AND KINROSS 9–3C

Monachyle Mhor £79 534

FK19 8PQ (01877) 384622

*A "romantic getaway six miles up a single-track road to nowhere", in the Trossachs National Park; with its "brilliant" locally sourced cuisine and "charming service", it's "definitely worth a detour". / **Details:** www.mhor.net; take the Kings House turning off the A84; 9 pm. / **Accommodation:** 14 rooms, from £195*

BAMPTON, DEVON 1–2D

The Swan £42 333

Station Rd EX16 9NG (01398) 332 248

*"A fantastic pub to stumble across on a wet day"; "brilliant value for money, and quality food in a great atmosphere" are to be found at this recently renovated hostelry (with features like the fireplace dating back to 1450). / **Details:** www.theswan.co; 9.30pm, Sun 8.45pm.*

BANGOR, COUNTY DOWN 10–1D

The Boat House £51 543

1a, Seacliff Rd BT20 5HA (028) 9146 9253

*On the marina, this sleekly converted former harbourmaster's building now offers an "unforgettable experience" for diners, taking in "exquisite wine pairings" and a "relaxed" fine dining ambience; staff are "fantastically cool" and "the chef/owner even delivers and explains some of his dishes to the table!" / **Details:** www.theboathouseni.co.uk; 10 pm; closed Mon & Tue.*

BARNET, HERTFORDSHIRE 3–2B

Savoro £46 332

206 High St EN5 5SZ (020) 8449 9888

*With its "brilliant" desserts and decent mains (especially meat), this pared-back hotel dining room "improves the high street"; even those who feel it's "solid" but "not inspirational" admit that it's "the best local restaurant" nonetheless. / **Details:** www.savoro.co.uk; 10 pm, Sun 9 pm; closed Sun D. / **Accommodation:** 9 rooms, from £75*

BARNSLEY, GLOUCESTERSHIRE 2–2C

The Village Pub £48 323

GL7 5EF (01285) 740 421

*A "charming" gastroboozer with "real log fires", "great beers" and a "well thought-out and varied menu"; "quirky rooms" ("get the four-poster bed!") mean that it's "perfect for a short break" too. / **Details:** www.thevillagepub.co.uk; 9.30 pm, Sun 9 pm. / **Accommodation:** 6 rooms, from £130*

BARNSTAPLE, DEVON 1–2C

Montys Caribbean Kitchen £29 443

19 Tuly Street EX31 1DH (01271) 372985

"Blooming delicious, fast Jamaican street food is served next to a car park" at this newcomer with "a pleasing, simple Caribbean interior, along with lilting reggae music". "Cocktails are top notch", and the "staggeringly good value" scoff is "cheap, yummy, pungent and worth the drive" – no wonder it's "always packed". "Generally no-one objects to sharing their table!" / **Details:** *www.montyscaribbeankitchen.co.uk; 3pm, Fri-Sat 11pm; No bookings.*

BARRASFORD, NORTHUMBERLAND 8–2A

Barrasford Arms £43 3 3 3

NE48 4AA (01434) 681237

Overlooking Northumberland National Park, Tony Binks's "always consistent" pub-with-rooms offers "warm service", and "straightforward cooking" that's "well above average" (and "takes pride in their homegrown ingredients from the garden"). / **Details:** *www.barrasfordarms.co.uk; 9 pm; closed Mon & Sun D; no Amex; children: 18+ in bar after 9.30 pm.* / **Accommodation:** *7 rooms, from £85*

BARTON-ON-SEA, HAMPSHIRE 2–4C

Pebble Beach £56 4 3 4

Marine Drive BH25 7DZ (01425) 627777

"Seafood, soufflées par excellence, and sea views" are all attractions at Pierre Chevillard's "tried and trusted" clifftop fish restaurant, offering a "wonderful view of the Isle of Wight from the windows overlooking the water" (as well as from the outside patio). / **Details:** *www.pebblebeach-uk.com; Mon - Fri 9.30 pm, Sat & Sun 10 pm.* / **Accommodation:** *4 rooms, from £100*

BARWICK, SOMERSET 2–3B

Little Barwick House £71 5 5 4

BA22 9TD (01935) 423902

Emma and Tim Ford's restaurant-with-rooms is a "very relaxing" spot, and "the location is lovely (next to Barwick House, with its park and follies)". While Tim's "good, classic British food" is "always on top form", "Emma really knows her wine": the "extraordinary" wine list is "full of good choices at reasonable prices" – and, "as well as numerous wines by the glass (thanks to their Verre de Vin apparatus), there are an unusual number of half-bottles, including some from the New World". / **Details:** *www.littlebarwickhouse.co.uk; take the A37 Yeovil to Dorchester road, turn left at the brown sign for Little Barwick House; 9 pm; closed Mon, Tue L & Sun; children: 5+.* / **Accommodation:** *6 rooms, from £69*

BASLOW, DERBYSHIRE 5–2C

Fischers at Baslow Hall £98 4 4 4

Calver Rd DE45 1RR (01246) 583259

Susan & Max Fischer's longstanding temple of gastronomy (est. 1989) occupies an Edwardian house built in the style of a 17th-century manor. Quibbles are raised by a few reporters – its elegance can at times seem "faded", and "both food and service show the occasional blip"; for the most part, however, reports are of the "top-quality, well-balanced cuisine and first-class service one might expect from a long-serving Michelin-starred establishment" (the tyre men's only award in the country), and fans say "it's less overbearing than some rivals, with an unhurried style and lovely gardens for a post-lunch stroll". / **Details:** *www.fischers-baslowhall.co.uk; on the A623; 8.30 pm, No trainers.* / **Accommodation:** *11 rooms, from £180*

Rowley's £54 3 4 2

Church Lane DE45 1RY (01246) 583880

A "pleasant brasserie", off the Chatsworth Estate, from the people behind Fischers of Baslow Hall; the "new menu provides a range from sandwiches to 3-course meals – all with an extra little touch", so you can "spend as little or as much as you like and still have excellent quality". / **Details:** *www.rowleysrestaurant.co.uk; Mon closed, Tue - Fri 9 pm, Sat 9.30 pm, Sun 3 pm; closed Mon & Sun D; no Amex.*

BASSENTHWAITE, CUMBRIA 7–3C

Bistro At The Distillery £49 3 2 3

Setmurthy CA13 9SJ (01768) 788850

"On the face of it, just an eatery at a tourist attraction" (a whisky distillery set in a former Victorian cattle parlour), Terry Laybourne's year-old venture is "in fact an excellent restaurant" – "much effort has been put into it and it's all top quality". / **Details:** *www.bistroatthedistillery.com; 9 pm.*

BATH, SOMERSET 2–2B

Acorn Vegetarian Kitchen £47 5 4 2

2 North Parade Passage BA1 1NX
(01225) 446059

"I've been vegetarian for over 20 years, and this is the best veggie I've ever eaten at!" – a cramped spot, in a cute city-centre alley, which is still remembered by some as Demuth's (long RIP). Foodwise "the quality just gets better and better" – "imaginative, seasonal menus" to suit carnivores and vegans alike. / **Details:** *www.acornvegetariankitchen.co.uk; 9.30 pm, Sat 10 pm.*

Allium Brasserie, Abbey Hotel £53 233

1 North Pde BA1 1LF (01225) 809380

Limited and polarised feedback on this four-year-old dining room, in a former Best Western Hotel, with Chris Staines (ex-of the Mandarin Oriental, Knightsbridge) at the stoves. Fans say that it's "a real pleasure dining here" (it was the winner of 'Top Restaurant' at the Bath Good Food Awards 2016) but sceptics would be "very loathe to go again". / **Details:** *abbeyhotelbath.co.uk/allium; 9 pm, Fri & Sat 10 pm.*

Bath Priory Hotel £111 333

Weston Rd BA1 2XT (01225) 331922

There's still the odd sceptic, for whom this plush but slightly "stuffy" Brownsword hotel dining room represents "very poor value for money", but the majority of reporters this year raved about its "extremely luscious food", "fabulous" wines and "lovely" (leafy) surroundings. / **Details:** *www.thebathpriory.co.uk; 9.30 pm; No jeans; children: 5+ L, 12+ D.* / **Accommodation:** *33 rooms, from £205*

Casanis £52 444

4 Saville Row BA1 2QP (01225) 780055

"A small bistro tucked away up a Bath side street, but worth the trudge for the very good French cuisine". Even a reporter who found the service "forbidding initially", said it "thawed as the night went on", ensuring a "very pleasant experience" overall. / **Details:** *www.casanis.co.uk; 9-9.30pm; closed Mon & Sun; no Amex.*

The Circus £49 343

34 Brock St BA1 2LN (01225) 466020

A "favourite", family-run (and "slightly cramped") bistro, near the Royal Crescent, that's the most commented-on destination in the city this year, on account of its "attentive" staff and "easy, café-style atmosphere", as well as its "excellent, well-presented modern European cooking". Top Tip – "try to book for upstairs". / **Details:** *www.thecircuscafeandrestaurant.co.uk; 10.30 pm; closed Sun; no Amex; children: 7+ at D.*

Clayton's Kitchen £56 442

15A, George St BA1 2EN (01225) 585 100

Rob Clayton's "small but buzzy eatery in the middle of town" is a "great deal", especially at lunchtime, and "fresh ingredients lend seasonal variety to the cooking"; nice bar upstairs too. / **Details:** *www.theporter.co.uk/claytons-kitchen; 10 pm, Fri & Sat 10.30 pm, Sun 9 pm.*

Colonna & Smalls £11 443

6 Chapel Row BA1 1HN (07766) 808067

An "amazing" minimal-chic café, by Queen Square, which "makes you realise how good coffee can taste"; forget soya lattes and frappucinos…it's a black filter coffee or espresso sort of place, where even an americano comes with "no sugar, milk or (more mysteriously) water allowed!" / **Details:** *www.colonnaandsmalls.co.uk; 5.30 pm, Sun 4 pm; no Amex; Booking max 6 may apply.*

Gascoyne Place £47 222

1 Sawclose BA1 1EY (01225) 445854

Mixed feedback this year on this relaxed Georgian dining room and Victorian pub; fans say that it's "still a decent choice", with some "scrumptious" dishes, but critics feel that the quality – both of food and service – has been rather "more variable of late". / **Details:** *www.gascoyneplace.co.uk; 10 pm; no Amex.*

Hare & Hounds £47 333

Lansdown Rd BA1 5TJ (01225) 482682

"A wonderful setting, just outside Bath" sets the scene at this "attractive" gastroboozer, consistently praised for its "great pub food and friendly staff"; it's "popular, so booking is a good idea, especially if you want a table with a view". / **Details:** *www.hareandhoundsbath.com; 9 pm, Sun 8 pm; no Amex.*

Indian Temptation £30 433

9-10 High Street (Cheap Street) BA1 5AQ (01225) 464631

"Fabulous authentic South Indian vegetarian food in a glorious 18th-century room with views of Bath Abbey" – one fan says it all about this first-floor subcontinental. / **Details:** *www.indiantemptation.com; 10.30pm.*

Menu Gordon Jones £74 542

2 Wellsway BA2 3AQ (01225) 480871

An "unmissable treat" on the outskirts of town (south of the city-centre) – this "highly innovative" venture delivers a "one-menu surprise for the whole room". Some feel that "the decor is a bit strange" ("basic and small"), but "you go for the fantastic creations of the clever Gordon Jones, who's always there, beavering away in the open kitchen". / **Details:** *www.menugordonjones.co.uk; 9 pm; closed Mon & Sun; no Amex.*

The Mint Room £38 433

Longmead Gospel Hall, Lower Bristol Rd BA2 3EB (01225) 446656

"Setting the standard" for a curry in Bath – a "contemporary Indian", on a busy road out of the city, praised for its "comfortable" interior and cooking with a "great balance of flavours". / **Details:** *www.themintroom.co.uk; 11 pm, Fri & Sat 11.30 pm; No shorts.*

The Olive Tree, Queensberry Hotel £65 533

Russell St BA1 2QF (01225) 447928

Chris Cleghorn's deft, classically inspired cuisine at this well-established basement hotel dining room put in a formidable showing in this year's survey; "excellent wines" too ("but then again we've come to expect that…"). / **Details:** *www.thequeensberry.co.uk; 22.00; Mon-Thu D only, Fri-Sun open L & D; no Amex, No shorts /* **Accommodation:** *29 rooms, from £125*

The Pump Room £49 2 2 5

Stall St BA1 1LZ (01225) 444477

"A real treat for foreign guests" – this 200-year-old Georgian landmark is a "wonderfully atmospheric" place ("especially with the string quartet" in full swing); perhaps unsurprisingly, food typically plays second fiddle – best to stick to breakfast or afternoon tea. / **Details:** *www.searcys.co.uk; 5.00pm; L only; Booking weekdays only.*

Scallop Shell £33 4 3 3

22 Monmouth Place BA1 2AY (01225) 420928

"Classy fish and chips (really good light, crispy butter), and many other tempting delights from the sea" win high approval ratings for this "fun and buzzy", no-bookings yearling, "well decked out with seaside-themed decor". / **Details:** *www.thescallopshell.co.uk; 9.30 pm; closed Sun; No bookings.*

Sotto Sotto £46 4 4 5

10 North Pde BA2 4AL (01225) 330236

A "charming restaurant set in brick-lined vaults", on North Parade, where the "superb atmosphere" is matched by "delightful" Italian food and "attentive, friendly service". "Children are made very welcome" too. / **Details:** *www.sottosotto.co.uk; 10 pm; Booking max 8 may apply.*

Yammo £38 3 4 2

66 Walcot St BA1 5BD (01225) 938328

"A little bit of Napoli in Bath", near the city-centre; while it's a "very small" spot with "basic tables and decor", the "great pizzas, tiramisu, espresso and lovely staff" make a visit to this well-situated Italian joint "really enjoyable!" / **Details:** *www.yammo.co.uk; 10.30 pm, Fri & Sat 11.30 pm, Sun 9 pm.*

BAUGHURST, HAMPSHIRE 2–3D

The Wellington Arms £60 4 4 4

Baughurst Rd RG26 5LP (0118) 982 0110

"It's a rare treat to find such a delightful pub/restaurant, set in beautiful countryside, and where everything makes for a wonderful eating experience"; Jason King and Simon Page are "enthusiastic owners", and "a lot of the food is sourced in the restaurant's own environs". "Be warned, it's very tiny; great for intimacy, but a little squashed (keeping out of serving staff's way can be an issue!), but it's worth it for some really memorable dishes." / **Details:** *www.thewellingtonarms.com; 9.30 pm; closed Sun D; no Amex. /* **Accommodation:** *4 rooms, from £130*

BEACONSFIELD, BUCKINGHAMSHIRE 3–3A

The Cape Grand Cafe & Restaurant £50 3 3 4

6a, Station Rd HP9 1NN (01494) 681137

"In a town where the chain gang rule, it's really nice to have somewhere that offers something a bit different" – namely South African food and wines, served in a "lovely", striking dining room. The best time to visit is brunch. / **Details:** *www.thecapeonline.com; 9.30 pm; closed Mon D, Tue D, Wed D, Thu D & Sun D; no Amex.*

Crazy Bear £65 2 2 4

75 Wycombe End HP9 1LX (01494) 673086

Glimmering with "gilt-laden and ostentatious interior" (the private dining rooms are "from another world"), this hybrid Anglo/Thai is certainly "a unique venue". It's a pricey one too, and results can still be "hit 'n' miss", but there were more fans this year who said that "once you get over the garish decor the food's pretty good". / **Details:** *www.crazybeargroup.co.uk/beaconsfield; 10 pm; closed Mon & Sun L; children: bar, not after 6pm. /* **Accommodation:** *19 rooms, from £220*

The Royal Standard of England £44 3 3 5

Forty Green HP9 1XT (01494) 673 382

"The oldest free pub in England" is a decidedly "lovely" spot, in a "wonderful setting" down a wooded country lane; "however busy, the staff are unruffled", and provide "top-quality dishes and cask ales". / **Details:** *www.rsoe.co.uk; Mon - Sat 10 pm, Sun 9 pm; no Amex.*

BEAMINSTER, DORSET 2–4B

Brassica £43 4 3 3

4 The Square DT8 3AS (01308) 538 100

Cass (ex-Canteen) and Louise Titcombe's "relaxed" yearling is a "real gem", combining "very interesting" food from "first-rate ingredients", with "a friendly welcome"; such are its strengths that it "would put many London restaurants to shame on price and quality". / **Details:** *www.brassicarestaurant.co.uk; Mon & Tue closed, Wed - Sat 9.30 pm, Sun 2.30 pm; closed Sun D.*

BEARSTED, KENT 3–3C

Fish On The Green £58 4 3 2

Church Ln ME14 4EJ (01622) 738 300

It's "a real delight to find a good restaurant in the Maidstone area" – this one specialising in "delicious", "very good value fish". Okay, the "shed-like" premises are "cramped", and it's a "shame about the acoustics", but "the food makes the visit very worthwhile". / **Details:** *www.fishonthegreen.com; 9.30 pm, Fri & Sat 10 pm; closed Mon & Sun D; no Amex.*

BEAULIEU, HAMPSHIRE 2–4D

The Terrace, Montagu Arms Hotel £104 343

SO42 7ZL (01590) 612324

"Time after time after time, they deliver great food with exceptional service" at this high-end New Forest inn, which also boasts "delightful" garden views; "yes, you pay for it, but it's still value for the (lots of!) money" by all accounts. / **Details:** *www.montaguarmshotel.co.uk; 9.30 pm; closed Mon & Tue L; No jeans; children: 11+ D. /* **Accommodation:** *22 rooms, from £143*

BEAUMARIS, ISLE OF ANGLESEY 4–1C

Ye Olde Bull's Head £43 334

Castle Street LL58 8AP (01248) 810329

A "light, airy and modern annexe behind the ye-olde-decor of the front of the pub, in the main street of pretty Beaumaris"; the food – polished classics in the downstairs brasserie, and "fine dining at its best" in the elegant upstairs dining room (the more expensive The Loft) – makes it "well worth the diversion on the way to Holyhead". / **Details:** *www.bullsheadinn.co.uk; on the High Street; Mon & Tue closed, Wed - Sat 9.30 pm, Sun closed; D only, closed Mon & Sun; No jeans; children: 7+ at D. /* **Accommodation:** *26 rooms, from £105*

BEELEY, DERBYSHIRE 5–2C

Devonshire Arms at Beeley £48 213

Devonshire Square DE4 2NR (01629) 733259

Very up-and-down reviews on this upscale pub-with-rooms, part of the Chatsworth Estate; fans praise its "consistently high standard", but cynics cite "disappointing" food and "offhand" service as proof of "a clear case of living off the memory of better times". / **Details:** *www.devonshirebeeley.co.uk; 9.30 pm; bookings for breakfast. /* **Accommodation:** *14 rooms, from £125*

BELFAST, COUNTY ANTRIM 10–1D

Deanes At Queens £49 344

1 College Gdns BT9 6BQ (028) 9038 2111

"A relaxed dining experience that always provides a tempting menu and an excellent wine list"; Michael Deane's large, popular bar/brasserie (with outside terrace), in the University Quarter, won consistently high ratings across the board this year, especially for business entertaining. / **Details:** *www.michaeldeane.co.uk; 10 pm, Mon & Tue 9 pm; closed Sun D.*

Hadskis £45 343

Commercial Ct BT1 2NB (02890) 325 444

This year-old eatery, in the Cathedral Quarter, has pedigree – being owned by Niall McKenna of James Street South fame; it's already winning attention for its contemporary European dishes, including "good lunchtime specials". / **Details:** *www.hadskis.co.uk; 9.30 pm, Thu-Sat 10 pm.*

James Street South £57 444

21 James Street South BT2 7GA
(028) 9043 4310

Niall McKenna's "excellent restaurant" remains at the forefront of the local dining scene, and was the site for many reporters' best meal of the year; "fantastic local produce is inventively served with great skill at affordable prices". / **Details:** *www.jamesstreetsouth.co.uk; 10.45 pm; closed Sun.*

Mourne Seafood Bar £43 534

34 - 36 Bank Street BT1 1HL (028) 9024 8544

"In what's becoming a very foodie city", this charming stalwart (with a fishmonger up front) "just goes on and on keeping up standards"; it's the "best place for fresh, well-cooked fish". / **Details:** *www.mourneseafood.com; 9.30 pm, Fri & Sat 10.30 pm, Sun 9 pm; No bookings at lunch.*

Ox £41 544

1 Oxford St BT1 3LA (028) 9031 4121

Launched by two chefs who met in some of Paris's finest kitchens, Stephen Toman and Alain Kerloc'h's acclaimed riverside three-year old wins raves for its "fantastic" food and "great eclectic wine list" (courtesy of their next-door wine bar the Ox Cave); "opt for a tasting menu with matching wines, or just sit in the Cave and nibble on amazing cheese and charcuterie". / **Details:** *www.oxbelfast.com; 8.30 pm.*

Tedfords Restaurant £54 443

5 Donegall Quay BT1 3EA (028) 90434000

"Surprisingly interesting and different dishes" (with a bias for seafood) justify a trip to this Victorian riverside building near Waterfront Hall. / **Details:** *www.tedfordsrestaurant.com; 9.30 pm; closed Mon, Tue L, Sat L & Sun.*

Zen £39 444

55-59 Adelaide St BT2 8FE (028) 9023 2244

This spacious, trendy Japanese has been satisfying the crowds for over a decade, and continues to elicit glowing (if limited) feedback. / **Details:** *www.zenbelfast.co.uk; 10.30pm; closed Sat L.*

BEMBRIDGE, ISLE OF WIGHT 2–4D

Best Dressed Crab 434
Fisherman's Wharf, Embankment Road, PO35 5NS (01983) 874 758
"Caught at 4am, cooked and served fresh for lunch" – the "seafood platter is outstanding" at this two-decades-old waterfront operation – "a floating café, with crab and lobster served fresh from the attached fishing boat". "Sit out on deck with the sea lapping against the side, or inside with the log burner to keep you warm." / ***Details:*** *www.thebestdressedcrabintown.co.uk; 8pm.*

The Crab And Lobster Inn £45 333
32 Forelands Field Rd PO35 5TR
(01983) 872244
"A lovely little inn ("if not cheap") by the sea, tucked into a small village near Chichester"; while the offerings can be "variable", and it strikes some as a "tourist trap", the majority insist it's "well worth a visit"... "stay the night if you can!" / ***Details:*** *www.crabandlobsterinn.co.uk; 9 pm, Fri & Sat 9.30 pm; no Amex. /* ***Accommodation:*** *5 rooms, from £80*

Fox's Restaurant £42 333
11 High St PO35 5SD (01983) 872626
"A real find in an area overrun with tourist traps" – an "unpretentious" and "exceptionally nice, simple village restaurant" serving "invariably excellently presented and tasty, fresh, 'real' food prepared by the chef-owner".

BENDERLOCH, ARGYLL AND BUTE 9–3B

Eriska Hotel £68 434
Isle of Eriska PA37 1SD (01631) 720371
This remote Relais & Chateaux property on a private island between lochs Linnhe and Creran lives up to the "cocooning" experience you might expect. The surroundings are "fabulous" and "superb Scottish produce" is "thoughtfully presented with interesting textures and flavours". / ***Details:*** *www.eriska-hotel.co.uk; 9 pm; D only; No shorts; children: 10. /* ***Accommodation:*** *25 rooms, from £340*

BERKHAMSTED, HERTFORDSHIRE 3–2A

The Gatsby £56 333
97 High St HP4 2DG (01442) 870403
"My favourite local" – an old picture-house foyer where service can be "a little variable", but where the "food's always good", and "the ambience of the '30s cinema decoration is always lovely"; "pre-cinema deals afternoon and evening also make it easily affordable". / ***Details:*** *www.thegatsby.net; 10.30 pm, Sun 9.30 pm; no Amex; Booking max 10 may apply.*

Porters Restaurant £44 333
Unit 3, 300 High Street HP4 1ZZ
(01442) 876666
Richard Bradford's airy modern brasserie bears little semblance to its origins (for many decades, he ran a venture of the same name in Covent Garden serving traditional British pies). With its large outside dining space (featuring summer BBQs), it offers a very flexible range of eating options, and is family-friendly too. / ***Details:*** *www.porters.uk.com; 10 pm.*

BEVERLEY, EAST YORKSHIRE 6–2A

Ogino £46 453
1st floor Beaver House, Butcher Row HU17 0AA (01482) 679500
"One of the most original food concepts in the area" – Julian & Rieko Ogino-Stamford's accomplished Japanese provides "excellent cuisine" and "exceptional service". "Two of our party of four thought that they didn't much like Japanese food until we went. The only complaint was that we had to ask for cutlery beyond chopsticks!" / ***Details:*** *ogino.co.uk.*

The Pipe & Glass Inn £58 444
West End HU17 7PN (01430) 810246
A "well-established East Yorkshire venue" located in "stunning countryside"; "James Mackenzie has really found his own style now, and his (and wife Kate's) pub stands as one of the best in the country" ("an absolute job, worthy of its Michelin star"). "Mouthwatering menus appeal to all the senses and feature the most delicious dishes using the very best fresh, seasonal, locally sourced ingredients, while the front-of-house team are professional and friendly; terrific accommodation too – just heavenly!" / ***Details:*** *www.pipeandglass.co.uk; Mon closed Tue - Sat 9.30 pm, Sun 4 pm; closed Mon & Sun D.*

The Westwood Restaurant £58 453
New Walk HU17 7AE (01482) 881999
Approaching its decennial next year, twins Matt and Michele Barker's modern brasserie in an old Georgian courthouse continues to win all-round praise: "we were special guests from the moment we walked through the door", and the "consistently good cooking is food you really want to eat". / ***Details:*** *www.thewestwood.co.uk; 9.30 pm; closed Mon & Sun D; no Amex.*

Whites £71 543
12-12a North Bar Without HU17 7AB
(01482) 866121
Chef John Robinson "doesn't get the respect he deserves" according to fans of this simply decorated restaurant-with-rooms – "a small and slightly sparse space, where any lack in atmosphere is made up for by the very attentive and welcoming service".

"Many unusual ingredients are superbly combined and accompanied to produce exquisite dishes." / **Details:** www.whitesrestaurant.co.uk; 9 pm; closed Mon & Sun D; no Amex. / **Accommodation:** 4 rooms, from £85

BIDBOROUGH, KENT 3–3B

Kentish Hare £52 433
95 Bidbourough Ridge TN3 0XB
(01892) 525709
While "not as old as many of the pubs nearby", this recently refurbed gastroboozer, in a rural setting with a pretty garden, is still a worthy destination thanks to its "relaxed" vibe and its "amazingly consistent" grub. / **Details:** *Mon closed, Tue - Sat 9.30 pm, Sun 5 pm; closed Mon.*

BIDDENDEN, KENT 3–4C

The West House £65 543
28 High St TN27 8AH (01580) 291341
"Graham Garrett and his family are champions!", say fans of this "quaint" little village restaurant, offering "top-drawer cooking and interesting wines". Having "built this up from nothing over the last 12 years", Garrett "deserves all the accolades" (including one from the tyre men). / **Details:** *www.thewesthouserestaurant.co.uk; Tue-Fri 9 pm, Sat 10 pm; closed Mon, Sat L & Sun D; no Amex.*

BIGBURY-ON-SEA, DEVON 1–4C

Burgh Island Hotel £93 335
TQ7 4BG (01548) 810514
"What could be more romantic than an island retreat from the 1930s?"..."dress up, enjoy the wonderful cocktails and then delve into the excellent menu"; even the odd sceptic, for whom the "food and service don't quite live up to expectations", can't fault the "marvellous" setting and "fabulous" cocktails at this serene Art Deco hotel (an old haunt of Agatha Christie). / **Details:** *www.burghisland.com; 8.30 pm; D only, ex Sun open L & D; no Amex; Jacket & tie required; children: 12+ at D.* / **Accommodation:** *25 rooms, from £400*

The Oyster Shack £50 434
Millburn Orchard Farm, Stakes Hills TQ7 4BE
(01548) 810876
"This hilltop restaurant reached along the river valley justifies its name" – expect "sensational oysters" from the beds nearby, plus "sublime lobsters and shellfish". The "cheap 'n' cheerful decor" is "no frills", but it's "a fun and friendly venue", and even the odd reporter who felt it "nothing remarkable in the way of food" conceded that "the setting is worth a detour". / **Details:** *www.oystershack.co.uk; 9 pm.*

BILDESTON, SUFFOLK 3–1C

The Bildeston Crown £61 423
104 High St IP7 7EB (01449) 740510
The "pleasant" dining room of this "beautiful old Suffolk coaching inn" is "back to its best now that the original team has returned", with longtime chef Chris Lee (and wife Hayley) replacing Zack Deakins after a two-year hiatus; it's now turning out "excellent" dishes in the main, though "service is still hit 'n' miss". / **Details:** *www.thebildestoncrown.com; from the A14, take the B115 to Bildeston; 9.45 pm, Sun 9 pm.* / **Accommodation:** *12 rooms, from £100*

BILLERICAY, ESSEX 3–2C

The Magic Mushroom £61 433
Barleylands Road CM11 2UD (01268) 289963
"An oasis in a culinary desert" – Darren Bennet's "pleasant" bistro remains a clear cut above the local competition with its "fresh ingredients" and "very good set lunch menu". / **Details:** *www.magicmushroomrestaurant.co.uk; next to "Barleylands Farm"; midnight; closed Mon & Sun D.*

BIRMINGHAM, WEST MIDLANDS 5–4C

Adam's £86 555
16 Waterloo St B2 5UG (0121) 643 3745
"Wow, wow, wow!" – Adam & Natasha Stokes's recently relocated city-centre venture is "a sensational experience reaching new heights" not only as "simply Birmingham's best fine dining" but also as one of the most notable gastronomic destinations in the UK (where is that second Michelin star?). At this new location, there's a "lovely, warm and stylish interior", complete with "beautifully designed bar" and chef's table (an "electric" experience). Meanwhile, "totally unpretentious, amenable and knowledgeable staff" provide tasting menus "with some similarities to the old set-up, but with so many new, exciting culinary ideas" – "every course is a trip on an amazing journey, every dish is packed full of flavours, it's an incredible happening from start to finish!" / **Details:** *www.adamsrestaurant.co.uk; 9.30 pm; Booking max 10 may apply.*

Al Frash £26 432
186 Ladypool Rd B12 8JS (0121) 753 3120
Perhaps the Balti Triangle's best-known veteran, serving splendid curries in a straightforward contemporary space where diners can BYO. / **Details:** *www.alfrash.com; 11 pm, Sun 10 pm.*

Asha's Indian Bar and Restaurant £50 333
12-22 Newhall St B3 3LX (0121) 200 2767
"Decades away from typical Balti-house standards"

– this city-centre branch of a Gulf States chain provides a "classy" Indian dining option, where "interesting cocktails, friendly staff and stylish decor all compliment the great cuisine". / **Details:** *www.ashasuk.co.uk; 10.30 pm, Thu-Sat 11 pm, Sun 10pm; closed Sat L & Sun L.*

Carters of Moseley **£72** **443**
20 Wake Green Rd B13 9EZ (0121) 449 8885
"An exceptional neighbourhood restaurant offering imaginative food in a relaxed setting" – but, "good luck getting a table, it's fabulous and very busy!" / **Details:** *www.cartersofmoseley.co.uk; 9.30 pm; closed Mon & Tue; children: 8+.*

Edmunds **£74** **332**
6 Central Sq B1 2JB (0121) 633 4944
"In a busy area of Birmingham, where most places pander to the needs of expense accounters and weekend revellers", this Brindleyplace venture is one of the better bets. Notwithstanding that some critics find the ambience "rather chilly and detached", fans say "Edmunds sets its sights far higher than its local rivals, and scores!" / **Details:** *www.edmundsrestaurant.co.uk; 10 pm; closed Mon, Sat L & Sun; no Amex.*

Gourmet Burger Company **£26** **422**
113-115 Wharfside Street B1 1RF
(01216) 338 564
Near the city-centre campus of Birmingham City University, Brum's answer to the burger revolution gets a big thumbs-up: "it's basic, not a place to go for a long meal, and the service is brisk", but there's "a wonderful choice of great burgers" which fans say "still can't be beaten" in the city. / **Details:** *www.gbk.co.uk.*

Jyoti **£23** **432**
1045 Stratford Rd B28 8AS (0121) 778 5501
"A cornucopia of tastes and textures" awaits at this "fantastic", Formica-topped South Indian veggie, in Hall Green; the menu is "large and tasty", and it's "still cheap, especially as it allows BYO". / **Details:** *www.jyotis.co.uk; 9 pm, Sun 7 pm; no Amex.*

The Karczma, Polish Millennium House **£43** **323**
Bordesley St B5 5PH (0121) 448 0017
"Hilarious…and I honestly have no idea whether it's intentional" – "an alpine shack, replete with sheepskins and thatch", and attached to Brum's Polish Centre. "I have never been in a restaurant with such kitsch and pastiche", but the "rib-sticking Polish scoff" is "as deliciously authentic as the decor is naff, and the portions titanic"…"and oh the vodka!" / **Details:** *www.thekarczma.co.uk; 10pm.*

Lasan **£58** **542**
3-4 Dakota Buildings B3 1SD (0121) 212 3664
"Down a dodgy-looking side street" in the Jewellery Quarter, this "upmarket Indian may not be a romantic venue, but it's of a quality found only rarely in the UK". "Unsung hero of Asian cuisine, Aktar Islam, cooks sincere and brilliant combinations that are superbly matched with the wine flight: it's a great culinary experience!" / **Details:** *www.lasan.co.uk; Mon - Sat 11 pm, Sun 9 pm; closed Sat L; No trainers.*

Opus Restaurant **£64** **343**
54 Cornwall Street B3 2DE (0121) 200 2323
A big, rather barn-like city-centre brasserie that attracted fewer reports this year; such as there are remain enthusiastic however, and all agree that it's "well located for business" (slap bang in the Colmore Business District). / **Details:** *www.opusrestaurant.co.uk; Mon - Sat 9.15 pm, Sun closed; closed Sun D; no Amex.*

Original Patty Men **£25** **[illegible]**
9 Shaw's Passage B5 5JG no tel
"The best burger ever" along with "a fine selection of craft beers" is provided at this Digbeth dive – or as they sell themselves 'Patty Pimps and Purveyors of Filth' – currently the top of the tree for a burger in Brum. / **Details:** *www.originalpattymen.com.*

Purecraft Bar and Kitchen **£38** **334**
30 Waterloo St B2 5TJ (0121) 237 5666
This industrial-chic two-year-old in the business district provides a "great experience pairing a superb range of beers, led by (Midlands brewery) Purity's own, with Simpsons-influenced cooking" (Simpsons being the venue's other backer). / **Details:** *11 pm, Fri & Sat midnight, Sun 10 pm.*

Purnell's Bistro **£52** **322**
11 Newhall St B3 3NY (0121) 200 1588
Glynn Purnell's "relaxed" spin-off in the city-centre is praised in all reports for its "delicious" cooking, but other aspects can be more mixed when it's full; the "enthusiastic service" can become "stretched", and when it comes to the "relaxing" interior, "the architecture of the room can amplify the hubbub to a deafening degree."

Purnells **£104** **333**
55 Cornwall St B3 2DH (0121) 212 9799
"Psychedelic wallpaper" is part of the more flamboyant look, since a summer 2015 revamp of Glynn Purnell's city-centre venture. Even those who say it's "brilliant" can find it "expensive" (or gripe that it's "recently been complacent"), but the overall picture is still of "tasting menus, with a succession of delicious and exciting dishes", served "by a phalanx of polished and very friendly young Brummies".

/ **Details:** *www.purnellsrestaurant.com; 9.30 pm; closed Mon, Sat L & Sun; children: 6+.*

Rofuto **£60** **344**
Park Regis Birmingham, 160 Broad Street B15 1DT (0121) 369 8888
"Another newcomer but already a winner!" – restaurateur Des McDonald (of London's Vintage Salt and Q Grill fame) set his sights outside of the capital for his latest venture – a big, Japanese izakaya-themed venue on the top (16th-) floor of the Park Regis in Birmingham, with DJs at the weekend. "Go with a group of friends and order everything to share – ribs, lamb chops, black cod favourites"; "if they can keep this up, it's great". / **Details:** *www.rofuto.co.uk; 10.30 pm, Fri & Sat 11.30 pm, Sun 4 pm; Booking max 8 may apply.*

San Carlo **£52** **223**
4 Temple Street B2 5BN (0121) 633 0251
This city-centre outlet of the glossy Italian chain, which was born in Brum in the 1990s, continues to do a fine trade with its "authentic" cuisine and service but, ironically, this "closely packed" fixture is one of the lowest-rated outposts nationally. / **Details:** *www.sancarlo.co.uk; 11 pm.*

Simpsons **£89** **332**
20 Highfield Road B15 3DU (0121) 454 3434
This "quiet and discreet" Edwardian villa in Edgbaston divides opinion since its major makeover in mid-2015, which has "increased space" and "given it more of a brasserie feel". Critics feel that "this once classy Georgian gem has had its heart ripped out with its new, contemporary Scandinavian look" (but "downgrading the ambience hasn't been match by lower prices!"), and say that "while the food is good it doesn't show the flair of years gone by". For fans though, "it just gets it right time after time" with "delightful and innovative (if expensive) cuisine". / **Details:** *www.simpsonsrestaurant.co.uk; Mon-Thur 9 pm, Fri & Sat 9.30 pm, Sun 4.30 pm; closed Sun D.* / **Accommodation:** *4 rooms, from £160*

Turners at 69 **£83**
69 High St B17 9NS (0121) 426 4440
In August 2016, acclaimed chef Richard Turner relaunched his well-known Harborne venture (adding the 'at 69' suffix), with the aim of ditching its fine dining style for a more approachable formula. He also has his eyes on a second opening in Sutton Coldfield, with more to follow around Brum. / **Details:** *www.turnersrestaurantbirmingham.co.uk; 9.30 pm; closed Mon, Tue L, Wed L, Thu L & Sun; no Amex.*

BISHOP'S STORTFORD, HERTFORDSHIRE 3–2B

Baan Thitiya **£37** **343**
102 London Rd CM23 3DS (01279) 658575
A 1930s pub with an attractive canal-view garden hosts this suburban venue, which fans proclaim the "best Thai in Hertford" (admittedly a limited field). / **Details:** *www.baan-thitiya.com; 10 pm, Fri & Sat 10.30 pm, Sun 9.30 pm; No bookings.*

BISHOPS TACHBROOK, WARWICKSHIRE 5–4C

Mallory Court **£69** **235**
Harbury Lane CV33 9QB (01926) 330214
This attractive Relais & Châteaux country house hotel put in another uneven performance this year. Reporters are generally well-disposed to the place but feedback is often mixed, describing service that's "patchy but still genuinely warm and welcoming", or food that's "good but not excellent, or outstanding and rather pricey". / **Details:** *www.mallory.co.uk; 2m S of Leamington Spa, off B4087; 9.30 pm, Sun 3.30 pm; closed Sat L; No trainers.* / **Accommodation:** *31 rooms, from £159*

BLACKBROOK, STAFFORDSHIRE 5–3B

Swan With Two Necks **£47** **344**
Nantwich Road ST5 5EH (01782) 680343
"Always fabulous!" – this "typical country pub" is a great boon in a poorly provided area; "you always get a warm welcome", and it provides a "busy, buzzy atmosphere", "excellent real ale", and "great home-cooked food". / **Details:** *www.theswanwithtwonecks.co.uk; 10 pm.*

BLAIRGOWRIE, PERTH AND KINROSS 9–3C

Kinloch House **£79** **344**
Blairgowrie PH10 6SG (01250) 884237
A "superb hotel-restaurant" – part of the Relais & Châteaux portfolio – with a "fantastic country house-style ambience" and solid, well-rated cuisine. / **Details:** *www.kinlochhouse.com; past the Cottage Hospital, turn L, procede 3m along A923, (signposted Dunkeld Road); 8.30 pm; no Amex; Jacket required; children: 6+ for dinner.* / **Accommodation:** *15 rooms, from £230*

BLAKENEY, NORFOLK 6–3C

The Moorings **£44** **433**
High Street NR25 7NA (01263) 740 054
In a "fantastic location overlooking the water", this "small" but "sensational" bistro offers a "seafood-oriented menu", which, "for the North Norfolk Coast, is staggering good". / **Details:** *www.blakeney-moorings.co.uk; Mon closed, Tue - Sat 10.30 pm, Sun closed; closed Mon & Sun; no Amex.*

BODIAM, EAST SUSSEX 3–4C

The Curlew **£59**
Junction Rd TN32 5UY (01580) 861 394
Polarised reports this year on this old coaching inn, set in the middle of nowhere. To fans it's a worthy winner of the Sussex Food and Drink Awards, but to a worrying number of critics it's "resting on its laurels" ("I so wanted to like it, but everything was disappointing"). Some kind of resolution may be afoot, however – the business was put up for sale in autumn 2016. / ***Details:*** *www.thecurlewrestaurant.co.uk; 9.30 pm, Sun 9 pm; closed Mon.*

BOLLINGTON, CHESHIRE 5–2B

The Lime Tree **£40** [3][4][3]
18-20 High St SK10 5PH (01625) 578182
"A bit of a perennial" – this "informal" yet "polished" venue combines "fantastic service" with "reasonable prices, great wine, and food all locally sourced from their farm in Macclesfield Forest"; okay, so it "never seems to hit the heights of its (famous Didsbury) sibling", but no one disputes that it's still a "great local". / ***Details:*** *www.limetreebollington.co.uk; 10 pm, Fri & Sat 11 pm, Sun 6pm; closed Mon.*

Lord Clyde **£58** [5][4][3]
36 Clarke Lane SK10 5AH (01625) 562123
"Remarkable food in a village pub, with imaginative, successful ingredient combinations and great service" elicit real raves for Ernest and Sarah van Zyl's very superior venture, which numbers a chef's table and tasting menus up to £165 per head amongst its many dining options. / ***Details:*** *www.thelordclyde.co.uk; 9 pm, Sun 5 pm; closed Mon & Sun D; cancellation charge for larger bookings.*

BOLNHURST, BEDFORDSHIRE 3–1A

The Plough at Bolnhurst **£53** [4][5][4]
MK44 2EX (01234) 376274
A "lovely country pub" with "absolutely delightful" front of house staff, a "superb menu which is changed daily, and a fairly solid wine list". "Prices are aimed at the middle ground and it's therefore immensely popular!" / ***Details:*** *www.bolnhurst.com; 9.30 pm; closed Mon & Sun D; no Amex.*

BOLTON ABBEY, NORTH YORKSHIRE 5–1B

Burlington, The Devonshire Arms **£93** [3][3][2]
BD23 6AJ (01756) 718 111
"For full romantic effect, you need to stay overnight, and preferably in winter with the fantastic open fires", at the Duke of Devonshire's graceful country house hotel. To critics its dining room is a tad "dated", and the food is "ordinary" at times, but for a majority the cooking can be "exceptional", and the cellar is legendary here. / ***Details:*** *www.thedevonshirearms.co.uk; 9.30 pm, Sat & Sun 10 pm; closed Mon; Jacket required; children: 7+. /* ***Accommodation:*** *40 rooms, from £250*

BOREHAMWOOD, HERTFORDSHIRE 3–2A

Kiyoto Sushi [3][3][2]
31 Shenley Rd WD6 1AE (020) 3489 6800
"In a Japanese desert" – the environs of Elstree & Borehamwood Station – this "very noisy" and "cramped" spot really stands out with its "super sushi and sashimi". / ***Details:*** *www.kiyotosushi.co.uk.*

BOUGHTON LEES, KENT 3–3C

The Manor Restaurant, Eastwell Manor **£71** [2][3][5]
Eastwell Pk TN25 4HR (01233) 213000
A "stylish" Elizabethan manor house hotel, nestled in rolling countryside, and with a "relaxed", "baronial hall-style restaurant". "While the food doesn't come up to the standard of the surroundings", it's still a good "establishment for that special occasion" (or a "very good afternoon tea"). / ***Details:*** *www.eastwellmanor.co.uk; 3m N of Ashford on A251; 9.30 pm; No jeans; Booking max 8 may apply. /* ***Accommodation:*** *62 rooms, from £180*

BOURNEMOUTH, DORSET 2–4C

Chez Fred **£29** [4][3][2]
10 Seamoor Rd BH4 9AN (01202) 761023
Fred Capel's upscale fixture is "still the best chippie in the area", and "the environment is more pleasant thanks to the long overdue expansion". Nonetheless, even fans "don't come to Chez Fred for the service or ambience" – "but for sitting on the sand eating fish 'n' chips in the sunshine", it's certainly "number one". / ***Details:*** *www.chezfred.co.uk; 9.00 pm, Sun 8.30 pm; closed Sun L; no Amex; No bookings.*

WestBeach **£52** [3][3][3]
Pier Approach BH2 5AA (01202) 587785
"Right on the beach and just a stone's throw away from the pier", this "fantastic gem" of an establishment offers "a view to die for"; on the menu? – "local catch galore". / ***Details:*** *www.west-beach.co.uk; 10 pm.*

BOURTON ON HILL, GLOUCESTERSHIRE 2–1C

Horse & Groom **£43** 4 4 4
GL56 9AQ (01386) 700413
*"Everything you could want in a gastropub" – "this Cotswold favourite on the hill above Moreton-in-Marsh" is "a beautiful pub, in the quintessential English village". "Excellent fare is charmingly served in a welcoming atmosphere, and there are splendid views from the garden too". / **Details:** www.horseandgroom.info; Mon - Thur 9 pm, Fri & Sat 9.30 pm; closed Sun D; no Amex. / **Accommodation:** 5 rooms, from £120*

BRACKLESHAM, WEST SUSSEX 3–4A

Billys On The Beach **£47** 3 3 3
Bracklesham Ln PO20 8JH (01243) 670373
*A "beautiful position on the beach" overlooking the Isle of Wight helps make this a bright and airy three-year-old café (sibling to Billy's On the Road) "well worth a visit"; "lovely breakfasts" are a big high point. / **Details:** 8.30pm, Sunday 4pm.*

BRADFORD ON AVON, WILTSHIRE 2–3B

Three Gables **£60** 3 4 4
1 St Margaret's St BA15 1DA (01225) 781666
*"An ideal option in this beautiful small town" – a "very pretty" 17th-century building, whose kitchen is headed by Bath Priory-trained chef Marc Salmon, and which delivers some "top-quality modern cuisine, plus an extensive wine list". / **Details:** www.thethreegables.com; 10 pm; closed Mon & Sun.*

BRADFORD, WEST YORKSHIRE 5–1C

Akbar's **£31** 4 4 3
1276 Leeds Rd BD3 8LF (01274) 773311
*Often acclaimed as the "best Indian" in town – or one of them – the big, busy, modern, original HQ of this popular northern chain (nowadays employing 400 people!) won solid ratings this year for its "good Asian food (as confirmed by my fellow Asian diners!)". / **Details:** www.akbars.co.uk; midnight, Sun 11.30 pm; D only.*

Karachi **£22** 4 3 1
15-17 Neal St BD5 0BX (01274) 732015
*"Don't expect cutlery, or a huge welcome" at this no-frills Bradford curry house...do expect "great authentic curries with chapatis" ("so fresh!") – and at a price that's "very cheap". / **Details:** 1 am, Fri & Sat 2 am; Cash only.*

Mumtaz **£29** 4 3 3
386-410 Great Horton Rd BD7 3HS
(01274) 571861
*This celebrated stalwart still offers the "best Indian food in the curry capital", making it "very popular with local Asians" (even if it's "relatively expensive by Bradford standards"); NB drinkers will have to stick to soft drinks and lassi, as the venue is alcohol-free. / **Details:** www.mumtaz.com; midnight, Fri & Sat 1 am.*

Zouk **£35** 4 3 2
1312 Leeds Rd BD3 8LF (01274) 258 025
*A large Pakistani, which fans say compares favourably to local rivals, only the food's "generally more interesting, the beer better, and the ambience more spacious and well appointed"; given that it "manages to cater to all groups – date night, stag parties, business and regulars" – it can get "noisy". / **Details:** www.zoukteabar.co.uk; 11.00 pm; no Amex; No shorts.*

BRADWELL, DERBYSHIRE 5–2C

The Samuel Fox Country Inn **£51** 4 5 4
Stretfield Rd S33 9JT (01433) 621 562
*"A hidden gem that's a real Peak District jewel!"; James Duckett produces "superb" seasonal food ("every course a taste sensation") at his fine country inn, served by "attentive but informal staff"; "smart decor and great views are a bonus" too. / **Details:** www.samuelfox.co.uk; 9 pm, Sun 8pm.*

BRANCASTER STAITHE, NORFOLK 6–3B

The White Horse **£51** 3 2 4
Main Rd PE31 8BY (01485) 210262
*"The views across the salt marshes are unbeatable" at this "excellent stalwart" near the North Norfolk coast, whose undistinguished exterior "conceals gastro-delights" – in particular "fantastically fresh fish and seafood". / **Details:** www.whitehorsebrancaster.co.uk; 9 pm; no Amex. / **Accommodation:** 15 rooms, from £94 / **Sustainability:** ★★★*

BRAY, BERKSHIRE 3–3A

Caldesi in Campagna **£71** 4 4 4
Old Mill Ln SL6 2BG (01628) 788500
"An oasis of Italian-ness in the quintessentially English environs of Bray" – Giancario Caldesi's Thames-side venture (also incorporating a cookery school) makes "a delightful find in a village dominated by culinary heavyweights". "It executes authentic, fine modern Italian cuisine at its best", and it's particularly splendid on a warm day, sitting

in the courtyard garden. / **Details:** *www.caldesi.com; 9.30 pm; closed Mon & Sun D.*

Crown Inn £54 [4][3][3]
High St SL6 2AH (01628) 621936
"Almost as good as the Hinds Head nearby but less fussy, and in more traditional pub style"; "try this if you want something in Bray owned by Heston Blumenthal which doesn't break the bank!" / **Details:** *www.thecrownatbray.com; 9.30 pm, Fri & Sat 10 pm, Sun 8 pm.*

The Fat Duck £323 [4][4][2]
High St SL6 2AQ (01628) 580333
"A theatrical and gastronomic event unlike any other"… Heston Blumenthal's re-launched extravaganza "has a new concept – they take you on a journey and even phone you in advance to ask you questions about your memorable experiences" – and on most accounts the result remains "a perfect balance of food and showmanship", with "attention to detail that's truly amazing and lots of fun"; but then there's the humungous cost. OK, it's always been an arm-and-a-leg job here, but "nigh on a grand for two!?" (if you go for the set menu and wine flights); while for a slim majority it's worth it for "a once-in-a-lifetime multi-sensory experience", for the first time in survey feedback on this famous venue there is very significant kickback against the quality/price equation, with two in five reporters finding that "whilst you can't help but praise the effort and the genius in the execution, it's all too much, and doesn't justify the stratospheric pricing". (Ironically, given all the recent investment in this converted pub, most regulars also "marginally preferred the old decor", or even find "the new, everything-grey look is like a prison!") / **Details:** *www.thefatduck.co.uk; 9 pm; closed Mon & Sun.*

The Hind's Head £67 [4][4][4]
High Street SL6 2AB (01628) 626151
"Consistently excellent interpretations of pub grub, delivered with flair and a sense of delight" win ringing endorsements for this "thankfully not over-Hestoned" gastropub (next door to The Fat Duck), which is "well worth making the foray down the M4 of a weekend to have a special lunch". It's an all-round "joy", "retaining its old-world feel (with classic wooden beams, uneven floors and walls and a roaring fireplace)", and with "courteous and prompt service" too. / **Details:** *www.hindsheadbray.com; 9.30 pm; closed Sun D.*

Waterside Inn £230 [4][5][5]
Ferry Rd SL6 2AT (01628) 620691
"On a fine summer's day, nothing can be more enchanting" than Alain Roux's Thames-side epic (founded in 1972 by his father Michel), whether you are "sipping pre-dinner cocktails on their electric launch (and looking forward to a sumptuous meal after you glide back to the dock)", or "sitting under the willow tree watching the boats go by as you sip a vintage champagne". A further boost is provided by its "absolutely impeccable" service ("nobody runs a better dining room than maître d' Diego!"). When it comes to the classic haute cuisine, however, there seemed to be "a number of question marks" this year and its rating sipped a notch; it has always been "eye-wateringly expensive", but even some who praise the food as "exquisite" can also find it "unimaginative" or "dated" in style ("like taking a time machine back to the '80s"). That's still a minority view however; on the vast majority of accounts this is a case of "perfect food in a perfect setting". / **Details:** *www.waterside-inn.co.uk; off A308 between Windsor & Maidenhead; 9.30 pm; closed Mon & Tue; No jeans; Booking max 10 may apply; children: 9+. /* **Accommodation:** *11 rooms, from £240*

BREARTON, NORTH YORKSHIRE 8–4B

The Malt Shovel £49 [3][3][3]
HG3 3BX (01423) 862929
"Consistently good service and food" make this quaint 16th-century rural pub "one of the best inns in which to eat" locally. / **Details:** *www.themaltshovelbrearton.co.uk; off A61, 6m N of Harrogate; 10 pm, Sun 4 pm; closed Mon & Sun D.*

BRECON, POWYS 2–1A

The Felin Fach Griffin £49 [4][4][3]
Felin Fach LD3 0UB (01874) 620111
"A real gem" in the Brecon Beacons that's long been a mainstay of the area's dining options, and whose food is "always imaginative without being pretentious". / **Details:** *www.eatdrinksleep.ltd.uk; 20 mins NW of Abergavenny on A470; 9 pm, Fri & Sat 9.30 pm. /* **Accommodation:** *7 rooms, from £115*

BRENTWOOD, ESSEX 3–2B

Alec's £66 [3][3][3]
Navestock Side CM14 5SD (01277) 375 696
Glitzy brasserie where "the fish is always extremely fresh" and it's "served by friendly staff"; while some "can't fault it", others feel that it's "pricey for what you get", or that the "ambience is somewhat OTT…unless you are a fan of TOWIE!" / **Details:** *www.alecsrestaurant.co.uk; 10 pm, Sun 4.30 pm; closed Mon, Tue L, Wed L & Sun D; no Amex; children: 12+.*

BRIDPORT, DORSET 2–4B

Riverside £55 [5][5][4]
West Bay DT6 4EZ (01308) 422011
"Superlative fresh fish and seafood in TV's

'Broadchurch' (West Bay)";Arthur Watson's "longstanding centre of excellence continues to attract a loyal following, unsurprisingly given its first-rate ingredients, not least supplies from the local catch". "We're getting worried that the many friends who come down to stay really come to go to the restaurant rather than to see us!" / **Details:** www.thefishrestaurant-westbay.co.uk; Mon closed, Tue - Sat 8.30 pm, Sun 2.30 pm; closed Mon & Sun D.

BRIGHTON, EAST SUSSEX 3–4B

Basketmakers Arms £41 434

12 Gloucester Rd BN1 4AD (01273) 689006

"Brighton's best pub food, year after year" is, say fans, to be found at this highly popular North Laine boozer. / **Details:** *www.basket-makers-brighton.co.uk; 9 pm; No bookings.*

Bincho Yakitori £33 432

63 Preston St BN1 2HE (01273) 779021

"Wonderful Yakitori at very reasonable prices" has made an instant hit of this "really good value" izakaya-style newcomer – one of the best arrivals of recent times. / **Details:** *www.binchoyakitori.com; 10 pm, Fri & Sat 10.30 pm.*

Burger Brothers £13 542

97 North Rd BN1 1YE (01273) 706980

Hip (and tiny) North Laine spot – essentially a take-away with a few seats – inspiring limited but excited feedback; "I almost don't want anyone else to know about it, as the queues are bad enough already, but the burgers are too good to stay quiet about!" / **Details:** *10 pm.*

The Chilli Pickle £46 533

17 Jubilee St BN1 1GE (01273) 900 383

Brighton's most commented-on dining destination this year; set in the recently built Arts Quarter, it's a "buzzing modern Indian with an open kitchen" and decor which is "about as far from the traditional flock-wallpaper look as you can get". Expect "stunning cooking from a varied and imaginative menu, a great range of craft beers, and amazing breads". / **Details:** *www.thechillipickle.com; 10.30 pm, Sun 10pm; closed Tue. /* **Sustainability:** ★

The Coal Shed £55 333

8 Boyces St BN1 1AN (01273) 322998

"A great place for steak-lovers" – this "upmarket, wood-floor bar/bistro" has a reputation as one of the city's better places and generally lives up to it. "The friendly staff will chat you through the various cuts and advise you (well) on what to go for". / **Details:** *www.coalshed-restaurant.co.uk; 10 pm, Fri & Sat 10.30 pm.*

Curry Leaf Cafe £39 333

60 Ship St BN1 1AE (01273) 207070

"Basic but friendly" Lanes café praised by fans of its "different" Indian dishes ("light and strong on veggie options"), although it also has its critics, who feel it's "nice enough" but "masquerading as something special". Also at the Temple Bar (121 Western Road, Brighton, BN1 2AD) and with a kiosk at the station. / **Details:** *www.curryleafcafe.com; 10 pm, Fri - Sat 10.30pm.*

Donatello £33 333

1-3 Brighton Pl BN1 1HJ (01273) 775477

This "huge" and "bustling" spot in the Lanes is an affordable and "fun place for all the family", where "kidlets always receive a great welcome"; "staff are great, plus the food's tasty and in vast portions". / **Details:** *www.donatello.co.uk; 11.00 pm.*

Drakes of Brighton, Drakes Hotel £69 353

43 - 44 Marine Parade BN2 1PE (01273) 696934

The "very good standards of cooking" again win plaudits for this small dining room in a Kemptown boutique hotel, on the seafront. "Pity that it's in the basement" – but on the plus side there's a "nice cocktail bar upstairs with sea views". / **Details:** *drakesofbrighton.com/restaurant; 9.45 pm. /* **Accommodation:** *20 rooms, from £115*

English's £54 443

29-31 East St BN1 1HL (01273) 327980

A "very long-established seafood restaurant" (est. 1890s), in the Lanes, where "the seafood is simply amazing", and service is "outstanding" too. While it has "had its ups and downs", and the interior "looks a bit 1980s" (notwithstanding the fin-de-siècle murals), it currently serves some of the "best seafood in Brighton". / **Details:** *www.englishs.co.uk; 10 pm, Sun 9.30 pm.*

Fatto A Mano £37 332

77 London Rd BN1 4JF (01273) 600621

A "nice, bright" yearling where the "fantastic" and "extremely good value" Neapolitan-style pizzas are the star of the show, but where there are also "yummy antipasti"; it added a Hove sibling in August 2016. / **Details:** *www.fattoamanopizza.com.*

Food for Friends £41 332

17-18 Prince Albert St BN1 1HF (01273) 202310

"They know what they're doing and do it well" at this "amazing" meat-free fixture on the Lanes; critics were notably absent this year, with even non-veggies finding the food "really interesting and tasty". / **Details:** *10 pm, Fri & Sat 10.30 pm; no booking, Sat L & Sun L.*

The Ginger Dog £54 333
12 College Pl BN2 1HN (01273) 620 990
"One of the 'Ginger'(man) family in Brighton" – this time in Kemptown, and with a "more relaxed gastropub atmosphere"; feedback included nothing but praise this year for its "excellent value" grub. / **Details:** *www.gingermanrestaurants.com; off Eastern Road near Brighton College; 10 pm.*

The Ginger Pig £53 333
3 Hove St BN3 2TR (01273) 736123
"Always dependable" – a Hove boozer that's a favourite component of the local Gingerman empire; "a very attractive place", it combines "very friendly staff" and "quality gastropub fare (rabbit, pâté, pies etc. all good, delicious desserts too)". / **Details:** *www.thegingermanrestaurants.com; 10 pm, Sun 9 pm; No trainers.*

Gingerman £56 554
21a Norfolk Sq BN1 2PD (01273) 326688
"Brighton's best 'fine dining'" is still – despite increased local competition – to be had at Ben Mckellar's "tiny", "utterly unpretentious" backstreet dining room, near the seafront – an "intimate" space, which "has been improved by its recent refurbishment" ("a win!"). Service is "totally charming", and the "increasingly inventive and adventurous dishes" are "fantastic and amazing value for the quality". / **Details:** *www.gingermanrestaurant.com; 9.45 pm; closed Mon.*

Indian Summer £45 444
69 East St BN1 1HQ (01273) 711001
"In recent times, having moved to larger premises a couple of doors away from their previous home", this "excellent" contemporary Indian in the Lanes maintains its high level of popularity with its "deft spicing and subtle culinary touches". / **Details:** *www.indiansummerbrighton.co.uk; 10.30 pm, Sun 10 pm; closed Mon L.*

Iydea £20 232
17 Kensington Gdns BN1 4AL
(01273) 667 992
A Brighton veggie where the food is "often raw", and often vegan, and where there's a "good choice" on the "good value" and "very healthy" menu; a Hove sibling caters to the dinner crowd. / **Details:** *www.iydea.co.uk; 5 pm; no Amex.*

Little Fish Market £73 543
10 Upper Market St BN3 1AS (01273) 722213
"Keep it bold and simple!"; in a "modern" former fishmonger's, ex-Fat Duck chef Duncan Ray turns out "fabulous" fish and seafood. Top Tip – "go for the tasting menu, which is reasonably priced and very good". / **Details:** *www.thelittlefishmarket.co.uk; Tue-Sat 10.30 pm; closed Mon, Tue L, Wed L, Thu L, Fri L & Sun*

Lucky Beach £29 444
183 King's Rd BN1 1NB (01273) 728280
With "a great location on the seafront", Mike Palmer's café in the arches provides "great homemade burgers, delicious chips, intelligent staff who know the menu, and great beer. On the beach on a sunny day, what better?" / **Details:** *www.luckybeach.co.uk; Mon-Fri 7 pm, Sat-Sun 8.15 pm.*

Market £42 333
42 Western Rd BN3 1JD (01273) 823707
"Love, love, love this place!" – a "laidback" yet "buzzy" yearling on the former site of Graze, with a "Spanish tapas bar-style ambience" and food that's "simple" but "really, really good". / **Details:** *www. market-restaurantbar.co.uk.*

Plateau £70 332
1 Bartholomews BN1 1HG (01273) 733 085
"A funky (even for Brighton) menu, and a natural-wine list could ring warning bells for hipster overload" – but this "very small French bistro close to The Lanes" is a "fun spot" combining "some interesting ingredients" into "delicious" dishes; service is distinctively Gallic. / **Details:** *www.plateaubrighton.co.uk; 10 pm.*

Polpo £48 333
20 New Rd BN1 1UF (01273) 697 361
Russell Norman and Richard Beatty take their Italian cicchetti formula outside of the capital (mind you, opening in 'London-on-Sea' isn't such a massive punt!). It's "frenetic and noisy" like its siblings, and its "scrummy little morsels" have helped make it "a good addition to Brighton". / **Details:** *www.polpo.co.uk; 11 pm, Sun 10.30 pm; Booking lunch only.*

The Regency £32 333
131 Kings Rd BN1 2HH (01273) 325014
A "great place for fish 'n' chips (plus seafood platters, etc.) right on the Brighton seafront". / **Details:** *www.theregencyrestaurant.co.uk; 10 pm. /* **Accommodation:** *30 rooms, from £50*

Riddle & Finns £49 434
12b, Meeting House Ln BN1 1HB
(01273) 323008
"Oyster, crab and fish pie are unbeatable" at this communal fish and seafood spot in The Lanes (nowadays less well-known than its beachside offshoot). "The catch of the day is always a good choice." / **Details:** *www.riddleandfinns.co.uk; 10 pm, Fri & Sat 11 pm; No bookings.*

Riddle & Finns On The Beach £49 444
139 Kings Road Arches BN1 2FN
(01273) 821218
"A lovely spot (if difficult to find) under the arches on Brighton Beach" – "you eat upstairs, and kitchen

and reception are below". The younger sibling to a spot on The Lanes, it's become one of the city's most popular destinations, not just on account of the super location, but also the "smiley and efficient" service, and most particularly its "enticing" range of "lip-smacking" fish and seafood. / **Details:** *www.riddleandfinns.co.uk; 10 pm.*

The Salt Room £58 344

106 King's Rd BN1 2FA (01273) 929 488

On an "A1 seafront site" overlooking the ruined West Pier, the Hilton Metropole's unexpectedly good yearling continues to grow in popularity; it provides "somewhat pricey" but "very accomplished" seafood and fish, "lots of atmosphere" in a "stripped-back" setting, and service that's "very cool and natural". Top menu tip – the 'Taste of the Pier' dessert: "boy do you need a sweet tooth, but it was ace; so much work in it!" / **Details:** *www.saltroom-restaurant.co.uk; Mon - Thur 10 pm, Fri & Sat 10.30 pm, Sun 10 pm.*

Semolina £46 454

15 Baker St BN1 4JN (01273) 697259

A "tiny husband-and-wife-run bistro tucked away on Baker Street"; the welcome is exceptional, and the French/European cuisine is "wonderful" and "amazingly good value". / **Details:** *www. semolinabrighton.co.uk.*

Set £49 433

33 Regency Sq BN1 2GG (01273) 855572

This former pop-up, newly rehoused in a "quirky" boutique hotel on Regency Square, scores high praise indeed for modern British cuisine that's "innovative without losing sight of what the dishes are all about"; "great service too". / **Details:** *www.thesetrestaurant.com; 9.30 pm; closed Mon & Sun.*

Silo £31 443

39 Upper Gardner St, North Laine BN1 4AN (01273) 674 259

"The composter isn't hidden away, it's in full view!" at this "eco-gourmet" venture in North Laine, where "local produce really is local", and owner Dougie McMaster "cultivates his own mushrooms in coffee grounds, ferments and pickles vegetables, and aims for zero waste". Practically all reporters are happy to "bear the risk of pretension" and uncomfy seats for the "lovely" grub… "please can we get more of this ethos into our towns!" / **Details:** *www.silobrighton.com; 11 pm, Sun & Mon 4 pm; closed Mon D, Tue D, Wed D & Sun D.*

64 Degrees £48 432

53 Meeting House Lane BN1 1HB (01273) 770 115

"A mecca for Brighton foodies" – Michael Bremner's "really splendid, inventive and deeply flavour-packed small-plate cooking" goes from strength to strength at his Lanes two-year-old ("try to sit at the counter and watch the chefs prepare an interesting array of goodies"). "But it's SO DAMN NOISY; when your food is this good, you don't need to crank up the volume guys!" / **Details:** *www.64degrees.co.uk; 9.45 pm.*

Small Batch Coffee £10 344

17 Jubilee St BN1 1GE (01273) 697597

This seven-strong local chain has built quite a following over the past decade owing to its "outstanding" small-batch coffee (plus sandwiches, cakes and pastries); this branch also wins praise for its "fun atmosphere" and "efficient service". / **Details:** *www.smallbatchcoffee.co.uk; 7 pm, Sun 6 pm.*

Terre à Terre £54 543

71 East St BN1 1HQ (01273) 729051

"Still the best vegetarian restaurant in Britain even after so many years!" – this "unfailing" Lanes "icon" as ever attracts a huge volume of commentary. "Dishes are unique, creative – look fantastic and taste amazing", and deliver "a spectacular array of flavours, incorporating so many different aspects of texture and smell." / **Details:** *www.terreaterre.co.uk; 10.30 pm, Sat 11 pm, Sun 10 pm; Booking max 8 may apply.*

24 St Georges £49 443

24-25 St Georges Rd BN2 1ED (01273) 626060

A "rather crowded" Kemptown spot, with "charming" service and "excellent" cooking (including notably "delicious vegetarian options"). / **Details:** *www.24stgeorges.co.uk; 9.30.*

Urchin £39 334

15-17 Belfast St BN3 3YS (01273) 241881

"Behind the Tesco Superstore", and atop the Brighton Gin distillery, this "unpretentious" pub is "by far Brighton's best for simple seafood impeccably presented" from a blackboard menu (plus "over a hundred different craft beers"); the grub comes in "generous" portions, and at an "unbelievably reasonable" cost to boot. / **Details:** *www.urchinpub.wordpress.com; 9.30pm, Fri - Sat 10pm.*

BRILL, BUCKINGHAMSHIRE 2–2D

Pointer £62 333

27 Church St HP18 9RT (01844) 238339

"In a fantastic Buckinghamshire village", a "lovely" beamed gastroboozer with a proper bar and plusher dining room; "exceptional food using locally sourced ingredients" (some from the owners' own farm) ensures that it's "thoroughly recommended" by all who comment on it. / **Details:** *www.thepointerbrill.co.uk; 11pm.*

BRISTOL, CITY OF BRISTOL 2–2B

Bell's Diner And Bar Rooms £50 554

1 York Rd BS6 5QB (0117) 924 0357

*"A local gem"; this beloved Montpelier veteran – once a greengrocer's, but operating (under several owners) as a ramshackle haunt since the '70s – is on sparkling form currently, serving up "a short menu" of "reliably superb" and "vibrant" small plates prepared by an ex-Moro chef. A jovial sibling, Bellita, arrived in Cotham Hill in 2015. / **Details:** www.bellsdiner.com; 10 pm; closed Mon L & Sun.*

Bellita £36 433

34 Cotham Hill BS6 6LA (0117) 923 8755

*On the former site of Flinty Red (RIP), a 'little sister' to the city's age-old Bell's Diner – a bright neighbourhood tapas bar, serving small plates of Spanish-, North African- and Middle Eastern-influenced cuisine. Early feedback is rapturous – "amazing food from the Bell's Diner gang (although it gets shouty and noisy as it's often very busy)". / **Details:** www.bellita.co.uk; 11pm..*

Birch £42 442

47 Raleigh Rd BS3 1QS (01179) 028 326

*Sam Leach & Beccy Massy, "who served their apprenticeships at many of Bristol's top restaurants", continue to win praise for their white-walled Southville venture, serving "exotic" small plates featuring "fascinating combinations of local ingredients". However, "more in the way of sound absorption" would go down well with some reporters. / **Details:** www.birchbristol.co; 10 pm; D only, closed Sun-Tue.*

Bordeaux Quay £55 333

Canons Way BS1 5UH (0117) 943 1200

*In a "great spot overlooking the waterfront", this multi-tasking brasserie, restaurant, deli and bakery – a "spacious" warehouse conversion – is a versatile destination with "food that's rather above average". / **Details:** www.bordeaux-quay.co.uk; Mon-Sat 10.30 pm, Sun 9.30 pm.*

Bosco Pizzeria £38 433

96 Whiteladies Rd BS8 2QX (01179) 737 978

*A casual, sophisticated-looking two-year-old that's built a massive local reputation for its "superb" Neapolitan pizza, but which serves other more substantial fare (grills, pasta) too. / **Details:** www.boscopizzeria.co.uk; 10 pm.*

Bravas £37 444

7 Cotham Hill BS6 6LD (0117) 329 6887

*"A total gem!"; all the essentials of a cosy, fun meal are to be had at this former pop-up – now a buzzy Cotham Hill bar: "authentic" dishes (the "closest to real tapas we have had in the UK, said our Spanish friend"), a "great gin menu and a perfect vibe". / **Details:** www.bravas.co.uk; 11 pm, Thu-Sat midnight; closed Mon & Sun.*

Bulrush £49 443

21 Cotham Road South BS6 5TZ (0117) 329 0990

*This "wonderful new locally sourced restaurant taking over from Juniper has made an impressive start". In a white-painted brick former grocery shop, George Livesey and Katherine Craughwell deliver a daring and mostly incredibly accomplished collection of eclectic dishes. / **Details:** www.bulrushrestaurant.co.uk; 9 pm.*

Casamia, The General £116 545

Guinea St BS1 6SY (0117) 959 2884

*"Casamia has moved with aplomb to a dramatic and beautifully designed dining room beneath the old General Hospital building in the heart of Bristol", and the new location clearly confirms it as the city's top culinary destination. Its cuisine (featuring multi-course tasting menus) "is every bit as epic as it was in its former premises" – "a carefully constructed, gorgeously presented, technically skilful and, above all, thoroughly flavoursome journey through a series of seasonal ingredients". "It couldn't have been any better, especially more so considering the challenges they have gone through in the last year" (namely the loss of co-proprietor Jonray Sanchez-Iglesias, brother of chef Peter Sanchez-Iglesias). / **Details:** www.casamiarestaurant.co.uk; 9.30 pm; closed Mon & Sun; no Amex.*

The Cowshed £49 332

44-46 Whiteladies Rd BS8 2NH (0117) 973 3550

*This "noisy" exposed-brick spot is clearly "not for vegetarians", but carnivores acclaim its "excellent steaks" and yummy burgers as some of the best in town (if at a cost). If you think you can do better, take home some meat from their butcher's next door. / **Details:** www.thecowshedbristol.com; 10 pm, Fri & Sat 10.30 pm, Sun 9.30 pm.*

Flour & Ash £37 333

38 High St BS9 3DZ (0117) 330 0033

*Trendy pizza purveyors expand from a single site in Bristol to take over the former home of the acclaimed Casamia in Westbury-on-Trym. "Great sourdough bases and interesting ice creams" feature in initial upbeat feedback, and one reporter "even enjoyed aubergines for the first time ever!" / **Details:** Mon-Wed 9.30pm, Thur-Sat 10pm, Sundays 9pm.*

Flour & Ash £37 332

230b Cheltenham Rd BS6 5QX (0117) 908 3228

A "popular" and "friendly" Clifton-chic venue specialising in "very good" wood-fired sourdough pizzas and ice-cream. The owners opened a

Westbury-On-Trym sibling in May 2016. / **Details:** www.flourandash.co.uk.

Lido £53 345
Oakfield Pl BS8 2BJ (0117) 933 9533
A "firmly established Bristol classic" – part of a "beautiful" old Victorian lido – where the Mediterranean/North African tapas-style food, by ex-Moro chef Freddie Bird, "is more than good enough" (indeed, for some fans, it's "remarkable"). "Eating upstairs whilst watching others swim is the real pleasure" ("like being on holiday!"). / **Details:** *www.lidobristol.com; 10.30 pm, Sun 10 pm; closed Sun D; no Amex.*

Lockside £33 332
No.1 Brunel Lock Road BS1 6XS
(0117) 9255 800
"The café under the underpass" in "the historic dock area"; this "very busy" polished-not-greasy-spoon (the venue for Sid's Café in 'Only Fools and Horses') serves "good wholesome" food, and is a particular hit for its "fab brunch";"nice outdoor deck for sunny days". / **Details:** *www.lockside.net; 4pm.*

Maitreya Social £40 333
89 St Marks Rd BS5 6HY (0117) 951 0100
Arty, pioneering veggie on Easton's bustling main strip; for some it's a gastronomic destination, for others "more like a café for a snack", but it garnered solid marks across the board. / **Details:** *www.maitreyasocial.co.uk; 11.30pm; closed Mon, Tue L, Wed L, Thu L & Sun D; no Amex; Booking evening only.*

The Mint Room £41 433
12-16 Clifton Rd BS8 1AF (01173) 291 300
The "classy" two-year-old sibling of the Bath original elicits real raves from reporters for former Tamarind chef Saravanan Nambirajan's "startlingly good" and "sophisticated" Indian cuisine; it "unfortunately follows the trend for echo-y restaurants but that is about its only fault". / **Details:** *www.themintroom.co.uk/bristol.*

Paco Tapas, The General
Lower Guinea St BS1 6SY (0117) 959 2884
A Spanish tapas and sherry bar from the Sanchez-Iglesias family will open in mid-November 2016, alongside the relocated Casamia in Bristol's new General development. / **Details:** *www.sanchez-brothers.co.uk.*

Pi Shop, The General
Guinea St BS1 6SY (0117) 925 6872
A sourdough pizza place, complete with open kitchen and wood-fired oven, from none other than Peter Sanchez-Iglesias (the chef behind Casamia). It sits alongside the relocated Casamia in Bristol's new General development, and while it opened too late for survey feedback, it has already scooped best pizza at the Bristol Good Food Awards 2016.

Primrose Café £47 443
1 Clifton Arcade BS8 4AA (0117) 946 6577
"Tucked away in a small cul-de-sac", this shabby-chic Clifton Village bistro has been "a favourite for over 20 years"; it's tipped for its yummy cakes, "great evening meals" (with a Med slant), and "great al fresco brunch on a sunny day!" / **Details:** *www.primrosecafe.co.uk; Mon 5 pm, Tue - Fri till late, Sat 5 pm, Sun 3 pm; Sun D; No bookings at lunch.*

The Pump House £52 443
Merchants Rd BS8 4PZ (0117) 927 2229
Pub downstairs, and high-end restaurant upstairs, this imposing waterside venue – as per the name, an old Victorian pumping house, by the docks – wins raves for its "amazing and good-value tasting menu":"bargain!" / **Details:** *the-pumphouse.com.*

River Cottage Canteen £46 223
St Johns Ct, Whiteladies Rd BS8 2QY
(0117) 973 2458
Patchy feedback (like last year) on HFW's three-year-old, in a restored Victorian church. No denying it's an "attractive" spot, and the cooking's generally well rated, but the menu can seem "unexciting", "inflexible", or too "pricey" for what it is. / **Details:** *www.rivercottage.net/canteens; 9.15 pm, Sun 4 pm.*

riverstation £50 335
The Grove BS1 4RB (0117) 914 4434
This striking-looking dockside landmark – a former river-police station – achieved solid feedback this year. Its most ardent fans say that it has been "constantly over-performing for over 20 years", but the general verdict is that it's more of a "good standby" for "perfectly acceptable and good value" food. Top Tip? – "a table on the terrace overlooking the river is a delight on a warm day". / **Details:** *www.riverstation.co.uk; 10.30 pm, Fri & Sat 11 pm; closed Sun D; no Amex.*

San Carlo £42 334
44 Corn St BS1 1HQ (0117) 922 6586
It's "always a pleasure" to eat at this "very reliable" (albeit expensive) Italian – part of the glossy national chain;"like the rest of the group it's a real 'see and be seen' place…great for WAGs"! / **Details:** *www.sancarlo.co.uk; 11 pm.*

Severnshed £46 213
The Grove, Harbourside BS1 4RB
(0117) 925 1212
This harbourside restaurant and cocktail lounge in Brunel's former boathouse on the docks doesn't fully exploit its potential; while the setting and ambience are "lovely", and the food and drink "decent", it's rather a "poorly managed" spot where "muddled" staff are seemingly constantly apologising. / **Details:** *www.severnshedrestaurant.co.uk; Sun-Thu 10.30 pm, Fri & Sat 11.30 pm.*

Souk Kitchen £38 433
277 North St BS3 1JP (0117) 966 6880
With its "interesting mix of dishes" and "bold" flavours, this Persian street food venue, opposite The Tobacco Factory, has built up a strong local following over the past few years; owners Darren & Ella Lovell recently opened a new Clifton sibling on the site of their popular former haunt, Rucola. / ***Details:*** *www.soukitchen.co.uk; 8.30pm.*

Spiny Lobster £56 333
128-130 Whiteladies Road BS8 2RS
(0117) 9737384
The "latest incarnation of Rockfish Grill"; "despite repeated name changes", Mitch Tonks's fishmonger and eatery is still a "must" for fish fans. The current New England-style vibe is "helped by nice booths with padded banquettes which are difficult to drag yourself off". / ***Details:*** *www.thespinylobster.co.uk; 10 pm, Fri & Sat 10.30 pm; closed Mon & Sun.*

The Thali Café £32 333
12 York Rd BS6 5QE (0117) 942 6687
This ever-"quirky", five-strong local chain has come a long way since its beginnings as a street food van at Glastonbury festival; the original Montpellier HQ still offers a "good buzz", and "excellent value" Indian cuisine. / ***Details:*** *www.thethalicafe.co.uk; 10 pm; closed weekday L; no Amex. /* ***Sustainability:*** ★★★

Wallfish Bistro £49 443
112 Princess Victoria St BS8 4DB
(01179) 735435
"Seldon Curry and Liberty Wenham have created a gem in Clifton" – a small site (home to Keith Floyd's first venture) which nowadays houses one of the city's most popular eateries. "Given its limited size (including the kitchen), Seldon produces the most wonderful array of interesting and innovative dishes". Top Tip – "the fantastic weekday lunch deal is unbelievable value". / ***Details:*** *www.wallfishbistro.co.uk; 10 pm, Sun 9 pm; closed Mon & Tue.*

Wilks £78 542
1 Chandos Rd BS6 6PG (0117) 9737 999
"James Wilkins is one of the best chefs in Bristol" and his backstreet Redland haunt "goes from strength to strength". The site is a modest one ambience-wise, but pepped up by its superb service ("welcoming, courteous, knowledgeable, efficient, discreet!") and "his cuisine is exceptional, both in presentation and combination of flavours". / ***Details:*** *www.wilksrestaurant.co.uk; 10 pm, sun 9 pm; closed Mon & Tue; no Amex.*

BROADSTAIRS, KENT 3–3D

Wyatt & Jones £47 444
23-27 Harbour St CT10 1EU (01843) 865126
An "excellent, quirky restaurant by the harbour" and "looking out over Broadstairs beach"; it's a "large, airy" sort of space, and, while "not faultless", the food manages to be both "family-friendly" and "grown-up", with a "good local beer list" to wash it down. / ***Details:*** *www.wyattandjones.co.uk; Wed & Thu 9 pm, Fri & Sat 10 pm, Sun 5 pm.*

BROADWAY, WORCESTERSHIRE 2–1C

Russell's £60 333
20 High Street WR12 7DT (01386) 853555
Located in grand premises at the entry to a pretty Cotswold village, this restaurant-with-rooms is lauded for its "pleasant setting" and "reasonable value fixed-price menu"; the owners' adjacent chippy is also worth considering. / ***Details:*** *www.russellsofbroadway.co.uk; Mon - Sat 9.15 pm, Sun 2.30 pm; closed Sun D. /* ***Accommodation:*** *7 rooms, from £110*

BROCKDISH, SUFFOLK 3–1D

Old Kings Head £38 344
50 The Street IP2 4JY (01379) 668843
"If you like pizza and pasta, this is the place to come!" – a new pub-conversion that "excels at what it does, and is always, always very busy"; a "really good gin menu" is also a feature. / ***Details:*** *www.kingsheadbrockdish.co.uk; 10pm, Fri - Sat 11pm, Sun 9pm.*

BROCKENHURST, HAMPSHIRE 2–4D

The Pig £56 344
Beaulieu Road SO42 7QL (01590) 622354
The Hotel du Vin founder's five-year-old country house – the first 'Pig' – is a "very good place to go for that special occasion". The mismatched decor creates an "engaging atmosphere" in which to enjoy some "interesting" cooking (mostly meat – and with "everything locally sourced a bonus"). / ***Details:*** *www.thepighotel.com; 9.30 pm. /* ***Accommodation:*** *26 rooms, from £139 /* ***Sustainability:*** ★★★

BROCKHAM, SURREY 3–3A

The Grumpy Mole £45 343
Brockham Green RH3 7JS (01737) 845 101
A bistro-style village gastroboozer offering "great service, lovely meat and nice people…what's not to like?" / ***Details:*** *www.thegrumpymole.co.uk; Mon - Sat 9.30 pm, Sun 8.30 pm; no Amex; No bookings.*

BROMESWELL, SUFFOLK 3–1D

The Unruly Pig £46 [3][3][3]
Orford Rd IP12 2PU (01394) 460 310
"After their disastrous fire so soon after opening, they've made an amazingly quick and confident return" at this "deservedly popular" gastropub, which has "reopened with an improved layout, and improved cooking!" / ***Details:*** *www.theunrulypig.co.uk; 9.30 pm, Fri & Sat 10 pm, Sun 8 pm, Closed Mon.*

BROMLEY, GREATER LONDON 3–3B

Cinnamon Culture £57 [3][3][3]
46 Plaistow Ln BR1 3PA (020) 8289 0322
"Given that it's in a part of the world where the branded norms prevail", this Indian independent "stands out as a local beacon" with its "smart surroundings", "friendly, attentive service" and "fabulously spiced" cuisine. / ***Details:*** *www.cinnamonculture.com; 10.30 pm, weekends 11 pm; closed Mon; no Amex.*

BROSELEY, SHROPSHIRE 5–4B

King And Thai £40 [5][3][3]
Broseley TF12 5DL (01952) 882004
"The good folk of Ironbridge and Broseley are very lucky having this converted pub on their doorstep"; "you think you're having something predictable, but the cooking is better than imagined" (namely Thai cuisine with a "superb use of fresh seasonal and regional ingredients"). / ***Details:*** *www.thekingandthai.co.uk/restaurant; 9 pm.*

BROUGHTON, LANCASHIRE 5–1A

Italian Orchard £41 [3][3][3]
96 Whittingham Ln PR3 5DB (01772) 861240
"Hard up against the M6", a "vast", "very busy", "Britalian" venue (part of a local mini-chain owned by the Braganini family), "serving hundreds of covers an hour". It offers "every sort of pizza and pasta, but the main culinary interest is on the specials board". / ***Details:*** *www.italianorchard.com; 10.30 pm.*

BROUGHTON, NORTH YORKSHIRE 8–4B

Bull at Broughton £44 [3][4][3]
BD23 3AE (01756) 792065
This spruced-up outpost of Ribble Valley Inns "has a menu with something for everyone", and is consistently well rated by reporters. / ***Details:*** *www.thebullatbroughton.com; 8.30 pm, Fri & Sat 9 pm; No bookings.*

BRUTON, SOMERSET 2–3B

At the Chapel £49 [3][2][4]
28 High St BA10 0AE (01749) 814070
A "delightful", "light and airy" converted chapel that's great "for weekend meals en famille"; the pizzas are "spectacular", the coffee "brilliant", and the room infused with "delicious smells from the in-house bakery". "If you stay overnight, the croissants are wonderful" too. / ***Details:*** *www.atthechapel.co.uk; 9.30 pm, Sun 8 pm. /* ***Accommodation:*** *8 rooms, from £100*

Roth Bar & Grill £39 [3][4][4]
Durslade Farm, Dropping Ln BA10 0NL
(01749) 814060
"Bruton is very lucky" to have this "striking", salvage-chic café, part of blue chip gallery Hauser & Wirth's West Country seat. Catherine Butler (of much-loved local eatery At The Chapel) oversees some "amazing" farm-to-table food, and "the atmosphere is great". / ***Details:*** *www.rothbarandgrill.co.uk; 9pm.*

BUCKFASTLEIGH, DEVON 1–3D

Riverford Field Kitchen £49 [4][3][4]
Wash Barn, Buckfast Leigh TQ11 0JU
(01803) 762074
"You do take pot luck not only on the menu (which depends upon what is fresh on the farm) but also on the companions sharing your table", yet it's "worth a visit to Devon" to eat the "yummy" food at this purpose-built communal-dining venue – and in particular its "most inventive use of fresh organic veg". "A walk around the farm in the drizzle is just what you need to round off your visit!" / ***Details:*** *www.riverford.co.uk; 8 pm; closed Sun D; Booking lunch only.*

BUNBURY, CHESHIRE 5–3B

The Dysart Arms £44 [3][4][4]
Bowes Gate Road CW6 9PH (01829) 260 183
A "typical Cheshire pub" owned by Brunning & Price, and garnering "high marks all round". Many reports note good visits and better ones ("one visit soufflés were ordinary, another perfect"... "an extensive menu that's reliable, with occasional flair"). / ***Details:*** *www.dysartarms-bunbury.co.uk; 9.30 pm, Sun 9 pm.*

BURTON BRADSTOCK, DORSET 2–4B

Hive Beach Cafe £43 [4][2][3]
Beach Road DT6 4RF (01308) 897 070
"Rickety tables, self service, draughty...but you won't find fresher fish", and "everyone including

the dog is welcome" – that's the equation at this "unbeatably situated" café. "Getting a spot on a sunny day requires application and guile" ("you find your own table", and "the ambience is not always great, because of the rush for seats"). / **Details:** *www.hivebeachcafe.co.uk; 5pm, 8 pm July & August only; L only; No bookings.* / **Accommodation:** *2 rooms, from £95*

Seaside Boarding House Hotel **£54** **345**
Cliff Road DT6 4RB (01308) 897205
This year-old venture from the people behind London media hangout The Groucho has a marvellous location (a chi-chi clifftop hotel overlooking Dorset's Jurassic Coast). Even a reporter who found the "menu a bit dull", rated the food well, "plus there are happy hour cocktails!" / **Details:** *www.theseasideboardinghouse.com; 10 pm.*

BURY ST EDMUNDS, SUFFOLK 3-1C

Maison Bleue **£56** **544**
30-31 Churchgate St IP33 1RG
(01284) 760 623
"Just lovely", "immense attention to detail", "beautiful fish dishes", "A1 service", "top-class environment"... the superlatives flow in feedback on Pascal and Karine Canavet's "very French" luminary, near the cathedral of this gorgeous town; its speciality is "fresh fish, cooked to perfection". / **Details:** *www.maisonbleue.co.uk; 9 pm, Sat 9.30 pm; closed Mon & Sun.*

1921 **£49** **543**
19-21 Angel Hill IP33 1UZ (01284) 704870
Zack Deakins's "fabulous" yearling "will get ever-busier and better known, because the quality and value this pedigree team are producing is first rate"; "tremendous care and attention to detail goes into every dish", and it delivers "Michelin star-style food at very reasonable prices" (if, perhaps, in "cheffy rather than Suffolk portion sizes"). "It's a lovely chilled venue too, with delightful staff". / **Details:** *nineteen-twentyone.co.uk; 9.30 pm; closed Sun; No bookings.*

The One Bull **£50** **344**
25 Angel Hill IP33 1UZ (01284) 848220
"The simple, effective and enjoyable food is a real surprise in terms of quality" but the big deal is the "cracking beer and wine" – "on a different level for an independent regional pub" – at this "absolutely buzzing" haunt (part of a group incorporating the local Brewshed Brewery). / **Details:** *www.theonebull.co.uk; 10pm.*

Pea Porridge **£55** **554**
28-29 Cannon St IP33 1JR (01284) 700200
"So unassuming, a real local eatery, but THE FOOD! – the food beats anything." This "small and delightful classic bistro" is "friendly, relaxed, informal... just what a neighbourhood restaurant should be". Foodwise, however, it's a major step up: Justin Sharp's "cracking and adventurous" fare is "fabulous, including unusual nose-to-tail options", and "his passion for natural wines and enthusiastic support of small producers makes for an intriguing list". There's an "absolutely first-class welcome" too, from staff overseen by Jurga, his wife. / **Details:** *www.peaporridge.co.uk; Mon closed, Tue - Thur 9 pm, Fri & Sat 9.30 pm, Su; closed Mon, Tue L & Sun; no Amex; No bookings.*

Voujon **£35** **343**
29 Mustow St IP33 1XL (01284) 488122
"The best Indian restaurant in the area bar none"; this "classy, well-run establishment" has "built up an excellent reputation" over the past few years for its "high-quality, reasonably priced food". / **Details:** *www.voujonburystedmunds.co.uk; 11.30 pm.*

BUSHEY, HERTFORDSHIRE 3-2A

St James **£46** **332**
30 High St WD23 3HL (020) 8950 2480
A "sustained and noticeable improvement" continues to be noted at this high street stalwart, presided over by "the affable Alonso"; "a longstanding fixture in the culinary desert that is the N London/Herts borderlands", nowadays it's "a proper restaurant" offering "especially good fish dishes" – and "the fact that the place is packed nightly is testament to its success". / **Details:** *www.stjamesrestaurant.co.uk; opp St James Church; 9 pm, Sun 2 pm; closed Sun D; no Amex.*

CAERNARFON, GWYNEDD 4-2C

Blas **£47** **443**
23 - 25 Hole in the Wall Street LL55 1RF
(01286) 677707
"What an unexpected find in Caernarfon!" – by the Royal Welch Fusiliers Museum, a venture whose "really delicious treatment of lovely local ingredients" makes it a particularly "popular" option in these parts. The only problem? – "too much choice on the menu" (which is much more ambitious at night than at lunchtime). / **Details:** *www.blascaernarfon.co.uk; 9 pm; closed Mon & Sun D.*

CAMBER, EAST SUSSEX 3-4C

The Gallivant **£52** **344**
New Lydd Rd TN31 7RB (01797) 225 057
A "great seafood place on an amazing beach"; this nautical-chic restaurant-with-rooms, converted

from an old motel, wins praise for its "fresh, locally caught fish well prepared, cooked and served". Being just metres from the dunes, it's especially "ideal for walking". / **Details:** *www.thegallivant.co.uk; 9.30 pm; Yes; children: under 12s 8.30. /* **Accommodation:** *20 rooms, from £115 /* **Sustainability:** ★★★

CAMBRIDGE, CAMBRIDGESHIRE 3–1B

Alimentum £77 331

152-154 Hills Rd CB2 8PB (01223) 413000

"The location isn't fab as it's on a busy road at a main junction, which you have to get across as the parking is on the far side", and "some criticise the rather stark red-and-black interior" too ("wonderful and modern" to fans, but "just doesn't work" to critics). Perhaps it's all part of "balancing innovation with a conservative local clientele"? Certainly the "unfussy" service was the least controversial point this year – "charming, and just the right side of attentive"; foodwise, Mark Poynton's brave venture is a 'Marmite' experience: for some it's bitterly disappointing ("I was so pleased when this restaurant got its Michelin star, but visiting after two years, I found it complacent and lazy"); for the majority it's "exciting as ever, precise, fun, and with great ingredients"; and for one fan it's "out of this world". / **Details:** *www.restaurantalimentum.co.uk; Mon-Thu 9.30 pm, Sat 10 pm, Sun 9 pm.*

The Cambridge Chop House £53 323

1 Kings Parade CB2 1SJ (01223) 359506

Whilst "it's mainly a pre-theatre standby", according to the general consensus, this operation opposite King's is worth remembering for its dependable (meat-focused) traditional British fare. / **Details:** *www.cambscuisine.com; 10.30 pm, Sat 11 pm, Sun 9.30 pm.*

Cotto £84 543

183 East Rd CB1 1BG (01223) 302010

Hans Schweitzer's "spectacularly good" cuisine is an "11/10" for practically all who report on this peripherally located spot (on a busy road, near the Grafton Centre). "Italian in inspiration, the food is simply gobsmackingly gorgeous and especially the desserts; lovely staff and a cosy feel to the place all add up to make this smallish restaurant a romantic highlight – and there aren't too many in Cambridge!" / **Details:** *www.cottocambridge.co.uk; 9.15 pm; D only, Wed-Sat; no Amex; need + to book.*

Fitzbillies £45 222

51 - 52 Trumpington Street CB2 1RG

(01223) 352 500

"A Cambridge institution" – a "cute little spot that holds on to its history" (including the original sign) and where, above all, "you have to try the Chelsea buns" ("but maybe take a friend and share!"). As a more serious place to eat, however, food journalist Tim Hayward's "upmarket café" can be a letdown, with food that's "no doubt very trendy, but quite strange", and service that – albeit "very friendly" – falls short. / **Details:** *www.fitzbillies.com; Mon - Thur 6 pm, Fri & Sat 7 pm, Sun 6 pm; closed Mon D, Tue D, Wed D & Sun D.*

Midsummer House £141 544

Midsummer Common CB4 1HA

(01223) 369299

"What a revelation to find this gastronomic oasis in Cambridge"; Daniel Clifford's Victorian villa – "fantastically located" on Midsummer Common, by the Cam – is nowadays one of the survey's top 5 most commented-on destinations outside London and, with the help of his team and continual investment in the property, it "radiates classy self-confidence". "An updating of the dining room with an open-plan kitchen has led to a far more relaxed atmosphere", there's "an upstairs bar overlooking the river", and the option to "end with coffee and petit fours in the walled garden" when the weather's fine. "Superb" staff deliver "a wonderful array" of "spectacular" dishes (plus "well-chosen wine pairings") "with just the right degree of theatre", and you choose from a series of "innovative tasting menus, with a choice as to the number of courses". No prize for guessing the catch! – even fans can choke on the "London prices in the provinces". / **Details:** *www.midsummerhouse.co.uk; Mon closed, Tue - Sat 9.30 pm, Sun closed; closed Mon, Tue L & Sun.*

Navadhanya £50 443

73 Newmarket Rd CB5 8EG (01223) 300583

"Not your regular curry house", but rather a refined two-year-old venture specialising in "amazing, beautifully cooked Indian food" which is "served with style". / **Details:** *www.navadhanya.co.uk.*

Oak Bistro £49 333

6 Lensfield Road CB2 1EG (01223) 323 361

"If you don't like chains, this is a good bistro halfway between the railway station and gown town"; "externally it looks relatively unpromising", but inside it's a "light and airy" room combining "a bit of character" with "reasonably priced" grub. / **Details:** *www.theoakbistro.co.uk; Mon - Thur 9.30 pm, Fri & Sat 9.45 pm, Sun closed; closed Sun; No bookings.*

Pint Shop £44 323

10 Peas Hill CB2 3PN (01223) 352 293

"An enviable range of ales and gins" adds vim to this "fun and fairly priced" gastropub two-year-old – an "energetic and welcoming" hang-out, serving "simple but excellent" cooking. When busy, though, it can be "super noisy and super slow". / **Details:** *www.pintshop.co.uk; 11 pm.*

The St John's Chop House — £50 232

21-24 Northampton St CB3 0AD
(01223) 353 110

Occupying a 19th-century brick building, this meat-centric eatery is worth remembering. Arguably "it's not as good as the main Chop House in Cambridge", but fans find it a useful option thanks to its "well-presented and tasty" fare. / **Details:** *www.cambscuisine.com/st-johns-chop-house; 10.30 pm, Sun 9 pm.*

Steak & Honour — £15 442

various locations CB2 1AA (07766) 568430

"If you can find out where they will be" – presumably easier now that "the secret's out", and they're "operating two vans" – then "make an effort to try one of their burgers: it doesn't get better than this!"; it's "far too popular though, so you have to queue". / **Details:** *www.steakandhonour.co.uk; 10 pm.*

Restaurant 22 — £56 [illegible]44

22 Chesterton Rd CB4 3AX (01223) 351880

Most (if not quite all) reporters "love everything" about this intimate riverfront villa with an elegant (prix fixe-only) Victorian dining room – particularly its "cosy atmosphere", but also its "lovely service" and "creative" cooking. / **Details:** *www.restaurant22.co.uk; Mon closed, Tue - Sat 9 pm, Sun closed; D only, closed Mon & Sun; children: 12+.*

Yippee Noodle Bar — £31 443

7-9 King St CB1 1LH (01223) 518111

"They do not come more cheap 'n' cheerful than this" – an "outstanding-value" joint, in the city centre, that's also noted for its "fast and boisterous atmosphere". / **Details:** *www.yippeenoodlebar.co.uk; 10 pm.*

CANTERBURY, KENT 3–3D

The Ambrette Canterbury — £48 433

14 - 15 Beer Cart Lane CT1 2NY
(01227) 200 777

Dev Biswal's converted pub (still with a bar for drinking) inspires just as much feedback as his Margate original. Gripes include "a slight lack of ambience" and "variable" standards, but most accounts are full of praise for its "airy" atmosphere and "expertly prepared Indian/British fusion dishes that are surprisingly good value". / **Details:** *www.theambrette.co.uk; Mon - Thur 9.30 pm, Fri - Sun 10 pm.*

Café des Amis — £42 434

95 St Dunstan's St CT2 8AD (01227) 464390

There's "always a fun and colourful atmosphere" at this long-running haunt by the Westgate; on the menu, "quality Mexican food (and the chocolate cake is great!)" / **Details:** *www.cafedez.com; 10 pm, Fri & Sat 10.30 pm, Sun 9.30 pm; Booking max 6 may apply.*

Cafe du Soleil — £43 333

4-5 Pound Lane CT1 2BZ (01227) 479999

A brick-walled riverside venue in a former 18th-century wool store; its "fantastic pizzas (courtesy of a proper wood-burning pizza oven)" continue to be the main event, and come "generously topped with tasty and quality produce". / **Details:** *www.cafedusoleil.co.uk; 10 pm.*

Cafe Mauresque — £42 434

8 Butchery Ln CT1 2JR (01227) 464300

"Very convenient for visiting the cathedral and city centre", this Andalucian/North African basement joint wins acclaim for its "great-tasting, authentic" food, backdropped by "suitable (Moorish) decor" / **Details:** *www.cafemauresque.com; 10 pm, Fri & Sat 10.30 pm.*

The Compasses Inn — £48 434

Sole Street CT4 7ES (01227) 700 300

A "charming country pub out in the wilds"; it's "not easy to access", but worth the hassle owing to its "consistently excellent" food and "great hosts". / **Details:** *www.thecompassescrundale.co.uk.*

County Restaurant, ABode Canterbury — £58 332

High St CT1 2RX (01227) 766266

This city-centre hotel dining room is well-rated on a number of fronts – from breakfast through to tasting menus with accompanying wines; "the lunch menu is a good reason to pause shopping whilst in Canterbury". / **Details:** *www.abodecanterbury.co.uk; 10.30 pm; closed Sun D. /* **Accommodation:** *72 rooms, from £125*

Deeson's British Restaurant — £51 342

25-27 Sun St CT1 2HX (01227) 767854

"Deeson's delivers time after time"; close to the cathedral and theatre, a "wonderful family-friendly restaurant" combining "very pleasant staff" and "food you can depend on" (in an "unfussy British style"). Small niggle? It might "benefit if they didn't cram in so many tables". / **Details:** *www.deesonsrestaurant.co.uk; 10 pm.*

Adam's, Birmingham

The Forest Side, Grasmere

The Painswick, Painswick

Goods Shed £50 335
Station Road West CT2 8AN (01227) 459153
"Eating over the permanent farmer's market creates a special ambience" at this foodie favourite, near Canterbury West station. "Sourcing is from the stalls" – "good quality ingredients plainly cooked and in fairly hearty portions" – and "if you're in Canterbury of a Saturday, brunch is a must, and you can also buy most of your weekend shopping!" / **Details:** *www.thegoodsshed.co.uk; 9.30 pm; closed Mon & Sun D.*

CARDIFF, CARDIFF 2–2A

Arbennig £45 333
6-10 Romilly Cr CF11 9NR (029) 2034 1264
On the site some still remember as Le Gallois (long RIP), John and Ceri Cook's "stark" no-tablecloth venture occupies a Pontcanna site long associated with being one of the city's top eating options. Some feedback this year was of the "OK but nothing special" variety, however. / **Details:** *www.arbennig.co.uk; 9.30 pm, Sat 10 pm, Sun 4 pm; closed Mon & Sun D.*

Casanova £47 332
13 Quay St CF10 1EA (029) 2034 4044
"A jewel of an old-fashioned Italian" which achieved very consistent support this year. / **Details:** *www.casanovacardiff.com; 10 pm; closed Sun.*

Fish at 85 £51 322
85 Pontcanna St CF11 9HS (029) 2023 5666
"If you don't mind eating in a shopping parade", or the "overpowering smell of fish", head to this "curiosity" – a "fish shop by day (not cheap) and a restaurant by night" where you "choose from the slab" hosting the day's catch, and results are "excellent". / **Details:** *www.fishat85.co.uk; Tue & Wed 8.30 pm, Thu-Sat 9 pm; closed Mon & Sun; no Amex.*

Moksh £38 433
Ocean Building, Bute Cr CF10 5AY
(029) 2049 8120
A nouvelle Indian, on the quayside, whose Goan-inspired dishes are "simply delicious", and "on an elevated level to your average curry house". / **Details:** *www.moksh.co.uk; 10.30 pm, Fri & Sat 11.30 pm; closed Mon.*

The Potted Pig £53 423
27 High Street CF10 1PU (029) 2022 4817
A location in underground bank vaults lends this dining room a certain drama; limited feedback on the cooking (which includes a selection of steaks) this year, but all of it positive. / **Details:** *www.thepottedpig.com; Mon closed, Tu - Thur 9 pm, Fri & Sat 9.30 pm, Sun; closed Mon & Sun D.*

Purple Poppadom £47 432
185a, Cowbridge Road East CF11 9AJ
(029) 2022 0026
"I visit as often as I can, and I have always said I don't like Indian cuisine!"; this popular curry house has a "slightly offputting location" ("over a shop on Cowbridge Road East") but many continue to reckon its "posh" Indian dishes "by far the best food in Cardiff". / **Details:** *purplepoppadom.com; Mon-Sat 11 pm, Sun 9 pm.*

Vegetarian Food Studio £21 442
115-117 Penarth Rd CF11 6JU
(029) 2023 8222
This beloved and simply decorated veggie by the Taff continues to inspire only the most positive feedback for its "huge, high quality portions" (and at "very low prices" too); "it really earns its place in your guide!" / **Details:** *www.vegetarianfoodstudio.co.uk; 9.30 pm, Sun 7 pm; closed Mon; no Amex.*

CARLISLE, CUMBRIA 7–2D

Alexandros £44 342
68 Warwick Road CA1 1DR (01228) 592227
A "deservedly popular" Greek deli/restaurant that "can always be relied upon for a good meal", be it comprised of "really fresh" fish or weekly specials "with a more modern twist"; "Aris, the owner, works extremely hard to ensure the quality of the food he serves and that everyone has a good time". / **Details:** *www.thegreek.co.uk; Mon - Fri 9.45 pm, Sat 10 pm, Sun closed; closed Mon L & Sun.*

CARTMEL FELL, CUMBRIA 7–4D

The Masons Arms £44 345
Strawberry Bank LA11 6NW (01539) 568486
"Magnificent views from the garden complement the first-class, imaginative food" (and in "ridiculously big portions") at this "truly excellent" timber-beamed Lakeland pub; add in "great warm fires" and a "friendly vibe" and it "can get very busy" – "get there early". / **Details:** *www.strawberrybank.com; W from Bowland Bridge, off A5074; 9 pm.* / **Accommodation:** *7 rooms, from £75*

CARTMEL, CUMBRIA 7–4D

L'Enclume £172 554
Cavendish St LA11 6PZ (01539) 536362
"Worth driving the length of the country for lunch!" – Simon Rogan's "beautiful old building in a stunningly romantic Lake District village" is "superb all round, and it's not hard to understand why it's such a powerful attraction" (the survey's third most commented-on restaurant outside of London).

*"Every course is a conversation starter", and the cooking delivers "pure theatre";"the most indulgent, understanding, fun, exciting, tasty gastronomic journey ever – 17 courses so perfectly balanced, and so packed with flavour that it left me fully satisfied yet begging for more!"The year has not been without its challenges – ex-head chef Mark Birchall's departure is noted by the odd regular (who feels the menu is more "stagnant" as a result), but Sam Ward's promotion from his post as maître d' has done little to dent the "impeccable", "almost choreographed" service, and for most guests this is "an astonishing, clever, occasionally challenging, and brilliant" experience. / **Details:** www.lenclume.co.uk; J36 from M6, down A590 towards Cartmel; 9 pm; closed Mon L & Tue L. / **Accommodation:** 16 rooms, from £119*

Rogan & Co **£59** 3 3 2
Devonshire Square LA11 6QD (01539) 535917
*"Rogan at accessible prices" is the aim of this "small and intimate" brasserie, near the mothership. The feeling lingers that "it used to be great, but has got a few things to work on to hit its original level" (and is "underwhelming if you compare it to L'Enclume"). That said, "for the same price as an ordinary meal in a Lakeland pub you get interesting and delicious food". / **Details:** www.roganandcompany.co.uk; Mon - Sat 9 pm, Sun 5 pm; closed Sun; no Amex.*

CASTLE COMBE, WILTSHIRE 2–2B

Bybrook Restaurant, Manor House Hotel **£104** 4 4 4
SN14 7HR (01249) 782206
*Given its gastronomic renown, this grand medieval house in a lovely Cotswolds village inspires surprisingly limited feedback; such as there is gives consistently very high ratings to Rob Potter's cuisine (he took to the stoves in February 2016) and to the romantic setting. / **Details:** www.exclusivehotels.co.uk; 9 pm, Fri & Sat 9.30 pm; closed Mon L & Tue L; No jeans; children: 11+. / **Accommodation:** 48 rooms, from £205*

CAVENDISH, SUFFOLK 3–1C

The George **£46** 3 3 3
The Green CO10 8BA (01787) 280248
*"An attractive timbered building in a pretty village, with a very nice 'Country Living' atmosphere, and whose clientele make it feel like the gastropub equivalent of Waitrose (all ages may be present, from babies to grandparents, plus dogs)". The food is "reliably well prepared" – "not always a gourmet choice, but a great spot for a relaxed family meal". / **Details:** www.thecavendishgeorge.co.uk; 9.30 pm, Sun 3 pm; closed Sun D. / **Accommodation:** 5 rooms, from £75*

CHADDESLEY CORBETT, WORCESTERSHIRE 5–4B

Brockencote Hall **£66** 4 3 4
DY10 4PY (01562) 777876
*The Eden Collection's "beautiful" Victorian country house hotel "in a lovely setting" is "back on form", say fans, with the cuisine "improving all the time". Former sous chef Tim Jenkins was appointed to the top job (post survey) in August 2016 – here's hoping it continues the good run. / **Details:** www.brockencotehall.com; on A448, outside village; 9 pm; No trainers. / **Accommodation:** 21 rooms, from £135*

CHAGFORD, DEVON 1–3C

Chagford Inn **£47** 4 4 2
7 Mill St TQ13 8AW (01647) 433109
*"Excellent hearty fayre from a brilliant nose-to-tail menu of local produce, served by very knowledgeable staff" make it worth truffling out this "pub-with-rooms in a pretty village" in the Dartmoor National Park. "They butcher the meat on site and we had the beef which was tasty and large!" / **Details:** www.thechagfordinn.com/.*

Gidleigh Park **£157** 5 5 5
TQ13 8HH (01647) 432367
*"Obviously everyone was nervous about the departure of Michael Caines, but fear not!" – "Michael Wignall is off to a fine start" at this famous Tudorbethan manor house discovered "after a terrifying drive up a narrow lane" on the fringes of Dartmoor. Once ensconced, there's the chance to "relax in the beautiful lounge and enjoy a warm welcome" amidst a setting of "country sophistication", before moving onto the main event in the dining room. The new kitchen's output is "utterly amazing – so quirky and gorgeous" and backed up by an "exceptional wine list". / **Details:** www.gidleigh.com; from village, right at Lloyds TSB, take right fork to end of lane; No jeans; children: 8+. / **Accommodation:** 24 rooms, from £350*

CHANDLER'S CROSS, HERTFORDSHIRE 3–2A

Colette's, The Grove **£105** 2 2 3
WD17 3NL (01923) 296015
*This tranquil but pricey country house hotel inspired relatively scant commentary this year for its main dining room, but – though it didn't impress all reporters – ex-Petrus chef Russell Bateman's ambitious tasting menus were generally well rated. / **Details:** www.thegrove.co.uk; 9.30 pm; D only, closed Mon & Sun; children: 16+. / **Accommodation:** 227 rooms, from £310*

The Glasshouse, The Grove **£70** **2 3 2**
WD3 4TG (01923) 296015
While there's the odd sceptic, for whom the "informal" second dining room of this lavish country house hotel is "overpriced", the general verdict is that it still offers a "great experience for a special occasion", where "the buffet format means that something is bound to appeal"; "let off some energy afterwards with a run around the grounds". / **Details:** *www.thegrove.co.uk; 9.30 pm, Sat 10 pm.* / **Accommodation:** *227 rooms, from £0*

Prime Steak & Grill, The Clarendon **£65** **3 2 3**
Redhall Lane WD3 4LU (01923) 264 580
The main event – sourced from an HRH-approved butcher's no less – is consistently "well cooked and tasty" at this former pub (nowadays an "always busy" country eatery). / **Details:** *www.primesteakandgrill.com/chandlers-cross.*

CHEADLE, CHESHIRE 5–2B

Indian Tiffin Room **4 4 3**
2 Chapel Street SK8 1BR (0161) 491 2020
A buzzing Indian street food spot whose "superb", "authentic" cuisine elicits raves from all who comment on it; "booking is essential as it's so popular, and rightly so". NB The owners opened an "interesting" new sibling in Manchester's gentrified First Street development in 2016. / **Details:** *www.indiantiffinroom.com; 10 pm.*

CHELMSFORD, ESSEX 3–2C

Galvin Green Man
Howe St CM3 1BG (01245) 408820
Set in 1.5 acres of riverside meadows, this bucolic country pub (dating back to the 14th century) is the first step outside London for the Galvin Bros new departure into pubs. Opening was set for November 2016.

CHELTENHAM, GLOUCESTERSHIRE 2–1C

L'Artisan **£59** **3 4 4**
30 Clarence St GL50 3NX (01242) 571257
The Ogrodzki's Gallic three-year-old is a real hit locally – "how wonderful to find a truly French restaurant in Cheltenham, serving satisfyingly traditional food". / **Details:** *www.lartisan-restaurant.com.*

Bhoomi **£53** **5 4 3**
52 Suffolk Rd GL50 2AQ (01242) 222 010
Experience "South Indian food at its best in this stunning, newly refurbished Cheltenham restaurant" – a plush dining room where the "faultless" Keralan dishes are invariably served "with care and attention to detail". / **Details:** *www.bhoomi.co.uk.*

Le Champignon Sauvage **£85** **5 5 3**
24-28 Suffolk Rd GL50 2AQ (01242) 573449
"Genuine food served by genuine people" is the essence of the ongoing success of the Everitt-Matthias's foodie legend – "celebrating 30 years next year, from a husband-and-wife team who have never missed a service... if the restaurant is open, they are always there". It's "a two-Michelin-star restaurant which has never rested on its laurels, with David's dishes constantly evolving and wowing guests and critics alike" ("foraging has become the norm these days, but David was doing it years before the rest caught up") and Helen's service coming with "total knowledge of the food and wines". The "pleasant" but low-key room is perhaps the weakest link, but "don't we make our own atmosphere? It was an amazing experience!" / **Details:** *www.lechampignonsauvage.co.uk; 8.30 pm; closed Mon & Sun.*

East India Cafe **£50** **3 3 3**
103 Promenade GL50 1NW (01242) 300850
"Unusual dishes inspired by The Raj" are "served with style" at this year-old basement, and the service "couldn't be more friendly and welcoming"; "the monthly cookery demos, with lunch and historical anecdotes are great fun and book up quickly". / **Details:** *www.eastindiacafe.com; 10 pm; closed Mon.*

Lumière **£83** **4 5 4**
Clarence Parade GL50 3PA (01242) 222200
"Enchanting service from the chef's wife Helen and her front of house team" adds further lustre to Jon Howe's "elegantly presented" cuisine at their "peaceful and relaxed" venture, where one reporter particularly appreciated the "exceptional care taken to accommodate all dietary requirements". / **Details:** *www.lumiere.cc; Mon closed, Tue - Sat 8.30 pm, Sun closed; closed Mon, Tue L, Wed L, Thu L & Sun; children: 8+ at D.*

No 131 **£64** **2 1 3**
131 Promenade GL50 1NW (01242) 822939
"Lovely interior design" – "jaw-droppingly impressive" to fans, but "a bit dead" to others – features in all reports on this Grade II-listed mansion on the promenade. Results from the "quirky menu" are likewise a bit mixed, but no disasters are reported, while service veers from "very attentive" to "truly amateur". / **Details:** *www.no131.com; 11 pm.*

Prithvi **£48** **5 5 3**
37 Bath Road GL53 7HG (01242) 226229
This "sensational 'haute cuisine' Indian" is one of the town's most notable culinary addresses thanks to its "very sophisticated approach with a modern twist to subcontinental cooking"; it's "a great treat,

*with delightful staff, delivering delicious and subtle flavours". / **Details:** www.prithvirestaurant.com; Mon closed, Tue - Sat 9.45 om, Sun closed; closed Mon & Tue L; no Amex.*

Purslane **£59** **4 4 4**
16 Rodney Rd GL50 1JJ (01242) 321639
*"Adding a touch more sparkle to the Cheltenham fine dining scene, Purslane has an added attraction in its unpretentiousness". The "intimate" venue is a "small", "quite plainly decorated" venture in a backstreet; on the menu, a good deal of "inventive, bright and surprising cuisine", and in particular "outstanding" fish. "Gareth Fulford is definitely (Michelin) star material". / **Details:** www.purslane-restaurant.co.uk; 9.30 pm; closed Mon & Sun.*

The White Spoon **£52** **3 3 3**
Well Wk GL50 3JX (01242) 228 555
*This "romantically lit" room overlooking a church makes "a fantastic addition to Cheltenham's dining choices". A "few bum notes" were reported – the "strange" flavour combinations bear witness to chef Christopher White's Fat Duck heritage – but, for early days, the majority found it "generally excellent". / **Details:** www.thewhitespoon.co.uk.*

CHESTER, CHESHIRE 5–2A

ABode Restaurant, ABode Hotels **£67** **4 3 3**
Grosvener Rd CH1 2DJ (01244) 347 000
*So far the exit of celeb chef Michael Caines, who has left the ABode Group to launch his own Devon hotel (Lympstone Manor) in February 2017, hasn't hurt this "fifth-floor hotel-restaurant with pleasant views" of the town and racecourse; while still sometimes considered "expensive", fans say that the "great, enthusiastic young team is cooking up a storm". / **Details:** www.michaelcaines.com; 9.45 pm, Sun 9 pm; No jeans. / **Accommodation:** 85 rooms, from £100*

Architect **£44** **2 2 3**
54 Nicholas Street CH1 2NX (01244) 353070
*Fans "love all the rooms, love the outside, and have never been disappointed" at this pretty Georgian-era gastropub by Chester Racecourse. For a growing band of cynics, though, "the quality has gone down" of late – "they seem to be adopting a standard menu replicated across most of the Brunning & Price pub group". / **Details:** www.brunningandprice.co.uk/architect; Mon - Sat 10 pm, Sun 9.30 pm; no Amex.*

La Brasserie, Chester Grosvenor **£67** **2 3 4**
Eastgate CH1 1LT (01244) 324024
*"Reasonable food and lots of buzz" are amongst the plus points of this swish haunt (which "recent refurbishment has made even more attractive"), by the city's famous clock. You choose from "a compact brasserie menu, with an affordable wine list to match". / **Details:** www.chestergrosvenor.com; 10 pm, Sun 9 pm. / **Accommodation:** 80 rooms, from £230*

The Chef's Table **£49** **4 4 3**
4 Music Hall Pas CH1 2EU (01244) 403040
*"Exceptional", conscientiously sourced dishes and "friendly staff" (plus second-hand cookery books, craft beers and superior cocktails) have made a big name for this low-key yearling, in a discreet city-centre passage; the "only downside is that it's a little too crowded". / **Details:** www.chefstablechester.co.uk; 9 pm, Fri & Sat 9.30 pm, Sun 3.45pm; closed Mon & Sun.*

1539 **£52** **3 3 4**
The Racecourse CH1 2LY (01244) 304 611
*"Fantastic views across the smallest racecourse in the country" are one excuse to visit this airy and attractive outfit; others include a dining room that's "perfect for business" (nice and quiet, with "plenty of space between tables)", plus "great food and quality wines". / **Details:** www.restaurant1539.co.uk; Mon-Sat 10pm, Sun 8pm; No bookings.*

Hickorys Smokehouse **£43** **3 3 4**
Souters Lane CH1 1SH (01244) 404000
*"A great location by the river (with outside tables available)" is a prime feature of this "American style BBQ" – one of a local chain along the North Wales coast. It's a "noisy, buzzy, slick operation" (and a notably kid-friendly one), serving "high quality burgers" and other meatylicious fare. / **Details:** www.hickorys.co.uk/chester; 11 pm.*

Joseph Benjamin **£50** **3 3 3**
140 Northgate St CH1 2HT (01244) 344295
*"Close to the city walls", a "small and intimate" deli-restaurant well rated for its imaginative fare. / **Details:** www.josephbenjamin.co.uk; 9.30 pm; closed Mon, Tue D, Wed D & Sun D.*

Moules A Go Go **£42** **3 3 3**
6-12 Cuppin St CH1 2BN (01244) 348818
*After 17 years on the city's medieval rows, this "reliable favourite" upped sticks to Cuppin Street, and the former site of La Tasca, in summer 2016; we've maintained its ratings, assuming continuity in its "gorgeous" cuisine – from steaks and rotisserie fare to the "divine" main event. / **Details:** www.moulesagogo.co.uk; 10 pm, Sun 9 pm.*

Simon Radley, The Chester Grosvenor **£106** **3 4 3**
56-58 Eastgate Street CH1 1LT
(01244) 324024
By the Eastgate Clock, the Duke of Westminster's gracious property is unusually grand for a

small-town hotel, and its "rather old-fashioned" dining room (a windowless space in the heart of the building) has long held a major culinary reputation under Simon Rudley. It drew a few critical reviews this year, and even some supporters say the food is "aiming slightly higher than it delivers". Overall, however, it scores high ratings for cuisine that "provides a kaleidoscope of taste and texture over a series of theatrical courses", and for its very heavyweight wine list (plus the "best bread board ever encountered"). / **Details:** *www.chestergrosvenor.com; Mon closed, Tue - Sat 9 pm, Sun closed; D only, closed Mon & Sun; No trainers; children: 12+.* / **Accommodation:** *80 rooms, from £230*

Sticky Walnut **£50** 454

11 Charles St CH2 3AZ (01244) 400400

Gary Usher's small bistro in Hoole, a little outside the city centre, has found fame not just because he's so adept at plugging himself on social media – but also because of its "decent value" cooking, "really interesting wine list", and "lovely" ambience. / **Details:** *www.stickywalnut.com; 9 pm, Fri & Sat 10 pm; Credit card deposit required to book.*

Upstairs at the Grill **£51** 443

70 Watergate St CH1 2LA (01244) 344883

"Excellent steaks" underpin the simple but successful formula of this split-level, Manhattan-style steakhouse and speakeasy bar, which remains one of the most popular destinations in town. / **Details:** *www.upstairsatthegrill.co.uk; 10.30 pm, Sun 9.30 pm; closed Mon L, Tue L & Wed L.*

CHEW MAGNA, SOMERSET 2–2B

The Pony & Trap **£62** 433

Chew Magna BS40 8TQ (01275) 332 627

"Great, great pub food" has won acclaim from the tyre men for Josh Eggleton's "friendly" gastroboozer, which enjoys "lovely views out over the country", helping to make it "the perfect way to break up a journey to Devon". He's opening in Bristol too (see Kensington Arms). / **Details:** *www.theponyandtrap.co.uk; 9.30 pm; closed Mon; no Amex.*

CHICHESTER, WEST SUSSEX 3–4A

Field & Fork **£45** 322

4 Guildhall St PO19 1NJ (01243) 789915

Sam and Janet Mahoney launched this conservatory venture in 2014; it's hailed (including for pre-theatre) as one of the better local options, with "reliable, light and imaginative" fare. / **Details:** *www.fieldandfork.co.uk; 10 pm; closed Mon, Tue D, Wed D, Thu D, Fri D, Sat D & Sun D.*

Pallant 323

East Pallant PO19 1TJ (01243) 770827

"Under new management and with a softer ambience" – the café has moved to another part of the building – as well as a "much improved menu", the restaurant attached to the "excellent" Pallant House Gallery is now "a very useful spot" indeed. / **Details:** *www.pallantrestaurantandcafe.co.uk; 9 pm.*

The Richmond Arms **£50** 443

Mill Road, West Ashling PO18 8EA (01243) 775537

A "lively" gastropub-with-rooms, on the Goodwood Estate, where the wine and food – including tapas and wood-fired pizzas – are "consistently interesting"; while "not cheap", it's "still excellent value for the quality and service". / **Details:** *www.therichmondarms.co.uk; 9 pm; closed Mon, Tue & Sun D.*

CHINNOR, OXFORDSHIRE 2–2D

The Sir Charles Napier **£68** 535

Spriggs Alley OX39 4BX (01494) 483011

"Cosy in winter", with the "lovely open fire in the bar", and particularly "beautiful in summer, when the wonderful garden and woodland make it possible to imagine you're on a terrace in the South of France", Julie Griffiths's "homely-yet-smart country pub-style restaurant" is "perfect for a lunch stop off the M40". Service is notably "charming" (even if it can be "distracted" and "slow"), and foodwise "this old favourite is going through a culinary purple patch" at present, serving "absolutely brilliant", "hearty" fare. Given the above, despite the fact that it's "in the middle of nowhere", and hard to find, it remains a top bucolic escape for jaded Londonites. / **Details:** *www.sircharlesnapier.co.uk; Tue-Fri 9.30 pm, Sat 10 pm; closed Mon & Sun D.*

CHIPPING CAMPDEN, GLOUCESTERSHIRE 2–1C

The Chef's Dozen **£61** 443

Island Hs, High St GL55 6AL (01386) 840598

A suitably "charming" restaurant in this chi-chi village, where chef Richard Craven turns out "locally sourced, in-season ingredients imaginatively prepared" and is ably abetted by "thoughtful service" from his wife Solanche. / **Details:** *www.thechefsdozen.co.uk; 9 pm; closed Mon, Tue L & Sun.*

The Ebrington Arms **£51** 334

GL55 6NH (01386) 593 223

This beamed B&B in a "lovely" village location is a "generally reliable" option for gastro fare and beers from the owners' microbrewery (they also run the

*Killingworth Castle, across the county border in Wootton). / **Details:** www.theebringtonarms.co.uk; 9 pm; no Amex.*

CHIPPING NORTON, OXFORDSHIRE 2–1C

Wild Thyme £53 343
10 New St OX7 5LJ (01608) 645060
*"Don't hold its Chipping Norton location against it!" – Sally and Nick Pullen's "lovely local" (a restaurant-with-rooms in the town centre) has an "interesting and quirky menu"; niggles about its execution were largely absent this year, with most reports saying it's "always a pleasure". / **Details:** www.wildthymerestaurant.co.uk; 9 pm, Fri & Sat 9.30 pm; closed Mon & Sun. / **Accommodation:** 3 rooms, from £75*

CHOBHAM, SURREY 3–3A

Stovell's £67 544
125 Windsor Road GU24 8QS
(01276) 858000
*"A real find in an area short of quality restaurants" – Fernando & Kristy Stovell's heavily beamed farmhouse, about a mile outside of Chobham, is widely extolled for its "consistently exceptional, innovative-yet-simple cuisine", its "excellent service" and its "delightful", "romantic" setting. "It must be only a matter of time before Michelin is knocking on the door!" / **Details:** www.stovells.com; Mon closed, Tue - Sat 10 pm, Sun 2.30 pm; closed Mon, Sat L & Sun D.*

The White Hart £47 232
High Street GU24 8AA (01276) 857 580
*There's still the odd dissenter, particularly on the food front, but the majority of reporters praise this Brunning & Price gastroboozer, in an increasingly foodie village, for its "good pub fare" and "great weekend brunch". / **Details:** www.whitehart-chobham.co.uk; Mon - Sat 10 pm, Sun 9.30 pm.*

CHOLMONDELEY, CHESHIRE 5–3A

Cholmondeley Arms £43 334
Wrenbury Road SY14 8HN (01829) 720 300
*In a converted Victorian schoolhouse on the Cholmondeley Castle Estate, this "good reliable gastropub" is a hit with all who comment upon it owing to its "warm and hearty" cuisine, as well as a "wide selection of ales, and a wider selection of gins" (they even run a summer 'ginfest'). / **Details:** www.cholmondeleyarms.co.uk; on A49, 6m N of Whitchurch; 10.30 pm; no Amex. / **Accommodation:** 6 rooms, from £80 / **Sustainability:** ★★*

CHRISTCHURCH, DORSET 2–4C

The Jetty £57 545
95 Mudeford BH23 3NT (01202) 400950
*"If the weather is good, there are few finer spots to spend the afternoon" than this "superb location" – "a small, contemporary glass-and-wood structure overlooking Christchurch harbour". "Alex Aitken has a winning formula here (even at the London prices!)", centring on his "fabulous" cooking, with "food sourced within 15 miles". / **Details:** www.thejetty.co.uk; 9.45 pm, Sun 7.45 pm. / **Sustainability:** ★★★*

The Kings Arms Hotel £55 433
18 Castle Street BH23 1DT (01202) 029900
*A stately restaurant-with-rooms in a restored Georgian building, overlooking the bowling green – "always an enjoyable place to stay and eat" thanks to "wonderful, winning food from Alex Aitken's kitchen". / **Details:** www.thekings-christchurch.co.uk; 11pm.*

CHURCHILL, OXFORDSHIRE 2–1C

Chequers £49 433
Church Ln OX7 6NJ (01608) 659393
*It may be "a bit pretentious" (it's a prime haunt of the Chipping Norton set), but even sceptics of the clubby vibe praise the "splendid" food at this cosy local pub – and you "can't beat" the weekday set menu. They've "just added some more outdoor space" so "it's all great for a spot of al fresco eating". / **Details:** www.thechequerschurchill.com; 9.30 pm, Fri & Sat 10.30 pm, sun 9.00pm; closed Sun D.*

CIRENCESTER, GLOUCESTERSHIRE 2–2C

Soushi £37 342
12 Castle St GL7 1QA (01285) 641414
*Tucked away in Cirencester's old post office, this rare, rural Japanese café, with glass doors opening onto a town-centre terrace, has filled a real gap in the market locally; it's a top destination for bento boxes, noodles and "excellent sushi". / **Details:** www.soushi.co.uk; 9.30pm, Fri - Sat 10.30pm.*

CLACHAN, ARGYLL AND BUTE 9–3B

Loch Fyne Oyster Bar £53 443
PA26 8BL (01499) 600264
With marvellous views over the loch, this remote waterside deli and restaurant (part of a well-established local shellfish business and smokery) is only loosely connected with the national chain which bears its name; it's a bracing venue for fresh

seafood and home-smoked salmon. / **Details:** *www.lochfyne.com; 10m E of Inveraray on A83; Mon - Thur 5 pm, Fri - Sun 6 pm.*

CLAYGATE, SURREY 3–3A

The Swan Inn £56

2 Hare Lane KT10 9BS (01372) 462 582
From restaurateur frères, Claude (Hibiscus, W1) and Cedric (The Charlton Arms, Ludlow) Bosi, a new pub-with-rooms close to Esher Common. The brothers have described the menu (overseen by Claude but delivered by head chef Justin West) as 'English food from a Frenchman' – one early report suggests that leads to "an uninspiring menu, but good cooking". / **Details:** *www.theswanesher.co.uk; 9.30 pm, Sun 8.30 pm.* / **Accommodation:** *0 rooms, from £6*

CLIFTON, CUMBRIA 8–3A

George & Dragon £50 333

CA10 2ER (01768) 865381
A "dogs-welcome-in-the-bar" kind of 18th-century inn, hailed for its "great atmosphere" and "the best pub food in the area" – the latter being "more imaginative than most" (and with an accent on local produce). / **Details:** *www.georgeanddragonclifton.co.uk; on the A6 in the village of Clifton; 9 pm; No bookings.* / **Accommodation:** *12 rooms, from £95*

CLIPSHAM, RUTLAND 6–4A

The Olive Branch £53 344

Main St LE15 7SH (01780) 410355
"I can't imagine driving down or up the A1 without stopping here!" – a Rutland-fringe pub which makes a "perfect stop-off". Though not as stellar as when it first opened over a decade ago, it remains one of the UK's best-known gastropubs, thanks to its "warm and engaging service", "very interesting menu and some great beers and wines". "We left replete and happy to carry on with our holiday!" / **Details:** *www.theolivebranchpub.com; 2m E from A1 on B664; 9.30 pm, Sun 9 pm; no Amex.* / **Accommodation:** *6 rooms, from £135*

CLITHEROE, LANCASHIRE 5–1B

The Assheton Arms £47 445

BB7 4BJ (01200) 441227
"The most gorgeous pub" – lead establishment of the ever-growing Seafood Pub Company – set in "the most gorgeous village location, where double-yellow lines, TV aerials, and any other 20th-century paraphernalia is banned". "From a family of fish merchants, you would expect good fish, and you'll not be disappointed", although simpler menu options are a better bet than the more "strange and exotic" choices. / **Details:** *seafoodpubcompany.com/the-assheton-arms/; 9 pm, Fri & Sat 10 pm, Sun 8 pm.* / **Accommodation:** *0 rooms, from £12*

Inn at Whitewell £55 335

Near Clitheroe BB7 3AT (01200) 448222
"The drive is always a treat (whatever the weather)" to this "sublime, tucked-away, romantic inn, set in the heart of the Forest of Bowland" (and one of the North West's best-known escapes). The former fishing lodge on the Duchy of Lancaster's estate "looks stunning, and there's a warm and welcome atmosphere" (helped by its large wine cellar, from which you can also buy retail). In recent times, the feeling has grown that "there's nothing wrong with the cooking, but that it's not inspiring", although some long-term fans insist you get the same "simple but outstanding fare" of yesteryear. / **Details:** *www.innatwhitewell.com; 9.30 pm; bar open L & D, restaurant D only; no Amex.* / **Accommodation:** *23 rooms, from £120*

CLYST HYDON, DEVON 1–3D

The Five Bells Inn £48 434

EX15 2NT (01884) 277288
"A real find"; in a "delightful rural location" amid the Kent Downs, this "tastefully furnished" thatched inn offers "competently executed traditional offerings sourced entirely from local farms and fisherman from Rye" – that, plus "a good deal of local atmosphere". / **Details:** *www.fivebells.uk.com; 9 pm.*

CLYTHA, MONMOUTHSHIRE 2–1A

Clytha Arms £50 333

NP7 9BW (01873) 840206
"Andrew and his staff make one feel like a king" at this well-established inn, where, for example, Sunday lunch can be "a joy! Slabs of tender pink sirloin, delicately golden Yorkshires, a stunning variety of fresh veg… all in front of a roaring log fire". / **Details:** *www.clytha-arms.com; on Old Abergavenny to Raglan road; 9.30 pm, Mon 9 pm; closed Mon L & Sun D.* / **Accommodation:** *4 rooms, from £80*

COBHAM, SURREY 3–3B

The Cricketers £49

Downside Common KT11 3NX
(01932) 862 105
This 17th-century Cobham inn by the common has been renovated and relaunched thanks to Brasserie Blanc's pub offshoot The White Brasserie Company; it serves French brasserie fare as well as British pub

*classics. / **Details:** www.cricketerscobham.com; 10 pm, Fri & Sat 10.30 pm, Sun 9 pm.*

La Rive £61 344
48 High Street KT11 3EF (01932) 862 121
*"Formerly La Capanna, this 'new' restaurant in a 16th-century house has been rebuilt in modern style, and the food and atmosphere updated along with the name" – even those who say it's now "overpriced by local standards" say the transformation is proving "very, very good". / **Details:** www.larivecobham.com; Mon closed, Tue - Sat till late, Sun closed.*

COLERNE, WILTSHIRE 2–2B

Lucknam Park, Lucknam Park Hotel £103 544
SN14 8AZ (01225) 742777
*A "beautiful" Palladian country house hotel where "the range of offerings on the menu is exceptional", and some of Hywel Jones's dishes are "downright extraordinary"; service is "attentive but not overbearing – we were allowed to have a meal at our own pace". Top Tip – "the hotel's brasserie is good too". / **Details:** www.lucknampark.co.uk; 6m NE of Bath; Tue-Sat 10 pm; closed Mon, Tue-Sat D only, closed Sun D; Jacket required; children: 5+ D & Sun L. / **Accommodation:** 42 rooms, from £360*

COLNE, LANCASHIRE 5–1B

Banny's Restaurant £27 432
1 Vivary Way BB8 9NW (01282) 856220
*While there are "not many good fish 'n' chippies in Lancashire", this purpose-built outfit – a former Harry Ramsden's attached to the Boundary Mill outlet – is certainly "an exception". / **Details:** www.bannys.co.uk; 8.45 pm; no Amex.*

COLWELL BAY, ISLE OF WIGHT 2–4C

Hut £40 333
Colwell Chine Road PO40 9NP
(01983) 898 637
*"Overlooking the beach, but far from a beach café" – this easygoing haunt boasts "excellent fish (and other dishes), plus a great view across the western entrance to the Solent to boot". / **Details:** www.thehutcolwell.co.uk; 9pm.*

CONGLETON, CHESHIRE 5–2B

Pecks £68 344
Newcastle Rd CW12 4SB (01260) 275 161
*"Still going strong" – an "unwavering" family-run fixture, whose "high standard of food" help make it, for fans, "the essential 'go-to' place for any special occasion", as does its "distinctive 5-course or 7-course 'Dinner at 8'" format. / **Details:** www.pecksrest.co.uk; off A34; Mon closed, Tue - Sat 8 pm, Sun closed; closed Mon & Sun D.*

COOKHAM, BERKSHIRE 3–3A

Bel & The Dragon £53 324
High St SL6 9SQ (01628) 521263
*Part of a small chain, this capacious gastroboozer remains especially of note for its "atmospheric country setting", spanning a "first-class garden" and "snug front rooms"; but the food – from a "diverse and changing menu" – also "rarely disappoints". / **Details:** www.belandthedragon-cookham.co.uk; 10 pm, Sun 9.30 pm.*

Maliks £43 534
High St SL6 9SF (01628) 520085
*"In a cosy, fire-lit old cottage" with "great character", this "gem" of a high street Indian maintains its renown for "lovely and unusual dishes" – "incredibly fresh, with generous use of herbs and spices". / **Details:** www.maliks.co.uk; from the M4, Junction 7 for A4 for Maidenhead; 11.30 pm, Sun 10.30 pm.*

The White Oak £43 343
The Pound SL6 9QE (01628) 523043
*"Everything a modern gastropub should be"; "the food is always good and innovative" and "the service is always charming, reliable and helpful" at this "well-renovated and -decorated old pub, just off the village green". / **Details:** www.thewhiteoak.co.uk; 9.30 pm, Sun 8.30 pm; no Amex.*

COPSTER GREEN, LANCASHIRE 5–1B

Yu And You £50 544
500 Longsight Rd BB1 9EU (01254) 247111
*"Whatever you pick it tastes wonderful every time" at this outstanding (especially for rural Lancashire) Chinese, in the Ribble Valley, whose "very blingy" decor lends a "'70s-takeaway-meets-Hakkasan" effect to "an unprepossessing building by the side of the A59 east of Preston". "Anyone looking for authenticity and weird bits of animals is going to be disappointed – the menu is fairly standard Cantonese; what marks it out is the high standard of cooking and even higher standard of ingredients". / **Details:** www.yuandyou.com; off the A59 7 miles towards Clitheroe; 11 pm; D only, closed Mon.*

CORSE LAWN, GLOUCESTERSHIRE 2–1B

Corse Lawn Hotel £55 343
GL19 4LZ (01452) 780771
"A rural idyll" – the Hine's "charming" country

house hotel, where "everyone is made to feel most welcome", even with "family members ranging from 8 to 80"; the dining room attracts acclaim for its "interesting wine list" and the food is "delicious too". / **Details:** www.corselawnhotel.com; 5m SW of Tewkesbury on B4211; 9.30 pm. / **Accommodation:** 18 rooms, from £120

COWBRIDGE, VALE OF GLAMORGAN 1–1D

Bar 44 £37 433

44c High St CF71 7AG (03333) 44 40 49

For a "top tapas selection with a good mix of meat and fish choices", washed down with "great sherry", head to this vibrant café-bar – part of a three-strong South Wales chain. / **Details:** www.bar44.co.uk; 11 pm (Food 9 pm), Fri-Sat Midnight (Food 10 pm); closed Mon D; no Amex.

CRASTER, NORTHUMBERLAND 8–1B

Jolly Fisherman £43 335

Haven Hill NE66 3TR (01665) 576461

This "brilliantly located" pub "with sea views (and a terrace) over the water" ("try to get a window seat") serves "the freshest fish imaginable, prepared with flair and obvious care"; "if you like crab, then pay a visit!" / **Details:** www.thejollyfishermancraster.co.uk; near Dunstanburgh Castle; 8.30 pm, Sun 7 pm; no Amex; No bookings.

CRATHORNE, NORTH YORKSHIRE 8–3C

Crathorne Arms £49 344

TS15 0BA (01642) 961402

"Now in its third year, Eugene and Barbara McCoy (ex-of the Cleveland Tontine) have certainly put this place on the map"; the rustic village pub-conversion is "always busy with good reason – an ever-changing menu well cooked and served, and including lovely tapas". / **Details:** thecrathornearms.co.uk; 11 pm, Sun 7 pm; No bookings.

CREIGIAU, CARDIFF 2–2A

Caesars Arms £50 343

Cardiff Rd CF15 9NN (029) 2089 0486

"Still a lovely place to go to", a jovial countryside pub-restaurant and farm shop where "the à la carte is a bit on the expensive side, but the specials are worth it"; "service is extremely good and you get the feeling that diners are regulars". / **Details:** www.caesarsarms.co.uk; beyond Creigiau, past the golf club; 10 pm; closed Sun D.

CROMER, NORFOLK 6–3C

No1 £34 443

1 New St NR27 9HP (01263) 512316

"Look out on a stunning view of the Cromer Pier and the North Sea" if you visit the upstairs of Galton Blackiston's seaside two-year-old. Downstairs "he puts his Michelin experience into fish 'n' chips" for take-away, and other dishes from a "straightforward menu". Up above "you can tickle your tastebuds with a changing menu of seasonal Norfolk produce, including tapas dishes to share". / **Details:** www.no1cromer.com; 9 pm, Sun 7pm.

CROSTHWAITE, CUMBRIA 7–4D

The Punch Bowl Inn £51 455

LA8 8HR (01539) 568237

"Giving some of the best restaurants in the Lake District a run for their money", this pub/hotel "beautifully located" in a tiny village provides "superb service and gorgeous food". In October 2016, chef for the last five years, Scott Fairweather, moved on (to be replaced by Arthur Bridgeman Quin) – we've maintained the rating on the basis of the "unceasingly delightful" performance this place has shown over very many years. / **Details:** www.the-punchbowl.co.uk; off A5074 towards Bowness, turn right after Lyth Hotel; 8.45 pm. / **Accommodation:** 9 rooms, from £105

CROYDON, SURREY 3–3B

Albert's Table £56 443

49c South End CR0 1BF (020) 8680 2010

"It's a treat to find a first-class, and very smart restaurant in Croydon" – and one which fans say is "the only place worth considering in this area"; it comes "highly recommended" for its superior cooking at "reasonable prices". / **Details:** www.albertstable.co.uk; 10.30 pm; closed Mon & Sun D.

Karnavar £40 433

62 Southend CR0 1DP (020) 8686 2436

"Classy" cooking – more "Cordon Bleu than bog-standard curry house" – again wins praise for this "good quality" two-year-old Indian. / **Details:** 10.30 pm, Sun 9 pm; closed Mon; No shorts; cancellation charge for larger bookings.

McDermotts Fish & Chips £29 532

5-7 The Forestdale Shopping Centre Featherbed Ln CR0 9AS (020) 8651 1440

Tony McDermott's stalwart chippy is "just simply the best for miles around"; "daily deliveries from the south coast ensure the fish is at its freshest", and it's served in "generous portions" too. Shame about the "scruffy location in a downtrodden shopping arcade", in the 'burbs, but "that is the only complaint". / **Details:** www.mcdermottsfishandchips.co.uk; 9.30 pm, Sat 9 pm; closed Mon & Sun.

CRUDWELL, WILTSHIRE 2–2C

The Potting Shed £47 324

The Street SN16 9EW (01666) 577833

*A "really pleasant country pub that does much better food than you'd expect"; fans say that it has "improved further under new management" (the latter responsible for a makeover a year or two ago). / **Details:** www.thepottingshedpub.com; 9.30 pm, Sun 9 pm; no Amex; No bookings. / **Accommodation:** 12 rooms, from £95*

CUCKFIELD, WEST SUSSEX 3–4B

Ockenden Manor £90 323

Ockenden Ln RH17 5LD (01444) 416111

*There's still the odd sceptic, for whom the cooking is "competent" rather than outstanding, but this Elizabethan country house hotel continues to please most of those who comment on it thanks to its "brilliant and original food, served in comfort and style". / **Details:** www.hshotels.co.uk/ockenden-manor-hotel-and-spa; 9.00pm; No trainers. / **Accommodation:** 28 rooms, from £190*

CUPAR, FIFE 9–3D

The Peat Inn £72 544

KY15 5LH (01334) 840206

*"For a special occasion, one of the best Scotland has to offer!" – Geoffrey and Katherine Smeddle's "marvellously relaxed and most comfortable" country inn (refurbished last year) may be "hard to find, but it's well worth the effort". Service is highly "professional", and the cooking – "using the freshest local ingredients" – is "superbly crafted". "Serious wine list", too, "with some real gems at reasonable prices". / **Details:** www.thepeatinn.co.uk; at junction of B940 & B941, SW of St Andrews; Mon closed, Tue - Sat 9 pm, Sun closed; closed Mon & Sun. / **Accommodation:** 8 rooms, from £180*

DALRY, NORTH AYRSHIRE 9–4B

Braidwoods £69 554

Drumastle Mill Cottage KA24 4LN

(01294) 833544

*"What a place!" – Keith & Nicola Braidwood achieve "year after year of perfect consistency" at their "gorgeous" converted croft restaurant, which combines "a fabulous and well-researched wine list" with "fantastic" food ("as good today as 20 years ago, with awards testimony to its high standards"). / **Details:** www.braidwoods.co.uk; 9 pm; closed Mon, Tue L & Sun D (open Sun L Oct-April); children: 12+ at D.*

DANEHILL, EAST SUSSEX 3–4B

Coach And Horses £50 333

School Ln RH17 7JF (01825) 740369

*A "totally unpretentious gastroboozer that serves really excellent pub grub", and whose "lovely gardens" also find favour with all reporters. / **Details:** www.coachandhorses.co; off A275; 9 pm, Fri & Sat 9.30 pm, Sun 3 pm; closed Sun D.*

DARSHAM, SUFFOLK 6–4D

Darsham Nurseries £43 223

Main Rd IP17 3PW (01728) 667022

*A hip and airy garden-centre café in a converted barn, where young chef Lola DeMille oversees locally sourced small plates, with "interesting" results. / **Details:** www.darshamnurseries.co.uk; 9.30 pm; closed Mon D, Tue D, Wed D, Thu D, Sat D & Sun D.*

DARTMOUTH, DEVON 1–4D

RockFish £40 433

8 South Embankment TQ6 9BH

(01803) 832800

*"Get there when they open or queue!" if you visit Mitch Tonks's upscale riverside chippie (the original of a growing chain) – "a very different fish 'n' chip restaurant, with all the normal options, plus a large selection of different fish (that can be grilled or pan-fried), plus as many chips as you can eat". What's more "children get real meals, not the usual bog-standard choices". / **Details:** www.rockfishdevon.co.uk/index.php; 9.30 pm.*

The Seahorse £68 534

5 South Embankment TQ6 9BH

(01803) 835147

*"The very best fish and seafood, simply but expertly treated" continue to win very high esteem for Mitch Tonks's acclaimed small dining room, right by the seafront. Service is "courteous and friendly too" (if at times "slow"). / **Details:** www.seahorserestaurant.co.uk; Mon closed, Tue - Sat 9.30 pm, Sun closed; closed Mon & Sun.*

Woodroast £13 443

2 Smith Street, TQ6 9QR (01803) 832115

"Another fantastic specialist coffee shop from Matteo, the founder of The Curator Café in Totnes,

*but with fewer crowds" and "really knowledgeable" staff who "know their provenance and grind"; they "always have delicious homemade cakes too". / **Details:** www.italianfoodheroes.com; No bookings.*

DATCHWORTH, HERTFORDSHIRE 3–2B

The Tilbury **£55** **344**
Watton Rd SG3 6TB (01438) 815 550
*"Nothing I can fault" – one reviewer encapsulates the enthusiastic tenor of reports on James and Tom Bainbridge's "lovely" village gastroboozer, where the food is "consistently imaginative" and service is "very attentive" too. / **Details:** www.thetilbury.co.uk; 9 pm, Fri & Sat 9.30 pm; closed Mon & Sun D; No bookings.*

DEDHAM, ESSEX 3–2C

Milsoms **£47** **214**
Stratford Rd CO7 6HW (01206) 322 795
*The setting of this Constable Country hotel is "still very nice", but that's where agreement ends. It does have fans for whom it's a "favourite", but its foes are vehement: "the same old menu, disappointing", "passionless staff couldn't care less" – "the only good thing is the garden is pleasant, so you can at least enjoy that as you get increasingly irritated!" / **Details:** www.milsomhotels.com; 9.30 pm, Fri & Sat 10 pm; No bookings. / **Accommodation:** 15 rooms, from £120*

The Sun Inn **£46** **324**
High St CO7 6DF (01206) 323351
*A "splendid convivial pub", in Constable Country, which wins solid feedback for its "rustic" cuisine, but where the star turn is the well-curated wine list (courtesy of the Tate's wine guru, Hamish Anderson). / **Details:** www.thesuninndedham.com; 9.30 pm, Fri & Sat 10 pm; no Amex. / **Accommodation:** 7 rooms, from £110*

Le Talbooth **£77** **345**
Gun Hill CO7 6HP (01206) 323150
*"Situated in Constable Country, Le Talbooth must be in one of the most picturesque sites in the country, especially on a sunny summer's day when lunching outside by the river is a delight" ("the wife's always in a good mood after lunch here!"). The cooking isn't quite as notable as the setting, but "well presented and full of flavour". ("More humble visitors should try not to be intimidated by the number of Bentleys and Ferraris in the car park.") / **Details:** www.milsomhotels.com; 5m N of Colchester on A12, take B1029; 9 pm; closed Sun D; No jeans.*

DEGANWY, CONWY 4–1D

Nikki Ips **£37** **332**
57 Station Road LL31 9DF (01492) 596611
*"An unusually quirky Chinese, plus bar" – a major rarity on the North Wales coast. One sceptical report dismisses the decor ("one decent table with a view of the estuary, otherwise dismal") and food ("nothing special despite rave reviews") but the majority say it's "really good". / **Details:** www.nikkiips.com; 9.30pm, Fri - Sat 10pm.*

Paysanne **£43** **332**
147 Station Road LL31 9EJ (01492) 582079
*The Ross family's "classic, intimate neighbourhood bistro" (nowadays run by son of the family, Cai) is a big favourite locally, owing to its "high standard of cooking" – Welsh fare with a strong Gallic accent. / **Details:** www.paysannedeganwy.co.uk; 9.00pm; No shorts.*

DENHAM, BUCKINGHAMSHIRE 3–3A

The Swan Inn **£47** **333**
Village Road UB9 5BH (01895) 832085
*"Popular, welcoming and atmospheric" gastroboozer whose "imaginative dishes" are "a cut or two above the usual pub food"; "a very enjoyable destination for Sunday lunch, with a large garden for summer days, and a beautiful village to explore, even though it's so close to London" (near the A40/M25 junction). / **Details:** www.swaninndenham.co.uk; Mon - Thur 9 pm, Fri & Sat 9.30 pm, Sun 8 pm.*

DERBY, DERBYSHIRE 5–3C

Darleys **£58** **445**
Darley Abbey Mill DE22 1DZ (01332) 364987
*In a "beautiful (World Heritage) setting in an old mill overlooking river and weir", an enduringly popular staple whose "accomplished cooking, complemented by excellent service makes it the place to eat around Derby". It's "now with a new terrace", too – just the spot for "watching black-headed gulls wheel around a large Derwent weir". / **Details:** www.darleys.com; 9 pm; closed Sun D; no Amex; children: 10+ Sat eve.*

Ebi Sushi **£40** **532**
59 Abbey St DE22 3SJ (01332) 265656
*"Book a long way in advance to get into this tiny Japanese café full of Derby's Toyota workforce"; once there you'll enjoy "truly delicious delicacies" which represent "fantastic value" too. / **Details:** 10 pm; D only, closed Mon & Sun; no Amex.*

The Wonky Table £44 333
32-33 Sadler Gate DE1 3NR (01332) 295 000
*A romantic family-run café with a handy location on one of the city's better shopping streets;"the food, if never exceptional, is also very rarely poor", making it a "solid" choice overall. / **Details:** www.wonkytable.co.uk; Mon - Sat 10 pm, Sun closed.*

DETLING, KENT 3–3C

Cock Horse Inn
39 The St ME14 3JT (01622) 737092
*Just outside Maidstone, this straightforward, family-run, rather 'olde worlde' inn offers a traditional menu of pub grub. / **Details:** www.cockhorseinn.co.uk.*

DINTON, BUCKINGHAMSHIRE 2–3C

La Chouette £60 423
Westlington Grn HP17 8UW (01296) 747422
*"A visit to (madcap chef) Freddie is always an adventure";"his Belgian cuisine never fails to bring a big smile to your face", and it's all "served in Freddie's inimitable style".The venue also offers "fun and informative" wine evenings. / **Details:** www.lachouette.co.uk; off A418 between Aylesbury & Thame; 9 pm; closed Sat L & Sun; no Amex.*

DODDISCOMBSLEIGH, DEVON 1–3D

The NoBody Inn £49 223
EX6 7PS (01647) 252394
*"The most idyllic setting" and an extensive wine list add to the charms of this out-of-the-way pub, near Exeter:"perfection on a sunny day".The food hits mostly highs with the odd low, but if solace is required, it's at hand in a huge wine list, and a range of 250 whiskies. / **Details:** www.nobodyinn.co.uk; off A38 at Haldon Hill (signed Dunchidrock); 9 pm, Fri & Sat 9.30 pm. / **Accommodation:** 5 rooms, from £60*

DONHEAD ST ANDREW, WILTSHIRE 2–3C

The Forester Inn £44 333
Lower Street SP7 9EE (01747) 828038
*A "typical West Country pub", with an exposed-beam dining room, that's "hidden away in the depths of the countryside"."They specialise in fish, which is always fresh and well executed", and – top tip – also garner praise for their "very good value" midweek prix fixe. / **Details:** www.theforesterdonheadstandrew.co.uk; off A30; Mon closed, Tue - Sat 9 pm, Sun 2 pm; closed Sun D.*

DORCHESTER, DORSET 2–4B

Sienna £67 443
36 High West Street DT1 1UP
(01305) 250022
*Encouraging feedback on this town-centre stalwart, which was taken over by MasterChef finalist Marcus Wilcox in May 2015, and where he's maintaining its gastro reputation with "fresh and inventive modern British food". If there's a caveat, it's that the tiny (16-cover) room can seem "too intimate". / **Details:** www.siennadorchester.co.uk; 9 pm; closed Mon, Tue L & Sun; no Amex; children: 12+.*

DORKING, SURREY 3–3A

Restaurant Two To Four £58 333
2 - 4 West Street RH4 1BL (01306) 889923
*"Charming beamed restaurant", on the edge of town, where the food's always "reliably good", with "excellent and unobtrusive" service to match. / **Details:** www.2to4.co.uk; Tue-Sat 10.15 pm; closed Mon & Sun.*

DREWSTEIGNTON, DEVON 1–3C

The Old Inn £70 453
EX6 6QR (01647) 281 276
*Dan Walker (ex-22 Mill Street) and Anthea Christmas's inn remains "excellent as always" – particularly its "very high standard" of cooking; for overnighters, the "wonderful welcome" and "touches like afternoon tea on arrival make the whole experience very special" ("we almost felt like we were staying with old friends"). / **Details:** www.old-inn.co.uk; 9 pm; closed Sun-Tue, Wed L, Thu L.; no Amex; children: 12+. / **Accommodation:** 3 rooms, from £90*

DUNBAR, EAST LOTHIAN 9–4D

The Rocks £46 343
Marine Rd EH42 1AR (01368) 862287
*Overlooking the Dunbar coast, this clifftop restaurant-with-rooms is a solid performer on all fronts, from its "very friendly atmosphere" to its "consistently good" cuisine. / **Details:** www.therocksdunbar.co.uk; 9 pm; no Amex; No bookings. / **Accommodation:** 11 rooms, from £75*

DUNMOW, ESSEX 3–2C

The Flitch of Bacon £62 423
The Street CM6 3HT (01371) 821 660
"At last – quality dining within a few miles, from the new pub outpost of Daniel Clifford!" ("Essex has

been in need of somewhere special to just go and eat, and this is it!") That said, this famous chef's new gastroboozer is "definitely not Midsummer!", and while "it serves good, flavoursome food, service is a bit disjointed". / **Details:** *www.flitchofbacon.co.uk; 9 pm, Sun 6.30 pm. /* **Accommodation:** *0 rooms, from £3*

DUNVEGAN, HIGHLAND 9–2A

The Three Chimneys £85 544

Colbost IV55 8ZT (01470) 511258

Despite its fame and ultra-remote setting, the Spears's old crofter's cottage "doesn't disappoint" thanks to its "fabulous seafood" ("locally sourced blah blah blah. Of course it's locally sourced in this part of the world. Where else could they get seafood so fresh?"). It has a "perfect" location by Loch Dunvegan, with "the great Isle of Skye to explore" – "heaven!" / **Details:** *www.threechimneys.co.uk; 5m from Dunvegan Castle on B884 to Glendale; 9.30pm; children: 8+. /* **Accommodation:** *6 rooms, from £345*

DYFED, PEMBROKESHIRE 4–4B

The Grove - Narberth £79 544

Molleston SA67 8BX (01834) 860915

"Deserves all the accolades it gets" – a "luxurious" country house hotel, where "fine food is served with finesse in a lovely setting", with beautiful views of the Preseli Hills. There's a high emphasis on sustainability with sourcing within a 50-mile radius (including from the kitchen's own garden and beehives), as well as a dedicated spring. / **Details:** *www.thegrove-narberth.co.uk; 9.30 pm.*

EAST CHILTINGTON, EAST SUSSEX 3–4B

Jolly Sportsman £50 333

Chapel Ln BN7 3BA (01273) 890400

It's "worth the trouble and the few wrong turns" (inevitable if you don't do sat nav) to get to Bruce Wass's "perfect" rural pub; it offers "above average" cuisine and there's a great outdoor playground for kids. / **Details:** *www.thejollysportsman.com; NW of Lewes; 9.30 pm, Fri & Sat 10 pm; closed Mon & Sun D; no Amex.*

EAST CHISENBURY, WILTSHIRE 2–3C

Red Lion £56 333

SN9 6AQ (01980) 671124

An "old-fashioned" ("but none the worse for that") thatched country pub, with "excellent" riverside rooms located across the road; the food is well rated, and comes "without any pretension". / **Details:** *www.redlionfreehouse.com; Mon - Sat 9 pm, Sun 8 pm; no Amex; No bookings. /* **Accommodation:** *5 rooms, from £130*

EAST CLANDON, SURREY 3–3A

Queen's Head £43 333

The Street GU4 7RY (01483) 222 332

A "friendly and comfortable" Surrey Hills spot that's part of a "lovely small chain of local food pubs" (the Red Mist Group); "quality cooking and service" make it "great for both couples and families". / **Details:** *www.queensheadeastclandon.co.uk; Mon-Thu 9 pm, Fri & Sat 9.30 pm, Sun 8 pm.*

EAST GRINSTEAD, WEST SUSSEX 3–4B

Gravetye Manor £97 334

Vowels Lane RH19 4LJ (01342) 810567

This "lovely country manor house with beautiful gardens" has been on an upward curve in recent years, winning ever-stronger ratings for "improved" cuisine under head chef George Blogg – "a wonderful surprise". / **Details:** *www.gravetyemanor.co.uk; 2m outside Turner's Hill; 9.30 pm; Booking max 8 may apply; children: 7+. /* **Accommodation:** *17 rooms, from £250*

EAST MOLESEY, SURREY 3–3A

Mezzet £35 454

43 Bridge Rd KT8 9ER (020) 89794088

"Lebanon brought to Hampton Court"; run by a "very experienced" team, this buzzing and smart Lebanese establishment's "delicious" cuisine makes it "all-round excellent for any occasion". (There's also a two-year-old sibling, Mezzet Dar, with a Spanish slant, a couple of doors down.) / **Details:** *www.mezzet.co.uk; 10 pm, Sun 9 pm.*

EAST WITTON, NORTH YORKSHIRE 8–4B

Blue Lion £50 334

DL8 4SN (01969) 624273

"Breathing confidence", this "classy" coaching inn, set in a beautiful rural location, continues to win praise for its "first-class" food and wine. / **Details:** *www.thebluelion.co.uk; between Masham & Leyburn on A6108; 9.15 pm. /* **Accommodation:** *15 rooms, from £94*

EASTBOURNE, EAST SUSSEX 3–4B

The Mirabelle, The Grand Hotel £67 343
King Edwards Parade BN21 4EQ
(01323) 412345
*An unabashedly "old-school" hotel-restaurant "with the sort of smooth, deferential, willing and professional service which is like gold-dust nowadays". The food is "always good, sometimes excellent" (not least "the best cream tea" in town). / **Details:** www.grandeastbourne.com; Mon closed, Tue - Sat 10 pm, Sun closed; closed Mon & Sun; Jacket required. / **Accommodation:** 152 rooms, from £199*

EASTON GREY, WILTSHIRE 2–2C

The Dining Room, Whatley Manor £141 433
SN16 0RB (01666) 822888
*A luxe hotel dining room where "Martin Burge is now showcasing three tasting menus each evening, of which you can mix and match"; fans say that "the food has never been as good as it is now" – and that it's "worth every penny for the whole experience" (just make sure that you "leave yourself plenty of time"). Stop Press – in November 2016, Martin Burge stepped down: no replacement has yet been announced. / **Details:** www.whatleymanor.com; 8 miles from J17 on the M4, follow A429 towards Cirencester to Malmesbury on the B4040; 9.30 pm; D only, closed Mon-Tue; No jeans; children: 12+. / **Accommodation:** 23 rooms, from £305*

EDINBURGH, CITY OF EDINBURGH 9–4C

Aizle £64 544
107-109 St. Leonard's Street EH8 9QY
(0131) 662 9349
*This "different and quirky" two-year-old neo-bistro, in student land, is one of Edinburgh's more interesting foodie fave raves. "There's no menu", but diners receive "a list of seasonal ingredients" starring on that night's five-course set – the "food does the talking", and it's notably "lovely" (not least fish). / **Details:** www.aizle.co.uk; 9.30 pm.*

Angels With Bagpipes £53 334
343 High St, Royal Mile EH1 1PW
(0131) 2201111
*In an ancient building on the Royal Mile, this two-floor operation (upstairs Halo, downstairs Chanters) is run by the family behind Valvona & Crolla. High ratings (if on limited feedback) for its modern Scottish cuisine (fairly trad dishes, plus a few more wacky ingredients). / **Details:** www.angelswithbagpipes.co.uk; 9.45 pm.*

Bell's Diner £31 333
7 St Stephen St EH3 5EN (0131) 225 8116
*"The very best burgers are well served in this small dining room in trendy Stockbridge"; "I've been going for 34 years, from a time when nobody bothered making 'gourmet' burgers: now the ersatz variety are everywhere?!" / **Details:** www.bellsdineredinburgh.co.uk; 10 pm, Mon 9 pm, Sun 9.30 pm; closed weekday L & Sun L; no Amex.*

Bia Bistrot £41 453
19 Colinton Rd EH10 5DP (0131) 452 8453
*"The local everybody would like to have" – alas, only Morningside residents can lay claim to this cosy bistro with French-Gaelic cuisine that's "just lovely". / **Details:** www.biabistrot.co.uk; 10 pm.*

Cadiz
George Street EH2 3EE (0131) 226 3000
*Above Café Andaluz (same owners), this well-located Summer 2016 newcomer opened too late for survey feedback. On the menu – Scottish fish and seafood cooked Mediterranean-style. / **Details:** www.cadizedinburgh.co.uk; 10pm.*

Café Marlayne £45 343
1 Thistle Street EH2 1EN (0131) 226 2230
*A "no-nonsense French bistro", in New Town, where the "great food" also comes at a "great price". There's an equally well-liked sibling on Antigua Street. / **Details:** www.cafemarlayne.com/thistle-street; 10 pm; no Amex.*

The Café Royal Bar £55 235
19 West Register St EH2 2AA
(0131) 556 1884
*A landmark, tile-adorned Victorian boozer, split between a buzzing bar and posher foodie outfit, where "the food is simple but delicious", and where fans say "the ambience is second to none". / **Details:** www.caferoyaledinburgh.co.uk; 9.30 pm; children: 5+.*

Café St-Honoré £50 334
34 NW Thistle Street Ln EH2 1EA
(0131) 226 2211
*"Tucked away like a touch of Paris in the 'Athens of the North'" – Neil Forbes's "very Gallic" brasserie in the New Town "does what it does with panache": "simple and effective" dishes are "helpfully" served in a "romantic" setting, and "all at very reasonable prices". / **Details:** www.cafesthonore.com; 10 pm. / **Sustainability:** ★★★*

The Castle Terrace £88 443
33-35 Castle Ter EH1 2EL (0131) 229 1222
Although the odd reporter again had an "underwhelming" trip to Tom Kitchin's castle-side dining room, it put in a strong performance this year, with high praise for its "top-notch food, expertly executed" and "excellent service" ("we were totally

spoiled!"). A £1m revamp has given the interior a lift too. / **Details:** *www.castleterracerestaurant.com; 10 pm; closed Mon & Sun.*

The Dogs **£40** **334**
110 Hanover St EH2 1DR (0131) 220 1208
Reporters "love this place" for a "cheap 'n' cheerful" bite – a "very friendly" and "really buzzy" pub, in the city centre, and which offers a "homely" menu. / **Details:** *www.thedogsonline.co.uk; 10 pm.*

L'Escargot Bleu **£51** **333**
56 Broughton St EH1 3SA (0131) 557 1600
"A really authentic French bistro in the heart of Edinburgh", combining "classic ("country-style") cooking and a lively, fun atmosphere" – "must be the effects of the Auld Alliance!" / **Details:** *www.lescargotbleu.co.uk; 10 pm, Fri & Sat 10.30 pm; closed Sun (except Festival); no Amex.*

Favorita **£45** **443**
325 Leith Walk EH6 8SA (0131) 554 2430
"I don't see how this terrific pizza joint could be any better!"; the Crolla family's "cosy" Leith Walk haunt lives up to its name with "superb pizza", "a decent supporting cast of prosecco and homemade ice-creams, plus lovely sharing platters to start". It's "very family-friendly and always full of happy people". / **Details:** *www.la-favorita.com; 11 pm.*

Field **£43** **332**
41 West Nicolson St EH8 9DB (01316) 677010
This elegant four-year-old, in Southside, turns out "ambitious" cooking using "top-notch" ingredients; prices are "incredibly good", with the set lunches "an absolute steal, meaning you can push the boat out". / **Details:** *www.fieldrestaurant.co.uk; 9 pm; closed Mon.*

Fishers Bistro **£53** **334**
1 The Shore EH6 6QW (0131) 554 5666
"Still an Edinburgh favourite" – "a harbourside building in Leith" that's "focused on expertly cooked Scottish fish and seafood". / **Details:** *www.fishersrestaurants.co.uk; 10.30 pm.*

Fishers in the City **£54** **223**
58 Thistle St EH2 1EN (0131) 225 5109
"Posh fish 'n' chips in a buzzy setting" has helped build a strong following for this bistro near the National Gallery; there's some feeling it's at its best on a quiet night. / **Details:** *www.fishersbistros.co.uk; 10.30 pm.*

Galvin Brasserie de Luxe, The Caledonian **£60** **233**
Princes St EH1 2AB (0131) 222 8988
The Galvin brothers' "buzzing, busy" four-year-old hotel-brasserie continues to elicit surprisingly middling feedback. While its "flexible menu choices make it great for business" and "it's open pleasantly late" ("big Edinburgh problem"), the food – "French classics with some great Scottish dishes in the mix" – strikes cynics as "nothing special" and "expensive" for what you get. / **Details:** *www.galvinbrasseriedeluxe.com; 10 pm, Sun 9.30 pm. /* **Accommodation:** *245 rooms, from £325*

Gardener's Cottage **£48** **343**
1 Royal Terrace Gardens EH7 5DX
(0131) 558 1221
In a 19th-century house kitted out with long communal tables, this self-consciously sustainably minded four-year-old, run by chef-owners Dale Mailley and Edward Murray (ex-Atrium), achieves high marks across the board. / **Details:** *www.thegardenerscottage.co; Mon 10 pm, closed Tue, Wed - Sun 10 pm; closed Tue & Wed.*

La Garrigue **£52** **343**
31 Jeffrey St EH1 1DH (0131) 557 3032
"The Auld Alliance at its best"; "Jean Michel Gauffre provides an attractive menu of characteristic dishes of south-west France" ("hearty rather than elegant"), "with a fascinating list of wines from the region", and a good dose of "charm", at his bustling "Old Town stalwart", behind Waverley Station – "one of the main reasons for my annual visit to the Edinburgh Fringe!" / **Details:** *www.lagarrigue.co.uk; 9.30 pm.*

Grain Store **£65** **323**
30 Victoria St EH1 2JW (0131) 225 7635
"Still a favourite" – a "welcoming and relaxed" warehouse, in the Old Town, whose traditional menu hasn't varied much over the years, and whose "service can be a bit hit and miss", but which remains an "excellent" destination for "authentic Scottish cooking". / **Details:** *www.grainstore-restaurant.co.uk; Mon - Sat 9.45 pm, Sun 9.30 pm; closed Sun L.*

Henderson's **£36** **232**
94 Hanover St EH2 1DR (0131) 225 2131
Established in 1963, Scotland's oldest veggie occupies a crypt beneath a New Town church. The food's not as radical as when it first opened its doors, but it's worth remembering if you're after a healthy snack that won't break the bank. / **Details:** *www.hendersonsofedinburgh.co.uk; 10 pm, Thu-Sat 11 pm; closed Sun; no Amex.*

The Honours **£70** **343**
58a, North Castle Street EH2 3LU
(0131) 220 2513
"A very good all-round experience" is to be had at star chef Martin Wishart's New Town bistro – "staff are attentive to every need" and the food's consistently highly rated. / **Details:** *www.thehonours.co.uk; Closed Mon, Tue - Sat 10 pm, Sun Closed; closed Mon & Sun.*

Kanpai **£36** 5 4 3
8-10 Grindlay St EH3 9AS (0131) 228 1602
"A real tribute to Japan"; with "prompt service, delicious food and lots of choice", this "tiny, modern, neat and clean little restaurant", opposite the Lyceum Theatre, is "a welcome and regular haunt", whose offering includes "exceptionally good sushi and sashimi". / ***Details:*** *www.kanpaisushi.co.uk; 10.30 pm; closed Mon.*

Karen's Unicorn **£33** 3 4 3
8b Aberecomby Pl EH3 6LB (01315) 566333
A smart New Town Cantonese again lauded for its "knowledgeable and helpful waiters", its "generous portions and individual flavours". / ***Details:*** *www.karensunicorn.com; 10 pm, Fri & Sat 11 pm; closed Mon.*

The Kitchin **£97** 4 3 4
78 Commercial Street EH6 6LX
(0131) 555 1755
"Incredible cooking perfectly matched with a very extensive wine list" underpins the huge satisfaction with Tom & Michaela Kitchin's "phenomenal" warehouse-conversion in Leith, whose ratings rivalled nearby Martin Wishart's this year. The couple took over the neighbouring premises a year ago, and although the odd purist gripes about "distracting elements (such as the waiters' kilts, the provenance map and handbag stools – attempts, clearly successful, to woo tourists!)", the change has boosted the ambience here. / ***Details:*** *www.thekitchin.com; Tue-Thu 10 pm, Fri & Sat 10.30 pm; closed Mon & Sun; children: 5+.*

Kyloe **£52** 4 3 2
1-3 Rutland Street EH1 2AE (0131) 229 3402
"Scottish steaks, with cuts of meat displayed on chopping boards and introduced" kick off a meal at what bills itself as 'Edinburgh's first gourmet steak restaurant', on the first floor of a hotel with castle views. The ambience can seem "slightly sterile", not so the "never-failing-to-please" Aberdeen Angus steaks and "lip-smacking wines". "I am considering making the journey from my home in the English Midlands to Edinburgh just to enjoy the experience again!" / ***Details:*** *www.kyloerestaurant.com; 10 pm.*

Locanda de Gusti **£40** 4 4 3
102 Dalry Road EH11 2DW (0131) 346 8800
Rosario & Maria Sartore's "classic, very italian neighbourhood restaurant"; service comes "with a personal touch", and the "ever-changing menu" provides "fresh-tasting" dishes ("the mixed Scottish seafood platter is particularly good"). / ***Details:*** *www.locandadegusti.com; 10pm.*

Mother India's Cafe **£34** 5 4 3
3-5 Infirmary St EH1 1LT (0131) 524 9801
"A great idea – small tapas-style dishes, perfect for ordering a few and sharing amongst friends" adds to the appeal of this ultra-reliable Glaswegian import, which has stormed the Scottish capital to become the survey's No. 1 Indian. It's a "bright and buzzy" outfit too, and "staff are lovely, even when the place is packed out...which it often is, and deservedly so!" / ***Details:*** *www.motherindiaglasgow.co.uk; 10.30 pm, Fri & Sat 11 pm, Sun 10 pm; no Amex.*

Norn **£62**
50-54 Henderson Street EH6 6DE
(0131) 629 2525
Chef Scott Smith, a protégé of Geoffrey Smeddle – owner of Cupar's Peat Inn – took over the site of The Plumed Horse (RIP) to open this ambitious new venture providing tasting menus centered on Scottish produce from local suppliers. It opened too late to attract survey feedback, but to say that early press reviews have been adulatory would be an understatement. / ***Details:*** *www.nornrestaurant.com; 9 pm.*

Number One, Balmoral Hotel **£98** 5 4 4
1 Princes Street EH2 2EQ (0131) 557 6727
Chef Jeff Bland doesn't deserve his name fortunately, but his "fantastic" cuisine – "with excellent, individual flavours", "imaginative presentation and lots of nice extra touches" – has long meant the basement of the city's grandest hotel arguably does justify its 'no. 1' moniker. "You might worry that the place would be pretentious, but it isn't" – "everything is done with a smile", and for somewhere that's underground the setting is surprisingly "special". / ***Details:*** *www.thebalmoralhotel.com; 10 pm; D only; No jeans. /* ***Accommodation:*** *188 rooms, from £360*

Ondine **£68** 3 2 4
2 George IV Bridge EH1 1AD (0131) 2261888
Mixed feedback this year on this "bustling seafood restaurant" – a "spacious and comfortable" operation, in an office block on the Royal Mile. Most reporters vaunt it as offering "Edinburgh's best seafood", but it was not without critics who found it "repeatedly underwhelming" and "expensive". / ***Details:*** *www.ondinerestaurant.co.uk; Mon - Sat 10 pm, Sun closed; closed Sun; Booking max 8 may apply.*

The Outsider **£44** 3 3 4
15 - 16 George IV Bridge EH1 1EE
(0131) 226 3131
With "good" castle views and smart, urban-chic decor, this Edinburgh institution remains of note for its "great atmosphere"; fans also praise the "accommodating staff" and "interesting" modern Scottish menu "with good specials". / ***Details:*** *www.theoutsiderrestaurant.com; 11 pm; no Amex; Booking max 12 may apply.*

The Pompadour by Galvin, The Caledonian £85 3 3 3
Princes Street EH1 2AB (0131) 222 8975
Entering its fifth year, the Galvin brothers' tenancy in this elegant chamber continues to receive a surprisingly mixed reception. Even those who say its cuisine is "faultless" can find the setting "pompous", whereas, by contrast, others find the room "delightful", but the food "a letdown", or "at high prices that may be increasingly hard to justify". It receives a majority of strong recommendations, though, especially for a "romantic" occasion. / **Details:** *www.thepompadourbygalvin.com; Mon closed, Tue - Sat 10 pm, Sun closed; D only, closed Sun-Tue.*

Restaurant Mark Greenaway £72 4 3 2
67 North Castle St EH2 3LJ (0131) 557 0952
The TV chef's "elegant" three-year-old, in a Georgian house in New Town, offers an "exciting" culinary experience. "Don't let the fancy-looking food fool you into thinking it's style over substance" – it's "anything but", and the staff are "impeccable" too. / **Details:** *markgreenaway.com; 10 pm.*

Restaurant Martin Wishart £96 4 4 3
54 The Shore EH6 6RA (0131) 553 3557
Martin Wishart's "brilliant Leith establishment" was again voted by reporters as Scotland's top gastronomic experience (despite taking rather more flak this year for punishing prices). "What makes it special is that isn't gimmicky" – food that's "adventurous but never wacky" is "just beautifully created from the best seasonal Scottish ingredients, and served by professionals in an ambience of calm and relaxation". / **Details:** *www.martin-wishart.co.uk; 9.30 pm; closed Mon & Sun; No trainers.*

Rhubarb, Prestonfield Hotel £76 3 4 4
Priestfield Rd EH16 5UT (0131) 225 1333
A "stunning" country house hotel, set in its own grounds, and fusing "Georgian baronial and modern OTT chic", including a sitting room with a "truly amazing density of posh bric-a-brac"; happily "the decor is matched by excellent service and flavours to entice". Top Tip – "classy" afternoon teas a highlight. / **Details:** *www.prestonfield.com; 10 pm; children: 12+ at D, none after 7pm.* / **Accommodation:** *23 rooms, from £295*

Scran & Scallie £43 3 4 4
1 Comely Bank Rd EH4 1DT (0131) 332 6281
"Ignore the hype! Just enjoy the food and ale served by incredibly friendly staff" at Tom Kitchin's "very relaxed" gastropub spin-off, which wins consistent support for its "very decent versions of classic pub grub"; "and it's child-friendly", too. / **Details:** *scranandscallie.com; 10 pm.*

The Stockbridge £54 4 4 4
54 St Stephen's St EH3 5AL (0131) 226 6766
This "elegant" basement has "an intimate ambience, with the feel of a private household, and thoughtful service"; it wins nothing but praise too for its "delicious" Scottish cuisine. / **Details:** *www.thestockbridgerestaurant.co.uk; 9.30 pm; D only, closed Mon; children: 18+ after 8 pm.*

Timberyard £76 5 4 4
10 Lady Lawson St EH3 9DS (01312) 211222
"The Radord family excel at this great space" – a converted warehouse with outside terrace near the Traverse Theatre. "Tastebuds are tantalised and challenged, but in a good way" by the "fascinating" Nordic-inspired cuisine, and it's an "exciting" venue – "lovely lighting, candles and woodburner" (and "great cocktails") – even if "you never feel hip enough to eat there". / **Details:** *www.timberyard.co; 9.30 pm; closed Mon & Sun.*

21212 £94 4 4 3
3 Royal Ter EH7 5AB (0845) 222 1212
If it wasn't all a bit "wacky" it wouldn't be a Paul Kitching restaurant. With "really weird decor (think Michelin handbook meets a mid-90s computer game!)", and food that provides "odd (sometimes inspired) combinations of flavours and ingredients", this Georgian townhouse is certainly a "quirky" venue; "there's a lot of fun here, however, including service which is far from stuffy" – even if at root this is a "textbook fine dining experience". "Expect to take a lovely long time over your meal – an amazing collection of different tastes." / **Details:** *www.21212restaurant.co.uk; 9.30 pm; closed Mon & Sun; children: 5+.* / **Accommodation:** *4 rooms, from £95*

Valvona & Crolla £39 2 2 3
19 Elm Row EH7 4AA (0131) 556 6066
No foodie visit of Auld Reekie would be complete without a trip to this wonderful 80-year-old deli and wine importer, at the start of the road to Leith. Its dining annexe serves some superb vintages at retail plus corkage, but achievement on the food front is surprisingly modest given the venue's potential. / **Details:** *www.valvonacrolla.com; Mon-Thur 6pm, Fri-Sat 6.30pm Sun 5pm.*

Wedgwood **£58** 4 4 2
267 Canongate EH8 8BQ (0131) 558 8737
*Paul Wedgwood's small contemporary basement, just off the Royal Mile, has a name for its highly accomplished cuisine, and again won solid ratings this year. Top Tip – "excellent value lunch, with some dishes that are remarkable at the price". / **Details:** www.wedgwoodtherestaurant.co.uk; 10 pm.*

The Wee Restaurant **£61**
61 Frederick Street EH2 1LH (0131) 225 7983
*Ten years after opening their North Queensferry restaurant of the same name, Craig and Vikki Wood opened a second outpost, this time in Edinburgh's New Town, taking over the site of Fleur de Sel. At the helm, chef Michael Innes (formerly of the much-lauded El Cellar de Can Roca in Girona, northern Spain). It opened too late for survey feedback. / **Details:** www.theweerestaurant.co.uk/edinburgh; 9 pm, Fri & Sat 10 pm.*

The Witchery by the Castle **£73** 2 3 5
Castlehill, The Royal Mile EH1 2NF
(0131) 225 5613
*This dark, dramatic gothic dining room near the castle – the building also hosts a brighter chamber, The Secret Garden – certainly provides a superbly "atmospheric" and "romantic" destination. Its cuisine and heavyweight wine selection continue to elicit slightly up-and-down reviews, however, and even its most ardent fans can find it "overpriced". / **Details:** www.thewitchery.com; 11.30 pm. / **Accommodation:** 8 rooms, from £325*

EGHAM, SURREY 3–3A

The Estate Grill, Great Fosters Hotel **£68** 3 4 4
Stroude Rd TW20 9UR (01784) 433 822
*"Eat unlimited sandwiches, and super scones and cakes (with refined teas) while feeling at home in exceptional comfort and subdued elegance", at this oak-beamed hotel dining room, in a "former Elizabethan hunting lodge"; it's "even better if you can sit outside and enjoy the beautiful gardens". / **Details:** www.greatfosters.co.uk/dining/estate-grill; Mon - Fri 9.30 pm, Sat 10 pm, Sun 9pm; No jeans; Booking max 12 may apply. / **Accommodation:** 43 rooms, from £155*

EGLWYS FACH, POWYS 4–3C

Gareth Ward at Ynyshir **£76** 5 5 4
SY20 8TA (01654) 781209
*"Gareth Ward (ex-Sat Bains) and team are first class" at this "wonderful" high-end hotel in a "lovely" setting "next to an RSPB reserve, across the road from the hills, and within easy reach of the beach". "We stayed for three nights, and amazingly they produced a different tasting menu each night!"; if you want to max out, "try booking the 15-course option at the Chef's Table". / **Details:** www.ynyshirhall.co.uk; signposted from A487; 8.45 pm; No jeans; Credit card deposit required to book; children: 9+. / **Accommodation:** 0 rooms, from £10*

ELDERSFIELD, GLOUCESTERSHIRE 2–1B

The Butcher's Arms **£68** 4 4 3
Lime St GL19 4NX (01452) 840 381
*James & Elizabeth Winter's "relaxed" pub has retained its 'local' feel while serving up "exceptional food". "Quirky" wine list, too – think bottles with "curiosity-arousing names (Kung Fu Girl!)". / **Details:** www.thebutchersarms.net; 9 pm; closed Mon, Tue L, Wed L, Thu L & Sun D; children: 10+.*

ELLASTONE, DERBYSHIRE 5–3C

The Duncombe Arms **£47** 4 4 3
Main Rd DE6 2GZ (01335) 324 275
*On the Derbyshire/Staffordshire border, this tranquilly located pub provides "lovely food using imagination, combined with tradition, decent beer, plus charming service". / **Details:** www.duncombearms.co.uk; 9.30pm, Fri - Sat 10.30pm, Sun 9pm.*

ELLEL, LANCASHIRE 5–1A

The Bay Horse **£46** 4 2 3
Bay Horse Ln LA2 0HR (01524) 791204
*Handy for the M6, "Craig Wilkinson's long-established gastropub continues to serve excellent food, cooked with care". The cuisine's "far from innovative (no gels, etc.)", but "fantastic fillet steak with textbook saucing" is a particular highlight of the well-grounded cooking. / **Details:** www.bayhorseinn.com; 9 pm, Sun 8 pm; closed Mon; no Amex.*

ELLON, ABERDEENSHIRE 9–2D

Eat on the Green **£66** 3 4 3
Udny Grn AB41 7RS (01651) 842337
*"Still as good as ever"; 'the kilted chef' Chris Wilkinson's long-running venture in a former inn continues to serve prime locally sourced food, with fans proclaiming it "a top place in Aberdeenshire for a dress-up dinner". / **Details:** www.eatonthegreen.co.uk; 9 pm, Sun 8 pm; closed Mon & Tue.*

ELY, CAMBRIDGESHIRE 3–1B

Old Fire Engine House **£46** 3 2 3
25 St Mary's St CB7 4ER (01353) 662582
*A venerable city-centre institution (est. 1968) and art gallery in a "pleasant" Georgian building with an "attractive garden"; there's the odd gripe, but even critics concede that the food – including "some local and obscure dishes" – is "perfectly acceptable", and for fans "it's the tops". / **Details:** www.theoldfireenginehouse.co.uk; 9 pm; closed Sun D; no Amex.*

EMSWORTH, HAMPSHIRE 2–4D

Fat Olives **£51** 5 5 4
30 South St PO10 7EH (01243) 377914
*Laurence & Julia Murphy's "truly fantastic small restaurant", in an old terraced house up the hill from the quay, continues to elicit raves. It combines "lovely food from local suppliers" and "personalised and friendly" service by Julia, who "makes you feel like a guest as well as a customer". / **Details:** www.fatolives.co.uk; 9.15 pm; closed Mon & Sun; no Amex; children: 8+, except Sat L.*

36 on the Quay **£83** 3 3 4
47 South St PO10 7EG (01243) 375592
*Ramon Farthing's "lovely quiet dining room", set right on the quay, continues to please most, if not quite all reporters, with its "very accomplished" food – and it's "so much better now the chef is providing three choices for each course". Top Tip? – "you can even make a night of it as it is possible to book a room". / **Details:** www.36onthequay.co.uk; off A27 between Portsmouth & Chichester; 9 pm; closed Mon & Sun; no Amex. / **Accommodation:** 5 rooms, from £100*

EPPING, ESSEX 3–2B

Haywards Restaurant **£63** 4 5 2
111 Bell Common CM16 4DZ
(01992) 577350
*"Exceptional for Essex!"; chef Jahdre Hayward creates some "very fine food, with lovely and unusual flavours", and "front of house is run to perfection by wife Amanda" at this "first-class" two-year-old. "Everything was very flavoursome, including the little spots of stuff, which looked as if they were solely for decoration!" / **Details:** www.haywardsrestaurant.co.uk; Mon & Tue closed. Wed & Thur 9.30 pm, Fri & Sat 10.*

EPSOM, SURREY 3–3B

Le Raj **£38** 4 3 4
211 Fir Tree Rd KT17 3LB (01737) 371371
*"Better than your normal local Indian", a stalwart subcontinental where "the (fine dining) food is very good… consistently". / **Details:** www.lerajrestaurant.co.uk; 11 pm; No jeans.*

ESHER, SURREY 3–3A

Good Earth **£56** 4 2 3
14 - 18 High Street KT10 9RT
(01372) 462489
*"A Chinese for a special occasion" – the most Outer London member of this family-owned chain provides "an elaborate experience, way above that of the average high street", with "wonderful freshly cooked Chinese food, that's tasty without being heavy". / **Details:** www.goodearthgroup.co.uk; Mon - Sat 11.15 pm, Sun 10.45 pm; Booking max 12 may apply.*

ETON, BERKSHIRE 3–3A

Gilbey's **£56** 2 3 3
82 - 83 High Street SL4 6AF (01753) 854921
*"Never failing to please" – a high street fixture with a well-stocked wine bar up front and a conservatory tucked to the rear; overnighters can enjoy prime Windsor Castle views from the top-floor studio suite. / **Details:** www.gilbeygroup.com; 5 min walk from Windsor Castle; Mon - Thur 9.45 pm, Fri & Sat 10 pm, Sun 9.45 pm.*

EVERSHOT, DORSET 2–4B

Summer Lodge Country House Hotel **£77** 5 4 5
9 Fore St DT2 0JR (01935) 482000
*"The perfect country retreat" – this "elegant" Relais & Châteaux country house hotel is "exceptional in every way", not least its "romantic" dining conservatory, overlooking beautiful gardens; chef Steven Titman produces "excellent" cuisine, backed up by a notable wine list. / **Details:** www.summerlodgehotel.co.uk; 12m NW of Dorchester on A37; 9.30 pm; No jeans. / **Accommodation:** 24 rooms, from £235*

EXETER, DEVON 1–3D

Rendezvous **£44** 2 3 3
38-40 Southernhay East EX1 1PE
(01392) 270 222
In Southernhay, a basement wine bar that's "slightly out of the centre but well worth finding" – not

least for its "super wine list" ("but the food's OK too"); the ambience is a tad schizophrenic... whilst one reporter found it "dead as a dodo", another felt "overwhelmed by the conversation of ultra-important-sounding office workers!" / **Details:** *www.winebar10.co.uk; Mon - Sat 9.15 pm, Sun closed; closed Sun.*

EXTON, HAMPSHIRE 2–3D

Shoe Inn **£43** 3 4 3
Shoe Ln SO32 3NT (01489) 877526
"Well situated in the village with tables overlooking a small stream/river", this "really nice pub on the South Downs Way" offers "good well-sourced cooking". / **Details:** *www.theshoeinn.moonfruit.com; 11 pm.*

EXTON, RUTLAND 6–3D

The Fox and Hounds Hotel **£52** 3 3 4
19 The Green LE15 8AP (01572) 812403
"Fire, candlelight, and the charm of a fine old building" are a highlight at this "romantic" inn, by Rutland Water, but its fairly traditional cooking is also consistently highly rated. / **Details:** *www.afoxinexton.co.uk.*

FAIRSTEAD, ESSEX 3–2C

The Square and Compasses
Fuller Street CM3 2BB (01245) 361477
Ten minutes' drive from Chelmsford, this converted 17th-century pub provides an attractive, rural destination, and has achieved a solid reputation for its gastropub fare. / **Details:** *www.thesquareandcompasses.co.uk.*

FALMOUTH, CORNWALL 1–4B

The Cove Restaurant & Bar **£49** 4 3 4
Maenporth Beach TR11 5HN (01326) 251136
"An unsung hero" with a "beautiful (sea-view) setting" by Maenporth Beach, and which serves "classic food that's bursting in flavour and well presented" (in "good-sized portions" too); that said, it inspired the odd letdown this year. / **Details:** *www.thecovemaenporth.co.uk; 9.30 pm; closed Sun D.*

Oliver's **£48** 4 4 3
33 High St TR11 2AD (01326) 218138
The food at this casual, funky venture is "as well cooked and presented as many a Michelin restaurant" – and comes at "fair prices" too; it's "difficult to get a booking as there are so few covers of an evening, but once you've snagged a table, you never feel rushed". / **Details:** *www.oliversfalmouth.com; 9 pm; closed Mon & Sun; no Amex.*

Rick Stein's Fish & Chips **£41** 4 3 2
Discovery Quay TR11 3XA (01841) 532700
For "posh fish 'n' chips", the TV chef's "casual" and "buzzy" outfit, near the Maritime Museum, continues to please with its "great range of traditional and innovative seafood at not too extravagant prices". / **Details:** *www.rickstein.com; 9 pm; no Amex; No bookings.* / **Sustainability:** ★★★

FARNBOROUGH, HAMPSHIRE 3–3A

Aviator **£56** 4 3 4
55 Farnborough Rd GU14 6EL
(01252) 555890
Solid marks this year for the sophisticated, mid-century-style brasserie of this trendy hotel overlooking Farnborough Airport; "the menu is always interesting and varied", and the "cocktails are sublime" – whether taken in the dining room or glamorous Sky Bar. / **Details:** *www.aviatorbytag.com; 10 pm, Fri & Sat 10.30 pm, Sun 9.30 pm.*

FAVERSHAM, KENT 3–3C

Read's, Macknade Manor **£84** 3 3 3
Canterbury Rd ME13 8XE (01795) 535344
"A lovely Georgian house with elegant dining rooms" provides the setting for David and Rona Pitchford's long-established venture. It's "a bit old-fashioned", but its regular local fan club say "it ticks all the boxes", with its "smart and comfortable" interior and "fine, classical standard of cooking". / **Details:** *www.reads.com; Mon closed, Tue - Sat 9.30 pm, Sun closed; closed Mon & Sun.* / **Accommodation:** *6 rooms, from £165*

Yard **£14** 3 3 3
10 Jacob Yd, Preston St ME13 8NY
(01795) 538265
In an historic mews, this "really high-quality café" has already made a name for itself locally owing to its "fabulous food" (spanning Kentish breakfasts, plus salads, sandwiches and soups) and "fabulous staff". / **Details:** *5 pm; L only, closed Sun; No bookings.*

FAWSLEY, NORTHAMPTONSHIRE 2–1D

Fawsley Hall **£65** **3 2 4**
NN11 3BA (01327) 892000
*"The hall is beautiful" and "in glorious surroundings", which "adds to the whole experience" of this luxurious hotel, especially for romance. Incidents of "shambolic service" can take the edge off the "beautifully presented" food, though. / **Details:** www.fawsleyhall.com; on A361 between Daventry & Banbury; 9.30 pm. / **Accommodation:** 58 rooms, from £175*

FENCE, LANCASHIRE 5–1B

White Swan at Fence **£41** **5 4 3**
300 Wheatley Lane Rd BB12 9QA
(01282) 611773
*It's "still relatively new, but this small kitchen is establishing a reputation for very fine cooking" by ex-Northcote chef Tom Parker, with another plus being that it's "the only Timothy Taylor-tied pub this side of the Pennines". ("Dishes are now priced à la carte", however – "and blimey, the prices!") / **Details:** www.whiteswanatfence.co.uk; 8.30 pm, Fri & Sat 9 pm, Sun 7 pm; closed Mon.*

FLAUNDEN, HERTFORDSHIRE 3–2A

The Bricklayers Arms **£56** **4 4 4**
Hogpits Bottom HP3 0PH (01442) 833322
*"Worth the drive!"; this rural pub maintains its high popularity, and "despite being very packed, the food is astonishingly good", considering – making it "the very best in the area for many years by miles and miles". / **Details:** www.bricklayersarms.com; J18 off the M25, past Chorleywood; 9.30 pm, Sun 8.30 pm.*

FLETCHING, EAST SUSSEX 3–4B

The Griffin Inn **£49** **3 2 4**
TN22 3SS (01825) 722890
*"The London pedigree (family links to the River Café) shows through" at this "very cosy" 16th-century inn, with views of the Ouse. The pub food is "excellent" (and comes in "delicious and generous portions"), and the garden is "lovely when the sun has got its hat on!" / **Details:** www.thegriffininn.co.uk; off A272; 9.30 pm, Sun 9 pm. / **Accommodation:** 13 rooms, from £85*

FOLKESTONE, KENT 3–4D

Rocksalt **£55** **4 4 4**
4-5 Fishmarket CT19 6AA (01303) 212 070
*"You can literally see the boats bringing in the catch" at Mark Sargeant's "classy" contemporary fish-restaurant where "you eat overlooking the old harbour, gazing out to sea". If it wasn't so darn expensive, it would be rated even higher given the "wonderfully inventive" cooking, "impeccable service" and "superb views". / **Details:** www.rocksaltfolkestone.co.uk; 10 pm; closed Sun D. / **Accommodation:** 4 rooms, from £85*

FOLLIFOOT, NORTH YORKSHIRE 5–1C

Horto Restaurant at Rudding Park

Rudding Park HG3 1JH (01423) 871350
This summer 2016 pop-up (above the golf shop) is now to find a permanent home in this luxury hotel's new spa development, when it opens in 2017. The focus of ex-Norse chef Murray Wilson is daily-changing tasting menus drawn from the hotel's extensive kitchen garden.

FONTHILL GIFFORD, WILTSHIRE 2–3C

Beckford Arms **£45** **3 3 4**
SP3 6PX (01747) 870 385
*"A hidden gem in the countryside that's worth finding"; "I'm not sure what more you could ask for in a country pub for Sunday lunch… it has a lovely relaxed atmosphere, an open fire, dogs sleeping, and EXCEPTIONAL roasts". / **Details:** www.thebeckfordarms.co.uk; 9.30 pm, Sun 9 pm; no Amex. / **Accommodation:** 10 rooms, from £95*

FORT WILLIAM, HIGHLAND 9–3B

Crannog **£55** **4 3 3**
Town Centre Pier PH33 6DB (01397) 705589
*In a "great location overlooking Loch Linnhe" – it's set on a pier next to the Fort William ferry, from which the fisherman owner runs cruises – a heavingly busy institution known for its good, simple seafood. / **Details:** www.crannog.net; 9 pm; no Amex.*

FRESSINGFIELD, SUFFOLK 3–1D

The Fox & Goose **£50** **3 4 4**
Church Rd IP21 5PB (01379) 586247
*"Paul Yaxley has got it nailed" at his "well-above-average gastropub in a delightful setting", which is "the best for miles around". "The ground floor has more of a buzz than the first-floor area, and the small bar with local real ales is a bit of a find". / **Details:** www.foxandgoose.net; off A143; 8.30 pm, Sun 8.15 pm; closed Mon; Yes; children: 9+ at D.*

FRILSHAM, BERKSHIRE 2–2D

The Pot Kiln £57 434

RG18 0XX (01635) 201366

"Definitely worth a visit" – a "very pretty", rather out of the way country pub with a "good garden and lovely setting". Game is particularly "excellent", but that's no surprise given that chef/director Mike Robinson, also connected with London's famed Harwood Arms, is something of a stalking authority. There are "great bar snacks" too (also available outside in summer), and regular pizza nights. / **Details:** *www.potkiln.org; between J12 and J13 of the M4; 9 pm, Sun 8 pm.*

FRITHSDEN, HERTFORDSHIRE 3–2A

The Alford Arms £49 334

HP1 3DD (01442) 864480

Following a fire and a six-month refurbishment, this "proper country pub" reopened its doors in August 2016; fans hope it "will be back to the usual standard" before long (ratings shown), serving "accomplished" and "interesting" food. / **Details:** *www.alfordarmsfrithsden.co.uk; near Ashridge College and vineyard; 9.30 pm, Fri & Sat 10 pm, Sun 9 pm; Booking max 12 may apply.*

FROXFIELD, WILTSHIRE 2–2C

The Palm £38 443

Bath Rd SN8 3HT (01672) 871 818

"A real find in deepest Wiltshire" – a swanky, and rather remote, South Indian off the A4, which "can get very busy" owing to its "good creative" food (especially curries). / **Details:** *www.thepalmindian.com; 11.30 pm.*

FULLER STREET, ESSEX 3–2C

Square And Compasses £33 333

CM3 2BB (01245) 361477

This 17th-century beamed country inn is "a bit hard to find but worth seeking out" thanks to its "excellent pub food, which usually includes a number of game dishes sourced from local estates"; the biggest complaint this year? – the "portions are too large!" / **Details:** *www.thesquareandcompasses.co.uk/.*

FYFIELD, OXFORDSHIRE 2–2D

White Hart £49 334

Main Road OX13 5LW (01865) 390585

The food at this 15th-century chantry – complete with vaulted dining room and large garden – is consistently rated as "well worth the drive to the middle of nowhere". / **Details:** *www.whitehart-fyfield.com; off A420; 9.30 pm, Sun 3 pm; closed Sun D.*

GATESHEAD, TYNE AND WEAR 8–2B

Eslington Villa Hotel £45 333

8 Station Rd NE9 6DR (0191) 487 6017

A "lovely little old-fashioned restaurant" ("close to, but fully screened from the Team Valley Trading Estate") where "the short menu is top quality" – and comes at "generous prices" too. / **Details:** *www.eslingtonvilla.co.uk; A1 exit for Team Valley Trading Estate, then left off Eastern Avenue; 9.30 pm; closed Sat L & Sun D.* / **Accommodation:** *18 rooms, from £90*

Six, Baltic Centre for Contemporary Arts £59 215

Baltic (Sixth Floor) NE8 3BA (0191) 440 4948

With "amazing views over the Newcastle quayside", this 6th-floor dining room is certainly a "great place to take visitors", and fans say that it's "also a reliable foodie destination in its own right"; there are dissenters, though – with incidents of "truly dire" service attracting particular ire. / **Details:** *www.sixbaltic.com; Mon - Sat 9.30 pm, Sun 3.30 pm; closed Sun D.*

GERRARDS CROSS, BUCKINGHAMSHIRE 3–3A

Maliks £44 423

14 Oak End Way SL9 8BR (01753) 880888

"Still the best curry in the area" – the spin-off from Cookham's favourite Indian gave the original a run for its money this year, thanks to its "lovely" ambience and the fact that "everything tastes great". / **Details:** *www.maliks.co.uk; 10.45 pm.*

Three Oaks £49 343

Austenwood Ln SL9 8NL (01753) 899 016

"Simple food is done very well" – "it always justifies the gastropub tag, and often goes beyond" – at this "lovely little gem, hiding away past the London borders". / **Details:** *www.thethreeoaksgx.co.uk; 9.15 pm.*

GILLINGHAM, DORSET 2–3B

Stock Hill Country House Hotel & Restaurant £62 454

SP8 5NR (01747) 823626

For "a delightful experience in beautiful peaceful surroundings", head to Peter Hauser's "splendid" old-school country house hotel. "Quality ingredients are respectfully prepared (with some hints of Austrian influences)" to an outstanding level, while "wife Nita is a consistently charming front of house". / **Details:** *www.stockhillhouse.co.uk; 8.30 pm; closed Mon L; no*

Amex; No jeans; children: 8+ at D in dining room. / **Accommodation:** 10 rooms, from £260

GLASGOW, CITY OF GLASGOW 9–4C

Atlantic Bar and Brasserie

Saint Vincent Place G1 2EU (0141) 221 0220

Launched at the end of 2015, this good-looking bar-restaurant (on the lower ground floor beneath The Anchor Line) majors in rotisserie chicken, but also serves a wide-ranging selection of Gallic dishes and steaks; a trendy gin list is a feature. / ***Details:*** *www.atlanticbrasserie.co.uk; 10pm.*

Babu £27 432

186 W Regent St G2 4RU (0141) 204 4042

"Amazing, fresh, spicy and authentic Mumbai-style street food" makes for "a quick and interesting snack when in central Glasgow", at this tiny, 3-table café. "Spot on recommendations from friendly staff", too. / ***Details:*** *www.babu-kitchen.com; 9 pm, Mon 4 pm; closed Mon D & Sun.*

The Bistro at One Devonshire Gardens £68 344

1 Devonshire Gdns G12 0UX
(0141) 339 2001

The restaurant of this luxe West End boutique hotel (nowadays part of the Hotel du Vin group) has a fine culinary history, having been, back in the day, a showcase for both Andrew Fairlie and Gordon Ramsay. Nowadays, it's still "a place to go for a special occasion", certainly in terms of plushness, and the "extremely comprehensive wine list", "expertly served by a very knowledgeable sommelier". Foodwise, fans say the cuisine is "second to none" too, and it was solidly rated this year. / ***Details:*** *www.hotelduvin.com.*

Black Dove £48 344

67 Kilmarnock Rd G41 3YR (0141) 231 1021

"The sort of place that the Southside of Glasgow has been waiting for" – "a new small-plates concept, of good quality and less expensive than equivalents in trendy Finnieston". A comprehensive list of cocktails and craft beers is part of its appeal. / ***Details:*** *www.blackdovedining.com; 11pm.*

Café Gandolfi £45 334

64 Albion St G1 1NY (0141) 552 6813

This Merchant City veteran (est. 1979) is something of a local institution, with a "relaxed", vaguely bohemian woody interior; it turns out dependable, straightforward Scottish scoff (haggis, neeps, tatties etc.), and has also spawned a number of spin-offs nearby. / ***Details:*** *www.cafegandolfi.com; 11.30 pm; Booking weekdays only.*

Crabshakk £53 533

Finnestone G3 8TD (0141) 334 6127

"The eponymous crab is superb" ("the crab cakes are real crab cakes"), at this "tiny, noisy, cramped little bar off a busy Glasgow street"; it serves "a limited but excellent selection" of "awesomely good fresh fish" – "I've never been disappointed with anything off the tattered menu!" / ***Details:*** *www.crabshakk.com; 10 pm; closed Mon; no Amex.*

The Fish People Cafe £48 332

350 Scotland Street G5 8QF (0141) 429 8787

"Despite its location" – opposite Shields Road subway station – this "tiny" and "buzzy" spot ("more restaurant than café") still "packs a punch with fresh, fresh fish presented in a range of different options". / ***Details:*** *www.thefishpeoplecafe.co.uk; Mon closed, Tue - Thu 9 pm, Fri & Sat 10 pm, Sun 8; closed Mon.*

Gamba £65 443

225a West George St G2 2ND
(0141) 572 0899

For a "unique experience with food to match", head to this acclaimed city-centre basement, that's long won renown for its "simple fish dishes, well cooked and well presented" – "I visited Glasgow in May 2016, and this was the best of the six restaurants I tried". / ***Details:*** *www.gamba.co.uk; 10 pm; closed Sun L.*

Gandolfi Fish £47 332

84 - 86 Albion Street G1 1NY
(0141) 552 9475

Café Gandolfini's fishy spin-off (near the original in the Merchant City) offers an "excellent set of seafood choices" including "particularly well-cooked local fish". / ***Details:*** *www.cafegandolfi.com; Mon - Sat 10.30 pm, Sun 9 pm.*

The Gannet £48 543

1155 Argyle St G3 8TB (0141) 2042081

This "cool and friendly" Finnestoun two-year-old, from an ex-ABode hotel team, is "definitely on the way up"; fans proclaim it a "true gem", where the small plates are "tasty and imaginative", and the "limited space is very well used to create a bustling, purposeful atmosphere". / ***Details:*** *www.thegannetgla.com; Mon closed, Tue - Sat 9.30 pm, Sun 7.30 pm.*

Hanoi Bike Shop £30 322

8 Ruthven Ln G12 9BG (0141) 334 7165

"Step straight off the Glasgow subway on a rainy night, and into a little piece of Vietnam", at this "funky", "Tardis-like" West End café (on a 2-floor site that was once Stravaigin 2, long RIP), and which provides "great, imaginative and tasty Vietnamese street food" ("including pheasant – believe it!"). / ***Details:*** *www.hanoibikeshop.co.uk; 11 pm, Fri & Sat 12.30 am.*

The Honours, Malmaison Glasgow £50 344

278 West George St G2 4LL (0141) 572 1001
In a "lovely" space at the foot of the Malmaison hotel, "the Martin Wishart empire's new outpost may not have quite the star quality of his Edinburgh and Loch Lomond establishments, but it is a very welcome addition to the Glasgow culinary scene". / ***Details:*** *www.thehonours.co.uk/glasgow.*

Mother India £38 433

28 Westminster Ter G3 8AD (0141) 339 9145
"Wonderful curries and tikkas" – some would say the best in town – help ensure it's "always busy" at this well-known West End fixture; the "charming upstairs room is candlelit and always filled with happy diners" (and may, therefore, be preferred to the noisy basement). / ***Details:*** *www.motherindiaglasgow.co.uk; 10.30 pm, Fri & Sat 11 pm, Sun 10 pm; Mon-Thu D only, Fri-Sun open L & D.*

Rogano £64 333

11 Exchange Place G1 3AN (0141) 248 4055
"Perfectly managed old-fashioned dining" awaits at this large Art Deco icon, in the city centre, where the decor – by the same team as the Queen Mary – is "worth seeing", and where the seafood, while "expensive", is "just about worth it" too. "If it was in London, the Caprice group would be snapping it up!" / ***Details:*** *www.roganoglasgow.com; 10.30 pm.*

Shish Mahal £40 442

60-68 Park Road G22 6DX (0141) 334 7899
"Continues as ever to be a favourite of Glaswegians – many of whom have been eating here for decades"; this "well-loved" curry house (which lays claim to the creation of chicken tikka masala) attracts nothing but bouquets for its "wonderful food" (albeit served in "not necessarily wonderful surroundings"). / ***Details:*** *www.shishmahal.co.uk; 11 pm, Fri, Sat 11.30pm, Sun 10 pm; closed Sun L; No bookings.*

Stravaigin £54 433

28 Gibson St G12 8NX (0141) 334 2665
Something of a local food hero, Colin Clydesdale's long-established world food pioneer in the West End inspires strong but mixed feelings; all agree the eclectic food is "good and interesting", but service can be a bit "cooler-than-thou". The ambience of the lively upstairs bar is sometimes preferred to that of the basement restaurant. / ***Details:*** *www.stravaigin.co.uk; 11 pm; no Amex.*

Two Fat Ladies at The Buttery £60 445

652 Argyle St G3 8UF (0141) 221 8188
Near the SECC, Ryan James's wood-panelled, business-friendly bastion with quiet booths inspired surprisingly little feedback this year for its seafood-focused cooking, but it remained extremely well rated. / ***Details:*** *www.twofatladiesrestaurant.com; 10 pm, Sun 9 pm.*

Ubiquitous Chip £59 335

12 Ashton Ln G12 8SJ (0141) 334 5007
"On the bustling Byres Road", this "fantastic Glaswegian institution" (est. 1971) is known for its "brilliant, relaxed atmosphere", particularly for a date in the cute conservatory. Gastronomically speaking, its famous wine list and one of Scotland's best whisky selections are at least an equal attraction to the modern Scottish cooking. / ***Details:*** *www.ubiquitouschip.co.uk; 11 pm.*

GOLDSBOROUGH, NORTH YORKSHIRE 8–3D

The Fox And Hounds Inn £61 343

YO21 3RX (01947) 893372
"In an area of outstanding beauty", Jason Davies's pub remains a real hit thanks to its "simple but really well-produced" Yorkshire food; "if it's open, and you can get a table, it's well worth going out into the wilds...." / ***Details:*** *www.foxandhoundsgoldsborough.co.uk; 8.30 pm; D only, closed Sun-Tue; no Amex.*

GORING-ON-THAMES, OXFORDSHIRE 2–2D

The Miller of Mansfield £52 322

High St RG8 9AW (01491) 872829
Taken over by Mary and Nick Galer, ex-of The Fat Duck Group, in 2014, this 18th-century coaching inn, in a pretty Thames-side village betwixt the Berkshire Downs and Chilterns, wins praise for its "fantastic" and "really well-presented food" (including a "perfect Sunday lunch"). / ***Details:*** *www.millerofmansfield.com.*

Rossini at The Leatherne Bottel £58 224

Bridleway House RG8 0HS (01491) 872667
"Just lovely on a summer's evening" – the "gorgeous riverside setting", with extensive al fresco seating in warmer weather, is the crown jewel of this Thames Valley fixture. There are few exaggerated claims made for its Italian cuisine, but on all accounts it's "fresh" and "reasonably priced". / ***Details:*** *www.leathernebottel.co.uk; Mon closed, Tue - Sat 10.30 pm, Sun 3pm; closed Sun D; children: 10+ for D.*

GRASMERE, CUMBRIA 7–3D

The Forest Side £74 555

Keswick Rd LA22 9RN (01539) 435 250
"A newcomer that will clearly reach the heights"; "this latest in Andrew Wildsmith's small collection of boutique hotels (Hipping Hall, etc.)" – "an imposing-looking Victorian building, a short walk

from Grasmere village" – is "fabulous in all respects" (seldom are reports quite so ecstatic). Decor-wise, "the formality-versus-informality, the luxury-versus-elegance are exceptionally well balanced, and the dining room itself is a gorgeous airy space (quite distinct from the style of the rest of the hotel) with a touch of the Scandi about it". "Kevin Tickle (ex L'Enclume) has devised a tasting menu that's clever without being overwrought and completely divine, showing off his foraging roots, and with many of the ingredients coming from the hotel's own kitchen garden". "It's only been open since January but already it's establishing itself as one of the best (if not the best) place to eat in this part of the Lakes." / **Details:** *www.theforestside.com; 9.30 pm.* / **Accommodation:** *0 rooms, from £20*

The Jumble Room £48 **334**
Langdale Road LA22 9SU (01539) 435 188
It's "always a delight to be able to revisit this gem in picture-perfect Grasmere" – from the "quirky interior" to the "diverse menu" it "scores all round". / **Details:** *www.thejumbleroom.co.uk; Mon & Tue closed, Wed - Sun 9.30 pm; closed Tue.* / **Accommodation:** *3 rooms, from £180*

GREAT GONERBY, LINCOLNSHIRE 5–3D

Harry's Place £84 **342**
17 High Street NG31 8JS (01476) 561780
"Unique: a bucket-list, must-visit experience!"; Harry and Caroline Hallam's "quaint" 10-seat venture, in their front room, continues to dazzle most reporters, owing to Caroline's "lovely" personal service, and Harry's "outstanding cooking", using whatever seemed good to buy that day. In such a tiny space, ambience can be elusive (and is somewhat dependent on fellow diners), and it also drew some unusual flak for being "overpriced" this year, amidst the odd accusation that it had "lost its sparkle somewhat". On most reports, however, this remains one of the UK's most individual of indies! / **Details:** *on B1174 1m N of Grantham; Tue-Sat 8.30 pm; closed Mon & Sun; no Amex; Booking essential; children: 5+.*

GREAT LIMBER, LINCOLNSHIRE 6–2A

The New Inn £46 **333**
2 High St DN37 8JL (01469) 569998
A two-year-old boutique hotel, run by Ian Matfin (whose pedigree includes Gordon Ramsay, Michael Caines and Raymond Blanc) and his wife, and based in the old village pub. Chef Chris Grist turns out "high-quality food rooted in local produce in season" (the latter sourced from the surrounding Brocklesby Estate). / **Details:** *www.thenewinngreatlimber.co.uk; 9 pm, Sun 6 pm.* / **Accommodation:** *0 rooms, from £10*

GREAT MILTON, OXFORDSHIRE 2–2D

Le Manoir aux Quat' Saisons £198 **555**
Church Road OX44 7PD (01844) 278881
"One of the most beautiful places in the UK"; Raymond Blanc has created "a jewel-like experience" (especially for couples who stay over in one of its rooms), at this "immaculately kept" Elizabethan manor, in a small village south of Oxford – "an iconic destination" (and the survey's most mentioned outside London). "From the moment you step out of the car", the "staff's welcome instantly makes you feel at ease", and a visit to the gardens – including the large kitchen garden that partly supplies the dining room – is an essential part of the trip; "even in the icy cold of February they are a pleasure to wander around", and "make one truly believe that fairy tales are indeed true!" For some reporters the atmosphere in the dining conservatory itself is exceeded by other elements of the experience, but quibbles in this respect are few. Meanwhile, if there's a gripe about the "beautiful and typically French haute cuisine", it's that some find it "slightly lacking innovation" – but for the vast majority of guests its "finesse" and "awe-inspiring attention to detail" contribute to an overall occasion that's "a benchmark for all things good in hospitality". Naturally it's best not to dwell on the prices, but the overwhelming verdict is that it's "worth it!" / **Details:** *www.manoir.com; from M40, J7 take A329 towards Wallingford; 9.30 pm; Booking max 12 may apply.* / **Accommodation:** *555 rooms, from £32* / **Sustainability:** ★★★

GREAT MISSENDEN, BUCKINGHAMSHIRE 3–2A

Wild Stawberry Cafe, Peterley Farm £19 **335**
Peterley Lane, HP16 0HH (01494) 863 566
"This pretty, characterful yurt on a Peterley Farm" is "always a lovely experience", and "it's the thoughtful little touches, like homegrown flowers, which make all the difference". It serves "gorgeous coffee, breakfast, lunch and tea", featuring "lots of locally produced ingredients (including fantastic sourdough bread made from grain grown in fields less than a mile away)". / **Details:** *www.peterleymanorfarm.co.uk/cafe/.*

GREETHAM, RUTLAND 5–3D

The Wheatsheaf £43 **432**
Stretton Rd LE15 7NP (01572) 812325
"A passion for cooking by Carol and the enthusiasm of her partner Scott for delivering front of house make this pub worth a detour again and again" –

*and don't miss the "brilliant" twice-cooked chips! / **Details:** www.wheatsheaf-greetham.co.uk; 9 pm; closed Mon & Sun D; no Amex.*

GRESFORD, WREXHAM 5–3A

Pant-yr-Ochain £47 345
Old Wrexham Road LL12 8TY
(01978) 853525
*A visit to this "very comfortable" and quaint manor house overlooking a lake is "like having your own country club!"; although the food can be "hit and miss", and there's little local competition, the "good beers" and "ever-changing" nosh makes it "one of the best Brunning & Price" spots. / **Details:** www.brunningandprice.co.uk/pantyrochain; 1m N of Wrexham; 9.30 pm, Sun 9 pm.*

GUILDFORD, SURREY 3–3A

Rumwong £42 344
18-20 London Rd GU1 2AF (01483) 536092
*"The best Thai outside Thailand" (well, nearly) say fans of this "always buzzing" veteran (est. 1978), which owes its high popularity to its "authentic cuisine" and "charming service". / **Details:** www.rumwong.co.uk; 10.30 pm; closed Mon; no Amex.*

The Thai Terrace £42 343
Castle Car Pk, Sydenham Rd GU1 3RW
(01483) 503350
*"Delightful food and great service" continue to win acclaim for this offbeat Thai, over a multi-storey car park; the "only downside is the slightly cramped" dining room ("very noisy") – best visit on a sunny day when the roof terrace offers "fabulous views over Guildford". / **Details:** thaiterrace.co.uk; 10.30 pm; closed Sun; no Amex.*

GULLANE, EAST LOTHIAN 9–4D

Chez Roux, Greywalls Hotel £59 344
EH31 2EG (01620) 842144
*A Roux empire outpost in a posh Lutyens-designed country house hotel; even sceptics of the "somewhat unchanging" menu award the food respectable marks – while fans feel that "of the Chez Roux restaurants in Scotland, this is the best by quite a margin". / **Details:** www.greywalls.co.uk; 10 pm; Jacket required. / **Accommodation:** 23 rooms, from £260*

GULWORTHY, DEVON 1–3C

The Horn of Plenty, Country House Hotel & Restaurant £73 344
Country House Hotel & Restaurant PL19 8JD
(01822) 832528
*This once-famous restaurant-with-rooms, "off the beaten track" and overlooking the Tamar Valley, continues its return to form; even the most sceptical reporter (who said the food is "nothing exceptional") rates it well overall, and the majority of reporters find that "splendid" food contributes to "a fine experience". / **Details:** www.thehornofplenty.co.uk; 3m W of Tavistock on A390; 9 pm; No jeans. / **Accommodation:** 10 rooms, from £95*

GWITHIAN TOWANS, CORNWALL 1–4A

Godrevy Beach Cafe £27 333
TR27 5ED (01736) 757999
*In a "quirky" (award-winning) building with a raised deck, this "cheap 'n' cheerful" modern beachside café is a reliable option for "high-quality home cooking" and "friendly service". / **Details:** www.godrevycafe.co.uk; 5 pm.*

HAMBLETON, RUTLAND 5–4D

Finch's Arms £45 224
Oakham Rd LE15 8TL (01572) 756575
*"With views over Rutland Water", a big garden and a "great ambience", this characterful village pub has all the ingredients for "a lovely day out"; the food can be "hit and miss", and service "can still be patchy", but it has its high points, and "it's always busy". / **Details:** www.finchsarms.co.uk; 9.30 pm, Sun 8 pm. / **Accommodation:** 10 rooms, from £100*

Hambleton Hall £92 554
LE15 8TH (01572) 756991
*"A beautiful country house hotel, with wonderful views over Rutland Water" provides the setting for Tim Hart's long-established East Midlands temple of gastronomy. It is "very expensive", and one or two reporters qualify their feedback with the odd reservation regarding the overall approach (which can seem a little "stiff and old-fashioned"), but these are minor concerns, as few restaurants can match its "old-school charm", or are as "consistently exceptional over the years". "Service is really spot-on (friendly but always professional)", and Aaron Patterson's "classic" cuisine is "always perfect in every respect", and matched with an "astonishing wine list" – "with many unusual items, ranging from everyday, affordable discoveries, to the most famous first-growths". / **Details:** www.hambletonhall.com; near Rutland Water; 9.30 pm; children: 5+. / **Accommodation:** 17 rooms, from £265*

HARDWICK, CAMBRIDGESHIRE 3–1B

The Blue Lion £47 343
74 Main Street CB23 7QU (01954) 210328
This 17th-century gastroboozer "has a lovely feel to it, with its cosy log fire and helpful and friendly staff"; "it caters for everyday diners as well as those wanting a more special evening out", and "the beer garden is nice in the summer too". / **Details:** *www.bluelionhardwick.co.uk; Mon - Fri 9 pm, Sat 9.30, Sun 8 pm; no Amex.*

HAROME, NORTH YORKSHIRE 8–4C

The Pheasant Hotel £62 444
YO62 5JG (01439) 771241
From its "very helpful" service to its "very good" food and excellent atmosphere ("a little Swiss chalet-style" in parts) there's no shortage of praise for this "lovely" establishment. As ever, fans insist that it's "better than its more famous neighbour, The Star Inn" (same owners). / **Details:** *www.thepheasanthotel.com; 9 pm; no Amex.* / **Accommodation:** *15 rooms, from £155*

The Star Inn £68 443
Harome YO62 5JE (01439) 770397
Fans of Andrew Pern's famous thatched inn hail "some of the best cooking in the country in a most beautiful setting" ("cosy in winter, gorgeous in summer") at this "rustic but refined" destination – "the pub all pubs want to be when they grow up", and "a brilliant, romantic experience". It doesn't win the highest ratings, though, due to some vocal refuseniks, who say "it's not worth the hype", and "hugely overrated". / **Details:** *www.thestaratharome.co.uk; 3m SE of Helmsley off A170; Mon - Sat 9.30 pm, Sun 6 pm; closed Mon L & Sun D; no Amex.* / **Accommodation:** *8 rooms, from £150*

HARPENDEN, HERTFORDSHIRE 3–2A

Lussmanns £46 233
20a Leyton Road AL5 2HU (01582) 965393
Numerous locals think of this branch of a well-known local group as "the best in the small chain" (although its ratings are, in fact, a tad lower than the St Albans original). Whatever the truth, it's "a happy spot", serving "mostly fish, but also a good carnivore selection". / **Details:** *www.lussmanns.com/restaurants/harpenden-res.* / **Sustainability:** ★★★

HARROGATE, NORTH YORKSHIRE 5–1C

Bettys £44 345
1 Parliament Street HG1 2QU
(01423) 814070
"You can't go to Yorkshire without eating at Betty's!"; for "the definition of an afternoon tea", and "classic old-world charm", head to these legendary tearooms – everything is "simply perfect". If there's a caveat, it's that you "can expect to queue most days", but it's "worth the wait". / **Details:** *9 pm; no Amex; No bookings.* / **Sustainability:** ★★

Bettys Garden Café, RHS Gardens Harlow Carr £36 444
Crag Lane, Beckwithshaw HG3 1QB
(01423) 505604
"The queues are testament to the success" of this "lovely modern pavilion" attached to the RHS Gardens at Harlow Carr (although some fans say it "avoids the crowding and parking problems of the famous Betty's tearooms in the centres of Harrogate and York"). "There's just the same menu: mouthwatering sandwiches, pastries and cakes", and what's more, "staff make you feel special" (and "are particularly good with people eating on their own"). / **Details:** *www.bettys.co.uk; Sun-Sat 9 pm.*

Clock Tower, Rudding Park £72 433
Follifoot HG3 1JH (01423) 871350
This chic hotel-restaurant with a conservatory and "pleasant" park view is a real "special occasion" place, where "the food, service and venue all aspire to the highest standards, and frequently achieve them" too. / **Details:** *www.ruddingpark.com; 10 pm.* / **Accommodation:** *49 rooms, from £170*

Drum & Monkey £46 434
5 Montpellier Gdns HG1 2TF (01423) 502650
"A Harrogate institution of great seafood"; this old Montpellier fixture, owned by the Carter family since 2013, has by and large "survived changes of ownership, and continues to offer top-quality fresh fare, with friendly and helpful service" – making it "a must for locals and visitors alike, even if tables are a little crammed together". / **Details:** *www.drumandmonkey.co.uk; 9 pm; closed Sun; no Amex; Booking max 10 may apply.*

Graveley's Fish & Chip Restaurant £45 342
8-12 Cheltenham Parade HG1 1DB
(01423) 507 093
Some reporters feel it's "not so cheap these days", but this authentic fixture – part of a small northern empire – still draws the crowds with some of the "best fish 'n' chips in Yorkshire". / **Details:** *www.graveleysofharrogate.com; Mon - Thur 9 pm, Fri & Sat 10 pm, Sun 8-9 pm.*

Norse £33 443

22 Oxford St HG1 1PU (01423) 202363

*"Just fantastic!" – café by day, and Nordic fine-dining haunt by night; "the new-wave Scandi cooking is great value", and "the homemade schnapps send you home with a glow". While "they could (frankly) charge much more for what they do", instead "they have introduced a demand-led pricing policy, so Tuesday night is discounted by 25%". / **Details:** www.norserestaurant.co.uk; 9 pm.*

Orchid £43 554

28 Swan Road HG1 2SE (01423) 560 425

*Harrogate's most enduring restaurant success-story – this "superb" pan-Asian favourite is "hard to beat for its food", and "you are always sure of a warm reception". Top Tip – "the Sunday lunch buffet is a fantastic chance to sample the menu". / **Details:** www.orchidrestaurant.co.uk; 10 pm; closed Sat L / **Accommodation:** 28 rooms, from £115*

Quantro £47 443

3 Royal Parade HG1 2SZ (01423) 503034

*An "ever-reliable" Harrogate fixture where the "simple, honest" food, "served from what appears to be a minuscule kitchen, is far better than the cost would suggest"; its "superb-value" weekday lunches in particular are a "bargain that cannot be beaten". / **Details:** www.quantro.co.uk; Mon - Sat 10 pm, Sun closed; closed Sun; children: 4+ at D.*

Sasso £47 343

8-10 Princes Square HG1 1LX
(01423) 508 838

*There's "always a good selection of more unusual Italian dishes" at this long-established local favourite, where "if you pick a good day, it's very good"; "very convenient for the shops too, with plenty of pay and display nearby!" / **Details:** www.sassorestaurant.co.uk; Mon - Thur 9.30 pm, Fri & Sat 10 pm, Sun closed; closed Sun.*

Stuzzi £45 444

46B Kings Road HG1 5JW (01423) 705852

*This "difficult-to-pigeonhole" venture occupies a hip (for Harrogate) hotel-brasserie, playing "cool music", and with flashes of funky decor. Its "limited but changing menu" of "Italian tapas" is a case of "simple food done really, really well", and there's "excellent wine" to go with it. / **Details:** 10pm.*

HARROW WEALD, MIDDLESEX 3–2A

The Hare £49 222

Old Redding HA3 6SD (020) 8954 4949

*"Formerly the site of a pub called The Hare, and then something called Blubreckers", this "very popular, busy and noisy" spot recently joined Raymond Blanc's fast-growing gastroboozer chain (The White Brasserie Co.); cynics claim it's "now catering for a much lower common-denominator, with undemanding grub", but for most reporters its very "decent". / **Details:** www.hareoldredding.com; 10 pm, Fri & Sat 10.30 pm, Sun 9 pm .*

HARROW, GREATER LONDON 3–3A

Incanto, The Old Post Office £52 344

41 High Street HA1 3HT (020) 8426 6767

*This "favourite local and top Italian" changed hands at the end of 2015. Ratings support those who say "it's still just as good...in fact, I would say even better as I prefer the more traditional menu". / **Details:** www.incanto.co.uk; Mon closed, Tue - Sat 10.30 pm, Sun closed; closed Mon & Sun D.*

HASELBURY PLUCKNETT, SOMERSET 2–3B

White Horse £45 333

North Street TA18 7RJ (01460) 78873

*In a 17th-century building, this "lovely local pub" turns out "some exceptional dishes", from "superb" fish to "particularly good" starters and "the best roast beef lunch". / **Details:** www.thewhitehorsehaselbury.co.uk; 11pm.*

HASSOP, DERBYSHIRE 5–2C

Hassop Hall £60 343

DE45 1NS (01629) 640488

*The Chapman family's romantic and "rather traditional" country house hotel is a good-value culinary destination. Perhaps a refreshing of the formula might be due, but overall there's strong praise for its "lovely" parkland setting and "welcoming service". / **Details:** www.hassophall.co.uk; on the B6001 Bakewell - Hathersage Road, Junction 29 of M1; 9 pm; closed Mon L, Sat L & Sun D. / **Accommodation:** 13 rooms, from £100*

HASTINGS, EAST SUSSEX 3–4C

Maggie's £24 443

Rock-a-Nore Road TN34 3DW
(01424) 430 205

*"Nothing fancy, just honest fresh fish 'n' chips well cooked" – the simple but unbeatable formula behind this modest café set in the Old Town, directly "amongst the fishing sheds", and boasting pleasant views of the sea. / **Details:** www.towncitycards.com/locations/hastings/ma; 9 pm; closed Mon D, Tue D, Wed D, Thu D & Sun; Cash only.*

The Pelican Diner £15 334

East Parade TN34 3AL (01424) 421555

"On Hastings Old Town seafront, with outdoor seating for those fine days", this quirky US

diner-style venue makes a "great breakfast or brunch spot"; "book upstairs for a view of the sea while you tuck into traditional burgers with the most divine side of coleslaw". / ***Details:*** *www.thepelicandiner.co.uk/coming_soon.html; 4 pm.*

Webbe's Rock-a-Nore £49 3 3 4
1 Rock-a-Nore Road TN34 3DW
(01424) 721650
"The fish comes straight from the fishermen on the beach across from the restaurant" at Paul Webbe's simple operation "opposite the Jerwood Gallery"; the seafood platters are "a gourmet delight for fish lovers" (there are also "all-day breakfasts, sarnies and a good menu for younger ones") and there are "wonderful views of the sea, the Old Town and towards Eastbourne" too. / ***Details:*** *www.webbesrestaurants.co.uk; 9.30 pm.*

HATCH END, GREATER LONDON 3–2A

Sea Pebbles £35 3 2 3
348-352 Uxbridge Rd HA5 4HR
(020) 8428 0203
For "good-quality fish every time" (including gluten-free fare on Mondays), head to this stalwart chippie; the diner-style premises were recently expanded and, post-makeover, its walls now bear jaunty illustrations of local history. / ***Details:*** *www.seapebbles.co.uk; 9.45 pm; closed Sun; May need 8+ to book.*

HATFIELD PEVEREL, ESSEX 3–2C

The Blue Strawberry £47 3 3 3
The Street CM3 2DW (01245) 381 333
This "good-quality country restaurant" within the village has long been one of the county's better culinary destinations, and remains consistently well rated all round. / ***Details:*** *www.bluestrawberrybistro.co.uk; 3m E of Chelmsford; Mon - Sat 10 pm, Sun 4 pm; closed Sun D.*

HAUGHTON MOSS, CHESHIRE 5–3B

The Nag's Head £43 3 3 3
Long Lane CW6 9RN (01829) 260 265
"One of the Ribble Valley Inns" – this "lovely, friendly gastropub" lives up to the brand with "good locally sourced cuisine" that's "served in great surroundings". / ***Details:*** *www.nagsheadhaughton.co.uk; Mon - Thur 9 pm, Fri & Sat 9.30 pm, Sun 9 pm.*

HAY ON WYE, POWYS 2–1A

St Johns Place £42 3 3 2
St. John's Chapel & Meeting Rooms, Lion Street, HR3 5AA (07855) 783799
"Only open part of the week, but worth the wait" – this café in an old chapel provides "a small, well-considered, weekly-changing menu, with good imaginative combos". / ***Details:*** *www.stjohnsplacehay.tumblr.com; 11 pm; Cash only.*

HAYWARDS HEATH, WEST SUSSEX 3–4B

Jeremy's at Borde Hill £57 4 4 4
Borde Hill, Borde Hill Gardens RH16 1XP
(01444) 441102
"Jeremy and his team have certainly not lost their touch", say fans of his "delightful dining room" – "a longtime favourite" that's "even better on the sun terrace overlooking the garden when weather permits". It again inspires one or two accusations of "living on past glories", but most reports say it's "excellent in all respects". / ***Details:*** *www.jeremysrestaurant.com; Exit 10A from the A23; 10 pm; closed Mon & Sun D.*

HEDLEY ON THE HILL, NORTHUMBERLAND 8–2B

The Feathers Inn £44 4 3 2
NE43 7SW (01661) 843 607
"Very popular" village gastroboozer – and "deservedly so", given its "interesting range of dishes" (including "excellent game and other local produce"). The interior's "a bit stark", and "it can feel cramped when busy (which is the norm)", but it's "well worth the effort to get out there". / ***Details:*** *www.thefeathers.net; Mon & Tue closed, Wed - Sat 8.30 pm, Sun 4.30 pm; closed Mon & Sun D; no Amex.*

HELMSLEY, NORTH YORKSHIRE 8–4C

Black Swan £67 4 3 3
Market Pl YO62 5BJ (01439) 770466
"Perfectly situated in this pleasant market town", an upscale boutique hotel dining room where chef Paul Peters delivers food that's "beautiful to look at" as well as to eat – from bold tasting menus through to "exceptional" breakfasts, and "fantastic gluten-free Yorkshire afternoon teas". Service is on the up of late too. / ***Details:*** *www.blackswan-helmsley.co.uk; 9.30 pm /* ***Accommodation:*** *45 rooms, from £130*

HEMINGFORD GREY, CAMBRIDGESHIRE 3–1B

The Cock £50 343
47 High St PE28 9BJ (01480) 463609
"It's always a pleasure to dine at The Cock" – "an absolute gem in a quintessential English riverside village". "You get a sense that it's there for the locals who love coming and really enjoy their food" – the latter from "a menu with character, individuality and quality" (plus top wines from the South of France). / **Details:** *www.thecockhemingford.co.uk; off the A14; follow signs to the river; 9 pm, Fri & Sat 9.30 pm, Sun 8.30 pm; Yes; children: 5+ at D.*

HENLEY IN ARDEN, WARWICKSHIRE 5–4C

Cheal's of Henley £72 443
64 High St B95 5BX (01564) 793 856
Matt Cheal, ex-head chef of Simpson's in Edgbaston set up shop in this old house on the high street towards the end of 2015. Feedback so far is limited, but full of praise for its "interesting menu and well-presented cuisine". / **Details:** *www.chealsofhenley.co.uk.*

HENLEY, WEST SUSSEX 3–4A

The Duke Of Cumberland £54 435
GU27 3HQ (01428) 652280
A "great English country pub serving wonderful food in an unpretentious manner", amid flagstone floors, log fires and vintage decor; the garden overlooking the South Downs is another major asset. / **Details:** *www.thedukeofcumberland.com; 10 pm.*

HENLEY-ON-THAMES, OXFORDSHIRE 3–3A

Luscombes at the Golden Ball £56 343
The Golden Ball, Lower Assendon RG9 6AH
(01491) 574157
In a lovely rustic setting, a "properly posh gastropub" ("the Chilterns set were turning up in droves") with a "nice garden" and "always cheerful service" (plus cooking that's "a cut above"). The "very cosy" upstairs may be preferred to the "buzzy" downstairs. / **Details:** *www.luscombes.co.uk; 10 pm; no Amex.*

Shaun Dickens at The Boathouse £66 444
The Boathouse RG9 1AZ (01491) 577937
"A fabulous location right on the Thames" sets the scene at Shaun Dickens's contemporary-style venture – "a gem of a restaurant serving high-quality and well conceived dishes in a sophisticated environment", and with "fantastic service" to boot. "Deserves its growing reputation." / **Details:** *www.shaundickens.co.uk; Wed - Sun 9.30 pm; closed Mon & Tue.*

Villa Marina £44 233
18 Thameside RG9 1BH (01491) 575262
For "excellent authentic Italian cooking", look no further than this smart sibling to Marlow's Villa d'Este, which has a great location next to the river. / **Details:** *www.villamarina-henley.com; opp Angel pub, nr Bridge; 10.30 pm, Sun 9 pm.*

HEREFORD, HEREFORDSHIRE 2–1B

Castle House Restaurant, Castle House Hotel £54 344
Castle St HR1 2NW (01432) 356321
Near the cathedral, this townhouse boutique hotel dining room is the "best restaurant in Hereford by a mile", combining "interesting locally sourced food and a warm welcome". / **Details:** *www.castlehse.co.uk; 9.30 pm, Sun 9 pm.* / **Accommodation:** *24 rooms, from £150*

HERNE BAY, KENT 3–3D

Le Petit Poisson £42 443
Pier Approach, Central Parade CT6 5JN
(01227) 361199
"Great to see a proper fish restaurant thriving in Herne Bay" – a seafront venue whose "small, ever-changing menu and reasonable prices" charm local fans ("I'd happily go every week"). / **Details:** *www.lepetitpoisson.co.uk; 9.30 pm, Sun 15.30 pm; closed Mon & Sun D; no Amex.*

HERSTMONCEUX, EAST SUSSEX 3–4B

The Sundial £64 444
Gardner St BN27 4LA (01323) 832217
"THE place to go in the Eastbourne area for a memorable meal", say fans of this "excellent", long-established (but contemporary-style) venture in a beamed building with marvellous views of the South Downs; its "stylish cooking" shows a strong Gallic slant. / **Details:** *www.sundialrestaurant.co.uk; centre of village; 9.30 pm Tue-Fri, Sat 10 pm; closed Mon & Sun D.*

HESWALL, MERSEYSIDE 5–2A

Burnt Truffle £48 423
104-106 Telegraph Road CH60 0AQ
(0151) 342 1111
Gary User's crowdfunded bistro yearling – a simply

*decorated two-storey building on the Wirral – has quickly won a strong fan club with its "novel, well thought-out dishes and cleverly selected wine in convenient volumes"; service, though sometimes "a little slow", is "cheerful and knowledgeable" too. / **Details:** www.burnttruffle.net; Mon - Thu 9 pm, Fri & Sat 10 pm, Sun 9 pm.*

HETHE, OXFORDSHIRE 2–1D

The Muddy Duck £55 344

Main St OX27 8ES (01869) 278099

*"Worth breaking your journey for if you're on the M40" (or visiting Bicester Shopping Village) – this four-year-old pub, in a tucked-away village, "feels really special as soon as you go inside to be greeted by the knowledgeable and charming staff, and the food's first class too". Large garden (with funky carvings) for the summer months. / **Details:** www.themuddyduckpub.co.uk; 9 pm, Sun 4 pm; closed Sun D.*

HETTON, NORTH YORKSHIRE 5–1B

The Angel Inn £49 434

BD23 6LT (01756) 730263

*"One of the UK's first gastropubs", this long-established Dales destination is "still always worth a visit for anything from a bar lunch all the way to a meal in the formal dining room (and the rooms are very comfortable too)". Its heavyweight wine list is an equal attraction to its robust country cooking. / **Details:** www.angelhetton.co.uk; 5m N of Skipton off B6265 at Rylstone; 9 pm; D only, ex Sun open L only. / **Accommodation:** 9 rooms, from £150*

HEXHAM, NORTHUMBERLAND 8–2A

Battlesteads £43 443

Wark on Tyne NE48 3LS (01434) 230 209

*"An eco-friendly inn with everything right" – a pub, hotel and restaurant with "a seasonal à la carte featuring produce from their own market garden, an extensive wine list, and several local cask beers"; "the attention to detail makes it a great pleasure to eat there at any time". A "superb 8-course tasting menu" is one of the many options ("the semifreddo and carpaccio of beetroot was worth driving miles to sample!"). / **Details:** www.battlesteads.com.*

Bouchon Bistrot £46 332

4-6 Gilesgate NE46 3NJ (01434) 609943

*"Like stepping into a restaurant in the heart of France" – a solid northern venture combining "agreeable" bistro fare and superior service ("the staff could not have been more attentive, and the maître d' was extremely knowledgeable"). / **Details:** www.bouchonbistrot.co.uk; 9.30 pm; closed Sun; no Amex.*

The Rat Inn £41 333

Anick NE46 4LN (014) 3460 2814

*"A charming, characterful pub between Hexham and Hadrian's Wall"; while the food "isn't haute cuisine by any means", dishes are nonetheless "cooked very well" (fish, in particular, comes in a "more modern idiom than meat"). / **Details:** www.theratinn.com; closed Sun D.*

HINTLESHAM, SUFFOLK 3–1D

Hintlesham Hall £68 224

Duke Street IP8 3NS (01473) 652334

*The setting of this famous old manor is "perfect for a romantic lunch or dinner". Its culinary standing has faded in recent times, but even fans who say it's "not inspiring", insist it's "well prepared". / **Details:** www.hintleshamhall.com; 4m W of Ipswich on A1071; 10 pm; Jacket required; children: 12+. / **Accommodation:** 33 rooms, from £99*

HINTON-ST-GEORGE, SOMERSET 2–3A

Lord Poulett Arms £47 434

TA17 8SE (01460) 73149

*A lovely, old village gastroboozer-with-rooms, whose "very atmospheric" interior is a big highlight. All aspects of the operation are well rated though – with "really imaginative food" matched by kitchen and dining room staff who "go out of their way to be helpful". / **Details:** www.lordpoulettarms.com; 9 pm; no Amex. / **Accommodation:** 4 rooms, from £85*

HOLKHAM, NORFOLK 6–3C

The Victoria at Holkham £49 324

.NR23 1RG (01328) 711008

*By one of the UK's most stunning beaches, The Vic – the Holkham Estate's coastal hotel – is "ideal for families in terms of location", and "service is great for dogs as well as humans". Most reports say it's "perfect in terms of welcome and food" too, but the odd cynic – irked by its prices – feels "the Earl of Leicester is taking his serfs for granted…it's just a pub serving pub grub. The note on the menu (from the Earl) encourages the diner to try unusual cuts we wouldn't normally consider. On the menu: pork belly; burger; roast chicken; venison sausages; duck breast!" / **Details:** www.holkham.co.uk; on the main coast road, between Wells-next-the Sea and Burnham Overy Staithe; 9 pm; no Amex. / **Accommodation:** 10 rooms, from £140*

HOLT, NORFOLK 6–3C

Wiveton Hall Cafe £45 333

1 Marsh Lane NR25 7TE (01263) 740525

*On a pick-your-own fruit farm with views over the marshes and out to sea, this "easygoing café with colourful tables" wins praise for its "good food in large portions" (be it offbeat tapas or wood-fired pizza); great "outside space for children to run around in" too. / **Details:** www.wivetonhall.co.uk/thecafe; 4.30 pm; closed Mon D, Tue D, Wed D, Thu D & Sun D.*

HONITON, DEVON 2–4A

The Holt £44 333

178 High Street EX14 1LA (01404) 47707

*"Consistent, genuine and sometimes inventive cooking of local ingredients" is the order of the day at this "convivial" pub, owned by the Otter Brewery; as well as substantial meals, British 'tapas' is served at the bar. / **Details:** www.theholt-honiton.com; Mon closed, Tue - Thu 9 pm, Fri & Sat 9.30 pm, Sun; closed Mon & Sun.*

HORDLE, HAMPSHIRE 2–4C

The Mill at Gordleton £48 335

Silver Street SO41 6DJ (01590) 682219

*In "a beautiful location" – a converted mill set amid gardens on the banks of the Avon – this elegant, ivy-clad boutique hotel is an "exceptionally friendly" spot, and its "competent cooking" does nothing to detract from the experience. / **Details:** www.themillatgordleton.co.uk; on the A337, off the M27; Mon - Sat 9.15 pm, Sun 8.15 pm; no Amex. / **Accommodation:** 8 rooms, from £150*

HORNDON ON THE HILL, ESSEX 3–3C

The Bell Inn £50 434

High Rd SS17 8LD (01375) 642463

*"A special place, on the top of the hill, where the bar is packed with lively conversation from locals and visitors alike"; some regulars prefer eating there to the restaurant ("same menu but also good-value, high-quality bar meals") – in either case the food's "very good". / **Details:** www.bell-inn.co.uk; signposted off B1007, off A13; 9.45 pm; Booking max 12 may apply. / **Accommodation:** 15 rooms, from £50*

HORSHAM, WEST SUSSEX 3–4A

Restaurant Tristan £67 543

3 Stans Way RH12 1HU (01403) 255688

*"New furniture and redecoration since the fire at Christmas has if anything spruced-up the atmosphere" at Tristan Mason's 16th-century building in the town centre. "Service is now very good, as his wife Candy has improved the front of house", and his "terrific and clever cuisine" continues to offer an "exceptional gastronomic experience". / **Details:** www.restauranttristan.co.uk; Tue-Sat 9.30 pm; closed Mon & Sun.*

HOUGH ON THE HILL, LINCOLNSHIRE 6–3A

Brownlow Arms £51 333

NG32 2AZ (01400) 250234

*A popular, scenically located village gastroboozer combining "restaurant-quality food" and solid service. / **Details:** www.brownlowarms.co.uk; on the Grantham Road; 9.15 pm; closed Mon, Tue-Sat D only, closed Sun D; no Amex; children: 10+. / **Accommodation:** 5 rooms, from £98*

HOWDEN, EAST YORKSHIRE 5–1D

Kitchen £24 433

38 Bridgegate DN14 7AB (01430) 430600

*"A simple tearoom (most of the eating area is upstairs)" and "fantastic deli" providing "a visual and tasty feast", from "brilliant breakfasts" to "light meals" and "excellent cakes and coffee"; "none of the dishes disappoint", and it's "a lovely little spot". / **Details:** www.kitchensnaith.co.uk; 5pm.*

HOYLAKE, MERSEYSIDE 5–2A

Lino's £39 444

122 Market St CH47 3BH (0151) 632 1408

*"An 'old reliable', yes, but the food has improved considerably over the past year or so" at this veteran Mediterranean venue, whose "friendly" service "makes you feel welcome and special every time". / **Details:** www.linosrestaurant.co.uk; 3m from M53, J2; 10 pm; D only, closed Mon & Sun; no Amex.*

HUDDERSFIELD, WEST YORKSHIRE 5–1C

Eric's £55 443

73-75 Lidget St HD3 3JP (01484) 646416

*"In what is a virtual wasteland for good eateries, Eric's restaurant shines a beacon with consistent offerings and quality food", as well as a "friendly and welcoming environment"; "it is to be hoped he does not spread his time too thin having opened a 'superior' burger joint a few doors down". / **Details:** www.ericsrestaurant.co.uk; 10 pm; closed Mon, Sat L & Sun D; no Amex.*

Med One **£42** 3 3 3
10-12 West Gate HD1 1NN (01484) 511100
*A cheap 'n' cheerful Lebanese favourite in the town centre, where "the quantities are large but the tastes never fail";"the main courses aren't quite as exciting, but the mezze starters are second to none"... "order 5 between 2 and eat tapas-style." / **Details:** www.med-one.co.uk; 10 pm.*

HULL, EAST YORKSHIRE 6–2A

1884 Dock Street Kitchen **£60** 2 3 4
Humber Dock Street, Marina HU1 1TB
(01482) 222260
*There were a couple of off-meals mentioned this year, but for the majority of reporters it's "always a treat" to dine at this "metropolitan" three-year-old, in a converted dock-side building with "lovely" views of the Humber and Hull Marina. / **Details:** www.1884dockstreetkitchen.co.uk/index.html; 9.30 pm; closed Mon & Sun D.*

HUNSDON, HERTFORDSHIRE 3–2B

The Fox And Hounds Restaurant & Bar **£43** 3 3 3
2 High Street SG12 8NH (01279) 843 999
*This "wonderful family-run gastropub" is a real "joy" that "caters for all age groups and diets";"their Black Angus côte de boeuf is always extremely good, but so is their fish, and and and...!" / **Details:** www.foxandhounds-hunsdon.co.uk; off the A414, 10 min from Hertford; Mon closed, Tue - Sat 9.30 pm, Sun 3.30 pm; no Amex.*

HUNTINGDON, CAMBRIDGESHIRE 3–1B

Old Bridge Hotel **£54** 2 3 3
1 High St PE29 3TQ (01480) 424300
*John Hoskins MW's "vast knowledge and cellar" are evident in the "stellar" wine list of this ivy-clad townhouse hotel dining room (with attached wine shop) – "a lovely spot for kicking backing in". Foodwise, it's more "variable", and the smaller dining room is preferred to the main restaurant. / **Details:** www.huntsbridge.com; off A1, off A14; 10 pm. / **Accommodation:** 24 rooms, from £160*

HURWORTH, COUNTY DURHAM 8–3B

The Bay Horse **£51** 4 4 4
45 The Grn DL2 2AA (01325) 720 663
*"Gorgeous food prepared with care, style, imagination and great technique" ("especially game") is to be found at this "cosy" gastropub; "choose a discreet table in the small dining room for an intimate dinner". / **Details:** www.thebayhorsehurworth.com; 9.30 pm, Sun 8 pm.*

HYTHE, KENT 3–4D

Hythe Bay **£46** 3 4 3
Marine Pde CT21 6AW (01303) 233844
*"If you enjoy fish (plus great views over Hythe Bay and "reasonable" wines) this place is a must" – a waterfront operation where service comes "with a smile";"they must be doing something right because they are opening their third fish restaurant" in Deal (following on from its Dover sibling). / **Details:** www.hythebay.co.uk; 9.30 pm.*

Saltwood On The Green **£49** 3 4 4
The Grn CT21 4PS (01303) 237 800
*In a former village store, where diners "sit amongst restored Edwardian shop fittings", this new solo venture from American-born chef Jeff Kipp (ex-Duck & Waffle) provides "imaginatively constructed" food, and its brunch is something of a "local institution". / **Details:** www.saltwoodrestaurant.co.uk; 11 pm, Sun 5pm; closed Mon, Tue & Sun D.*

ILKLEY, WEST YORKSHIRE 5–1C

Bettys **£47** 4 5 5
32 The Grove LS29 9EE (01943) 608029
*This "very elegant" outpost of the much-loved tearooms offers an experience that's simply "first class", be it for "fabulous cakes and pastries" or a spot of lunch;"it was exceptionally busy, but staff didn't falter and we never felt rushed to leave". / **Details:** www.bettys.co.uk/tea-rooms/locations/ilkle; 5.30 pm; no Amex; No bookings. / **Sustainability:** ★★*

Bistro Saigon **£41** 3 3 2
1A, Railway Rd LS29 8DE (01943) 817999
*Near the railway, this tiny Vietnamese bistro has built up quite the local fanbase, with weekend tables snapped up far in advance; the reason? – "excellent food, well prepared and served". / **Details:** www.bistrosaigon.co.uk; 10 pm, Sun 8.30 pm; closed Mon.*

The Box Tree **£79** 5 4 5
35-37 Church St LS29 9DR (01943) 608484
"The Box Tree is class, and exudes it from its every pore!"; Simon and Rena Gueller's "special and quirky" institution is "that very rare thing these days: a posh restaurant (jackets for men, tablecloths for tables, sculpted butter, eau de toilette in the gents, etc.) serving classic food in the French tradition... might one call it the Gavroche of the North?" Results are generally "faultless" – from Lawrence Yates's "meticulously prepared", "classic-style cuisine", to the "amazing and extensive wine list

(you could spend some serious money getting into very rare wine here)", and the "wonderfully relaxed yet civilised ambience". / **Details:** *www.theboxtree.co.uk; on A65 near town centre; 9.30 pm; closed Mon, Tue L, Wed L, Thu L & Sun D; No jeans; children: 10+.*

IPSWICH, SUFFOLK 3–1D

Mariners at Il Punto £48 335
Neptune Quay IP4 1AX (01473) 289748
A revamped 100-year-old Belgian gunboat makes an unusual setting for this unconventional venue, run by the Crépy family on the waterfront; fans suggest there's not much to say about the Gallic food, it's "just very good". / **Details:** *www.marinersipswich.co.uk; Tue- Sat 9.30 pm; closed Mon & Sun; no Amex.*

Trongs £34 453
23 St Nicholas St IP1 1TW (01473) 256833
Year after year this "family-run" stalwart "maintains its standard", from the "delightful service" to the fine Chinese cuisine (with a Vietnamese accent) – indeed its loyal army of fans "love everything about it". / **Details:** *www.trongs.co.uk; 10.30 pm; closed Sun.*

IRBY, MERSEYSIDE 5–2A

Da Piero £51 442
5-7 Mill Hill Rd CH61 4UB (0151) 648 7373
"Every dish is a winner" at this "out-of-the-way" Sicilian; on the downside, "ambience can be lacking", but it's partly compensated for by the "welcoming and friendly" staff. / **Details:** *www.dapiero.co.uk; 9 pm; D only, closed Mon & Sun; no Amex.*

JERSEY, CHANNEL ISLANDS –

Bohemia, The Club Hotel & Spa £85 544
Green St, St Helier JE2 4UH (01534) 876500
"The food here is at the top end of the excellent scale, and there's great attention to detail in respect of everything" at Stephen Smith's famous St Helier dining room, whose ambience received a much-needed boost a couple of years ago, making it a very strong all-rounder nowadays. / **Details:** *www.bohemiajersey.com; 10 pm; No trainers. /* **Accommodation:** *46 rooms, from £185*

Longueville Manor £84 444
Longueville Rd, St Saviour JE2 7WF
(01534) 725501
This "beautiful" and "romantic" 16th-century Relais & Châteaux manor house makes a "very pleasant place for a relaxed Sunday lunch", a "wonderful" seafood supper, or "lovely" afternoon tea featuring "dainty little cakes plus endless pots of tea". / **Details:** *www.longuevillemanor.com; head from St. Helier on the A3 towards Gorey; less than 1 mile from St. Helier; 10 pm; No jeans. /* **Accommodation:** *31 rooms, from £170*

Mark Jordan at the Beach £51 444
La Plage, La Route de la Haule, St Peter JE3 7YD (01534) 780180
"An ideal beachside location with pleasant outdoor space" makes this glass-walled St Aubin's Bay restaurant a particularly popular choice on sunny days; the food's relatively accomplished – fish in particular. / **Details:** *www.markjordanatthebeach.com; 9.30 pm; closed Mon.*

The Oyster Box £58 434
St Brelade's Bay JE3 8EF (01534) 850 888
In a "beautiful location overlooking the sea" (at St Brelade's Bay), this "very relaxed" New England-style bistro continues to win acclaim for its "fantastic fish" – fans have "never had a bad meal there"… "and how could you beat eating grade one oysters with that view!" / **Details:** *www.oysterbox.co.uk; Mon - Thur 9 pm, Fri & Sat 9.30 pm, Sun 9 pm; closed Mon L & Sun D; no Amex.*

Suma's £60 334
Gorey Hill, Gorey JE3 6ET (01534) 853291
A "small but delightfully formed restaurant on Jersey's eastern coast overlooking the bay and Gorey Castle"; on the food front, "local produce features across the menu" and there's "always something to please". Top Tip – snap up a "romantic" balcony table (they've "added more shelter" to the outdoors this year). / **Details:** *www.sumasrestaurant.com; underneath castle in Gorey Harbour; 9.30 pm, Sun 3.30 pm; closed Sun D; Booking max 12 may apply.*

KELHAM ISLAND, SOUTH YORKSHIRE 5–2C

The Milestone £47 433
84 Green Lane At Ball Street S3 8SE
(0114) 272 8327
This Victorian gastroboozer, set amid one of the city's oldest industrial sites (parking can be "tricky") is a "fun" sort of place offering "locally sourced and delicious" food (not least brunch). / **Details:** *www.the-milestone.co.uk; 10 pm; no Amex.*

KENDAL, CUMBRIA 7–4D

Castle Dairy £54 544
26 Wildman St LA9 6EN (01539) 733946
"The unique setting in Kendal's oldest building, and the fact that it is mostly staffed by apprentice chefs, makes the standard of the fine dining experience even more impressive" at this "quirky" Grade I-listed

property – "run by the local catering college as an apprentice training operation". Closed as a result of Storm Desmond flooding in December, it is set to re-open in late 2016 with Chris O'Callaghan (most recently at Linthwaite House) as head chef. We've rated it assuming a maintenance of its former outstanding level of "modern British cooking, with a certain magpie tendency" (including "a real treat of a tasting menu"). "It's the best eating in Kendal, and lest that sound like damning with faint praise, I find it worth the journey from Lancashire!" / **Details:** *www.castledairy.co.uk; 9 pm.*

KENILWORTH, WARWICKSHIRE 5–4C

Bosquet £56 543

97a Warwick Rd CV8 1HP (01926) 852463

A visit to Bernard and Jane Lignier's "sublime" Gallic stalwart is "like being transported to a small town in the Midi", June "is attentive, friendly and efficient", while Bernard oversees a "great gastronomic experience" – "the difficulty is choosing, with every dish being so inviting". / **Details:** *www.restaurantbosquet.co.uk; 9.15 pm; closed Mon, Sat L & Sun; closed 2 weeks in Aug.*

The Cross at Kenilworth £71 532

16 New St CV8 2EZ (01926) 853840

'Great British Chef' Adam Bennett "goes from strength to strength" at this "informal" pub – hailed by fans as "200% improved!" since it was relaunched by Andreas Antona (ex- of Simpson's, Brum) two years back; let's just "hope the chef's ambition and obvious talent do not outgrow the attractions of this pleasant hostelry". / **Details:** *www.thecrossatkenilworth.co.uk; 10 pm; closed Sun L.*

KENTISBURY , DEVON 1–2C

The Coach House, Kentisbury Grange £65 544

EX31 4NL (01271) 882 295

"North Devon's finest dining experience by far" – this two-year-old collaboration with the ex-Gidleigh chef is firing on all cylinders currently. The scenic spot sits in a stylish converted coach house on the grounds of a boutique hotel, and "every mouthful of food is exciting". / **Details:** *www.kentisburygrange.com/; 10pm.*

KESWICK, CUMBRIA 7–3D

The Cottage In The Wood £73

Whinlatter Forest CA12 5TW

(01768) 778409

"A little gem hidden away" in a boutique hotel "with lovely views down the valley"; "eating here is always a memorable occasion" owing to the "well thought-out menu (with lesser cuts made interesting)" and "excellent wine pairings". Stop Press – in October 2016 the owners put the business on the market in preparation for their retirement, and the following month chef Chris Archer announced his departure (so we've left it unrated). / **Details:** *www.thecottageinthewood.co.uk; 9 pm; closed Mon & Sun; no Amex.* / **Accommodation:** *10 rooms, from £96*

Lyzzick Hall Country House Hotel £58 333

Underskiddaw CA12 4PY (017687) 72277

"A real find in the northern Lakes" – Dorothy & Alfredo Fernandez's 35-year-old country house hotel has a "lovely location" on extensive parkland near Keswick, and "very accommodating staff". The new monthly-changing tasting menu makes "a welcome addition", but the star of the show for gastronauts remains the acclaimed wine list – "a real treat for Iberian fans", with "old wines that are still in good condition and at remarkable prices". / **Details:** *www.lyzzickhall.co.uk; 9 pm; no Amex.* / **Accommodation:** *30 rooms, from £148*

KETTLESHULME, CHESHIRE 5–2B

The Swan Inn £46 323

Macclesfield Rd SK23 7QU (01663) 732943

Out in the sticks, a "lovely" old pub whose "popular" bar "complements the new, light and pleasant dining room" – the latter offering a "full view of the kitchen and Josper oven from which superb fish and meat dishes" emerge. / **Details:** *8.30 pm, Thu-Sat 7 pm, Sun 4 pm; closed Mon; no Amex.*

KEYSTON, CAMBRIDGESHIRE 3–1A

The Pheasant at Keyston £52 322

Loop Rd PE28 0RE (01832) 710241

This thatched pub is "a bit of an Old Bridge, Huntingdon lookalike" – no surprise since it's "in the same group of course". "The country pub atmosphere seems largely to have gone", but on the upside, it's "consistent" in its service of "fine gastropub food". / **Details:** *www.thepheasant-keyston.co.uk; 1m S of A14 between Huntingdon & Kettering, J15; Mon closed, Tue - Sat 9.30 pm, Sun 3.30 pm; closed Mon & Sun D; no Amex.*

KIBWORTH BEAUCHAMP, LEICESTERSHIRE 5–4D

The Lighthouse £48 423

9 Station Street LE8 0LN (0116) 279 6260

It may be "about as far as you can get from the sea

on this island, but the fish and seafood are excellent" at the Boboli family's Anglo follow-up to their hit (and more haute) Italian venue, Firenze; if there's a tiny quibble it's that service can be "rushed" or relaxed. / **Details:** *www.lighthousekibworth.co.uk; Mon closed, Tue - Sat 9.30 pm, Sun closed; D only, closed Mon & Sun; no Amex.*

KILLIECRANKIE, PERTH AND KINROSS 9–3C

Killiecrankie House Hotel £62 454

PH16 5LG (01796) 473220

"The welcome and service from Henrietta and her team (plus the "good ambience") make this small country house hotel a special place to stay", while the kitchen also wins plaudits for its "good-quality cooking"; away from the dining room, simpler meals are served in the conservatory bar. / **Details:** *www.killiecrankiehotel.co.uk; 8.30 pm; no Amex; No shorts. /* **Accommodation:** *10 rooms, from £150*

KINGHAM, GLOUCESTERSHIRE 2–1C

Daylesford Café £45 324

Daylesford near Kingham GL56 0YG
(01608) 731700

This yummy mummy-beloved farmshop café remains "a great option in the country" for diners (and brunchers) seeking a faux-rustic organic idyll, and prepared to pay for it; "such a pain to wait for a table though!" and "when busy" (which is often) "standards can slip". / **Details:** *www.daylesfordorganic.com; Mon-Wed 4.30 pm, Thu 7pm, Fri & Sat 9 pm, Sun 3 pm; L only. /* **Sustainability:** ★★★

KINGHAM, OXFORDSHIRE 2–1C

The Kingham Plough £61 444

The Green OX7 6YD (01608) 658327

Emily Watkins (a Blumenthal protégé) "was one of the first to bring such heights of cookery to the Cotswolds", and this village pub is "more akin to a high-class restaurant". The cooking – "big on sous vide and doesn't compromise on quality of ingredients or creative execution" – "manages to put a special touch on everything including the basics (like perfect bread and butter)". / **Details:** *www.thekinghamplough.co.uk; 9 pm, Sun 8 pm; closed Sun D; no Amex. /* **Accommodation:** *7 rooms, from £95*

The Wild Rabbit £66 324

Church St OX7 6YA (01608) 658 389

"A bit too Notting-Hill-in-the-country" for some tastes, Lady Bamford's hotel and restaurant has for some time been "trying hard to get a Michelin star", and finally pulled it off in October 2016. Even fans can find it "expensive", and for some sceptics the perceived push for culinary recognition means "everything is very, very showy nowadays, and you need to take out a mortgage for food not much different to cheaper options nearby". Even so, it does win consistently "safe" ratings for its "stylish and tasty" cuisine. / **Details:** *www.thewildrabbit.co.uk; 10 pm.*

KINGSTON UPON THAMES, SURREY 3–3A

The Canbury Arms £44 323

49 Canbury Park Road KT2 6LQ
(020) 8255 9129

"Appetising menus and food you really want to eat" – all "in surroundings you feel at home in" – help make this a "great community pub"; "I wouldn't exchange it for any of the flush, plush, trumperies of Mayfair!" / **Details:** *www.thecanburyarms.com; Mon - Sat 10 pm, Sun 8.30 pm.*

Jin Go Gae £46 432

272 Burlington Rd KT3 4NL (020) 8949 2506

This "out-of-the-way place (unless you live in SW London)" is "a cut above all the many other local Korean" venues – but "shhh, don't tell anyone!"; the main event is the "fantastic, authentic" cuisine (mainly BBQ, and coming at a "decent price") – indeed "you're not really here for anything else". / **Details:** *www.jingogae.co.uk; 11 pm.*

Roz ana £45 322

4-8 Kingston Hill KT2 7NH (020) 8546 6388

A superior Norbiton Indian – the venue is split between a casual downstairs or smarter, colonial-style upstairs room – with "very good" adventurous cooking. / **Details:** *www.roz-ana.com; 10.30 pm, Fri & Sat 11 pm, Sun 10 pm; no Amex; No bookings.*

KINGUSSIE, HIGHLAND 9–2C

The Cross £79 334

Tweed Mill Brae, Ardbroilach Rd PH21 1LB
(01540) 661166

With its super-scenic location, amid the Cairngorms National Park, this 18th-century inn (originally built as a watermill) is "a great place for gastronomic retreat" thanks to David Skiggs's high quality, ambitious cuisine (with the option of a 6-course taster menu). / **Details:** *www.thecross.co.uk; 8.30 pm; children: 9+. /* **Accommodation:** *8 rooms, from £100*

KIRKBY LONSDALE, CUMBRIA 7–4D

Hipping Hall £77 444
Cowan Bridge LA6 2JJ (01524) 271187
*This "flagship" of the Wildsmith Hotels boutique hotel chain "maintains very high all-round standards", including in its "old country-house-style dining hall", where Oli Martin creates "stunning and very, very clever dishes". / **Details:** www.hippinghall.com; 9.30 pm; closed weekday L; no Amex; No trainers; children: 12+. / **Accommodation:** 10 rooms, from £239*

KIRKCALDY, FIFE 9–4C

Amritsar £24 432
274 High St KY1 1LB (01592) 267 639
*'Indian Cuisine Of World Renown' is the promise of the home page of this family-run tandoori. That might be over-egging it a bit, but it is consistently highly rated for its "expertly prepared" dishes. / **Details:** Yes.*

KNOWSTONE, DEVON 1–2D

The Mason's Arms £64 533
South Molton EX36 4RY (01398) 341231
*Chef Mark Dodson's "Waterside Inn pedigree shines through" at this "pub-style" spot in a "quaint little mid-Devon village". While more "modest" than his former haunt, the "first-class" dishes strike a "perfect balance between the hearty and pretty" – "I always know I'll enjoy a meal here, menu unseen". / **Details:** www.masonsarmsdevon.co.uk; Mon closed, Tue - Sat 9 pm, Sun closed; closed Mon & Sun D; children: 5+ after 6pm.*

KNUTSFORD, CHESHIRE 5–2B

Belle Époque £54 213
60 King St WA16 6DT (01565) 633060
*"Clearly the ambience is the main draw" to this long-running, town-centre veteran, in a celebrated Art Nouveau building. As for the food? – "incidental" ("many years ago, this was the area's go-to place, now it's a shadow of that former self"). / **Details:** www.thebelleepoque.com; 1.5m from M6, J19; 9.30 pm; closed Sun D; Booking max 6 may apply. / **Accommodation:** 7 rooms, from £110*

KYLESKU, HIGHLAND 9–1B

Kylesku Hotel £44 445
IV27 4HW (01971) 502231
*"It takes a while to get to" this "jewel" of a hotel dining room in a remote corner of the Highlands, where diners are richly rewarded by "wonderful New England décor" (if a somewhat "basic" one), "amazing" loch views and some "excellent" catch (one reporter actually "saw the seafood being landed and entering the kitchen!") / **Details:** www.kyleskuhotel.co.uk; on A894, S of Scourie, N of loch inver; 9 pm; no Amex. / **Accommodation:** 8 rooms, from £55*

LANGAR, NOTTINGHAMSHIRE 5–3D

Langar Hall £50 335
Church Ln NG13 9HG (01949) 860559
*This "sumptuous" country house – "old-fashioned in ambience and setting, and second-to-none for and comfort" – has won renown for its "quirky" style, matched with "wonderful" cooking. It was the family seat and creation of splendidly idiosyncratic owner, Imogen Skirving, who, aged 78, tragically died (post-survey) in a car accident in June 2016. We've maintained the ratings in the hope that 22-year-old Lila Skirving, who has taken the reins, can follow successfully in her grandmother's footsteps. / **Details:** www.langarhall.com; off A52 between Nottingham & Grantham; 9.30 pm; no Amex; No trainers. / **Accommodation:** 12 rooms, from £100*

LANGFORD FIVEHEAD, SOMERSET 2–3A

Langford Fivehead 434
TA3 6PH (01460) 282020
*"An imposing 15th-century manor house tucked away in the Somerset Levels" is nowadays a restaurant-with-rooms, run by Olly and Rebecca Jackson, and inspires promising reports on the food front; a more 'bistro'-style menu is also available for lunch Wed-Fri (booking essential). / **Details:** thelangford.co.uk/.*

LANGHO, LANCASHIRE 5–1B

Northcote £98 554
Northcote Rd BB6 8BE (01254) 240555
*"A major decor upgrade for the better" (completed 2-3 years ago) still features in reports on the North West's most commented-on country house hotel – "a class act" in all respects. "Nigel Haworth (chef/patron) and Lisa Allen (head executive chef) have created the most wonderful menus – world-class yet true to their local roots" – delivered by "excellent but unfussy service". "I have been visiting Northcote for over 20 years, and have never been disappointed." / **Details:** www.northcote.com; M6, J31 then A59; 10 pm, Sun 9 pm; No trainers. / **Accommodation:** 18 rooms, from £280 / **Sustainability:** ★★★*

LAVENHAM, SUFFOLK 3–1C

Great House £64 554
Market Pl CO10 9QZ (01787) 247431
"Regis Crepy's brilliant restaurant in the heart of Lavenham never falters" and wins praise in many reports for a "perfect meal from start to finish". It occupies an "exquisite" timbered building, and provides "classic French cuisine, locally sourced, served in style, plus a great place to stay". What's more, "being taken into another room to peruse the amazing cheeseboard is always a treat to be relished!" / **Details:** *www.greathouse.co.uk; follow directions to Guildhall; 9.30 pm; closed Mon & Sun D; closed Jan; no Amex.* / **Accommodation:** *5 rooms, from £95*

Lavenham Greyhound £43 333
97 High Street CO10 9PZ (01787) 249553
The Melford Swan team's "refurbed local pub" is a "most enjoyable" spot, offering a "great new (small plates) menu concept" of the kind "usually found in London but not in Suffolk!"; for more conservative types, there are "good old pub favourites as well". / **Details:** *10 pm.*

Number Ten £39 433
10 Lady St CO10 9RA (01787) 249438
In an attractive 15th-century house in an old market town, this three-year-old establishment garners plaudits for its "interesting" and "well-executed" dishes (including pizza), and "reasonably priced wine". / **Details:** *www.ten-lavenham.co.uk; 9 pm.*

Swan Hotel £60 335
High St CO10 9QA (01787) 247477
This 15th-century inn at the heart of a pretty town provides a "fabulous setting", and even a reporter who says "the food is sometimes unadventurous" says it's "very good". Top Tip – "a truly indulgent afternoon tea". / **Details:** *www.theswanatlavenham.co.uk; 9 pm; No jeans; children: 12+ at D.* / **Accommodation:** *45 rooms, from £195*

LEAMINGTON SPA, WARWICKSHIRE 5–4C

La Coppola £50 333
86 Regent St CV32 4NS (01926) 888 873
"Very popular", quirkily styled Italian – a "reliable" spot with "very good food and service"; the owners also run two local coffee shops, Bar Angeli and Corleone Caffe, which are "fantastic too". / **Details:** *www.lacoppola.co.uk; 10 pm, Sun 9 pm; no Amex.*

Oscars French Bistro £47 344
39 Chandos Street CV32 4RL (01926) 452807
"You could be in France" at this "authentic" bistro – "cramped tables included!"; its "old-fashioned but delicious and comforting" country cooking has "no surprises but many pleasures", making it a contender for the "best place to eat in Leamington". / **Details:** *www.oscarsfrenchbistro.co.uk; 9.30 pm; closed Mon & Sun.*

Restaurant 23 £66 344
34 Hamilton Ter CV32 4LY (01926) 422422
Locals say "a big YES" to this "London-style" eatery in a Victorian house in the 'burbs, complete with cocktail bar and food that's "stunning" for the area. / **Details:** *www.restaurant23.co.uk/#!; 9.30 pm; closed Mon & Sun; children: 12+.*

LECHLADE, GLOUCESTERSHIRE 2–2C

The Five Alls £50 324
Filkins GL7 3JQ (01367) 860875
Sebastian Snow's (anyone remember 'Snows on the Green'?) village gastropub "just goes from strength to strength", winning consistent high ratings for its approach and cuisine: "better beers would be the only way to improve it!" / **Details:** *www.thefiveallsfilkins.co.uk; 9.30 pm, Fri & Sat 10 pm; closed Sun D; no Amex.*

LEEDS, WEST YORKSHIRE 5–1C

Aagrah £36 333
Aberford Rd LS25 2HF (0113) 2455 667
There's "always an enjoyable dining experience" to be had at this "very reliable and consistent performer" – a Garforth Kashmiri that's part of a well-established northern chain. / **Details:** *www.aagrah.com; from A1 take A642 Aberford Rd to Garforth; midnight, Sun 10.30 pm; D only.*

Aagrah £35 443
St Peter's Sq LS9 8AH (0113) 2455667
"Still one of the best modern Indian restaurants"; this plush city-centre outpost of the celebrated northern chain "ticks every box and more" – "great curry and great value!" / **Details:** *www.aagrah.com; midnight, Sun 1030 pm.*

Akbar's £34 433
16 Greek St LS1 5RU (0113) 242 5426
"The window into the kitchen makes for interesting viewing" at this popular Indian, where there's "no messing about: just great grills, breads and curries". In particular "watch the man making the monster naans… he does have pride in the job!" / **Details:** *www.akbars.co.uk; midnight; D only.*

Art's £43 333
42 Call Lane LS1 6DT (0113) 243 8243
Launched in the 1990s, this arty café and bar near the Corn Exchange remains a staple on the local scene ("when I'm in Leeds I never fail to call") owing to its "consistently high-class food"

(and at "very reasonable" prices too). / ***Details:*** *www.artscafebar.com; Mon - Thur 10 pm, Fri & Sat 10.30, Sun 10 pm.*

Bottega Milanese 3 4 3
4 Russell St LS1 5PT awaiting tel
"Easily the best coffee in Leeds" is one reason to visit this "very pleasant" city-centre café – others being "great nibbles" and a "mouthwatering range of cakes and sandwiches"... "why anyone goes to Costa next door is baffling!"

Bundobust £26 4 2 3
6 Mill Hill LS1 5DQ (01234) 567 890
A "cracking collaboration between local craft ale types (The Sparrow) and Prashad", an acclaimed local Indian; the two-year-old joint features simple wood-chip communal tables and a deck, while the street-food-style cuisine is "so good and tasty no one notices it's veggie too". / ***Details:*** *www.bundobust.com; Mon-Thur 9:30pm, Fri, Sat 10pm, Sun 8pm.*

Crafthouse, Trinity Leeds £64 3 3 4
Level 5 LS1 6HW (0113) 897 0444
Perched atop a new shopping centre, D&D London's first out-of-town opening is certainly a "stylish", glass-box-style spot. Not everyone is convinced by the cooking ("go for the views from the upstairs bar but not the food… if blindfolded, you'd not know what you'd eaten!"), but the majority laud "excellent food and ambience" – "great for a city meet-up with a friend or business!" / ***Details:*** *www.crafthouse-restaurant.com; 10.30 pm, Sun 9.30 pm.*

Fazenda, Waterman's Place £52 3 4 3
3 Wharf Approach, Granary Whf LS1 4GL (0113) 247 1182
The original branch of this expanding northern chain offers the successful all-you-can-eat rodizio formula for which the group has become known: eat your fill of meats brought to your table, then show the red card when you're at bursting point! / ***Details:*** *www.fazenda.co.uk/leeds/.*

Fourth Floor Café, Harvey Nichols £46 2 4 3
107-111 Briggate LS1 6AZ (0113) 204 8000
Atop the chi-chi shopping store, this attractive modern British brasserie remains a solid destination for "well-cooked and presented food"; "excellent value fixed price menu". / ***Details:*** *www.harveynichols.com/restaurant/leeds-dini; Mon 3 pm, Tue - Sat 10 pm, Sun 3.45 pm; L only, ex Thu-Sat open L & D; No bookings.*

Fuji Hiro £26 5 4 2
45 Wade Ln LS2 8NJ (0113) 243 9184
"The portion sizes are huge and damn tasty" at this basic but "wonderful" city-centre ramen bar offering a "proper 'cantina' feel". / ***Details:*** *10 pm, Fri & Sat 11 pm; May need 5+ to book.*

Hansa's £32 5 4 2
72-74 North St LS2 7PN (0113) 244 4408
Mrs Hansa Dabhi's city-centre stalwart serves "some of the most interesting Gujarati food you could wish to taste", and "the colours that emerge from the kitchen are an Instagrammer's dream". Even for a "devoted meat-eater", the place is a real "haven" ("my veggie friends can feel good, and I don't feel short-changed!") / ***Details:*** *www.hansasrestaurant.com; 10 pm, Sat 11 pm; D only, ex Sun L only.*

Kendells Bistro £45 3 4 4
St Peters Square LS9 8AH (0113) 2436553
A dark, "romantic", candle-lit French bistro with a "good choice of dishes, some of them excellent". / ***Details:*** *www.kendellsbistro.co.uk; Mon closed, Tue - Thur 9 pm, Fri & Sat 10 pm, Sun; D only, closed Mon & Sun; no Amex.*

The Man Behind The Curtain £98 5 4 3
Top Floor Flannels LS1 7JH (0113) 2432376
Amongst the most notable restaurants in the UK – Michael Hare's "unforgettable and must-visit" city-centre venue is "truly unique and improving exponentially". It's "a barn of a room" – a rooftop space over a men's clothes store, bizarrely entered through a shop – but service is "exemplary" and in any case you are here for the cooking: "a tour de force of whimsical and exciting food" ("some dishes reduced us to giggling schoolchildren at their brilliant audacity") from an "utterly beguiling" menu that "superficially looks gimmicky, but what it delivers is just remarkably delicious". / ***Details:*** *www.themanbehindthecurtain.co.uk; Sun - Tue closed, Wed - Sat 9.30 pm; closed Mon, Tue & Sun.*

MEATliquor £37 4 3 3
Bank St LS1 5AT (01138) 346 090
This "subterranean haven" of "great burgers, cocktails and really cool music" has "a great vibe" (even if "the dive bar ambience can be a bit trying at times") – "what more do you want from a burger joint?" / ***Details:*** *www.meatliquor.com/leeds; Fri & Sat 12.30am, Thurs 23.30pm, 23.30pm; May need + to book.*

Pintura £40 3 3 4
1 Trinity St LS1 6AP (0113) 4300 915
"Riding the current San Sebastian craze"; this "lively cocktail/pintxo place" – a huge three-floor operation with a "great gin bar" – "decent plates of appetising fare (not the absolute best but far better

than most!)" / **Details:** *www.pinturakitchen.co.uk; Mon - Sun, Late.*

Prashad £42 443
137 Whitehall Rd BD11 1AT (0113) 285 2037
This Gujarati stalwart continues to provide some "outstanding" food, with "beautiful spicing" and "lovely, unusual regional dishes" a highlight; they moved out of the centre a couple of years ago to these new premises, near the motorway. / **Details:** *www.prashad.co.uk; 11 pm; closed Mon, Tue L, Wed L & Thu L; no Amex.*

Red Chilli £41 433
6 Great George St LS1 3DW (01132) 429688
A centrally located basement, with a "good range" of dishes, including "some fiery cooking" (the Sichuanese options attract the most positive reports); it "can get very busy" at times, but crowds are well handled by the "accommodating" staff. / **Details:** *www.redchillirestaurant.co.uk; 10.30 pm, Fri & Sat 11.30 pm; closed Mon.*

Reds True Barbecue £42 334
Cloth Hall St LS1 2HD (0113) 834 5834
For a "fun American-style BBQ experience with pit masters who know their stuff!", this original branch of an 8-strong, mostly northern chain is just the job. / **Details:** *www.trucebarbecue.com; 11 pm, Fri & Sat midnight, Sun 10 pm.*

The Reliance £39 334
76-78 North St LS2 7PN (0113) 295 6060
"Hearty fare" – "simple ingredients, well-prepared from a menu full of good ideas", including "good, home-produced charcuterie" – plus "always-interesting beers and wines" and "friendly" staff win praise for this tucked-away but "very busy" boozer. / **Details:** *www.the-reliance.co.uk; 10 pm, Thu-Sat 10.30 pm, Sun 8.30 pm; No bookings.*

Salvo's £48 443
115 & 107 Otley Road LS6 3PX
(0113) 275 2752
"Still the best Italian place to eat in Leeds after 36 years" according to fans of this Headingley stalwart. With its "tasty, interesting" grub and "friendly, efficient service", this "noisy" staple "could teach some fine dining places a lesson or two". "They keep reinventing themselves and now have a wonderful salumeria a couple of doors away, which is a great all-day café with lots of Italian products to buy." / **Details:** *www.salvos.co.uk; Mon - Thur 10 pm, Fri & Sat 10.30 pm, Sun 9 pm; No bookings at diner.*

Sous le Nez en Ville £46 332
Quebec Hs, Quebec St LS1 2HA
(0113) 244 0108
"For a really lazy and boozy business lunch" this "lovely basement" stalwart is just the ticket; the Gallic menu can cause consternation, but only because "there are so many good things on it", and "the noise level can be high" (not helped by low ceilings) but "this reflects its enormous popularity". / **Details:** *www.souslenez.com; 9.45 pm, Sat 10.30 pm; closed Sun.*

Sukhothai £42 553
8 Regent St LS7 4PE (0113) 237 0141
Still the "best Thai in Leeds"; the original, Chapel Allerton outpost of this four-strong northern chain is "unmissable for food" (for added theatre, "sit at the correct tables and you can see the cooks at work!") Upbeat reviews for the city-centre branch, too. / **Details:** *www.sukhothai.co.uk; 10.45pm; Mon-Thu D only, Fri-Sun open L & D; no Amex.*

Tharavadu £38 543
7- 8 Mill Hill LS1 5DQ (0113) 244 0500
"Taking the city by storm since it first opened its doors" – this incredibly popular and "efficient" venue "may not look much from the outside, but is a really different sort of Indian restaurant" due to the Keralan focus on its menu, providing particularly "excellent fish mains" and "great for vegetarians" too. / **Details:** *www.tharavadurestaurants.com; 10 pm, Fri - Sat 10.30pm; closed Sun.*

Zaap £28 333
16 Grand Arcade LS1 6PG (0113) 243 2586
"If you want fast Thai street food that's cheap and delicious, you can't do better than Zaap" – a "bustling" new "city-centre favourite", set in the Grand Arcade, from the people behind Sukhothai; "kids love it"... after all, "what kid wouldn't enjoy dinner in a tuk tuk?" / **Details:** *www.zaapthai.co.uk/zaap-leeds; 11 pm; No bookings.*

Zucco £44 443
603 Meanwood Road LS6 4AY
(01132) 249679
"Always spoken of in revered terms amongst Leeds foodies" – a Meanwood Italian serving "small plates, beautifully crafted", plus an "interesting regional Italian wine list"; whilst "a little bit out of town", it's "absolutely worth the trip". / **Details:** *www.zucco.co.uk; 10 pm, Fri & Sat 10.30 pm, Sun 8.30 pm.*

LEICESTER, LEICESTERSHIRE 5–4D

Bobby's £24 321
154-156 Belgrave Rd LE4 5AT
(0116) 266 0106
"The best in Leicester's Golden Mile!", say fans of this ancient sweet shop and canteen, whose bargain basement Gujarati cuisine has made it a mainstay of the area since 1976. / **Details:** *www.eatatbobbys.com; 10 pm; no Amex.*

Hotel Maiyango £51 444
13-21 St Nicholas Pl LE1 4LD
(0116) 251 8898
*"The best choice in Leicester" (especially not of an Asian variety) offering "adventurous" cuisine – this "quirky" restaurant in a town-centre boutique hotel "just gets better" under newish head chef Nick Wilson (a Jean-Christophe Novelli protégé). / **Details:** www.maiyango.com; 9.30 pm, Sun 9 pm; closed Mon L & Sun L. / **Accommodation:** 14 rooms, from £90*

Kayal £36 432
153 Granby St LE1 6FE (0116) 255 4667
*A "great" and "charming" spot, near the railway station, where the Keralan cuisine makes a "welcome change from the standard Bangladeshi fare";"there is a lot of good choice in Leicester for Indian food but Kayal is head and shoulders above the rest". / **Details:** www.kayalrestaurant.com/; 11 pm, Sun 10 pm.*

LEWANNICK, CORNWALL 1–3C

Coombeshead Farm
Coombeshead Farm PL15 7QQ
(01566) 782009
*From Tom Adams (of Pitt Cue Co fame) and April Bloomfield (of NYC's Spotted Pig fame), comes a farm-to-table guesthouse in the Cornish countryside.The pair snapped up this Georgian dairy farm in spring 2016 and have renovated it into a guesthouse, dining room and working farm.There are just six bedrooms and the dining room accommodates up to 14 guests, who eat communally. No survey feedback yet, but if you can't get a decent meat dish here, where can you? / **Details:** www.coombesheadfarm.co.uk. / **Accommodation:** 0 rooms, from £6*

LICKFOLD, WEST SUSSEX 3–4A

Lickfold Inn £65 333
Highstead Ln GU28 9EY (01798) 861285
*"The London foodie prophet behind Story", Tom Sellers's "charming, comfortable" pub "in the (very quiet) depths of the countryside" inspires a mixed rep. While it's "arrogant" to some tastes ("the sense is that they're overcharging by tapping into the local wealthy clientele"), others proclaim the "superb", "metropolitan-standard" cooking as proof that, as per Story, it's "really going for a star". / **Details:** www.thelickfoldinn.co.uk; 3m N of A272 between Midhurst & Petworth; 9.30 pm, Sun 4 pm; closed Mon & Sun D; no Amex.*

LINCOLN, LINCOLNSHIRE 6–3A

Browns Pie Shop £46 233
33 Steep Hill LN2 1LU (01522) 527330
*"Extremely comforting on a winter's day", this old vaulted cellar is "just perfect" to its fans. The odd critic is dismissive ("surprisingly bland pies served in a poky back room"), but on most accounts this is "a taste of old England". / **Details:** www.brownspieshop.co.uk; 9.30 pm, Sun 8.30 pm; no Amex.*

Jew's House Restaurant £55 334
15 The Strait LN2 1JD (01522) 524851
*Fans of this long-established beamed dining room, in an atmospheric 12th-century building, hail it as "THE place to eat in Lincoln". The odd let-down is also reported, but most feedback is of "seriously thought-through cooking and a general sense of competence". / **Details:** www.jewshouserestaurant.co.uk; Mon closed, Tue - Sat 9.30 pm, Sun closed; closed Mon, Tue L & Sun; no Amex.*

The Old Bakery £57 334
26-28 Burton Road LN1 3LB (01522) 576057
*Near the cathedral, a rustic restaurant-with-rooms (plus a "lovely, sunny conservatory") where Italian chef Ivano de Serio turns out "excellent, interesting food" (including a tasting menu with a "well-chosen wine accompaniment"). / **Details:** www.theold-bakery.co.uk; Tue - Sat 8.30 pm, Sun 1.30 pm; closed Mon; No jeans. / **Accommodation:** 4 rooms, from £65*

LITTLE ECCLESTON, LANCASHIRE 5–1A

The Cartford Inn £43 322
Cartford Lane PR3 0YP (01995) 670 166
*"A good solid gastropub, which shines in an area that has very few decent places to eat" – "this quirky, comfortable pub/ restaurant-with-rooms, with beautiful views over the river from the picture window" is "a particularly valuable option in the hinterland of Blackpool". Some reports are of "variable quality", but most say its "pub classics, French classics, and more typical gastro-fare" are "well done", and regulars tip the fish specials – "ultra-fresh and perfectly cooked". / **Details:** www.thecartfordinn.co.uk; Mon-Thur 9 pm, Fri & Sat 10 pm, Sun 8.30 pm; closed Mon L.*

LITTLE WILBRAHAM, CAMBRIDGESHIRE 3–1B

The Hole In The Wall £50 444
2 High St CB21 5JY (01223) 812282
MasterChef winner "Alex Rushmer has done an amazing job" with this "impressive" and "calm" gastroboozer on the outskirts of Cambridge; fans say that it "gets better each time" (marks rose a

*notch this year) from the newly "comfy" bar lounge to food that's "sublime". As such, it's now "essential to book in advance, even midweek". / **Details:** www.holeinthewallcambridge.com; 9 pm; closed Mon & Sun D.*

LITTLEFIELD GREEN, BERKSHIRE 3–3A

The Royal Oak **£65** 2 2 3
Paley Street SL6 3JN (01628) 620541
*Parkie's country gastropub is "the kind of pub you could imagine having a beer in". We – like one or two reporters – are "not sure about the Michelin star": at the price, the food is "perfectly competent". / **Details:** www.theroyaloakpaleystreet.com; Mon - Thur 9.30 pm, Fri & Sat 10 pm, Sun closed; closed Sun D; children: 3+.*

LITTLEHAMPTON, WEST SUSSEX 3–4A

East Beach Cafe **£44** 3 3 3
Sea Road BN17 5GB (01903) 731 903
*"Situated on the estuary at Littlehampton", and with a "great view" of the English Channel, this "very buzzy" café – in a strikingly modern, driftwood-style building – provides a "limited menu" of "fresh and succulent" fish and seafood. Minor cavil? – the "acoustics need taming". / **Details:** www.eastbeachcafe.co.uk; 8.30 pm; closed Mon D, Tue D, Wed D & Sun D.*

LIVERPOOL, MERSEYSIDE 5–2A

The Art School **£50** 4 5 4
Sugnall St L7 7DX (0151) 230 8600
*Just across the road from the Liverpool Philharmonic, Paul Askew's year-old venture is "getting better all the time". "It's a beautiful, airy room with the kitchen visible through a long window", service is "wonderful", and there was more consistent praise this year for the "fantastic" cuisine. / **Details:** www.theartschoolrestaurant.co.uk; 9 pm; closed Mon & Sun.*

Etsu **£43** 4 4 3
25 The Strand L2 0XJ (0151) 236 7530
*Tucked into an unpromising concrete and glass edifice, this pleasingly minimal room just off the Strand is one of the city's better bets – a "great little authentic Japanese restaurant", which draws fans from across the area. / **Details:** www.etsu-restaurant.co.uk; off Brunswick street; Mon closed, Tue - Thur 9 pm, Fri & Sat 10 pm, Sun ; closed Mon, Wed L & Sat L.*

Fazenda **£51** 3 4 4
Unit B, Horton Hs L2 3YL (0151) 227 2733
*A "fabulous (Brazilian all-you-can-eat-style) rodízio in Liverpool"; the "amazing" salad bar attracts particular acclaim, but the meats are also "excellent". It's a natural choice for a big get-together. / **Details:** www.fazenda.co.uk/liverpool; 9.30 pm, Sun 8.30 pm.*

Fonseca's **£43** 3 3 3
12 Stanley St L1 6AF (0151) 255 0808
*In the buzzing Stanley St Quarter, the original Delifonseca – renamed after the launch of a Dockside sibling in 2010 – is "really handy for the city centre" and continues to be well rated; these days, besides a booth-lined dining room, its downstairs deli has made way for a cosy, vintage-style bar. / **Details:** www.delifonseca.co.uk; 9 pm, Fri & Sat 10 pm; closed Mon & Sun.*

Hanover Street Social **£39** 2 3 4
16-20 Hanover St L1 4AA (0151) 709 8764
*A "buzzy atmosphere", and "good variety of dishes", help win fans for this lively hang-out, as does the "lovely Liverpool gin!" / **Details:** www.hanoverstreetsocial.co.uk; 6 pm, Sat 5 pm.*

Host **£40** 3 3 2
31 Hope St L1 9XH (0151) 708 5831
*This 60 Hope Street spin-off near the Phil is an "excellent all-rounder", whose "extensive" pan-Asian fare is "a little unusual compared to chains like Wagamama" – "always reliable, quick, simple and well done". / **Details:** www.ho-st.co.uk; 11 pm, Sun 10 pm.*

The Italian Club Fish **£45** 3 3 3
128 Bold St L1 4JA (0151) 707 2110
*A "great little" Italian, near Central Station, with a "café-like feel"; top menu billing goes to the "superb oysters" and enjoyable fish dishes. / **Details:** www.theitalianclubfish.co.uk; 10 pm, Sun 9 pm; no Amex.*

The London Carriage Works, Hope Street Hotel **£62** 3 3 2
40 Hope Street L1 9DA (0151) 705 2222
*The city's pioneering design hotel continues to divide views. To cynics, it's "nowhere near as good as it thinks it is", "efficient without being special" and with "very little ambience" – to fans, "very grand and beautiful", with "very welcoming staff" and "very creative" cuisine. (The hotel must be doing something right though, as in October 2016 they announced an expansion.) / **Details:** www.thelondoncarriageworks.co.uk; 10 pm, Sun 9 pm; No shorts. / **Accommodation:** 89 rooms, from £150*

Lunya £45 4 3 3

18-20 College Ln L1 3DS (0151) 706 9770

*"You can visit for a snack, or pig out on the full gourmet experience" at this Latino, shopping-mall mecca – nowadays the most commented-on eatery in 'The Pool'. "The modern tapas just gets better and better" and "there's a good, short wine list" in what's a "laid-back, café-style place" (with a "brilliant deli" attached). "Now open in Manchester too." / **Details:** www.lunya.co.uk; 9 pm, Wed & Thu 9.30 pm, Fri 10 pm, Sat 10.30 pm,.*

Maray £43 4 2 3

91 Bold Street L1 4HF (0151) 709 5820

*Comparisons with London's Palomar and Ottolenghi crop up in reports on this "very noisy, crowded and tightly packed" member of the Bold Street scene ("advertised as a cocktail bar, but the food's the best bit"). All feedback says its "eclectic" sharing plates of "unusual Middle-Eastern-leaning, seasonal food" are a wow! "Not since Paddy and Dave opened the Everyman Theatre Bistro in 1968 has Liverpool seen a more exciting development in its restaurant scene!" / **Details:** www.maray.co.uk; 10 pm, Fri & Sat 11 pm, Sun 9 pm.*

The Monro £42 3 2 3

92-94 Duke St L1 5AG (0151) 707 9933

*"A pleasant surprise" – a "relaxing, welcoming" gastroboozer whose "sound pub menu" earns its popularity. / **Details:** www.themonro.com; 9.30 pm, Sun 7.30 pm; no Amex; No trainers.*

Mowgli £31 3 3 3

69 Bold St L1 4EZ (0151) 708 9356

*"Interesting Indian street food" bites ("I'm not sure it is in fact street food, but whatever it is, it's very well done") win ongoing praise for this "relatively recent arrival on Bold Street", which offers a selection of tapas dishes, many in tiffin boxes. In December 2016, Nisha Katona is opening a second bigger site, just off Castle Street. / **Details:** www.mowglistreetfood.com; 9.30 pm, Thu-Sat 10 pm.*

Panoramic 34, West Tower £63 3 5

Brook Street L3 9PJ (0151) 236 5534

*"Obviously the views are an important part of the overall experience" at this 34th-floor venue, but the food gains respectable feedback too; service has been up-and-down in the past, but more than one reporter now finds it "superb". Top Tip – afternoon tea here has a "certain sense of occasion". / **Details:** www.panoramic34.com/; Mon closed, Tue - Sat 9.30 pm, Sun 8 pm; closed Mon; no Amex; No trainers.*

Pen Factory £37 3 3 4

13 Hope St L1 9BQ (0151) 709 7887

*"Paddy (Byrne) goes from strength to strength" at this "little gem" – a "good approximation of the original Everyman bistro, run by the original owner, and just next door". While the excellent "buzz" is similar, he "has really improved the food" – "quirky" small plates offering "quality but without the fuss" – and this time there's a garden too. / **Details:** www.pen-factory.co.uk/; midnight; closed Mon & Sun.*

Puschka £52 3 2 3

16 Rodney St L1 2TE (0151) 708 8698

*"A great little restaurant" in the Georgian Quarter whose "short menu" is "supplemented by a specials board"; a couple of reporters found it a tad "ordinary", but on most accounts it's well-rated. / **Details:** www.puschka.co.uk; 10 pm, Sun 9 pm; D only.*

Salt House £37 3 4 3

Hanover Sq L1 3DW (0151) 706 0092

*For "lip-licking tapas in a low-lit industrial atmosphere", this split-level venue is just the place: staff are "fantastically attentive" and "the prices aren't outrageous" (especially the "good lunchtime deal"). / **Details:** www.salthousetapas.co.uk; 10.30 pm.*

Salt House Bacaro £36 3 3 3

47 Castle St L2 9UB (0151) 665 0047

*In the business district, a "buzzy Italian tapas/small plates place, opened by the owners of Salt House Tapas"; "they have kept their standards high, and it's a great place to sit at the bar (or dining room), have a cocktail and work your way through the menu". / **Details:** www.salthousebacaro.co.uk/; 10.30 pm.*

San Carlo £47 2 2 3

41 Castle St L2 9SH (0151) 236 0073

*A "good busy Italian in the heart of the business district" – an outpost of the ever-better-known national chain. While it's arguably a tad "overpriced", even sceptics laud the "great atmosphere" (often animated by local WAGs) and the "vast" menu usually has something to suit. / **Details:** www.sancarlo.co.uk; 11 pm.*

60 Hope Street £59 4 3 3

60 Hope St L1 9BZ (0151) 707 6060

*In a townhouse near the Anglican Cathedral, this "sophisticated but not over-fussy" modern British venture was a pioneer for the city when it opened, and still "never fails to deliver top-quality cooking" based on "interesting seasonal ingredients"; fans also love the "relaxed metropolitan atmosphere". / **Details:** www.60hopestreet.com; 10.30 pm, Sun 8 pm.*

Spire £48 4 4 2

1 Church Road L15 9EA (0151) 734 5040

"Some of the best cooking in Liverpool" awaits at this "always busy" Wavertree restaurant; while the location, just off Penny Lane, is "not the place to expect a top-class meal", and the food is "served on

café-style plates in a café setting", the main event is nonetheless "delicious and refined". / **Details:** www.spirerestaurant.co.uk; Mon - Thu 9 pm, Fri & Sat 9.30 pm, Sun closed; closed Mon L, Sat L & Sun.

LLANARTHNE, CARMARTHENSHIRE 4–4C

Wrights Food Emporium £36 443

Golden Grove Arms SA32 8JU

(01558) 668929

"Quite a find"; one-time AA chief inspector (and Y Polyn owner) Simon Wright's "very casual" year-old deli/café – a former pub – is "an asset for the area". A "diverse" menu encompasses "good rustic cooking", "an excellent choice of vegetarian dishes", brunch options, and "the best cakes in south-west Wales". / **Details:** *maryann@wrightsfood.co.uk; 11 pm; closed Mon D, Tue D, Wed D, Thu D & Sun D; No bookings.*

LLANDEWI SKIRRID, MONMOUTHSHIRE 2–1A

The Walnut Tree £65 533

Llanddewi Skirrid NP7 8AW (01873) 852797

"The simplicity and precision of the cuisine marks a true understanding of food", at Shaun Hill's acclaimed inn (made famous in the '70s by Franco and Ann Taruschio), whose "honest, imaginative and creative" dishes maintain it as the survey's most commented-on destination in Wales. Where there are gripes it's generally over the odd "rustic" dish that has "lacked subtlety", but according to nearly all reports this modest venue is "always a treat and well worth the journey". / **Details:** *www.thewalnuttreeinn.com; 3m NE of Abergavenny on B4521; 9.30 pm; closed Mon & Sun.* / **Accommodation:** *5 rooms, from £300*

LLANDRILLO, DENBIGHSHIRE 4–2D

Tyddyn Llan £80 545

LL21 0ST (01490) 440264

"To recharge your batteries" or "let your loved one know you care", Susan and Bryan Webb's ever-popular country house hotel "in the former hunting lodge of the Duke of Westminster" is just the job. The "excellent" level of cuisine is matched by a "well-chosen" wine list "with something for everyone, and some real bargains". / **Details:** *www.tyddynllan.co.uk; on B4401 between Corwen and Bala; 9 pm; (Mon-Thu L by prior arrangement only); Credit card deposit required to book.* / **Accommodation:** *12 rooms, from £180*

LLANDUDNO, CONWY 4–1D

Bodysgallen Hall, Dining Room £72 335

The Royal Welsh Way LL30 1RS

(01492) 584466

This "wonderful" National Trust-owned Elizabethan manor house hotel certainly has a "great location" (a leafy 200-acre plot). While not, perhaps, an equal attraction to the setting, "the food is always good as well (but can't they ever change the menu?)" / **Details:** *www.bodysgallen.com; 2m off A55 on A470; 9.15 pm, Fri & Sat 9.30 pm; closed Mon; No trainers; children: 6+.* / **Accommodation:** *31 rooms, from £179*

LLANGOLLEN, DENBIGHSHIRE 5–3A

Corn Mill £47 335

Dee Ln LL20 8PN (01978) 869555

"Superbly located, on the side of the River Dee rapids", this "high quality" Brunning & Price gastropub provides "really good food and views". / **Details:** *www.cornmill-llangollen.co.uk; 9.30 pm, Sun 9 pm.*

LLANWRTYD WELLS, POWYS 4–4D

Carlton Riverside £53 433

Irfon Cr LD5 4SP (01591) 610248

It's 'all change' at Alan & Mary Ann Gilchrist's much-loved mid-Wales inn, recently taken over by Mary Ann's protégé Luke (kitchen) and his partner Rosie (front of house). Service is "effective" and the menu "well executed", but there's a slight sense that the "overall charm might be suffering… however, early days; maybe they'll blossom once they get the basics sorted". / **Details:** *www.carltonriverside.com; 8.30 pm; closed Mon L & Sun; no Amex.* / **Accommodation:** *4 rooms, from £60*

LLYSWEN, POWYS 2–1A

Llangoed Hall £102 324

LD3 0YP (01874) 754525

A "beautiful" Wye Valley setting and "wonderful dining room" help create the "romantic" ambience at this well-known country house hotel – "a special place, offering fare served in a style long gone elsewhere". Nick Brodie's "arty" dishes took some flak for "style over substance", but most reporters think his food is "fabulous". / **Details:** *www.llangoedhall.com; 11m NW of Brecon on A470; 8.45 pm; no Amex; Jacket required.* / **Accommodation:** *23 rooms, from £210*

LOCH LOMOND, DUNBARTONSHIRE 9–4B

Martin Wishart, Cameron House **£108** 444
Cameron House G83 8QZ (01389) 722504
*Martin Wishart's "lovely restaurant in an amazing setting on Loch Lomond" has beautiful views and is extremely "romantic" ("we felt like we were the only people on Earth!") Prices and/or portion size inspired flak in some reports this year, but most feedback is rapturously positive, describing "food and service that's always fantastic". / **Details:** www.mwlochlomond.co.uk; over Erskine Bridge to A82, follow signs to Loch Lomond; Mon & Tues closed, Wed - Sun 9.45 pm; Mon, Tues. / **Accommodation:** 134 rooms, from £215*

LOCHINVER, HIGHLAND 9–1B

The Albannach **£68** 544
IV27 4LP (01571) 844407
*An "unfailingly excellent" (and very remote) hotel with "views to Suilven from the lounge and dining room across Lochinver harbour"; the fixed 5-course menu is "brilliant", and there's a "sensibly priced wine list with an emphasis on France". "We have been 9 times even though it's 600 miles away!" Top Tip – the owners recently "opened another pub (The Caberfeidh) in the village". / **Details:** www.thealbannach.co.uk; closed Mon, Tue, Wed L, Thu L, Fri L, Sat L & Sun L; no Amex; children: 12+. / **Accommodation:** 5 rooms, from £295*

LOCKSBOTTOM, KENT 3–3B

Chapter One **£61** 432
Farnborough Common BR6 8NF
(01689) 854848
*"Who cares whether or not they still have a Michelin star?" – this well-known rural eatery on the fringes of the metropolis still satisfies most reporters with its "fine quality, out-of-town dining", producing food that's "imaginative and respectful of its ingredients". Service does not seem as accomplished as it once was however, and this "busy and animated" ("slightly suburban") venue can give a "somewhat soulless" impression – "the food is stunning, but I can't help thinking it is the non-food areas that are holding Chapter One back from its previous glories?" – "In a finer housing they could charge twice as much and still be booked for months!" / **Details:** www.chaptersrestaurants.com; Mon-Thu 9.30 pm, Fri & Sat 10.30 pm; No trainers; Booking max 12 may apply.*

LONG CRENDON, BUCKINGHAMSHIRE 2–2D

The Angel **£51** 323
47 Bicester Rd HP18 9EE (01844) 208268
*A 16th-century inn, set in a "lovely country setting", on the Oxfordshire borders, where "the food is usually very reliable". / **Details:** www.angelrestaurant.co.uk; 2m NW of Thames, off B4011; 9.30 pm; closed Sun D. / **Accommodation:** 4 rooms, from £110*

The Mole & Chicken **£53** 334
Easington Lane HP18 9EY (01844) 208387
*Near the M40, and "very convenient for breaking the journey from north to south", this gastropub-with-rooms offers "good quality locally sourced food" and a terrace with "lovely views across Oxfordshire". / **Details:** www.themoleandchicken.co.uk; follow signs from B4011 at Long Crendon; 9.30 pm, Sun 9 pm. / **Accommodation:** 5 rooms, from £110*

LONG MELFORD, SUFFOLK 3–1C

Melford Valley Tandoori **£31** 443
Hall St CO10 9JT (01787) 311 518
*A "great Indian", where the "authentic dishes" are "excellent", and there's "good service" to match. Top Tip – they "offer a waist watcher's menu, and will cook items with as little fat as possible if you're on a diet". / **Details:** www.melfordvalley.com; 11 pm, Fri & Sat 11.30 pm.*

Swan **£57** 353
Hall St CO10 9JQ (01787) 464545
*"The Swan goes from strength to strength under the guidance of the Macmillan family"; "a lot of money has been spent on refurbishment", and "the food gets better and better" – "now into the fine dining category", with a more "sophisticated" à la carte, plus a 6-course tasting option with "wine flights galore". "Even more great boutique rooms are being added", too. / **Details:** www.longmelfordswan.co.uk; Mon-Thu 9 pm, Fri-Sat 10 pm; closed Sun D.*

LOWER BEEDING, WEST SUSSEX 3–4B

The Pass Restaurant, South Lodge Hotel **£109** 443
Brighton Road RH13 6PS (01403) 891711
"The set-up of the dining room is something of an unexpected contrast with the traditional style and elegance of the rest of the hotel – elevated banks of seats and high chairs designed to allow full visibility of the open kitchen opposite, and where the chefs serve and explain dishes." Having won renown with his "superb tasting menus", Matt Gillan left after a decade at the stoves in spring 2016 to be replaced by ex-Samling maestro, Ian Swainson. Early reports

*after the switch are of some "fine creativity" – "our thoughts did, inevitably, turn to wondering how the new chef will put his stamp on The Pass", but "everything was very competently done and most enjoyable" – hence for the time being we have maintained its ratings. / **Details:** www.exclusive.co.uk; Mon & Tue closed, Wed - Sun 8.30 pm; closed Mon & Tue; children: 12+. / **Accommodation:** 89 rooms, from £235*

LOWER BOCKHAMPTON, DORSET 2–4B

Yalbury Cottage £54 554

DT2 8PZ (01305) 262382

*"Worth a huge detour"; reporters have "absolutely no complaints" about Ariane & Jamie Jones's "tiny" yet "charming" and exceptionally "welcoming" cottage-restaurant, in a village on the outskirts of town. "Every delicious item is home made" and comes "in very generous portions, and at good-value prices". / **Details:** www.yalburycottage.com; 9 pm; Tues to Sat L - booking only; no Amex; practically no walk-ins – you must boo. / **Accommodation:** 8 rooms, from £120*

LOWER FROYLE, HAMPSHIRE 2–3D

The Anchor Inn £50 324

GU34 4NA (01420) 23261

*"With plenty of charm and interesting decor", this rural 16th-century inn (with rooms) makes a very attractive destination, and one with "high quality cooking". / **Details:** www.anchorinnatlowerfroyle.co.uk; 9pm, Fri - Sat 9.30pm, sun 8pm. / **Accommodation:** 5 rooms, from £120*

LOWER ODDINGTON, GLOUCESTERSHIRE 2–1C

The Fox Inn £48 323

GL56 0UR (01451) 870 862

*A "very good country pub" in a "lovely village setting"; "the standard dishes are well-cooked and good value" and served alongside some "decent real ales". / **Details:** www.foxinn.net; on A436 near Stow-on-the-Wold; 9.30 pm; no Amex. / **Accommodation:** 3 rooms, from £85*

LOWER SLAUGHTER, GLOUCESTERSHIRE 2–1C

The Slaughters Manor House £90 433

COPSEHILL RD GL54 2HP (01451) 820456

*This Gidleigh Park-affiliated hotel (fka Lower Slaughter Manor) reopened in March 2016 after a country-chic refurb and a slight change of name; according to early reports it's "still great, if not as casually elegant as before", and you can't beat the "marvellous" countryside setting. / **Details:** www.lowerslaughter.co.uk; 2m from Burton-on-the-Water on A429; Sun - Thur 9 pm, Fri & Sat 9.30 pm; No jeans. / **Accommodation:** 19 rooms, from £310*

LUDLOW, SHROPSHIRE 5–4A

Bistro 7 £45 333

7 Corve St SY8 1DB (01584) 877412

*"A good addition for Ludlow" – this "friendly" two-year-old bistro, named for its address (in the town's old Post Office) and also the fact that it's its owners James & Beverley Croft-Moss's seventh venture, wins praise for "reliable everything". / **Details:** www.bistro7ofludlow.co.uk.*

The Charlton Arms, Charlton Arms Hotel £47 334

Ludford Bridge SY8 1PJ (01584) 872813

*"Hurrah! Ludlow finally has a pub worth eating in!" – a new gastroboozer-with-rooms from Cedric Bosi (sibling to Claude of Hibiscus and soon-to-be Bibendum fame). The cooking "goes from strength to strength", and a "superb location overlooking the river" lends it "far and away the best view" in town. / **Details:** www.thecharltonarms.co.uk; Mon - Sat 9.30 pm, Sun 8.30 pm.*

The Clive Restaurant With Rooms £54 332

Bromfield SY8 2JR (01584) 856565

*A "firm favourite" set in an 18th-century farmhouse handy for the castle, with an attractive red-brick façade and a B&B annexe, scoring solid feedback for its "consistently good" cuisine. / **Details:** www.theclive.co.uk; 2m N of Ludlow on A49 to Shrewsbury; 9.30 pm. / **Accommodation:** 15 rooms, from £70*

The Fish House £30 443

51 Bullring SY8 1AB (01584) 879790

*"Only open Wednesday to Saturday, this is a fishmonger's serving cold fish dishes (including seafood platters) at lunch times"; "seating around barrels is limited and not the most comfortable, but despite this it is well worth a visit". / **Details:** www.thefishhouseludlow.co.uk; Sat 4 pm; closed Mon, Tue, Wed D, Thu D, Fri D, Sat D & Sun; Booking weekdays only.*

The French Pantry £41 333

15 Tower St SY8 1RL (01584) 879133

*"An unexceptional exterior hides a truly exceptional menu and wine list" at this petite French bistro on a side street in the centre of town; "it's cosy, but that adds to the charm". / **Details:** www.thefrenchpantry.co.uk/; 8.30 pm; closed Sun.*

Green Café, Ludlow Mill On The Green £36 554

Dinham Millennium Green SY8 1EG
(01584) 879872

*"I've simply never not loved any dish served here in all the years I've been going!" With a "superb location looking across the River Teme", chef Clive Davis's "wonderful" café ("sit outside and watch the kids fishing") offers "simple and uncomplicated" food, whose "deftness and assurance means it's always brilliant" (and "at these affordable prices, you can afford to spend extra petrol to get there"). "I had foie gras the night before at a Michelin-starred joint and it was good. The next day I had Clive Davis's chicken liver paté for lunch, and it was ridiculously 10 times better!" / **Details:** www.thegreencafe.co.uk; 8pm; closed Mon, L only Tue-Sun.*

Mortimers £61 444

17 Corve St SY8 1DA (01584) 872 325

*"Early days are very promising" at Claude Bosi protégé, Wayne Smith's accomplished yearling, on the famous foodie site that was formerly La Bécasse (RIP). "The cooking is going from strength to strength, and the lunch menu is particularly good value." / **Details:** www.mortimersludlow.co.uk.*

Smoke House Deli And Cicchetti £33 343

10 Broad St SY8 1NG (07890) 412 873

*"The best coffee shop in Ludlow by a long way" is "a great antidote to samey-ness" – modelled on a Venetian bàcaro, it "serves great brews, and varied breakfast and lunch menu" of cicchetti. / **Details:** www.ludlowcicchettibar.wordpress.com; 5 pm; L only; Cash only.*

LUPTON, CUMBRIA 7–4D

The Plough Inn £45 333

Cow Brow LA6 1PJ (01539) 567 700

*This "spacious" pub-with-rooms, in a "beautiful setting" just off the M6, continues to win the thumbs up for its "terrific" cooking (a mixture of pub classics with a twist, and more ambitious dishes). / **Details:** www.theploughatlupton.co.uk; 9 pm. / **Accommodation:** 6 rooms, from £115*

LUTON HOO ESTATE, BEDFORDSHIRE 3–2A

Luton Hoo, Luton Hoo Hotel £52 344

The Mansion House LU1 3TQ
(01582) 734437

*For a "special occasion", there's no beating this stately country house hotel – nowadays a five star, plus spa and golf course – in a lush parkland setting. "The food usually (but not always) matches the setting", and "the wine list is comprehensive" ("though not exactly bargain basement"). Top Tip – the "classy afternoon tea, matched by the classy surroundings" is one of the most popular in the survey. / **Details:** www.lutonhoo.co.uk; Mon & Tues closed, Wed - Fri 10 pm, Sat 10.30 pm; L only.*

LYDFORD, DEVON 1–3C

The Dartmoor Inn £51 333

Moorside EX20 4AY (01822) 820221

*Philip Burgess and Andrew Honey continue to serve "exceptional" locally sourced food, at this "lovely" old coaching inn set in the National Park. / **Details:** www.dartmoorinn.com; on the A386 Tavistock to Okehampton road; 9.30 pm; closed Mon L & Sun D. / **Accommodation:** 3 rooms, from £95*

LYDGATE, GREATER MANCHESTER 5–2B

The White Hart £51 333

51 Stockport Rd OL4 4JJ (01457) 872566

*After a major contemporary makeover in 2015, the grey-walled dining room of this "fab pub" on a hillside not far from the Peak District now offers a stylish stage for chef Mike Shaw's "excellent value" cooking. / **Details:** www.thewhitehart.co.uk; 2m E of Oldham on A669, then A6050; 9.30 pm. / **Accommodation:** 12 rooms, from £120*

LYME REGIS, DORSET 2–4A

Hix Oyster & Fish House £56 324

Cobb Rd DT7 3JP (01297) 446910

*"Such a beautiful setting looking over the harbour in this candlelit room" helps inspire many rapturous reviews for Mark Hix's cliff-top venture, which at its best delivers "sparklingly fresh and simple fish and seafood"; and "a great choice of indigenous drinks (Dorset sparkling wine, local apple brandy)" too. Even some who say "it's a great spot" fear "it has become a little complacent" however, and one or two reports were of "dull and un-special" cooking this year. / **Details:** www.restaurantsetcltd.co.uk; 10 pm.*

LYMINGTON, HAMPSHIRE 2–4C

Elderflower £57 444

Quay St SO41 3AS (01590) 676908

*"Local ingredients are handled with a classy touch" at Andrew & Marjolaine Du Bourg's restaurant-with-rooms, on a cobbled street opposite the Pier – "the exiting food is a brilliant: there's always a surprise of some sort". / **Details:** www.elderflowerrestaurant.co.uk; Wed & Thu 9.30 pm, Fri & Sat 10 pm.*

LYMM, CHESHIRE 5–2B

La Boheme **£43** 4 4 3

3 Mill Lane WA13 9SD (01925) 753657

"If you don't mind eating with a fair number of Cheshire's more mature citizens", this "slightly old-fashioned" Gallic operation is just the place for "difficult-to-reproduce French-style cooking". / ***Details:*** *laboheme.co.uk; Mon-Sat 10 pm, Sun 9 pm; closed Mon L & Sat L.*

LYMPSTONE, DEVON 1–3D

Lympstone Manor

Courtlands Lane EX8 3NZ awaiting tel

Ex-Gidleigh chef Michael Caines is set to open this 21-bedroom hotel, a short drive from Exeter, in spring 2017. It promises three dining rooms (complete with a separate wine tasting space) overlooking the Exe estuary, of which a 60-seater fine dining room will be the flagship.

LYNDHURST, HAMPSHIRE 2–4C

Hartnett Holder & Co, Lime Wood Hotel **£73** 3 2 2

Beaulieu Rd SO43 7FZ (02380) 287177

For fans, Angela Hartnett's New Forest hotel "oozes unpretentious style", with a drinks list that's "second to none" and "absolutely delicious" Italian-ish cuisine. For sceptics, though, albeit only three years old, it's "not as good as it used to be by a long chalk" – bugbears being "awkward" seating, and a feeling it's "pricey". / ***Details:*** *www.limewoodhotel.co.uk; 11 pm.*

LYTHAM ST ANNES, LANCASHIRE 5–1A

Novello **£49** 5 3 2

9 Clifton St FY8 5EP (01253) 730278

"A small, ordinary Italian, which has jumped on the cicchetti bandwagon… the odd thing here is that it's exceptionally good." "I've been going for years, and Sal the chef has seriously picked up his game in the past 12 months", cranking out some "fabulous" dishes. "The old-school service improves as the owner recognises you." / ***Details:*** *Tues - Sat 10.00pm, Sun 9.00pm.*

MADINGLEY, CAMBRIDGESHIRE 3–1B

Three Horseshoes **£52**

High St CB23 8AB (01954) 210221

Long beloved of varsity students and their doting parents, this "picturesque thatched dining pub in a pretty village", known for its "lovely" conservatory setting, has put in an uneven performance for many years. But – Stop Press – in October 2016, erstwhile owners, John & Julia Hoskins re-acquired the property after the latest regime ceased trading, and initiated a major re-building programme – so a return to form may well be on the cards at this old favourite. / ***Details:*** *www.threehorseshoesmadingley.co.uk; 2m W of Cambridge, off A14 or M11; 9.30 pm,.*

MAIDENHEAD, BERKSHIRE 3–3A

Boulters Riverside Brasserie **£51** 2 2 4

Boulters Lock Island SL6 8PE (01628) 621291

"One of the best locations in the South East" (hugging the Thames at Boulters Lock) is the undeniable highlight of a trip to this Home Counties haunt, with an expansive terrace. The food escapes criticism, but if it were better this could be a major destination. / ***Details:*** *www.boultersrestaurant.co.uk; 9.30 pm; closed Sun D.*

MAIDSTONE, KENT 3–3C

Frederic Bistro **£42** 3 4 4

Market Buildings, Earl St ME14 1HP (01622) 297414

"A touch of France in the middle of Maidstone"; reporters praise the "true Gallic cooking" at this "lovely little bistro" whose "extremely good value" cuisine and "very good portions" ensure that it's "always packed with happy diners!" / ***Details:*** *www.fredericbistro.com; 10 pm.*

MALMESBURY, WILTSHIRE 2–2C

The Old Bell Hotel **£55** 3 2 3

Abbey Row SN16 0AG (01666) 822344

Near the Abbey, a beautiful wisteria-clad hotel and coach house dating back to 1220 in parts; there are "lots of lounges for privacy" and the restaurant is uniformly rated as "very good". / ***Details:*** *www.oldbellhotel.com; Mon - Thur 9 pm, Fri & Sat 9.30 pm, Sun 9 pm. /* ***Accommodation:*** *33 rooms, from £115*

MANCHESTER, GREATER MANCHESTER 5–2B

Adam Reid at The French, Midland Hotel **£98**

Peter St M60 2DS (0161) 236 3333

In October 2016, a couple of weeks after it failed to win a Michelin Star, Simon Rogan severed his links with this famous dining room (where Mr Rolls first met Mr Royce in days gone by), so we've left it un-rated, even though head chef Adam Reid remains in place. Perhaps under the management of the hotel, this operation will sort itself out, because reports this year suggested the former set-up "just hadn't got it right". Fans were very enthusiastic, extolling "adventurous food and a wonderful, wonderful overall experience", but even some of them could find the ambience "uptight", and a worrying number of harsher critics "were hugely disappointed on so many levels" finding it "very fancy, but neither memorable nor exceptional". Perhaps by next year it will have settled down a bit? / **Details:** *www.the-french.co.uk; 9.00 pm; closed Mon, Tue L & Sun; No jeans; children: 9+.* / **Accommodation:** *312 rooms, from £145*

Akbar's **£34** 5 2 3
73-83 Liverpool Rd M3 4NQ (0161) 834 8444
"It's well worth the horrific wait!" to eat at this "mentally busy" Pakistani. "You queue outside, before being penned in to the front bar area to wait for your buzzer to go off!" Once seated, you're in an "echoey and noisy cavern" – "a bit shabby and cheap" – but "great if you like buzzy", and "fantastic value" for "a particularly tasty curry". / **Details:** *www.akbars.co.uk; 11 pm, Fri & Sat 11.30 pm; D only; May need 10+ to book.*

Albert's **£46** 2 2 2
120-122 Barlow Moor Rd M20 2PU
(0161) 434 8289
A "buzzing, always busy brasserie in smart Didsbury" combining a "fun, noisy atmosphere" and a "menu that runs the gamut from burgers to steaks via pasta and pies". ("There's a sister restaurant – Albert's Shed – at Castlefields too.") / **Details:** *www.albertsdidsbury.com; 10 pm; no Amex.*

Albert's Worsley **£46** 2 3 2
East Lancashire Rd M27 0AA (0161) 794 1234
Brunch and the "excellent value" set lunch (running until a very leisurely 6pm) win most recommendations for this Swinton three-year-old – the latest addition to a small northern chain named after the owner's uncle. / **Details:** *www.albertsworsley.com; 10 pm, Fri 10.30 pm, Sat 11 pm, Sun 9.30 pm; Booking max 9 may apply.*

Almost Famous **£30** 3 2 3
100-102 High St M4 1HP no tel
"Great burgers, fries, cocktails etc" – that's the simple but powerful pull of the Northern Quarter original of this small NW chain of 'dirty' food pitstops. / **Details:** *www.almostfamousburgers.com; 10 pm, Fri & Sat 11 pm; No bookings.*

Australasia **£61** 3 3 4
1 The Avenue Spinningfields M3 3AP
(0161) 831 0288
"An excellent bar and cocktails" help drive the "always busy, always bubbly" vibe at this "slick", subterranean operation (from Living Ventures), just off Deansgate, where "enjoyable", eclectically sourced small plates provide "bursts of flavour". / **Details:** *www.australasia.uk.com; 10.45 pm.*

La Bandera **£51** 3 3 3
2 Ridgefield M2 6EQ (0161) 833 9019
Off Deansgate, Basque chef Josetxo Arrieta's über-modern (or "rather garish", depending on taste) two-year-old has already made quite a name for itself. Yet while some fans cite "exceptional" food as proof that it's "probably the best of the new tapas venues" in town, critics felt that it's rather "ho hummm-y" – "fine", but "nothing that captivates". / **Details:** *www.labandera.co.uk; midnight; no Amex.*

Bar San Juan **£32** 3 3 4
56 Beech Rd M21 9EG (0161) 881 9259
"You really feel you could be in Spain", according to fans of this diminutive tapas bar – a "cheap 'n' cheerful" choice in Chorlton. / **Details:** *barsanjuan.com; 11.30 pm, Fri & Sat midnight, Sun 11 pm.*

Burger & Lobster **£45** 3 2 2
Ship Canal Hs, King St M2 4WU
(0161) 832 0222
The Mancunian outpost of the fast-growing Russian-owned surf 'n' turf chain is "a vast, largely dark space", whose "surprisingly good" food is "better than the service and ambience". / **Details:** *www.burgerandlobster.com/home/; 22.30pm, Fri - Sat 23.00pm, sun 22.00pm.*

Chaophraya **£48** 3 3 4
19 Chapel Walks M2 1HN (0161) 832 8342
"Still the premium destination for Thai food in Manchester" – this well-known operation (part of the growing, UK-wide Thai Leisure Group) continues to win praise for its "all-round good dining experience". / **Details:** *www.chaophraya.co.uk; Mon - Sat 10.30 pm, Sun 10 pm.*

Croma **£36** 3 4 4
1-3 Clarence St M2 4DE (0161) 237 9799
"Slick and professional", incredibly popular pizzeria, near the Town Hall, that "can always be relied on for a good and quick meal" and in particular is "ideal for pre-concert or theatre". Choose from "an exceptional range of tasty toppings". / **Details:** *www.cromapizza.co.uk; 10 pm, Fri & Sat 11 pm.*

Evuna **£44** 3 4 4
277 – 279 Deansgate M3 4EW
(0161) 819 2752
"Always busy" brick-walled bar in the city-centre with a "relaxed and friendly" vibe – "even if the tapas is not particularly surprising it's well executed and consistent" and there are "fantastic wines". A Northern Quarter sibling is equally acclaimed – indeed, for one reporter, "the NQ has the slight edge as it feels more like Madrid or Barcelona inside!" / ***Details:*** *www.evuna.com; Mon 9 pm, Tue - Sat 10 pm, Sun 8 pm.*

Fazenda **£53** 3 4 3
The Ave M3 3AP (0161) 834 1219
This branch of this Brazilian 'rodizio' chain offers its trademark, all-you-can-eat meat-feast and fans say "it's the best of this type of experience" in Manchester. Consistently well-rated, it's a natural choice in a group. / ***Details:*** *www.fazenda.co.uk/manchester; 22.00pm, 21.00pm Sun.*

El Gato Negro **£47** 4 4 5
52 King Street M2 4LY (0161) 694 8585
"Manchester's gain is Ripponden's loss" and after less than a year, Simon Shaw is already looking to expand his "slick, very large city centre operation" (adding 50 covers in the rooftop level), as it proves "a fantastic addition" and one "offering a different experience on each of its three floors". "It being Manchester, there is a serious bar-element to the business", and "it's a great place to eat or just enjoy a glass of wine and nibbles". "Scaling up the food production from Ripponden to King Street does not seem to have been a problem" – "the majority of the tapas are not merely correct, but excellent" – and overall this is "a successful transfer to a cracking new site". / ***Details:*** *www.elgatonegrotapas.com; Mon - Thur 10 pm, Fri & Sat 11 pm, Sun 9.30 pm.*

Glamorous **£40** 4 2 2
Wing Yip Bus' Centre, Oldham Rd M4 5HU
(0161) 839 3312
This "premier eating warehouse", atop Wing Yip supermarket, is perennially "crammed with Chinese" come the weekend. "Authentic dim sum" is the main event ("other items only rate as good"); "Sundays and Mondays are when you get the trolleys, but the selection seems pretty comprehensive during other lunchtimes too". "Service is chaotic but friendly enough, if you smile and speak a few words of Cantonese!" / ***Details:*** *www.glamorous-restaurant.co.uk; 11.30 pm, Fri & Sat midnight, Sun 11 pm.*

Great Kathmandu **£37** 4 2 3
140-144 Burton Rd M20 1JQ (0161) 434 6413
"Why go to the curry mile?" say fans of this West Didsbury spot, whose fanclub hail it as "the best Indian in Manchester"; it may be "getting ever bigger", but the food is "just as good" as ever, and these days there's a "more comfortable" dining room to enjoy it in. / ***Details:*** *www.greatkathmandu.com; midnight.*

Greens **£44** 3 2 3
43 Lapwing Ln M20 2NT (0161) 434 4259
"Meat eaters love it as well as veggies!" – a "pleasant" West Didsbury operation serving well-rated vegetarian cooking. / ***Details:*** *www.greensdidsbury.co.uk; Mon - Wed 9.30 pm, Thu-Sat 10 pm, Sun 9.30 pm; closed Mon L; no Amex.*

Grill on the Alley **£55** 2 3 3
5 Ridgefield M2 6EG (0161) 833 3465
A "great steak restaurant in central Manchester, with a good atmosphere" – the verdict on this polished bare-brick operation located off Deansgate. / ***Details:*** *www.blackhouse.uk.com; 11 pm.*

Hawksmoor **£65** 4 3 3
184-186 Deansgate M3 3WB (0161) 836 6980
No-one doubts the quality of this cult, London steakhouse chain: "amid all the bling of aspirational dining and the dirty burgers of Manchester, Hawksmoor stands quietly and reassuringly expensively head and shoulders above the rest in terms of pure class – the meat is first-rate" and they serve "amazing cocktails". The ratings of this operation "in an old court house, full of nooks and crannies" (a bit "cavernous" and "gloomy"), are coming under pressure though: "trying to be metropolitan in Manchester doesn't always work" and "the elephant in the room is of course, the prices… they just make you wince". / ***Details:*** *www.thehawksmoor.com; Mon - Thurs 10 pm, Fri & Sat 10.30 pm, Sun 9.30 pm.*

Hispi Bistro **£46**
1c School Lane M20 6RD awaiting tel
Opened in autumn 2016 – a new neighbourhood bistro from Sticky Walnut (Chester) and Burnt Truffle (Heswall, Wirral) proprietor, Gary Usher, on the former site of Didsbury's Jem & I. The venture has been part crowd-funded and will serve a similar style of food to the chef's other sites, and has inspired ecstatic early write-ups in the regional press. / ***Details:*** *9pm, Fri - Sat 10pm.*

Home 3 3 4
2 Tony Wilson Pl, First St M15 4FN
(0161) 200 1500
Opened in May 2015, "Manchester's new centre for art, theatre and film" also hosts this "beautiful" café with "a good selection of local micro-brewery ales, passable pizza, and a buzzy atmosphere in this most metropolitan of Manchester buildings". For afters? – "five great cinemas showing the very latest movies at a third of London prices".

Ibérica, Spinningfields £47 222
14-15 The Avenue M3 3HF (01613) 581 350
"A great lavish interior (if you can forgive the dodgy bull's head)" sets the scene at this year-old northern outpost of the London-based modern tapas chain, and it's a "lively" hang out. Feedback is mixed however – some of the criticism is sharp ("waste of time…";"very let down…";"lost its way…"), but fans hail its "great quality" ("I was a bit sniffy as it's a chain, but they proved me very wrong!") / **Details:** *www.ibericarestaurants.com; Mon - Thur 11 pm, Fri & Sat 11.30 pm, Sun 11 pm.*

Indian Tiffin Room 422
Isabella Banks St, First St M15 4RL
(0161) 228 1000
The brand new sibling of the popular Cheadle establishment occupies a striking glass-fronted building amid the city's new cultural hub First Street; as per the original, the MO is Indian street food that's "interesting great and cheap" – and so "different from just about anything else in Manchester". / **Details:** *www.indiantiffinroom.com/manchester-restaur.*

James Martin £54 443
2 Watson St M3 4LP (0161) 828 0345
"Don't let the unusual location in a casino put you off" – despite its "odd setting", the TV chef's city-centre venture serves some "fantastic food, particularly the starters", and "at truly reasonable prices" too. / **Details:** *www.jamesmartinmanchester.co.uk; Mon - Thur 10 pm, Fri & Sat 11 pm, Sun 5 pm.*

Katsouris Deli £14 332
113 Deansgate M3 2BQ (0161) 819 1260
You get "tasty food and great value" – particularly at breakfast – at this "cheap 'n' cheerful" city-centre feature (whose main menu majors in mezze).
/ **Details:** *www.katsourisdeli.co.uk; L only; no Amex.*

The Lime Tree £50 454
8 Lapwing Ln M20 2WS (0161) 445 1217
This "brilliant, relaxed" Didsbury brasserie continues to deliver some of "the most consistent food in Manchester", as it has for decades – "much of it from (chef-patron) Patrick Hannity's farm" – along with an "excellent wine list" and "superb staff".
/ **Details:** *www.thelimetreerestaurant.co.uk; 10 pm; closed Mon L & Sat L.*

Lunya £45 333
7 Barton Sq M3 2BB (0161) 413 3317
"Offshoot of the well-regarded Liverpool original", this new two-floor venture in the Barton Arcade is a similar mix of deli and dining-area. Reports suggest it too supplies "excellent tapas and lovely wine", although the odd report says it's "good but not up to the standard of the original".

Manchester House £90 434
18-22 Bridge St M3 3BZ (0161) 835 2557
"Buzz buzz buzz", there's "always a buzz" at this Manc-bling venue in an office block, combining a 12th-floor cocktail lounge, with a very contemporary 2nd-floor restaurant, where you can watch the chefs in the open kitchen. Some reporters do find it "overpriced" but on most accounts "Aiden Byrne's cooking keeps going from strength to strength", delivering "top class complex dishes with clean flavours". / **Details:** *www.manchesterhouse.uk.com; 9.30 pm; closed Mon.*

Mowgli £31 333
37 Exchange St M4 3TR (0161) 832 0566
"Offshoot of the Liverpool original, bringing its Indian tapas/small plate concept here (Manchester is being spoilt for newish openings of Indians recently). Some dishes were merely ok, others very good: expect to see it rolled out at a high street near you, which IHMO is no bad thing!"

Mr Cooper's House & Garden, The Midland Hotel £51
Peter St M60 2DS (0161) 236 3333
"What a wonderful space – one part garden, one part house" – The Midland's more accessible brasserie is a very high-ceilinged and atmospheric venue, complete with its own tree. Previously run by Simon Rogan, he cut his ties with it in October 2016, hence we've left it un-rated. Chef Robert Taylor, who joined in March 2016, remains however, and survey reports here were of "food that seems to have stepped up a notch, service that's a real strength, and a bar that should not be missed".
/ **Details:** *www.mrcoopershouseandgarden.co.uk; 10 pm, Sun 8 pm.*

Mughli £31 333
30 Wilmslow Rd M14 5TQ (0161) 248 0900
"I'd given up on Rusholme but then I found this place!" This superior Curry Mile Indian offers "brilliant" street food alongside "pretty ordinary curries". "Lamb chops, grilled over the charcoal pit, are just outstanding, and almost worth a 100 mile round-trip on their own, particularly combined with their 'gunpowder chips'". / **Details:** *www.mughli.com; 11.45 pm, Fri 12.15 am, Sat 2.45 am, Sun 10.45 pm.*

Red Chilli £40 422
70-72 Portland St M1 4GU (0161) 236 2888
For "large quantities of tasty, spicy, no-holds-barred Sichuanese food", you can't beat this ever-popular Chinatown outfit; lunch is an "absolute bargain" too!
/ **Details:** *www.redchillirestaurant.co.uk; 11pm, Fri & Sat midnight; closed Mon.*

Rose Garden £45 453
218 Burton Road M20 2LW (0161) 478 0747
Fans say it "rivals the Lime Tree": in fact ratings are higher nowadays at William Mills's rather

"sparse" Didsbury spot – arguably "Manchester's best mid-range restaurant". / **Details:** *www.therosegardendidsbury.com; Mon - Thur 9 pm, Fri & Sat 10 pm, Sun 8.30 pm; no Amex.*

Rosso £67 334
43 Spring Gardens M2 2BG (0161) 8321400
"Take a footballer (Rio Ferdinand), sprinkle on some Italian style, spend some money on some bling, and you have a restaurant to be seen in"… "but as a place to eat?" – some "would not give it another try", others are more positive but say "we ate early before the chaos…" / **Details:** *www.rossorestaurants.com; 10 pm; closed Sun.*

Rudys Pizza £24 443
9 Cotton St M4 5BF (07931) 162059
"Five minutes' walk north of the Northern Quarter (where parking's quite easy)", this "minimalist", "industrial-concrete" yearling – an erstwhile pop-up run by a graduate of local pizza heroes Honest Crust – "has got it absolutely right", with its simple but winning formula of "authentic Neapolitan-style pizzas married with local beer". / **Details:** *www. rudyspizza.co.uk.*

Sam's Chop House £46 333
Back Pool Fold, Chapel Walks M2 1HN
(0161) 834 3210
A well-known, local-favourite bar-restaurant (est. 1872), whose LS Lowry statue pays tribute to one of its famous former regulars; no fancy south'n nonsense here: black pud', Lancs Butter Pie, Barnsley Chop… / **Details:** *www.samschophouse.com; 9.30 pm, Sat 10.30 pm, Sun 8 pm.*

San Carlo £43 325
40 King Street West M3 2WY
(0161) 834 6226
"Love San Carlo!" – this "big, bold and brash" footballer-favourite is "always amazingly busy", and its Italian fare "can be very good, if you pick the right dish". "Service gets a bad rap" from some, but others insist that "nobody creates your night like Marcello!" / **Details:** *www.sancarlo.co.uk; 11 pm.*

San Carlo Cicchetti £49 322
42 King Street West M3 2QG
(0161) 839 2233
"A reliable go-to Italian" – a "busy, bustling place" where the small plates "virtually always hit the mark"; that the food is "served quickly" is a pluspoint to some, but to others leads to "a feeling of being rushed through the meal". / **Details:** *www.sancarlocicchetti.co.uk; 11 pm, Sun 10 pm; Booking evening only.*

Siam Smiles £29 421
48a George St M1 4HF (0161) 237 1555
A "terrific Thai-street-food-style café" in a Chinatown basement, producing some seriously "authentic" cuisine; "be prepared to eat in a supermarket, with most of your fellow patrons being Thai", and "most of all, be prepared to SWEAT!" / **Details:** *www.facebook.com/SiamSmilesCafe; 7.30 pm, Fri & Sat 9.30 pm.*

63 Degrees £71 343
20 Church St M4 1PN (0161) 832 5438
Limited commentary of late on the Moreau family's "tucked away venture in the Northern Quarter", although all of it – even critical reports – thought the modern French cuisine was good. In early 2016, it moved just a stone's throw from its original site on Church Street to a bigger, more prominent, two-storey building on the corner of Edge Street and High Street (hence for the time being we've left it unrated). / **Details:** *www.63degrees.co.uk; 10.30 pm, Fri 11 pm; closed Mon & Sun.*

Solita £42 323
37 Turner St M4 1DW (0161) 839 2200
"If you're not bearded you might feel out of place" at this "achingly hip" Northern Quarter hang-out: "one of the most innovative outposts of the north west's 'dirty food' movement". "There's no doubt their burgers are amongst the best", even if "some items are over-complicated and trying a bit hard to be too exciting". Also in Didsbury, Prestwich and most recently Preston. / **Details:** *www.solita.co.uk; 10 pm, Fri-Sat 11 pm, Sun 9 pm.*

Tai Pan £36 433
81-97 Upper Brook St M13 9TX
(0161) 273 2798
"A favourite with Chinese students from the university and local restaurateurs, so it can't be bad!" – this cavernous Longsight spot turns out "excellent dim sum" and is a handy "cheap 'n' cheerful option". / **Details:** *www.taipanmanchester.co.uk; 10.30 pm, Sun 9.30 pm.*

Tampopo £33 333
16 Albert Sq M2 5PF (0161) 819 1966
"Still the just about the best for a quick street-food type meal" – a "longstanding noodle bar where you are seated on benches", and where, despite the speed of delivery, "you may have to queue"; the "original underground branch" is still "better than their new ones" by most accounts. / **Details:** *www.tampopo.co.uk; 11 pm, Sun 10 pm; May need 7+ to book.*

This & That £12 522
3 Soap St M4 1EW (0161) 832 4971
"In a slightly dubious (Northern Quarter) location", this canteen-style Indian "remains a bastion of cheap heartiness" ("get well fed for a fiver!") – and it's "even better with the new Scandi-influenced décor" ("new Formica tops!" and "the prices haven't gone up…"); on the menu? – "great, enormo-flavoursome, home-style dishes". / **Details:**

www.thisandthatcafe.co.uk; 4 pm, Fri & Sat 8 pm; closed Mon D, Tue D, Wed D, Thu D & Sun D; Cash only.

Whitworth Art Gallery £22 **3 2 5**
The University of Manchester, Oxford Rd M15 6ER (0161) 275 7511
"A beautiful glass café overlooking the park" and attached to the recently rejigged Whitworth Gallery; while the room is clearly "wonderful", the food, from a "tapas-style menu", is "quite good as well", spanning "delicious veggie breakfasts", "lovely cakes" and a "great lunch deal". / ***Details:*** *www.whitworth.manchester.ac.uk; 5 pm Thu 9 pm; closed Mon D, Tue D & Wed D.*

Wing's £51 **4 5 5**
1 Lincoln Sq M2 5LN (0161) 834 9000
"Lots of Man-U clientele" have driven the fame of Wing Shing Chu's fairly intimate Chinese, at the foot of a city-centre office building. "Not only is it a place to be seen in Manchester, more importantly it's a great place to eat!" – "it's taken the standard of service first developed hereabouts by Yang Sing to a new level" and the cooking itself is "always brilliant". / ***Details:*** *www.wingsrestaurant.co.uk; 11.30 pm, Sun 10.30 pm; closed Sat L; children: 11+ after 8 pm Mon-Fri.*

Yang Sing £53 **4 2 2**
34 Princess Street M1 4JY (0161) 236 2200
"An institution the city can be proud of" – the Yeung family's epic Chinatown landmark is more often rated "very good" than "exceptional" nowadays, but still earns impressively consistent praise from reporters, and deserves its reputation as one of the UK's foremost Chinese restaurants, whatever Giles Coren may say. Often recommended for its banquet "blow-outs", there's no doubting that it's "the dim sum that's the star turn". / ***Details:*** *www.yang-sing.com; Mon - Thur 11.30 pm, Fri 11.45 pm, Sat 12.15 am, S.*

Yuzu £40 **5 3 2**
39 Faulkner St M1 4EE (0161) 236 4159
A "charming, little, wood-covered Japanese bolthole" which "continues to impress at every visit with its clarity of flavours", its "precision of cooking, and its uncompromising no-sushi policy (as they haven't done the 7 years' training)"; even so, "their rice continues to be some of the best around" – but "expect to share a table or counter space" to enjoy it. / ***Details:*** *www.yuzumanchester.co.uk; 9.30 pm; closed Mon & Sun.*

MANNINGTREE, ESSEX 3–2C

Lucca Enoteca £39 **3 4 3**
39-43 High St CO11 1AH (01206) 390044
A "true focus on ingredients" helps inspire fans of this crowded Italian, run by the owners of the nearby Mistley Thorn; even those not usually enamoured of pizza proclaim its Neapolitan-style dishes to be "the real deal" ("excellent" daily specials too). / ***Details:*** *www.luccafoods.co.uk; 9.00pm, Weds - Thurs 9.30 pm, Fri & Sat 10 pm.*

MARAZION, CORNWALL 1–4A

Ben's Cornish Kitchen £49 **5 4 3**
West End TR17 0EL (01736) 719200
"Fish is perfectly cooked and presented" at Ben Prior's seaside bistro, with great views – "wonderful food at reasonable prices" ("worth travelling to the other end of the country for…") / ***Details:*** *www.benscornishkitchen.com; 8.30 pm; closed Mon & Sun.*

MARGATE, KENT 3–3D

The Ambrette £52 **5 4 3**
44 King St CT9 1QE (01843) 231 504
"A sort of cross between Indian and 'haute cuisine'" – "Div Biswal's expertly-prepared, exceptional Indian and British-fusion dishes" at his original venture (it now also has a Canterbury spin-off). "It's really good to see care and attention paid to Indian cuisine in this way!" Top Tip – "excellent value lunch". / ***Details:*** *www.theambrette.co.uk; 9.30 pm, Fri-Sun 10 pm.*

GB Pizza £31 **4 4 3**
14a Marine Drive CT9 1DH (01843) 297 700
"Damn good pizza" – "super-thin" and with "lots of original toppings" – again inspires mega-enthusiastic reviews for this seafront spot. "No cutlery. Help yourself to wine (they have both types: red & white) from the barrel!" / ***Details:*** *www.greatbritishpizza.com; 9.30 pm; closed Sun D.*

Mullins Brasserie £37 **3 3 3**
6 Market Pl CT9 1EN (01843) 295603
In the Old Town, and run by a Bajan chef, this venue in a "beautifully furnished" former butcher's wins plaudits for its "interesting", Caribbean-inspired cuisine – a "casual" and "noisy" sort of spot, where "the sound of chatter and laughing adds to the enjoyment". Top Tip – the bi-monthly Caribbean evening is "not to be missed". / ***Details:*** *www.mullinsbrasserie.co.uk; 9pm, Fri, Sat 9:30pm.*

MARLBOROUGH, WILTSHIRE 2–2C

The Harrow at Little Bedwyn £78 **5 5 4**
Little Bedwyn SN8 3JP (01672) 870871
"Sue & Roger Jones have created a stunning restaurant with some of the very best food in the country", at this converted inn, located "in the

*middle of nowhere but well worth seeking out". Roger is well-known for his knowledge of wine, which evidences itself in a "fabulous" and "unexpectedly wide range of excellent and well-priced wines". All this plus "spot-on service". / **Details:** www.theharrowatlittlebedwyn.co.uk; 9 pm; closed Mon, Tue & Sun; No trainers; Credit card deposit required to book.*

MARLOW, BUCKINGHAMSHIRE 3–3A

The Coach £43 444
3 West Street SL7 2LS (01628) 483013
*Tom Kerridge's second venture (now a year old) is "not quite a pub and not quite a cafe" – "a no booking outlet" serving "very creative small plates" ("prices are high for the portions"). "Don't take a cat to swing (it gets mammothly busy)", but some feel the "food's better than the Hand & Flowers" and it's also great "fun". / **Details:** www.thecoachmarlow.co.uk; 10.30 pm, Sun 9 pm.*

Hand & Flowers £89 433
West Street SL7 2BP (01628) 482277
*"You wait a year but it's worth it" according to most reports on Tom Kerridge's Thames-valley legend, which owes its packed reservation book and huge fame (one of the top-10 most commented-on restaurants outside London in our survey) to being the only UK pub to hold two Michelin stars. "Any high-end restaurant where jeans are OK, and you can order a pint of top ale with your 2-star food gets my vote" – indeed, it is still a "proper pub" ("although if you only want to drink, you'll have to go in the side room") and "where else is such great food eaten in so buzzing and boisterous an environment?" There are inevitable gripes – for some the "mismatch of high-end food and low-key pub interior doesn't work" and quite a sizeable disgruntled minority "love Tom on TV" but find the cooking "disappointing for all its stars and rosettes". Given the huge expectations here however, what's most striking is the proportion loving "the happiest staff" and "somewhere to enjoy with friends and family!" / **Details:** www.thehandandflowers.co.uk; 9.45 p, Sat closed; closed Sun D. / **Accommodation:** 4 rooms, from £140*

Marlow Bar & Grill £53 233
92-94 High Street SL7 1AQ (01628) 488544
*In the centre of town, a contemporary bar and steak restaurant with booths and an open kitchen; the odd cynic feels that the food has slipped a tad of late, but the majority cite its "reliable" cuisine and "good atmosphere" as proof that it still has "one up on the likes of Brasserie Blanc". / **Details:** www.individualrestaurants.com; towards the river end of the High Street; 11 pm, Sun 10.30 pm.*

The Royal Oak £48 333
Frieth Road SL7 2JF (01628) 488611
*"A warm welcome" sets the tone at this "solid" pub-restaurant (with garden), where "robust and tasty dishes are very well-presented in a cosy setting". / **Details:** www.royaloakmarlow.co.uk; Mon - Thur 9.30 pm, Fri & Sat 10 pm, Sun 9 pm.*

Sindhu, Macdonald Compleat Angler Hotel £65 433
The Compleat Angler SL7 1RG
(01628) 405 405
*That is has a "superb location on the river" with "lovely views" is the one undisputed highlight of Atul Kochhar's famous Thames Valley landmark. A few critics find it "over-priced", and feel that the cuisine "while good, doesn't quite hit the spot". For most reporters though, "it's such a shock to find an exciting Indian restaurant in the home counties!", and most reports are of "outstanding" cooking. / **Details:** www.sindhurestaurant.co.uk; Mon - Sat 10.30 pm, Sun 10 pm.*

The Vanilla Pod £67 543
31 West St SL7 2LS (01628) 898101
*Perhaps Michelin should take one of the stars from the nearby Hand & Flowers and give it to Michael Macdonald's "wonderful" venture? "It's like having a world class chef invite you to his house" – "the dining room is tiny and it can feel like eating in a home" – but the "exciting" cuisine is "always brilliant", and "staff are attentive and knowledgeable too". / **Details:** www.thevanillapod.co.uk; 10 pm; closed Mon & Sun.*

MASHAM, NORTH YORKSHIRE 8–4B

Samuel's, Swinton Park Hotel & Spa £80 445
Swinton Park HG4 4JH (01765) 680900
*An "impressive dining room in a grand and beautiful hotel", set on "extensive grounds", where some guests "arrive by helicopter". Stephen Bulmer's food is "not cheap" but "for the (spectacular-fine-dining) standard very good value" (and when it comes to afternoon tea, there's "no competition" – "an example of how to do it for all"). / **Details:** www.swintonpark.com; 9.30 pm; closed weekday L; No jeans; children: 8+ at D. / **Accommodation:** 31 rooms, from £31 / **Sustainability:** ★★★*

Vennells £52 [4][4][3]
7 Silver St HG4 4DX (01765) 689000
*Jon Vennell and his wife Laura "have steadily built a fine reputation in North Yorkshire for good food" at this "most enjoyable" spot (est. 2005), with views of the town's lovely market square. "The décor has improved considerably" since a recent-ish refurb, and "there is now an attractive, if small, bar with seating". / **Details:** www.vennellsrestaurant.co.uk; 9.30 pm; closed Mon, Tue?Sat D only, closed Sun D.*

MATLOCK, DERBYSHIRE 5–2C

Stones £52 [4][4][4]
1C Dale Rd DE4 3LT (01629) 56061
*"Tucked down steps near the river", the Stone family's "superb, little restaurant" boasts "a lack of pretension and a loyal following" thanks to its "serious" cooking and "informal yet informed" service. / **Details:** www.stones-restaurant.co.uk; 8.30pm; closed Mon, Tue L & Sun; no Amex; No shorts.*

MELBOURNE, DERBYSHIRE 5–3C

Bay Tree £51 [3][3][3]
4 Potter St DE73 8HW (01332) 863358
*The "very popular champagne breakfast" continues to draw particular shout-outs at this stylish, contemporary restaurant in this pretty little town; at other times it offers a prix fixe menu focussing on New World cuisine. / **Details:** www.baytreerestaurant.co.uk; 9.30 pm; closed Mon, Tue & Sun D; no Amex.*

MELLS, SOMERSET 2–3B

The Talbot Inn £46 [3][4][4]
Selwood St BA11 3PN (01373) 812254
*A "splendid country inn" near Glasto' – split between a restaurant and casual brasserie – a "perfectly managed" spot and "a real joy to visit". / **Details:** www.talbotinn.com; 9.30 pm. / **Accommodation:** 0 rooms, from £8*

MENAI BRIDGE, GWYNEDD 4–1C

Dylan's Restaurant £44 [3][3][4]
St George's Road LL59 5EY (01248) 716 714
*"The best in casual seaside dining"; with its "wonderful sea views" and "informal but slick service", this "family-friendly" venue offers a "very enjoyable" experience, with the "view over the Menai Straits another plus". "Fabulous fresh fish" is the menu highlight (but they also serve pizza). / **Details:** www.dylansrestaurant.co.uk; 10 pm .*

Sosban And The Old Butchers £63 [5][4][4]
1 High St, Menai Bridge LL59 5EE
(01248) 208 131
*"Anglesey's hidden gem"; in an old butcher's, this "amazing and exciting" fine dining spot continues to inspire adulation for its "clever combination of ingredients and painstaking presentation" ("saved from pretension by the quiet, friendly service and plain furnishings"). "It's only a matter of time for this special place to gain recognition all over the UK and even the world!". / **Details:** www.sosbanandtheoldbutchers.com; Thu-Sat midnight.*

MILFORD-ON-SEA, HAMPSHIRE 2–4C

La Perle £48 [3][3][2]
60 High Street SO41 0QD (01590) 643 557
*A "pleasant albeit rather cramped restaurant", in an attractive seaside village, where chef Lionel Sené turns out "good quality cooking" (including a "good value" fixed menu at lunch). / **Details:** www.laperle.co.uk; Mon closed, Tue - Sat 9.30 pm, Sun 2.30 pm; closed Mon L & Sun.*

Verveine Fishmarket Restaurant £67 [5][3][3]
98 High St SO41 0QE (01590) 642 176
*"Wow!" David Wykes "shows real imagination and skill in both cooking and presentation" at this "small" venture, behind a fishmonger. "Garnishes and flourishes galore, plus the freshest fish" deliver "a wonderful meal, full of surprises". / **Details:** www.verveine.co.uk; 9.30 pm; closed Mon & Sun; no Amex.*

MILTON KEYNES, BUCKINGHAMSHIRE 3–2A

Jaipur £37 [3][3][3]
599 Grafton Gate East MK9 1AT
(01908) 669796
*There are some "very enjoyable" and "good value" meals to be had at this landmark Indian – a lavish, purpose-built venue near the station; service is notably accommodating ("one item I didn't particularly like, and although there was nothing wrong with it, they took it off the bill!") / **Details:** www.jaipur.co.uk; 11.30 pm, Sun 10.30 pm; No shorts.*

MINSTER, KENT 3–3D

Corner House £49 [3][3][3]
42 Station Rd CT12 4BZ (01843) 823000
A three-year-old village restaurant (with two rooms) run by Matthew Sworder, ex-of Gordon Ramsay; while critics felt that it "was pleasant enough, but overall didn't live up to the ('Kent Restaurant of the

Year') hyperbole", fans insist that it's still "worth travelling to". A Canterbury sibling opened in July 2016 (the Flying Horse pub in Dover Street). / **Details:** *www.thecornerhouseminster.co.uk; 9.30 pm, Sun 3.30; closed Sun D.*

MISTLEY, ESSEX 3–2D

The Mistley Thorn Hotel £50 [3][2][3]
High St CO11 1HE (01206) 392 821
This gastropub-with-rooms (a former stomping ground of Witchfinder General, Matthew Hopkins), is "very good all-round", "with nice views of the river". / **Details:** *www.mistleythorn.com; 9.30 pm.* / **Accommodation:** *11 rooms, from £100*

MONTGOMERY, POWYS 5–4A

Checkers £74 [5][4][3]
Broad St, Powys SY15 6PN (01686) 669 822
"You don't expect to find such sophisticated and refined food in the wilds of Wales", but prepare to be wowed at Stéphane Borie & Sarah Francis's "beautiful" inn. "They have stopped doing à la carte and now only offer a tasting menu" – the latter is "truly outstanding". / **Details:** *www.thecheckersmontgomery.co.uk; 9 pm; closed Mon, Tue L, Wed L, Thu L & Sun; no Amex; children: 8+ at D.* / **Accommodation:** *5 rooms, from £125*

MORECAMBE, LANCASHIRE 5–1A

Midland Hotel, English Lakes hotels and venues £53 [4][3][5]
Marine Road west LA4 4BU (01524) 424000
A "gorgeous Art Deco hotel" whose "beautiful" dining room boasts "uninterrupted views of the sea" from the promenade; even if "it is the vista that raises this to a special experience", the food is "lovely" too. Top Tip – the "best afternoon tea ever". / **Details:** *www.englishlakes.co.uk; 9.30 pm.* / **Accommodation:** *44 rooms, from £94*

MORETON-IN-MARSH, GLOUCESTERSHIRE 2–1C

Horse & Groom £53 [3][4][4]
Upper Oddington GL56 0XH (01451) 830584
In an attractive Cotswold stone building, this "stylish" hilltop venue – a gastroboozer with "very comfortable" rooms – makes a "great place for a romantic meal or night out" thanks to its "consistently good food". / **Details:** *www.horseandgroom.uk.com; 9 pm; no Amex.* / **Accommodation:** *7 rooms, from £89*

MORSTON, NORFOLK 6–3C

Morston Hall £94 [4][4][4]
Main Coast Rd NR25 7AA (01263) 741041
"Exquisite tasting menus (a taste explosion!), with wines setting each course off to perfection", won renewed enthusiastic endorsements for Galton Blackiston's acclaimed country house hotel, near the coast. The odd niggle is raised – "not particularly innovative"... "too many rich sauces and not enough vegetable to balance (this is 2016!)" – but all reports on the cuisine are fundamentally very upbeat and most are "fantastic", while "staff try to accommodate all requests". / **Details:** *www.morstonhall.com; between Blakeney & Wells on A149; 8 pm; D only, ex Sun open L & D; practically no walk-ins – you must boo.* / **Accommodation:** *13 rooms, from £330*

MOTHERWELL, NORTH LANARKSHIRE 9–4C

Glass House, Alona Hotel £44 [3][2][3]
Strathclyde Country Park ML1 3RT
(01698) 333 888
"Excellent for lunch – it's a great deal!"; if you're prepared to act as a gastronomic guinea pig, you can enjoy a meal that's interesting and good value, at the training restaurant for Hospitality and Culinary Arts at Salford City College (plus a local sixth form centre). / **Details:** *www.alonahotel.co.uk; 9 pm.*

MOULSFORD, OXFORDSHIRE 2–2D

The Beetle & Wedge Boathouse £52 [2][3][4]
Ferry Ln OX10 9JF (01491) 651381
With its "beautifully calming views", this "romantic" ex-boathouse-turned-restaurant has a picture book setting on the Thames (quite literally, as it was the stretch of water that inspired The Wind in the Willows); the food plays something of a supporting rôle. / **Details:** *www.beetleandwedge.co.uk; on A329 between Streatley & Wallingford, take Ferry Lane at crossroads; 8.45 pm.* / **Accommodation:** *3 rooms, from £90*

MOULTON, CAMBRIDGESHIRE 3–1C

The Packhorse Inn £53 [2][2][3]
Bridge St CB8 8SP (01638) 751818
An "attractive restaurant-with-rooms in a picturesque setting" in "the middle of nowhere" (not that this deters the "London foodie brigades who inhabit the place at weekends"). While some feel the "food doesn't quite match the

expensive surroundings", even mild cynics would be "quite happy to dine and stay again". / **Details:** *www.thepackhorseinn.com; 10 pm.*

MOUNTSORREL, LEICESTERSHIRE 5–3D

John's House £65 443

139 - 141 Loughborough Road LE12 7AR (01509) 415569

"The website makes it feel like a sort of farm kitchen but that's not the character!" – John Duffin's "off-the-beaten-track" venture on the family farm in Mountsorrel has won high foodie acclaim in its two years of operation and is "definitely a destination restaurant". Even the most sceptical report of a "very pleasant but ultimately unexciting" meal said the place is "hard to find, but worth going", and on most accounts it's "a great gastronomic experience that does not melt your credit card!" / **Details:** *www.johnshouse.co.uk; 9 pm.*

MOUSEHOLE, CORNWALL 1–4A

The Old Coastguard £45 323

TR19 6PR (01736) 731222

With a "lovely setting looking out to sea", this "cosy" yet "spacious" hotel dining room – offering "gorgeous" fish-centric cuisine – feels "more south of France than Cornwall";"come here during the day and sit outside to enjoy the wonderful views towards St Michael's Mount". / **Details:** *www.oldcoastguardhotel.co.uk; 9 pm;The Old Coastguard. /* **Accommodation:** *20 rooms, from £170*

2 Fore Street Restaurant £45 433

2 Fore St TR19 6PF (01736) 731164

"An excellent bistro-style restaurant, in this small fishing village", set in a street a little way from the harbour. Fish and seafood is the highlight "as it ought to be" – "wonderful, fresh and expertly cooked". / **Details:** *www.2forestreet.co.uk; 9.30 pm. /* **Accommodation:** *2 rooms, from £250*

MURCOTT, OXFORDSHIRE 2–1D

The Nut Tree Inn £66 434

Main Street OX5 2RE (01865) 331253

"Michael North and Imogen Young set a very high bar indeed for how to balance running an exemplary village pub with stunning food", at this rural thatched pub (about 10 minutes' drive from Bicester Shopping Village), which has "a superb focus on local produce, much of which is grown or reared on site (including 'pick-your-own' rare breed pigs)". Top Menu Tip – "they have a Michelin star, but their legendary soufflés are worth three stars!" / **Details:** *www.nuttreeinn.co.uk; Mon & Tue closed, Wed - Sat 9 pm, Sun 3 pm.*

MUTHILL, PERTH AND KINROSS 9–3C

Barley Bree £62 434

6 Willoughby St PH5 2AB (01764) 681451

In a rural spot near Gleneagles, this cosy restaurant-with-rooms serves "excellent, French-bistro-type food made with local Scottish ingredients". Chef/patron "Fabrice (Bouteloup) is also an amazing baker and pastry chef", so "fantastic" bread is par for the course, while "head waitress Alma is always attentive". / **Details:** *www.barleybree.com; 9 pm Wed-Sat, 7.30pm Sun; closed Mon & Tue; no Amex. /* **Accommodation:** *6 rooms, from £110*

NAILSWORTH, GLOUCESTERSHIRE 2–2B

Wild Garlic £51 433

3 Cossacks Sq GL6 0DB (01453) 832615

Matthew Beardshall oversees "consistently innovative cooking using excellent ingredients" at this petite restaurant-with-rooms, which is "now doing tapas" too;"service occasionally wobbles, but it's a fine local" nonetheless. / **Details:** *www.wild-garlic.co.uk; 9.30 pm, Sun 2.30 pm; closed Mon, Tue & Sun D; no Amex. /* **Accommodation:** *3 rooms, from £90*

NANTGAREDIG, CARMARTHENSHIRE 4–4C

Y Polyn £46 444

Capel Dewi SA32 7LH (01267) 290000

A "bit tricky to find", and "the (former tollhouse) exterior is unprepossessing", but this "wonderfully understated pub" does "food that is way better than lots of much flashier urban restaurants" – "no wonder the trophy cabinet is full of culinary accolades!" / **Details:** *www.ypolyn.co.uk; 9 pm; closed Mon & Sun D.*

NETHER BURROW, CUMBRIA 7–4D

The Highwayman £45 333

Burrow LA6 2RJ (01524) 273 338

"Not pretentious, just good" – the verdict on this "very popular" and welcoming Ribble Valley Inn, acclaimed for an "interesting menu with regular seasonal specials" and "chips to die for". / **Details:** *www.highwaymaninn.co.uk; Mon -Thur 9 pm, Fri & Sat 9.30 pm, Sun 9 pm.*

NETHER WESTCOTE, OXFORDSHIRE 2–1C

The Feathered Nest Inn £80 5 4 4
OX7 6SD (01993) 833 030
*"Off the beaten track in an outstandingly beautiful location", this Cotswolds gastropub is a stunning all-rounder (and you can sit outside when it's fine). Enjoy "fabulously delicious" food of a kind that's "occasionally adventurous but never faddish". / **Details:** www.thefeatherednestinn.co.uk; 9.15 pm; closed Mon & Sun D. / **Accommodation:** 4 rooms, from £150*

NEW MILTON, HAMPSHIRE 2–4C

Chewton Glen £92 2 2 2
Chewton Glen Rd BH23 5QL (01425) 282212
*This "very stylish" country house hotel, set in marvellous grounds on the edge of the New Forest, again split reporters on predictable lines this year. For fans it's "still very special", "setting a high standard (if at a price)" for "beautiful food, wonderfully presented". Foes, though, in particular, just can't get over the requirement for a second mortgage. (Given how grand the place is however, "it's great the way they cater to small kids without hassle".) / **Details:** www.chewtonglen.com; on A337 between New Milton & Highcliffe; 10 pm; No trainers. / **Accommodation:** 70 rooms, from £325 / **Sustainability:** ★★*

NEWARK, NOTTINGHAMSHIRE 5–3D

Koinonia £35 4 4 3
19 St Marks Ln NG24 1XS (01636) 706230
*The "unlikely location" – in "a strange little passageway" – "should not put you off" a trip to this "super" south Indian restaurant; the "warm and genuine" welcome, and "wonderful tastes" offer some reporters "a new slant on Indian food", and others "an experience that lived up to a recent gastronomic tour of Kerala!" / **Details:** www.koinoniarestaurant.com; 11 pm, Sat 11.30 pm, Sun 7.30 pm.*

NEWBOROUGH, ISLE OF ANGLESEY 4–1C

The Marram Grass £47 5 3 3
White Lodge LL61 6RS (01248) 440 077
*"A potting shed, of all bizarre places" houses this "impossibly cute, disarmingly snug" Anglesey five-year-old, whose "lovely owners" serve a "small but interesting menu of locally sourced, seasonal produce". Even cynics carping at "high prices to sit cheek-by-jowl with neighbouring diners" give top marks to the food; "a real find". / **Details:** www.themarramgrass.com.*

NEWBURY, BERKSHIRE 2–2D

The Crab & Boar £57 3 2 2
Wantage Rd RG20 8UE (01635) 247550
*Renamed and expensively refurbed, this country pub-with-rooms (fka The Crab at Chieveley) now offers a "very pleasant interior", including an "excellent pub grub area"; "the menu (as the name) espouses both fish and meat now", with the fish in particular "restoring the high standards" achieved in the past. / **Details:** www.crabandboar.com; M4 J13 to B4494 – 0.5 mile on right; 9.30 pm. / **Accommodation:** 14 rooms, from £90*

Woodspeen £69 5 4 4
Lambourn Rd RG20 8BM (01635) 265 070
*John Campbell's "seriously impressive" cooking goes from strength to strength at this "lovely newish restaurant in the countryside near Newbury – an ex-pub modernised to create a New-World-style atmosphere" with open kitchen. "Highly recommended", and there's an adjoining cookery school too. / **Details:** www.thewoodspeen.com; 9.30 pm, Sun 4 pm; closed Mon.*

NEWCASTLE UPON TYNE, TYNE AND WEAR 8–2B

21 £51 4 4 3
Trinity Gdns NE1 2HH (0191) 222 0755
*They've dropped the word "Café" from the name of Terry Laybourne's "oldest and probably best venture" – "a great city-centre all-rounder" that's been the most commented-on restaurant in these parts for as long as we can remember. Its "creative bistro-style food" has likewise "shown consistent quality for many years now"; but some old regulars "are not sure about the summer 2015 refurb – it feels a bit more stark, and we're not quite sure what they were aiming for". / **Details:** www.cafetwentyone.co.uk; 10.30 pm, Sun 8 pm.*

artisan, The Biscuit Factory £52 3 2 2
Stoddard St NE2 1AN (0191) 260 5411
*David Kennedy's oft-renamed spot – in the UK's largest arts and craft gallery – continues to elicit solid marks for former 'North East Chef of the Year' Andrew Wilkinson's locally sourced bistro fare. / **Details:** www.artisannewcastle.com; 9 pm, Fri & Sat 9.30 pm; closed Sun D.*

Blackfriars Restaurant £50 3 3 5
Friars St NE1 4XN (0191) 261 5945
The "aggressively local" (in a good way!) cuisine is "well-prepared" and the "ambience in particular can't be faulted" at this romantic venue in a "lovely" 13th-century building with a cloister. As of late 2016, owner Andy Hook plans to expand this 15-year-old

*venture into the neighbouring space. (In fact, he also, apparently, has his eyes on the 21 Queen Street site, most recently trading as Pan Haggertys, RIP.) / **Details:** www.blackfriarsrestaurant.co.uk; 10 pm; closed Sun D.*

Broad Chare £43 333
25 Broad Chare NE1 3DQ (019) 1211 2144
*A gastroboozer combining a "good pubby atmosphere", "lovely" staff, and "very fresh local produce with a traditional British slant"; it's particularly "handy for a pre-theatre meal if you are off to Gateshead Sage or the Live Theatre". / **Details:** www.thebroadchare.co.uk; 10 pm; closed Sun D; no Amex.*

Café Royal £46 333
8 Nelson St NE1 5AW (0191) 231 3000
*"A regular stop for coffee and light lunch" – this well-known grand café by Grainger Market "gets very crowded, particularly at weekends, when service gets a bit slow". Even so, generally "consistent standards make it a safe bet". / **Details:** www.sjf.co.uk; 5.30 pm, Sun 3.30 pm; L only; Booking weekdays only.*

Caffé Vivo £41 444
29 Broad Chare NE1 3DQ (0191) 232 1331
*"Laybourne's Italian" is a "very reliable" destination for a "good value pre-theatre" meal, but it's "also a great place for a sociable night out" – "especially the regular Wednesday BYO" events. / **Details:** www.caffevivo.co.uk; 10 pm; closed Sun.*

Dabbawal £37 443
69-75 High Bridge NE1 6BX (0191) 232 5133
*"Lunch, dinner time, on a date, a family meal or a quick pre-film bite – I love it!" This "very different" and "buzzing" outfit, near the Theatre Royal, remains the city's most popular Indian. High ratings too for its Jesmond sibling. / **Details:** www.dabbawal.com; 10pm , Fri - Sat - Sun -10.30 pm; closed Sun.*

Francesca's £36 343
134 Manor House Rd NE2 2NE
(0191) 281 6586
*"Always the place to go for a cheap, vaguely Italian meal if you can stand the queues" – an "old-school" Jesmond institution specialising in pizza and pasta; fans cheerfully admit that its "best suit is nostalgia" (right down to the "Hilda Ogden-style posters of the Colosseum"). / **Details:** www.francesca.com; 9.30 pm; closed Sun; no Amex; No bookings.*

House of Tides £77 543
28-30 The Close NE1 3RN (0191) 2303720
*Kenny Atkinson's two-year-old in an old building on the Quayside ("ask for a window table") put in a "brilliant" performance this year, justifying its foodie renown with "fast class", "exciting" cuisine, with great "clarity of flavour", and "cheerful, knowledgeable and helpful staff" – "a total delight!" / **Details:** www.houseoftides.co.uk; Mon closed, Tue - Fri 9.30 pm, Sat 10 pm; closed Mon, Tue L & Sun.*

Jesmond Dene House £75 344
Jesmond Dene Rd NE2 2EY (0191) 212 6066
*Tucked away in a wooded gorge, Terry Laybourne's boutique hotel certainly has a "lovely country house setting". The odd "erratic performance" is noted, but all reports are fundamentally positive and most are out-and-out "superb". Top Tip – "they do a really good afternoon tea". / **Details:** www.jesmonddenehouse.co.uk; 9.30 pm. / **Accommodation:** 40 rooms, from £120*

Osaka £28 342
69 Grey St NE1 6EF (0191) 2615300
*"A total surprise" – an "authentic Japanese" opposite the Theatre Royal, offering "many classic dishes" (and at "very reasonable" prices for the "tremendous quality"). / **Details:** www.osakanewcastle.co.uk; 10 pm, Fri & Sat 10.15 pm.*

Pani's £32 354
61-65 High Bridge NE1 6BX (0191) 232 4366
*"Staff treat everyone as friends" at this "fab, fab, fab", "cheap 'n' cheerful" Sardinian favourite – "still, after many years, one of Tyneside's most reliable venues for a value-for-money get-together". / **Details:** www.paniscafe.co.uk; 10 pm; closed Sun; no Amex; No bookings at lunch.*

Paradiso £42 343
1 Market Ln NE1 6QQ (0191) 221 1240
*"Our own Italian restaurant in the heart of the city"; there's "always a warm welcome" at this "unbelievably cheerful" local, and, whilst the offering "rarely changes", it "never results in menu fatigue" owing to the "exceptional value" food. / **Details:** www.paradiso.co.uk; 10.30 pm, Fri & Sat 10.45 pm; closed Sun.*

Peace & Loaf £58 444
217 Jesmond Road NE2 1LA (0191) 281 5222
*"Just sensational" – a stylish, split-level venue in Jesmond that "goes from strength to strength", offering MasterChef: The Professionals finalist, Dave Coulson's "superbly presented food, with tastes to match". / **Details:** www.peaceandloaf.co.uk; Mon - Sat 9.30 pm, Sun 3.30 pm; closed Sun D.*

Sachins £39 443
Forth Banks NE1 3SG (0191) 261 9035
*Bob and Neeta Arora's extremely well-established Indian, near Central Station, continues to win very solid ratings as one of the town's curry favourites. / **Details:** www.sachins.co.uk; 10.45pm; closed Sun L.*

A Taste of Persia £32 432
14 Marlborough Cr NE1 4EE (0191) 221 0088
On the city outskirts, this local favourite "continues to impress" with its "deliciously spiced Middle

André Garrett At Cliveden, Cliveden House, Maidenhead

The Cricketers, Cobham

Mr Cooper's, Manchester

Eastern cuisine (part-Persian, part-Turkish)" and in "substantial portions" too; for new converts, it's something of "a revelation… how did we miss this before?!" / **Details:** www.atasteofpersia.com; 10 pm; closed Sun.*

Tyneside Cinema Bar Cafe £31 334

10 Pilgrim St NE1 6QG (0191) 227 5522

*Launched in August 2014, this cinema café-bar combines a "good vibe", an "interesting selection of specials" and an "unusual" weekend brunch – and, should you choose, all "accompanied by movies on the big screen" (which is sectioned off from the rest of the space). / **Details:** www.tynesidecinema.co.uk/food-drink/tynesi.*

Tyneside Coffee Rooms, Tyneside Cinema £31 355

10 Pilgrim St NE1 6QG (0191) 227 5520

*In a Grade II listed Art Deco cinema, this "bustling, happy" spot is "a part of Tyneside folklore" turning out "comfort food at its best". The place "has managed to retain the best of the past" – indeed, it's the UK's last surviving newsreel theatre in full-time operation – while adding "modern favourites too" ("they now do gluten-free sandwiches"!) / **Details:** www.tynesidecinema.co.uk; 9 pm; closed Sun D; no Amex.*

NEWPORT, ISLE OF WIGHT 2–4D

Thompsons £66 543

11 Town Lane PO30 1JU (01983) 526118

*"Robert Thompson is now on his own, having left The Hambrough in Ventnor" and "his first venture as chef/owner has made a great start" ("the islanders are queueing up to eat there"). A "light and warming" café-like space, "if you have a coveted table in the downstairs area by the open kitchen, then you are really close to the action". "There are some amazing taste and texture combinations to be had and the taster menu is a must." / **Details:** www.robertthompson.co.uk.*

NEWPORT, PEMBROKESHIRE 4–4B

Llys Meddyg £51 444

East St SA42 0SY (01239) 820008

*From the food to the service, this "wonderfully warm and welcoming" restaurant-with-rooms offers "a very good overall experience"; one reporter made a "special mention of the local, seasonal vegetables" (the owner runs foraging trips along the coast). / **Details:** www.llysmeddyg.com; 9 pm; D only, closed Sun; no Amex. / **Accommodation:** 8 rooms, from £100*

NEWQUAY, CORNWALL 1–3B

Fish House £43 333

Headland Road TR7 1EW (01637) 872085

*"Don't visit on a grey day (when it seems a bit utilitarian and lacking atmosphere)", but this converted unit, with terrace overlooking Fistral beach, is tipped for its "friendly service and great seafood". / **Details:** 9.30 pm.*

NEWTON-IN-BOWLAND, LANCASHIRE 5–1B

The Parkers Arms £44 554

Hall Gate Hill BB7 3DY (01200) 446236

*"It looks like a typical local inn, set in a pretty village in the Forest of Bowland", but Stosie Madi's cooking "is on another level" – "it's simply the best food ever" – at this "just amazing" destination, which is "worth travelling over the Pennines for". "Exceptional ingredients are cooked with skill and flair" from "a constantly-changing, hyper-locally-sourced menu" and Kathy Smith oversees "the friendliest, efficient service". "While the real gems come in the dishes with Middle Eastern inspiration" (reflecting the chef's heritage), it would be wise not to ignore the pub classics, especially pies. Top Menu Tip – "the wild garlic custard tart was probably the best thing I have ever eaten!" / **Details:** www.parkersarms.co.uk; Mon & Tue closed, Wed - Fri 8.30 pm, Sat 9 pm, Sun; closed Mon. / **Accommodation:** 4 rooms, from £77*

NOMANSLAND, WILTSHIRE 2–3C

Les Mirabelles £52 554

Forest Edge Rd SP5 2BN (01794) 390205

*"A piece of France in the New Forest"; from its "superb" location ("overlooking a green, where ponies frequently wander by"), to the "very well-cooked and well-presented French cuisine at reasonable prices", and a wine list "full of unusual South African rarities", Claude Laage's Gallic operation is a real "gem" and "terrific value". / **Details:** www.lesmirabelles.co.uk; off A36 between Southampton & Salisbury; Mon closed, Tue - Sat 10 pm, Sun closed; closed Mon & Sun; no Amex.*

NORDEN, LANCASHIRE 5–1B

Nutter's £52 433

Edenfield Road OL12 7TT (01706) 650167

"Run by indefatigable (local celeb chef) Andrew Nutter" – this "slightly barn-like" manor house hotel dining room is "easy to mock for its formal setting and rather '90s approach". But this is, in fact, a "serious restaurant turning out serious, classical food", and desserts, as ever, remain knock-out. Top Tip – afternoon tea here is of "exceptional quality".

/ **Details:** www.nuttersrestaurant.com; between Edenfield & Norden on A680; Mon closed, Tue - Thur 9 pm, Fri & Sat 9.30 pm, Su; closed Mon.

NORTH SHIELDS, TYNE AND WEAR 8–2B

Irvins Brasserie £45 333

Irvin Building NE30 1JH (0191) 296 3238

*"A great find" – a spacious, laid-back brasserie, in the former HQ on the North Shields Fish Quay of fishing pioneer Richard Irvin (whose steam-powered trawlers were once the world's envy), and with a menu of well-priced, fishy cuisine. / **Details:** www.irvinsbrasserie.co.uk; Mon & Tue closed, Wed & Thur 10 pm, Fri & Sat 11 p; closed Mon & Tue.*

River Cafe £38 343

51 Bell Street, Fish Quay NE30 1HF (0191) 296 6168

*"You can see the boats unloading or getting ready for sea" at this rather smart bistro (tablecloths!), tipped for its "ultra-fresh fish" (in particular from the "seafood themed lunch and early evening menu (Wed-Fri) , which is fantastic value"). / **Details:** www.rivercafeonthetyne.co.uk; Tues - Sat 9.30pm, Sun 4.00pm,.*

Staith House £46 332

57 Low Lights NE30 1JA (0191) 270 8441

*MasterChef finalist John Calton's "understated" quayside two-year-old is "an unexpected delight" offering an "ever-changing menu" majoring in "very fresh fish and seafood". "You'd never think North Shields would have a great pub with friendly service, coastal ambience and winning food, but it does!" / **Details:** www.thestaithhouse.co.uk; 9 pm, Fri & Sat 9.30 pm, Sun 4 pm.*

NORTHALLERTON, NORTH YORKSHIRE 8–4B

The Cleveland Tontine £46 333

Staddlebridge DL6 3JB (01609) 882 671

*This stylish boutique hotel-restaurant has passed through a couple of hands since it was known as McCoy's at the Tontine. It pleases locals with its "quality" cooking (including an "excellent afternoon tea"), and the latest owners continue to invest in the property, with a £1m expansion coming soon. / **Details:** www.theclevelandtontine.co.uk; near junction of A19 & A172; 9 pm, Sat 9.30 pm. / **Accommodation:** 7 rooms, from £130*

NORTHLEACH, GLOUCESTERSHIRE 2–1C

Wheatsheaf Inn £50 343

West End GL54 3EZ (01451) 860244

*The Lucky Onion empire's village gastroboozer offers "the best country pub food in the area, bar none"; there are critics of the "unlovely" room, while the food "varies from good pub standard to much better than that". / **Details:** www.cotswoldswheatsheaf.com; 3pm, Sun 3.30pm. / **Accommodation:** 14 rooms, from £140*

NORTHWICH, CHESHIRE 5–3B

The Fishpool Inn £46 323

Fishpool Rd CW8 2HP (01606) 883277

*On the edge of Delamere Forest, "a modernised country gastropub", dating from the 18th century, with "great staff" and a "wonderful menu" based on "good reliable" grub (spanning wood-fired pizzas and classics). / **Details:** thefishpoolinn.co.uk; 9.30 pm, Fri & Sun 10 pm, Sun 9 pm.*

NORTON, WILTSHIRE 2–2B

The Vine Tree £47 343

Foxley Road SN16 0JP (01666) 837 654

*"Another great gastropub worth a visit" – this "small-but-perfectly-formed" hostelry is well-placed for the A4, and praised for its "beautifully prepared meals". / **Details:** www.thevinetree.co.uk; Mon - Sat 9.30 pm, Sun 3.15pm; closed Sun D.*

NORWICH, NORFOLK 6–4C

Benedicts £53 432

9 St Benedicts St NR2 4PE (01603) 926 080

*"If there was a new restaurant deserving culinary gongs it's this one!", say fans of Great British Chef, Richard Bainbridge's assured newcomer. Some reports note "a tension between the kitchen's ambition, and the local bistro setting" – and there's the odd gripe about "dreary, MasterCheffy cooking" – but most reporters are delighted with the "remarkable modern cuisine in a beautifully simple, yet elegant environment". / **Details:** www.restaurantbenedicts.com/home; just off the city centre (2 doors up from Pizza Express); 10pm; closed Mon & Sun.*

The Gunton Arms £49 345

Cromer Rd, Thorpe Mkt NR11 8TZ (01263) 832010

*The "amazing grounds" ("a wonderful setting in a deer park") and "quirky and original interior" are undisputed attractions of this countryside "gem". Sceptics say the cooking's "OK, but nothing special" or "not up to past best", but most reporters say it's "worth the train from London" for its "first-rate fare" (including beef cooked on an open fire). / **Details:** www.theguntonarms.co.uk; 10.00pm. / **Accommodation:** 8 rooms, from £95*

Iron House £43 444
1 St John Maddermarket NR2 1DN
(01603) 763388
"An undiscovered gem in the heart of Norwich" ("tucked away near the central market"); all the food is "bloody good" (for the price, "amazing") at this simply decorated five-year-old, and a top attraction is "the excellent breakfast choices" (plus "if you can get a seat by St John Maddermarket you can people-watch to your heart's content"). / **Details:** *www.theironhouse.co.uk/contact/; Mon - Sat, 11.00pm.*

Last Wine Bar & Restaurant £47 344
70 - 76 St Georges Street NR3 1AB
(01603) 626 626
"Probably the best wine bar in Norwich" – a veteran venue spread across an old Victorian shoe factory (hence the name); it's best known for its "really good selection of wines" served by the glass or carafe, but the food is also "a pleasure". / **Details:** *www.thelastwinebar.co.uk; Mon - Sat 10.30 pm, Sun closed; closed Sun.*

Roger Hickman's £68 544
79 Upper St. Giles St NR2 1AB
(01603) 633522
"Definitely outstanding in Norwich!" – Roger Hickman's "first-class restaurant" is still being buoyed along by the addition of a bar and a more contemporary look a year or two ago. "Staff clearly take pride in what they do", and results from both à la carte meals and taster menus with matching wine flights are "really exceptional". / **Details:** *www.rogerhickmansrestaurant.com; 10 pm; closed Mon & Sun.*

NOSS MAYO, DEVON 1–4C

The Ship Inn £44 344
PL8 1EW (01752) 872 387
A "perfect riverside pub" approached along narrow lanes, and with a "great location" by the water; "good fish and traditional meals, plus lots of outside seating in summer". / **Details:** *www.nossmayo.com; 9.30 pm.*

NOTTINGHAM, NOTTINGHAMSHIRE 5–3D

Annie's Burger Shack £16 443
5 Broadway NG1 1PR (07463) 033255
For an "amazing array" of "fabulous burgers", look no further than this "busy" spot; the "only trouble is trying to get a table… it is just much too popular"; now serving breakfast too. / **Details:** *www.anniesburgershack.com.*

Baresca £34 324
9 Byard Ln NG1 2GJ (0115) 948 3900
"A fantastic new addition to Nottingham's emerging dining scene on the edges of the vibrant Creative Quarter". This "much more urban" sibling to West Bridgford's Escabeche mostly inspires approval for its "diverse" and affordable tapas. Top Tip – "very good value" lunches and early bird offers. / **Details:** *www.baresca.co.uk.*

Cafe Roya £40 342
130 Wollaton Rd NG9 2PE (0115) 922 1902
"Imaginative vegetarian food served up with cheer" has made this "very popular" spot "a great addition to the local restaurant scene"; it has an unusual layout, with numerous rooms spread over two floors. / **Details:** *11 pm.*

Chino Latino, Park Plaza Hotel £39 422
41 Maid Marian Way NG1 6GD
(0115) 947 7444
"Exciting" pan-Asian cuisine has long been an unexpected find in this once-trendy dining room off the foyer of a dull business hotel, where for years it's been "a shame about the sterile décor", which is now "looking very tired". / **Details:** *www.chinolatino.co.uk; 10.30 pm; closed Sun.*

The Cumin £40 452
62-64 Maid Marian Way NG1 6BQ
(0115) 941 9941
"The setting is not that appealing", but that's about the only caveat with this "warm" Indian "on Nottingham's curry strip". While "traditional" in style, its dishes are "cleaner-flavoured than the norm", while "pleasant" and "personal" service also elevates it above the competition. / **Details:** *www.thecumin.co.uk; 11 pm, Fri & Sat 11.30 pm; D only, closed Sun.*

French Living £43 323
27 King St NG1 2AY (0115) 958 5885
Offering "French bistro food at its best", this stalwart venue "has many fans, of all ages, not least because it is always good value, and the house wine is very swill-able"; and "you can almost believe you're in Paris". / **Details:** *www.frenchliving.co.uk; 10 pm; closed Mon & Sun; no Amex.*

Hart's £66 332
Standard Hill, Park Row NG1 6GN
(0115) 988 1900
Tim Hart's "modern", '90s brasserie near the castle is one of the city's culinary linchpins and remains the most commented-upon place in the city centre. A "slick" operation, it's still seen by many reporters as a "reliable" favourite, but ratings waned this year amidst complaints from one or two regulars of increasingly "predictable" cooking, and a "lack of atmosphere". / **Details:** *www.hartsnottingham.co.uk;*

10 pm, Sun 9 pm. / ***Accommodation:*** *32 rooms, from £125*

Iberico **£43** **444**

The Shire Hall, High Pavement NG1 1HN
(01159) 410410

"A cosy historic cellar in the Lace Market" ("we walked past twice before we found it") provides the "romantic" setting for this "hidden gem" – one of the town's most commented-on eateries – on account of its "tapas dishes prepared with panache", and "efficient but un-rushed" service. With success is coming expansion – a new 'Bar Iberico' is on the cards on Carlton Street in Hockley. / ***Details:*** *www.ibericotapas.com; 10 pm; closed Sun; no Amex; children: 12+ D.*

Junkyard **£32** **433**

12, Bridlesmith Walk NG1 2FZ
(0115) 9501758

"One of the coolest places to grab lunch" – a "craft beer bar serving creative and interesting small plates". "They import beer direct from California, and accompany it with brilliant food inspired by America's West Coast". Owners Nigel Garlick and Sam Dean must be doing something right as in June 2016 they annexed the neighbouring building to open The Herbert Kilpin pub, with which Junkyard shares a beer garden. / ***Details:*** *Mon - Sat 10.00pm, Sun 9.00pm.*

Masala Junction **£40** **444**

301-303 Mansfield Road, Carrington NG5 2DA
(0115) 9622366

Well-known Notts restaurateur, Nel Aziz's new venture – "a converted Nat West, with a beautiful, very tastefully refurbished dining area" – provides "wonderful contemporary Indian food in a classical environment". "I just love the energy that has gone into project, from the restoration of the building, to the menu and the wine list." / ***Details:*** *masalajunction.co.uk/; 10.30pm, Sat 11.30pm.*

MemSaab **£42** **444**

12-14 Maid Marian Way NG1 6HS
(0115) 957 0009

"The best Indian in Nottingham" – this prized city-centre venue is "hard to fault for quality and taste" and service is very "friendly" too. / ***Details:*** *www.mem-saab.co.uk; near Castle, opposite Park Plaza Hotel; 10.30 pm, Fri & Sat 11 pm, Sun 10 pm; D only; No shorts.*

Restaurant Sat Bains **£128** **533**

Lenton Lane NG7 2SA (0115) 986 6566

"Sat is a genius", and the "edgy" and "amazingly executed" cuisine at his fringe-of-Nottingham HQ can be "beyond delicious", both within the main dining room, or – if you want to push the boat out further – at 'Nucleus', a new six-seater chef's table within his development kitchen. True "it is difficult to get away from the fact that it is a '70s, brick, motel-like structure, in an industrial setting" amidst pylons and "under a ring road", but for most reporters the "exceptional food more than compensates for the bizarre location". Other niggles this year? – that it is "so expensive" seemed to grate a little more, and service – on most accounts "hugely professional" – also showed instances of being "a little automated", or in the odd case even dictatorial. / ***Details:*** *www.restaurantsatbains.com; Mon & Tue closed, Wed & Thur 9 pm, Fri & Sat 9.45 ; closed Mon & Sun; no Amex; children: 8+. /* ***Accommodation:*** *8 rooms, from £129*

Shanghai Shanghai **£32** **532**

15 Goose Gate NG1 1FE (0115) 958 4688

Expect "great flavours with few compromises" at this ace Sichuanese in the heart of the Lace Market, serving a "fantastic selection of authentic, regional Chinese dishes at surprisingly reasonable prices"; no one begrudges what's a "fairly basic café ambience". / ***Details:*** *www.shanghai-shanghai.co.uk; Sun-Wed 10 pm, Thu-Sat 11 pm.*

200 Degrees **£12** **334**

Heston Hs, Meadow Lane NG2 3HE
(0115) 837 4849

With its "great, great" coffee and "very tempting" cakes, this "lovely" two-year-old café and roastery is "by the far the best independent coffee house" in these parts – and it's also "great for lunch". Just in – summer 2016 saw a new branch open by the railway station, as well as in Birmingham's old Grand Hotel. / ***Details:*** *www.200degs.com; 8pm, Sat 7pm, Sun 6 pm.*

Victoria Hotel **£37** **334**

Dovecote Ln NG9 1JG (0115) 925 4049

Near Beeston station, this "highly recommended" boozer supplies a "huge range of good pub food", with "something to suit everyone", plus "very good real ale"; "getting a seat for eating can be difficult", though – especially in the garden come summer. / ***Details:*** *www.victoriabeeston.co.uk; 9.30 pm, Sun-Tue 9.00 pm; closed Mon for food; no Amex; Yes; children: 18+ after 8 pm.*

The Wollaton **£43** **333**

Lambourne Drive NG8 1GR (0115) 9288610

Especially "excellent for families with children", this gastroboozer by Wollaton Park earns praise for its "monthly changing menu reflecting fresh, local produce". / ***Details:*** *www.thewollaton.co.uk; 9 pm, Sun 5 pm; closed Sun D.*

World Service **£58** **334**

Newdigate Hs, Castlegate NG1 6AF
(0115) 847 5587

Themes have remained consistent over the years in feedback on this quirky haunt, near the castle – it's "relaxed, and not too formal", its adventurous *cuisine has its highpoints and low points, it can seem "expensive", but locals in particular often tip it as "one of the best restaurants in Nottingham". / **Details:** www.worldservicerestaurant.com; 10 pm; closed Sun D, except bank holidays; children: 10+ at D.*

Zaap **£31** **[4][4][4]**
Unit B, Bromley Place NG1 6JG
(0115) 947 0204
*A "wonderful, authentic setting" ("you feel like you are on the streets of Thailand", with "tuk tuks and all things Thai") and "very flavoursome fresh cooking in a street food style" make this colourful, rather kitsch yearling "a great substitute for the real thing". / **Details:** www.zaapthai.co.uk; Sat, Sun, Mon, Tues, Wed, Thurs, Fri, 11.00pm.*

OARE, KENT 3–3C

The Three Mariners **£42** **[3][3][4]**
2 Church Rd ME13 0QA (01795) 533633
*"Lovely and attentive" staff, "clean, cheerful interiors" (including "lots of little rooms" to hide away in) and "interesting and tasty" food make this village gastropub a "favourite for family occasions". / **Details:** www.thethreemarinersoare.co.uk; Mon-Thu 9 pm, Fri-Sat 9.30 pm, Sun 9 pm; no Amex.*

OBAN, ARGYLL AND BUTE 9–3B

Ee-Usk (Seafood Restaurant) **£51** **[4][2][3]**
North Pier PA34 5QD (01631) 565666
*"Eating fresh oysters, lobster or fruits-de-mer with the sun going down over Oban Bay is an experience that everyone ought to have at least once in their life" – perhaps at this "very popular" seafront café, noted for its "great buzz" and "superbly prepared fish straight out of the sea". / **Details:** www.eeusk.com; 9-9.30 pm; no Amex; children: 12+ at D.*

OLD HUNSTANTON, NORFOLK 6–3B

The Neptune **£79** **[5][5][4]**
85 Old Hunstanton Rd PE36 6HZ
(01485) 532122
*"Always a wonderful all-round experience" – "this family-run, old coaching inn, on the edge of town, is in the perfect location", "the ambience is friendly and intimate", "staff are welcoming and attentive without being intrusive", and chef-owner Kevin Mangeolles provides "fantastic cuisine to savour" (including the option of a 9-course tasting menu). "Comfortable rooms" if you stay too. / **Details:** www.theneptune.co.uk; 9 pm; closed Mon, Tue-Sat D only, Sun open L & D; children: 10+. / **Accommodation:** 6 rooms, from £120*

OLDSTEAD, NORTH YORKSHIRE 5–1D

Black Swan **£83** **[5][5][4]**
YO61 4BL (01347) 868 387
*"A long way off the beaten track, charmingly located in a very quiet hamlet", Tommy Banks's converted pub, near Byland Abbey, again wins one of the highest ratings in the survey. "Excellent tasting menus" make a big effort to feature home-grown produce, plus locally farmed and foraged foods, and the result is "quite exceptional, with a tendency to the dramatic and theatrical" and served in a simple dining room "with such humour and attention to detail". / **Details:** www.blackswanoldstead.co.uk; 9 pm; closed weekday L; no Amex. / **Accommodation:** 4 rooms, from £270*

ONGAR, ESSEX 3–2B

Smith's Brasserie **£57** **[4][4][3]**
Fyfield Rd CM5 0AL (01277) 365578
*"Essex at its best!" – this "always reliable" fixture is "a lively and enjoyable" operation ("it's busy even midweek!"), with "very thoughtful and friendly staff"; on the menu, "tip top" fish and seafood. / **Details:** www.smithsrestaurants.com; left off A414 towards Fyfield; Mon-Fri 10 pm, Sat 10.30 pm, Sun 10 pm; closed Mon L; children: 12+.*

ONICH, HIGHLAND 9–3B

Loch Leven Seafood Café **£48** **[4][3][3]**
PH33 6SA (01855) 821 048
*"Rather like what Loch Fyne used to be 30+ years ago?" – a straightforward waterside café, with a "buzzing ambience" and "great" seafood (there's a "nice shop too"). / **Details:** www.lochlevenseafoodcafe.co.uk; 9 pm; no Amex.*

ORFORD, SUFFOLK 3–1D

Butley Orford Oysterage **£39** **[5][4][3]**
Market Hill IP12 2LH (01394) 450277
*"A beautiful, simple fish restaurant that sticks religiously to what it knows how to deliver perfectly!" This 50-year-old venture has spawned a local fish and seafood empire but its "no frills", "school-dining-room feel never changes" and it continues to offer "the freshest of fish, delivered daily from Bill Pinney's own boats"; plus "excellent smoked fish from Pinney's of Orford's own local smokehouse". "A fish-eater's paradise": "you get twice the freshness at half the price, served with double the charm of any fancy London joint!" / **Details:** www.butleyorfordoysterage.co.uk; on the B1078, off the A12 from Ipswich; 9 pm; no Amex.*

The Crown & Castle £56 333
IP12 2LJ (01394) 450205
*Erstwhile 'The Hotel Inspector' star, Ruth Watson's "lovely small hotel" by the sea combines "fascinating" rooms with "very well-cooked, flavoursome food you want to eat";"relaxed" service too,"there's no sense of rushing you out". / **Details:** www.crownandcastle.co.uk; on main road to Orford, near Woodbridge; 8 pm, Fri & Sat 9 pm; no Amex; Booking max 10 may apply; children: 8+ at D. / **Accommodation:** 21 rooms, from £135*

ORPINGTON, KENT 3–3B

Xian £38 543
324 High St BR6 0NG (01689) 871881
*"Victor and his team continue to serve up exceptional Chinese food" at this High Street fixture, whose "good prices" represent "fantastic value for money". / **Details:** 11 pm; closed Mon & Sun L.*

OSWESTRY, SHROPSHIRE 5–3A

Sebastian's £62 453
45 Willow Street SY11 1AQ (01691) 655444
*"Another scintillating year for this outstanding local" – a "French-influenced" restaurant-with-rooms, which is "supplying increasing amounts of food to the Orient Express", and where food and service achieve the "highest level"; it's certainly consistent ("in 20 or more years of visiting we have never had a poor meal!") / **Details:** www.sebastians-hotel.co.uk; 9.30 pm; D only, closed Mon & Sun; no Amex. / **Accommodation:** 5 rooms, from £75*

OXFORD, OXFORDSHIRE 2–2D

Al-Shami £29 343
25 Walton Cr OX1 2JG (01865) 310066
*A "wonderfully reliable" Jericho Lebanese particularly of note for its superior mezze;"it's the antithesis of fine dining, and much the better for it!" / **Details:** www.al-shami.co.uk; midnight; no Amex. / **Accommodation:** 12 rooms, from £60*

Ashmolean Dining Room £52 334
Beaumont St OX1 2PH (01865) 553 823
*"Great views across the Oxford rooftops" are a major draw to the patio of this "English, eccentric and lovely" venue (indeed rather "too many tourists come to photograph from it"); it strikes the odd critic as "less than the sum of its parts", but the food is "very good" by all accounts. / **Details:** www.ashmoleandiningroom.com; 10 pm; closed Mon, Tue D, Thu D & Sun D.*

Atomic Burger £30 333
92 Cowley Rd OX4 1JE (01865) 790 855
*"The most fun burger place in the galaxy!" (well, nearly) – "so much better value than the ubiquitous chains" and with "excellent cocktails". / **Details:** www.atomicburger.co.uk; 10.30 pm; no Amex.*

Branca £43 332
111 Walton St OX2 6AJ (01865) 556111
*A Jericho staple offering "good Italian-inspired food in airy surroundings". It's "not very sophisticated", perhaps, but all "Oxford eats here, with students and profs alongside yummy mummies and their progeny, and proud parents with slightly embarrassed sons and daughters";"lovely deli attached" too. / **Details:** www.branca.co.uk; 11 pm; no Amex.*

Brasserie Blanc £52 223
71-72 Walton St OX2 6AG (01865) 510999
*"Reliable, but short of flair" is a harsh but fair verdict on M Blanc's city-centre brasserie (the original of the chain), with its "comforting" (but "standard") Gallic menu. / **Details:** www.brasserieblanc.com; 10 pm, Sat 10.30 pm, Sun 9.30 pm.*

Cherwell Boathouse £47 235
Bardwell Road OX2 6ST (01865) 552746
*"Outdoor seating in the summer is lovely, and you can go boating before you eat!" at this superbly-located stalwart,"on the banks of the River Cherwell", where "watching the punts either skilfully or comically handled" provides an amusing backdrop to a meal. It's "a delight", with "lovely" wine in particular – the food is dependable nowadays too. / **Details:** www.cherwellboathouse.co.uk; Mon - Thur 9 pm, Fri & Sat 9.30 pm, Sun 9 pm.*

Chiang Mai £45 433
Kemp Hall Passage, 130A High Street OX1 4DH (01865) 202233
*This "quirky staple", hidden just off the High Street in a rather amazing Tudor building, has long been a top tip locally for its superior Thai cuisine; it "gets very busy in the evening when quality can suffer, but visit at lunchtime and the food is brilliant". / **Details:** www.chiangmaikitchen.co.uk; 10.30 pm, Sun 10 pm.*

La Cucina £38 332
39-40 St Clements OX4 1AB (01865) 793811
*"Proper Italian pizza" ("cooked in a fierce oven"), and other "good, honest", "clean-tasting" Italian dishes ("love the rotating specials") have "maintained very high standards from day one" at this "very popular local". / **Details:** www.lacucinaoxford.co.uk; 10.30 pm.*

The Fishes £45 344
North Hinksey Village OX2 0NA
(01865) 249796
*"Well-sourced, thoughtful cooking, careful service and a great choice of puds" are three reasons why "you always leave The Fishes feeling cheerful" – others being the attractive waterside setting and pleasant garden. / **Details:** www.fishesoxford.co.uk; Mon -Thur 11 pm, Fri & Sat midnight, Sun 10.30 pm.*

Gee's £54 334
61 Banbury Rd OX2 6PE (01865) 553540
*"Gee's is always relaxing and enjoyable"; "despite the staff turnover each time, the service and the overall atmosphere remain friendly and welcoming" at this north Oxford venture in a striking Victorian glasshouse. The food was consistently well-rated this year. / **Details:** www.gees-restaurant.co.uk; 10 pm, Fri & Sat 10.30 pm.*

The Magdalen Arms £44 4[illegible][illegible]
243 Iffley Road OX4 1SJ (01865) 243 159
*It may be "a little bit out of Oxford town centre", but "it's worth the walk" to this "comfortable", if somewhat "dark", gastroboozer – sibling to London's Hope & Anchor – specialising in "good British pub food, cooked to a high standard" (not least the "stunning Sunday roast" and steaks). / **Details:** www.magdalenarms.com; Mon - Sat 10 pm, Sun 9 pm; closed Mon L; no Amex; No bookings.*

My Sichuan £42 533
The Old School, Gloucester Grn OX1 2DA
(01865) 236 899
*"Go once and – if you like Sichuan cooking – you'll be hooked" on this "really interesting", if "slightly Spartan" old schoolhouse, near the Ashmolean, which is "always bursting with diners". "It's not for the faint of heart" – "dishes are heavy on grease (as in China), and definitely heavy on chillies too", and include "unusual" ingredients (duck tongues, pig tripe, frogs legs), but if you can take it, results are "brilliant and exciting". / **Details:** www.mysichuan.co.uk; 11 pm.*

Oli's Thai £31 554
38 Magdalen Rd OX4 1RB (01865) 790223
*"Brilliant", "just brilliant", "wow, wow, wow!"; this "tiny" Thai café may have a "small menu that never changes dramatically", and "you do have to book two to three months in advance", but the "sublime" and "astonishing" flavours are "worth all the waiting" – so "if at first you don't succeed in getting a table, try, try again!" / **Details:** www.olisthai.com; 9 pm; closed Mon, Tue L & Sun.*

The Oxford Kitchen £54 332
215 Banbury Rd OX2 7HQ (01865) 511 149
*"A surprise find in Oxford's restaurant desert" – a smart, modern British venue, set on Summertown's main drag, and offering "real quality and imagination" ("I won't forget the blue cheese lollipop for a long time"). / **Details:** www.theoxfordkitchen.co.uk; 7 pm.*

The Perch £48 334
Binsey Ln OX2 0NG (01865) 7228891
*"A wonderful pub" near Oxford which is particularly "lovely on a warm evening", when "you can sit in the beautiful garden, either outside or undercover". "Willing staff serve a wide range of homely dishes". / **Details:** www.the-perch.co.uk; 10:00pm, 9pm Sun.*

Pierre Victoire £43 333
Little Clarendon St OX1 2HP (01865) 316616
*Who doesn't have a "soft spot for this traditional, bistro-type-of-outfit"? – this "buzzy" survivor of the once-national group actually "seems like a genuine French restaurant" in its own right. The food is "not out of this world", but "efficient, friendly service" and "excellent value" contribute to what's a "pleasant informal experience" overall. / **Details:** www.pierrevictoire.co.uk; 11 pm, Sun 10 pm; no Amex.*

Quod, Old Bank Hotel £46 233
92-94 High St OX1 4BJ (01865) 202505
*Some dishes are "particularly successful" – others a little "middle of the road" – at this "decent but unexciting" brasserie, but its "pleasant and convenient position on the High" ensures it's "always buzzy and packed". / **Details:** www.oldbank-hotel.co.uk; 11 pm, Sun 10.30 pm; Booking max 10 may apply. / **Accommodation:** 42 rooms, from £140*

Sojo £41 532
6-9 Hythe Bridge St OX1 2EW
(01865) 202888
*Vying with My Sichuan for the crown of "best Chinese food in Oxford" – this "superb" outfit offers "an excellent and unusual range of mainly Cantonese dishes"; not only are they "wonderful", they're also "sensibly priced". "The back room is good for those who want less noise." / **Details:** www.sojooxford.co.uk; 11 pm, Sun 10 pm; No bookings.*

Turl Street Kitchen £40 334
16 Turl St OX1 3DH (01865) 264 171
*"If visiting Oxford, this is a place on the to-do list!" – a trendy non-profit venture whose "excellent" local/seasonal grub "has just about kept up with the hype" (and comes at prices which are "better than reasonable"). Okay, it's "pretty Spartan, but that's just in keeping with its style and ethos". / **Details:** www.turlstreetkitchen.co.uk; 10 pm, Fri & Sat 10.30 pm, .*

The Vaults And Garden Cafe £20 333
University Church of St Mary the Virgin, Radcliffe Sq OX1 4AH (01865) 279112
A "cheap 'n' cheerful place milling with tourists and

students", and set in the chapter house of a 14th-century church with a garden; it's "self-service only" and there's a "modest choice, but you will find plenty to appeal" – just "get there early to grab a seat!" / **Details:** www.thevaultsandgarden.com; 6 pm; L only.

Zheng **£37** 3 3 1
82 Walton St OX2 6EA (01865) 51 11 88
*A "proper-basic", "cramped" pan-Asian, which "might put you off by covering three different Chinese cuisines, along with Malaysian and Singaporean", but whose results can be truly "excellent". That said, more than one reporter thinks that "there may have been a little too much gushing" about it (not least by Giles Coren), and "while good, it's not grrrrrr-eat"! / **Details:** www.zhengoxford.co.uk; 10.45 pm, Sun 10.15 pm; closed Tue L.*

OXTON, CHESHIRE 5–2A

Fraiche **£109** 5 5 4
11 Rose Mount CH43 5SG (0151) 652 2914
*"Mark Wilkinson seems to be taking the cuisine to another level" at his "small but perfectly formed" 12-cover foodie Mecca, on the fringe of Birkenhead. His "dazzling, flavour-packed and perfect" dishes are married with "playful" décor and "superb and attentive" service. "Hard to get a booking, but worth the hassle!" / **Details:** www.restaurantfraiche.com; 8.30 pm, Sun 7 pm; closed Mon, Tue, Wed L, Thu L, Fri L & Sat L; no Amex.*

PADSTOW, CORNWALL 1–3B

Paul Ainsworth at Number 6 **£84** 5 4 4
6 Middle St PL28 8AP (01841) 532093
*"Easily the best fine-dining restaurant in Padstow" – and some would say even better than Nathan Outlaw down the coast in Port Isaac – Paul Ainsworth's tiny old townhouse "makes you feel special" and delivers "a short menu" of "absolutely superb" cuisine – "tried and tested dishes sit alongside new and interesting offerings and the attention to detail is phenomenal". Top Menu Tip – "the bread 'n' butter pudding has star quality". / **Details:** www.number6inpadstow.co.uk; Mon closed, Tue - Sat 10 pm, Sun closed; closed Mon & Sun; no Amex; children: 4+.*

Rojanos **£49** 3 4 3
9 Mill Sq PL28 8AE (01841) 532796
*Paul Ainsworth (of No. 6 in Padstow) seems to have the formula right at this vibrant and stylish Italian in the heart of town – a "good lunch stop" which, amongst other dishes, is "still serving the best pizza ever". / **Details:** www.rojanos.co.uk; 10 pm.*

St Petroc's Hotel & Bistro **£55** 3 4 3
4 New Street PL28 8EA (01841) 532700
*While it usually attracts some flak, this outpost of the all-conquering Jill & Rick Stein empire received (almost) uniformly positive reports this year – from the "lovely informal atmosphere" to the "classic refined cooking" and "comfortable beds"... "but oh, the size of those tables!" (dinky and packed like sardines). / **Details:** www.rickstein.com/stay/st-petrocs-hotel/; 10 pm; no Amex. / **Accommodation:** 10 rooms, from £150 / **Sustainability:** ★★★*

Seafood Restaurant **£86** 3 3 3
Riverside PL28 8BY (01841) 532700
*The Stein empire's original flagship by this small Cornish fishing town's harbour is a UK dining institution, and for many fans "it's still one of the great places to eat the freshest fish from around the British Isles, with influences of cuisines from around the world". It's a "huge" operation nowadays though, and some regulars say that while "there's nowhere nicer on quiet nights", that when busy "they cram you in, and the noise is oppressive". Likewise, food that, at best, is "not over-complicated and respecting the ingredients" can – when the kitchen is stretched – seem "slightly underwhelming and rather costly for a relatively simple meal". / **Details:** www.rickstein.com/eat-with-us/the-seafood-; 9.45 pm; ; no Amex; Booking max 14 may apply; children: 3+. / **Accommodation:** 16 rooms, from £150 / **Sustainability:** ★★★*

PAINSWICK, GLOUCESTERSHIRE 2–2B

The Painswick **£57**
Kemps Lane GL6 6YB (01452) 813 688
*From the Calcot Collection of hotels, a self-professed 'country cool restaurant-with-rooms' featuring a first-floor restaurant, bar and lounge, as well as private dining facilities and 16 bedrooms. Early feedback hails "a great makeover and super food at reasonable prices". / **Details:** www.thepainswick.co.uk; 9.30 pm. / **Accommodation:** 0 rooms, from £16*

PEEBLES, SCOTTISH BORDERS 9–4C

Cringletie House **£55** 4 3 4
Edinburgh Rd EH45 8PL (01721) 725750
*Despite its Scottish baronial styling, complete with turrets, this is a "superb country house hotel with a homely feel to it" (it's owned by a couple who live in the grounds). "It maintains a good standards of cooking", including "excellent tasting menus with matching wines". / **Details:** www.cringletie.com; between Peebles and Eddleston on A703, 20m S of*

Edinburgh; 9 pm; D only, ex Sun open L & D; children: 4. / **Accommodation:** 15 rooms, from £99

PENALLT, MONMOUTHSHIRE 2–2B

Inn at Penallt £50 4 3 3

NP25 4SE (01600) 772765

In a "lovely" countryside location, a "great" yet "hard-to-find" inn whose "cosy" bar may be preferred to the dining room. The new owners are "trying hard to maintain the previous standards whilst also learning and aiming to improve the experience" – and so far it's working, with reports of "excellent" cuisine of late. / **Details:** *www.theinnatpenallt.co.uk/; 9 pm; closed Mon, Tue L & Sun D.* / **Accommodation:** *4 rooms, from £75*

PENARTH, VALE OF GLAMORGAN 1–1D

Restaurant James Sommerin £78 4 3 3

The Esplanade CF64 3AU (07722) 216 727

From the ex-chef of the Crown at Whitebrook, this two-year-old restaurant-with-rooms gains praise for its "exceptional quality" cuisine, in particular "great seafood". Niggles remain that "the ambience doesn't quite match the food", but others say it's improved since opening. "The (waterside) views are spectacular too (although the layout of the restaurant doesn't maximise that benefit)." / **Details:** *www.jamessommerinrestaurant.co.uk; Mon closed Tue - Sun 9.30 pm.*

PENRITH, CUMBRIA 7–3D

Four & Twenty £47 4 3 3

42 King St CA11 7AY (01768) 210231

A converted former bank with open kitchen, and mix-and-match furniture houses this "great little restaurant", which goes easy on the wallet. / **Details:** *www.fourandtwentypenrith.co.uk; 9 pm, Fri & Sat 9.30 pm.*

PENSFORD, SOMERSET 2–2B

The Pig, Hunstrete House £45 3 5 5

Hunstrete BS39 4NS (01761) 490 490

While perhaps not the pick of the 'Pig' litter, there's nothing but praise for the "relaxing" Somerset sibling of this shabby chic mini-chain. It's particularly of note for its excellent rooms, but it "also does very decent food" and service is "impeccable" – "the perfect blend of efficient, welcoming and cheerful!" / **Details:** *www.thepighotel.com/near-bath; 9.30 pm.*

PENZANCE, CORNWALL 1–4A

Tolcarne Inn £41 3 2 2

Tolcarne Pl TR18 5PR (01736) 363074

Reporters "loved the mismatch of shabby tables and seating at Ben Tunnicliffe's buzzy, very popular inn", and the food continued to win solid marks. Scores were generally lower this year though – the pressure of opening Sennen Cove? / **Details:** *www.tolcarneinn.co.uk; 10 pm.*

PERSHORE, WORCESTERSHIRE 2–1C

Eckington Manor £64 3 2 3

Hammock Road WR10 3BJ (01386) 751600

MasterChef winner Mark Stinchcombe cooks and his wife Sue serves at this farm-to-table spot in a medieval manor. The odd sceptic feels the "rather canteen-like" decor "doesn't chime with the rest of the set-up", or that the food, while "enjoyable", is "lacking in the sort of adventure demonstrated in winning the prized trophy on display in reception". The majority though, feel it's tipped for great things.

PERTH, PERTH AND KINROSS 9–3C

Cafe Tabou £50 3 3 2

4 St John's Pl PH1 5SZ (01738) 446698

"Very dependable", "French-bistro-style, comfort food" can come as "a real surprise" at this authentically Gallic spot (especially when you know the chef is actually Polish!). "It's busy and atmospheric at lunchtime, a bit quieter at night but always good." / **Details:** *www.cafetabou.com; 9.30 pm, Fri & Sat 10 pm; closed Mon D & Sun; no Amex.*

Pig'Halle £49 3 4 4

38 South St PH2 8PG (01738) 248784

"A real find in Perth that's authentically French down to the pigs' trotters!" – a simple and genuine bistro praised for its enjoyable fare. / **Details:** *www.pighalle.co.uk; Tues - Wed 9.30 pm, Thu-Sat 10 pm, Sun & Mon 9 pm.*

Post Box £43 3 4 3

80 George Street PH1 5LB (01738) 248 971

"A stylish room near the river Tay in Perth" – a corner site that was once the town's first post office. "They are trying very hard and succeeding: great modern food with a French twist." / **Details:** *www.thepostboxperth.co.uk; Tues - Sat 9.30.*

63 Tay Street £63 3 3 2

63 Tay St PH2 8NN (01738) 441451

Down by the banks of the Tay, Graeme Pallister's low-key but refined operation, now approaching its first decade, continues to set the bar locally with its "interesting meals prepared with skill". / **Details:** www.63taystreet.com; on city side of River Tay, 1m from Dundee Rd; 9 pm; D only, closed Mon & Sun; no Amex.

PETERBOROUGH, CAMBRIDGESHIRE 6–4A

Clarkes £60 343
10 Queen St PE1 1PA (01733) 892681
"A decent oasis in a gastronomic desert" – this smartish (tablecloths, etc), family-run neighbourhood restaurant benefits from "great service" and provides really quite "ambitious" cuisine, plus "an interesting wine list with modest mark-ups". / **Details:** *www.clarkespeterborough.co.uk; 9 pm, Sat 10 pm.*

PETERSFIELD, HAMPSHIRE 2–3D

JSW £74 422
20 Dragon Street GU31 4JJ (01730) 262030
Jake Saul Watkin "sure can cook", and his tasting menus in particular are "absolutely superb", say fans of this venue in a former coaching inn. Service, however, is "still below the standard the food deserves", and the interior can feel a tad too "quiet" ("a bit like a funeral parlour"). / **Details:** *www.jswrestaurant.com; on the old A3; 8 min walk from the railway station; 9 pm; closed Mon, Tue & Sun D; children: 5+ D. /* **Accommodation:** *4 rooms, from £95*

PETTS WOOD, KENT 3–3B

Indian Essence £49 433
176-178 Petts Wood Rd BR5 1LG
(01689) 838 700
"The name says it all!" Ratings recovered this year at Atul Kochhar's "high-end Indian dining room in a most unlikely suburban setting" in Petts Wood – "a little gem" extolled by a huge fanclub from across the Kent/London borders for its "superb cuisine, a world away from 'normal' Indian food". / **Details:** *www.indianessence.co.uk; 10.45 pm, fri & sat 11 pm, sun 10.30 pm; closed Mon L; No trainers.*

PETWORTH, WEST SUSSEX 3–4A

The Leconfield £66 332
New St GU28 0AS (01798) 345111
This upmarket bar-restaurant is "a great addition to Petworth" by most, if not all, accounts; although for sceptics it's "not up to the local hype", fans praise its "serious cooking" and an "unexpectedly good experience". / **Details:** *www.theleconfield.co.uk; Tue-Sat 11 pm, Sun 4 pm.*

Meghdoots £36 343
Mystique Masala, East St GU28 0AB
(01798) 343217
A local institution, in the town centre, offering the "best Indian food in the area – very different indeed from the usual standard fare (e.g. game in season)". / **Details:** *www.mystiquemasala.co.uk; 10 pm.*

The Noahs Ark Inn £47 345
Lurgashall GU28 9ET (01428) 707 346
"Set in English countryside overlooking a picturesque cricket green", this "classic" pub is "a beautiful place where everything feels just right" (with "log fires inside" in winter); all this, plus "consistently good cooking". / **Details:** *www.noahsarkinn.co.uk; Mon - Sat 9.30 pm, Sun 3.15 pm; closed Sun D.*

PICKERING, NORTH YORKSHIRE 8–4C

The White Swan £52 333
Market Pl YO18 7AA (01751) 472288
A traditional coaching inn with an "attractive" new extension out back, and a short menu (including vegetarian options); fans say it's "a real benchmark for gourmet pub food" ("long may it remain family-owned!") / **Details:** *www.white-swan.co.uk; 9 pm. /* **Accommodation:** *21 rooms, from £150*

PINNER, GREATER LONDON 3–3A

Friends £56 454
11 High St HA5 5PJ (020) 8866 0286
Terry Farr's "lovely, intimate" stalwart, occupying a 500-year-old, half-timbered cottage, is simply a "perfect local". The food is "altogether surprising – not at all what you'd expect in such a suburban location" – while "service is charming too". / **Details:** *www.friendsrestaurant.co.uk; 9.30 pm; closed Mon & Sun D.*

PLEASINGTON, LANCASHIRE 5–1B

Clog & Billycock £48 333
Billinge End Rd BB2 6QB (01254) 201163
"Another top-quality venue from Ribble Valley Inns" is the majority verdict on this "friendly and good value" pub, which has "a great location on the 'Yellow Hills'". / **Details:** *www.theclogandbillycock.com; 9 pm, Fri & Sat 9.30 pm.*

PLUMTREE, NOTTINGHAMSHIRE 5–3D

Perkins £51 433
Old Railway Station NG12 5NA
(0115) 937 3695
"At a former Victorian railway station in the rolling Nottinghamshire countryside", this unusually located restaurant "never disappoints with its good tasty

food" (including "superb afternoon teas"). / **Details:** *www.perkinsrestaurant.co.uk; off A606 between Nottingham & Melton Mowbray; 9.30 pm; closed Sun D.*

PLYMOUTH, DEVON 1–3C

Chloe's, Gill Akaster House £58 3 4 3
27 Princess St PL1 2EX (01752) 201523
A consistently popular city-centre bistro offering "lovely French cooking" in a small, smartly decorated room; a location just around the corner from the Theatre Royal makes it a particularly good pre-theatre option. / **Details:** *www.chloesrestaurant.co.uk; 9 pm; closed Sun.*

River Cottage Canteen £46 3 2 4
Royal William Yd PL1 3QQ (01752) 252702
"A really nice option in Plymouth's King William Yard"; HFW's canteen in a former navy yard warehouse "has a certain buzz about it", and, even if some feel the food is "adequate but not exciting", all reports are fundamentally positive. / **Details:** *9.30 pm.*

Rock Salt £47 3 2 3
31 Stonehouse St PL1 3PE (01752) 225522
"Good restaurants are hard to come by in Plymouth, but this one breaks the chain/burger/kebab shop mould" with its "fantastic, imaginative" locally sourced food; "located in a formerly rather seedy pub" – and in the "former red-light area" – it's "not a place you'll find by accident", but worth the effort. / **Details:** *www.rocksaltcafe.co.uk; 9.30 pm; Booking max 6 may apply.*

Salumi £47 4 4 4
18 Milbay Road PL1 3LH (01752) 267538
A "welcome addition to a more gritty party of the city"; it's early days, but Rock Salt chef Dave Jenkins's "new kid on the block" – featuring a beer garden and "quirky", shabby chic decor – is already "incredibly popular" owing to its "really good menu", "impeccable service" and vivid atmosphere ("with all the fun of a buzzy night out"). / **Details:** *www.eatsalumi.co.uk/; Mon - Sun, 9.30pm.*

Samphire Bush £44 4 3 2
36 Admiralty Street, Stonehouse PL1 3RU (01752) 253 247
"An exceptional value prix-fixe menu" is a feature of this modestly sized, simply decorated indie two-year-old, where Martin Benjamin's seafood cooking often wins outstanding ratings. / **Details:** *www.thesamphirebush.co.uk; Tues, Wed, Thurs, Fri, Sat, 21.00.*

POLKERRIS, CORNWALL 1–3B

Rashleigh Inn £33 3 3 4
The Inn on the Beach PL24 2TL (01726) 81 3991
Calling itself 'The Inn on the Beach' in an old stone building by the sands, "you can eat on a terrace outside overlooking the sea, or in the bar or restaurant". "Thick pieces of cod in light batter and great thick-cut crunchy chips – yum!" (although the menu is by no means just fish). / **Details:** *therashleighinnpolkerris.co.uk/; Mon - Sun 9.00pm.*

Sams on the Beach £46 3 2 4
PL24 2TL (01726) 812255
With a "great location" in a converted lifeboat station, this beachside café in a tiny village is a firm family favourite ("you can watch the kids playing on the beach while you enjoy your lunch"); it serves a simple menu based on "good pizzas and very fresh fish". / **Details:** *www.samscornwall.co.uk; 9 pm; no Amex.*

POOLE, DORSET 2–4C

Branksome Beach £52 3 4 4
Pinecliff Rd BH13 6LP (01202) 767235
"Good food and value for money" are "not always associated with Sandbanks" – but, happily, this "glass box on the beach", reputed for its Sunday breakfast, is one exception. / **Details:** *www.branksomebeach.co.uk; 5 pm; L only.*

Guildhall Tavern £52 4 4 4
15 Market Street BH15 1NB (01202) 671717
A "long-running favourite with fantastically fresh fish the order of the day, accompanied by smashing wine and great attention to detail"; the "understated, charming" venue also benefits from a "lovely French ambience". / **Details:** *www.guildhalltavern.co.uk; Mon closed, Tue - Sat 10 pm, Sun closed; closed Mon & Sun; no Amex.*

South Deep £34 3 3 5
Parkstone Bay Marina, Turks Ln BH14 8EW (01202) 733155
The "view is a bonus" at this rustic café with an outdoor deck, in a marina on the edge of Poole Harbour; on the menu, "good fresh ingredients" which are "served simply" – and the "lunch and tapas evenings are great". / **Details:** *www.facebook.com/southdeepcafe; 9 pm, Fri & Sat 9.30 pm; closed Mon D, Tue D & Sun D.*

PORT APPIN, ARGYLL AND BUTE 9–3B

Airds Hotel £81 443
PA38 4DF (01631) 730236
"Extremely comfortable in an old-school (good) way"; this "very intimate" Relais & Châteaux dining room, set in a former ferry inn with "traditional lounges and wonderful views to Loch Linnhe", maintains "continually high standards", with "local seafood well represented on the tempting menu". / **Details:** *www.airds-hotel.com; 20m N of Oban; 9.30 pm; No jeans; children: 8+ at D.* / **Accommodation:** *11 rooms, from £290*

Pierhouse Hotel £59 534
PA38 4DE (01631) 730302
"Exceptionally located" by the harbour, and occupying the Pier Master's former residence, this acclaimed, family-run hotel boasts wonderful views of Loch Linnhe; "superbly fresh seafood and perfectly good service" round out its appeal. / **Details:** *www.pierhousehotel.co.uk; just off A828, follow signs for Port Appin & Lismore Ferry; 9.30 pm.* / **Accommodation:** *12 rooms, from £100*

PORT ISAAC, CORNWALL 1–3B

Fresh From The Sea £25 432
18 New Road PL29 3SB (01208) 880849
"Superb crab straight from the trawler" ("you can see their boat in the harbour") "prepared, cooked and served on the premises" helps enthuse fans of this "family-run, chaotic cafe, with real soul and vibe – simplicity at its very best, and great value!" / **Details:** *www.freshfromthesea.co.uk; 5pm; No bookings.*

Outlaw's Fish Kitchen £36 455
1 Middle St PL29 3RH (01208) 881138
Nathan Outlaw's "crushed, tiny, no-bookings" venture has a "gorgeous", "quaint" location in this "busy, touristy village", and inspires adulation for its "cracking" small, seafood dishes. When it comes to the portions though, "for small read minuscule!" / **Details:** *www.outlaws.co.uk; 9 pm; closed Mon & Sun.*

Restaurant Nathan Outlaw £147 545
6 New Rd PL29 3SB (01208) 880 896
"Easily the best seafood in the region, if not the UK". Nathan Outlaw's HQ, relocated from Rock two years ago, is going from strength to strength in its new home in this picture-book Cornish fishing village: a "most relaxing" venue, which boasts "tremendous views" over the coast. "Friendly and incredibly well-informed staff" deliver "the freshest dishes you can imagine": "a masterclass in gastronomic delight – so simple, so perfect", and with "an amazing intensity of flavour". / **Details:** *www.nathan-outlaw.com; Mon & Tue closed, Wed - Sat 9 pm, Sun closed; practically no walk-ins – you must boo.*

PORTHGAIN, PEMBROKESHIRE 4–4B

The Shed £42 334
SA62 5BN (01348) 831518
A "rustic" yet "reliable" fish 'n' chip bistro, "right by the quay", where the seafood is "fresh, basic and great", and there are "old-fashioned chips" to go with it. / **Details:** *www.theshedporthgain.co.uk; 9 pm; no Amex.*

PORTHLEVEN, CORNWALL 1–4A

Kota £56 433
Harbour Head TR13 9JA (01326) 562407
"The food is always excellent, the service is first class and the ambience is warm and inviting" at this winning Cornish/Asian fusion restaurant in a "lovely harbour setting". Fans NB – the owners also run a relaxed sibling, Kota Kai, at the head of the harbour. / **Details:** *www.kotarestaurant.co.uk; 9 pm; D only, closed Sun-Tue; no Amex.* / **Accommodation:** *2 rooms, from £70*

Rick Steins Seafood Restaurant 334
Mount Pleasant TR13 9JS (01326) 565636
"The food is not five star, like the original Seafood Restaurant, but then it doesn't pretend to be", at this two-year-old outpost of the Stein empire – good cooking, with twists, using excellent local produce from the sea. "This one wins over his Padstow HQ in at least one way – it looks over the wonderful harbour rather than a car park!" / **Sustainability:** ★★★

The Square at Porthleven £42 443
7 Fore Street TR13 9HQ (01326) 573 911
"Fine food for reasonable prices in a foodie town with lots of competitors" is the pay-off at this brasserie-style venture, overlooking the town's picturesque harbour. / **Details:** *www.thesquareatporthleven.co.uk; Sun - Sat 9.00pm.*

PORTMAHOMACK, HIGHLAND 9–2C

The Oystercatcher £56 422
Main Street IV20 1YB (01862) 871560
"A highpoint of the Highlands" – a small, casual coastal bistro whose "wine list reads like a telephone directory" (in a good way) and whose food is "exceptional too". / **Details:** *www.the-oystercatcher.co.uk; Mon & Tues closed, Wed - Sat 10 pm, Sun 2.45 pm; closed Mon, Tue, Wed, Thu L & Sun D.* / **Accommodation:** *3 rooms, from £82*

PORTMEIRION, GWYNEDD 4–2C

Portmeirion Hotel **£62** **334**
LL48 6ET (01766) 772440
*"There's backdrop and scenery in abundance", at this estuary-side hotel dining room at the heart of Sir Clough Williams-Ellis's fantastical homage to Portofino. Gastronomically speaking, it's been less stellar in recent years, but this year's (fairly limited) feedback reports that its "classical cuisine" is "vastly improved over a few years ago, and overall the place offers a winning combination". / **Details:** www.portmeirion-village.com; off A487 at Minffordd; Mon - Sat 9.30 pm, Sun 2 pm. / **Accommodation:** 14 rooms, from £185*

PORTSMOUTH, HAMPSHIRE 2–4D

abarbistro **£42** **343**
58 White Hart Rd PO1 2JA (02392) 811585
*"The independent answer to the chains in Gunwharf";"consistently reliable on all fronts", this "always cheerful" bistro gains particular praise for its "interesting wines" – no surprise given that "they have their own wine business (Camber Wines) above the restaurant". / **Details:** www.abarbistro.co.uk; 11 pm.*

Restaurant 27 **£63** **343**
27a Southsea Parade PO5 2JF
(023) 9287 6272
*This Southsea local is often said to be the best bet in town; not to over-egg it though – even a reporter who acknowledges that "by all accounts this is Portsmouth's finest by some distance" feels the food is "OK but not exceptional on a national scale". / **Details:** www.restaurant27.com; Mon & Tue closed, Wed - Sat 9.30 pm, Sun 2.30 pm; closed Mon, Tue, Wed L, Thu L, Fri L, Sat L & Sun D.*

Rosie's Vineyard **£44** **233**
87 Elm Grove PO5 1JF (02392) 755944
*A cosy French bistro, incorporating a cellar bar and a conservatory; reviews are positive if often qualified ("fully priced", "excellent but a bit heavy"), and this remains one of the few decent non-chain options in this underserved town. / **Details:** www.rosies-vineyard.co.uk; S from M275 towards Southsea. At roundabout turn left into King's Rd, leading to Elm Grv; 10 pm; D only, ex Sun open L & D. / **Sustainability:** ★★★*

PRESTON BAGOT, WARWICKSHIRE 5–4C

The Crabmill **£46** **322**
B95 5EE (01926) 843342
*A "very popular gastropub" with "good pub grub and draught ales", especially recommended as a pitstop that's "convenient for the M40". / **Details:** www.thecrabmill.co.uk; on main road between Warwick & Henley-in-Arden; 9.30 pm, Sun 4 pm; closed Sun D; no Amex.*

PRESTON CANDOVER, HAMPSHIRE 2–3D

The Purefoy Arms **£47** **333**
RG25 2EJ (01256) 389 777
*"Wish I lived in this village!" So say fans of this "cosy" local, known for its "frequently changing, Spanish-inspired menu" that's "well cooked and served, alongside an incredible Iberian wine list". / **Details:** www.thepurefoyarms.co.uk; 11 pm, Sun 4 pm; closed Mon & Sun D.*

PRESTON, LANCASHIRE 5–1A

Bukhara **£35** **442**
154 Preston New Rd PR5 0UP
(01772) 877710
*"Authentic Indian food cooked fresh as you watch" (including "awesome baked breads") is served at this family-run, alcohol-free venue, "popular with young and old from all sections of the community"; okay, so there's "no special ambience, but the food is what matters". ("I always try to visit with Asian friends who know exactly what to order".) / **Details:** www.bukharasamlesbury.co.uk; 11 pm; closed weekday L.*

PWLLHELI, GWYNEDD 4–2C

Plas Bodegroes **£68** **445**
Nefyn Rd LL53 5TH (01758) 612363
*It's all change at this landmark restaurant-with-rooms, set in a "glorious" country location; after nearly three decades in business, longtime owners the Chown family made way for husband-and-wife-team Chris (ex- Cotswold 88) & Camille Lovell in April 2016. Here's hoping they can keep up the impeccable standards. / **Details:** www.bodegroes.co.uk; on A497 1m W of Pwllheli; 9.00 pm; closed Mon, Tue-Sat D only, closed Sun D; no Amex; children: 12+ at D. / **Accommodation:** 10 rooms, from £130*

QUEENSBURY, MIDDLESEX 3–3A

Regency Club **£37** **433**
19-21 Queensbury Station Pde HA8 5NR
(020) 8952 6300
*"Real, honest Indian food" is "enhanced with an East African touch" at this Edgware fixture: "an intriguing fusion of pub and curry house". / **Details:** www.regencyclub.co.uk; 10.30 pm, Fri & Sat 11 pm, Sun 10 pm; closed Mon L; Yes; children: 18+.*

RAMSBOTTOM, LANCASHIRE 5–1B

Baratxuri £44 444
1 Smithy St BL0 9AT (01706) 559090
"It's a cliché, but it's like finding yourself in the Basque Country", at this spin-off from Levanter (same owners, just round the corner), which fans say "has taken everything to the next level" providing "a proper pintxos bar in a fairly undistinguished northern town". "You sit at the counter, which has four or five trays of different pintxos waiting to be picked, and there's a short blackboard of dishes that are cooked to order. And, as they say round there, by gum it's all proper good and astounding value". At least that's the majority stellar view, but ratings are brought slightly down-to-earth by those who say "it's not there yet, even if it's good". / **Details:** *www.levanterfinefoods.co.uk/baratxuri; 9 pm.*

Levanter £36 544
10 Square St BL0 9BE (01706) 551530
Albeit "tiny, cramped and invariably crowded", the "food is worth the squash" at Fiona & Joe Botham's back-street venue – a former barber's – which serves "an exceptionally good range of tapas" at "bargain" prices. (It's "more family-friendly than its (bar-like) sibling, Baratxuri, 100 yards around the corner".) / **Details:** *www.levanterfinefoods.co.uk; 10 pm, Sun 7.30 pm; closed Mon & Tue.*

RAMSGATE, KENT 3–3D

Albion House £49 334
Albion Place CT11 8HQ (01843) 606630
In a stunning Regency-era townhouse on the East Cliff, and with prime views of the beach and Royal Harbour, the restaurant at this year-old boutique hotel is tipped as a "chic, comfortable venue for brunch, dinner and drinks". / **Details:** *www.albionhouseramsgate.co.uk; 9.30 pm.*

Flavours By Kumar £36 442
2 Effingham St CT11 9AT (01843) 852631
This celebrated year-old establishment by Anir Kumar (ex-Ambrette, Margate) is "a real treat"; the setting is not particularly glam, but it's worth a visit for the food – "on a par with a top London Indian, but at a quarter of the price!" / **Details:** *10.30 pm.*

RAMSGILL-IN-NIDDERDALE, NORTH YORKSHIRE 8–4B

Yorke Arms £94 544
HG3 5RL (01423) 755243
"A sophisticated experience right in the heart of Nidderdale" is to be found at this famous "old coach house / shooting lodge which enjoys a fabulous, picturesque setting" – one of the UK's best dining destinations. The kitchen – overseen by Frances Atkins – produces "wonderfully prepared, beautifully presented" cuisine "using the finest ingredients the Dales terroir can offer", while "nothing is too much trouble for the attentive staff". / **Details:** *www.yorke-arms.co.uk; 4m W of Pateley Bridge; 8.45 pm; closed Mon & Sun.* / **Accommodation:** *16 rooms, from £200*

RAVENGLASS, CUMBRIA 7–3C

Inn At Ravenglass £37 433
Main St, Ravenglass Cumbria CA18 1SQ
(01229) 717230
"Slap bang on the coast" and "looking as if it could just as well be on some Scottish isle, as (not quite) in the shadow of Sellafield", this Lakeland inn comes "highly recommended" for its fish and seafood. Dishes are a mix of the "old-fashioned (like your parents enjoyed)", and newer ideas (vanilla-salting or Thai influences), but all result in "sublime tastes" for "very reasonable prices". / **Details:** *www.theinnatravenglass.co.uk/; 9pm; closed Sun.*

READING, BERKSHIRE 2–2D

Caprice Restaurant Holiday Inn Reading
Wharfedale Road, Winnersh Triangle RG4 5TS
(01189) 440444
Off the M4, next to the Winnersh Triangle, this modern hotel dining room (with outside terrace) is an extremely convenient stopping-off point, serving a wide range of affordable menus. / **Details:** *www.hireadinghotel.com; 10 pm.* / **Accommodation:** *174 rooms, from £174*

Forbury's £68 433
1 Forbury Sq RG1 3BB (0118) 957 4044
A "very welcoming" hotel dining room, in the city-centre; even the most dismissive report on it ("menu a bit 1990s"), said the food is "a bit safe but usually pretty good", with "a great choice of wine" ("fun wine evenings" are a regular feature) to wash it down. / **Details:** *www.forburys.co.uk; 9.30 pm; closed Sun D.*

London Street Brasserie £58 333
Riverside Oracle RG1 4PN (0118) 950 5036
"A gem in the centre of Reading" – "a local restaurant with consistently great food" from "an extensive menu", and a "nice location with a riverside terrace for summer days". / **Details:** *www.londonstbrasserie.co.uk; 10.30 pm, Fri & Sat 11 pm.*

REIGATE, SURREY 3–3B

La Barbe £53 [2][3][3]

71 Bell St RH2 7AN (01737) 241966
*"Still a good brasserie" offering "very French" and "very enjoyable" cuisine; it did, however, rub a few reporters up the wrong way this year – whether because it "tries too hard" to be Gallic ("couldn't bear the corny, and noisy, accordion!") or because the "wine prices are ridiculously high". / **Details:** www.labarbe.co.uk; 9.30 pm; closed Sat L & Sun D.*

REYNOLDSTON, SWANSEA 1–1C

Fairyhill £67 [4][4][5]

SA3 1BS (01792) 390139
*Having been run by Andrew Heatherington and Paul Davies since 1993, this quiet and peaceful restaurant-with-rooms, lost in a maze of lanes on the Gower Peninsula, was acquired in November 2016 by a local wedding venue company (Oldwalls). The aim is apparently to build on its current performance, which, judging on its survey results (we've maintained the rating), is extremely positive all-round. / **Details:** www.fairyhill.net; 20 mins from M4, J47 off B4295; 9 pm; no Amex; children: 8+ at D. / **Accommodation:** 8 rooms, from £180*

RIDGEWAY MOOR, SOUTH YORKSHIRE 5–2C

The Old Vicarage £91 [3][2][2]

S12 3XW (0114) 247 5814
*Similar themes to last year's in feedback on this well-known stalwart, where "OTT pricing" and "indifferent service" can be sticking points. Not everyone's 100% convinced on the culinary front either, although fans say it "seems to be back on form, despite (or because of?) the loss of its Michelin star". Afternoon tea is a recent innovation. / **Details:** www.theoldvicarage.co.uk; Mon closed, Tue - Sat 9.30 pm, Sun closed; closed Mon, Sat L & Sun; no Amex; children: call in advance.*

RIPLEY, SURREY 3–3A

Anchor £53 [3][2][4]

High St GU23 6AE (01483) 211866
*A recent "offshoot of Drakes", set "just across the road" from that establishment, and offering "brilliant food but fewer pub facilities" than in its former, less glamorous, incarnation. / **Details:** 11 pm, Sun 9 pm; closed Mon.*

Drakes £85

The Clock Hs, High St GU23 6AQ
(01483) 224777
*The future is a little unclear regarding this acclaimed restaurant, as it was awarded to Serina Drake in a divorce settlement in summer 2016. Husband Steve Drake was awarded the Anchor pub opposite, but will no longer be at the stoves here (and Michelin removed their star in October). In November 2016 he announced a new venture, Sorrel, but its location is still not confirmed. / **Details:** www.drakesrestaurant.co.uk; 9.30 pm; closed Mon, Tue L & Sun; no Amex.*

Pinnocks £13 [4][4][4]

High St GU23 6AF (01483) 222419
*The "best in the area by a country mile" – a "great local coffeehouse" ("using locally roasted beans"), serving "excellent" cakes and "great value lunches". / **Details:** www.pinnockscoffeehouse.com; 6 pm, Sun 5 pm.*

ROCK, CORNWALL 1–3B

Dining Room £62 [4][3][2]

Pavilion Buildings, Rock Rd PL27 6JS
(01208) 862622
*"A hidden star on the way into Rock"; "husband-and-wife team Fred and Donna are a great partnership", say fans of this restaurant in a roadside parade of shops; "it can be a little quiet" (maybe the "difficult shape of the premises"), but the standard of food overcomes any niggles… "try it, you'll be surprised!" / **Details:** www.thediningroomrock.co.uk; 9 pm; closed Mon, Tue, Wed L, Thu L, Fri L, Sat L & Sun L; no Amex; children: 10+.*

Mariners £42 [4][2][3]

PL27 6LD (01208) 863 679
*This pub overlooking the Camel Estuary from the heart of the town is a joint venture between famous local chef, Nathan Outlaw and Sharp's Brewery. "Nathan Outlaw's input carries into the food quality" – gripes include service that's "friendly but can be slow at busy times" and "one too many Hooray Henries". / **Details:** www.themarinersrock.com/; Mon - Sat 09.30pm, Sun 04.30pm.*

St Enodoc Restaurant, St Enodoc Hotel £66 [5][4][3]

St Enodoc Hotel, Rock Road PL27 6LA (\N)
01208 863394
*MasterChef winner "James Nathan only took over in March 2016", after Nathan Outlaw shifted focus to his Port Isaac HQ, "but he has made a hit with both locals and tourists already" thanks to "amazing" and "well-priced" food that by no means represents an obvious step down from that of his famous predecessor. The interior is perhaps a tad "bland", but the overall setting – with a "terrace overlooking the Camel Estuary" – remains "heavenly". / **Details:** www.enodoc-hotel.co.uk/food.html; 9 pm.*

ROCKBEARE, DEVON 1–3D

Jack in the Green Inn £49 443
London Rd EX5 2EE (01404) 822240
A quarter of a century in its current guise, and this "consistently excellent" gastropub is still combining "friendly, efficient" service with "good value" nosh. / **Details:** *www.jackinthegreen.uk.com; On the old A30, 3 miles east of junction 29 of M5; 9.30 pm, Sun 9 pm, Fri 10pm; no Amex.*

ROSEVINE, CORNWALL 1–4B

Driftwood Hotel £78 444
TR2 5EW (01872) 580644
"A hidden gem on the Roseland Peninsula offering a constantly superb dining experience" – this cliff-top dining room has a "lovely" and "romantic" setting, with magnificent views, and makes "a great place to stay and eat" thanks to Chris Eden's very accomplished cooking. / **Details:** *www.driftwoodhotel.co.uk; off the A30 to Truro, towards St Mawes; 9.30 pm; D only; children: 7. /* **Accommodation:** *15 rooms, from £170*

ROWSLEY, DERBYSHIRE 5–2C

The Peacock at Rowsley £72 443
Bakewell Rd DE4 2EB (01629) 733518
A country house hotel "in the heart of the beautiful Peak District" which provides "great food and so much more" (think white-gloved service and roaring fires). / **Details:** *www.thepeacockatrowsley.com; 9 pm, Sun 8.30 pm; Booking max 8 may apply; children: 10+ at D. /* **Accommodation:** *15 rooms, from £160*

RUTHIN, DENBIGHSHIRE 4–3A

On The Hill £42 444
1 Upper Clwyd Street LL15 1HY
(01824) 707736
"An exceptional find" – this beamed bistro in a 16th century house, set in a picturesque town, provides "superb" straightforward dishes; and "at the price it's almost too good to be true". / **Details:** *onthehillrestaurant.co.uk/; Sun - Sat 09.00pm.*

RYDE, ISLE OF WIGHT 2–4D

Three Buoys £51 333
Appley Lane PO33 1ND (01983) 811212
Panoramic views "of the beach and overlooking the Solent" are a big highpoint of this straightforward, seaside fixture, whose food is well-rated in (nearly) all reports. / **Details:** *www.threebuoys.co.uk; 9 pm.*

RYE, EAST SUSSEX 3–4C

The Ambrette at Rye £50 433
6 High St TN31 7JE (01797) 222 043
"Revelatory Indian regional food with a European influence" continues to win enthusiastic endorsements for Dev Biswal's nouvelle Indian (which moved a year or so ago to this new home on the High Street). / **Details:** *www.theambrette.co.uk; 9.30 pm, Fri - Sun 10 pm; closed Mon L.*

Landgate Bistro £45 322
5 - 6 Landgate TN31 7LH (01797) 222829
A small bistro of over two decades' standing, set in adjoining Georgian shops, and offering "excellent" local, foraged food. / **Details:** *www.landgatebistro.co.uk; Mon & Tue closed, Wed - Sat 9 pm, Sun 3 pm; closed Mon, Tue, Wed L, Thu L, Fri L & Sun D; no Amex.*

Tuscan Rye 543
8 Lion St TN31 7LB (01797) 223269
"Previous owners Franco and Jen have returned to loud acclaim" at this "first-class, genuine Italian" ("like a mini River Café") and "life is now sweet in Rye". The victuals – "authentic Tuscan regional dishes with superb wines" – make it "well worth booking for" (not least as "their clientele have flocked back en masse"). / **Details:** *www.tuscankitchenrye.co.uk; 11.30 pm; closed Mon, Tue, Wed L & Sat L.*

Webbe's at The Fish Cafe £45 322
17 Tower Street TN31 7AT (01797) 222 226
"Another of Paul Webbe's establishments" – this one located in a "bustling" converted warehouse in the town centre; it garners plaudits for its "great range of imaginative fish and seafood dishes" (and at "great value" prices too). / **Details:** *www.webbesrestaurants.co.uk/the-fish-cafe/; 9.30 pm.*

SALCOMBE, DEVON 1–4C

South Sands Hotel £61 345
Bolt Head TQ8 8LL (01548) 845900
"A stunning location" – on the beach in South Sands bay, just outside Salcombe – helps create "the perfect atmosphere to relax" at this modern seaside hotel. "The food is rooted in the expected classics with a contemporary twist", and tips include Sunday lunch, afternoon tea, and regular special evenings. / **Details:** *www.southsands.com; 9pm. /* **Accommodation:** *75 rooms, from £27*

SALISBURY, WILTSHIRE 2–3C

Anokaa £43 432
60 Fisherton St SP2 7RB (01722) 414142
"Salisbury's top spot, and constantly packed" – "an

Indian that tries (and succeeds) with contemporary cuisine", consistently producing food that's "high quality and completely different from the norm". / **Details:** *www.anokaa.com; 10.30 pm; No shorts.*

SALTAIRE, WEST YORKSHIRE 5–1C

Salts Diner £35 2 3 4
Salts Mill, Victoria Rd BD18 3LA
(01274) 530 533
This gallery café in the UNESCO-listed Salts Mill "still delivers a great food experience", including pizza (and not every restaurant has a logo designed by David Hockney); ignore the din and it's a "great place for lunch". / **Details:** *www.saltsmill.org.uk; 2m from Bradford on A650; 5.30, Sat and Sun 6pm; L & afternoon tea only; no Amex; No bookings.*

SALTHOUSE, NORFOLK 6–3C

Dun Cow £39 3 3 4
Purdy St NR25 7XA (01263) 740467
In a "great setting" overlooking the marshes, this wood-beamed venture has transformed its fortunes under the newish management – it's "now a thriving gastropub" serving up "outstanding food in generous portions". / **Details:** *www.salthouseduncow.com; 9pm.*

SANDBANKS, DORSET 2–4C

Rick Stein £67 4 4 3
10-14 Banks Rd BH13 7QB (01202) 283 000
"Stunning views of the sea (if you're lucky enough to get a table with a view)" set the scene at the new Stein empire outpost on this plutocratic peninsula – a big operation that's "a great improvement on its predecessor, Café Shore" (RIP). It's a good spot in which to enjoy some "perfect fruits de mer", and initial reports on its "delicious" fish are uniformly upbeat. / **Details:** *www.rickstein.com/eat-with-us/rick-stein-sandbanks; 10 pm; children: 3.*

SANDIACRE, NOTTINGHAMSHIRE 5–3D

La Rock £65 4 4 3
4 Bridge Street NG10 5QT (0115) 939 9833
A "small, stylish restaurant" tucked away on a side street, whose notably "adventurous menu" and "professional feel" make a big impression on many local reporters, who say that "prices are high, but worth it!" / **Details:** *www.larockrestaurant.co.uk; Mon & Tue closed, Wed - Sun 9 pm; closed Mon, Tue & Wed L.*

SANDSEND, NORTH YORKSHIRE 8–3D

Estbek House £60 4 4 4
East Row YO21 3SU (01947) 893424
A Georgian restaurant-with-rooms, on the seafront, where "prices are towards the high end for North Yorks", but where "the (seafood-centric) cooking is precise". / **Details:** *www.estbekhouse.co.uk; 9 pm; D only; no Amex; No bookings at diner.* / **Accommodation:** *5 rooms, from £125*

SAPPERTON, GLOUCESTERSHIRE 2–2C

The Bell at Sapperton £49 2 3 4
GL7 6LE (01285) 760298
This "delightful pub in a very pretty part of the world" has quite a foodie reputation, but inspires slightly mixed reports: most (but not all) are upbeat, but even those who say the food's "great" can find it "a little overpriced" or that "the enthusiastic team are trying hard to improve". / **Details:** *www.bellsapperton.co.uk; from Cirencester take the A419 towards Stroud, turn right to Sapperton; 9.30 pm, Sun 9 pm.*

SAUNDERSFOOT, PEMBROKESHIRE 4–4B

Coast £65 4 4 5
Coppet Hall Beach SA69 9AJ (01834) 810800
A "stunning" setting – with "fabulous views over the sea from every table" – add lustre to this coastal venue, overlooking the famous beach. Cooking is from chef/patron, Will Holland, the Craft Guild of Chefs' 'UK Restaurant Chef of the Year' – "simple food is the hardest to do well, here it's great food!" / **Details:** *www.coastsaundersfoot.co.uk; 9 pm; closed Mon & Tue.*

SAWLEY, LANCASHIRE 5–1B

The Spread Eagle £49 3 3 3
BB7 4NH (01200) 441202
On the edge of the Ribble Valley, by the river opposite a ruined abbey, "one of the most popular pub-restaurants" in the region, thanks to its "always excellent food" and "great beer". / **Details:** *www.spreadeaglesawley.co.uk; 9.30 pm, Sun 7.00 pm.* / **Accommodation:** *7 rooms, from £80*

SCARBOROUGH, NORTH YORKSHIRE 8–4D

Lanterna £54 5 5 3
33 Queen Street YO11 1HQ (01723) 363616
A "small, comfortable" and pleasingly "old-fashioned" Italian "serving exceptionally fresh, locally sourced fish dishes"; "try the lobster or

take a few extra pennies and go during the 'truffle' weeks – you won't regret it!" / **Details:** www.lanterna-ristorante.co.uk; Mon closed, Tue - Sat 9.30 pm, Sun closed; D only, closed Sun; no Amex.

SCAWTON, NORTH YORKSHIRE 8–4C

Hare Inn £49 554
YO7 2HG (01845) 597769
"A charming inn, tucked away in glorious countryside close to Helmsley and Rievaulx Abbey" – and what "astonishing food to find in the middle of nowhere essentially" from chef Paul Jackson ("beautifully prepared local ingredients, with game a highlight"). Service is a highpoint too, with "serious attention to detail and guests". / **Details:** www.thehare-inn.com; off A170; 9 pm, Sun 4pm; closed Mon, Tue & Sun D; Credit card deposit required to book.

SEER GREEN, BUCKINGHAMSHIRE 3–3A

The Jolly Cricketers £50 433
24 Chalfont Rd HP9 2YG (01494) 676308
"Top-flight food in a proper local's local" – that's the deal at this incredibly popular pub that's "well worth a drive out!". Service is "friendly with genuine smiles"; and the ambience is "buzzy and traditional in a positive way". / **Details:** www.thejollycricketers.co.uk; 11.15 pm, Fri & Sat 11.30, Sun 10.30.

SENNAN COVE, CORNWALL 1–4A

Sennan Cove
TR19 7BT (01736) 871191
Ben Tunnicliffe (of the Tolcarne Inn in Newlyn) took on this beachside café "overlooking a beautiful beach" in 2015. "The location is fantastic", and one early reporter lauds the "stylish presentation, excellent service and perfectly cooked fish". Feedback is too limited for a rating, however.

SEVENOAKS WEALD, KENT 3–3B

Giacomo £50 233
Morleys Road TN14 6QR (01732) 746200
A "family-run Italian" with a "lovely atmosphere"; for the odd cynic its approach is "quaint-going-on-dated (the last time I consumed a flambé was 40 years ago!)", but even they concede "there's evidently a market for it", and for fans its "consistently good food and delightful service" carry the day. / **Details:** www.giacomos.uk.com; 9 pm.

SEVENOAKS, KENT 3–3B

Little Garden £44 443
1-2 Bank St TN13 1UN (01732) 469397
This tucked-away two-year-old, from the owners of Chipstead's acclaimed George & Dragon, "continues to be a bright spot in the banal dining scene of Sevenoaks". "The menu hasn't developed much since they opened, but the staples cooked in the Josper oven continue to please" and there's an "excellent selection of local beer and wine to boot!" / **Details:** www.littlegardensevenoaks.com/; Mon -Sat 10 pm, Sun 9 pm.

SHALDON, DEVON 1–3D

Ode £60 543
Fore Street TQ14 0DE (01626) 873977
In a quaint village, this "small and intimate" venture has an outspoken local/seasonal ethos with "suppliers and food miles on the back of the menu". Whilst "all very commendable", it's "what's on the plate that really counts"... and it's "more than impressive, with value that's second to none". (It has a nearby café sibling too). / **Details:** www.odetruefood.com; Mon - Thur closed, Fri & Sat 9 pm, Sun closed; D only, closed Sun-Tue; no Amex; children: 8+ after 8pm.

SHEFFIELD, SOUTH YORKSHIRE 5–2C

Arusuvai £39 322
74 Abbeydale Road S7 1FD (0114) 255 0779
"Not the nicest location", "service is sometimes a little chaotic", but this Hillsborough curry house serves "very good South Indian / Sri Lankan dishes". / **Details:** www.arusuvai.co.uk; 10 pm.

Nonna's £48 433
535 - 541 Eccleshall Road S11 8PR
(0114) 268 6166
Long "one of the best Italians in Sheffield", if not the best – this Eccleshall fixture provides a "real Italian atmosphere" ("generally busy and bustling, sometimes even a little chaotic") plus "consistently great" and "authentic" home-style cooking.
/ **Details:** www.nonnas.co.uk; Mon - Sat 11 pm, Sun 10.30 pm; no Amex.

Rafters £62 454
220 Oakbrook Rd, Nether Grn S11 7ED
(0114) 230 4819
"In a leafy suburb, set above a shop – hence the name", this "small, friendly" Ranmoor staple is "still one of the best", "whether you are there for a romantic meal for two or a big family get-together". Chef-patron Tom Lawson "continues to innovate" and there's "knowledgeable wine help from (FOH)

Alistair Myers". / **Details:** *www.raftersrestaurant.co.uk; Wed & Thu 8.30 pm, Fri & Sat 9 pm; D only, closed Tue & Sun; children: 8.*

Silversmiths **£40** 2 3 2
111 Arundel St S1 2NT (0114) 270 6160
Handy for the University and Lyceum Theatre, this "enjoyable" spot is "great for pre-theatre food and cocktails". / **Details:** *www.silversmiths-restaurant.com; 9.30 pm, Fri & Sat 9.45; D only, closed Mon & Sun.*

Street Food Chef **£7** 3 4 3
90 Arundel St S1 4RE (0114) 275 2390
A "quick, authentic Mexican" with "communal tables" and a "great atmosphere"; why not try the £15 'Bastardo' burrito? – "eat it in under half an hour and it's on the house" (although "the challenges might actually kill you…") / **Details:** *www.streetfoodchef.co.uk; 10 pm, Sun 9 pm.*

Vero Gusto **£65** 4 5 3
12 Norfolk Row S1 2DA (0114) 276 0004
A candidate for "the best Italian in Sheffield (with Nonna's?)" – a "small and intimate" indie, whose food and "fascinating" wine list "knock spots off many a London restaurant". It's "close to the Crucible Theatre, so perfectly located for a pre-theatre meal, but clearly worth settling down for a full dinner". / **Details:** *www.verogusto.com; 10 pm; closed Mon & Sun.*

Wong Ting 4 3 2
6-8 Matilda St S1 4QD (0114) 275 7392
"The most authentic Chinese cooking in Sheffield" awaits at this "exceptionally good" city-centre venue; the menu is "not very varied, but very consistent" ("Top Tip – you need to ask for the Chinese menu if you want the real McCoy)".

SHEFFORD, BEDFORDSHIRE 3–1A

Black Horse at Ireland **£53** 3 3 3
SG17 5QL (01462) 811398
Nestled in a small hamlet, a pretty, 17th-century pub-with-rooms; the "bar offers a light snack or there are two dining rooms serving classic-style food" – the latter "excellent". / **Details:** *www.blackhorseireland.com; 9.30 pm, Fri & Sat 10 pm; closed Sun D. /* **Accommodation:** *2 rooms, from £55*

SHELLEY, WEST YORKSHIRE 5–2C

Three Acres **£58** 2 3 4
Roydhouse HD8 8LR (01484) 602606
"Set high up on the hills" – near the Emley TV transmitter – "it can be wind-swept and bitter" at this renowned, moor-top inn "but when you go in it's as snug as anyone could want". "It's trading on its past reputation", though, nowadays – the food's still "reliable", but "not as good as it used to be", and with "toppy bills" – "you can get better at this price elsewhere". / **Details:** *www.3acres.com; 9.30 pm; no Amex. /* **Accommodation:** *16 rooms, from £125*

SHERBORNE, DORSET 2–3B

The Green **£58** 4 4 3
3 The Green DT9 3HY (01935) 813821
In a picture-postcard building in the town-centre, a well-rated all-rounder, combining "fantastic food, plus lovely service and atmosphere". / **Details:** *www.greenrestaurant.co.uk; Mon closed, Tu - Sat 9.30 pm, Sun closed; closed Mon & Sun.*

SHERE, SURREY 3–3A

Kinghams **£56** 4 4 4
Gomshall Ln GU5 9HE (01483) 202168
"In a beautiful old building" with exposed-wood beams, Paul Baker's "longstanding favourite" where the cooking is "right up there with the very best". It "can get very noisy when busy (most of the time), but it's worth it" by all accounts. / **Details:** *www.kinghams-restaurant.co.uk; off A25 between Dorking & Guildford; 11 pm; closed Mon & Sun D.*

SHINFIELD, BERKSHIRE 2–2D

L'Ortolan **£97** 3 2 3
Church Ln RG2 9BY (0118) 988 8500
"Wonderfully located, in an old rectory" (a little off the M4, near the Reading turn-off), this well-known foodie bastion put in a more uneven performance this year. A vociferous minority described "poor" service and judged the food "overpriced and overhyped", but the majority still applaud Tom Clarke's "superb standard of cuisine" and "an amazing experience rather than just a meal". / **Details:** *www.lortolan.com; 8.30 pm; closed Mon & Sun.*

SHIPBOURNE, KENT 3–3B

The Chaser Inn **£44** 3 3 4
Stumble Hill TN11 9PE (01732) 810 360
The "food continues to deliver time after time" at this well-presented country pub – the founding member of the south-eastern Whiting & Hammond Group; regulars also "love the new courtyard area with the retractable roof". / **Details:** *www.thechaser.co.uk; Mon - Sat 9.30 pm, Sun 9 pm.*

SHIPLAKE, OXFORDSHIRE 2–2D

Orwells £65 543

Shiplake Row RG9 4DP (0118) 940 3673

"Best by far in the Reading/Henley area" – this "very upmarket" gastropub is carving an ever-increasing reputation. Service is "warm, friendly and informed" and "more awards are surely coming" for the "memorable", "exquisitely presented" cooking from chefs Ryan Simpson & Liam Trotman: the tyre men haven't elevated the place yet but this is "Michelin star cuisine at very reasonable prices". / **Details:** *www.orwellsatshiplake.co.uk; 9.30 pm; closed Mon, Tue & Sun D.* / **Sustainability:** ★★★

SHIPLEY, WEST YORKSHIRE 5–1C

Aagrah £36 332

4 Saltaire Rd BD18 3HN (01274) 530880

The headquarters of this popular local Kashmiri chain has long been of note for its vibrant atmosphere and upstairs buffet – even a reporter who found it "could be uninspiring" says it's "reliable". / **Details:** *www.aagrah.com; 11.30 pm, Fri-Sat midnight, Sun 10.30 pm; D only.*

SHIRLEY, DERBYSHIRE 5–3C

The Saracen's Head £41 333

Church Ln DE6 3AS (01335) 360 330

It's "well worth going out of your way" to get to this "consistently good country pub", combining a "friendly and cosy environment" with gastro fare that "can't be beat". Try it – "you won't be disappointed". / **Details:** *www.saracens-head-shirley.co.uk; 9 pm; no Amex.*

SHREWSBURY, SHROPSHIRE 5–3A

Haughmond £47 433

Upton Magna SY4 4TZ (01743) 709918

"An exceptional village pub-with-rooms serving beautiful British food" – you can opt for the bar menu ("fantastic, fresh burger with superb relish and brioche"), but the "adjoining restaurant offers fine dining" – "the chef is self-taught, which is astonishing considering the standard of cuisine". / **Details:** *www.thehaughmond.co.uk; 8.45 pm, Sun 6.30 pm.*

Number Four £36 344

4 Butcher Row SY1 1UW (01743) 366691

A "really friendly and always busy" café, in the city-centre, which may be "a little cramped" but serves some "brilliant" dishes – a particular shout-out goes to the "great range of breakfast items". / **Details:** *www.number-four.com; 11 pm; closed Mon D, Tue D & Wed D.*

SLEAT, HIGHLAND 9–2B

Kinloch Lodge £95 434

Sleat IV43 8QY (01471) 833333

The Macdonald of Macdonalds's old hunting lodge – converted by Lord Godfrey and his food writer wife, Claire, into a hotel – has won renown for its "first-class" cuisine. There was the odd sceptical report this year – "on a return visit after several years, despite the acquisition of a Michelin star and leap in price, standards had declined" – but on most accounts "it's a wonderful spot and a great experience to stay and eat". / **Details:** *www.kinloch-lodge.co.uk; 9 pm; no Amex.* / **Accommodation:** *19 rooms, from £99*

SNAPE, SUFFOLK 3–1D

The Crown Inn £41 324

Bridge Rd IP17 1SL (01728) 688324

A "cosy", 15th-century smugglers' inn, "particularly on a winter's night", when "you can sit on huge high-backed settles around an open fire"; the food is "mainly meat-based", but no less "excellent" for that – and there's a particular shout-out for the "porky platter" (the pigs being reared on site). / **Details:** *www.snape-crown.co.uk; off A12 towards Aldeburgh; 9.30 pm, Sat 10 pm, Sun 9.30 pm; no Amex.* / **Accommodation:** *2 rooms, from £90*

The Plough and Sail £37 333

Snape Bridge IP17 1SR (01728) 688413

A "large" and "lively" pub/dining room launched four years ago by local brothers Alex & Oliver Burnside; the "food is usually good" – not least the "amazing ploughman's". / **Details:** *www.theploughandsailsnape.com/; 10 pm.*

SNETTISHAM, NORFOLK 6–4B

Rose & Crown £40 222

Old Church Rd PE31 7LX (01485) 541382

On the moors, this "busy" pub sits at the centre of a bucolic village. Its advocates say its cooking is "better than average", but there are sceptics for whom "it doesn't really work" – "not bad, but just not as good as you'd hope for with the price and plaudits" (the latter heavily on display). / **Details:** *www.roseandcrownsnettisham.co.uk; 9 pm, Fri - Sat 9.30pm; no Amex.* / **Accommodation:** *16 rooms, from £90*

SONNING-ON-THAMES, BERKSHIRE 2–2D

The French Horn £82 335

RG4 6TN (0118) 969 2204

"Old fashioned but still worth a visit" – this unreformed '70s survivor occupies a "wonderful

location" on the Thames, and its dining room is "maintained to a high standard". When it comes to the old-school victuals, "first-class ingredients are prepared with no fuss, and there's an extraordinary wine list, with prices below auction prices for first growths of a few years ago." / **Details:** *www.thefrenchhorn.co.uk; 9.30 pm, Sun 9 pm; Booking max 10 may apply.* / **Accommodation:** *21 rooms, from £160*

SOUTH FERRIBY, LINCOLNSHIRE 6–2A

Hope And Anchor £46 443

Sluice Rd DN18 6JQ (01652) 635334

TV chef Colin McGurran's "great new pub" (expansively refurbed after a 2013 flood) wins raves for its "absolutely fantastic food" (not least meats showcased in the snazzy MaturMeat fridge). There are "stunning views over the River Humber", and service is "spot on" too. / **Details:** *www.thehopeandanchorpub.co.uk; 9 pm, Fri & Sat 10 pm, Sun 6 pm.*

SOUTH SHIELDS, TYNE AND WEAR 8–2B

Colmans £34 544

182-186 Ocean Rd NE33 2JQ
(0191) 456 1202

"The best chippie in the North East!" has been "a great institution since 1926" – "an excellent, well-organised operation", with "top quality fish 'n' chips", "super-friendly hosts" and offering "unbeatable value for money". (The business is also pitching to turn a local seaside landmark, 'Ghandi's Temple', into another outlet, with cocktail bar.) / **Details:** *www.colmansfishandchips.com; 6.00pm; L only; no Amex; No bookings.* / **Sustainability:** ★★★

SOUTHAMPTON, HAMPSHIRE 2–3D

Kuti's £37 443

37-39 Oxford St SO14 3DP (023) 8022 1585

"Delicious curries that make you want to come back for more!", make it worth remembering this well-established Indian: one of Southampton's few culinary sparks. / **Details:** *www.kutis.co.uk; 11.30 pm.*

Lakaz Maman £24 433

22 Bedford Place SO15 2DB (023) 8063 9217

Is this new "friendly and informal, Mauritian street food eaterie of MasterChef winner Shelina Permalloo" the most exciting thing ever to happen to Southampton foodwise? Reporters say "it's still finding its feet, but is good and interesting and will undoubtedly get better!" / **Details:** *www.lakazmaman.com; Tue- Sat 10.00pm, Sun 6.00pm.*

SOUTHPORT, MERSEYSIDE 5–1A

Bistrot Vérité £48 333

7 Liverpool Road PR8 4AR (01704) 564 199

"Just as a French bistro should be" – this "great little neighbourhood restaurant", in a converted shop in Birkdale village, "attracts a loyal following" for its "excellent, Gallic classic dishes (as well as fish 'n' chips)". / **Details:** *www.bistrotverite.co.uk; Mon closed, Tue 5.30 pm Wed - Sat 10 pm, Sun close; closed Mon & Sun.*

The Vincent Hotel V-Cafe £48 333

98 Lord Street PR8 1JR (0843) 509 4586

"Very good Japanese options" are the distinctive feature at this "very popular hotel restaurant", which serves "everything from coffee and breakfasts to afternoon teas… plus excellent sushi" to boot; while the odd sceptic finds the concept "muddled", the majority insist that the food "never disappoints", and that the venue is "good for people-watching at weekends". / **Details:** *www.thevincenthotel.com; 10 pm.* / **Accommodation:** *60 rooms, from £93*

SOUTHROP, GLOUCESTERSHIRE 2–2C

The Swan at Southrop £51 333

GL7 3NU (01367) 850205

Set on a country estate with a boutique hotel and cookery school, this well-heeled, ivy-covered Cotswold gastroboozer draws praise for well-sourced cuisine that's well rated by the locals. / **Details:** *www.theswanatsouthrop.co.uk; Mon-Thurs 9 pm, Fri-Sat 9.30 pm; closed Sun D; no Amex.*

SOUTHWOLD, SUFFOLK 3–1D

Coasters £45 333

Queen St IP18 6EQ (01502) 724734

With the "feel of a converted tearoom", this diminutive outfit makes "a great alternative to Southwold's prestigious but pricey hotel kitchens"; "excellent local fish" dominates the modestly priced menu, and there's a "well-chosen wine list" to go with it. / **Details:** *www.coastersofsouthwold.co.uk; 2 min walk from seafront and Market square; 9 pm; closed Mon & Sun D; no Amex.*

The Crown, Adnams Hotel £55 223

90 High St IP18 6DP (01502) 722275

This noted Adnams pub has been up and down over the past few years, and while fans of the "beautifully fresh, locally sourced food" and "exceptional wines" insist that "what had appeared for some time to be a rudderless ship" is "vastly improved" after the recent arrival of a new manager, others find it "hard to believe how far this one-time destination has plummeted". One fixed point: "there's a great buzz no matter which day you go". / **Details:** *www.adnams.co.uk/stay-with-us/the-crown; 9 pm; no Amex. /* **Accommodation:** *14 rooms, from £160*

Sole Bay Fish Company **£30** **534**
22e Blackshore IP18 6ND (01502) 724241
"Dickensian shed from the outside" – inside this "harbourside shack" is a "wonderfully quirky restaurant and wet fish counter", whose "superb" fish dinners and "fabulous" cold seafood platters mean that it's "one of the worst-kept secrets" in town! NB These days they also have a smokehouse and wine license, so it's no longer BYO. / **Details:** *www.solebayfishco.co.uk; 3 pm; closed Mon.*

Sutherland House **£50** **333**
56 High St IP18 6DN (01502) 724544
The Bank family's B&B in a 15th-century building doubles as a "consistently good" fish restaurant "with many changes of menu to reflect the best fish available"; even the most critical reporter who "expected better", still "enjoyed the experience". / **Details:** *www.sutherlandhouse.co.uk; 9.30 pm; closed Mon (winter). /* **Accommodation:** *3 rooms, from £150*

The Swan **£53** **123**
The Market Pl IP18 6EG (01502) 722186
There are many old fans of this famous, Adnams-run "grand hotel"; and its dining room, while "stuffy", certainly "looks the part". For critics, though, too many incidents of "less-than-competent" service and "form-over-substance" cooking take the shine off the experience. "It's the worst we have experienced in many years of staying at The Swan – hopefully the new chef will improve matters." / **Details:** *www.adnams.co.uk/stay-with-us/the-swan; 9 pm; no Amex; No jeans; children: 5+ at D. /* **Accommodation:** *42 rooms, from £185*

SPARKWELL, DEVON 1–3C

Treby Arms **£58** **543**
PL7 5DD (01752) 837363
"Since winning MasterChef Anton Piotrowski has gone from strength to strength" at this "quality gastropub on the edge of Dartmoor" (originally built for workers on Brunel's Royal Albert Bridge). The odd reporter finds the food "over-fussy", but such reports are overwhelmed by the vast majority applauding the "exquisite dishes, particularly fish" that "amuse the mind, eyes and taste buds with every course. Oh yes, and the charming and down-to-earth service was lovely too". / **Details:** *www.thetrebyarms.co.uk; 9 pm; closed Mon.*

SPARSHOLT, HAMPSHIRE 2–3D

The Plough Inn **£49** **324**
Woodman Lane SO21 2NW (01962) 776353
A "rural" gastroboozer – "more of a restaurant than a local" – serving "reliably good" food; "the service can be slow when it's busy... and it does always seem to be busy for very good reason". / **Details:** *www.ploughinnsparsholt.co.uk; 9 pm, Sun & Mon 8.30 pm, Fri & Sat 9.30 pm; no Amex.*

ST ALBANS, HERTFORDSHIRE 3–2A

Barrissimo **£12** **353**
28 St Peters St AL1 3NA (01727) 869999
"A pleasant change to all the chains!" – a "good local indie coffee shop" where "everything's freshly prepared and served with a smile"; despite the departure of much-loved former owners Angelo & Rosa, it's "surviving well under new management". / **Details:** *5.30 pm, Sun 4 pm; L only; Cash only.*

The Cock Inn **£39** **234**
48 St Peters St AL1 3NF (01727) 854 816
Handily located between the cathedral and the river, this very traditional 17th-century inn offers fairly predictable, but enjoyable, pub grub, while the setting – with its wood-beamed ceiling, log fire and garden – is just the ticket. / **Details:** *www.thecockinnstalbans.co.uk; 10.30pm; no Amex.*

Lussmanns **£45** **233**
Waxhouse Gate, High St AL3 4EW
(01727) 851941
"A reliable St Albans stand-by" that's "situated right by the cathedral in a lovely location" and is "a dependable fall-back for simple classics" ("steak-frites is a sure-fire winner"). Not only did it win the Sustainable Restaurant's Association 'People's Favourite' award in 2016, but also backing from private equity impresario, Luke Johnson, with the aim of pushing its further expansion (there are 4 other branches in nearby towns). / **Details:** *www.lussmanns.com; 9.30 pm, Fri & Sat 10 pm, Sun 9 pm. /* **Sustainability:** ★★★

Prime Steak & Grill **£69** **333**
83 - 85 London Road AL1 1LN
(01727) 840 309
"A top town-centre steakhouse" also serving "genuinely good burgers" – like so many of others of its ilk, it's "a little pricey". / **Details:** *www.primesteakandgrill.com/st-albans; Mon - Sat 11 pm, Sun 10 pm.*

Tabure **£42** **333**
6 Spencer St AL3 5EG (01727) 569068
Opened in spring 2015 by a husband-and-wife team, this "very friendly" tiled venue, in the city centre, is already "a real favourite" thanks to its

"delicious modern take on Turkish tapas". / **Details:** *www.tabure.co.uk/; 10:30pm.*

Thompson £73 322

2 Hatfield Rd AL1 3RP (01727) 730 777
"The best in St Albans" – ex-Auberge du Lac chef Phil Thompson's three-year-old venue in the town centre "continues to improve", offering food that's "always outstanding and full of creativity". / **Details:** *www.thompsonstalbans.co.uk; 9 pm, Fri & Sat 9.30 pm.*

ST ANDREWS, FIFE 9–3D

Seafood Restaurant £75 435

The Scores KY16 9AB (01334) 479475
"Heaven in a glass box": a "delightful" seaside establishment "with beautiful views" and "food to match" (i.e. "the freshest seafood"). / **Details:** *www.theseafoodrestaurant.com; 9.30 pm; children: 12+ at D.*

Vine Leaf £48 343

131 South Street KY16 9UN (01334) 477497
This "go-to favourite", "hidden away" off the main street, "has a fantastic location that's perfect for romance". "Ian always looks after his guests, while Morag cooks up a storm", and the result is "some of the best value in the area". / **Details:** *www.vineleafstandrews.co.uk; Mon closed, Tue - Sat 9.15 pm, Sun closed; D only, closed Mon & Sun.*

ST AUSTELL, CORNWALL 1–4B

Austells £50 432

10 Beach Rd PL25 3PH (01726) 813888
"The location is a little off-putting" – set amid grotty suburban shops, it's a bit "like an estate café" – but reporters "can't complain about the food" at Brett Camborne-Paynter's establishment; not only does it taste "wonderful", "you can tell the chef has experience in fine dining from the presentation". / **Details:** *www.austells.co.uk; 9 pm; closed Mon.*

ST BRELADE, CHANNEL ISLANDS –

Ocean Restaurant, Atlantic Hotel £90

Le Mont de la Pulente JE3 8HE
(01534) 744101
"His food is so good we travelled to Jersey to eat it!" – Mark Jordan's cuisine inspires limited (too few reports for a rating) but hugely enthusiastic feedback for this contemporary dining room, with fine views of the bay. / **Details:** *www.theatlantichotel.com; 10 pm; No jeans.* / **Accommodation:** *50 rooms, from £150*

ST DAVIDS, PEMBROKESHIRE 4–4A

Cwtch £50 333

22 High St SA62 6SD (01437) 720491
With chef Andy Holcroft at the pass, this "relaxed, good value" option in the town centre is a "lovely little place delivering much better than it needs to in order to be number one in St Davids". / **Details:** *www.cwtchrestaurant.co.uk; 10.30 pm; D only, ex Sun open L & D.*

ST HELIER, CHANNEL ISLANDS –

Ormer £76 322

7-11 Don Street JE2 4TQ (01534) 725 100
A restaurant, bar and deli from TV star Shaun Rankin (ex-Bohemia), with "high-quality" cooking, and an "excellent" bar, which ensures a "great range of wines and cocktails". It does have the odd critic though, and even fans can cite food that's "pleasant but unremarkable". / **Details:** *www.ormerjersey.com; Mon - Sat 10 pm, Sun closed; closed Sun.*

ST HELIER, JERSEY –

Bistro Rosa 544

19-22 Beresford Street Fish Mkt JE2 4WX
(01534) 729559
"Situated in St Helier fish market" this "quaint little bistro" delivers "fabulous fish, and service-with-a-smile", with "the minimum of fuss, in simple surroundings, without an astronomical price tag. A seafood lover's dream!"

ST IVES, CORNWALL 1–4A

Alba Restaurant £49 334

The Old Life Boat Hs, Wharf Rd TR26 1LF
(01736) 797222
A "friendly" fish-centric outfit in a "lovely location" overlooking the harbour; the worst anyone had to say about it? – "everything from the food to service was good". / **Details:** *www.thealbarestaurant.com; 10 pm.*

Porthgwidden Beach Café £43 245

Porthgwidden Beach TR26 1PL
(01736) 796791
This relaxed fish and seafood café – right on the beach and with uninterrupted views across the bay to Godrevy Lighthouse – is just "perfect for breakfast"; more generally however, "it was more disappointing this year, in common with its sister restaurant, Porthminster Café". / **Details:** *www.porthgwiddencafe.co.uk; 9.30 pm; no Amex; Booking max 10 may apply.*

Porthmeor Beach Cafe **£40** 4 4 5
Porthmeor Beach TR26 1JZ (01736) 793366
"If the weather's good, there's nowhere better" to be than this café, with a "lovely location right on the beach", and near the Tate. The food, including "fantastic" seafood tapas, is "divine", and the "view over to the island is amazing". Top Tip – brunch: "get yourself into one of the pods that looks out onto the sands, turn on the heaters, and cosy up on not so sunny days." / ***Details:*** *www.porthmeor-beach.co.uk; 9 pm; D only. Closed Nov-Mar.; no Amex.*

Porthminster Café **£58** 3 2 5
Porthminster Beach TR26 2EB
(01736) 795352
This "lovely beach restaurant" just yards from the sea is marvellously located. "It's relying on its fame and ambience" nowadays, though – "the food, although good, seems overhyped and service at peak times can be incredibly slow" or "distracted". / ***Details:*** *www.porthminstercafe.co.uk; 9.30 pm; no Amex.*

ST JAMES STREET, SOMERSET 2–3A

Augustus **£47** 4 5 3
3 The Courtyard TA1 1JR (01823) 324 354
"The favourite of Taunton"; the ex-Castle Hotel team's "outstanding" bistro serves up "truly wonderful", "French-inspired seasonal food", delivered by seriously "welcoming staff". / ***Details:*** *www.augustustaunton.co.uk; Mon closed, Tue - Sat 9.30 pm, Sun closed; closed Mon & Sun; no Amex.*

ST LEONARDS-ON-SEA, EAST SUSSEX 3–4C

Half Man Half Burger **£29** 3 3 2
7 Marine Court TN38 0DX (01424) 552332
A "newly opened (and markedly hipster) burger house", in a cruise liner-style building on the seafront, where the main event is "monstrously good". / ***Details:*** *www.halfmanhalfburger.com; No bookings.*

St Clement's **£49** 4 4 2
3 Mercatoria TN38 0EB (01424) 200355
"New venues are opening up on the seafront, but St Clements continues to be the top venue in St Leonards". It's an "unexpected neighbourhood bistro" in a backstreet, serving "high-quality cuisine" in a "cosy dining room". / ***Details:*** *www.stclementsrestaurant.co.uk; 9 pm, Sat 10 pm; closed Mon & Sun D.*

ST MARGARETS, SURREY 3–3A

The Crown **£47** 3 3 4
174 Richmond Rd TW1 2NH (020) 8892 5896
A fine Georgian tavern – nowadays a very "commendable" gastroboozer that's "the best in the area"; "it's dog-friendly too, so you can go with the hound!" / ***Details:*** *www.crowntwickenham.co.uk.*

ST MAWES, CORNWALL 1–4B

Hotel Tresanton **£67** 3 5 5
27 Lower Castle Road TR2 5DR
(01326) 270055
"One of the best views in England" over St Mawes and the bay, "from the delightful and sheltered setting of the terrace at the Tresanton make this an idyllic venue for lingering". You would expect an establishment owned by TV's 'The Hotel Inspector', Olga Polizzi, to be pretty good, and – with its "light and well-prepared dishes" – it does provide "a really lovely experience", if not an especially foodie one. / ***Details:*** *www.tresanton.com; 9.30 pm; Booking max 10 may apply; children: 6+ at dinner. /* ***Accommodation:*** *40 rooms, from £250*

ST MERRYN, CORNWALL 1–3B

The Cornish Arms **£41** 4 2 3
Churchtown PL28 8ND (01841) 520288
Now with a "beautifully executed" extension out back, Rick Stein's "family-friendly" inn scores warm reports for "food that – while very pubby – is all of it delicious and well-sourced". Service can be "chaotic", and it's "probably best to avoid if you don't like dogs hanging around your table", but these are the only complaints. / ***Details:*** *www.rickstein.com; 8.30 pm; no Amex. /* ***Sustainability:*** ★★★

ST PETER PORT, CHANNEL ISLANDS –

Da Nello **£48** 3 3 3
46, Le Pollet GY1 1WF (01481) 721 552
In a 500-year-old building with a pretty courtyard dining area and an atrium-topped restaurant, this veteran St Peter Port trattoria (est. 1978) has maintained "constant standards over the years". / ***Details:*** *www.danello.gg; 10 pm.*

Le Petit Bistro **£53** 4 2 4
56 Lower Pollet GY1 1WF (01481) 725055
"Perfect!" – a cosy Gallic favourite overlooking the harbour in St Peter Port; admittedly service "can be slow, but it's worth the wait!" / ***Details:*** *www.petitbistro.co.uk; Mon - Thur 10 pm, 10.30 pm Fri & Sat, Sun closed; closed Sun.*

ST TUDY, CORNWALL 1–3B

St Tudy Inn £50 443
Bodmin PL30 3NN (01208) 850 656
*"Chef/patron Emily Scott (ex-Harbour Inn, Port Isaac) is a star" with a "deft touch for local produce", say fans of her excellent year-old tenure at this "lovely country pub, in the middle of nowhere", in the back lanes of north Cornwall. / **Details:** www.sttudyinn.com; 9 pm; closed Mon & Sun D; no Amex.*

STADHAMPTON, OXFORDSHIRE 2–2D

The Crazy Bear £69 233
Bear Ln OX44 7UR (01865) 890714
*This once-excellent Anglo-Thai (one dining room each) had seemed to be back on the up last year, but this year it starkly divided reporters. Fans still report a "lovely" experience with "terrific" cuisine, but cynics were "very disappointed", finding the funky interior "jaded", the cooking "a fraction as good as it was", and the bill "humungous for the quality". / **Details:** www.crazybeargroup.co.uk; 10 pm; children: 12+ at Fri & Sat D. / **Accommodation:** 16 rooms, from £169*

STAMFORD, LINCOLNSHIRE 6–4A

The George Hotel £69 334
71 St Martins PE9 2LB (01780) 750750
*"This unique and beautiful old coaching inn" (standing on what used to be the A1, before this gorgeous Georgian town was by-passed) is a "classic" – "a refreshing venue to relax in and recharge the batteries". It has a "lovely dining room" of the old-school variety, though often the cuisine is no better than "sound" ("I felt let down after the big build up") – other eating options include the popular Garden Room bistro, or, in summer, "an excellent lunch in the courtyard". / **Details:** www.georgehotelofstamford.com; 9.30 pm; Jacket required; children: 8+ at D. / **Accommodation:** 47 rooms, from £190*

STANHOE, NORFOLK 6–3B

The Duck Inn £46 443
Burnham Rd PE31 8QD (01485) 518 330
*This "warm and friendly", spruced-up, village gastroboozer-with-rooms won acclaim this year for its "really exciting" cuisine – "great local produce", showcasing "original and surprising" flavour combinations that nonetheless "just work". / **Details:** www.duckinn.co.uk; 9 pm, Sun 7.45 pm.*

STANTON, SUFFOLK 3–1C

Leaping Hare Vineyard £56 325
Wyken Vineyards IP31 2DW (01359) 250287
*"A romantic 'wow' of an oak-framed barn" ("Martha Stewart would be proud") provides a "serene and well-spaced setting" for the café of the acclaimed Wyken Vineyards. It's a "wonderful location" with, of course, "fabulous wine". Foodwise it's "good, sometimes excellent" and "the whole package is well worth the drive: cute llamas and lambs in the fields, lovely gardens, very appealing Country Store (like walking into Country Living magazine), Farmers' Market on Saturdays…" / **Details:** www.wykenvineyards.co.uk; 9m NE of Bury St Edmunds; follow tourist signs off A143; 5.30 pm, Fri & Sat 9 pm; L only, ex Fri & Sat open L & D.*

STATHERN, LEICESTERSHIRE 5–3D

Red Lion Inn £45 334
2 Red Lion Street LE14 4HS (01949) 860 868
*"Never failing to please" – this old-school rural pub near Belvoir Castle (sister to the Olive Branch at Clipsham), is "always popular", owing to its "good food" and "excellent atmosphere" (both in the bar and adjacent dining room). / **Details:** www.theredlioninn.co.uk; Mon - Sat 9 pm, Sun 6 pm; closed Sun D (and Mondays during Winter); no Amex.*

STOCKBRIDGE, HAMPSHIRE 2–3D

Clos du Marquis £56 343
London Rd SO20 6DE (01264) 810738
*"In farmhouse-type surroundings" – and "in the middle of nowhere" – this former pub, now under a South African owner, wins raves for its "astoundingly good" French cuisine ("slightly weird" as the concept may be)! / **Details:** www.closdumarquis.co.uk; 2m E on A30 from Stockbridge; 9 pm; closed Mon & Sun D.*

Greyhound £64 333
31 High Street SO20 6EY (01264) 810833
*This "pleasant, popular" gastropub-with-rooms in a building dating from the 1800s was taken over by an ex-Peat Spade team a couple of years ago; feedback remains a tad muted – no doubt because, as one reporter puts it, "the hype [it was a recent Michelin Pub of the Year] had let me to expect more" – but it's still "pretty good for down in the sticks". / **Details:** www.thegreyhoundonthetest.co.uk; 9.30 pm; Booking max 12 may apply. / **Accommodation:** 7 rooms, from £100*

Thyme & Tides £32 332
The High St SO20 6HE (01264) 810101
"Finding a table is the only problem" at this "upmarket" deli, café and "excellent" fishmonger, with a smattering of tables and a courtyard sitting

area. There's a "constantly changing lunchtime menu of tasty plates" and "Friday night fish 'n' chip suppers are another great reason to visit". / **Details:** *www.thymeandtidesdeli.co.uk; 2.30 pm, Sat 3 pm; closed Mon; no Amex.*

STOCKCROSS, BERKSHIRE 2–2D

The Vineyard at Stockcross £95 333

RG20 8JU (01635) 528770

"A cornucopia of New World wines" ("particularly strong on California") has always been the 'crown jewel' feature of Sir Peter Michael's contemporary-style property (which is not now so far off being 20 years old). Daniel Galmiche moved on at the start of 2016 to be replaced at the stoves by Robby Jenks (from Amberley Castle) – overall ratings however so far seem to have held up after the changeover. / **Details:** *www.the-vineyard.co.uk; from M4, J13 take A34 towards Hungerford; 9.30 pm; No jeans.* / **Accommodation:** *49 rooms, from £194*

STOCKPORT, GREATER MANCHESTER 5–2B

Brassica Grill £45 434

27 Shaw Rd SK4 4AG (0161) 442 6730

Paul Faulkner (ex-Albert Square Chop House) has a hit on his hands with this "lovely" yearling, in an "unexpected location" in suburban Heaton Moor. It wins praise for its "excellent cooking" from a "small menu of seasonal produce", plus a "great (Med-style) ambience". / **Details:** *www.brassicagrill.com; 10 pm, Sun 7pm; closed Mon.*

Damson £54 444

113 Heaton Moor Rd SK4 4HY
(0161) 4324666

It's all-change at this "relaxed and easygoing" Heaton Moor spot, which recently lost its newer Media City sibling, and where half of these premises are – since autumn 2016 – now surfing the tapas trend, and branded La Cantina. Half the site still trades, however, as this "favourite of many years", and we've rated it for its "high standards maintained over time, friendly service and good seasonal menu". / **Details:** *www.damsonrestaurant.co.uk; 9.30 pm, Sun 7 pm; closed Mon L, Sat L & Sun D.*

Easy Fish Company £43 343

117 Heaton Moor Road SK4 4HY
(0161) 442 0823

"A real find!" – a "very popular" mini-restaurant "at the back of a fishmonger", where the open kitchen means that "everyone is at the chef's table". While there's the odd sceptic of what "looks like a café, and feels like a café" ("I want it to be brilliant, but I find it hard to like"), most laud its "fabulous fresh fish" and "great atmosphere". / **Details:** *www.theeasyfishco.com; 11:30pm.*

STOKE HOLY CROSS, NORFOLK 6–4C

The Wildebeest Arms £53 533

82-86 Norwich Rd NR14 8QJ (01508) 492497

This diminutive village spot "has been a good buzzing gastropub for years, but is now up a couple of leagues" after being taken over by ex-Le Gavroche chef Daniel Smith's group G&D Ventures, also behind the Ingham Swan; the improvement does come "with prices that match", however. / **Details:** *thewildebeest.co.uk/; from A140, turn left at Dunston Hall, left at T-junction; 9 pm.*

STOKE ROW, OXFORDSHIRE 2–2D

The Crooked Billet £54 445

Newlands Ln RG9 5PU (01491) 681048

"Tucked away in the Chiltern Hills between Reading and Henley", Paul Clerehugh's "wonderful, out-of-the-way pub/restaurant" is "still a favourite after many years". The food is "gorgeous", staff are "very friendly and cheerful" and the oak-beamed interior is "just lovely" (there's also "the option of eating in the secret garden area" at the back). Top Tip – "great music nights". / **Details:** *www.thecrookedbillet.co.uk; off the A4130; 10 pm, Sat 10.30 pm.*

STOKE-BY-NAYLAND, SUFFOLK 3–2C

The Crown £44 335

Park Street CO6 4SE (01206) 262 001

A "buzzy, modern" gastropub that's "light, airy and cheery in winter" – with a "useful walk-in wine cellar, characterful exposed beams and a wood fire" – and that also offers "great courtyard dining in summer"; on the menu a "great range of brasserie favourites and new creations, normally including 10 fish choices". / **Details:** *www.crowninn.net; on B1068; Mon-Thur 9.30 pm, Fri & Sat 10pm, Sun 9 pm.* / **Accommodation:** *11 rooms, from £11*

STOW ON THE WOLD, GLOUCESTERSHIRE 2–1C

The Old Butchers £46 333

Park St GL54 1AQ (01451) 831700

Near the main square, and true to its name, Peter & Louise Robinson's contemporary venue is a real bastion of nose-to-tail cooking, turning out "thoughtful" and "always delicious" plates from the "very best menus"; Louise is a "charming hostess", too! / **Details:** *www.theoldbutchers.com; on the main road heading out of Stow on the Wold towards Oddington; 9.30 pm, Sat 10 pm; closed Mon & Sun; Booking max 12 may apply.*

STRACHUR, ARGYLL AND BUTE 9–4B

Inver £49 [5][4][4]
Stracthlachlan PA27 8BU (01369) 860 537
*Taken over and rebaptised by Pam Brunton & Rob Latimer in 2015, this "cool" dining room (fka Inver Cottage) wins raves for its "bold"-going-on-"extraordinary" new-Nordic-style cuisine – "inspired and novel" while avoiding fine-dining-style "death by foam!". "It's a long, long way to drive" – being "out-of-the-way on the gorgeous Cowal Peninsula" – but the pay-off includes "beautiful views". / **Details:** www.inverrestaurant.co.uk; 8.30 pm; closed Mon & Tue.*

STRATFORD UPON AVON, WARWICKSHIRE 2–1C

The Fuzzy Duck £49 [3][3][3]
Ilmington Rd CV37 8DD (01608) 682635
*In a pretty north Cotswolds hamlet not far from Stratford, this understated brick-clad pub is now a classy boutique inn, combining four upscale bedrooms and a dining room, serving sophisticated gastro fare, which was again consistently well-rated. / **Details:** www.fuzzyduckarmscote.com/; 9 pm, Fri & Sat 9.30 pm, Sun 3pm; closed Mon & Sun D.*

Lambs £48 [2][2][3]
12 Sheep Street CV37 6EF (01789) 292554
*"Pre-theatre is still very good" and remains much of the raison d'être of this buzzy city-centre stalwart. / **Details:** www.lambsrestaurant.co.uk; 9 pm; closed Mon L; no Amex.*

No. 9 £50 [4][3][2]
9 Church Street CV37 6HB (01789) 415 522
*This "small" spot is "excellent value pre-theatre", and there are also takers for the "interesting tasting menus with good wine matches"; even those who feel that it "lacks a little atmosphere", are confident that it "won't disappoint". / **Details:** no9churchst.com; Mon closed, Tue - Sat 9.30 pm, Sun closed; no Amex.*

The Oppo £47 [3][3][2]
13 Sheep Street CV37 6EF (01789) 269980
*This stalwart bistro is "a safe bet for a pre-theatre meal" – "probably the best in town". / **Details:** www.theoppo.co.uk; Mon - Thur 9.30 pm, Fri & Sat 11 pm, Sun closed; closed Sun; no Amex; Booking max 12 may apply.*

Rooftop Restaurant, Royal Shakespeare Theatre £42 [3][3][4]
Waterside CV37 6BB (01789) 403449
*Set in "fascinating" and "iconic" surroundings – the gods of the old theatre – the RSC's rooftop venue is a real "treat" offering "very thoughtful service and well-above-average food" for an arts venue. Try for an outside table in summer to enjoy splendid views across the river. / **Details:** www.rsc.org.uk/eat; 9.45 pm; no Amex.*

The Vintner £49 [2][2][3]
4-5 Sheep St CV37 6EF (01789) 297259
*Fans highlight the "interesting menu" and "great service" at this "excellent value" fixture, occupying a half-timbered building in the city centre; the sceptical view? – "the setting is pleasant, the rest is adequate but not outstanding". / **Details:** www.the-vintner.co.uk; 9 pm; no Amex.*

STUCKTON, HAMPSHIRE 2–3C

The Three Lions £60 [3][4][3]
Stuckton Rd SP6 2HF (01425) 652489
*Continued praise for Mike & Jayne Womersley's New Forest restaurant-with-rooms; front of house Jayne "always seems to be cheerful and welcoming", and chef Mike (ex-Lucknam Park) turns out food which is "invariably of a high standard". / **Details:** www.thethreelionsrestaurant.co.uk; off the A338; 9 pm, Fri & Sat 9.30 pm; closed Mon & Sun D; no Amex. / **Accommodation:** 7 rooms, from £105*

STUDLAND, DORSET 2–4C

Pig on the Beach £53 [3][3][5]
Manor House, Manor Road BH19 3AU
(01929) 450 288
*With its "utterly tranquil location, overlooking Studland Bay towards Poole and Sandbanks" from an old clifftop hotel, this "wonderful" representative of Robin Hutson's 'Pig' brand is "the nicest place ever" for fans. Dining itself takes place in a "well-heeled", very "romantic" conservatory, where "classic British fare is served in generous portions". Local sourcing is a feature: "all ingredients come from both its own walled garden and within 25 miles". The catch? – it ain't cheap. / **Details:** 9.30 pm.*

Shellbay £48 [4][2][4]
Ferry Road BH19 3BA (01929) 450363
*"The most perfect beach setting, with views across Poole Harbour towards Brownsea Island and Sandbanks" is the highlight of a visit to this "very cheerful, relaxed" venue with a minimal conservatory; on the menu? – "delicious fresh local seafood". / **Details:** www.shellbay.net; near the Sandbanks to Swanage ferry; 9 pm.*

SUDBURY, SUFFOLK 3–2C

Secret Garden £38 [3][3][3]
21 Friars Street CO10 2AA (01787) 372 030
"A great little piece of France in this small market town" – a "friendly, cosy and comfortable" spot where "the food is always delicious" (and sometimes

*even "exceptional"). Stop Press – the café is due to close in November 2016, for a major expansion into the neighbouring 15th century Buzzards Hall, with a view to "putting Sudbury on the [culinary] map". / **Details:** www.tsg.uk.net; 9 pm.*

Shillingfords, The Quay Theatre **£40** 544
Quay Lane CO10 2AN (01787) 211328
*"Carl Shillingford's pop-up restaurant at the Quay theatre, only opens Friday and Saturday night". "The menu is small, but delicious" – "wonderful foraged and locally sourced food, with three options to choose from: meat, veggie and fish". Importantly "prices don't break the bank". / **Details:** www.quaysudbury.com/shillingfords-quay; 11 pm.*

SUMMERHOUSE, COUNTY DURHAM 8–3B

Raby Hunt **£109** 554
DL2 3UD (01325) 374237
*James Close's "hidden gem is now getting the accolades it deserves": in October 2016 it was the only establishment to be elevated to two Michelin stars in this year's crop of awards. He runs "a really down-to-earth team" who make "wonderful use of local ingredients" to create food that's "delicious, subtle and well-presented, but also honest and wholesome rather than 'too-clever-by-half'". To cap it all, this restaurant with rooms is "beautifully located" too, in the Durham Dales. / **Details:** www.rabyhuntrestaurant.co.uk/; Mon & Tue closed, Wed - Sat 9.30 pm, Sun closed; closed Mon, Tue & Sun. / **Accommodation:** 2 rooms, from £125*

SUNBURY ON THAMES, SURREY 3–3A

Indian Zest **£44** 543
21 Thames Street TW16 5QF
(01932) 765 000
*"Definitely not the average Indian restaurant" – Manoj Vasaikar's "distinctive" colonial-style villa provides "courteous" service, and "delicious, beautifully presented", nouvelle-style dishes; "easy parking" too! / **Details:** www.indianzest.co.uk; midnight.*

SUNNINGDALE, BERKSHIRE 3–3A

Bluebells **£67** 343
Shrubs Hill SL5 0LE (01344) 622 722
*"From the outside, Bluebells looks very quiet and low-key, the sort of place which might provide a bog-standard family meal"… but, make no mistake – "the reality is far different" at this humble-looking roadhouse, boasting "polished" décor, "competent" service and "excellent food" (all at a "very reasonable" price). / **Details:** www.bluebells-restaurant.com; 9.45 pm; closed Mon & Sun D.*

SUNNINGHILL, BERKSHIRE 3–3A

Carpenter's Arms **£57** 444
78 Upper Village Rd SL5 7AQ (01344) 622763
*"French owners have turned what was an average, traditional pub into this Gallic heaven" – "you feel you are in France!" – offering "superb" cooking. / **Details:** www.laclochepub.com; 10 pm.*

SURBITON, SURREY 3–3A

The French Table **£60** 453
85 Maple Rd KT6 4AW (020) 8399 2365
*This "ever popular French gem lost in suburbia", delivers "a really enjoyable experience every time". The interior is "slightly poky", but that's the sole caveat: service is "with grace and kindness" with "excellent attention by owner Sarah" and the cuisine is both "faultless and sensibly priced". / **Details:** www.thefrenchtable.co.uk; 10.30 pm; closed Mon & Sun.*

SUTTON GAULT, CAMBRIDGESHIRE 3–1B

The Anchor **£47** 323
Bury Ln CB6 2BD (01353) 778537
*"On a (slightly "bleak") cut of the River Great Ouse", this "friendly and efficient" inn is "one of those places that is so remote you have to know about it"; those who do, praise its "slightly unusual menu options", which are "well cooked and presented". / **Details:** www.anchorsuttongault.co.uk; 7m W of Ely, signposted off B1381 in Sutton; Mon- Fri 9 pm, Sat 9.30 pm, Sun 8.30 pm; no Amex. / **Accommodation:** 4 rooms, from £80*

SWANSEA, SWANSEA 1–1C

Didier And Stephanie **£47** 442
56 Saint Helen's Rd SA1 4BE (01792) 655603
*Gallic cuisine that's "good, and good value for money" wins praise for Didier Suvé and Stephanie Danvel's city-centre outfit (although the ambience of this tiny, 20-seat room, took some flak this year). / **Details:** 9 pm; closed Mon & Sun; no Amex.*

Hanson At The Chelsea Restaurant **£49** 433
17 St Marys St SA1 3LH (01792) 466200
*"A family-run restaurant which never fails to please", and where chef/owner Andrew Hanson's pedigree – including a stint at The Ritz – "shows in the quality of the (fish-centric) food". / **Details:** www.hansonatthechelsea.co.uk; 9.30 pm; no Amex.*

Patricks With Rooms £46 [3][3][2]
638 Mumbles Rd SA3 4EA (01792) 360199
A chi-chi restaurant-with-rooms, overlooking Mumbles Bay, where a "warm welcome" is the prelude to some "excellent" food ("in spite of the price rises"); to sidestep the latter, why not try the "good value" lunch? / ***Details:*** *www.patrickswithrooms.com; in Mumbles, 1m before pier; 9.50 pm; closed Sun D. /* ***Accommodation:*** *10 rooms, from £110*

SYCHDYN, FLINTSHIRE 5–2A

Glasfryn £45 [3][3][4]
Raikes Lane CH7 6LR (01352) 750 500
"Another Brunning & Price but you know what you're getting"; this member of the characterful gastroboozer chain puts in a typically solid performance, combining "good value" food with expansive views of the town. "Handy for meals pre-Theatr Clwyd". / ***Details:*** *www.glasfryn-mold.co.uk; Mon - Sat 9.30 pm, Sun 9 pm.*

TAPLOW, BERKSHIRE 3–3A

The Astor Grill £75
Clivedon Road SL6 0JF (01628) 607 107
This newcomer in the Stable Block is the less formal eatery that has for so long seemed an opportunity at this famous country seat. Or at least it might be, were it not so brutally expensive. It opened mid-survey, and one early report – rather in line with negative newspaper reviews – suggests that in terms of value it's ferociously bad. / ***Details:*** *www.clivedenhouse.co.uk; 9.30 pm.*

André Garrett At Cliveden, Cliveden House £107 [3][3][5]
Cliveden Rd SL6 0JF (01628) 668561
"The glamour associated with Cliveden is in evidence in this atmospheric dining room": a "grand and stately" chamber with chandeliers, plus "amazing views" over the "gorgeous, groomed grounds", and – last but not least – fine cuisine from star chef, André Garrett. Reports are overwhelmingly positive, but in one or two there's a slight whiff of opportunity missed: "very promising, but didn't follow through"… "tried hard but a little lacking". Still the overall verdict is often of "one of the most memorable dining experiences in the UK". / ***Details:*** *www.clivedenhouse.co.uk; 9.45 pm; No trainers. /* ***Accommodation:*** *48 rooms, from £445*

TEDDINGTON, MIDDLESEX 3–3A

Imperial China £41 [3][1][2]
196-198 Stanley Rd TW11 8UE
(020) 8977 8679
"The local Chinese community flock" to this remote spot, long of note for its "fabulous" and "very reasonably priced" dim sum – but also for its "woeful" service; reports on the food were a tad more muted this year, however, with several finding it "a big disappointment after all the rave reviews". / ***Details:*** *www.imperialchinalondon.co.uk; 11 pm, Fri & Sat 11.30 pm, Sun 10 pm.*

Retro £58 [3][3][3]
114-116 High St TW11 8JB (020) 8977 2239
"A good place to celebrate in Teddington" – a Gallic fixture whose "great maître d' and staff" create a "very welcoming atmosphere", and where the bistro fare is "always good" – even one critic of "slightly self-conscious plating" says results are "very tasty". / ***Details:*** *www.retrobistrot.co.uk; Tue-Sat 11 pm; closed Mon & Sun D.*

TEIGNMOUTH, DEVON 1–3D

Crab Shack £42 [5][4][4]
3 Queen St TQ14 9HN (01626) 777956
"The husband catches it and the wife cooks it" at this seaside shack, "in a fantastic location on Teignmouth's back beach" ("get a seat on the terrace for a great sunset"). "The catch from the owner's fishing boats is exceptional" and "doesn't get any fresher" – "the crab is so good!!!!!" – and "you're by the water, and it smells amazing". ("The only problem is getting a table" and "they do observe the time allocation rather religiously…") / ***Details:*** *www.crabshackonthebeach.co.uk/; 9 pm; closed Mon & Tue; no Amex.*

TETBURY, GLOUCESTERSHIRE 2–2B

Gumstool Inn, Calcot Manor £49 [2][3][4]
GL8 8YJ (01666) 890391
A "delightful" and rather well-heeled hotel-brasserie offering "wonderful pub food" in "hearty portions"; even those not wowed by the cooking praise a "fabulous overall package" which "ticked all the boxes". / ***Details:*** *www.calcotmanor.co.uk; crossroads of A46 & A41345; 9.30 pm, Sun 9 pm; No jeans; No bookings; children: 12+ at dinner in Conservatory. /* ***Accommodation:*** *35 rooms, from £240*

THORNHAM, NORFOLK 6–3B

Eric's Fish & Chips £24 433
Drove Orchard, Thornham Rd PE36 6LS
(01485) 525 886
Titchwell Manor chef Eric Snaith's industrial-chic chippy makes "a superb addition to the coast": it serves "quite stunning (pearl-like) fish, the chips more than pass muster, and those battered gherkin slices are freakin' genius!" / ***Details:*** *www.ericsfishandchips.com; 9 pm.*

The Orange Tree £51 333
High St PE36 6LY (01485) 512 213
"Great after a morning on the marshes!" This jazzed-up coastal gastropub-with-rooms has a "buzzy" vibe fuelled by "interesting and substantial pub grub" – a minority find it "too complicated" but for most reporters it's "brilliant and inventive". / ***Details:*** *www.theorangetreethornham.co.uk; 9.30 pm; no Amex. /* ***Accommodation:*** *6 rooms, from £89*

THORNTON CLEVELEYS, LANCASHIRE 5–1A

Twelve Restaurant & Lounge Bar £49 443
Marsh Mill Village, Fleetwood Road North FY5 4JZ (01253) 821212
"One of the best places to eat near Blackpool, with good solid cooking that gets better with each visit." An "enforced refurbishment (after a lorry crashed into it) has helped soften what was always a cavernous barn of a place, and the food distinguishes itself by the clarity and cleanness of its flavours". / ***Details:*** *www.twelve-restaurant.co.uk; closed Mon, Tue-Sat D only, closed Sun D.*

THORNTON HOUGH, MERSEYSIDE 5–2A

The Lawn, Thornton Hall Hotel & Spa £62 444
Neston Rd CH63 1JF (0151) 336 3938
A "stunning" hotel dining room with "wood panelling, glittering chandeliers, stained-glass windows, a mosaic-style leather ceiling and quirky monkey wallpaper" – plus a "great soundtrack" (at least for Westlife fans!). New chef Ben Mounsey (ex-Fraiche) joined in spring 2016 – early signs are that he's maintaining the "incredible" standards set by his predecessor Matt Worswick. / ***Details:*** *www.thorntonhallhotel.com; 11 pm; need + to book.*

Red Fox £48 334
Liverpool Road CH64 7TL (0151) 353 2920
Riffing on a "typical Brunning & Price theme" – namely a "stunning location" (in a former country club) and a "good menu and selection of beers" – this pleasing link yearling "retains its individuality", with "lots of nooks and crannies to sit in". / ***Details:*** *www.brunningandprice.co.uk/redfox; Mon - Sat 10 pm, Sun 9.30 pm.*

THURNHAM, KENT 3–3C

Black Horse £47 323
Pilgrims Way ME14 3LD (01622) 737185
"The food is always great – fresh, inventive and of restaurant standard" at this characterful 18th-century inn with a "light-filled conservatory"; even reporters who found "all specials deleted and a chef-wanted sign" on their visit, received a "very creditable pub lunch with no signs of stress"! / ***Details:*** *www.blackhorsekent.co.uk.*

TILLINGTON, WEST SUSSEX 3–4A

The Horse Guards Inn £48 445
Upperton Rd GU28 9AF (01798) 342 332
"Breathing countryside rusticity" – this "lovely" informal inn (with rooms) is a real "gem" (The Good Pub Guide's 2017 Pub of the Year), with "adventurous" cuisine, based on "hyper-local sourcing". / ***Details:*** *www.thehorseguardsinn.co.uk; 9 pm, Fri & Sat 9.30 pm; no Amex.*

TITCHWELL, NORFOLK 6–3B

Titchwell Manor £55 433
PE31 8BB (01485) 210 221
In a "great setting" on the "beautiful" north Norfolk coast, the Snaith family's Victorian boutique hotel (est. 1988) provides an "inventive" fine dining experience; "maybe there are one or two elements too many in just a few dishes, but this is generally good food cooked with passion." / ***Details:*** *www.titchwellmanor.com; 9:30pm. /* ***Accommodation:*** *29 rooms, from £27*

TITLEY, HEREFORDSHIRE 2–1A

Stagg Inn £52 334
HR5 3RL (01544) 230221
*In a tiny village in Herefordshire, this popular pub has a big fanclub, despite being quite remote. There were some gripes this year about the prices ("the food may be good, but when we got the bill we felt it's not *that* good!"), but the main picture is of "consistently high-quality cooking". /* ***Details:*** *www.thestagg.co.uk; on B4355, NE of Kington; 9 pm; closed Mon & Tue. /* ***Accommodation:*** *7 rooms, from £100*

TOBERMORY, ARGYLL AND BUTE 9–3A

Cafe Fish Tobermory £47 442

The Pier PA75 6NU (01688) 301253
"Brilliant, fresh seafood" is the hallmark of this "small, very busy, noisy, but great" venue on the harbour; "try to get a table with a view of the sea" (but you'll "need to book well in advance"). / **Details:** *www.thecafefish.com; 10 pm; Closed Nov-Mar; no Amex; children: 14+ after 8 pm.*

TORQUAY, DEVON 1–3D

Elephant Restaurant & Brasserie £57 543

3-4 Beacon Ter, Harbourside TQ1 2BH
(01803) 200044
"The name suggests a sense of humour", but there's no mocking Simon Hulstone's "beautifully cooked and presented" cuisine ("most ingredients come from the Hulstone farm, and the freshness is quite evident"). For good buzz mid-week, Wednesday is 'free wine' day. / **Details:** *www.elephantrestaurant.co.uk; 9 pm; closed Mon & Sun; children: 14+ at bar.*

No 7 Fish Bistro £51 543

7 Beacon Terrace TQ1 2BH (01803) 295055
For an "amazing fish dinner" based on "top-notch" ingredients, this well-established harbour-view restaurant is just the ticket; even those who had "a long way to go" felt that it was "worth every mile". / **Details:** *www.no7-fish.com; 9.45 pm.*

TREEN, CORNWALL 1–4A

The Gurnard's Head £46 324

TR26 3DE (01736) 796928
It's "worth travelling past the many culinary delights of St Ives" to the "end of Cornwall" where this famous, "bright yellow" venue, in a "fabulous" cliff-top setting, offers "tasty cooking", "cheerful service", and "super pub atmosphere" ("particularly good on a cold and windy day, with the weather howling outside"). / **Details:** *www.gurnardshead.co.uk; on coastal road between Land's End & St Ives, near Zennor B3306; 9.15pm; 2015; no Amex. /* **Accommodation:** *7 rooms, from £7*

TROON, SOUTH AYRSHIRE 9–4B

MacCallum's Oyster Bar £41 433

The Harbour, Harbour Rd KA10 6DH
(01292) 319339
"The freshest, finest seafood for miles around" (plus "wonderful fish 'n' chips") wins an enduring fanclub for this local institution. / **Details:** *www.maccallumsoftroon.co.uk; 9.30 pm; closed Sun.*

TRURO, CORNWALL 1–4A

Tabb's £53 434

85 Kenwyn St TR1 3BZ (01872) 262110
"Nigel Tabb has been part of the local scene for a long time now", and continues to impress at this "special occasion" fine dining haunt, offering "beautifully cooked and presented" food, and a "romantic atmosphere". / **Details:** *www.tabbs.co.uk/; 9 pm; closed Mon & Sun D; no Amex.*

TUDDENHAM, SUFFOLK 3–1C

Tuddenham Mill, Tuddenham Mill Hotel £60 344

High St IP28 6SQ (01638) 713 552
"A little gem" in a "romantic" old mill overlooking a large pond; even those who quibble that the cooking is a "mite too clever for its own good" say it's "a beautiful location with good food". / **Details:** *www.tuddenhammill.co.uk; 9.15 pm. /* **Accommodation:** *15 rooms, from £205*

TUNBRIDGE WELLS, KENT 3–4B

Abergavenny Arms £45 444

Frant Road TN3 9DB (01892) 750233
"Recently refurbished at considerable expense, this imposing 15th-century former coaching house has been vastly improved by its new owner, retired jeweller Richard Burrell. There are three dining areas plus room for further diners on the split-level deck". "New head chef Giles Fulchester is doing great things in the kitchen, retaining traditional pub classics, alongside modern British cuisine with familiar yet unique flavour combinations." / **Details:** *www,abergavennyarms.co.uk; 10 pm.*

The Beacon Kitchen £43 434

Tea Garden Lane TN3 9JH (01892) 524252
"Pete the owner has created an exceptional destination" in his two years at this "superbly located" re-launched local pub, whose outside terrace boasts brilliant views over Tunbridge Wells. With food that's "fresh and beautifully cooked" plus "attentive" (and child-indulgent) staff, it's a "rare, all-rounder". / **Details:** *www.the-beacon.co.uk; Mon 5.00pm, Tues -Sat 11.30pm, Sun 6.00pm. /* **Accommodation:** *3 rooms, from £97*

The Black Pig £44 333

18 Grove Hill Road TN1 1RZ
(01892) 523 030
"A bit more grungy and laid-back than the slew of yummy mummy joints you find everywhere else here" – and none the worse for it – this ramshackle joint is "more like a country food pub than one in town"; solid marks, too, for its "tasty" and "good

*value" cuisine. / **Details:** www.theblackpig.net; Mon - Thur 9.30 pm, Fri & Sat 10 pm, Sun 9 pm; no Amex.*

Hotel du Vin et Bistro £62 233
Crescent Road TN1 2LY (01892) 320 749
*A Georgian-era former mansion, with a lovely, airy interior and the chain's hallmark Gallic-influenced fare and superior wine list; its ratings remain rather middling – like so many HdVs – but one regular insists "management here are pushing boundaries for the group and go to every effort". / **Details:** www.hotelduvin.com/locations/tunbridge-wel; 10 pm, Fri & Sat 10.30 pm; Booking max 10 may apply. / **Accommodation:** 34 rooms, from £120*

Sankey's Champagne & Oyster Bar, The Old Fishmarket £49 333
39 Mount Ephraim TN2 5TN (01892) 511422
*"Fresh, well-presented and tasty seafood" is the unsurprising forte of this intimate venture – the second outpost of a well-known local foodie empire, set in a bijou old fishmarket building in the heart of the Pantiles. / **Details:** www.sankeys.co.uk; 10pm, sun 8pm; closed Mon D & Sun D.*

Thackeray's £74 433
85 London Rd TN1 1EA (01892) 511921
*Why have Michelin taken a star from Richard Phillips's well-known Regency villa near the centre – by far the best-known place in town? All reports this year are of "good" or "excellent" cuisine, with the feeling that it's "on top form" currently. Top Tip – "the set lunch is incredible value for cooking of this complexity and has all the extras you'd expect at evening service." / **Details:** www.thackerays-restaurant.co.uk; 10.30 pm; closed Mon & Sun D.*

TYNEMOUTH, TYNE AND WEAR 8–2B

Longsands Fish Kitchen £41 333
27 Front St NE30 4DZ (0191) 272 8552
*"A great addition to the thriving Tynemouth street restaurant scene"; this "posh" fish 'n' chippie serves some "awesome" grub – either taken away, or enjoyed in the hip yet "crowded" dining room. / **Details:** www.longsandsfishkitchen.com/; 8pm.*

Riley's Fish Shack £32 535
King Edward's Bay NE30 4EB (0191) 257 1371
*"A unique location" – "an old shipping container with the side removed to give fantastic views onto the beach and sea at King Edward's Bay" (with "outdoor seating for the brave") – provides an enjoyably "hip" setting for this "well-executed concept". On the menu – "large portions of seafood, accompanied with bread or wraps and delicious salads", including "the best fish ever!" (well, nearly) with "amazing wood-fired-oven options". It's "fully licensed but expect plastic glasses" plus "cardboard plates and wooden forks". / **Details:** www.rileysfishshack.com; 10 pm.*

TYTHERLEIGH, DEVON 2–4A

Tytherleigh Arms £45 443
EX13 7BE (01460) 220214
*"Everything is cooked with flair" at this rural, family-run 16th century coaching inn, whose "lovely service" and "relaxing" style mean it's always "a joy to go there, whether for a special occasion, or every day". / **Details:** www.tytherleigharms.com; 9 pm, Fri & Sat 9.30 pm, Sun 8.30 pm; children: 5. / **Accommodation:** 0 rooms, from £6*

ULLSWATER, CUMBRIA 7–3D

Sharrow Bay £94 435
CA10 2LZ (01768) 486301
*This seminal country house hotel (often thought to be the UK's first) "still reigns". "Memorable cooking, with grace and flavour" is served from "a well-balanced menu", and "the dining experience is enhanced by the individual tables" – set in private alcoves with "breathtaking" views over Ullswater. / **Details:** www.sharrowbay.co.uk; on Pooley Bridge Rd towards Howtown; 9 pm; No jeans; children: 8+. / **Accommodation:** 17 rooms, from £355*

UPPER SLAUGHTER, GLOUCESTERSHIRE 2–1C

Lords of the Manor £101 323
Stow-on-the-Wold GL54 2JD (01451) 820243
*"A lovely place for a weekend or just a night away" – this Olde Englishe hotel in an archetypal Cotswolds setting is a natural choice for a "romantic" occasion (if not a budget one), with Richard Picard-Edwards's "delightful", traditional-ish cooking "from the canapés in the bar, to the petits fours". / **Details:** www.lordsofthemanor.com; 4m W of Stow on the Wold; 8.45 pm; D only, ex Sun open L & D; No jeans; children: 7+ at D in restaurant. / **Accommodation:** 26 rooms, from £199*

USK VALLEY, GWENT 2–2A

Cen, Celtic Manor Resort £52
Coldra Woods NP18 1HQ (01633) 410 262
*Former MasterChef finalist Larkin Cen launched his first restaurant at the Celtic Manor Resort in Newport in early 2016, serving pan-Asian dishes, from trendy steamed bao buns and Korean fried chicken to Peking duck. Scant early feedback, but all-round positive. / **Details:** www.celtic-manor.com/cen; 10 pm; Booking max 9 may apply.*

WADEBRIDGE, CORNWALL 1–3B

Bridge Bistro £43 332
4 Molesworth St PL27 7DA (01208) 815342
"Simplicity is key" at this husband-and-wife-owned bistro, where "the menu's short-ish, but the food's always good"; it recently expanded into the next door shoe shop, "but although the number of tables has pretty much doubled, it doesn't feel like they've over-extended". / ***Details:*** *www.bridgebistro.co.uk/; 9 pm; closed Sun D; no Amex.*

WALBERSWICK, SUFFOLK 3–1D

The Anchor £44 332
Main Street IP18 6UA (01502) 722 112
This gastroboozer-with-rooms, in a 1920s building near the beach, wins praise for its "very extensive beer list" (with "over 100 brews to choose from") and "very fresh" fish. / ***Details:*** *www.anchoratwalberswick.com; 9 pm. /* ***Accommodation:*** *10 rooms, from £110*

WARLINGHAM, SURREY 3–3B

Chez Vous £58 323
432 Limpsfield Rd CR6 9LA (01883) 620451
A hotel dining room acclaimed as the "best of its type in the area"; this said, even some fans feel that it's "becoming expensive for what it is" – with "further work needed on service and greeting" too. / ***Details:*** *www.chezvous.co.uk; 9.30 pm, Fri & Sat 10 pm; closed Mon & Sun D.*

WARWICK, WARWICKSHIRE 5–4C

The Art Kitchen £47 343
7 Swan St CV34 4BJ (01926) 494303
A "well-rounded, popular" Thai, in the city centre, "with excellent food, well prepared and beautifully served". / ***Details:*** *www.theartkitchen.com; 10 pm.*

Micatto £49 333
62 Market Pl CV34 4SD (01926) 403053
"Real Italian food, cooked with passion" and "served with a smile" is the reason why reporters "always love to visit" this town-centre spot, with open kitchen. / ***Details:*** *www.micatto.com; 10.30 pm, Sun 9 pm.*

Tailors £57 533
22 Market place CV34 4SL (01926) 410590
The "best meal in town" awaits at this compact venue – in days gone by a tailor's shop, but also at other times a fishmonger, butcher and casino! – offering a real "gourmet experience", with "beautifully presented, fresh cuisine". / ***Details:*** *www.tailorsrestaurant.co.uk; 9 pm; closed Mon & Sun; no Amex; No bookings; children: 12+ for dinner.*

WATERGATE BAY, CORNWALL 1–3B

The Beach Hut, Watergate Bay Hotel £46 333
On The Beach TR8 4AA (01637) 860543
"Anticipate sand on the floor, kids and a few dogs" (plus "wonderful sea views") at this "relaxed venue right on the beach". "The food is really excellent, beautifully cooked and so much better than you'd expect from a place of this size." / ***Details:*** *www.watergatebay.co.uk; 9 pm; no Amex. /* ***Accommodation:*** *69 rooms, from £105*

Fifteen Cornwall, Watergate Bay Hotel £78 345
TR8 4AA (01637) 861000
"You can't beat the view", at Jamie O's "lovely modern dining room", which has a "fantastic position", "overlooking the beach". One or two reports repeat the grumble that the place "trades on his name", but most accounts say it's "brilliant on every level, for breakfast, lunch or dinner, with amazing food, and connected staff who are superb with children". / ***Details:*** *www.fifteencornwall.co.uk; on the Atlantic coast between Padstow and Newquay; 9.15 pm; children: 4+ at D.*

WATERMILLOCK, CUMBRIA 7–3D

The Lake
CA11 0LP awaiting tel
Opening in spring 2107, what was formerly the Rampsbeck Hotel – a country house gem on the shore of Ullswater – will re-open having been totally redeveloped and expanded by the Another Place group (owners of Cornwall's Watergate Bay Hotel). Under chef Neil Haydock, food options will include a restaurant, The Living Space bar, plus a range of 'off-the-grid' options – we think that means picnics.

WATERNISH, HIGHLAND 9–2A

Loch Bay £53 544
1 Macleods Terrace IV55 8GA (01470) 592235
Talented chef Michael Smith, formerly of the acclaimed The Three Chimneys, took over this wee seafront venue in March 2016; according to early reports it's "an excellent new home for this well-known chef" – combining "fabulous" surroundings with "marvellous food". / ***Details:*** *www.lochbay-seafood-restaurant.co.uk; 22m from Portree via A87 and B886; 8m from Dunvegan; Mon closed, Tue - Sat 11 pm, Sun closed; closed Mon, Tue L, Wed L, Thu L, Fri L, Sat & Sun; no Amex; children: 8+ at D.*

WATH-IN-NIDDERDALE, NORTH YORKSHIRE 8–4B

Sportsman's Arms £51 434
HG3 5PP (01423) 711306
"This is not a 'here today, gone tomorrow' sort of place", but rather a solid country pub – in a beautiful, quite remote setting – which "has maintained high standards for many years", and which this year won praise for its "brilliant bar food". / ***Details:*** *www.sportsmans-arms.co.uk; take Wath Road from Pateley Bridge; 9 pm; closed Sun D; no Amex. /* ***Accommodation:*** *11 rooms, from £120*

WELLAND, WORCESTERSHIRE 2–1B

Inn at Welland £40 233
Hook Bank, Drake St WR13 6LN
(01684) 592317
Reporters are evenly divided on this "former pub in the middle of nowhere", which inspires a good deal of interest; while fans say that it's a "very relaxed" spot, where the frequently changing menu "never disappoints", critics find it merely "mediocre", and are "sad to think this is regarded as one of the best in the Malvern area". / ***Details:*** *www.theinnatwelland.co.uk/; 12.00 -2.30pm Lunch 6.00-9.30pm Dinner.*

WELLS, SOMERSET 2–3B

Goodfellows £56 443
5 - 5 B Sadler Street BA5 2RR
(01749) 673866
There's some "excellent cooking" (not least fish) to be had, if from a "limited menu", at Adam Fellows's diminutive modern European restaurant, near the cathedral. / ***Details:*** *www.goodfellowswells.co.uk; Mon & Tue closed, Wed & Thur 9.30 pm, Fri & Sat 10; closed Mon, Tue D & Sun.*

WELWYN, HERTFORDSHIRE 3–2B

Auberge du Lac, Brocket Hall £90 345
AL8 7XG (01707) 368888
After a rocky 2015, when it went into administration, Lord Palmerston's erstwhile estate now has new Chinese backers. This former hunting lodge by the lake, with al fresco table in summer, continues to enjoy a "unique setting" and has the potential to rebuild its position as a major dining destination. Feedback on the new régime is limited, but is extremely enthusiastic all round. / ***Details:*** *www.brocket-hall.co.uk; on B653 towards Harpenden; 9.30 pm; closed Mon & Sun L; No jeans; children: 12+. /* ***Accommodation:*** *16 rooms, from £175*

WEST BRIDGFORD, NOTTINGHAMSHIRE 5–3D

Larwood And Voce £45 333
Fox Road NG2 6AJ (0115) 981 9960
A "lively pub-restaurant, adjoining Trent Bridge cricket ground", where the gastro fare is "a cut above other pub menus" and "good value for money" too; the Sunday lunch attracts particular praise. / ***Details:*** *www.molefacepubcompany.co.uk/the-larwood-an; Mon - Sat 9 pm, Sun 5 pm; closed Sun D.*

WEST BYFLEET, SURREY 3–3A

London House £55 432
30 Station Approach KT14 6NF
(01932) 482026
MasterChef semi-finalist Ben Piette's popular five-year-old relocated to West Byfleet (Station Approach) in April 2016; reports during the soft opening praised the "amazing food" and "low-key and very stylish environment". / ***Details:*** *www.londonhouseoldwoking.co.uk; 10 pm.*

WEST CLANDON, SURREY 3–3A

The Onslow Arms £46 333
The Street GU4 7TE (01483) 222447
The "straightforward" food is a cut above basic pub fare, and portions are "generous without being OTT" at this "unpretentious" village pub, which has a "lovely garden". / ***Details:*** *www.onslowarmsclandon.com; 9.30 pm, Fri & Sat 10 pm; children: 18+ after 7.30pm.*

WEST HOATHLY, WEST SUSSEX 3–4B

The Cat Inn £46 443
North Lane RH19 4PP (01342) 810369
In a "beautiful" village location, a "very welcoming" pub-with-rooms where the staff "always seem to go that extra mile"; "the food is pretty good too!" – "very popular, and deservedly so." / ***Details:*** *www.catinn.co.uk; 9 pm, Fri-Sat 9.30 pm; closed Sun D; no Amex; children: 7+. /* ***Accommodation:*** *4 rooms, from £110*

WEST MALLING, KENT 3–3C

The Swan £54 322
35 Swan St ME19 6JU (01732) 521910
A 15th-century coaching inn, with a stylish, muted interior, numerous private dining rooms and a "really comfortable courtyard"; the menu can play it safe, "it's clearly working really hard, and on the up". / ***Details:*** *www.theswanwestmalling.co.uk; 11 pm, Sun 7 pm.*

WEST MERSEA, ESSEX 3–2C

The Company Shed £36 523
129 Coast Rd CO5 8PA (01206) 382700
"Don't expect anything except very fresh fish and shellfish" ("incredible oysters"), if you visit this "really fun, if unconventional" little seaside legend (it really is a shed), where you "bring your own bread/wine etc" – an experience that's "worth every penny". "Order a day ahead for the prepared crab". / ***Details:*** *www.thecompanyshed.co; 4 pm; L only, closed Mon; No bookings.*

West Mersea Oyster Bar £38 433
Coast Rd CO5 8LT (01206) 381600
"Slightly more salubrious than the rickety old (and more famous) Company Shed just down the road", this nonetheless rustic spot enjoys a "real seaside buzz"; "order a plate of oysters and sit back smug in the knowledge that people in London are paying four times the amount" for the same thing! / ***Details:*** *www.westmerseaoysterbar.co.uk; 8.30 pm; Sun-Thu closed D; no Amex; No shorts.*

WEST WITTON, NORTH YORKSHIRE 8–4B

The Wensleydale Heifer £63 323
Main St DL8 4LS (01969) 622322
"An aquatic food oasis some 80 miles from the sea!" "If you can't get to the Yorkshire coast this little gem is a worthy substitute" – "a relaxed and friendly" village pub (with rooms). It can feel "crammed in" and one or two doubters find it "decidedly average", but most reports are full of praise for its "exciting and creative" cooking, notably of fish. / ***Details:*** *www.wensleydaleheifer.co.uk; 9.30 pm.* / ***Accommodation:*** *13 rooms, from £130*

WESTFIELD, EAST SUSSEX 3–4C

The Wild Mushroom £47 443
Woodgate House TN35 4SB (01424) 751137
Offering "fresh local food cooked beautifully" and a "lovely garden for drinks and coffee", this outpost of Paul Webbe's empire in a converted farmhouse is a notably consistent sort of place; "interesting events" too – some in keeping with the foraging ethos. / ***Details:*** *www.webbesrestaurants.co.uk; Mon & Tue closed, Wed - Sat 9.30 pm, Sun 2 pm; closed Mon, Tue & Sun D.*

WESTLETON, SUFFOLK 3–1D

The Westleton Crown £46 322
The Street IP17 3AD (01728) 648777
In "the heart of the charming village of Westleton, the Crown has a vibrant menu and lovely old rooms" – plus, for dining, "a large conservatory tacked on to the back". Aside from some gripes about "over-ambitious dishes" and "toppish prices", fans say that "everything about the place is good", even if "the beige-trouser-brigade do tend to take over a bit!" / ***Details:*** *www.westletoncrown.co.uk; 9.30 pm.* / ***Accommodation:*** *0 rooms, from £34*

WESTON SUPER MARE, SOMERSET 2–2A

Cove £43 334
Birnbeck Road BS23 2BX (01934) 418 217
This "friendly", fish-centric venture is "definitely a culinary high point for WSM"; it's no criticism to say, though, that "the biggest winner is the location (a quiet stretch of the promenade) with views across the sea out to the islands of Steep Holm and Flat Holm". / ***Details:*** *9 pm, Sun 5 pm; closed Mon.*

WETHERBY, WEST YORKSHIRE 5–1C

Piccolino 443
Wetherby Rd LS22 5AY (01937) 579797
"No garlic bread, no pizzas, just completely authentic cuisine" – is a surprise find at this "splendidly Italian" branch of the national chain where "everthing is carefully sourced, from the olive oil to the coffee", to the "inexplicably cheap wine", and run with "idiosyncratic passion" by a husband-and-wife team. / ***Details:*** *www.piccolinorestaurants.co.uk; 11 pm.*

WEYBRIDGE, SURREY 3–3A

Osso Buco £42 353
23 Church St KT13 8DE (01932) 849949
Service often scores highly at this well-regarded local, offering "great Italian food" (including the nippers' menu), and at very "good value" prices too. / ***Details:*** *www.ossobuco.co.uk; 10.30 pm, Fri & Sat 11 pm; closed Sun.*

WEYMOUTH, DORSET 2–4B

Crab House Café £48 444
Ferrymans Way DT4 9YU (01305) 788 867
"Perennially good, fresh and imaginative fish dishes" (not least the "best oysters") are the hallmark of this atmospheric spot in a "fabulous" village location. "Pick a warm summer day and you're in paradise", sitting in the lush garden overlooking the oyster beds. / ***Details:*** *www.crabhousecafe.co.uk; overlooking the Fleet Lagoon, on the road to Portland; Mon & Tue closed, Wed & Thur 8.30 pm, Fri 9 pm, Sa; closed Mon, Tue & Sun D; no Amex; 8+ deposit of £10 per head.*

Les Enfants Terrible £41 **4 3 4**
19 Custom House Quay DT4 8BG
(01305) 772270
"Beautifully situated next to the Old Harbour", Eric Tavernier's straightforward bistro provides "very well prepared and very affordable" Gallic cooking, especially "fish that's as fresh as it gets, straight from the fishermen!" / ***Details:*** *www.les-enfants-terribles.co.uk/; 11 pm.*

WHALLEY, LANCASHIRE 5–1B

Benedicts of Whalley £35 **4 3 3**
1 George St BB7 9TH (01254) 824 468
A bustling, continental-style café and deli in a charming village – "always busy" ("you may have to queue"), especially around brunch and teatime, thanks to its "great range of savoury snacks, as well as the usual sandwiches and cakes". / ***Details:*** *www.benedictsofwhalley.co.uk; 7.30 pm, Sun 4 pm.*

Food by Breda Murphy £43 **5 4 4**
41 Station Rd BB7 9RH (01254) 823446
Breda Murphy's marvellous deli/café serves up "anything from fine dining to delicious delicatessen goodies – all with an Irish twist". It's "always busy" (sometimes "invaded by ladies in tweed"), but the victuals are "very edible", and the terrace is an especially "nice place to spend time when the sun shines on the Ribble Valley". / ***Details:*** *www.foodbybredamurphy.com; 5.30 pm; closed Mon & Sun, Tue-Sat D; no Amex.*

The Three Fishes £47 **3 4 3**
Mitton Rd BB7 9PQ (01254) 826888
The first of the Ribble Valley Inns – "this lovely, ancient village pub set in the North Lancashire valley" provides "interesting, locally sourced food in comfortable surroundings" and "staff who have a warm and friendly attitude". / ***Details:*** *www.thethreefishes.com; 9 pm, Fri & Sat 9.30 pm.*

WHITBY, NORTH YORKSHIRE 8–3D

Magpie Café £40 **5 3 2**
14 Pier Rd YO21 3PU (01947) 602058
"Best fish 'n' chips in the country!" – this seaside café is the UK's most famous chippy, and on all of the many accounts we receive on it, remains on "magnificent" form. Some regulars feel "the secret is to go for the specials (which reflect the chef's interests and the catch-of-the-day)", but others declare that although "there's a huge choice of locally caught fish, I've never had anything other than the brilliant cod or haddock!" "You're rather squashed in, and the queue can be a pain", but no-one cares. / ***Details:*** *www.magpiecafe.co.uk; 9 pm; no Amex; No bookings at lunch.*

Star Inn The Harbour
Langborne Rd YO21 1YN awaiting tel
The Star Inn The Harbour – part of Andrew Pern's well-known group – will be a brasserie-style seafood restaurant located overlooking the town's harbour, with views up to Whitby Abbey.

Trenchers £41 **4 3 3**
New Quay Rd YO21 1DH (01947) 603212
Though with nothing like the profile of the Magpie, this "comfortable", "efficient" and "friendly" fixture, with boothed seating, "scores highly in every department", and – being "less than a cricket pitch away from the quay" – the choice of fish is "magnificent". / ***Details:*** *www.trenchersrestaurant.co.uk; 8.30 pm; May need 7+ to book.*

WHITE WALTHAM, BERKSHIRE 3–3A

Beehive £55 **3 3 2**
Waltham Rd SL6 3SH (01628) 822877
Newly taken over by Dominic Chapman, ex-of the acclaimed Royal Oak nearby, and now turning out some "delicious food", this red-brick venture is "much improved on the old pub" that formerly stood here. / ***Details:*** *www.thebeehivewhitewaltham.com; 2.30pm for lunch and 9.30pm for dinner Mon-Fri, 9..*

WHITEBROOK, MONMOUTHSHIRE 2–2B

The Whitebrook, Restaurant with Rooms £83 **4 4 3**
NP25 4TX (01600) 860254
"Tucked away in the Monmouthshire countryside", Chris Harrod's long-famous inn (he dropped 'The Crown' from its name in recent times) is "not the easiest place to find, but worth the effort". "It's ordinary-looking from the outside, but evidently older once you get in", and the food is "superb, with subtle flavours that are utterly delicious". "Along with its craft ales and fine wines, it's a perfect bolt-hole after a busy week – pure comfort for the soul!" / ***Details:*** *www.thewhitebrook.co.uk; 2m W of A466, 5m S of Monmouth; 9 pm; closed Mon; children: 12+ for D. /* ***Accommodation:*** *8 rooms, from £145*

WHITSTABLE, KENT 3–3C

Crab & Winkle £46 **3 3 4**
South Quay, Whitstable Harbour CT5 1AB
(01227) 779377
"Ideally located for a seafood restaurant", with "amazing views of the harbour from its huge windows", this café-style spot is "highly recommended" by reporters owing to its "excellently prepared and presented" fish. / ***Details:*** *www.crabandwinklerestaurant.co.uk; 9.30 pm, Sun 4.30 pm; closed Mon & Sun D; no Amex; children: 6.*

East Coast Dining Room £50 433
101 Tankerton Rd CT5 2AJ (01227) 281180
"A local gem" in a row of shops in Tankerton with a major following from Kent and into London. "Simple food is transformed into something special" in a "beautifully relaxed environment". Top Tip – "great value set lunch". / **Details:** *www.eastcoastdiningroom.co.uk; 9 pm, Fri-Sat 9.30 pm; closed Mon, Tue, Wed D & Sun D.*

Elliots @ No.1 Harbour Street £44 332
1 Harbour Street CT5 1AG (01227) 276608
"In a town full of good restaurants", this popular and understated café near the beach is "one of the best options for brunch/lunch" locally, courtesy of the solid food from ex-Dove-Inn-at-Dargate-chef Phill MacGregor. / **Details:** *Mon-Wed 4 pm, Thu-Sat 11 pm, Sun 4pm.*

JoJo £37 554
2 Herne Bay Rd CT5 2LQ (01227) 274591
"Exquisite tapas-style food" with "fantastic combinations and flavours" is the main draw to this easy-going cliff-top restaurant, which is also noted for its "lovely" staff; minor caveat? – it can seem a bit "noisy" ("the music's annoying if you're sitting by the speaker"). / **Details:** *www.jojosrestaurant.co.uk; 11pm; closed Mon, Tue, Wed L & Sun D; Cash only.*

Krishna £28 432
49 Old Bridge Road CT5 1RD
(01227) 282639
It's rather "out of the way by Whitstable train station", and the exterior is unprepossessing, but this "real Indian" wins raves from locals for its "expertly cooked food, with dishes not seen elsewhere". / **Details:** *www.krishnarestaurant.co.uk; 9.30 pm, Fri & Sat 10.30 pm.*

Lobster Shack £23 323
East Quay CT5 1AB (01227) 771923
"Share a native lobster when in stock", "fantastic line-caught fish", or "an amazing value plateau of fruits de mer" – all "served right on the sea front" (there's "a great view") – at this descriptively named outfit. / **Details:** *www.eqvenue.com/restaurant; 9 pm.*

Pearson's Arms £49 324
The Horsebridge, Sea Wall CT5 1BT
(01227) 272005
In a "fantastic location overlooking the Thames Estuary", and with "fabulous" views from the upstairs room, Richard Phillips's combined pub and fine dining spot continues to garner praise, particularly (Top Tip) for its "excellent value set lunch". / **Details:** *www.pearsonsarmsbyrichardphillips.co.uk; 9 pm, Fri & Sat 9.30 pm, Sun 8.30 pm; closed Mon D.*

Samphire £47 443
4 High Street CT5 1BQ (01227) 770075
This "very busy" bistro, in the town centre, combines "superb service", an "interesting menu using locally sourced products", and "reasonable prices"; "not unique... but very special". / **Details:** *www.samphirewhitstable.co.uk; 10 pm; no Amex.*

The Sportsman £54 555
Faversham Road CT5 4BP (01227) 273370
"From the outside you would think you had arrived at a run down pub", but Stephen Harris's legendary, if "shabby looking" coastal tavern – "on the North Kent marshes near Whitstable" – is nigh on "the perfect pub". Few establishments can match its consistency – "they get it spot on, every time, all of the time" – be it the "chilled-out" atmosphere; the utterly "charming" service; or his "inspired", "honest", "strongly-flavoured" cooking – most particularly "out-of-this-world fish dishes". "Go – just go!" Top Menu Tips – "magnificent native oysters" and his "pitch-perfect slip sole with seaweed butter: the most delicious fish dish ever... and he makes his own butter!" / **Details:** *www.thesportsmanseasalter.co.uk; Mon closed, Tue - Sat 9 pm, Sun 2.45 pm; closed Mon & Sun D; no Amex; children: 18+ in main bar.*

Wheelers Oyster Bar £47 555
8 High Street CT5 1BQ (01227) 273311
"Like eating in Granny's parlour... if Granny cooked fish to perfection"; the town's oldest restaurant (est. 1856) is "one of the funkiest places you can eat in" – "a tiny room with only 14–16 seats" serving an "interesting menu of excellent seafood", and "BYO helps make it a very good-value experience". Let's hope they don't wreck it with a mid-2016 refurbishment, bringing a cocktail bar and "allegedly even toilets on site". / **Details:** *www.wheelersoysterbar.com; Mon & Tue 9 pm, Wed closed, Thur 9 pm, Fri 9.30 pm; closed Wed; Cash only.*

Whitstable Oyster Fishery Co. £61 434
Royal Native Oyster Stores, Horsebridge CT5 1BU (01227) 276856
"Fresh, succulent seafood in an atmospheric, old, timbered shed – love it!" This famous haunt is "fantastically located on the beach" and makes a wonderfully "quirky" destination for some of the "freshest oysters around". / **Details:** *www.whitstableoystercompany.com; 8.45 pm, Fri 9.15 pm, Sat 9.45 pm, Sun 8.15 pm.*

WILLIAN, HERTFORDSHIRE 3–2B

The Fox £49 333
SG6 2AE (01462) 480233
After a recent refurb, this "well located" village gastroboozer is now a "very attractive" place to be; on the food front, "everything is always of a

*high standard" – a combination ensuring that it's invariably "very busy" ("and deservedly so"). / **Details:** www.foxatwillian.co.uk; 1 mile from junction 9 off A1M; 9 pm; closed Sun D. / **Sustainability:** ★★★*

WINCHCOMBE, GLOUCESTERSHIRE 2–1C

5 North Street £67 5 4 3

5 North St GL54 5LH (01242) 604566

*Marcus & Kate Ashenford's "tiny gastronomic haven" in an "intimate" old building (a former tea room) is a classic "husband cooks and wife is front of house" kind of place, and consistently delivers an "unpretentious" yet "fabulous" experience. Service is "friendly and welcoming" and the food is "honest, generous, creative, and stylishly plated" ("even from the reassuringly limited menu, we still found choosing difficult!") / **Details:** www.5northstreetrestaurant.co.uk; 9 pm; closed Mon, Tue L & Sun D; no Amex.*

WINCHESTER, HAMPSHIRE 2–3D

The Black Rat £57 4 4 4

88 Chesil St SO23 0HX (01962) 844465

*"Always interesting food, without being over-fussy or pretentious" achieves consistently above-average ratings for this acclaimed pub conversion, on the outskirts of the city-centre. / **Details:** www.theblackrat.co.uk; 9.30 pm; closed weekday L; children: 18+ except weekend L.*

The Chesil Rectory £59 3 4 4

1 Chesil St S023 0HU (01962) 851555

*In terms of elegance, this "beautiful" and "romantic" destination is arguably the town's best, and "friendly" service and highly rated food complete a positive picture. Top Tip – "the pre-theatre fixed price menu is very good indeed". / **Details:** www.chesilrectory.co.uk; 9.30 pm, Sat 10 pm, Sun 9 pm; children: 12+ at D.*

Hotel du Vin et Bistro £55 2 2 4

14 Southgate Street SO23 9EF
(01962) 896 329

*HdV's original outpost continues to put in an up-and-down performance – even fans concede that service is still a "bit hit and miss", and reports on the food are likewise mixed; one constant as you might hope – some good finds on the wine list. / **Details:** www.hotelduvin.com; Mon - Thur 10 pm, Fri & Sat 10.30 pm, Sun 9.30 am; Booking max 12 may apply. / **Accommodation:** 24 rooms, from £145*

The Avenue, Lainston House Hotel £83 3 3 3

Woodman Ln SO21 2LT (01962) 776088

*Chef Olly Rouse (late of Coworth Park) turns out "excellent" tasting menus and "the heartiest, tastiest breakfast bar none" at this "very comfortable" country house hotel and adjoining cookery school; prices do, however, remain a sticking point. / **Details:** www.lainstonhouse.com; 9.30 pm, Fri & Sat 10 pm. / **Accommodation:** 50 rooms, from £245*

The Old Vine £45 3 3 3

8 Great Minster Street SO23 9HA
(01962) 854616

*This beamed 18th-century inn, near the cathedral, makes a cosy place for a local real ale; the food elicited scant commentary this year, though one reporter claimed that the bar snacks compared favourably to the dining room's bistro-style fare. / **Details:** www.oldvinewinchester.com; Mon - Sat 9.30 pm, Sun 9 pm; children: 6+. / **Accommodation:** 5 rooms, from £100*

Rick Stein £58 3 3 2

7 High Street SO23 9JX (01962) 353535

*Fans are "absolutely delighted not to have to go all the way to Padstow for delicious seafood" now that the Stein empire has an outpost in the town. It's not as highly rated as when it first opened last year – inevitable criticisms are creeping in that it's "cashing in on its name: OK but nothing special" – but, for the most part, it earns kudos for "at last providing a local restaurant that has really fresh fish and knows how to cook it". / **Details:** www.rickstein.com; 10 pm. / **Sustainability:** ★★★*

River Cottage Canteen £46 3 2 3

Abbey Mill, Abbey Mill Gardens SO23 9GH
(01962) 457747

*"It's Hugh Fearnley-Whittingstall personified!" – "noisy", "casual", but all about "interesting (local) food" – say fans of his venture, in a striking mill near the cathedral. Some reviews are more reserved: "I found it variable: strange, imaginative combinations in dishes, but made with no finesse". / **Details:** www.rivercottage.net/canteens/winchester; Mon closed, Tue - Sat 9.15 pm, Sun 4 pm.*

Wykeham Arms £54 3 2 5

75 Kingsgate St SO23 9PE (01962) 853834

*"A good, old pub like it should be!" – this "old-fashioned Victorian hostelry near the cathedral" has a "unique ambience" and it's "always busy with a great mix of locals and visitors". "Delicious food" and "sometimes amateur service" complete the picture. / **Details:** www.wykehamarmswinchester.co.uk; between Cathedral and College; 9.15 pm; children: 14+. / **Accommodation:** 14 rooms, from £139*

WINDERMERE, CUMBRIA 7–3D

First Floor Café, Lakeland Limited £34 332
Alexandra Buildings LA23 1BQ (015394) 47116
*"Attuned to the psychology of the middle-class shoppers who want a break from their status-enhancing kitchen products" – bought in the downstairs cookware shop – this mountain-view café, helmed by ex-Gavroche chef Steven Doherty, mixes a "solid range of light lunches and snacks" with a "nice sofa area to read the papers" afterwards. / **Details:** www.lakeland.co.uk; 6 pm, Sat 5 pm, Sun 4 pm; L only; no Amex.*

Gilpin Hotel £88 433
Crook Rd LA23 3NE (01539) 488818
*A well-established Lakeland hotel with several small dining areas; fans say that it's "definitely worthy of awards" from chef Hrishikesh Desai's "absolutely outstanding food" to the "very good" service and ambience, while others are a tad more measured in their praise. / **Details:** www.thegilpin.co.uk; 9.15 pm; No jeans; children: 7+. / **Accommodation:** 20 rooms, from £255*

Holbeck Ghyll £94 224
Holbeck Lane LA23 1LU (01539) 432375
*"With wonderful views across Windermere", this "formal" dining room is part of an old-fashioned hunting lodge – nowadays a luxurious country house hotel. Despite being one of the better-known culinary destinations in the Lakes, it inspired strikingly little feedback this year: such as there was however, avoided the critiques of last year, praising its "romantic" style and "creative menu". / **Details:** www.holbeckghyll.com; 3m N of Windermere, towards Troutbeck; 9.30 pm; No jeans; children: 7+ at D. / **Accommodation:** 33 rooms, from £190*

Hooked £47 542
Ellerthwaite Square LA23 1DP (01539) 448443
*For "superb fish, simply cooked and served fresh", head to this "unpretentious" spot, where the "small menu" is "cooked with precision", and where "the bonhomie of the (Antipodean) owner adds to the experience". / **Details:** www.hookedwindermere.co.uk/; Mon closed, Tue - Sun 10.30pm; D only, closed Mon; no Amex.*

Linthwaite House £77 333
Crook Rd LA23 3JA (015394) 88600
*Change may be in the air at this Edwardian country house hotel – set in 14 acres, with a fine Lakeland location overlooking Lake Windermere – which achieved solid ratings in this year's survey. In April, it was acquired by a South African group (the Leeu Collection), and August 2016 saw the appointment of a new chef, David Aspin. / **Details:** www.linthwaite.com; near Windermere golf club; 9 pm; No jeans; children: 7+ at D. / **Accommodation:** 30 rooms, from £180*

The Samling £94 444
Ambleside Road LA23 1LR (01539) 431922
*"New Chef. New Menu. WOW!" This well-known culinary hotspot overlooking Windermere is maintaining its foodie reputation under new chef, Nick Edgar, and although it did again inspire the odd 'off' report, a majority of "divine" meals from the "tasting menus" ("generous helpings" too) bolstered ratings here this year. Further change is afoot as "the current dining room will be greatly extended in late 2016". / **Details:** www.thesamlinghotel.co.uk; take A591 from town; 9.30 pm. / **Accommodation:** 11 rooms, from £300*

WINDSOR, BERKSHIRE 3–3A

Al Fassia £42 443
27 St Leonards Rd SL4 3BP (01753) 855370
*"They've done their best to 'Moroccan-ise" the shop-shaped space" at this well-established, "no-frills" north African – "a little oasis away from the crowds of the tourist trail", providing "warm and welcoming service and "flavourful food in substantial portions". / **Details:** www.alfassiarestaurant.com; 10.15 pm, Fri & Sat 10.30 pm, Sun 9.45 pm; closed Mon L.*

Meimo £37 343
69-70 Peascod St SL4 1DE (01753) 862 222
*"It's like being back in Morocco… without the warmth" – this "buzzy" spot provides "obliging service" and "excellent" north African and Mediterranean dishes. / **Details:** www.meimo.co.uk; 10pm, Fri - Sat 10.30pm.*

WINTERINGHAM, LINCOLNSHIRE 5–1D

Winteringham Fields £107 554
1 Silver St DN15 9ND (01724) 733096
*"We travel miles, spend hundreds on trains and taxis to get there, but it's worth it!" – Colin McGurran's "comfortable and stylish" retreat, near the banks of the Humber, is "back to its best after a few years in the wilderness". In particular, its 7-course and 9-course tasting menus are "exceptional", with "a fabulous wine selection" and "staff are very professional, knowledgeable, and charming". "We love it and just wish we lived nearer!" / **Details:** www.winteringhamfields.co.uk; 4m SW of Humber Bridge; 9 pm; closed Mon & Sun; no Amex; practically no walk-ins – you must boo. / **Accommodation:** 11 rooms, from £180*

WISWELL, LANCASHIRE 5–1B

Freemasons at Wiswell £65 554
8 Vicarage Fold Clitheroe BB7 9DF
(01254) 822218
"Steve Smith continues to lead the vanguard of haute gastronomy in the Ribble Valley", at this nationally notable and "attractive pub", "in a tiny village alley" – "a brilliant gourmet destination high on the moors of East Lancashire", which local cognoscenti feel "knocks Northcote into second place". While the style is "unpretentious, with wooden tables", this is "a class act all round": "service is exemplary with a sommelier on hand", and the dishes are "well thought out", "skilfully executed" and highly "memorable". / ***Details:*** *www.freemasonswiswell.co.uk; Tue-Thu 9 pm, Fri & Sat 9.30 pm, Sun 8 pm; closed Mon & Tue; no Amex; 8+ have to pre-order.*

WITHYHAM, EAST SUSSEX 3–3B

Dorset Arms £48 334
Buckhurst Park TN7 4BD (01892) 770278
A "lovely old pub" (ex-Harveys) which was recently re-acquired and revamped by longtime owners the Sackvilles; from the "brilliant food, service and charm" to the "great views" it's really "a must!" / ***Details:*** *Mon - Sat 9 pm, Sun 8 pm.*

WITNEY, OXFORDSHIRE 2–2D

Eynsham Hall £48 333
OX29 6PN (01993) 885200
"Worth a visit for the splendour of the setting!" – this "large 18th century Cotswolds country house (and erstwhile police training centre)" is a "fantastic" old pile. Compared with all the grandeur, its brasserie (in the former billiard room) is very straightforward, with affordable bistro cooking that's not at all bad. / ***Details:*** *www.eynshamhall.com/; 10pm.*

WIVETON, NORFOLK 6–3C

Wiveton Bell £46 322
Blakeney Rd NR25 7TL (01263) 740 101
"Quirky", "crowded" gastroboozer with a good garden, which continues to please all who comment on it with its "fantastic local food", and "lovely" location on the village green. / ***Details:*** *www.wivetonbell.co.uk; 9 pm; no Amex. /* ***Accommodation:*** *4 rooms, from £75*

WOBURN, BUCKINGHAMSHIRE 3–2A

Birch £49 332
20 Newport Rd MK17 9HX (01525) 290295
"A very good country restaurant" – a converted pub with modern décor and a conservatory, which has built up a solid reputation for its "imaginative" menu and "excellent" cooking. / ***Details:*** *www.birchwoburn.com; between Woburn and Woburn Sands on the Newport rd; 9.30 pm; closed Sun D.*

Paris House £123 333
Woburn Park MK17 9QP (01525) 290692
"An absolutely fantastic setting" – a Tudor building on the Woburn Estate – adds to the charms of Phil Fanning's well-established dining room, especially for romance. It inspired surprisingly limited feedback this year (and also saw the loss of its Michelin star in October 2016), but the few reports we have are full of nothing but praise of "superb" cuisine. / ***Details:*** *www.parishouse.co.uk; on A4012; Mon & Tue closed, Wed & Thur 8.30 pm, Fri & Sat 9 ; closed Mon, Tue & Sun D.*

WOKING, SURREY 3–3A

The Inn West End £52 334
42 Guildford Rd GU24 9PW (01276) 858652
"A recent makeover has improved the ambience of this great inn". "Once a pub with pretensions, this is now an upwardly-aspiring restaurant-with-rooms, with a wine business attached". Perhaps it's "a little on the expensive side", but this is "quality food, closer to fine dining than pub grub". / ***Details:*** *www.the-inn.co.uk; Mon - Sat 9.30 pm, Sun 9 pm; No trainers; Yes; children: 5+.*

WOLLATON, NOTTINGHAMSHIRE 5–3D

Cods Scallops £27 532
170 Bramcote Ln NG8 2QP (0115) 985 4107
An award-winning chippie with a wet fish counter, which defies its nondescript, suburban setting with "first-class food", incorporating "a very large selection of fish and shellfish". In summer 2016 it opened a larger spin-off in Carrington. / ***Details:*** *www.codsscallops.com; 9 pm, Fri & Sat 9.30 pm; closed Sun.*

WOLVERCOTE, OXFORDSHIRE 2–2D

The Trout Inn £46 224
195 Godstow Rd OX2 8PN (01865) 510930
"Location, location, and location" underpin the popularity of this riverside pub – an old haunt of Inspector Morse ("but he would not like the crowds and busy-ness"); it serves "generous

*pub grub that's not too expensive". / **Details:** www.thetroutoxford.co.uk; 2m from junction of A40 & A44; 10 pm, Sat 10.30 pm, Sun 9 pm.*

WOLVERHAMPTON, WEST MIDLANDS 5–4B

Bilash £52 443
2 Cheapside WV1 1TU (01902) 427762
*It's been going for over 20 years, but Sitab Khan's well-run, traditional stalwart remains a beacon of "always reliable and interesting" Indian cooking in the Wolverhampton area. / **Details:** www.thebilash.co.uk; 10.30 pm; closed Sun.*

WOODBRIDGE, SUFFOLK 3–1D

The Table £42 334
Quay St IP12 1BX (01394) 382428
*A "lively, laidback venue" where the food is consistent (if a trifle "average" for sceptics) and whose courtyard garden makes it "very popular on a sunny day". / **Details:** www.thetablewoodbridge.co.uk; 9.30 pm, Sun 3 pm.*

WOODLANDS, HAMPSHIRE 2–4C

Terravina, Hotel Terravina £72 353
174 Woodlands Rd, Netley Marsh, New Forest SO40 7GL (023) 8029 3784
*Wine guru, "Gerrard Bassett has chosen an extensive wine list with many vintages from small producers": this, plus "lovely, attentive but relaxed service" (overseen by wife Nina), are the twin highlights at their New Forest hotel dining room (which will be 10 next year). The food – not the main point – can seem a tad "over-fussy and pricey" – but is uniformly thought to be "well-cooked". / **Details:** www.hotelterravina.co.uk; 9.30 pm. / **Accommodation:** 11 rooms, from £165*

WOODSTOCK, OXFORDSHIRE 2–1D

The Feathers Hotel
Market St OX20 1SX (01993) 812291
*In this gorgeous town and near the gates of Blenheim, this luxurious boutique hotel has perennially disappointed in the food department. Perhaps until now, with the October 2016 announcement of a new venture here overseen by Dominic Chapman (Beehive, ex-Royal Oak). / **Details:** www.feathers.co.uk; 8m N of Oxford on A44; 9 pm; No jeans. / **Accommodation:** 21 rooms, from £199*

WOOTTON, OXFORDSHIRE 2–1D

The Killingworth Castle £50 343
Glympton Rd OX20 1EJ (01993) 811 401
*This 17th-century inn (and youthful sibling to the Ebrington Arms) provides a "good standard of cooking" to match its "excellent" home-brewed ales and "beautiful garden"; there are now stylish boutique rooms too. / **Details:** www.thekillingworthcastle.com; 9 pm, Fri & Sat 9.30 pm, Sun 8.30 pm.*

WORTHING, WEST SUSSEX 3–4A

The Fish Factory £39 432
51-53 Brighton Rd BN11 3EE (01903) 207123
*A notably consistent performer, this relaxed seafood restaurant and chippy (with a Littlehampton sibling) draws plaudits for its "really good fish". / **Details:** www.protorestaurantgroup.com; 10 pm.*

WRINEHILL, CHESHIRE 5–2B

The Hand & Trumpet £48 223
Main Rd CW3 9BJ (01270) 820048
*"In the culinary desert in this part of the UK, the Hand & Trumpet shines, particularly since they started taking orders at the table"; even some fans, however, "do not expect too much" of the typical Brunning & Price fare, but focus their attention on the "fine range of real ales". / **Details:** www.brunningandprice.co.uk/hand; 10 pm, Sun 9.30 pm.*

WRINGTON, SOMERSET 2–2B

Ethicurean £49 435
Barley Wood Walled Garden, Long Ln BS40 5SA (01934) 863713
*"You feel you are going back to the roots of good eating" at this "very different" ethical establishment in a "relaxed" Victorian walled garden – "stunning fresh food" is "grown in the gardens" just beyond, and there's an "unbeatable view from the full-wall window". / **Details:** www.theethicurean.com; 8.30 pm, Sun 5 pm; closed Mon & Sun D.*

WYMESWOLD, LEICESTERSHIRE 5–3D

The Hammer & Pincers £50 443
5 East Rd LE12 6ST (01509) 880735
Long popular for its "varied and interesting menu", this "relaxed", beamed village gastropub continues its upward march. Fans say that "it is now offering a level of cuisine not matched by many restaurants" – "without the gimmicks of a starred Nottingham

restaurant", and "at a fraction of London prices" ("this is MasterChef meets The Great British Menu!") / **Details:** *www.hammerandpincers.co.uk; 9.30 pm, 4pm Sun; closed Mon & Sun D; no Amex.*

WYMONDHAM, LEICESTERSHIRE 5–3D

The Berkeley Arms £46 3 3 3

59 Main St LE14 2AG (01572) 787 587
A "cosy" country gastroboozer that "retains its bar and the ambience of a pub", but where "the draw is very good food and service from the Hambleton-Hall-trained husband and wife"; while he's at the pass, creating "excellent dishes from the freshest, well-sourced ingredients", she's front of house "running everything with great efficiency". / **Details:** *www.theberkeleyarms.co.uk; 9 pm, Fri & Sat 9.30 pm, Sun 3 pm; closed Mon & Sun D; no Amex.*

YORK, NORTH YORKSHIRE 5–1D

Ambiente £27 2 2 4

31 Fossgate YO1 9TA (01904) 638 252
The "industrial", "warehouse-style" location provides a lively (if "squashed" and "noisy") setting for tapas, wines and sherries at this bigger sibling to the Goodramgate original. Service can be "slow", and foodwise, results are "variable" – "some dishes are like misguided experiments, some are OK, some are good". / **Details:** *www.ambiente-tapas.co.uk; 10 pm.*

Bettys £44 3 4 4

6-8 St Helen's Square Y01 8QP
(01904) 659142
An "incomparable" institution and "time warp delight" that's "so good you won't mind the queue" – these epic tearooms "never disappoint for afternoon tea" (featuring "outstanding cakes" and "cream teas to die for"), and are also "worth remembering for a light meal, and in particular a very good breakfast". / **Details:** *www.bettys.co.uk/tea-rooms/locations/york; 9 pm; no Amex; no booking, except Sun.*

Cafe No. 8 Bistro £46 4 4 3

8 Gillygate YO31 7EQ (01904) 653074
It may be home to "one of the smallest kitchens in York", but this diminutive café (with "recently overhauled garden") just outside the city walls turns out some "gorgeous" food, including "exceedingly good" puds. It's "now also in the Art Gallery (100 metres away) where the queues are huge", making the original HQ "a better choice". / **Details:** *www.cafeno8.co.uk; 10 pm; no Amex.*

Le Cochon Aveugle £53 5 4 4

37 Walmgate YO1 9TX (01904) 640222
Ex-Waterside Inn chef, Josh Overington's "tiny" (seven-table) venture, a follow-up to the Blind Swine, is "excellent on all levels". "The most important thing you have to do is trust" – "there's no menu", so you just choose "six or nine courses of whatever the kitchen is preparing that day" – and "you will get the most extraordinary meal". It's a "bloody bargain", too! / **Details:** *www.lecochonaveugleyork.com; Sun & Mon closed, Tue - Sat 9 pm.*

Il Paradiso Del Cibo £37 4 4 3

40 Walmgate YO1 9TJ (0190) 461 1444
It "looks unprepossessing on the outside", but this is in fact a "very welcoming and jolly" Sardinian, which sets the tone with an "enormous painting of Paolo the owner in the first room". Its many merits include "divine and inventive homemade pasta", and service in a "buzzy, undersized room by Italian family members". / **Details:** *www.ilparadisodelciboyork.com; 10pm; closed Mon D, Tue D, Wed D, Thu D & Fri D.*

Melton's £55 4 4 3

7 Scarcroft Rd YO23 1ND (01904) 634 341
"Away from the tourist-filled centre" (just outside the city walls), "this super restaurant maintains high standards year after year", and wins a hymn of praise for "interestingly different" cooking that's "always consistent". / **Details:** *www.meltonsrestaurant.co.uk; Mon closed, Tue - Sat 9.30 pm, Sun closed; closed Mon & Sun; no Amex.*

Middlethorpe Hall £75 3 3 5

Bishopthorpe Road YO23 2GB
(01904) 641241
"Enjoy your tea in spacious Georgian lounges" and "feel like the lord of the manor" at this "very special" country house hotel with "lovely" gardens. The victuals – "wonderful" cake and "excellent" Sunday lunch – attract praise, but "it's the ambience that makes this place worth a visit" ("you could be on Downton!") / **Details:** *www.middlethorpe.com; 9.30 pm; No shorts; children: 6+.* / **Accommodation:** *29 rooms, from £199*

Mumbai Lounge £34 3 3 3

47 Fossgate YO1 9TF (01904) 654 155
A spacious and polished city-centre venue whose offbeat menu helps make it a favourite local Indian; solid food ratings again this year and "staff really try to make you welcome". / **Details:** *www.mumbailoungeyork.co.uk; 11.30 pm, Fri & Sat midnight; closed Fri L.*

Pig And Pastry 4 4 4

35 Bishopthorpe Road YO23 1NA
(01904) 675115
"A lovely café near the centre of York". "It's a bit of a squash, but once you've fought your way in, you'll get some excellently prepared local stuff" ("fab range of cooked breakfasts and lush baked goods"); "all cafe/bistro food should be as good as this!" / **Details:** *Mon - Sat 5.00pm.*

Rattle Owl **£49** 4 4 2

104 Micklegate YO16 6JX (01904) 658658

"It's tiny – a bit like eating in a corridor, and with service that's a little strained at times… but the food is excellent", at this "up-and-coming", somewhat eco-inspired venture, where the seasonally inspired cooking features "interesting combinations". / **Details:** *www.rattleowl.co.uk.*

Star Inn the City **£60** 1 1 3

Lendal Engine House, Museum Street YO1 7DR (01904) 619208

It may have "a superb location by the river" ("perfect in summer"), but this "city cousin of the Star Inn at Harome" is "definitely not on the same planet as the original Star" – "the food isn't a patch on that of its sibling" and this operation "doesn't seem to have decided what it wants to be": even fans can find that "the pricing's a bit aggressive", "service struggles" and the food "tries too hard to be trendy" – "please make it simpler and less expensive!" / **Details:** *www.starinnthecity.co.uk; 10 pm.*

The Whippet Inn **£41** 3 4 3

15 North St YO1 6JD (01904) 500660

This trendy, brick-walled pub conversion, tucked-away in the city centre, draws praise for its "well-informed staff", and "consistent" – largely meat-centric – cooking, which takes in an "excellent Sunday lunch, and the 'dog's burger' is also good!" / **Details:** *www.thewhippetinn.co.uk.*

UK MAPS

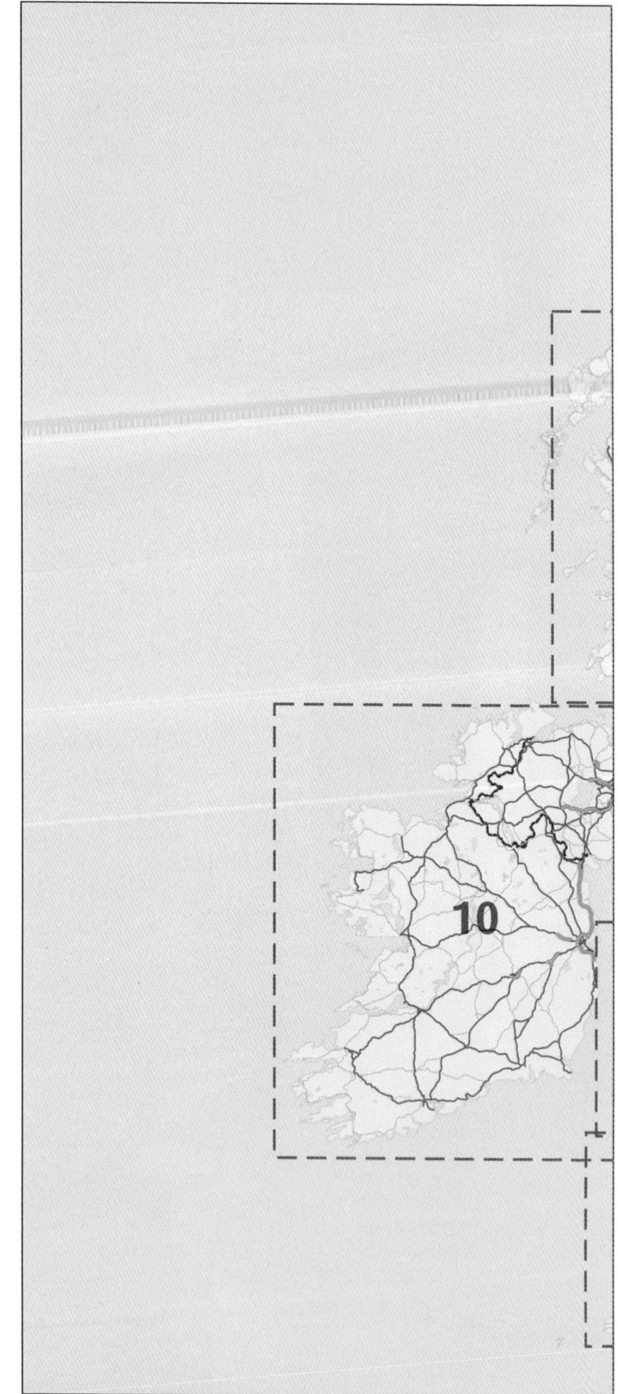
10

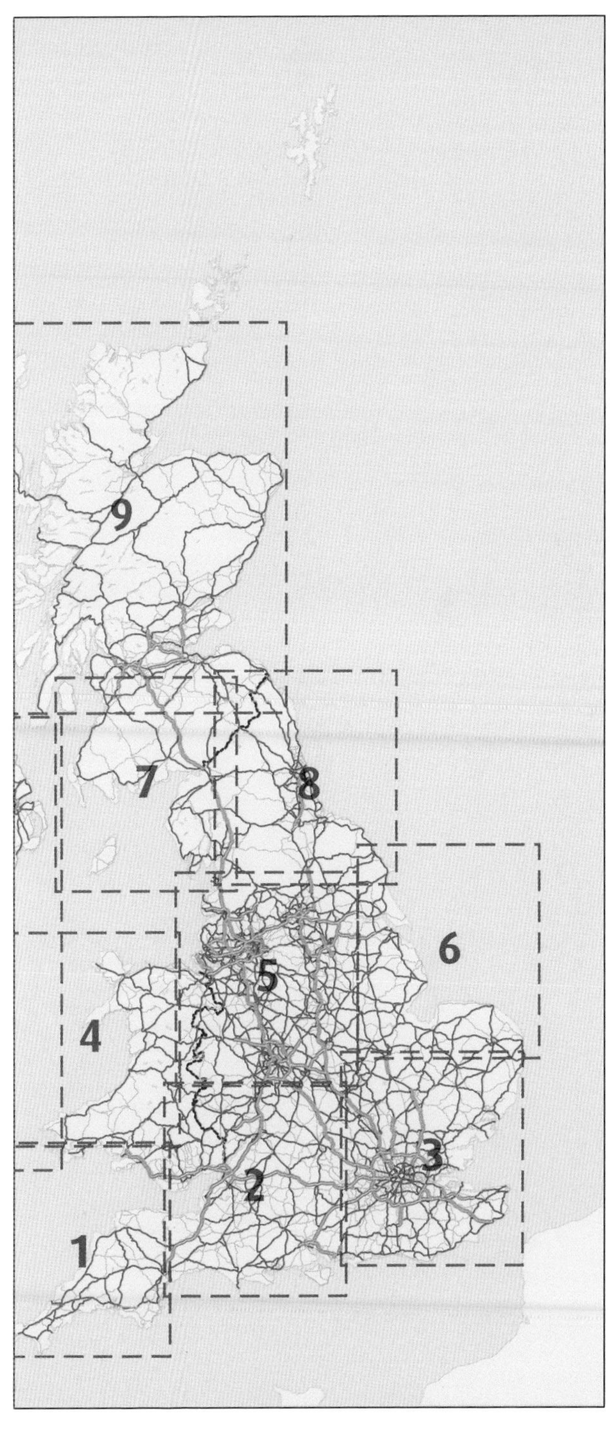
9
7
8
6
5
4
3
2
1

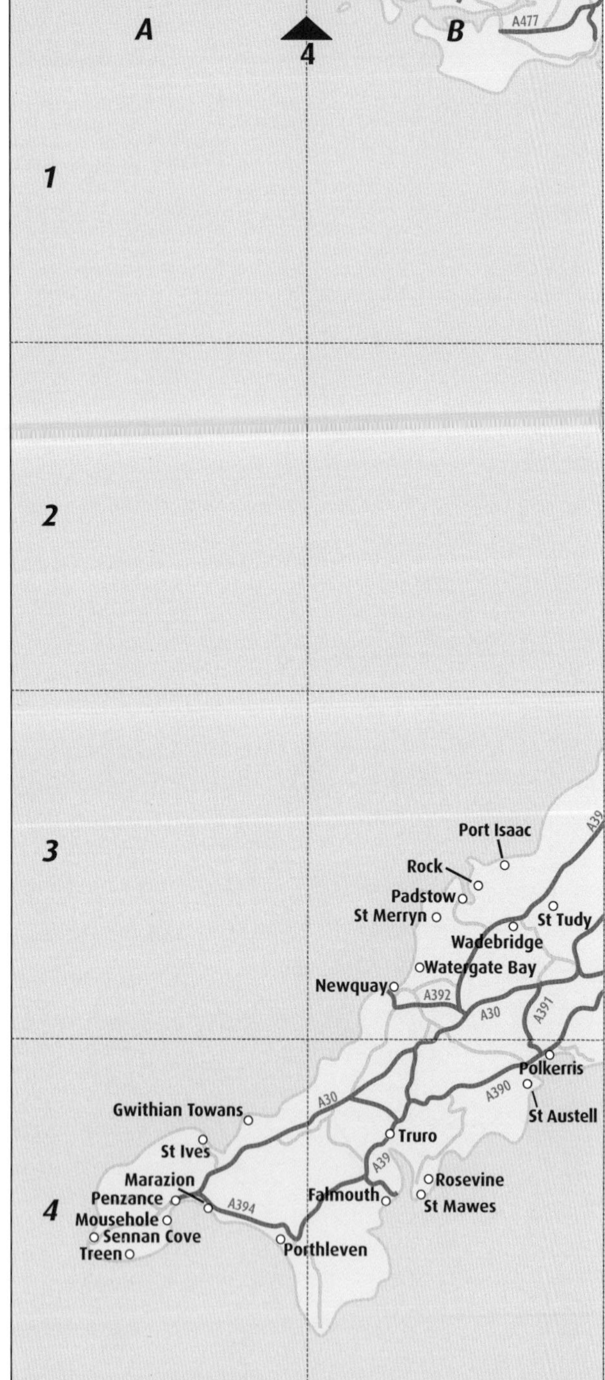
A
B
4
A477
1
2
3
4
Port Isaac
A39
Rock
Padstow
St Merryn
St Tudy
Wadebridge
Watergate Bay
Newquay
A392
A30
A391
Polkerris
A390
St Austell
Gwithian Towans
A30
Truro
St Ives
A39
Marazion
Rosevine
Penzance
Falmouth
St Mawes
A394
Mousehole
Sennan Cove
Treen
Porthleven

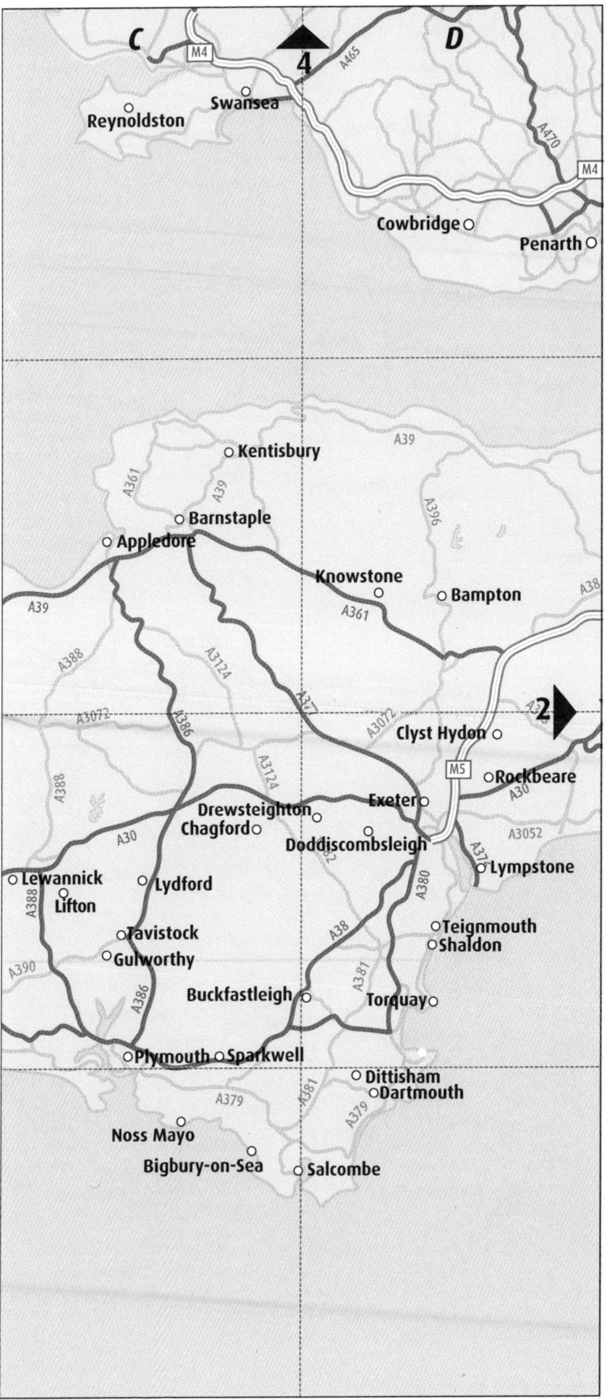
C
D
4
M4
A465
Swansea
Reynoldston
A470
M4
Cowbridge
Penarth
Kentisbury
A39
A361
A39
A396
Barnstaple
Appledore
Knowstone
Bampton
A38
A39
A361
A388
A3124
A377
2
A3072
A3072
A386
Clyst Hydon
M5
Rockbeare
A388
A3124
A30
Exeter
Drewsteighton
Chagford
Doddiscombsleigh
A30
A3052
A376
Lympstone
Lewannick
Lydford
Lifton
A388
A380
Teignmouth
Shaldon
Tavistock
A38
Gulworthy
A390
A381
A386
Buckfastleigh
Torquay
Plymouth
Sparkwell
Dittisham
Dartmouth
A379
A381
A379
Noss Mayo
Bigbury-on-Sea
Salcombe

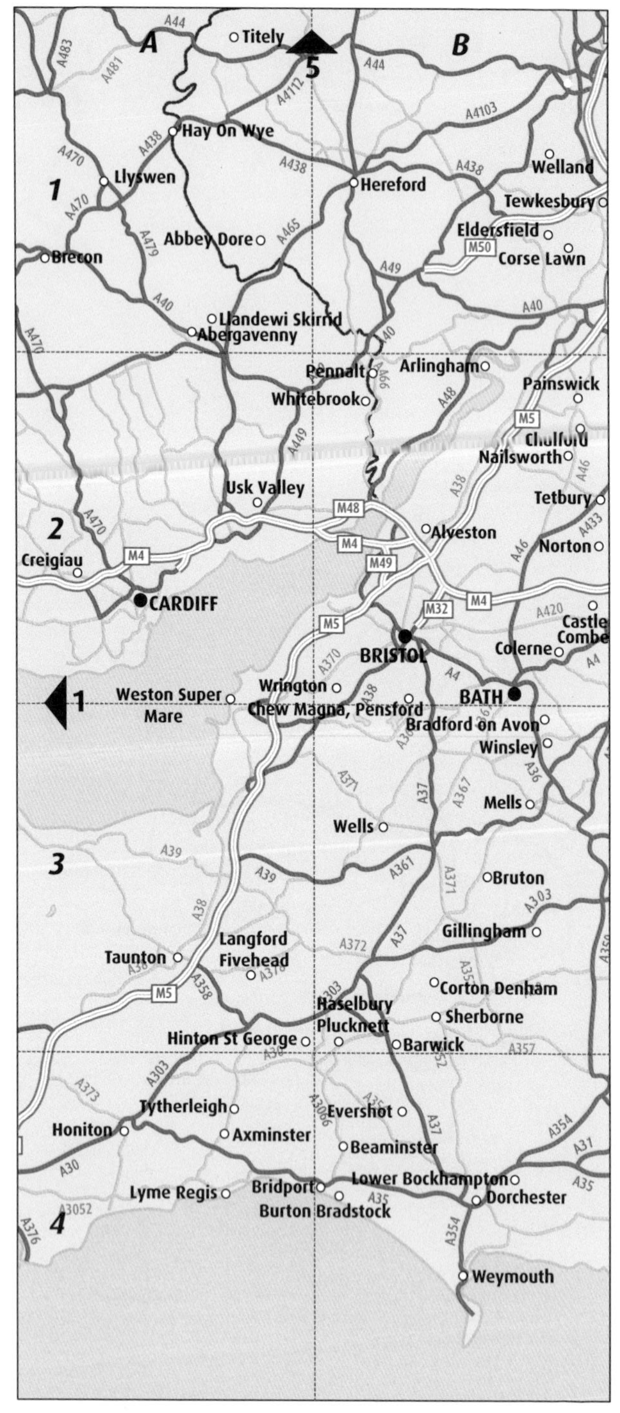

A
B
5
1
Titely
Hay On Wye
Llyswen
Hereford
Welland
Tewkesbury
Eldersfield
Corse Lawn
Abbey Dore
Brecon
Llandewi Skirrid
Abergavenny
Pennalt
Arlingham
Painswick
Whitebrook
Chulford
Nailsworth
Usk Valley
Tetbury
2
Alveston
Norton
Creigiau
CARDIFF
Castle Combe
BRISTOL
Colerne
BATH
Weston Super Mare
Wrington
Chew Magna, Pensford
Bradford on Avon
Winsley
Mells
Wells
3
Bruton
Gillingham
Langford Fivehead
Taunton
Corton Denham
Haselbury Plucknett
Sherborne
Hinton St George
Barwick
Tytherleigh
Evershot
Honiton
Axminster
Beaminster
Lower Bockhampton
Lyme Regis
Bridport
Dorchester
Burton Bradstock
4
Weymouth
M4
M48
M49
M32
M5
M50
A44
A4103
A438
A470
A465
A49
A40
A48
A46
A38
A4
A37
A39
A361
A303
A372
A373
A30
A35
A354
A31
A357

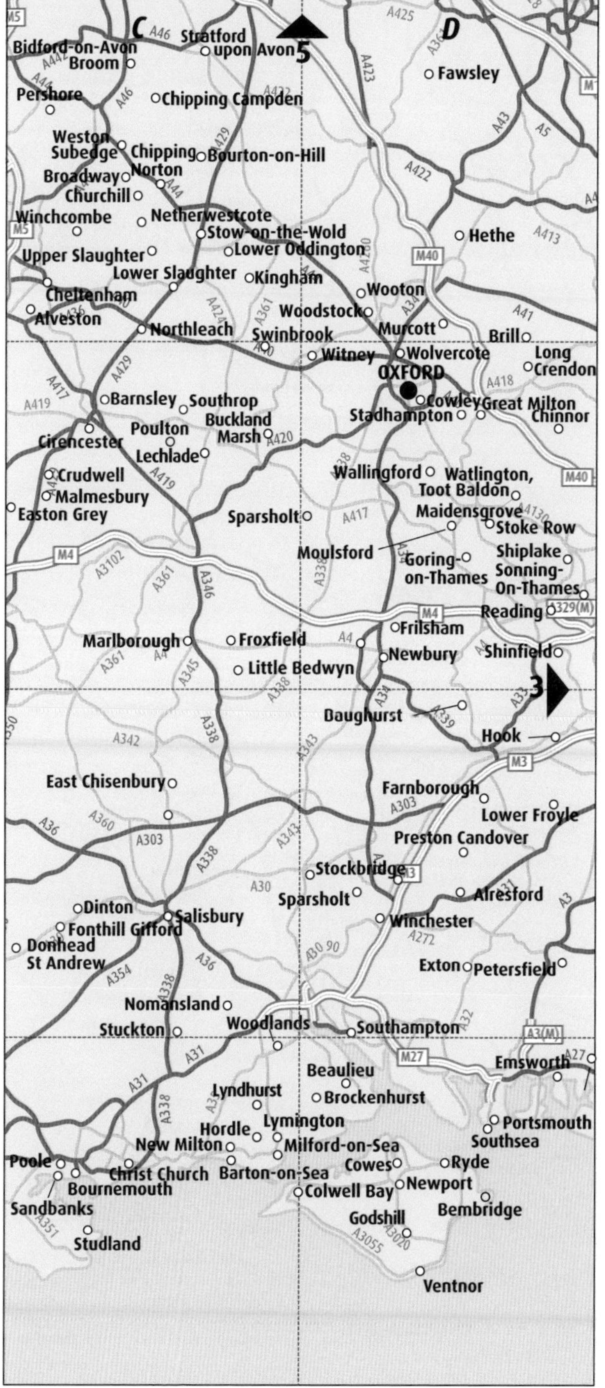
C
D
5
3
Bidford-on-Avon
Broom
Stratford upon Avon
Fawsley
Pershore
Chipping Campden
Weston Subedge
Chipping Norton
Bourton-on-Hill
Broadway
Churchill
Winchcombe
Netherwestcote
Stow-on-the-Wold
Hethe
Upper Slaughter
Lower Oddington
Lower Slaughter
Kingham
Wooton
Cheltenham
Woodstock
Alveston
Northleach
Swinbrook
Murcott
Brill
Witney
Wolvercote
Long Crendon
OXFORD
Barnsley
Southrop
Cowley
Great Milton
Stadhampton
Chinnor
Poulton
Buckland Marsh
Cirencester
Lechlade
Crudwell
Wallingford
Watlington,
Toot Baldon
Malmesbury
Easton Grey
Sparsholt
Maidensgrove
Stoke Row
Moulsford
Goring-on-Thames
Shiplake
Sonning-On-Thames
Reading
Frilsham
Marlborough
Froxfield
Newbury
Shinfield
Little Bedwyn
Daughurst
Hook
East Chisenbury
Farnborough
Lower Froyle
Preston Candover
Stockbridge
Sparsholt
Alresford
Dinton
Salisbury
Winchester
Fonthill Gifford
Donhead St Andrew
Exton
Petersfield
Nomansland
Stuckton
Woodlands
Southampton
Emsworth
Beaulieu
Lyndhurst
Brockenhurst
Lymington
Portsmouth
Hordle
Southsea
New Milton
Milford-on-Sea
Poole
Cowes
Ryde
Christ Church
Barton-on-Sea
Bournemouth
Newport
Colwell Bay
Sandbanks
Bembridge
Godshill
Studland
Ventnor
M5
M4
M40
M3
M27
M1
A3(M)
A329(M)
A46
A44
A429
A40
A34
A338
A4
A303
A36
A31
A354
A3

A
B
1
2
3
4
6
Sutton Gault
Ely
St Ives
Keyston
Huntingdon
Hemingford Grey
Madingley
CAMBRIDGE
Bolnhurst
Hardwick
Little Wilbraham
Shefford
Milton Keynes
Woburn
Willian
Stevenage
Bishop's Stortford
St Ippolyts
Luton
Welwyn
Aylesbury
Harpenden
Hunsdon
Dinton
Frithsden
Berkhamstead
St Albans
Datchworth
Great Missenden
Flaunden
Epping
Ongar
Amersham
Chandlers Cross
Bushey
Harrow Weald
Barnet
Brentwood
Seer Green
Hatch End
Borehamwood
Marlow
Gerrards Cross
Beaconsfield
Denham
Queensbury
Bovingdon Green
Cookham
Harrow
Taplow
Henley-on Thames
Maidenhead
Teddington
Bray
White Waltham
Eton
Windsor
St Margarets
Littlefield Green
Sunningdale
Kingston upon Thames
Sunninghill
East Molesley
Petts Wood
Egham
Orpington
Ascot
Weybridge
Surbiton
Sunbury on Thames
Esher
Croydon
Bagshot
Claygate
Cheam
Wallingham
Chobham
Cobham
Locksbottom
West Byfleet
Epsom
Woking
West Clandon
Farnborough
Ripley
Guildford
East Clandon
Westerham
Shipbourne
Brockham
Shere
Dorking
Sevenoaks Weald
Bidborough
East Grinstead
Tunbridge Wells
Horsham
West Hoathly
Withyham
Lickfold
Lower Beeding
Danehill
Cuckfield
Henley
Haywards Heath
Fletching
Tillington
Petworth
Strettington
Amberley
Albourne
East Chiltington
Herstmonceux
Chichester
Arundel
BRIGHTON & Hove
Worthing
Littlehampton
Eastbourne
Bracklesham
A1(M)
M1
M10
M25
M11
M4
M23
M26
M20
A14
A10
A428
A6
A1
A505
A507
A1307
A120
A5
A10
A414
A12
A13
A205
A232
A23
A22
A26
A24
A25
A31
A281
A325
A272
A27
A267
A427
A605
A6116
A43
A45
A509
A421
A413
A11
A1198

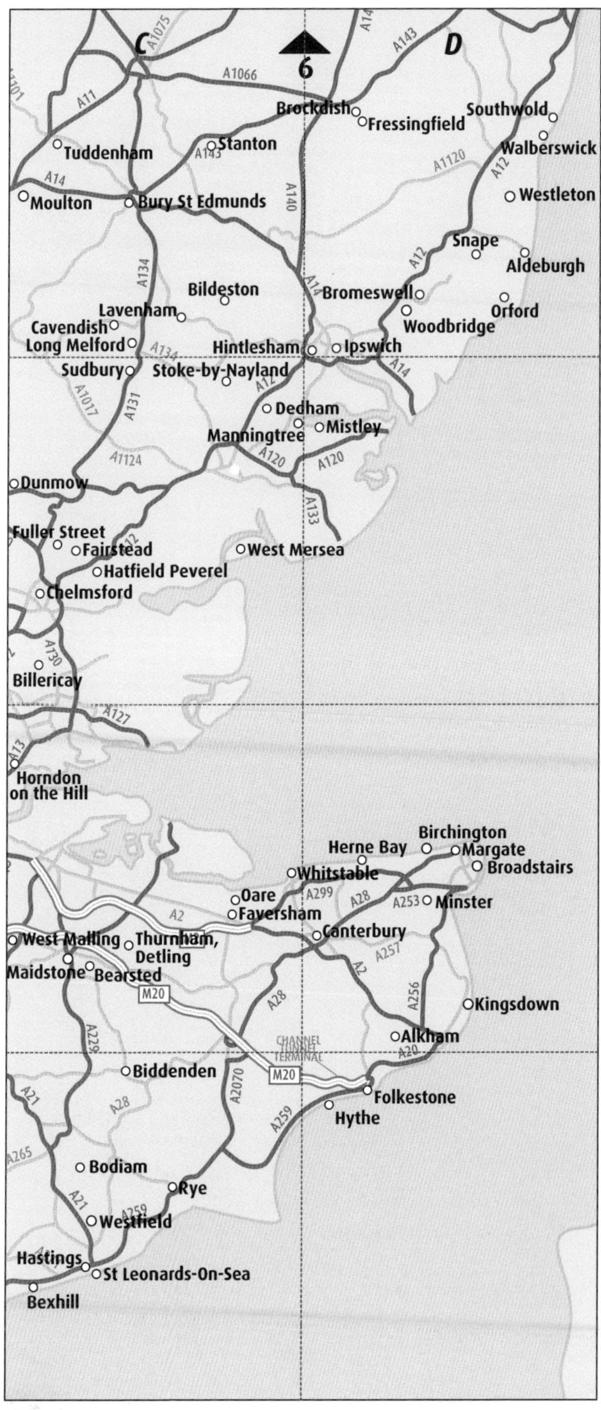
C
6
D
Brockdish
Fressingfield
Southwold
Walberswick
Tuddenham
Stanton
Moulton
Bury St Edmunds
Westleton
Snape
Aldeburgh
Bildeston
Bromeswell
Orford
Lavenham
Woodbridge
Cavendish
Long Melford
Hintlesham
Ipswich
Sudbury
Stoke-by-Nayland
Dedham
Manningtree
Mistley
Dunmow
Fuller Street
Fairstead
West Mersea
Hatfield Peverel
Chelmsford
Billericay
Horndon on the Hill
Birchington
Herne Bay
Margate
Broadstairs
Whitstable
Oare
Minster
Faversham
Canterbury
West Malling
Thurnham, Detling
Maidstone
Bearsted
Kingsdown
Alkham
CHANNEL TUNNEL TERMINAL
Biddenden
Folkestone
Hythe
Bodiam
Rye
Westfield
Hastings
St Leonards-On-Sea
Bexhill

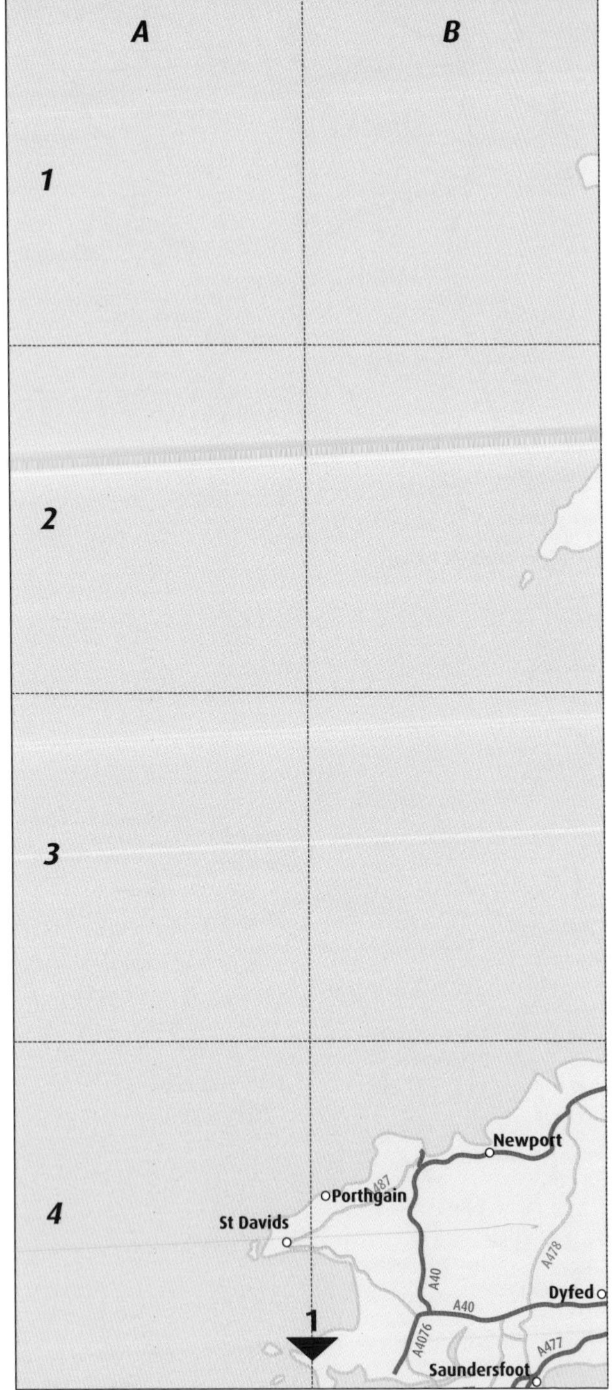

A
B
1
2
3
4
Newport
Porthgain
A487
St Davids
A478
A40
Dyfed
A40
1
A4076
A477
Saundersfoot

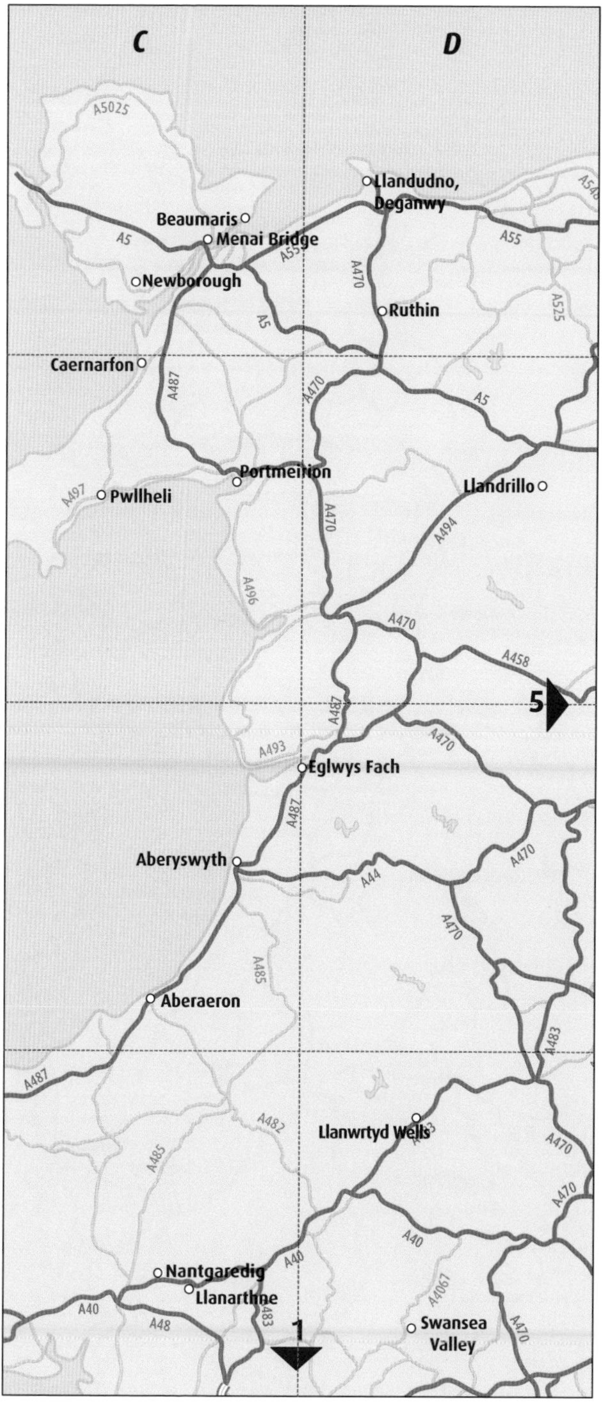

C
D
A5025
Llandudno,
Deganwy
Beaumaris
Menai Bridge
A5
A55
A470
A55
Newborough
Ruthin
A525
A5
Caernarfon
A487
A470
A5
Portmeirion
A497
Pwllheli
A470
Llandrillo
A494
A496
A470
A458
5
A487
A470
A493
Eglwys Fach
A487
Aberyswyth
A44
A470
A470
A485
Aberaeron
A483
A487
A482
Llanwrtyd Wells
A485
A470
A470
A40
A40
Nantgaredig
A4067
Llanarthne
A40
A48
A483
1
Swansea
Valley
A470

MAP 4

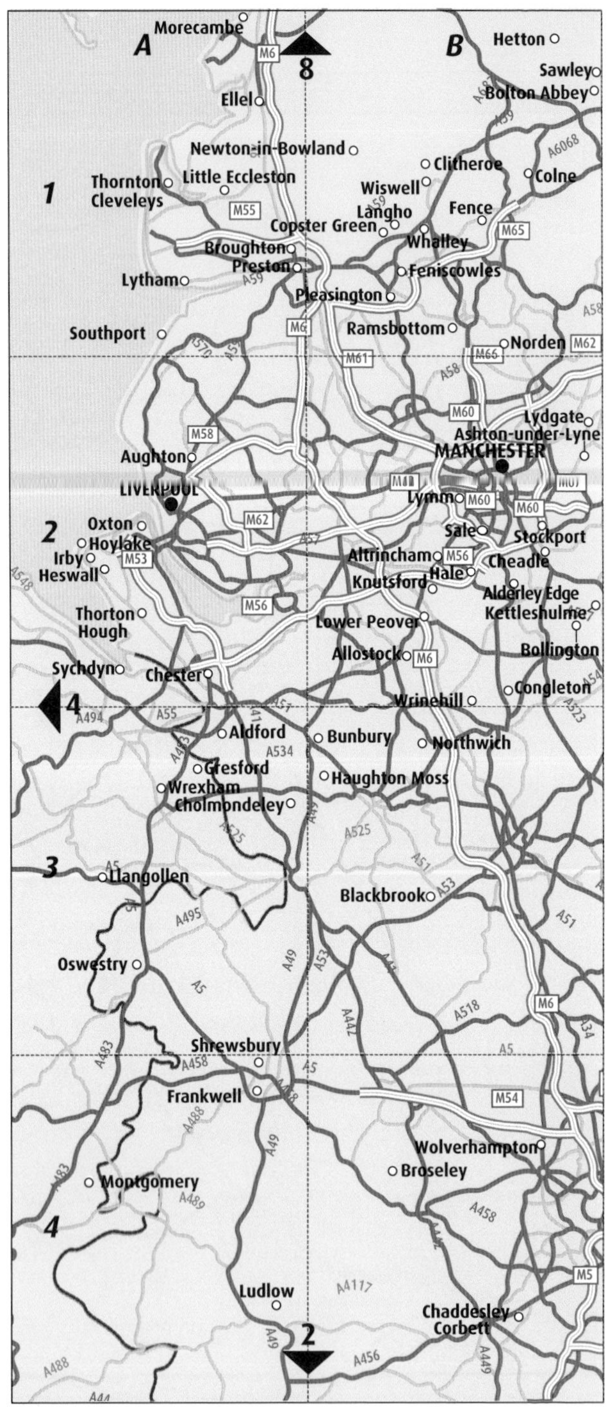
A
B
8
1
2
3
4
Morecambe
Hetton
Sawley
Bolton Abbey
Ellel
Newton-in-Bowland
Clitheroe
Colne
Thornton Cleveleys
Little Eccleston
Wiswell
Langho
Fence
Copster Green
Whalley
Broughton
Preston
Feniscowles
Lytham
Pleasington
Southport
Ramsbottom
Norden
Lydgate
Ashton-under-Lyne
MANCHESTER
Aughton
LIVERPOOL
Lymm
Oxton
Hoylake
Irby
Heswall
Sale
Stockport
Altrincham
Hale
Cheadle
Knutsford
Alderley Edge
Kettleshulme
Thorton Hough
Lower Peover
Allostock
Bollington
Sychdyn
Chester
Congleton
Wrinehill
Aldford
Bunbury
Northwich
Gresford
Haughton Moss
Wrexham
Cholmondeley
Llangollen
Blackbrook
Oswestry
Shrewsbury
Frankwell
Wolverhampton
Broseley
Montgomery
Ludlow
Chaddesley Corbett
M6
M55
M65
M61
M66
M62
M58
M60
M53
M56
M54
M5
A59
A6068
A58
A570
A57
A55
A494
A548
A534
A483
A525
A5
A495
A49
A53
A51
A41
A442
A518
A458
A488
A489
A4117
A456
A449
A523
A34
A44

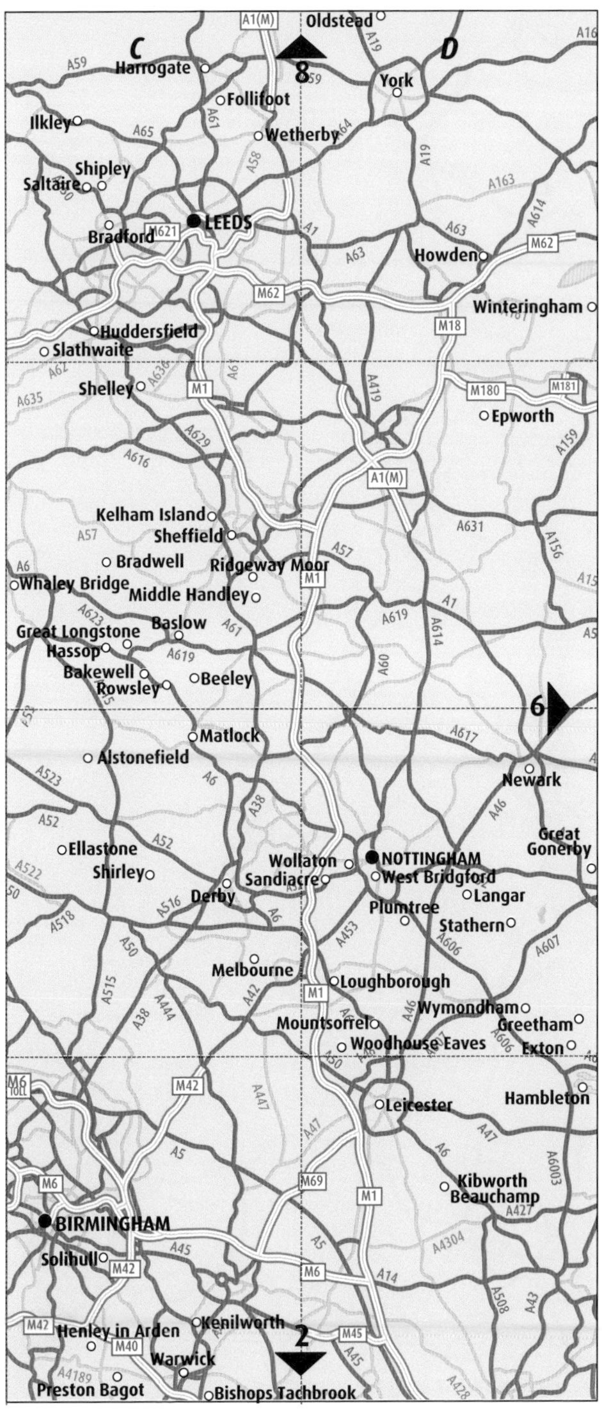
C
D
8
Oldstead
Harrogate
York
Follifoot
Ilkley
Wetherby
Shipley
Saltaire
LEEDS
Bradford
Howden
Winteringham
Huddersfield
Slathwaite
Shelley
Epworth
Kelham Island
Sheffield
Bradwell
Ridgeway Moor
Whaley Bridge
Middle Handley
Great Longstone
Baslow
Hassop
Bakewell
Beeley
Rowsley
6
Matlock
Alstonefield
Newark
Great Gonerby
Ellastone
Wollaton
NOTTINGHAM
Shirley
Sandiacre
West Bridgford
Derby
Langar
Plumtree
Stathern
Melbourne
Loughborough
Wymondham
Mountsorrel
Greetham
Woodhouse Eaves
Exton
Leicester
Hambleton
Kibworth Beauchamp
BIRMINGHAM
Solihull
Henley in Arden
Kenilworth
2
Warwick
Preston Bagot
Bishops Tachbrook

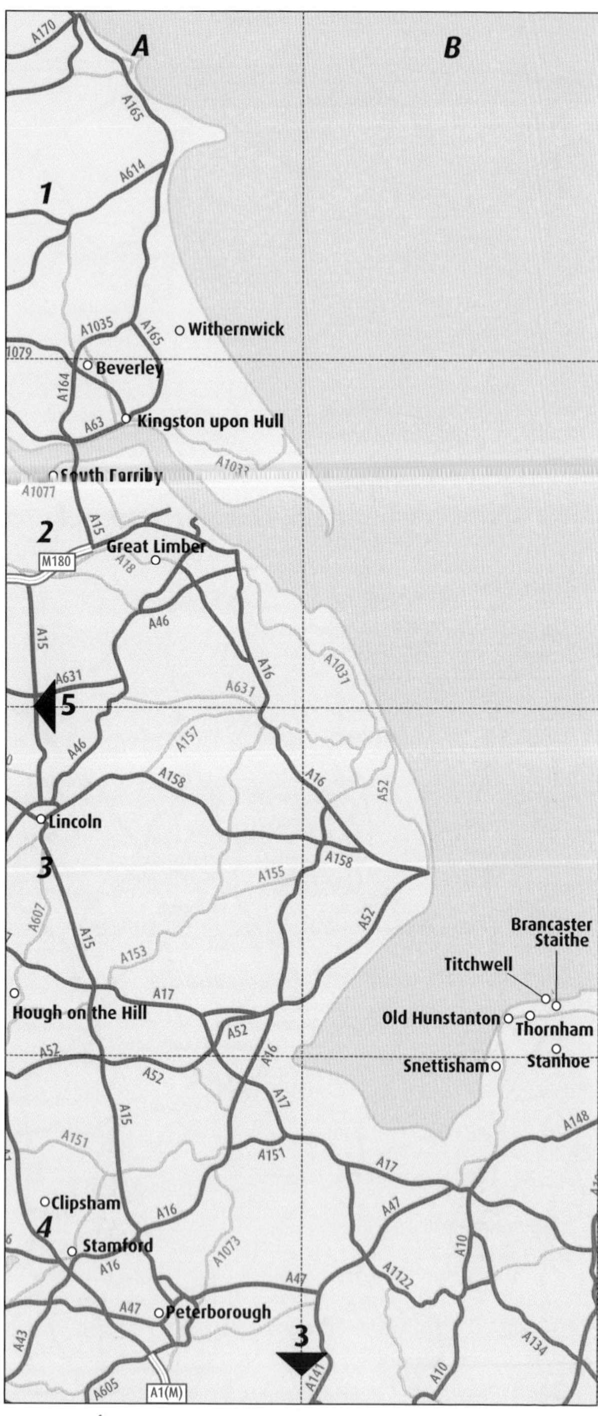
A
B
1
2
3
4
5
3
Withernwick
Beverley
Kingston upon Hull
South Ferriby
Great Limber
Lincoln
Hough on the Hill
Clipsham
Stamford
Peterborough
Brancaster Staithe
Titchwell
Old Hunstanton
Thornham
Snettisham
Stanhoe
A170
A165
A614
A1035
A1079
A164
A63
A1077
A15
M180
A18
A46
A631
A16
A1031
A157
A158
A52
A155
A607
A153
A17
A151
A148
A47
A10
A1073
A1122
A134
A43
A605
A1(M)
A141

C
D
Holkham
Morston
Blakeney
Wiveton
Holt
Cromer
A148
A140
A149
A1067
A47
Norwich
A47
Stoke Holy Cross
Darsham
A146
A143
A11
3
A1075
A140
A143

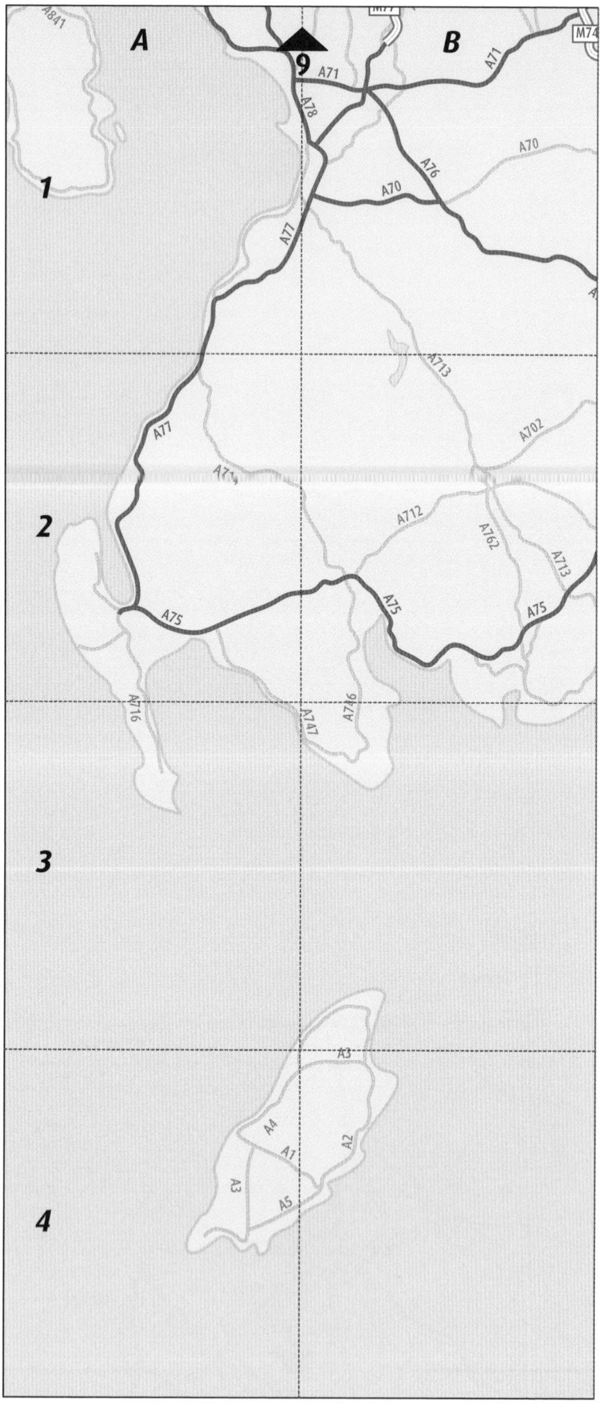
A841
A
B
9
A71
M74
A71
A78
A70
A76
A70
1
A77
A713
A702
A77
A71
2
A712
A762
A713
A75
A75
A75
A716
A747
A746
3
A3
A4
A1
A2
A3
A5
4

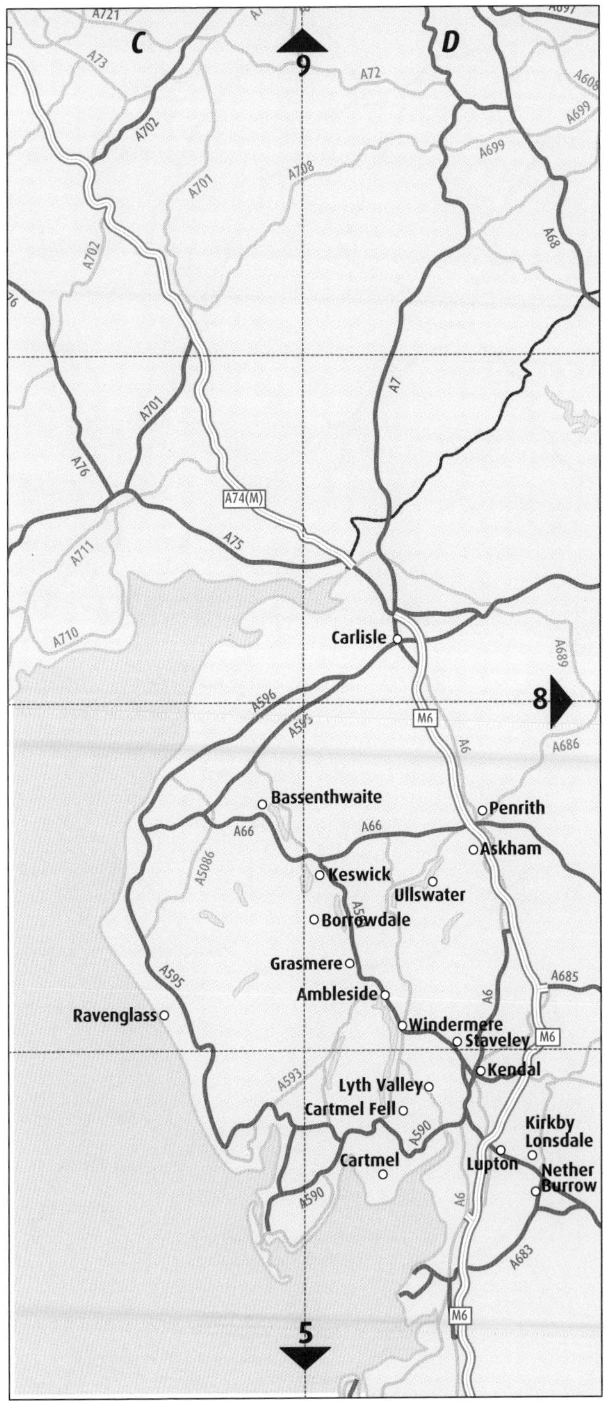
C
D
9
8
5
Carlisle
Bassenthwaite
Penrith
Askham
Keswick
Ullswater
Borrowdale
Grasmere
Ambleside
Ravenglass
Windermere
Staveley
Kendal
Lyth Valley
Cartmel Fell
Kirkby Lonsdale
Cartmel
Lupton
Nether Burrow
A721
A73
A72
A702
A701
A708
A699
A608
A68
A7
A76
A74(M)
A75
A711
A710
A689
A596
A595
M6
A6
A686
A66
A5086
A685
A593
A590
A683

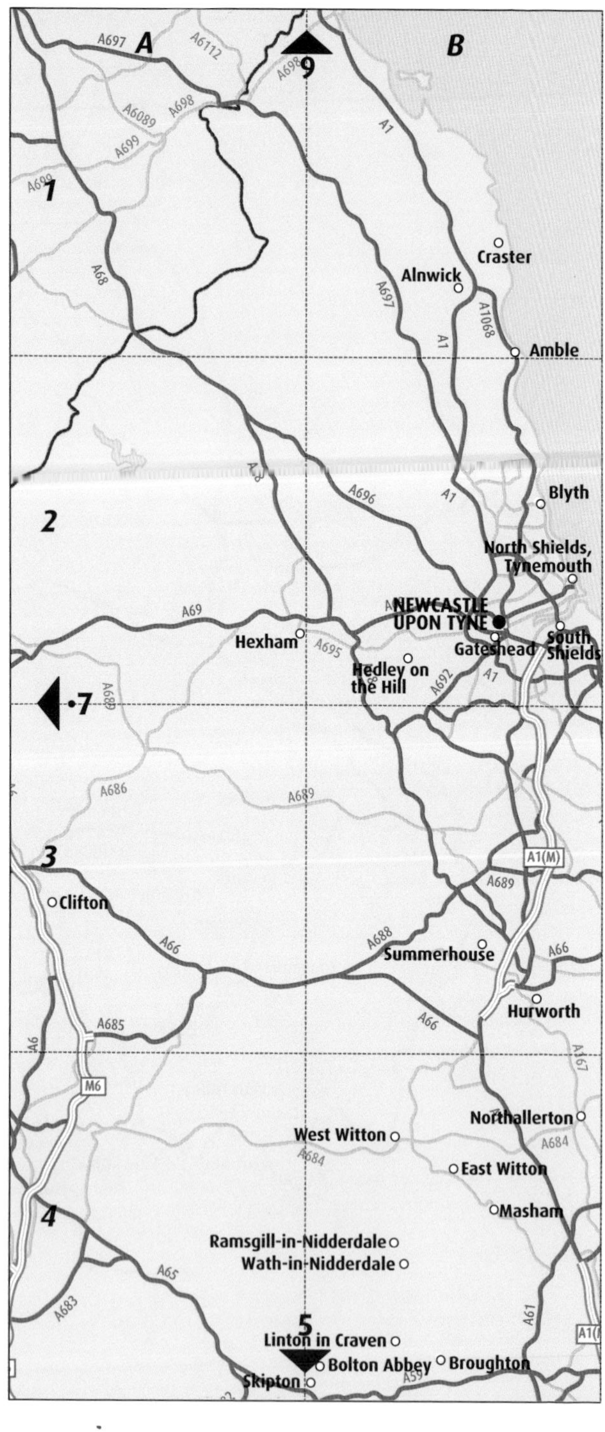

A
B
9
1
2
3
4
5
7
A697
A6112
A698
A6089
A699
A68
A1
A1068
A696
A69
A695
A689
A692
A686
A1(M)
A688
A66
A685
A6
M6
A167
A684
A65
A683
A61
A59
Craster
Alnwick
Amble
Blyth
North Shields, Tynemouth
NEWCASTLE UPON TYNE
Gateshead
South Shields
Hexham
Hedley on the Hill
Clifton
Summerhouse
Hurworth
Northallerton
West Witton
East Witton
Masham
Ramsgill-in-Nidderdale
Wath-in-Nidderdale
Linton in Craven
Bolton Abbey
Broughton
Skipton

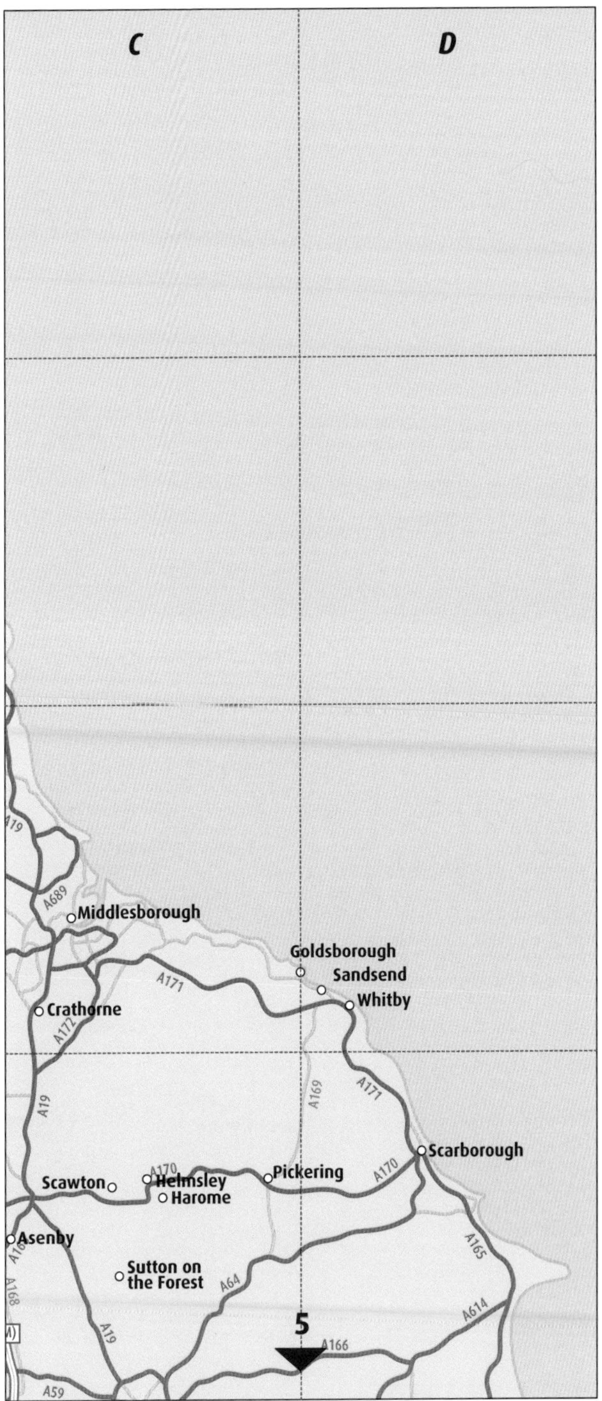
C
D
A19
A689
Middlesborough
Goldsborough
Sandsend
Whitby
A171
Crathorne
A172
A19
A169
A171
Scarborough
A170
Helmsley
Pickering
A170
Scawton
Harome
Asenby
Sutton on
the Forest
A64
A165
A168
A19
5
A166
A614
A59

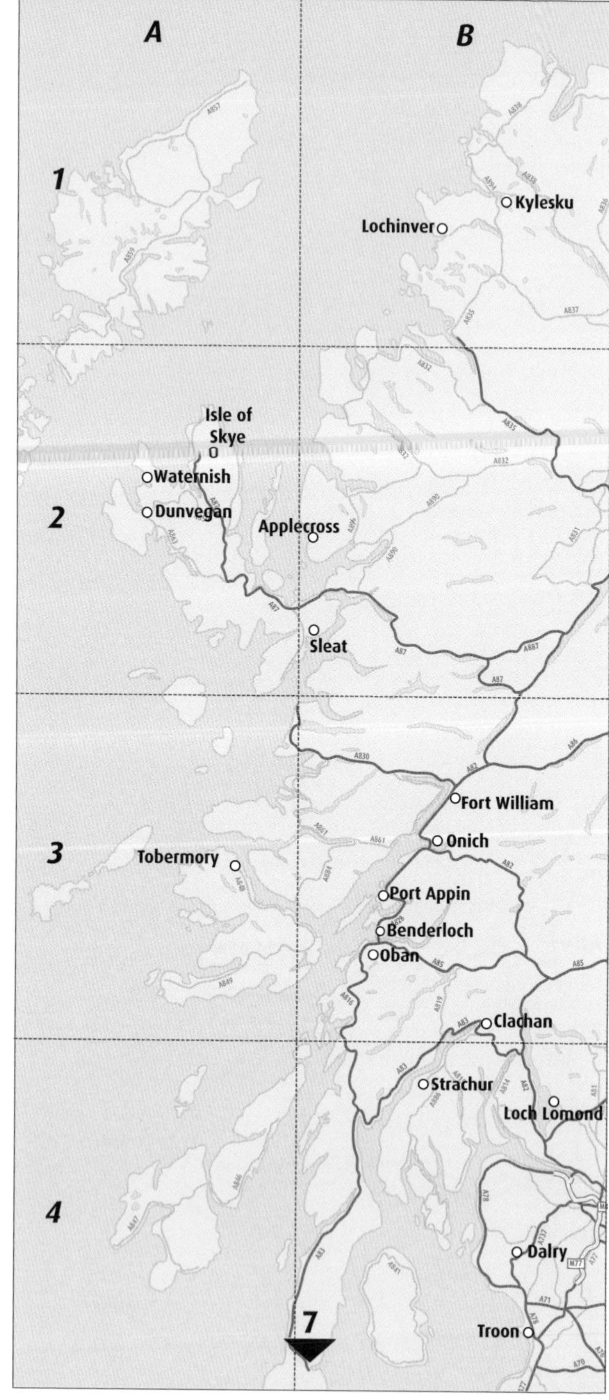
A
B
1
2
3
4
Kylesku
Lochinver
Isle of Skye
Waternish
Dunvegan
Applecross
Sleat
Fort William
Onich
Tobermory
Port Appin
Benderloch
Oban
Clachan
Strachur
Loch Lomond
Dalry
Troon
7

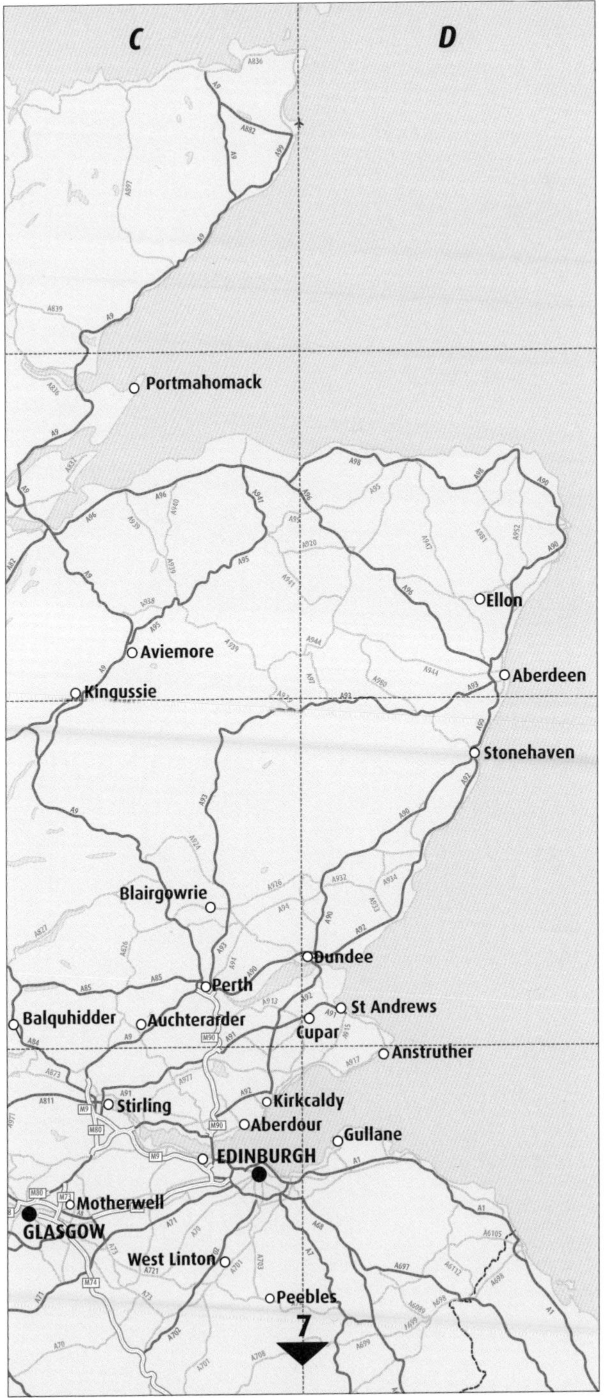
C
D
Portmahomack
Ellon
Aviemore
Aberdeen
Kingussie
Stonehaven
Blairgowrie
Dundee
Perth
St Andrews
Balquhidder
Auchterarder
Cupar
Anstruther
Kirkcaldy
Stirling
Aberdour
Gullane
EDINBURGH
Motherwell
GLASGOW
West Linton
Peebles
7

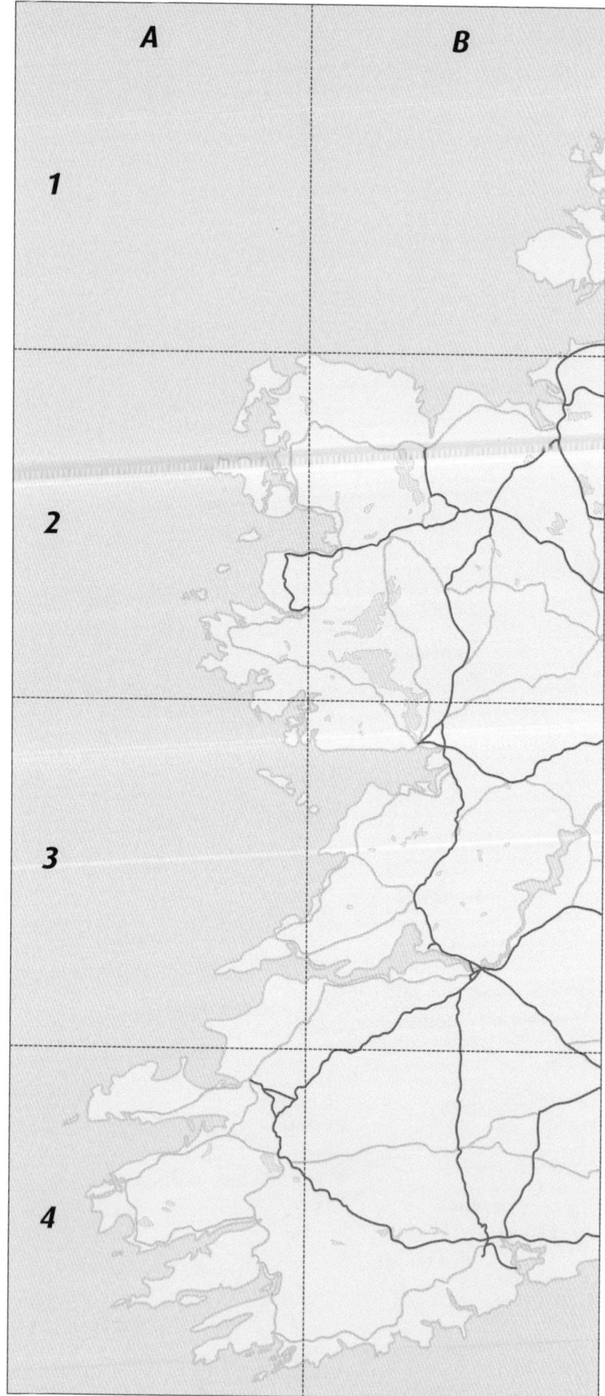
A
B
1
2
3
4

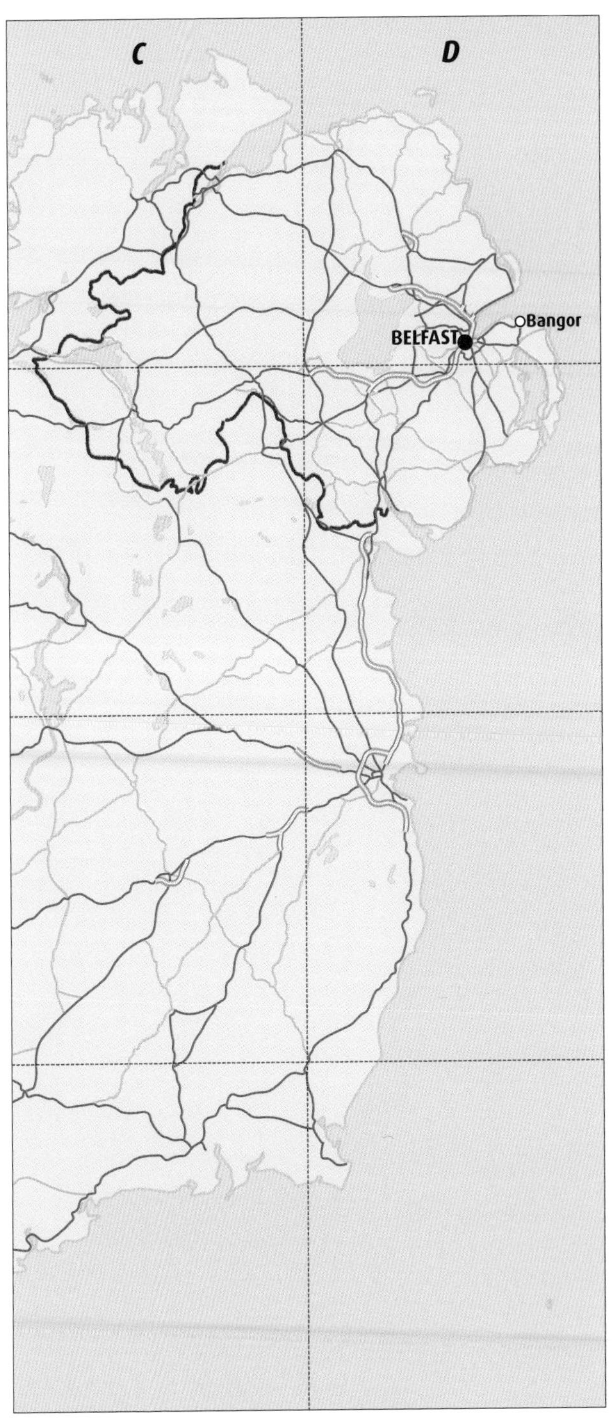
C
D
BELFAST
Bangor

ALPHABETICAL INDEX

ALPHABETICAL INDEX

ALPHABETICAL INDEX

ALPHABETICAL INDEX

ALPHABETICAL INDEX

ALPHABETICAL INDEX